THE ROUTLEDGE COMPANION TO LATIN AMERICAN CINEMA

The Routledge Companion to Latin American Cinema is the most comprehensive survey of Latin American cinemas available in a single volume. While highlighting state-of-the-field research, essays also offer readers a cohesive overview of multiple facets of filmmaking in the region, from the production system and aesthetic tendencies, to the nature of circulation and reception. The volume recognizes the recent "new cinemas" in Argentina, Brazil, Chile, and Mexico, and, at the same time, provides a much deeper understanding of the contemporary moment by commenting on the aesthetic trends and industrial structures in earlier periods. The collection features essays by established scholars as well as up-and-coming investigators in ways that depart from existing scholarship and suggest new directions for the field.

Contributors: Gonzalo Aguilar, Salomé Aguilera Skvirsky, Luisela Alvaray, Jens Andermann, María Fernanda Arias Osorio, Josetxo Cerdán, Maite Conde, Amalia Córdova, Nilo Couret, Andrea Cuarterolo, Gerard Dapena, Luis Duno-Gottberg, Tamara L. Falicov, Miguel Fernández Labayen, Silvana Flores, Geoffrey Kantaris, Alejandro Kelly Hopfenblatt, Mariana Lacunza, Horacio Legrás, Adrián Pérez Melgosa, Mariano Mestman, Rielle Navitski, María Luisa Ortega, Roberto Carlos Ortiz, Joanna Page, Juan Poblete, Victoria Ruétalo, Masha Salazkina, Ignacio M. Sánchez Prado, Freya Schiwy, Laura Isabel Serna, Lisa Shaw, Niamh Thornton, Dolores Tierney, David Wood.

Marvin D'Lugo is Research Professor at Clark University, USA. He has written extensively on Hispanic transnational cinema, focusing on "audio politics" in Latin American film. He is currently completing a book on the digital cinema revolution in Mexico.

Ana M. López is Director of the Cuban and Caribbean Studies Institute at Tulane University, USA. Her research is focused on Latin American and Latino film and cultural studies. She is currently the editor of *Studies in Spanish and Latin American Cinemas*.

Laura Podalsky has authored *The Politics of Affect and Emotion in the Contemporary Latin American Cinema* (2011) and *Specular City: Transforming Culture, Consumption, and Space in Buenos Aires, 1955–1973* (2004). She teaches Latin American film and cultural studies at the Ohio State University, USA.

THE ROUTLEDGE
COMPANION TO LATIN
AMERICAN CINEMA

Edited by Marvin D'Lugo, Ana M. López,
and Laura Podalsky

Routledge
Taylor & Francis Group

LONDON AND NEW YORK

First published 2018
by Routledge
2 Park Square, Milton Park, Abingdon, Oxon OX14 4RN

and by Routledge
711 Third Avenue, New York, NY 10017

Routledge is an imprint of the Taylor & Francis Group, an informa business

British Library Cataloguing-in-Publication Data
A catalogue record for this book is available from the British Library

Library of Congress Cataloging-in-Publication Data
Names: D'Lugo, Marvin editor. | Lopez, Ana M. editor. | Podalsky, Laura,
1964- editor.
Title: The Routledge companion to Latin American cinema /
edited by Marvin D'Lugo, Ana M. Lâopez and Laura Podalsky.
Description: New York : Routledge, 2017.
Identifiers: LCCN 2017016053 | ISBN 9781138855267 (hardback)
Subjects: LCSH: Motion pictures—Latin America—History and criticism.
Classification: LCC PN1993.5.L3 R68 2017 | DDC 791.43098—dc23
LC record available at https://lccn.loc.gov/2017016053

ISBN: 978-1-138-85526-7 (hbk)
ISBN: 978-1-315-72044-9 (ebk)

Typeset in Goudy Std
by Swales & Willis Ltd, Exeter, Devon, UK

To our families, with gratitude for all they put up with.

CONTENTS

Contents

FIGURES

CONTRIBUTORS

Gonzalo Aguilar is Professor of Brazilian and Portuguese Literatures at the University of Buenos Aires. Among his books are *Otros mundos. Un ensayo sobre el nuevo cine argentino* (2006) and *Más allá del pueblo. Imágenes, indicios y políticas del cine* (2015).

Salomé Aguilera Skvirsky is Assistant Professor in the Cinema and Media Studies Department at the University of Chicago. Her articles have appeared in *Cinema Journal, Journal of Latin American Cultural Studies*, and *Social Identities*.

Luisela Alvaray is an Associate Professor at DePaul University. Her research explores globalization and media, cultural studies, documentary studies, and film historiography. Her articles have appeared in *Cinema Journal, Transnational Cinemas*, and *Studies in Hispanic Cinemas*, among other publications.

Jens Andermann is Professor of Spanish and Portuguese at New York University and editor of the *Journal of Latin American Cultural Studies*. Among his recent books are *The Optic of the State: Visuality and Power in Argentina and Brazil* (2007) and *New Argentine Cinema* (2011).

María Fernanda Arias Osorio holds a Ph.D. in Film and Media Studies from Indiana University. She is Associate Professor at the University of Antioquia (Colombia). Her areas of research are the social history of Latin American cinema, and film and media audiences.

Josetxo Cerdán is Associate Professor of Media Studies at Universidad Carlos III de Madrid and member of the research group TECMERIN. He is part of the editorial board of the *Aproximaciones a las culturas Hispánicas* series (Iberoamericana Vervuert).

Maite Conde is University Lecturer in Brazilian Culture at the University of Cambridge. Her books include *Consuming Visions: Cinema Writing and Modernity in Rio de Janeiro* (2011) and a translation of Marilena Chauí's *Between Conformity and Resistance: Essays on Politics Culture and the State* (2011).

Amalia Córdova is Latino Curator for Digital and Emerging Media at the Smithsonian Institution's Center for Folklife and Cultural Heritage, where she has developed video programs for their Museum of the American Indian. She teaches at New York University's Gallatin School of Individualized Study.

Nilo Couret is an Assistant Professor at the University of Michigan. He is currently completing his book manuscript *Mock Classicism* on interwar Latin American popular culture and film comedy. He has published in *SubStance*, *Social Identities*, and forthcoming in *Discourse*.

Andrea Cuarterolo is a full-time researcher specializing in the study of Argentine and Latin American photography and cinema. She is the author of *De la foto al fotograma: Relaciones entre cine y fotografía en la Argentina 1840–1933* (2013) and the co-editor of *Pantallas transnacionales* (2017).

Gerard Dapena is a scholar of Hispanic Cinemas and Visual Culture. He has authored articles and book chapters on various aspects of Spanish and Latin American film and art history. He has taught at New York University, Bard College, Macalester College, and the New School.

Luis Duno-Gottberg is Associate Professor and Chair at the Department of Spanish, Portuguese, and Latin American Studies at Rice University. He has authored/edited eight books and many articles on Caribbean culture, with emphasis on race and ethnicity, politics, violence, and visual culture.

Tamara L. Falicov is Professor in the Department of Film and Media Studies at the University of Kansas. She is the author of *The Cinematic Tango: Contemporary Argentine Film* (2007). Her forthcoming book is entitled *Latin American Film Industries*.

Miguel Fernández Labayen is Associate Professor in the Department of Journalism and Media Studies at Universidad Carlos III de Madrid and member of the research group TECMERIN. His articles appear in journals such as *Transnational Cinemas* and the *Journal of Spanish Cultural Studies*.

Silvana Flores is author of *El Nuevo Cine Latinoamericano y su dimensión continental: Regionalismo e integración cinematográfica* (2013) She has co-edited *Cine y Revolución en América Latina: Una perspectiva comparada de las cinematografías de la región* (2014). She currently teaches at UBA XXI.

Geoffrey Kantaris is Reader in Latin American Culture at the University of Cambridge. He specializes in modern Latin American film and literature, with interests in urban film, popular culture, and the cultures of globalization. He recently co-edited *Latin American Popular Culture* (2013).

Alejandro Kelly Hopfenblatt has a postdoctoral appointment with CONICET in Buenos Aires, where he does research on Latin American cinema. In 2013, he was awarded First

Prize in the "Concurso de Ensayos Domingo di Núbila" organized by ASAECA and the Mar del Plata Film Festival.

Mariana Lacunza holds a PhD from the Ohio State University. She is Chair of the Communications Department at the Universidad Privada Boliviana; and has taught courses in literature and film in the United States and Bolivia.

Horacio Legrás teaches Latin American literature, film, and critical theory at the University of California Irvine. He is the author of *Literature and Subjection* (2008) and *Culture and Revolution: Violence, History and the Making of Modern Mexico* (2017).

Adrián Pérez Melgosa, Associate Professor of Hispanic Languages and Literature at Stony Brook University, works on the transnational and cross-cultural dynamics in Latin American and Spanish cinemas. He is the author of *Cinema and Inter-American Relations: Tracking Transnational Affect* (2012).

Mariano Mestman is a Researcher at the National Council of Scientific Research and at the University of Buenos Aires. His published works include studies of the working class on-screen and the relations between Latin American and Third World filmmakers.

Rielle Navitski is Assistant Professor of Film Studies at the University of Georgia. She is the author of *Public Spectacles of Violence: Sensational Cinema and Journalism in Early Twentieth-Century Mexico and Brazil* (2017) and the co-editor of *Cosmopolitan Film Cultures in Latin America, 1896–1960* (2017).

María Luisa Ortega is Professor of Audiovisual Communication at the Universidad Autónoma de Madrid. She is on the editorial board of the journal *Secuencias* and has co-authored *Cine documental en América Latina* (2003) and *The Grierson Effect: Tracing Documentary's International Movement* (2014).

Roberto Carlos Ortiz is an independent scholar based in Mexico City. He has written about the intersection of film stardom, Hispanic/Latino images, and queer identities, and is completing a manuscript about the female stars of classic Mexican cinema.

Joanna Page is Director of the Centre of Latin American Studies at the University of Cambridge. She has published several books on literature and cinema from Argentina and is currently working on the graphic novel in Latin America.

Juan Poblete is Professor of Latina/o American Literature and Cultural Studies at the University of California, Santa Cruz. Most recently, he co-edited *Sports and Nationalism in Latin America* (2015) and *Humor in Latin American Cinema* (2015).

Victoria Ruétalo is Associate Professor of Latin American Studies at the University of Alberta. She has co-edited *Latsploitation, Exploitation Cinemas, and Latin America* (2009), and is completing a manuscript about censorship in Argentina and the sexploitation films by Armando Bó and Isabel Sarli.

Masha Salazkina has authored *In Excess: Sergei Eisenstein's Mexico* (2009). She was co-editor of *Sound, Speech, Music in Soviet and Post-Soviet Cinema* (2014) and edited a special issue of *Framework* (2015) on the geopolitics of film. She teaches at Concordia University, Montreal.

Ignacio M. Sánchez Prado is Professor of Spanish and Latin American Studies at Washington University in St. Louis. He has authored and edited various books on Mexican and Latin American literature and cinema, including *Screening Neoliberalism: Transforming Mexican Cinema 1988–2012* (2015) and *A History of Mexican Literature* (2016).

Freya Schiwy is Associate Professor at the University of California, Riverside. She is the author of *Indianizing Film: Decolonization, the Andes, and the Question of Technology* (2009) and *Adjusting the Lens: Community and Collaborative Video in Mexico* (2017).

Laura Isabel Serna is Associate Professor of Cinema and Media Studies at the University of Southern California. She is the author of *Making Cinelandia: American Films and Mexican Film Culture before the Golden Age* (2014). Her research focuses on Mexican and Latina/o film culture.

Lisa Shaw is Reader in Portuguese and Brazilian Studies at the University of Liverpool. She is the author of books on *Brazilian Samba* (1999) and *Carmen Miranda* (2013). She is the co-author of *Popular Cinema in Brazil* (2004) and *Brazilian National Cinema* (2007).

Niamh Thornton is Reader in Latin American Studies at the University of Liverpool. Her books include *Revolution and Rebellion in Mexican Cinema* (2013), *International Perspectives on Chicana/o Studies: This World is My Place* (2013), and *Ghosts: Memory and Trauma in Mexican Visual Culture* (forthcoming).

Dolores Tierney is Senior Lecturer in Film Studies at the University of Sussex. She has published widely on Latin(o/a) American film, authored a monograph on *Emilio Fernández* (2007), and co-edited *Latsploitation: Exploitation Cinema and Latin America* (2009) and *The Transnational Fantasies of Guillermo del Toro* (2014).

David Wood is a film scholar based at UNAM in Mexico City. He is the co-editor of *Cine mudo latinoamericano: inicios, nación, vanguardias y transición* (2015) and the author of *El espectador pensante: el cine de Jorge Sanjinés y el Grupo Ukamau* (forthcoming).

INTRODUCTION
Troubling histories

Marvin D'Lugo, Ana M. López, and Laura Podalsky

Though film production in Latin America can trace its history back over more than a century, Latin American film studies as a serious field of intellectual and artistic inquiry is still fairly young. It has only been a little over 50 years since critics and scholars began to write about Latin American cinemas with systematic rigor (Paranaguá 2000: 11–17). Initially, many critics crafted local studies offering overviews of the types of films produced in their own country of origin in specific periods or throughout the twentieth century (DiNubila 1959; Viany 1959; Agramonte 1966; Mahieu 1966; Ayala Blanco 1968; García Riera 1969–1971, 1974; Ossa Coo 1971; Chanan 1976; Mesa 1979; Salcedo Silva 1981). By the 1980s, others began to tackle filmmaking trends in the region as a whole (Hennebelle and Gumucio Dagron 1981; Paranaguá 1984; Schnitman 1984; Burton 1986, 1990; Schumann 1987; King 1990). The latter group often utilized the radical challenges of the New Latin American Cinema as a point of departure to analyze the structure of the region's film industries within the context of larger political and economic dynamics. Leaving aside for the moment the geopolitics of these critical tendencies, it is important to note that, taken together, these efforts began to shape Latin American film studies as a new field of inquiry that, almost from the start, lensed the region's cinema from a multiplicity of cultural and critical positions.

Gradually, the new field became stabilized as scholars in some countries were able to find institutional support. In Mexico in the mid-1980s, Spanish-born historian Emilio García Riera established the CIEC through the Universidad de Guadalajara to gather together researchers dedicated to the delineation of Mexican film history. In Brazil, Fernão Ramos assembled a team of young scholars to write a definitive history of Brazilian cinema in the mid-1980s (Ramos 1987). In Argentina, through the auspices of the Universidad de Buenos Aires, Claudio España collaborated with a group of scholars to map Argentine cinema—its recent history in the aftermath of dictatorship as well as its more distant past (España 1994, 2000, 2005) (see Kriger 2014 for a more detailed account of this trajectory). Such efforts to construct comprehensive historical accounts of domestic filmmaking were perhaps only possible in places such as Mexico, Brazil, Argentina, and Cuba, where public (and some private) institutions provided the necessary backing and resources (e.g. universities, film archives, and state film institutes such as Argentina's Instituto Nacional de Cine y Artes

1

Audiovisuales [previously the Instituto Nacional de Cine, INC] and the Instituto Cubano del Arte e Industria Cinematográfricos [ICAIC]).

Outside the region, institutional support for scholarship on Latin American film emerged in various guises, including the broadening interests of established film journals and publishers, the emergence of university-level training, and the rise of professional interest groups. Starting in the 1970s, politically engaged English-language film journals such as *Jump Cut* and *Screen* began to publish articles on contemporary figures such as Glauber Rocha, Fernando Solanas, and Tomás Gutiérrez Alea, whose films, at this time, were viewed as contributing to a "tricontinental" political project. In France, the UK, Canada, and Spain, critical studies on films and national film traditions in the region began to appear in the 1980s (Hennebelle and Gumucio Dagron 1981; Chanan 1985, 2004; Barnard 1986; Paranaguá 1987, 1992a, 1992b; King 1990; Elena and Díaz López 1999, 2006), and in the 1990s the Filmoteca Española partnered with the publishing house Cátedra to underwrite a series on singular directors: Tomás Gutiérrez Alea (Evora 1996), Patricio Guzmán (Ruffinelli 2001), and Glauber Rocha (Avelar 2002). During this same period, young scholars in the US found some support within film studies programs and even in departments of Spanish and Portuguese or Romance Languages. In 1990, there was enough of a critical mass of Latino/a American film specialists to establish the Latino/a Caucus within the Society for Cinema Studies (now known as the Society for Cinema and Media Studies), the premiere professional organization in the field. A decade later, in 2002, the Latin American Studies Association (LASA) approved a Film Section.

Since that time, there has been an even greater flourishing of Latin American film scholarship—both within and outside the region. In ways analogous to what happened in the aftermath of the New Latin American Cinema, recent scholarship has been spurred on by the effervescence of filmmaking itself in countries such as Chile, Brazil, Argentina, Mexico, Bolivia, and Peru, and numerous tomes have been dedicated to the "new new" national cinemas of Latin America. Along with the increased interest of publishers and the appearance of the specialized journal *Studies in Spanish and Latin American Cinemas* (est. 2004, initially as *Studies in Hispanic Cinemas*), online platforms have proliferated in ways that have been absolutely essential to the dissemination of scholarship coming from Latin America in journals such as Mexico's *El Ojo que Piensa* (*Nueva época*, est. 2010), Brazil's *Revista Digital de Cinema Documentario* (est. 2006) and *Revista Brasileira de Estudos de Cinema e Audiovisual/REBECA* (est. 2012), Cuba's *Revista Enfoco* (est. 2007), and Argentina's *Imagofagia* (est. 2010) and *Revista Cine Documental* (est. 2010). Some of these publications have been the direct outgrowth of newer, Latin American-based professional organizations such as SEPANCINE (Mexico, est. 2005) and AsAECA (Argentina, est. 2008) that emerged alongside the older SOCINE (Brazil, est. 1996). They also benefit from the dynamism of online research networks such as RICiLa (Red de Investigadores de Cine Latinoamericano, est. 2011) and REDIC (Red de Investigadores de Cine) that have fortified exchanges between scholars living in different countries and working within a variety of institutional frameworks. Finally, blogs have offered a new format to engage with a wider public—from the single-authored *Cine cubano: La pupila insomne* (by Cuban scholar Juan Antonio García Borrero) to the multi-authored *Mediático* (edited by Dolores Tierney and Catherine Grant, with the help of Juan Ramos, through the auspices of the University of Sussex).

Against this rich scholarly backdrop, and in the immediate context of the recent 'boom' in new cinema initiatives throughout the region, *The Routledge Companion to Latin American Cinema* offers a unique, multidimensional approach to the rigorous study of film from Latin America. The volume acknowledges a range of cross-border contexts in which particular films, film-related institutions, and scholarly traditions function. Despite the challenges of providing a comprehensive map of the field (given its current dynamism; the multiple sites of production in Latin America, the US, the UK, Spain, and Germany; and the complex intellectual geneal-ogies that inform scholarship in different locales), the current scholarly effervescence demands critical reflection on the state of the field. This mapping exercise, however imperfect, serves as a useful means to acknowledge more clearly the conceptual frameworks and methodologies that have been employed to produce certain types of critical discourse (historical, formalist, intermedial, etc.). This meta-critical exercise has, in turn, a generative value, functioning as a point of departure to chart new approaches, identify unexamined or under-studied topics, and reconsider dominant critical concepts, paradigms, and categories—from the notions of realism(s) and art cinema(s), to the apparent "dividing line" between film and photography (often understood as "proto"-filmic within the context of cinema studies).

Among the many concerns of Latin American film scholarship, there are two concep-tual axes that have been particularly influential, and thus merit particular attention: a spatial-territorial axis, rooted in the geopolitical identity of Latin American cinema; and a temporal axis, involving questions of periodization and historicity. The spatial-territorial axis has been debated in at least two ways: (i) in arguments about the medium's national and/or transnational tendencies that recognize cinema as local(ized) practice and/or as an art and industry that connects across broader territories; and (ii) in (often unstated) claims about the scope and nature of the very category of "Latin American cinema" made by multiple social agents, from festival organizers and scholars to filmmakers. Long left to the side in such debates is how any attempt to link film with a particular territory involves assumptions about audiences. To whom are films directed and who actually sees them? And how do films' modes of address encourage the formation of imagined communities, whether class-based, nation-based, or transnational?

The second conceptual axis is temporal, involving questions of periodization and histo-ricity. While generally agreeing that Latin American film history can be divided into several semi-discrete periods (e.g. the silent period, transition to sound, New Latin American Cinema of the 1960s), scholars have held ongoing debates about the reach of given eras (e.g. debates in the 1980s about whether or not the New Latin American Cinema was over). More recently, some film historians and critics have begun to question whether the standard periodization adequately reflects the complexity of film culture or merely reduces film history to successive modes of production and stylistic changes. This line of thought also encourages us to pursue a more thorough (re)conceptualization of the *timeliness* of Latin American film. On the one hand, how should we understand its relationship to the histori-cal context from which it emerges and to which it responds (as representational system, as industrial form, as technology)? On the other, how does (and has) film contribute(d) to temporal notions of past, present, and future—in particular to the characterization of Latin America or certain nations as modern? As the volume's contributors address these concep-tual axes in ways that are implicit and explicit, it will be useful to provide a fuller overview of each of them here in the Introduction.

The spatio-temporal axis of Latin American film scholarship

National cinema/cinema as transnational

Some critical approaches have favored one side or the other of the national/transna-tional dyad. As suggested earlier, nation-based approaches dominated much of the early critical discussion of film in the region, and often continue to do so for a variety of reasons. For some scholars, this approach offers what appears to be a self-evident explanation of how film production and reception are shaped around notions of (a unified) national culture. That film festivals identify a film's nation of production often reinforces this scholarly perspective and disseminates it among wider publics. Publications on film auteurs—Emilio Fernández, Leopoldo Torre Nilsson, Glauber Rocha, Tomás Gutiérrez Alea, Patricio Guzmán, María Luisa Bemberg—that align the filmmaker with the national context of his or her production provide further buttressing. Other scholars recognize the national as a contentious identity claim, and yet nonetheless call for its continued utility as a critical category. For those working on contemporary "new" cinemas in Latin America (Poblete, Page, Sánchez Prado), the national optic is the only one to adequately acknowledge the importance of state initiatives to the relative health of given domestic industries and/or the role of domestic audiences in sustaining local domestic production of commercial fare (comedies, romantic comedies, horror films).

This "nation-centric" approach has been challenged by the view of other scholars that Latin American film production has been involved in transborder, cross-cultural dynamics. In the 1980s, some studies focused on the emergence of an oppositional cinematic practice, which had reached a high degree of visibility through New Latin American Cinema of the 1960s and 1970s (Burton 1986, 1990; Pick 1993). Such political and ideological projects stressed the unity of regional liberation movements, and the critical literature echoed the filmmakers' perspective by focusing on the films' shared sociopolitical goals, collective modes of production, and aesthetic tendencies (e.g. the influence of Italian neorealism, the promotion of active spectatorship through formal experimentation). More recently, scholars have developed this optic in new directions by suggesting that Latin American cinemas in all eras have been constituted by transnational linkages on all levels—from financing arrangements such as co-production, to the transnational circulation of narrative conventions, to the professional trajectory of particular directors, cinematographers, and actors (who worked in several domestic industries), to the cross-border business of distribution and marketing of films.

At first glance, these two critical tendencies (cinema as national or transnational) may appear to delineate two distinct ways of looking at film. Rather than encouraging readers to choose a side, this volume promotes an awareness of how national/transnational dynamics embedded within film (as art form, as commercial product, as sociopolitical project, as industry, as social practice) informs a range of political, artistic, social, and commercial activities. Several of the "cluster chapters" in which collaborators address a common topic from the perspective of different countries (e.g. screen culture in Chapter 5; stardom in Chapter 11; community filmmaking in Chapter 14; digital technologies in Chapter 24) enable advanced students and scholars to engage in comparative and contrastive views of developments across the region in terms that duly appreciate the continuities and discontinuities that coexist in the region's cinema. At the same time, some single-author chapters (e.g. on cosmopolitan nationalism in Chapter 9; radical ruptures in Chapter 12; transnational financing networks in Chapter 17; and film festivals in Chapter 18) and some cluster chapters (e.g. hybridization between film and photography in Chapter 20) allow readers to trace how scalar shifts between local/provincial, national, and transnational influences and imperatives have shaped industrial dynamics, filmmaking practices, and habits of spectatorship throughout Latin America from the silent period to the present.

What do we mean when we speak of Latin American cinema?

For defenders of the transnational view, claims about the cross-border nature of film from the region go to the heart of the argument for the continuity and coherence of Latin American cinema as a discrete body of works and criticism. An often-unexamined proposition (subtending course offerings, syllabi, conference papers, and book titles), the category itself merits greater attention—among other things, by raising a number of questions about what it does and does not include. How, for instance, does Portuguese-speaking Brazilian cinema, with a cultural heritage distinct from that of Spanish America "fit" into the view of Latin America? Until recent decades, there has been little effort by historians of Spanish-speaking Latin America to consider Brazilian cinema. Similarly, until the rise of political cinema of the 1960s, Brazilian cinema seldom saw itself within the broad Latin American context (Paranaguá 2000: 10). What Stephanie Dennison euphemistically terms "Luso-exceptionalism" (Dennison 2013: 9–14) raises fundamental questions about the field that need to be addressed at the outset. And what about films from Haiti or Trinidad and Tobago? Despite linguistic differences, these francophone and anglophone cinemas often comment on sociocultural and political dynamics that result from a shared history of European colonialism (involving the massive forced immigration of African peoples), as experienced in the Caribbean's "repeating islands" (Benítez Rojo 1989). Beyond the issue of which countries' filmic traditions should be included under the umbrella of "Latin American cinema/s," it is also vital to recognize subnational dynamics. As noted in Chapter 14 (on community-based practices), in recent decades an increasing number of films are being made by indigenous filmmakers/collectives and/or in indigenous languages. What are the advantages and disadvantages of classifying (and perhaps subsuming) these efforts into the category of "Latin American film"? Rather than settling on or promoting a singular definition of "Latin American cinema/s," it will be useful to recognize how the category itself is rooted in various institutions, involving the practices of film festivals and the projects of filmmakers and critics, among other things.

The festival "packaging" and positioning of films from Latin America tells us much about the recent history of global perspectives on Latin American cinema. For the organizers of the Category A film festivals such as Cannes, Latin American cinema has largely been part of a broader artistic category that aligns auteurs with political thematics—a topic taken up in different ways by Juan Poblete in Chapter 1, Nilo Couret in Chapter 16, and Tamara L. Falicov in Chapter 18. As many of these authors note, this tendency goes back several decades. The Quinzaine des Réalisateurs/Directors' Fortnight became formalized as part of the Cannes' competitive cycles in the aftermath of the 1968 upheavals. One of the first films to receive broad accolades at that event was the 1971 screening of Paul Leduc's *Reed, México insurgente* (*Reed: Insurgent Mexico*) about the famous U.S. journalist's role in the Mexican Revolution. Over the years, other Latin American films, including Pablo Larraín's recent *Neruda* (2016), have achieved recognition at this sidebar. Other Category A European festivals, most conspicuously Berlin, have highlighted political films from Latin America as part of their general fare, thereby solidifying the notion that films from the region come with a necessary political charge, yet seldom address the complex social or political contexts out of which those "political" films have arisen.

For their part, film festivals in Spain do not always recognize "Latin American film" as a distinct category. Rather, several have promoted a notion of a borderless community that includes Spain and Portugal alongside Spanish- and Portuguese-speaking America. This is evident in the naming of the annual festival held in the Spanish port city of Huelva, near where Columbus set sail, the Festival de Cine Iberoamericano. According to some, the incorporation of films from Latin America into that more capacious classification often downplays divergent multilingual and multicultural aspects of cinema from the region in ways that are immensely problematic. Paulo Antonio Paranaguá calls out the San Sebastián Film Festival for labeling its Latin American film cycles "Made in Spanish." He sees the exclusion of Portuguese-speaking Brazilian cinema as symptomatic of the sloppy intellectual practices that often accompany the promotion of films from the region in venues outside of it, or worse yet as a reflection of a profound cultural myopia about the underlying nature of Latin American film.

In Latin America itself, there has been an important evolution in thinking about the definition as well as the place of Latin American film. Early efforts to not isolate Latin American films as different or "other" led to the wide use of "*internacional*" to describe the remit of festivals at Mar de Plata. This followed the pattern of festivals in Europe and Asia that were established in the 1950s. The term "international" appeared to normalize films from the region as one other source of cinema around the globe. The Havana Film Festival, founded in 1979, is the first to insist on the historical specificity of New Latin American Cinema (NLAC) with its general rubric of *Festival del Nuevo Cine Latinoamericano*. Other festivals flirted with the category of the "iberoamericano" in certain periods; Guadalajara's Festival de Cine Mexicano e Iberoamericano now calls itself Festival Internacional de Cine de Guadalajara (FICG). Others eschew these issues in their titles while still implicitly staking a territorial claim. Founded in the mid-2000s, the Trinidad and Tobago Film Festival began as an effort to showcase English-language films made on the islands, but quickly incorporated films made elsewhere, paying particular attention to those made in the Spanish- and Portuguese-speaking countries in the larger region. All of these branding and programming strategies need to be understood historically as ways to denote "our" cinema. As such, they reflect the deeper effort to establish the identification between communities in the region with the global cinema community as constituted through the international film festival circuit. As Falicov notes in Chapter 18, the networks linking together Latin American-based festivals with those elsewhere have become much more complex since the early 2000s.

Of course, film festivals are not the only sites in which Latin American cinema has been demarcated in particular ways. In addition to (certain) festival programmers, there are other stakeholders that wish to hold it up as a unique category—most notably filmmakers and scholars. In her 1993 book *The New Latin American Cinema: A Continental Project*, Zuzana Pick argued for the extended reach of the politically militant, aesthetically experimental project of the 1960s and 1970s into the 1980s by identifying in the latter works a shared commitment to sociopolitical engagement—including the questioning of patriarchal norms and dominant racializing tactics by contemporaneous female directors. Only a few years later, in an impassioned foreword to one anthology on Latin American cinema, Cuban critic Ambrosio Fornet rejected the hegemony of national cinemas in favor of a regional conception: "Latin American cinema, from its origins, has been multinational and transcultural" (Fornet 1997: xvii). In making such a claim, Fornet formulates a model that downplays the significance of national cinema, to the point of seeing it as historically irrelevant. Echoing the claims of NLAC directors as well as the earlier Bolivarian dream of "continental" liberation, Pick and Fornet make a deeply rooted political-historical argument for a borderless South American cinema congruent with the notion of a borderless Latin American transnation.

Such scholarly arguments often dovetail with institutional dynamics within universities and film schools. In the US, film studies programs may include a "Latin American

Film" course, as a parallel offering to others on "Asian Film" or "European Film," and occasionally a course on a single "national" cinema (e.g. "Mexican Cinema"). For their part, Departments of Spanish and Portuguese (or Foreign or Modern Languages) often began by teaching a course on film that included works from both Spain and Spanish America. Since the late 1990s, the expansive appeal of such courses has encouraged curricular growth. Nowadays, many of those departments have individual course numbers dedicated to Latin American Film, Spanish (Peninsular) Film, and Latino/a Film, and perhaps to Lusophone Film and/or Brazilian Film and Portuguese Film. The proliferation of such courses certainly responds to "internal" imperatives—namely, the search for increased enrollments in "languages and cultures" departments. At the same time, this trend also has the effect of influencing U.S. and U.K. publishing companies that are looking to sell books to "captive" academic markets, and, by (indirect) extension, the work of academics who hope to publish their scholarly monographs. Without suggesting any simple, deterministic feedback loop, the recognition of such dynamics helps us to acknowledge the institutional parameters that help to shape territorialized conceptualizations of cinema in the Spanish and Lusophone worlds.

What do we mean when we talk about Latin American film audiences?

In considering the evolving dynamics of Latin American cinema studies, it is impossible not to take into account the question of audience. Until recently, most studies identified a simple distinction between popular cinema directed at mainstream or mass audiences, and an art cinema targeting (a smaller sector of) cultural elites. Whereas the former has been associated with commercial cinema made by private companies seeking maximum financial returns (whether in the 1940s or the 1990s) from domestic (or "national") audiences (and perhaps in foreign markets), the latter often has been tied to films made by individuals or small groups looking for personal expression and/or artistic recognition (often seen as emerging in the late 1950s as a notable tendency) from cultural elites at home, and particularly abroad.

In marking this distinction, scholars frequently have deduced the implicit audience through the analysis of the films themselves (e.g. arguing that the use of formulaic, easily understood plots and well-known performers in the roles of everyday people appealed to the "masses"). More specifically, critics have suggested that films deployed musical forms, historical references, timely wordplay linked to current events, and particular accents to call on (and appeal to) the cultural and linguistic competencies of audiences tied to specific territories and geo-cultural formations. In other words, this line of thought characterized domestic commercial production as (primarily) targeting the domestic market and a somewhat homogenous "national" audience composed of both working- and middle-class people. Conversely, scholars have characterized art films as those works that are less reliant on widely shared competencies, and more dependent on tightly circumscribed knowledge and tastes that often *exceed* the national (whether elite visual culture traditions such as painting, or foreign films from *particular* countries such as Italy and France). Such demarcations between popular and art cinema often confirm arguments about films' *implicit* audience through discussion of films' circulation in particular exhibition circuits—i.e. within a wide national circuit (in rural and urban areas, in the city center as well as neighborhood theaters), or within a reduced national-urban circuit and a reduced international (i.e. European) circuit, particularly after the rise of European film festivals in the post-World War II period.

Recently, scholars have begun to question this binary breakdown of audiences (and films). This has occurred, in part, through methodological innovation. Instead of utilizing textual analysis to extrapolate about implicit audiences, film historians have studied specific theaters, exhibition circuits, and alternative screening facilities and practices. In their analysis of off-screen culture in Brazil, Mexico, and Colombia during three crucial decades (Chapter 5), Maite Conde, Laura Isabel Serna, and María Fernanda Arias Osorio look to the vast array of cultural practices that surround and inform filmgoing, from fan magazines and popular fashion, to the social meaning of the architecture of film theaters, to the political and aesthetic interventions made by film clubs. Through textured accounts, the authors reveal how film culture has provided a nodal point for social encounters of differential publics, divided by gender, class, and educational norms. Their essay encourages us to recognize multiple audiences within any given country and to understand not only how films address audiences, but also how audiences *practice* filmgoing.

Other scholars have reconsidered textual evidence to argue against the notion that films interpellate spectators in singular or univocal ways—as *either* "national" *or* cosmopolitan subjects. In Chapter 9, Adrián Pérez Melgosa suggests that, from the earliest sound films, filmmakers and producers in Argentina, Brazil, Chile, and Mexico eschewed formulations that would limit the appeal of films. Given their own experiences as immigrants or having worked abroad, these cultural producers constructed films to appeal to spectators as cosmopolitan nationals (e.g. at home listening to tango, while also keeping up to date with the latest consumer trends being imported from abroad). In Chapter 10, Gerard Dapena offers a corollary argument about the doubled or layered mode of address of genre films. He reminds us that by drawing on and reformulating widely recognized narrative formulas, for many decades Latin American filmmakers have addressed their films to audiences at home, *while at the same time* seeking commercial success with audiences abroad.

The delineation of the multiple audiences of Latin American cinema also becomes more complex as we trace intermedial connections—beginning with film's interfaces with the record industry and radio in the 1930s, then with television after the 1960s, and finally with the rise of digital technologies at the end of the twentieth century. According to Marvin D'Lugo, film's early interweavings with the record industry and radio allowed for the circulation of musical forms beyond national borders, the emergence of a transnational community across the region, and the box-office success of Carlos Gardel films and *Allá en el Rancho Grande* (*Over at the Big Ranch*, Fernando de Fuentes, 1936) in multiple countries (D'Lugo 2010). As he notes in Chapter 22, these dynamics take on a particular force after the 1950s, given a number of material changes, including rapid urbanization and the establishment of a festival circuit, that reconfigure and diversify audiences. It is from that decade forward that more films—from *Víctimas del pecado* (*Victims of Sin*, Emilio Fernández, 1951) to *Tangos el exilio de Gardel* (*Tangos: The Exile of Gardel*, Fernando Solanas, 1985) and *Suite Habana* (Fernando Perez, 2003)—begin to recognize their own inclusion of musical forms from diverse origins via reflexive moments. Josetxo Cerdán and Miguel Fernández Labayen (Chapter 23) offer a slightly different take on the constitution of audiences by different media. In analyzing film's relationship with television, they argue that the latter managed something that the former never could: the consolidation of a national imaginary ("an idea of nation") through shared viewing habits of domestic publics.

Other scholars recognize in the more recent dissemination of digital technologies not only the emergence of new producers of audiovisual materials (Schiwy et al. in Chapter 14; Mariana Lacunza in Chapter 24), but also new online exhibition platforms and new audiences. As noted by Niamh Thornton in Chapter 24, companies such as Netflix, MUBI and

Amazon have made it possible for films made in Latin America to reach audiences outside the region—including those who would not tend to seek out such films in their local theaters. How those international companies classify such films (as well as others made outside the region) as "Argentine," "Chilean," or "Mexican" points to the need for further study of contemporary industrial dynamics that target niche audiences in both domestic markets as well as in multiple foreign countries.

Timelines, timeliness, and histor(icit)y

The other conceptual axis that has helped to orient the study of Latin American film in fundamental ways relates to historiographical tendencies as well as to questions of history and temporality. On the most direct level, film history is an extremely important subfield— particularly in Latin American universities and institutions where scholars have mined film industry journals, fan magazines, newspapers, state regulations, and other primary sources to write rich, detailed accounts of the practices of specific production companies, filmmaking trends, the professional trajectories of particular filmmakers, changing film laws, and exhibition trends (of both domestic and imported films), among other things. For example, we can point to the work of Aurelio de los Reyes and Angel Miquel in Mexico, Ricardo Bedoya (1992) in Peru, Hernando Martínez Pardo (1978) in Colombia, and Arturo Agramonte and Luciano Castillo in Cuba (Agramonte 1966; Agramonte and Castillo 2011–2016).

While quite rich on many levels, film histories traditionally have tended to favor the delineation of domestic production and the identification of aesthetic trends in particular national contexts over other potential topics. In response, as noted above, younger researchers have looked to broaden the scope of Latin American film histories by examining, among other things, the history of theaters (Serna, Chapter 5), reception practices (Conde and Arias Osorio, Chapter 5), and intermedial connections with the illustrated press and formal trends in photography (Navitski, Chapter 2; Cuarterolo, Chapter 19).

Another area ripe for interrogation is the standard periodization of Latin American film history in four major horizons: the silent era (1896–1920s), the industrial era (1930s–1950s), the New Latin American Cinema (late 1950s–1970s), and the contemporary era (1980s to the present). As noted by Laura Podalsky (Chapter 4), scholars have tended to "break . . . down Latin American cinema into successive historical periods separated by watershed moments of aesthetic and/or industrial rupture" measured in terms of technological innovations (e.g. sound, digital), aesthetic tendencies, modes of production (studio vs. independent, collective projects), and/or a relationship with the state. Such criteria also allow for subdivisions within those four major periods. For example, whereas the 1980s marked the rise/return of more conventional narratives (including genres) and less experimental aesthetics in many countries (i.e. a break from the NLAC), many critics point to the implementation of new film laws and new financing arrangements (stimulating film production levels and wider distribution) in the mid-1990s or early 2000s as the key to the rise of new (new) cinemas in Brazil, Argentina, and Mexico (Johnson 2000, 2006: Alvaray 2008; Page 2009; Rêgo 2011; MacLaird 2013; Sánchez Prado 2014).

Within this standard periodization, the New Latin American Cinema often has been singled out as initiating particularly profound changes. While generally agreeing with that perspective, several authors within this volume call for a more nuanced understanding of the period. In Chapter 12, Mariano Mestman insists on the importance of recognizing the complex and diverse forms of experimentation, along with the subnational and

9

regional networks that emerged at this time. In Chapter 13, Masha Salazkina promotes a more intricate understanding of the theoretical foundations of the New Latin American Cinema, by tracing circuits of influences—from post-revolutionary Soviet filmmakers and theorists, to intellectual debates within post-World War II Italy, to post-revolutionary Cuban filmmakers. Mestman and Salazkina's extensive historical research complicates existing scholarship that perhaps has underrepresented the tensions between different cultural producers within this period and offered an overly streamlined aesthetic genealogy from Soviet montage and Italian neorealism (characterized as monolithic tendencies) to the New Latin American Cinema.

Silvana Flores and Gerard Dapena complicate our understanding of the NLAC by, respectively, examining intermedial connections and placing it within a larger film industry context. In Chapter 20, Flores contributes to the rethinking of this era by tracing linkages between film and photography in Argentina, Chile, and Bolivia. She reveals how filmmakers incorporated archival photographs to freeze, momentarily, the flow of the present, and to utilize this re-presencing of past injustices to further animate the call for contemporary change. For his part, Dapena (Chapter 10) recalls that despite the NLAC's explicit rejection of film genres, several directors overtly toyed with the western and the *chanchada*, as well as with adventure and action films. Moreover, the overarching characterization of the late 1950s–1970s as the era of politicized filmmaking frequently overlooks the substantive commercial output during those same decades, from youth films, to crime thrillers and *sexy-comedias*.

Other contributors rethink the continuities or analogies between the 1960s–1970s and later periods. In Chapter 7, María Luisa Ortega interrogates the category of the *film-ensayo* or essay-film, arguing for a more expansive definition that includes not only widely recognized politically militant films such as *La hora de los hornos* (*The Hour of the Furnaces*, Cine Liberación, 1966–1968), but also lesser-known works such as like *Carlos, Cine-retrato de un caminante* (Mario Handler, 1965) and *Por la vuelta* (Cristian Pauls, 2002). In so doing, she identifies potential commonalities between the New Latin American Cinema and contemporary nonfiction from the 2000s, in terms of a shared interest in the personal and intimate (within larger socioeconomic structures) (i.e. two periods that are often cast as quite distinct). Her essay, along with that of Marvin D'Lugo (Chapter 22), suggests that the influential experiments that took place in the 1960s extended beyond the grossly political. In his essay, D'Lugo identifies another, less recognized innovation of the New Latin American Cinema—namely, the sound experiments that facilitated the rise of a new aural imaginary that transcended national borders.

Such efforts to complicate our understanding of particular periods and the relationship between them acknowledge the broad implications of periodization itself for certain subfields. Scholars often utilize those temporal breakdowns as points of departure to study topics ranging from the changing representation of women to the rise and fall or particular genres/modes. For example, film critics have compared "classic" melodramas (e.g. *Flor silvestre* [*Wild Flower*, Emilio Fernández, 1943] or *Madreselva* [*Honeysuckle*, Luis César Amadori, 1938]) from the "industrial era" in the 1940s to the mode's redeployment in the contemporary period (*Camila* [María Luisa Bemberg, 1984], *Como agua para chocolate* [*Like Water for Chocolate*, Alfonso Arau, 1992]) to evaluate how the latter relate to a new generation of filmmakers (including women directors such as Maria Luisa Bemberg) or new sociocultural conditions. Often interested in delineating the marked differences between the two periods, such assessments tend to trace narratives of progress by asserting, for instance, that the presence of women directors behind the camera makes possible a more complex, nuanced representation of female subjectivity located within larger repressive social and political structures. Or that the new sociopolitical position of women in the 1980s and 1990s, and the accompanying shifts in expectations about gender roles, demanded/determined the increasing depiction of women as social agents—even in historical films. This scholarly tendency to look for change and to trace narratives of progress (e.g. the "improved" representation of female characters in more recent films) is not necessarily wrong. It does, however, presuppose a faith in a particular model of historical change that may lead to overlooking (or under-studying) elements of Latin American film that do not readily fit that paradigm—in this case, the continued cultural legibility today of the standard models of female representation that circulated in the 1940s and 1950s.

Recognizing this, several contributors to this volume offer alternate temporal frameworks that do not reify rupture and innovation. Some scholars working outside of the subfield of film history (per se) challenge the identification of particular (documentary) forms such as the essay-film or particular aesthetic modes such as realism with singular eras—in this case, with the New Latin American Cinema—by offering compelling accounts of their deployment in other periods (Ortega, Chapter 7; Aguilera Skvirsky, Chapter 8). For her part, film historian Andrea Cuarterolo (Chapter 19) contests periodizing schemes that overestimate a film's ability to break with established formal tendencies present in preexisting visual technologies and traditions from photography to theater and painting. In Chapter 21, Ana M. López similarly questions suppositions about any univocal relationship between radio and film, arguing that the two media "grew up" together as radio became consolidated as a culture industry much later than previously believed. In contrast to previous scholarship that traced how film simply appropriated performers and formulas associated with radio, López insists on charting the intersections and rivalries between the two media as they developed from the 1930s to the 1940s. For her part, Laura Podalsky (Chapter 4) argues for a more thorough accounting of the temporal undergirding of periodization itself "because it *still* influences how Latin American cinemas are positioned in relation to filmmaking traditions elsewhere"—often gauging the fluctuations/ temporalities in that region in terms of Hollywood-based or Eurocentric chronologies (e.g. Deleuzian approaches).

Other scholars have sought more complicated models for understanding the "timeliness" of Latin American film—in other words, how it forms part of and responds to larger sociopolitical and economic dynamics and structures within given historical periods (as a system of representation, as an evolving set of technologies, as a commercial product). For example, several recent studies of historical films have jettisoned any simplistic notion of progress. Rather than suggesting that recent films about a particular moment (e.g. the *Proceso de Reorganización Nacional*, 1976–1983) have become more complex (in line with presumably more nuanced scholarly work on the period by professional historians), scholars such as Cuarterolo and Verónica Garibotto have traced how sequential depictions of the Argentine dictatorship resonate with the dominant public discourses as well as the horizons of expectations within given periods (Cuarterolo 2011; Garibotto 2012). In terms of the latter, Garibotto argues that we must acknowledge how many such films address themselves to a particular generation of film-goers with a de/limited understanding of the past; in soliciting a given market sector, filmmakers make assumptions about the implicit audience's knowledge (and lack of knowledge) about the past, which in turn influences how the film depicts that historical moment. The above-mentioned studies encourage us to eschew direct comparison of the representational conventions of individual films within different historical periods in favor of multi-tiered studies that place formal analysis alongside considerations about mode of address and the changing configuration of audiences and their cultural competencies. This work also suggests the utility of engaging in a more sustained way with the recent reflections of Latin American historians about historiographical trends.

Even as some scholars rethink the historical valences of film's re-presentational politics, others encourage us to reconsider the medium's role in *producing* space and place—including the very notion of "Latin America" itself— during particular moments in the twentieth and twenty-first centuries. In this volume, Jens Andermann (Chapter 15) examines how contemporary films from Argentina, Brazil, and Chile deploy framing and editing in innovative ways in order to trouble how audiences locate themselves in relation to the profilmic. He argues that the films' reflexive questions about the delineation of screen space demonstrate a meta-critical sensibility that examines the adequacy of imagining "Latin America" as singular and particular in a globalized era. Geoffrey Kantaris's Chapter 6 takes a more diachronic view, analyzing film as a commodity form in three different historical horizons (1920s, 1950s, 2010s). Rather than characterizing the films as part of a cohesive timeline within a given territory (Latin America), he examines how particular films have helped to interrogate the socio-spatial and economic configurations that emerged during given periods, as well as the underlying claims about modernity and about Latin America as modern. Both Andermann's and Kantaris's contributions suggest that considerations of space/place "in" Latin America cinema always already involve considerations of Latin America as a spatial *and temporal* category.

Strategies for navigating this volume

In light of the complex dynamics that have shaped critical discourses about Latin American cinema, we have sought to embody in the organization of this volume, and in the individual sections and chapters, the importance of approaching the topic in ways that reflect and embody the multifaceted, transnational, transdisciplinary, and transhistorical nature of the evolution of film industry and culture in the region. The four parts—"Historiographies," "Interrogating Critical Paradigms," "Business Practices," and "Intermedialities"—are designed to reflect on questions of art and industry; the shifting positioning of Latin American film and its multiple audiences; the commercial underpinnings that have enabled cinema to flourish in the region; evolving notions of audiences that take into account geopolitical, class, and cultural diversity; and, finally, the range of cross-media, cross-disciplinary affinities that underpin the more obvious cross-border tendencies of Latin American film.

The anthology seeks to provide a multiple range of views. Not only does this principle guide the variety of perspectives presented in each of the volume's four sections, but also in the inclusion of multi-authored chapters. The latter treat topics that demanded a multi-perspectival approach and the collaboration of several scholars specializing in different geographic, historical, and/or cultural dimensions of the same subject matter. Each of these cluster chapters depended upon an ongoing exchange among the various authors over a period of many months; those generative encounters allowed the co-authors to hammer out a shared conceptual framework and to utilize the interventions of their colleagues to further hone their individual contributions.

Finally, in an effort to chart the multiple touchpoints linking together different chapters, we have included an editors' introduction in each. Aside from recognizing how a given chapter takes up issues and topics discussed elsewhere in the volume, our initial remarks attempt to map the field in ways that develop and deepen the remarks in this general introduction. Our comments also sketch out some of the broader implications of the arguments in a given chapter, paying particular attention to pointing to future lines of inquiry. While we recognize that there were many additional topics and cases that could have been included in the anthology (through the work of many other fine scholars), our goal has never been total coverage. Rather, we hope the anthology will serve as a useful overview of the state of the field of Latin American film studies and a stimulus for further study.

References

Agramonte, A. (1966) *Cronología del cine cubano*. Havana: ICAIC.
—— and Castillo, L. (2011–2016) *Cronología del cine cubano*, vols. 1–4. Havana: ICAIC.
Alvaray, L. (2008) "National, Regional, and Global: New Waves of Latin American Cinema." *Cinema Journal*, 47(3): 48–65.
Avelar, J.C. (2002) *Glauber Rocha*. Madrid: Cátedra/Filmoteca Española.
Ayala Blanco, J. (1968) *La Aventura del cine mexicano, 1931–67*. Mexico City: Era.
Barnard, T. (1986) *Argentine Cinema*. Toronto: Nightwood Editions.
Bedoya, R. (1992) *100 años de cine en el Perú: una historia crítica*. Lima: Universidad de Lima/Instituto de Cooperación Iberoamericana.
Benítez Rojo, A. (1989) *La isla que se repite: el Caribe y la perspectiva posmoderna*. Hanover, NH: Ediciones del Norte.
Burton, J. (1986) *Cinema and Social Change in Latin America: Conversations with Filmmakers*. Austin, TX: University of Texas Press.
—— (1990) *The Social Documentary in Latin America*. Pittsburgh, PA: University of Pittsburgh Press.
Chanan, M. (1976) *Chilean Cinema*. London: BFI.
—— (1985) *The Cuban Image: Cinema and Cultural Politics in Cuba*. London: BFI.
—— (2004) *Cuban Cinema*. Minneapolis, MN: University of Minnesota Press.
Cuarterolo, A. (2011) "La memoria en tres tiempos. Revisiones de la última dictadura en la ficción industrializada de los inicios de la democracia (1983–1989)." In A.L. Lusnich and P. Piedras (eds.), *Una historia del cine político y social en Argentina (1969–2009)*. Buenos Aires: Nueva Librería, pp. 339–363.
D'Lugo, M. (2010) "Aural Identity, Genealogies of Sound Technologies, and Hispanic Transnationality on Screen." In N. Ďurovičová and K. Newman (eds.), *World Cinemas, Transnational Perspectives*. New York: Routledge, pp. 160–185.
Dennison. S. (2013) *Contemporary Hispanic Cinema: Interrogating the Transnational in Spanish and Latin American Film*. London: Tamesis.
DiNubila, D. (1959) *Historia del cine argentino*, vols. 1–2. Buenos Aires: Cruz de Malta.
Elena, A. and Díaz López, M. (1999) *Tierra en trance: el cine latinoamericano en 100 películas*. Madrid: Alianza.
—— (2006) *The Cinema of Latin America*. London/New York: Wallflower.
España, C. (ed.) (1994) *Cine argentino en democracia, 1983–1993*. Buenos Aires: Fondo Nacional de las Artes.
—— (ed.) (2000) *Cine argentino: industria y clasicismo, 1933–1956*. Buenos Aires: Fondo Nacional de las Artes.
—— (ed.) (2005) *Cine argentino: modernidad y vanguardia 1957/1983*, vols. 1–2. Buenos Aires: Fondo Nacional de las Artes.
Evora, J.A. (1996) *Tomás Gutiérrez Alea*. Madrid: Cátedra/Filmoteca Española.
Fornet, A. (1997) "Foreword." In A.M. Stock (ed.), *Framing Latin American Cinema: Contemporary Critical Perspectives*. Minneapolis, MN/London: University of Minnesota Press, pp. ix–xx.

García Riera, E. (1969–1971) *Historia documental del cine mexicano*, vols. 1–8. Mexico City: Era.

—— (1974) *El cine y su público*. Mexico City: Fondo de Cultura Económica.

Garibotto, V. (2012) "Iconic Fictions: Narrating Recent Argentine History in Post-2000 Second-Generation Films." *Studies in Hispanic Cinemas*, 8(2): 175–187.

Hennebelle, G. and Gumucio Dagron, A. (1981) *Les Cinémas de l'Amérique Latine*. Paris: L'Herminier.

Johnson, R. (2000) "Departing from *Central Station*: Notes on the Reemergence of Brazilian Cinema." *The Brazil e-Journal*. Available at: www.brasilemb.org/br_ejournal/cinebras.htm (accessed September 28, 2000).

—— (2006) "Post-*Cinema Novo* Brazilian Cinema." In L. Badley, R. Barton Palmer, and S.J. Schneider (eds.), *Traditions in World Cinema*. New Brunswick, NJ: Rutgers University Press, pp. 117–129.

King, J. (1990) *Magical Reels: A History of Cinema in Latin America*. London/New York: Verso.

Kriger, C. (2014) "Estudios sobre cine clásico en Argentina: De la perspectiva nacional a la comparada." *AdVersuS: Revista de Semiótica*, 26: 133–150.

MacLaird, M. (2013) *Aesthetics and Politics in the Mexican Film Industry*. New York: Palgrave Macmillan.

Mahieu, J.A. (1966) *Breve historia del cine argentino*. Buenos Aires: EUDEBA.

Martínez Pardo, H. (1978) *La historia del cine colombiano*. Bogotá: Librería y Editorial América Latina.

Mesa, C. (ed.) (1979) *Cine boliviano: del realizador al crítico*. La Paz: Gisbert.

Ossa Coo, C. (1971) *Historia del cine chileno*. Santiago: Quimantú.

Page, J. (2009) *Crisis and Capitalism in Contemporary Argentine Cinema*. Durham, NC: Duke University Press.

Paranaguá, P.A. (1984) *O cinema na América Latina: longe de Deus e perto de Hollywood*. Porto Alegre, Rio Grande do Sul: L&PM.

—— (ed.) (1987) *Le Cinéma brésilien*. Paris: Centre Georges Pompidou.

—— (ed.) (1992a) *Le Cinéma cubain*. Paris: Centre Georges Pompidou.

—— (ed.) (1992b) *Le Cinéma mexicain*. Paris: Centre Georges Pompidou.

—— (2000) "Entre modernismo y modernidad." *Archivos de la Filmoteca*, 36 (October): 4–17.

Pick, Z. (1993) *The New Latin American Cinema: A Continental Project*. Austin, TX: University of Texas Press.

Ramos, F. (1987) *História do Cinema Brasileiro*. São Paulo: Art Editora.

Rêgo, C. (2011) "The Fall and Rise of Brazilian Cinema." In C. Rêgo and C. Rocha (eds.), *New Trends in Argentine and Brazilian Cinema*. Bristol: Intellect, pp. 35–49.

Ruffinelli, J. (2001) *Patricio Guzmán*. Madrid: Cátedra/Filmoteca Española.

Salcedo Silva, H. (1981) *Crónicas del cine colombiano (1897–1950)*. Bogota: Carlos Valencia Editores.

Sánchez Prado, I. (2014) *Screening Neoliberalism: Transforming Mexican Cinema, 1988–2012*. Nashville, TN: Vanderbilt University Press.

Schnitmann, J. (1984) *Film Industries in Latin America: Development and Dependency*. Norwood, NJ: Ablex.

Schumann, P. (1987) *Historia del cine latinoamericano*. Buenos Aires: Legasa.

Viany, A. (1959) *Introducão ao cinema brasileiro*. Rio de Janeiro: Instituo Nacional do Livro.

PART I

Historiographies

1

NATIONAL CINEMA

Juan Poblete

Editors' introduction

National cinema has been a defining concept for film criticism, frequently determining the scope of given studies. As noted in the introduction to this volume, the
earliest monographs aimed to delineate the historical development of films made
within given countries, and since that period there have been numerous books on
Mexican cinema, Bolivian cinema, Cuban cinema, etc. Yet, starting in the late 1980s,
numerous theorists began to question the underlying (and often unacknowledged)
parameters that have been used to delineate the category itself (Higson 1989, 2006;
Crofts 2006). Does national cinema refer to *all* films made within specific countries,
or does it refer *primarily* to those films that uphold a (given) notion of national identity? Could the term refer to something other than domestic productions?

In a chapter that resonates with the contributions of other authors in this volume,
Juan Poblete begins by examining the larger geopolitical dynamics and scholarly tendencies (both within and outside of Latin America) that have underwritten existing
conceptualizations of "national cinema" before turning to an examination of contemporary Chilean cinema. Anticipating Niamh Thornton's questioning of national
categories on online servers such as Netflix in Chapter 24, Poblete recognizes the
precariousness of any rigid definition of national cinema. At the same time, like the
co-authors of Chapter 3, he argues for the category's ongoing viability. Yet, whereas
Lisa Shaw, Luis Duno-Gottberg, Joanna Page, and Ignacio M. Sánchez Prado address
the topic by offering a historical overview of the different social agents (e.g. filmmakers, government officials) who have staked a claim to the category of national cinema,
Poblete creates a four-pronged model for identifying different types or forms of national
cinema. This framework illuminates the importance of rethinking "national cinema"
to recognize not only how the cinema participates in the discursive construction of an
imagined community, but also how audiences within given countries are constituted
as interpretive communities based on shared practices of reception, cultural competencies, and vernacular sensibilities.

In most countries (including those in Latin America), the idea of a "national" cinema has long been more an aspiration than a reality. With the implacable economic reality of the medium, even when budgets are kept very low, it takes a minimum number of spectators for the film's producers to recoup their investment. Most domestic audiences do not, on a regular basis, offer such a minimum for most locally produced films to be commercially profitable. Thus, a homegrown production often requires the help of international markets to be at least viable, if not financially successful. The locally produced film in the region thus inevitably makes the national dependent on the international for its sustained viability.

Throughout history, national cinemas have been connected to the international in at least three key respects. First, film technologies, advanced financing, technical expertise, and, crucially, access to circuits of distribution and exhibition have all depended, in one way or another, on foreign actors and foreign circumstances. Second, as a modern invention, cinema has often depicted historical and cultural processes directly relating to internationally spreading modernity: rural migration to the cities, the life of the newly arrived in the city, transformations in the backcountry, the formation of the urban middle class, and the impact of mass media itself. Third, Hollywood, heavily involved in the global control of screen traffic, and responsible for the production of its naturalized visual narrative styles, has dominated the world scene since the early twentieth century. In sum, despite the protestations of autonomy and cultural specificity of its supporters, national cinema is a concept haunted by its international (repressed or less visible) dimension.

Furthermore, it can be critiqued along the same lines as national literature, a related and older concept. Until relatively recently, most national cinemas in Latin America (i.e. most critically acclaimed and often state-sponsored cinema) have served as an echo chamber for the lettered elite that has produced them. This is evident in the elitist orientation of their high modernist texts, the exclusive use of the dominant language of (national) culture (overwhelmingly Spanish and Portuguese) in often deeply multilingual countries, and the problematic representation of the poor and indigenous along with other *others* of elite-led national culture. If, for instance, the concept of national cinema were to be systematically subjected to the same scrutiny subaltern studies has provided for national literatures, it would certainly be found wanting. National cinema would have an additional difficulty justifying its expansive claim to speak to/for domestic audiences within a given territory. Unlike various national literatures, which were incorporated by Latin American states into their educational curricula at some point in the early to mid twentieth century, national cinema was never really adopted as a crucial part of school lessons. Instead, it was left to fend for itself when facing Hollywood, a formidable competitor that excelled at socializing massive audiences in its ways of understanding and consuming cinema and encompassing populations well beyond the national school system's reach. Thus, critical canonization of film at the national level never enjoyed the benefits of the formal and systematic cultural inculcation nor the training in (national) ways of reading or seeing, that school provided for literary texts. In other words, national cinema has had no mediating agent capable of bridging the distance between its texts and those mass national publics that such texts are said to be addressed to, and of which they are said to be representative. By way of comparison, Latin American television may be seen as recently awakening to this function of mediation between national cinema and a national community that has long been so crucial in the European model of TV that sponsors and widely broadcasts national cinema. Efforts to broadcast the national visual patrimony on a regular basis on TV include current and proposed national audiovisual channels in Argentina (INCAA TV), Brazil (TV Brasil and TV Cultura), and Chile (Canal de Televisión Cultural, proposed).

If literature belongs to the Gutenberg(ian) modernity that closely linked the book, literary discourse, and the state inside the territory of a national culture, then film may be seen to inhabit a world of visual and electronic media whose technologies, markets, circulation, and consumption are, at least partially, international (and now transnational) in orientation. Nonetheless, I want to put forward a concept of national cinema as a necessary category of analysis that cannot be sidelined by the realization of how inter- and transnational film culture has become or has always been. The category of national cinema is needed for the simple reason, if nothing else, that for most films, that is the only accurate sphere of real distribution, exhibition, and consumption. Those films only seen nationally (the majority) coexist with a more selective group of often internationally circulating films that different actors inside and outside the nation recognize, too, as defining national cinema. I begin with a few general comments on the concept of national cinema and its relation to Hollywood; then I expand that discussion to the more specific Latin American context; and, finally, I develop one case study, Chilean national cinema, as a concrete example of some of those complexities.

The discussion on national cinema

In an often-cited article, "The Mass Production of the Senses" (1999), Miriam Hansen revisits the issue of modernity and film in relation to one of the field-structuring divides in film studies: that between classical or hegemonic Hollywood cinema and high modernist film. If the first type of film had been defined by the very effective marriage of a production mode (the studio) and a style (realism), both "rooted in neoformalist poetics and cognitive psychology" (Hansen 1999: 63), the second depended for its efficacy precisely on the undoing of all those classical and bourgeois aesthetic principles, emphasizing instead ruptures and discontinuities.

This binary has had immense repercussions, underwriting scholarly distinctions between Hollywood productions and cinemas made elsewhere in the post-World War II period, and classifying the latter as "national." If what defined Hollywood films was their direct popular orientation and the modern experience they provided their spectators (through theater attendance and often subject matter), national cinemas could claim the unclaimed territory of high cultural sophistication as defined by the national bourgeoisies.

Rather than trying to fully distinguish the clear territory of national film, it is more useful to recognize the term as a category through which various stakeholders (scholars, and also the state and filmmakers) make claims. Methodologically, declaring a film as national has meant, in brief, a context for and a direction in which any analysis of such a film should proceed. Analytically, the national as a category has provided for the cinematic work in question: (a) a historical context, and thus an inscription within a historical process connected to the evolution of such sociopolitical and cultural entity (the nation); (b) a cinematically specific tradition (movements, directors, themes, aesthetics) within which the work is to be inscribed and against which it must be measured; (c) an intended audience, and thus an encyclopedia of pertinent references (shared knowledges, languages, experiences); (d) a comparative perspective with other national film traditions; and (e) the reduction of all relevant external factors to stylistic influences or details of production that do not affect the centrally national core of the film.

In the 1970s and 1980s, this scholarly framework privileged a certain type of Latin American cinema—the politically militant and aesthetically experimental New Latin American Cinema—as exemplary of national cinemas in the region and as quintessentially non-Hollywood. However, before the notion of national culture was radicalized as revolutionary and anti-capitalist in the 1960s by Third World anti-colonial movements, it had had a decades-long life in Latin America as national-popular culture. The latter was promoted by a series of populist governments involving popular front-like formations in Chile, Argentina, Brazil, and Mexico. Between the 1930s and the 1950s, these cultures produced both the first incarnation of national cinemas in Latin America (Mexican, Brazilian, and Argentine cinemas) and created, also for the first time, a continental market for some of its products, especially comedies, musicals, and melodramas (Noble 2005; Shaw and Dennison 2007).

This dominance of genres was no accident. It prevailed—as Martín-Barbero (1987), Monsiváis (1995, 2000), and Ortiz (1988) have demonstrated—because it presented a high degree of continuity between pre-mass media forms of popular entertainment, such as the comedy-circus, the vaudeville show, the carnival, and their mass media inheritors, such as radio and film. For these three authors, popular cinema functioned in these decades as a highly influential and educational medium, helping Latin Americans become simultaneously national, urban, and modern. Along with Hollywood, and not just simply against Hollywood, national-popular cinemas, following Hansen's argument, produced vernacular modernities in the region.

Film comedies and melodramas are types of film in which the national products, can compete with Hollywood on a much more level field. The difference in budgets and production values—seen as paltry or amateurish in other genres compared to Hollywood products—is offset in the more modest settings of the comedy or the melodrama by what elsewhere I have called a vernacular advantage, or the advantage of the vernacular in Latin American film comedies (Poblete 2015a). In these genres, the settings are often simple, the actors are frequently already well-known nationally for their work in national radio or TV shows, and a significant portion of the primary material is itself the national situation and the national language (i.e. something that Hollywood can do best only for the American context). These genre films were, and still are, very popular with their respective national audiences and (in the case of many Mexican films of the golden era) with Latin American audiences, then and now (through endless programming in TV and cable, including Latino channels in the US).

Until relatively recently, many scholars dismissed these popular films as not artistic enough and too commercial, and defined national cinema around the New Latin American Cinema of the 1960s and 1970s based on its radical opposition (as Third Cinema, imperfect cinema, or cinema of hunger) to the capitalist industrialism and aesthetic conservatism of Hollywood. Indeed, somewhat paradoxically in light of the binary outlined by Hansen, the New Latin American Cinema achieved the status of the classic or natural form of Latin American cinema, the golden rule against which all other film products in the continent were deemed wanting or irrelevant, too commercial or not political enough, and thus insignificant. Michael Chanan is highly representative of this critical tendency. Referring to the New Latin American Cinema in 2006, he felt it was still possible to write: "Forty years ago—*after decades of low-level commercial production*, Latin American cinema underwent an astonishing rebirth as a vanguard film movement with objectives both political and aesthetic" (Chanan 2006: 38, emphasis added). The assertion reveals more about scholarly inclinations (favoring socially critical, formally experimental films over commercial success) than about film history. These *decades of (supposedly) low-level commercial production* included most of Cantinflas, Luis Sandrini, and Niní Marshall's comedy classics, most of Mexico's classic melodramas and musical films, the work of Fernando de Fuentes, Emilio Fernández, and Lucas Demare, and 30 years of film experience by spectators throughout the continent.

There is then a fork in the road in the Latin American critical tradition about national cinemas (López 1994, 1998, 2002a, 2002b). In one model, Carlos Monsiváis and others credit classic golden age Latin American cinema with a nationalizing effect, an effect that would have occurred mostly when the Mexican industry focused on the commercial production of popular *comedias rancheras* and melodramas. In this view, even while emulating the Hollywood model of commercial production, these films resonated with domestic audiences and were integral to the modernizing and nationalizing project—at least in Mexico, Argentina, and Brazil. In the other model, scholars such as Chanan followed filmmakers such as Fernando Solanas and Octavio Getino to envi-sion a new form of the popular as the basis of a national cinema. Solanas and Getino's 1969 "Hacia un Tercer Cine" ("Towards a Third Cinema") (Solanas and Getino 1997) proposed a new articulation between the artistic medium, its producers and publics, and their political aspirations based on revolutionary premises of radical social *transformation* rather than on the populist ones of social *representation* that had linked the golden age classics to their respective political regimes in the 1930s–1950s. These two models of national cinema employ different criteria. Cinema could be *national* because it involved a domestic industry in the production, distribution, and exhibition of nationally pro-duced commercial products, such as comedies and melodramas, as occurred in the golden age of Brazilian, Mexican, and Argentine cinema in the 1930s, 1940s, and even 1950s; or it could be national because it used the radical critique of a dependent nation-state and bourgeois nationalism as ideological platforms to denounce both the international hegemony of dominant Hollywood cinema and its forms and that of national dominant oligarchies and their power, as it did in the new Third Cinema and Cinema Novo (see Burton-Carvajal 1998a, 1998b; Paranaguá 2003; and especially López 1994, 1998, 2002a, 2002b, 2006 about the critical relationship between Hollywood and Latin American cinema; see D'Lugo 2010; Newman 2010; Smith 2012; Dennison 2013; Shaw 2013 for transnational models that attempt to displace a binary model opposing national cinema to Hollywood).

Regardless of the other criteria, any effort to define a national cinema confronts the task of constituting a primary corpus. This implies recognizing what, following Franco Moretti, we could call "the great unseen" (i.e. the great number of films that are not available and thus not considered in critical evaluations). This problem is not exclusive to the Latin American film tradition, but given the limited efforts, up until recently, to archive and preserve older films, it has been particularly consequential in that region. This difficulty of grappling with "the great unseen" is compounded by the always restrictive process of select-ing a few films—oftentimes those that have successfully been shown internationally—to stand for the whole of that national film trajectory. A national cinema is then always the result of a theoretical effort positing it as a relatively unified object, even when the goal is showcasing its complexity (Rosen 2006). The issue of the constitution of the corpus (what is in) and the canon (what is best) of national film traditions lends itself—through the concept of masterpieces endowed with great depth—to a mostly metonymic presenta-tion of national film trajectories, which in turn lends itself easily to much faster critical apprehension (and reduction) by metropolitan critics interested in world cinema. Both are restrictive and selective processes.

Contemporary scholarly accounts of national cinema are therefore always caught between the pressures of dynamics that are national (demanding more inclusion) and international (based on greater selectivity). Within given countries, the category's coherence and even its right to exist is questioned both by those who claim it is not representative enough of the regional, ethnic, cultural diversity of the nation and by those who doubt its quality vis-à-vis Hollywood or European auteur cinema. In the international context, domestic productions from a given country rarely register as a distinctive national cinema under the pressure of world cinema dynamics that select a few international auteurs as representatives of the world beyond Hollywood, or that, when recognizing a cinema as "national," choose from its complex trajectory only a few works that travel well internationally. So, while annual domestic film production in the region is now generally much more significant than in the past—an increase facilitated by the globalization of exhibition venues, the rise of streaming services, and the decrease in the cost and democratization of access to highly professional digital equipment—at the level of metropolitan film studies, Latin American films are still mostly represented by a select number of auteurs and films with international circulation, often recognized as examples of world cinema.

The Chilean case

The trajectory of modern Chilean national film is clearly and tragically condensed in the story of *El Día del Cine Chileno* (*The Day of Chilean Cinema*). This celebration originated under the Pinochet dictatorship in the mid-1970s as an effort by friends and colleagues to commemorate the day of the disappearance of two young Chilean filmmakers: Jorge Muller, who had worked with Raúl Ruiz, and in the making of *La Batalla de Chile* (*The Battle of Chile*, Patricio Guzmán, 1975–1979); and his girlfriend, Carmen Bueno, an actress in *La Tierra prometida* (*The Promised Land*, Miguel Littín, 1973). The two young professionals had been detained in November 1974, the day after they had participated in the debut of one of the few Chilean films released during the Pinochet dictatorship: *A la sombra del sol* (*In the Shadow of the Sun*, Silvio Caiozzi and Pablo Perelman, 1974). Muller and Bueno were Chilefilms (an intermittent state-funded effort to produce a Chilean film industry running first from 1944 to 1973) employees and were headed to the studios that morning. Two decades later, in the 1990s under democracy, this "Day of Chilean Cinema" was taken up by commercial interests and sponsored by the Chilean state. Since then it has floated around different dates in which, annually, Chilean cinema is made available to its potential local public at discounted prices (Cine underground chileno n.d.; González n.d.).

This story condenses the trajectory of Chilean cinema in at least three ways: first, it links contemporary Chilean cinema to the work of a (national) studio and (national) auteurs, in this case Chilefilms and canonical directors such as Ruiz, Guzmán, and Caiozzi; second, it places the brutal interruption of the 1973 coup and its violent aftermath as one of the repressed but paradoxically central elements of that trajectory; finally, it pits social memory against market and industrial dynamics in ways that announce some of the issues facing post-dictatorship cinema, and that were and still are showcased by some of those films to position themselves as examples of national cinema in the global context.

The story will also allow me to propose four trajectories in Chilean cinema as emblematic of the tensions it encompasses, as well as those defining Chilean and national cinemas more broadly. Before discussing those four pathways, it is necessary to delineate the two sociological realities involved and intertwined in the definition of most national cinemas. On the one hand, most cinema is national in the sense that most films only circulate within national or subnational markets. That is the norm. On the other, there is another

Figure 1.1 Poster for the 2016 "Day of Chilean Cinema."

national cinema defined more often than not by a tiny selection of films that circulate internationally.[1] In other words, at the heart of the concept of national cinema, there is a seeming paradox of dual recognitions, a tension between the local and the global that sustains it. Like nations themselves, national cinemas can only be national if they are specific enough to that cultural context and so recognized by a correspondingly specific (national) audience. But that national cinema is incomplete without some further recognition provided to at least some of its vernacular films by an international or global audience. Only then, in an international context and granted international recognition, is a national cinema truly and fully national (both singular and distinct from others, and seen by others as such). What makes it specific nationally has to be not just culturally thick, but also, at least sometimes, translatable in terms both legible and recognized as distinctive by that international community. This mediation connecting the local with the national and the latter with the international or global is constitutive of national cinemas, and it is clearly exemplified by the case of Chilean cinema (see Burton-Carvajal 1998b for a similar situation in Venezuela).

Chilean cinema belongs historically to that second tier of Latin American film industries Paulo Antonio Paranaguá has identified as "intermittent." That is, those countries below Argentina, Mexico, and Brazil in the quantity and frequency of their output, a group that also includes Venezuela, Peru, and Colombia (Paranaguá 2003: 23). The story of Chilean cinema begins in 1910 with *Manuel Rodríguez*, a 10-minute film. From then on, and until 1973, it produced an average of almost three films per year, with certain spike-years in the periods 1924–1926 (a total of 44 films), 1944–1947 (26 films), and 1973 (six films) (Schnitman 1984: 116–117). Then, during the Pinochet dictatorship, Chilean national cinema produced just ten films in the 17 years between 1973 and 1990 (Trejo 2009: 82). In contrast, however, Chilean filmmakers in exile produced 56 feature films between 1973 and 1980 (Ossa 1971; Mouesca and Orellana 2010). From the restoration of democracy in 1990 to 2014, Chile has produced 237 theatrical releases for an average of 16 films per year, with its highest point in 2014 with 42 releases. While the number of films has steadily increased in the last decade, and the international accolades continue to accumulate, the main obstacle in the development of Chilean cinema is its still low and fluctuating market share in the country. The problem is vividly illustrated by the excellent *Matar a un hombre* (*To Kill a Man*, Alejandro Fernández, 2014), which received the best film award in the World Cinema category at Sundance in 2014. That year, the film was seen by a grand total of 4,425 spectators in Chile (González 2015).

Chilean cinema presents at least four basic ways—two more directly commercial and two more artistically inclined—in which non-Hollywood national cinemas can develop. On one end of the spectrum are films such as those of Nicolás López that seek to use, imitate, parody, or improve (at least by significantly reducing production costs) some of contemporary Hollywood's defining genres: youth-oriented comedies and horror films, in his case. The resulting product can then be shown in theaters nationally and its theatrical and, above all, international video-on-demand rights sold to distributors or outfits such as Netflix or HBO. On the other end, exemplified by Patricio Guzmán's documentary *oeuvre* and illustrated here by the work of Pablo Larraín, are high art films, or so-called festival films, whose forms and topics are legible both nationally and internationally (Crofts 2006: 53). Based on the prestige thus garnered, the film can then be shown in theaters nationally and internationally. In between these two different directorial trajectories are two other forms of Chilean national cinema. On the commercial end, alongside those made by López, are other films that exploit a locally known connection between film and other media such as radio or TV (a certain program, a set of telenovela actors, a current event of significant national coverage). In this case, form and cinematic language take a back seat to the prominence of the originating facts or news, and the scope of the film's distribution is more often than not exclusively national. Here, the thickness of local specificity and local language are crucial to the forms of spectatorial identification and recognition. Humor is often the central focus, although historical figures, crimes, national scandals, or sports events can also make an appearance. Good examples here are the series of comedies by radio personality El Rumpy, *Radio Corazón* (2007), *Grado 3* (2009), and *Paseo de oficina* (2012), and films such as *Sexo con amor* (2003), *Super, Todo Chile adentro* (2009), and *Ojos Rojos* (2010). On the artistic side of the spectrum, alongside works such as those of Larraín, is a final type of national cinema in Chile, defined below as a subtype of the so-called festival film. Let us now examine each of these four pathways in greater detail.

Nicolás López (born 1983) embodies a very comfortable relation with both regular Hollywood films and commercial American indies, as exemplified by his production partner Eli Roth's horror flicks (*Cabin Fever*, *Hostel*). López and Roth have in fact entered into a production deal in which they alternate writing, directing, and producing roles.

Figure 1.2 Qué pena tu vida (*F*ck My Life*, Nicolás López, 2010): Chilean upper middle class
mediated by technology.

López has christened his efforts Chilewood. Chilewood is both an idea of what films
should be about and a certain mode of production. The idea is "to make genre movies
that we want to see for the entire world," says Eli Roth (cited in Fragoso 2015). Genres—
horror films for both Roth and López, and comedies and superhero flicks for López—provide
the language and the playful formats for these Spanish, English, and sometimes bilingual
efforts. As a mode of production, Chilewood is defined by cheap Chile-based locations,
flexible labor (unencumbered by the limitations and protections generated by American
film unions), and an efficient use of the latest visual technologies (including commercial
releases filmed entirely with digital cameras.) It is also fast: at 32 years of age, López has
already directed eight feature films (including the very successful *Qué pena* trilogy), written
or co-written nine, and produced six. His Sobras International production company produces both Spanish-based films for Chilean consumption that are then released on Netflix
(a partner in the *Qué pena* series) and English-based efforts in collaboration with Roth and
Uruguayan Guillermo Amoedo, including *The Green Inferno* (2013), *Knock, Knock* (2014),
and *The Stranger* (2015).

Qué pena tu vida (*F*ck My Life*, 2010), the first film in López's comedy trilogy, was
the most seen film of the year in Chile (beating *The Social Network*), and depicted the
complicated love life of a Chilean young couple living in the cinematic equivalent of
MacOndo: a Latin America in which almost every social interaction occurs within a
middle- or upper-middle-class environment and is significantly mediated by modern
technologies (the film itself has been widely credited with being the first ever commercial release filmed entirely with a Canon 7D digital camera). Like the Chilean authors
Alberto Fuguet and Sergio Gómez who coined the term MacOndo to define their literary generation, López was in fact interested in a counter-representational depiction of
Latin America:

Most of the movies people made in Latin America were about poor people with guns [...] All the movies were showing a version of Latin America that had nothing to do with my Latin America [where] everybody had Wi-Fi and iPods and was watching movies on IMAX. [...] I wanted to make a movie that had more to do with John Hughes than City of God.

(cited in Kay 2014)

Aftershock (2012) was directed by López (using a Canon EOS 5D digital camera), co-written by Roth, Amoedo, and López, and stars Roth as Gringo, one of the three male travelers, who, along with their international female friends, will wind up in Valparaíso the night a major earthquake hits Chile. While the film cleverly plays with the issues of translation and cultural (mis)understanding of its international set of characters, its broad global legibility is ensured by the use of the dominant conventions of the youth-oriented horror film.

López's career is both an example of one of the modes of national cinema as defined by its playful use of Hollywood's most commercial genres, and a case blurring that and other distinctions. After all, it is becoming increasingly difficult to tell what the nationality of some of his films is, and some of them have been celebrated at Cannes, Toronto, and other international film festivals.

The two forms of Chilean national cinema on the artistically inclined end of the spectrum correspond to two varieties of the art house film, or festival film. According to Paul Julian Smith, such films "employ little camera movement and extended takes without edits; they tell casual or oblique stories, often elliptical and inconclusive; and they often cast non-professionals whose limited range restricts their performance to a consistently blank or affectless acting style" (Smith 2012: 72). For Smith, festival films are one of three categories of transnational film. The other two are the genre film, such as Fernando Meirelles and Kátia Lund's *Cidade de Deus* (*City of God*, 2002) (whose allegedly more universal generic language compensates, in the international context, for its national linguistic specificities) and the 'prestige film', which is a transnational blockbuster done in English by a multinational cast and creative team, such as Alejandro González Iñárritu's *21 Grams* (2003) and *Babel* (2006). According to Smith, festival films are oftentimes shown first in international film festivals and only afterwards in their local or national context, and they regularly "receive significant foreign input into their development and production process" (p. 71). David Martin-Jones and María Soledad Montañez have gone one step further and discussed "the aesthetics and politics of auto-erasure" (Martin-Jones and Montañez 2013: 26), the disappearance of small cinemas' national characteristics in their national industry as the price they pay for their own existence as "intercultural translations of the nation for global consumption" (p. 30).

The first subtype of festival cinema in the Chilean case fits—formally, semantically, and industrially—the small story and small budget, auteur-driven, very detailed, individual story-oriented film, for which the setting, national or otherwise, is less important than the slice of life at the center of the script. In such films, narrative development is much less crucial than a certain intensity of affective depth. Here, one could mention as emblematic the films of Alicia Scherson, *Play* (2005), *Turistas* (*Tourists*, 2009), and Matías Bize, *En La cama* (*In Bed*, 2005), *La Vida de los peces* (*The Life of Fish*, 2010), and *La Memoria del agua* (*The Memory of Water*, 2015).

Pablo Larraín's work, especially his trilogy on the Pinochet dictatorship (*Tony Manero* [2008], *Post Mortem* [2010], and *No* [2012]), is both better known and part of the second subtype of festival cinema. While Larraín's four films so far (a fifth, *El Club*, has just won the Silver Bear at the Berlin film festival) do not fit Smith's description of the formal style of a festival film, they have tended to be shown first at international festivals and only then theatrically in Chile and abroad. I would add one more defining characteristic that in my view makes them part of a second kind of festival film: their forms and topics must be legible and interesting both nationally and internationally. While this trait is obviously shared by both subtypes of festival films, its predominance over the formal features listed by Smith would define this second kind. In fact, I would argue that Larraín's trilogy's broad legibility resides in the fact that it has as its central subject the specific forms of violence imposed in Chile by the Pinochet dictatorship and its aftermath (which resonates nationally), and the transition itself from one form of social world to another as a result of the much broader and more significant global imposition of neoliberal regimes (which resonates with international audiences) (Poblete 2015b).

In this context, Larraín's *Tony Manero* can be read as one of the most radical Latin American film explorations of the deep social violence involved in the continental implantation of neoliberalism. While seemingly inscribed as yet another Third World reflection on the world of fandom, *Tony Manero* ends up offering a trenchant critique of neoliberalism, as represented by the arrival in Chile of both a new model of society and a form of mass mediated modernity that found in global Hollywood one of its main vehicles of reproduction. Along these lines, too, *No* is a melancholy meditation and a historical media reconstruction of the forms (mainly advertisement and consumption as key practices) through which the basic transformation of neoliberal globalization as epochal change was imposed (in Chile and elsewhere), and how it has involved the compulsion into new forms of subjectification determined by an economic understanding of society qua market society, as well as,

Figure 1.3   Pablo Larraín's *No* (2012) has been able to engage both national and international audiences.

as a side effect, the nostalgic remembrance of a previous historical moment of the social (Poblete 2015b). In other words, Larraín's films have been made simultaneously viable as national films and world cinema, at least in part because of their depiction of one nationally and globally defining transformation: the dual nature of neoliberal globalization, which has imposed both a new political economy (oftentimes referred to as neoliberal trickle-down economics), and a new libidinal economy (based on the stimulation of individual consumption and debt), and above all their imbrication (and, as a result, their contrast with previous forms of structuring the social and individual experience). This capacity of a nationally specific film to intervene in the global public cultural sphere by representing a transformation, an event, or a process nationally defining and internationally significant may be one of the signal contributions of national cinema to the global history of the medium. It is also one of the main reasons why I insisted on putting forward a concept of national cinema that considered it a necessary category of analysis that cannot be sidelined by the realization of how inter- and transnational film culture has become or has always been.

Note

1 Web-based distribution and access is changing this picture in some important respects. See, for example, the full-length films archived online on YouTube and many national websites such as Cinechile.cl and Cinepata.com. See also Castillo (2008).

References

Burton-Carvajal, J. (1998a) "South American Cinema." In J. Hill and P. Church Gibson (eds.), *The Oxford Guide to Film Studies*. Oxford: Oxford University Press, pp. 578–594.

—— (1998b) "Araya across Time and Space: Competing Canons of National and International Film History." In J. Burton-Carvajal (ed.), *Revisión del cine de los cincuenta*, Special Issue of *Nuevo Texto Crítico*, 21(22): 207–234.

Castillo, D. (2008) "The New New Latin American Cinema: Cortometrajes on the Internet." In C. Taylor and T. Pitman (eds.), *Latin American Cyberculture and Cyberliterature*. Liverpool: Liverpool University Press, pp. 39–49.

Chanan, M. (2006) "Latin American Cinema: From Underdevelopment to Postmodernism." In S. Dennison and S. Hwee Lim (eds.), *Remapping World Cinema*. London: Wallflower, pp. 38–54.

Cine underground chileno (n.d.) "Jorge Müller y Carmen Bueno." Available at: http://cineundergroundchileno.blogspot.com (accessed June 1, 2017).

Crofts, S. (2006) "Reconceptualising National Cinema/s." In V. Vitali and P. Willemen (eds.), *Theorising National Cinema*. London: BFI, pp. 44–58.

Dennison, S. (ed.) (2013) *Contemporary Hispanic Cinema: Interrogating the Transnational in Spanish and Latin American Film*. Woodbridge: Tamesis.

D'Lugo, M. (2010) "Aural Identity, Genealogies of Sound Technologies, and Hispanic Transnationality on Screen." In N. Durovicova and K. Newman (eds.), *World Cinemas*. London: Routledge, pp. 160–184.

Fragoso, S. (2015) "How a Movement in Chile Is Transforming Film Worldwide." Wired.com, June 12, 2015. Available at: www.wired.com/2015/06/chilewood-primer-the-stranger/ (accessed June 1, 2017).

González, F. (n.d.) "El día del cine chileno en memoria de Carmen Bueno y Jorge Müller." Available at: http://cinechile.cl/crit&estud-389 (accessed June 1, 2017).

González, M. (2015) "El Cine chileno: un éxito de exportación sin espectadores." Latercera.com, February 20, 2015. Available at: www.latercera.com/noticia/el-cine-chileno-un-exito-de-exportacion-sin-espectadores/ (accessed June 1, 2017).

Hansen, M. (1999) "Mass Production of the Senses: Classical Cinema as Vernacular Modernism." *Modernism/Modernity*, 6(2): 59–77.

Higson, A. (1989) "The Concept of National Cinema." *Screen*, 30(4): 36–46.

—— (2006) "The Limiting Imagination of National Cinema." In E. Ezra and T. Rowden (eds.), *Transnational Cinema: The Film Reader*. London: Routledge, pp. 15–25.

Kay, J. (2014) "Welcome to Chilewood." Screendaily.com, October 16, 2014. Available at: www.screendaily.com/features/welcome-to-chilewood/5078735.article (accessed June 1, 2017).

López, A.M. (1994) "A Cinema for the Continent." In C. Noriega and S. Ricci (eds.), *The Mexican Cinema Project*. Los Angeles, CA: UCLA Film and Television Archive, pp. 7–12.

—— (1998) "Historia nacional, historia transnacional." In J. Burton-Carvajal, P. Torres, and A. Miquel (eds.), *Horizontes del Segundo siglo. Investigación y pedagogía del cine mexicano, latino-americano y chicano*. Guadalajara: Universidad de Guadalajara, pp. 75–81.

—— (2002a) "Are All Latins from Manhattan? Hollywood, Ethnography, and Cultural Colonialism." In A. Williams (ed.), *Film and Nationalism*. New Brunswick, NJ: Rutgers University Press, pp. 195–214.

—— (2002b) "Facing up to Hollywood." In C. Gledhill and L. Williams (eds.), *Reinventing Film Studies*. London: Arnold, pp. 419–437.

—— (2006) "Early Cinema and Modernity in Latin America." In V. Vitali and P. Willemen (eds.), *Theorising National Cinema*. London: BFI, pp. 209–225.

Martín-Barbero, J. (1987) *De los medios a las mediaciones*. Barcelona: Gustavo Gili.

Martin-Jones, D. and Montañez, M. (2013) "Uruguay Disappears: Small Cinemas, Control Z Films, and the Aesthetics and Politics of Auto-Erasure." *Cinema Journal*, 53(1): 26–51.

Monsiváis, C. (1995) "All the People Came and Did Not Fit Onto the Screen: Notes on the Cinema Audience in Mexico." In P.A. Paranaguá (ed.), *Mexican Cinema*. London: BFI, pp. 145–151.

—— (2000) *Aires de familia. Cultura y sociedad en América Latina*. Barcelona: Anagrama.

Mouesca, J. and Orellana, C. (2010) *Breve historia del cine chileno. Desde sus orígenes hasta nuestros días*. Santiago: Lom.

Newman, K. (2010) "Notes on Transnational Film Theory: Decentered Subjectivity, Decentered Capitalism." in N. Durovicova and K. Newman (eds.), *World Cinemas, Transnational Perspectives*. London: Routledge, pp. 3–11.

Noble, A. (2005) *Mexican National Cinema*. London: Routledge.

Ortiz, R. (1988) *A Moderna tradição brasileira*. São Paulo: Brasiliense.

Ossa, C. (1971) *Historia del cine chileno*. Santiago: Quimantú.

Paranaguá, P.A. (2003) *Tradición y modernidad en el cine de América Latina*. Madrid: FCE.

Poblete, J. (2015a) "Introduction." In J. Poblete and J. Suárez (eds.), *Humor and Latin American Cinema*. New York: Palgrave, pp. 1–28.

Poblete, J. (2015b) "The Memory of the National and the National as Memory." *Latin American Perspectives*, 202, 42(3): 92–106.

Rosen, P. (2006) "History, Textuality, Nation: Kracauer, Burch and Some Problems in the Study of National Cinemas." In V. Vitali and P. Willemen (eds.), *Theorising National Cinema*. London: BFI, pp. 17–28.

Schnitman, J.A. (1984) *Film Industries in Latin America*. Norwood, NJ: Ablex.

Shaw, L. (2013) "Deconstructing and Reconstructing Transnational Cinemas." In S. Dennison (ed.), *Contemporary Hispanic Cinema: Interrogating the Transnational in Spanish and Latin American Film*. Woodbridge: Tamesis, pp. 47–65.

Shaw, L. and Dennison, S. (eds.) (2007) *Brazilian National Cinema*. London: Routledge.

Smith, P.J. (2012) "Transnational Cinemas: The Cases of Mexico, Argentina, and Brazil." In L. Nagib, C. Perriam, and R. Dudrah (eds.), *Theorizing World Cinema*. London: I.B.Tauris.

Solanas, F. and Getino, O. (1997) "Towards a Third Cinema." In M. Martin (ed.), *New Latin American Cinema. Volume I*. Detroit, MI: Wayne State University Press, pp. 33–58.

Trejo, R. (2009) *Cine, neoliberalismo y cultura. Crítica de la economía política del cine chileno contemporáneo*. Santiago: Arcis.

Further reading

Hjort, M. and Mackenzie, S. (eds.) (2000) *Cinema and Nation*. London: Routledge.

Hjort, M. and Petrie, D. (eds.) (2007) *The Cinema of Small Nations*. Bloomington, IN: Indiana University Press.

Martin, M. (ed.) (1997) *New Latin American Cinema*. Detroit, MI: Wayne State University Press.

Monsiváis, C. (1985) "De las relaciones literarias entre alta cultura y cultura popular." *Texto Crítico*, 33: 48–61.

Nagib, L. (2006) "Towards a Positive Definition of World Cinema." In S. Dennison and S. Hwee Lim (eds.), *Remapping World Cinema*. London: Wallflower, pp. 30–37.

Nagib, L., Perriam, C., and Dudrah, R. (eds.) (2012) *Theorizing World Cinema*. London: I.B.Tauris.

2

SILENT AND EARLY SOUND CINEMA IN LATIN AMERICA

Local, national, and transnational perspectives

Rielle Navitski

Editors' introduction

As new audiovisual technologies have emerged over the past three decades, film historians have increasingly turned their attention to the early twentieth century, a moment when cinema and recorded sound sparked equally profound transformations of popular culture. In the context of this so-called "historical turn," research on silent and early sound cinema in Latin America has been shaped by persistent challenges as well as new opportunities. Due to the discontinuous character of film production in the region and other obstacles to film preservation, only a small percentage of Latin American silent films have survived, and many early sound features have also been lost, making print publications the primary source for early film histories. The growing availability of digitized newspapers and magazines, along with the rediscovery, restoration, and video/digital release of silent and early sound films, has opened up new avenues for exploring cinema's profound impact in early twentieth-century Latin America.

Providing an overview of key developments in Latin American film culture between 1896 and 1936, Navitski's essay also interrogates dominant critical tendencies in Latin American film historiography—in particular, the use of "national cinema" as an organizing framework and a focus on production (especially of fiction features) to the detriment of other aspects of film culture. Throughout, she emphasizes the potential of engaging more deeply with distribution, exhibition, and fan culture, and highlights some of the insights yielded by studies that adopt a geographic scope above or below the level of the nation, ranging from a focus on a single city to complex networks of cross-border exchange.

Beginning with the first surveys published in the late 1950s (Di Núbila 1959; Viany 1959; García Riera 1969), most historians of Latin American cinema have focused on analyzing— or recovering the traces of—film production within the borders of a single nation. These accounts have implicitly framed filmmaking as an affirmation of cultural identity in the face of North American and European cinema's dominance of local screens. Recuperating histories of production took on particular urgency in the case of the silent and early sound eras, given the dismal survival rate for Latin American films produced in the absence of self-sustaining industries or government policies to foster preservation. Yet recent scholarship on Latin American film culture, rather than treating imported cinema solely as an agent of cultural colonization, has begun to offer more nuanced accounts of how audiences, industry workers, critics, and exhibitors, as well as filmmakers, reacted to its presence on local screens (Serna 2014a). By shifting focus to the site-specific (and often overlooked) practices of distribution, exhibition, and fan culture, these histories open up fresh approaches that attend not only to the social meanings inscribed within a film text at the site of production, but also to the renegotiation of these meanings in the course of a film's circulation within and beyond national borders. In this vein, scholars have highlighted the complexities of intra-regional exchanges—such as the significant presence of Mexican cinema throughout Latin America and beyond from the 1930s through the 1950s (Castro Ricalde and McKee Irwin 2011, 2013)—as well as the variety of film cultures outside national capitals, which tends to be obscured by the "national cinema" framework. At the same time, nationalist imaginaries undeniably shaped filmmaking across the region in the first decades of the twentieth century. Providing an overview of key developments in Latin American film culture between 1896 (when moving images were first projected for audiences in the region) and 1936 (often viewed as the end of a period of experimentation with sound film, as it marks the consolidation of Mexico's sound film industry with the sweeping success of Fernando de Fuentes' *Allá en el Rancho Grande* [*Over at the Big Ranch*]), this essay outlines the possibilities and limitations of national, local, regional, and transnational approaches to Latin American cinema.

While the past two decades have witnessed an explosion of critical interest in the transnational dimensions of moving-image production and consumption, in Latin American cultural criticism, local and national experiences have long been interpreted through a continental framework. Scholars have debated the extent to which the region's diverse countries share a common relationship to (neo)colonial powers and Euro-American models of modernity. Néstor García Canclini has argued that Latin American nations possess "hybrid cultures" marked by "multitemporal heterogeneity," an uneasy coexistence of modernity and tradition (García Canclini 1995: 3). This emphasis on the multiplicity of experiences of modernization productively highlights disparities within and between nations. Films were screened in Rio de Janeiro, Buenos Aires, and Montevideo only six months after the first public exhibition of the Lumière Cinématographe in Paris in December 1895, with other major cities in the region close behind, yet the first confirmed screenings in Bolivia did not occur until 1904 (Paranaguá 1984: 11). Fairly complex narrative films were being produced in Argentina and Brazil by 1908 and 1909, while no fiction features were shot in Bolivia or Peru until the latter half of the 1920s (López 2000: 65). The transition to sound widened the gaps between the filmic output of Latin American nations; Argentina, Mexico, and Brazil established profitable industries in the early 1930s, while sound features were not made in Peru until 1937 with the founding of Amauta Films (Bedoya 2009b: 33).

Arguing that silent-era filmmakers across the region shared a common practice of navigating between local cultural referents and international trends in film style and narrative, Paul Schroeder Rodríguez proposes a periodization for Latin American silent film that mirrors developments in the United States and Western Europe (Schroeder Rodríguez 2008: 40–44). He distinguishes between a period dominated by actualities (short, topical nonfiction films), which corresponds closely to the early cinema period as defined in the United States (1897–1907), a transitional era (1908–1915) characterized by experiments with narrative film formats, and a period marked by the dominance of feature-length fiction films (1915–1930). While useful as a guide, this periodization does not address the lasting significance of nonfiction filmmaking in early twentieth-century Latin America. It also minimizes the sheer heterogeneity of genres and styles evident between and even within individual films. For example, Juan Sebastián Ospina León (2013) notes the use of both static, tableau-style framing associated with early cinema, and the internationally dominant continuity editing conventions forged in Hollywood, in the Colombian melodrama *Alma provinciana* (*Provincial Soul*, Félix J. Rodríguez, 1926). Elements of what Tom Gunning calls the "view aesthetic" of early cinema, which "captur[es] and preserv[es] a look or vantage point" on a seemingly unstaged subject (Gunning 1997: 14), persist in both non-fiction and fiction films made in Latin America through the end of the silent era, allowing spectators to contemplate familiar locales and events on-screen.

In her influential essay "Early Cinema and Modernity in Latin America," Ana M. López cautions against "any attempt to directly superimpose the developmental grid of U.S. and European early film history (albeit with its own discontinuities and heterogeneity) on the Latin American experience," emphasizing that "the history of filmmaking in Latin America is too profoundly marked by differences in global position, forms of social infrastructure, economic stability, and technical infrastructure" (López 2000: 50). Instead, López recasts Euro-American accounts of silent cinema's development by attending to local conditions of reception and production. She argues that upon cinema's initial reception in the region, a fascination with cinematic technology and its images of modern life positioned audience members as both "voyeurs" of imported modernity and avid consumers of "whatever forms of modernity . . . were available locally" (p. 53). While imported films continued to dominate, filmmakers also produced their own visions of local modernization and narratives that exalted national identities.

In his analysis of early fiction features, Schroeder Rodríguez critiques nationalistic narratives aligned with dominant ideals of modernization, suggesting these films embody a "criollo aesthetic . . . directly linked to the political project of inserting the young republics into a Euro-American modernity" (Schroeder Rodríguez 2008: 38). He attributes this "Eurocentric worldview and . . . correspondingly Europeanized aesthetics" to the upwardly mobile ambitions of filmmakers, most of whom were members of the emerging middle classes, European immigrants eager to align themselves with their adopted country, or both. Yet many filmmakers moved frequently across national borders, complicating the issue of national allegiances. Italian immigrant Pedro Sambarino worked in Argentina, Bolivia, and Peru, Cuban filmmaker Ramón Peón in Mexico, and Chilean Alberto Santana in his home country, in Ecuador, in Peru (where he directed the silent wartime drama *Yo perdí mi corazón en Lima* [*I Lost My Heart in Lima*] in 1933), and later in Colombia, Paraguay, Costa Rica, and Panama. Schroeder Rodríguez's analysis also glosses over the complexities of film financing prior to the emergence of industries. Funding schemes ranged from private investment in fiction features to sponsorship of nonfiction films by government or business interests, such as Silvino Santos' *No país das Amazonas* (*In the Land of the Amazon*, Brazil, 1922) and a group of comparable films highlighting the "civilizing" efforts of wealthy landowners and Catholic missionaries in the rubber-producing regions of Peru (Bedoya 2009a: 150–152).

Cinema was thus linked to a diverse series of modernizing projects, both local and national in scope. For example, the working-class filmmakers active in the city of Recife in the Brazilian Northeast in the 1920s were arguably more invested in using filmmaking to demonstrate the modernity of their city and region—increasingly imagined as drought-stricken, impoverished, and decadent (Cunha Filho 2010: 160–170; Muniz de Albuquerque Jr. 2014)—than in fulfilling the ambitions for a Hollywood-style national cinema articulated by Rio de Janeiro fan magazines such as *Cinearte, Selecta,* and *Para Todos.* On the opposite extreme of the class spectrum, elite women's organizations in Uruguay produced feature-length documentary and fiction films promoting social hygiene in the late 1920s, asserting the relevance of their charity efforts in the context of an expanding welfare state (Ehrick 2006). Cinema's initial presence in Latin America was certainly marked by close links to state power, as the presence of presidents Porfirio Díaz of Mexico and Nicolás de Piérola of Peru at early film screenings suggests (de los Reyes 1995: 123; Bedoya 2009a: 26). Yet the ideological projects that shaped filmmaking were diverse and sometimes conflicting, complicating their relationship to hegemonic nationalism and positivist notions of progress.

As Paranaguá (1984: 9) and others have noted, moving-image technology arrived in Latin America as a foreign import, rather than an outgrowth of broader technological and economic shifts. Since the Lumière Cinématographe (one among several competing apparatuses) could be used both to capture and to project moving images, the Lumières' agents filmed actualities that were then added to the company's catalog. Gabriel Veyre produced the earliest films made in Mexico, including a number of actualities featuring Díaz. He then traveled to Cuba, where he shot the first known film produced there, the 1897 *Simulacro de un incendio* (*Simulacrum of a Fire*), a document of training exercises by local firefighters, before moving on to Venezuela and Colombia. Veyre, like other exhibitors of imported film technologies, holds an uneasy place in national film histories as a representative of the foreign companies that dominated Latin American screens from cinema's earliest days. Earlier Latin American film scholars often presented the interests of filmmakers and exhibitors as diametrically opposed, with the latter viewed as complicit with foreign interests (Salles Gomes 1995). Indeed, after 1910, when permanent movie theaters were well established in many large Latin American cities, impresarios came to rely on steady supplies of European and later North American productions. Yet, as noted in more recent histories addressing the activities of film exhibitor-producers in Mexico and Brazil, production and exhibition remained closely intertwined throughout the silent era (de los Reyes 1983; Miquel 1997; Melo Souza 2003).

During the so-called "bela época" of Brazilian cinema (1908–1911) in Rio de Janeiro and São Paulo, film exhibitors were pivotal in film production, producing short, topical "local films" (Jung 2002) that showed the elites engaging in leisure activities or at public events, offering these spectators the pleasure of recognizing themselves and their social world on-screen (Melo Souza 2003: 154). Producer-exhibitors such as Antônio Leal and Júlio Ferrez also made short comedies, reconstructions of sensational crimes, and *filmes falados e cantantes* (talking and singing films). Accompanied by live performances by actors behind the screen, these locally made adaptations of operettas and the *teatro de revista* (musical revue) attained incredible popularity. A film based on the satirical musical *Paz e amor* (*Peace and Love*), financed by impresario William Auler and filmed by Alberto Botelho, was screened over 1,000 times in Rio in 1910 (Melo Souza 2003: 291). In Havana, behind-the-screen performances were used at screenings of imported films as early as 1906 and as late as 1920, helping to ground imported images in their exhibition context, often through locally specific humor (Agramonte and Castillo 2011: 82–87).

Brazilian producer-exhibitors' success was short-lived, especially as the powerful distribution and exhibition company owned by Spanish immigrant Francisco Serrador crowded out other theater owners beginning in 1911. Yet exhibitors continued to play an important

Figure 2.1   A still from the "cinematic operetta" *The Geisha*, shot by Júlio Ferrez and exhibited in Rio de Janeiro's Cinema Rio Branco, accompanied by vocal performances from behind the screen. *Fon-Fon* (Rio de Janeiro), November 13, 1909. Hemeroteca Digital Brasileira.

role in film production across Latin America. The Buenos Aires-based distribution/ exhibition network owned by Austrian immigrant Max Glucksmann produced most of Uruguay's actualities between 1913 and 1931 (López 2000: 66), while in Peru, a rivalry between the Teatros y Cinemas and Compañía Cinematográfica Mundial companies prompted them to produce competing newsreels between 1923 and 1926 (Bedoya 2009a: 229–234). In Colombia, the Italian-born di Doménico family, whose exhibition and distribution empire stretched across Venezuela, Central America, and the Caribbean, ventured into production in 1915 with *El drama del 15 de octubre* (*The Drama of the 15th of October*), which reconstructed the assassination of politician Rafael Uribe Uribe and documented its aftermath. Although the film provoked controversy and proved a commercial disappointment, the di Doménicos went on to produce four fiction features in the 1920s.

As exhibitors experimented with production, other enterprising filmmakers sought to tap into nationalistic sentiments. In Argentina, Italian immigrant Mario Gallo dramatized national history in films such as *La revolución de mayo* (*The May Revolution*, 1909) and *El fusilamiento de Dorrego* (*The Execution of Dorrego*, 1910). In Cuba, Enrique Díaz Quesada directed adventure films set during national independence struggles, including *Manuel García o el Rey de los campos de Cuba* (*Manuel García or the King of the Cuban Countryside*, 1913) and *El capitán mambí o libertadores y guerrilleros* (*The Revolutionary Captain or Liberators and Guerillas*, 1914). Mexico's earliest known fiction feature, *1810 o los libertadores* (*1810 or the Liberators*, Carlos Martínez Arredondo, 1917), filmed in Mérida, Yucatán, also capitalized on patriotic themes, while *El húsar de la muerte* (*The Hussar of Death*, Pedro Sienna, 1925) narrated the exploits of Manuel Rodríguez, a hero of Chile's

Figure 2.2 Immigrant impresarios whose business spanned national borders, such as the di Doménico family in Colombia and the Circum-Caribbean, and Max Glucksmann (pictured) in Argentina and the Southern Cone, played a pivotal role in the development of film exhibition, distribution, and production in Latin America. *Caras y Caretas* (Buenos Aires), January 3, 1914.

wars of independence. Other silent-era features invoked national patron saints: *Tepeyac* (Carlos E. Gónzalez, Mexico, 1917) and *La Virgen de la caridad* (*The Virgin of Charity*, Ramón Peón, Cuba, 1930).

Beyond overtly nationalistic themes, Latin American silent cinema displayed and affirmed emerging urban modernity, often in counterpoint to rural life. This strategy was perhaps exploited most successfully in *Nobleza gaucha* (*Gaucho Nobility*, Humberto Cairo,

Eduardo Martínez de la Pera, and Ernesto Gunche, 1915). The film's plot—a gaucho rescues his innocent love interest after she is kidnapped by a wealthy, unscrupulous city dweller—framed the countryside as a space of purity. At the same time, the film displayed Buenos Aires' broad avenues, historic buildings, and modern public transportation system. After reportedly being seen by over 50,000 spectators in Buenos Aires in 1915 (*La Prensa* 1915: 18), *Nobleza gaucha* screened in Barcelona (Batlle 1916: 395), Rio de Janeiro (*Fon-Fon* 1916), and Santiago de Chile (*El Mercurio* 1917: 6). Yielding a $200,000 profit in its first year of release (Ortega 1917: 437), *Nobleza gaucha* was exhibited into the late 1910s, playing in Lima three years after its premiere (Derteano 1918: 582).

In the wake of *Nobleza gaucha*, Gunche and Martínez de la Pera directed *Hasta después de muerta* (*Until after Her Death*, 1916), one of several Argentine melodramas that explored the ultramodern yet corrupting environment of rapidly growing cities. The prolific Afro-Argentine director José Agustín "El Negro" Ferreyra explored related themes into the sound era. In a similar vein, the 1918 adaptation of Federico Gamboa's naturalist novel *Santa* (Luis G. Peredo) linked Mexico City's modernization with moral decay through the tale of an innocent country girl who becomes a high-class courtesan. Other early features drew on what Doris Sommer (1991) calls "foundational fictions"—literary works that allegorized national unification through the formation of heterosexual couples across political parties, ethnicities, and regional groups—including *Amalia* (Enrique García Velloso, Argentina, 1914), based on José Mármol's novel, and the multiple silent-era versions of José de Alencar's *O guarani*.

Figure 2.3   The display of urban space and modern transportation technologies take center stage in a fragment from the 1918 version of *Santa*, whose title character's transformation from innocent village girl to courtesan allegorizes the temptations of big-city life. Actress Elena Sánchez Valenzuela crosses an avenue in Mexico City's upscale western districts, with Chapultepec Castle in the background.

O guarani, which portrays the chaste love between the young white settler Cecilia and her indigenous protector Peri, exemplifies a region-wide fascination with romanticized images of indigenous peoples, decimated by the Conquest and marginalized within Latin American societies. In Argentina, *El último malón* (*The Last Indian Attack*, Alcides Greca, 1916) documented the dismal living conditions of the Mocoví tribe in an ethnographic mode, while consigning them to the nation's past (Tompkins 2014: 104–105). In Chile, *La agonía del Arauco* (*The Agony of the Arauco*, Gabriela von Bussenius and Salvador Giambastiani, 1917) lamented the impending disappearance of the Mapuche tribe, while also trivializing it through parallels to the suffering of a grieving mother from the city (Donoso 1994: 34). In Bolivia, *Corazón aymara* (*Aymara Heart*, Pedro Sambarino, 1925) portrayed a virtuous native woman victimized by the supposedly rigid sexual morality of indigenous communities, while José María Velasco Maidana's *La profecía del lago* (*The Prophecy of the Lake*, 1925) and *Wara Wara* (1929) depict troubled romances between white and indigenous characters (Gumucio Dagron 1983: 63–68, 104–119).

In contrast to the dominance of the fiction feature in Argentina, Brazil, and Cuba beginning in the early 1910s, filmmaking in Mexico was shaped by a collective fascination with the violent events of the Revolution (1910–1920). Cameramen such as Enrique Rosas, Salvador Toscano, Jesús H. Abitia, the Alva Brothers, and others documented the final years of Porfirio Díaz's dictatorship, the uprising led by defeated presidential candidate Francisco I. Madero, and the bitter struggles between military factions that marked the later phases of the conflict. Very few fiction films were produced before 1917, when enthusiasts such as variety actress Mimí Derba, together with Rosas, began to film high-society melodramas. These were modeled on popular Italian "diva films," which starred celebrated actresses such as Pina Menichelli and Francesca Bertini.

Mexico's distinctive tradition of nonfiction filmmaking fostered unique exhibition practices, as camera operators combined their footage with images shot by others in compilation films that reviewed recent events. These images were often repurposed in later years: Rosas incorporated a scene showing the 1915 execution of members of the infamous "Gray Automobile Gang" into his 1919 crime serial *El automóvil gris* (*The Gray Automobile*). From the 1910s through the 1930s, Toscano assembled multiple versions of *Historia completa de la Revolución Mexicana, 1910–1920* (*Complete History of the Mexican Revolution, 1910–1920*) and *Los últimos treinta años en México* (*The Last Thirty Years in Mexico*) (Miquel 2010). In the 1930s, Félix Padilla, an itinerant exhibitor active in the US-Mexico borderlands, combined U.S. and Mexican newsreels, original footage, and images from U.S. serials to create *La venganza de Pancho Villa* (*Pancho Villa's Revenge*), which contested both racist Hollywood images of Mexicans and official versions of revolutionary history (Serna 2012: 12–13). Rooted in representational practices linked to the Revolution, the cases of Padilla and Toscano suggest the rich afterlives of moving images in their circulation across time and space, underlining the "multitemporal heterogeneity" of Latin American cultural formations.

The "delayed" circulation of imported films also proved generative for filmmaking outside major cities across Latin America. In 1920s Brazil, where films were exhibited in the North and Northeast months and even years after their releases in Rio de Janeiro and São Paulo, Hollywood westerns and crime serials of the 1910s inspired dynamic adventure films that showcased local transportation infrastructure and industry, including *Retribuição* (*Retribution*, Gentil Roiz, 1925), made in Recife, and *Tesouro perdido* (*Lost Treasure*, 1927), made in Cataguases, Minas Gerais, by Humberto Mauro, later a pivotal figure of Brazil's early sound cinema. A similar fascination with physical action and modern transportation technologies is evident in the adventure films *El tren fantasma* (*The Ghost Train*, 1927) and *El puño de hierro* (*The Iron Fist*, 1928), directed by Gabriel García Moreno in Orizaba in the Mexican state of Veracruz. The Colombian regional productions *Bajo el cielo antioqueño* (*Beneath the Skies of Antioquia*, Arturo Acevedo, 1925) and *Alma provinciana* (*Provincial Soul*, Félix J. Rodríguez, 1926) showcased both agriculture and industry through scenes that displayed coffee plantations and cigarette factories, testifying to the productivity of local economies.

The multiplicity of local production practices is paralleled by the heterogeneity of film audiences in Latin America. Far from constituting a unified national public, spectators were segmented by geographic location, ethnicity, and class. Given elites' early embrace of the cinema, working-class spectators were barred from early exhibitions of Edison's Vitascope in Lima (Bedoya 2009a: 29). In turn-of-the-century Rio de Janeiro, a society columnist advocated for "soirées da moda" ("fashionable screenings") intended for the affluent (Melo Souza 2003: 143). Ticket prices that varied by seating area reinforced internal divisions within exhibition spaces, and in capitals such as Rio de Janeiro and Mexico City, neighborhood venues catering to working-class spectators emerged quickly (de los Reyes 1983: 31–32, 66–67; Gonzaga 1996: 90, 102; Serna 2014a: 58–67). Yet class-segregated venues failed to quell the anxieties generated by the new medium, including concerns that movie theaters' dark environment encouraged pickpocketing and sexual advances (both welcome and uninvited). Critics' descriptions of "unruly" film audiences also indicate they were far from passive in the face of imported films. Particularly in neighborhood theaters, spectators read intertitles aloud for the benefit of illiterate audience members and reacted to the on-screen action with aplomb (*El Universal* 1920: 16).

Attempting to account for the unique dynamics of spectatorship outside Euro-American contexts, Hamid Naficy (1996) argues that rather than being "hailed" by imported films (recognizing themselves as subjects within the ideological order established by these texts), "Third World" spectators engage in "haggling," asserting their ability to produce meaning at the site of consumption through oral commentary and other practices. This negotiation with the purveyors of imported images took on literal form in some cases. Juan Sebastián Ospina León (2017) notes that the tradition of the *ñapa* ("extra gift")—a film added to the program at the audience's request—prevailed in Colombian movie theaters in the 1910s, signaling an active exchange between spectators and exhibitors. Vocal protests by audience members who stamped or whistled to express their displeasure could also influence a key aspect of the moviegoing experience: musical accompaniment. Ranging from full orchestras in movie palaces to lone piano players in neighborhood theaters, film music drew on Latin American genres such as marimba, danzón, and tango, as well as North American rhythms such as foxtrot and jazz (*El Universal* 1920: 16; Serna 2014a: 15, 60). Film music could complement projected images with familiar melodies, or render it thrillingly cosmopolitan.

Many of the strategies used to domesticate imported films for local consumption, including musical accompaniment, would be eliminated by the sweeping changes wrought by the transition to sound. Debuting in major cities in 1929, synchronized sound established new barriers to the international distribution of films, which had previously required relatively inexpensive—though often transformative—adjustments such as the translation of inter-titles (Serna 2014b: 122–123). Initially, Hollywood studios tried to cater to the lucrative Spanish-speaking market, among others, by producing multiple-language versions. Usually remakes of English-language productions shot with actors fluent in Spanish, multiple-language versions generated controversy among Latin American critics and spectators. Many objected to the studios' choice of a Castilian accent as the standard for Spanish-language dialogue, as well as to casting practices that combined actors from multiple countries with varying accents in a single film (Gunckel 2008: 333–334). Foreign-language versions also disappointed audiences accustomed to the high production values and recognizable stars of English-language productions (Vasey 1997: 96). Yet Lisa Jarvinen (2012: 10) suggests that critics' negative reception of Hollywood Spanish-language versions overshadowed their considerable success with audiences. Furthermore, Hollywood productions that proved popular with Latin American spectators—in particular, the seven Paramount films starring tango legend Carlos Gardel (D'Lugo 2008; Navitski 2011)—provided a model for Latin American sound film industries: a "basic combination of comedy, melodrama, and good songs" (King 2000: 37). Although improvements in dubbing and subtitling allowed Hollywood studios to recapture and even increase their global market share, Argentina and Mexico proved powerful competitors in Spanish-language markets.

Early Latin American sound films capitalized on the continent-wide popularity of musical genres increasingly viewed as embodying national identity: the Argentine tango, Brazilian samba, and Mexican ranchera. Following the early successes of *Tango!* (directed by Luis Moglia Barth for Argentina Sono Film) and *Los tres berretines* (*The Three Amateurs*, directed collectively by the Lumiton studio's founders) in 1933, Argentina's industry developed melodramatic formulas that dramatized class conflict, exemplified by the series of films starring tango singer Libertad Lamarque (Karush 2012: 108–118). Early Brazilian sound films also capitalized on radio performers' popularity in Carnival-themed *chanchadas* such as *Alô, alô Brasil* (*Hello, Hello Brasil*, Wallace Downey, João de Barro, and Alberto Ribeiro, 1935) and *Alô, alô Carnaval* (*Hello, Hello Carnaval*, Adhemar Gonzaga, 1936). In Mexico, the pessimistic tone of fallen-woman films such as *Santa* (Antonio Moreno, 1931) and *La mujer del puerto* (*The Woman of the Port*, Arcady Boytler, 1934) and revolutionary dramas such as Fernando de Fuentes' *El prisionero 13* (*Prisoner Number 13*, 1933), *El compadre Mendoza* (*Godfather Mendoza*, 1934), and *Vámonos con Pancho Villa* (*Let's Go with Pancho Villa*, 1936) gave way to the light-hearted *comedia ranchera Allá en el Rancho Grande* (*Over at the Big Ranch*, Fernando de Fuentes, 1936), a huge hit in Mexico and beyond. Latin American industries increasingly resorted to "exaggerating the national," packaging popular customs and music to appeal to domestic and overseas markets alike (Jarvinen 2012: 139).

While sound cinema fostered industries in Argentina, Mexico, and Brazil, its increased cost and technological complexity also prolonged silent filmmaking and gave rise to creative exhibition practices. Arguably the only Latin American examples of modernist silent cinema premiered in Brazil after sound cinema's debut in local movie theaters: *São Paulo, sinfonia da metrópole* (*São Paulo, Symphony of the Metropolis*, Rodolfo Lustig and Adalberto Kemeny, 1929) and Mário Peixoto's *Limite* (*Limit*, 1931). Other filmmakers and exhibitors improvised solutions in the absence of synch-sound equipment. Unable to afford the costs of conversion, some movie theater owners used phonograph records to loosely "synchronize" film screenings (Freire 2011). In 1930, filmmaker Jota Soares accompanied showings of his silent film *No cenário da vida* (*On the Stage of Life*, co-directed with Luiz Maranhão) with prerecorded sound effects (Cunha Filho 2006: 33). Also in Brazil, Antonio Tibiriçá recorded sound-on-disc accompaniment for his 1926 film *Vício e beleza* (*Vice and Beauty*) (Cinemateca Brasileira 1930). Even *Acabaram-se os otários* (*No More Suckers*, Luiz de Barros, 1929), considered the first Brazilian synch-sound feature, used existing phonograph records as the basis for musical scenes (Freire 2013: 109), while in Ecuador, *Guayaquil de mis amores* (*Guayaquil of My Loves*, Francisco Diumenjo, 1930) was accompanied live with the popular title song. The transition to sound thus fostered production and exhibition practices that, while ephemeral, challenge any straightforward account of Hollywood dominance tested then quickly reaffirmed.

Figure 2.4   An announcement of the temporary closure of Rio de Janeiro's Cinema Pathé for the installation of Western Electric sound equipment in August 1929. Less prosperous exhibitors in the city often improvised cheaper alternatives to imported sound technologies. Arquivo Nacional (Brasil), Coleção Famíla Ferrez. Reference number FF_FMF_6_1_0_7_4.

As the examples discussed above suggest, Latin American film cultures of the silent and early sound period diverge from linear accounts of stylistic and industrial change developed in other contexts, as well as the stark opposition between moving-image producers and consumers that structure many previous histories of Latin American cinema. The medium's complex trajectories in the region also confound clear divisions between early and classical cinema and between fictional and nonfictional modes. Furthermore, practices that blur the distinction between production and exhibition—the conjunction of film projection with vocal performances or ad hoc "synchronization" with recorded sound in Brazil and Cuba, the continual reworking of the compilation films that circulated through Mexico and its borderlands—challenge the notion of the cinematic text as a fixed, bounded entity that can be understood in isolation from the context of its reception. These insights help highlight the impact of distributors, exhibitors, fans, and critics—along with individuals whose activities exceed these retrospectively defined roles—in negotiating the range of meanings and values attached to cinema in early twentieth-century Latin America. Film production and consumption articulated the interests of foreign film companies, local impresarios, filmmakers, government representatives, elites, intellectuals, and audience members in configurations that defy binary oppositions between neocolonial powers and national interests. Filmmaking was linked with nation-building projects (both in its iconographies and themes, and in public discourses that framed it as a marker of modernity and progress), but the circulation and consumption of cinema intersected with heterogeneous experiences and ideals of modernization inflected by regional, racial, and class differences. Attending to cinema's links to national imaginaries, as well as to the circulation of filmmakers and films on local, regional, and transnational scales, generates fresh perspectives on the politics of the moving image in early twentieth-century Latin America.

References

Agramonte, A. and Castillo, L. (2011) *Cronología del cine cubano vol. I: 1897–1936*. Havana: Ediciones ICAIC.

Batlle, J.L. (1916) "De la ciudad condal." *Cine-Mundial*, September: 395–396.

Bedoya, R. (2009a) *El cine silente en Perú*. Lima: Universidad de Lima.

—— (2009b) *El cine sonoro en Perú*. Lima: Universidad de Lima.

Castro Ricalde, M. and McKee Irwin, R. (2011) *El cine mexicano se impone: mercados internacionales y penetración cultural en la época dorada*. Mexico City: Universidad Nacional Autónoma de México.

—— (2013) *Global Mexican Cinema: Its Golden Age*. London: Palgrave Macmillan.

Cinemateca Brasileira (1930) Annotated photograph, reference number FB_1410_019. Available at: www.bcc.org.br/ (accessed February 19, 2017).

Cunha Filho, P.C. (2006) *Relembrando o cinema pernambucano: Dos arquivos de Jota Soares*. Recife: Editora Massangana.

—— (2010) *A utopia provinciana: Recife, cinema, melancolia*. Recife: Editora Universitária— Universidade Federal de Pernambuco.

de los Reyes, A. (1983) *Cine y sociedad en México vol. I: Vivir de sueños*, 2nd ed. Mexico City: Filmoteca de la UNAM.

—— (1995) "Gabriel Veyre y Fernand Bon Bernard, representantes de los Hermanos Lumière en México." *Anales del Instituto de Investigaciones Estéticas*, 67: 119–137.

Derteano, R. (1918) "Crónica del Perú." *Cine-Mundial*, September: 582.

Di Núbila, D. (1959) *Historia del cine argentino*, vol. I. Buenos Aires: Ediciones Cruz de Malta.

D'Lugo, M. (2008) "Early Cinematic Tangos: Audiovisual Culture and Transnational Film Aesthetics." *Studies in Hispanic Cinemas*, 5(1/2): 9–23.

Donoso, E.J. (1994) *Cine mudo chileno*. Santiago: Imprenta los Héroes.

Ehrick, C. (2006) "Beneficent Cinema: State Formation, Elite Reproduction and Silent Film in Uruguay, 1910s–1920s." *The Americas*, 63(2): 205–224.

Fon-Fon. (1916) "Nobreza gaúcha," May 13.

Freire, R. de L. (2011) "Truste, músicos e vitrolas: A tentativa de monopólio de Western Electric na chegada do cinema sonoro ao Brasil e seus desdobramentos." *Imagofagia*, 5. Available at: www.asaeca.org/imagofagia/index.php/imagofagia/article/view/193 (accessed February 19, 2017).

—— (2013) "*Acabaram-se os otários*: Compreendendo o primeiro longa-metragem sonoro brasileiro." *Revista brasileira de estudos de cinema e audiovisual*, 2(3): 104–128.

García Canclini, N. (1995) *Hybrid Cultures: Strategies for Entering and Leaving Modernity*, trans. C.L. Chiappari and S.L. López. Minneapolis, MN: University of Minnesota Press.

García Riera, E. (1969) *Historia documental del cine mexicano*, vol. I. Mexico City: Ediciones Era.

Gonzaga, A. (1996) *Palácios e poeiras: 100 anos de cinemas no Rio de Janeiro*. Rio de Janeiro: FUNARTE.

Gumucio Dagron, A. (1983) *Historia del cine boliviano*. Mexico City: Filmoteca de la UNAM.

Gunckel, C. (2008) "The War of the Accents: Spanish Language Hollywood Films in Mexican Los Angeles." *Film History*, 20(3): 325–343.

Gunning, T. (1997) "Before Documentary: Early Non-Fiction Films and the 'View' Aesthetic." In D. Hertogs and N. de Klerck (eds.), *Uncharted Territory: Essays on Early Non-Fiction Film*. Amsterdam: Nederlands Filmmuseum, pp. 9–24.

Jarvinen, L. (2012) *The Rise of Spanish-Language Filmmaking: Out from Hollywood's Shadow, 1929–1939.* New Brunswick, NJ: Rutgers University Press.

Jung, U. (2002) "Local Views: A Blind Spot in the Historiography of Early German Cinema." *Historical Journal of Radio, Film and Television*, 22(3): 253–273.

Karush, M. (2012) *Culture of Class: Radio and Cinema in the Making of a Divided Argentina, 1920–1946.* Durham, NC: Duke University Press.

King, J. (2000) *Magical Reels: A History of Cinema in Latin America.* London: Verso.

López, A.M. (2000) "Early Cinema and Modernity in Latin America." *Cinema Journal*, 40(1): 48–78.

Melo Souza, J.I. (2003) *Imagens do passado: São Paulo e Rio de Janeiro nos primórdios do cinema.* São Paulo: Editora Senac.

El Mercurio (1917) June 10, p. 6.

Miquel, Á. (1997) *Salvador Toscano.* Mexico City: Filmoteca de la UNAM.

—— (2010) "Las historias completas de la Revolución de Salvador Toscano." In P. Ortiz Monasterio (ed.), *Fragmentos: Narración cinematográfica compilada y arreglada por Salvador Toscano, 1900–1930.* Mexico City: Conaculta, pp. 23–37.

Muniz de Albuquerque Jr., D. (2014) *The Invention of the Brazilian Northeast*, trans. J.D. Metz. Durham, NC: Duke University Press.

Naficy, H. (1996) "Theorizing 'Third World' Film Spectatorship." *Wide Angle*, 18(4): 3–26.

Navitski, R. (2011) "The Tango on Broadway: Carlos Gardel's International Stardom and the Transition to Sound in Argentina." *Cinema Journal*, 51(1): 26–49.

Ortega, F.G. (1917) "Film Export Notes." *Moving Picture World*, April 21: 437.

Ospina León, J.S. (2013) "Discursos, práticas, historiografía: continuidad y tableau en el cine silent colombiano." *Imagofagia*, 8. Available at: www.asaeca.org/imagofagia/index.php/imagofagia/article/view/487 (accessed February 19, 2017).

—— (2017) "Films on Paper: Early Colombian Cinema Periodicals, 1916–1920." In R. Navitski and N. Poppe (eds.), *Cosmopolitan Visions: The Transnational Horizons of Latin American Film Culture, 1896–1960*, 39–65.

Paranaguá, P.A. (1984) *Cinema na América Latina: Longe de Deus e perto de Hollywood.* Porto Alegre: LP&M Editores.

La Prensa (1915) August 23, p. 18.

Salles Gomes, P.E. (1995) "Cinema: A Trajectory within Underdevelopment." In R. Johnson and R. Stam (eds.), *Brazilian Cinema.* New York: Columbia University Press, pp. 245–255.

Schroeder Rodríguez, P.A. (2008) "Latin American Silent Cinema: Triangulation and the Politics of Criollo Aesthetics." *Latin American Research Review*, 43(3): 33–57.

Serna, L.I. (2012) "*La venganza de Pancho Villa*: Resistance and Repetition." *Aztlán: A Journal of Chicano Studies*, 37(2): 11–42.

—— (2014a) *Making Cinelandia: American Films and Mexican Film Culture before the Golden Age.* Durham, NC: Duke University Press.

—— (2014b) "Translations and Transportation: Towards a Transnational History of the Intertitle." In J. Bean, A. Kapse, and L. Horak (eds.), *Silent Cinema and the Politics of Space.* Bloomington, IN: Indiana University Press, pp. 121–146.

Sommer, D. (1991) *Foundational Fictions: The National Romances of Latin America.* Berkeley, CA: University of California Press.

Tompkins, C. (2014) "*El último malón de Alcides Greca*: Repetición y cine de atracciones." *Studies in Latin American Popular Culture*, 32: 97–119.

El Universal (1920) "El reino del ridículo: Los que van al cine," p. 16.

Vasey, R. (1997) *The World According to Hollywood, 1918–1939.* Madison, WI: University of Wisconsin Press.

Viany, A. (1959) *Introdução ao cinema brasileiro.* Rio de Janeiro: Ministério da Educação e Cultura.

3

NATIONAL CINEMAS (RE)IGNITED

Film and the state

*Lisa Shaw, Luis Duno-Gottberg, Joanna Page,
and Ignacio M. Sánchez Prado*

Editors' introduction

National cinema has long been about "selling" the nation—whether in the 1930s with the rise of more consolidated domestic industries interested in staking out market shares at home and abroad, the 1960s during the apogee of explicitly avant-garde, politicized filmmaking, or the present moment. Eschewing the earlier paradigm of national cinemas defined exclusively through cultural and artistic specificities, this chapter focuses on the range of common strategies through which, since at least the 1930s, producers and filmmakers have been encouraged, guided, or incentivized by the agencies that act on behalf of various nation-states to develop modern forms of national cinema. Lisa Shaw, Luis Duno-Gottberg, Ignacio M. Sánchez Prado, and Joanna Page provide a valuable historical narrative of the evolution of that complex relation between state agencies and culturally defined film industries in the region. In their comparative and contrastive views of the relation of historical and more recent national film industries, they underscore the trans-regional nature of the role of the state in guiding, protecting, financially sustaining, and even coercing local national cinema. Implicitly, this essay encourages us to reconceptualize national cinema less as a unified, homogenous entity than as a plural, often tension-filled set of claims by different groups who invest in the cinema and sell the national (understood in a variety of ways), and to recognize how those varied claims involve the medium's dual status as representational form and as commodity.

Beyond the particular case studies presented, two interconnected points are especially noteworthy about this approach to the national in Latin American cinema. The first is the way discussions of national cinema only reaffirm the transborder nature of the national cinematic project. In this, the chapter echoes positions that figure prominently in Juan Poblete's inquiry into Chilean cinema in Chapter 1 and in Mexico and Brazil in Chapter 2 by Rielle Navitski. National cinema, understood as part of a national state-invested project, enables us to appreciate the ways in which cinema seems always to have operated on levels that transcend what Andrew Higson (2000) famously termed the "limiting imagination of national cinema." This is, indeed, the point of Masha Salazkina's discussion of intellectual border crossings and exchanges in Chapter 13.

The second point relates to how previous studies of the national as a political construction have largely ignored the dynamics of audiences. Sánchez Prado and Page shine an important light on the ways in which the shifts in the cultural politics of the state in the contemporary neoliberal moment have reshaped Latin American markets and audiences. Film's former role as a mass medium that educated domestic audiences in how to be citizens of the nation (per Carlos Monsiváis) has been taken over by television, as argued by Cerdán and Fernández Labayen in Chapter 23. Today, through the interplay of state initiatives and the expansion of global art cinema, the audience of much Latin American cinema is now shaped around a peculiar mix of a middle-brow, middle-class audience at home and an art cinema and alternative audience abroad, as documented by Gerard Dapena's discussion of the international appeal of Latin American genre films. In these reconfigurations of audience, it is essential to note the way technology has impacted notions of audience and film reception. The impact of revolutionary digital technologies on film viewing, as discussed in Chapter 24, complements the thrust of this chapter by pointing to the limits of the presumed hegemony of the state's claim to sovereignty over "national cinema" in an age when the very idea of national audiences has been diminished, if not made entirely irrelevant, by new audiovisual technologies.

This chapter argues for the essential role of state support for the ongoing production of films within national spaces, and recognizes its various manifestations, including direct and indirect funding mechanisms, screen quotas, and government-sponsored distribution networks and exhibition venues. In charting historical trajectories, the sections track the "stop-and-go development" of individual film industries as governments oscillated between liberal economic models and moderate-to-strong state intervention (Tompkins 2013: 21). At some historical junctures, governments would not only facilitate production (through grants, tax breaks, or the creation of state-owned production facilities), distribution, and even exhibition, but also fund national film archives. The opposite often occurred when governments liberalized their economies and retracted such support, generating a significant contraction of the domestic film industry.

The sections track a shift in funding models and in the relationship between private investments and state support. In the silent period, private entrepreneurship underwrote domestic production and exhibition. Starting in the 1930s, governments began to act as a vital stakeholder and invest public resources towards crafting a certain configuration of national cinema. If the 1980s witnessed the dismantling of state support, the 1990s initiated more heterogeneous funding models drawing on international support, private domestic investment (often encouraged by legislation), and other forms of indirect state support. In tracing these general patterns, the authors observe the variability of government initiatives in different countries and underscore how state intervention necessarily entails a disciplinary function to one degree or another. Some countries benefited significantly from protectionist legislation and funding (Mexico, Argentina, Brazil, Colombia, Venezuela, and Cuba); others did not (Peru, Bolivia). While some filmmakers suffered tremendous repression (Chile, Argentina, Brazil, Cuba), those in other countries experienced it to a lesser extent (Venezuela, Mexico).

As we underscore the vital role of government support, we identify the state as one stakeholder (among others) with a vested interest in the cinema as both an ideological and economic "engine" of national development. The last two sections recognize how, in the present moment, the investments of other sectors have helped to reconfigure the story of national cinema—including a new generation of filmmakers who have fostered a more vibrant commercial cinema, the middle-class audiences in the domestic market-place to whom such films are directed, and foreign entities (from European film festivals to Hollywood studios) that have begun to provide new sources of financing.

The emergence of film industries and the role of the state in Mexico, Brazil, and Argentina in the early sound era

LISA SHAW

With the advent of the talkies in the 1930s, film production gathered momentum in Mexico, Brazil, and Argentina, Latin America's traditional "big three" film industries, stimulated by governments keen to "sell" a vision of domestic progress and modernity to national audiences, and in some cases those of neighboring countries. In Mexico various state initiatives arose to foster the growth of private enterprise in the form of a variety of small production companies. The government of President Lázaro Cárdenas (1934–1940) took an active role in the development of the industry, introducing a protectionist policy for domestic film production, which included tax exemptions for local producers and a screen quota for Mexican films. This policy of state support, which was mirrored to some extent in Brazil, continued under the administration of Manuel Avila Camacho (1940–1946), which backed the Banco Cinematográfico, a bank created in 1942 with the sole purpose of financing national film production and distribution. In Argentina, however, the state was not *initially* a major stakeholder in the nascent film industry, and the first film studios remained largely in private hands during the 1930s and early 1940s, producing "national" films for domestic audiences and for export to most Latin American countries (Falicov 2007: 21). Ironically, privately produced Argentine cinema suffered during the war as a direct consequence of the government's support for the Axis powers, which resulted in film stock from the US being redirected to Mexico as a reward for that country's support for the Allied cause. Although until the outbreak of the war Mexican cinema had been trailing that of Argentina in terms of technical quality and the scale of production (Falicov 2007: 24), the US's embargo on Argentina turned the tables in Mexico's favor. By 1943, the Mexican film industry had established itself as the most important in Latin America. With the election to the presidency of Juan Perón in 1946, there was more intensive government intervention in the Argentine film industry, and the Peronist postwar years saw a partial recovery and a more overt attempt to create a national cinema that would increase Argentina's status and market share abroad.

The situation in Brazil was slightly different in the early sound period, with the state and private entrepreneurs staking out alternate visions for national cinema. The regime of Getúlio Vargas (1930–1945) believed that cinema could transmit a nationalist ideology and promote a sense of belonging to the wider national community, but concentrated its efforts on the educational and patriotic potential of filmmaking rather than on fostering a commercial film industry. Vargas's provisional government (1930–1933) passed the first legislation in support of national cinema, making it compulsory to screen one Brazilian short film in every cinema program, and giving a tremendous boost to short film production. The INCE (*Instituto Nacional de Cinema Educativo*—National Institute of Educational Cinema) was established on January 13, 1937, in response to fears that the unfettered growth of commercial film threatened to erode moral and educational standards. The INCE films, some of which were of feature length, were exhibited in schools, cultural centers, sporting associations and workers' organizations, and provided regular work for actors and technical staff, as well as helping Brazilian cinema fulfill the quota system introduced by the Vargas regime. These state-sponsored films represented a vision of "national" cinema as a way of fostering a sense of belonging and celebration of modernity for domestic audiences. This intensified with the establishment of the authoritarian *Estado Novo* (New State) in November 1937; the incentives that had previously been suggested to stimulate the involvement of private enterprise in the production of educational films were scrapped in favor of an overwhelming emphasis on the INCE, particularly in association with the talented director Humberto Mauro.

In the 1930s and 1940s, enterprising businessmen such as Adhemar Gonzaga supported a different vision of "national" cinema as an up-to-date industrial system that could exemplify the country's technological advances. Gonzaga founded the Cinearte studios in 1930 to tie in with his eponymous film magazine. Renamed Cinédia, this studio remained in continual operation until 1951, and was consciously modeled on the Hollywood majors. In São Paulo in the late 1940s, a group of bourgeois intellectuals founded the Vera Cruz film company. Although the studio system was by then in decline in Hollywood, Vera Cruz looked to the MGM studios for inspiration with regard to its structure, employing contract stars and directors on generous salaries, in spite of the absence of any sound economic infrastructure.

Private and public efforts to expand domestic film production (given the medium's economic and/or ideological potential) went hand in hand with developing representational conventions that could imagine the nation in particular ways. In order to lay claim to the domestic market, private entrepreneurs had to find repeatable formulas to distinguish their films from imports and to attract local audiences. This often entailed drawing on the power of local musical and performance traditions and established domestic stars, and placing these elements within Hollywood genres already familiar to Latin American audiences. In Argentina, Mexico, and Brazil, films capitalized on the existing reputations of local performers such as Carmen Miranda in Brazil, Libertad Lamarque in Argentina, and Pedro Infante and Jorge Negrete in Mexico, many of whom were well known to radio listeners.

Popular comedies were particularly central to the Brazilian and Mexican industries because of their ability to draw on the linguistic and sociocultural competencies of local audiences. Films starring comic performers such as Cantinflas and Tin Tan delighted Mexican audiences from the 1930s until the 1960s. Like the *chanchada* tradition in Brazil, these films poked fun at the nation's elite and middle classes, highlighting the artificial nature of the distinctions within Mexico's social hierarchy, and humorously represented the underdog— often a rural-urban migrant—in a constant battle with the modern, industrialized world. In Mexico and Brazil, the films of Cantinflas and the *chanchada*, respectively, addressed one of the principal social concerns of the 1940s: mass migration to the capital city.

These comic movies were a hit with working-class audiences throughout the nation, thus helping Mexicans and Brazilians to imagine a national community during a decade in flux, reflecting "national" cinema's dual status as both commodity and representational form, and selling a critical vision of national modernity to those who least benefited from it. They were naturally favored by the semiliterate and illiterate masses over subtitled Hollywood imports, and appealed to rural-urban migrants who could identify with the characters and predicaments presented on screen.

In Brazil, popular genres, chiefly musical comedies that drew on the theme and music of carnival, became the mainstay of Cinédia's productions in the 1930s and 1940s. Gonzaga astutely realized that this tried-and-trusted formula was the key to the commercial viability of his studio. It was thus at Cinédia that the *chanchada* tradition coalesced in the form of *Alô, alô, carnaval!* (*Hello, Hello, Carnival!*, 1936), directed by Gonzaga and starring Carmen Miranda, which definitively established the paradigms of Brazilian musical comedy with its pioneering combination of carnival music and festivity, a backstage plot, and a liberal dose of satire, particularly directed at foreign cultural forms. *Alô, alô, carnaval!* proved an unprecedented success at the box office in spite of its lack of sophistication in relation to imported Hollywood movies. In fact, Gonzaga's film celebrated the limitations of the Brazilian film industry to great comic effect, establishing a vein of self-deprecating humor and lack of pretension that would run through the *chanchada* tradition and guarantee its enduring popularity. It was with the founding of the Atlântida Cinematográfica studio in Rio de Janeiro in 1941 that the *chanchada* came to exemplify the multivalent notions of "national" cinema. The genre was a product sold to domestic audiences, promoted a vision of modernity—albeit a satirical one—for the benefit of those it had left behind, and served as a site of identification and belonging for the masses. Despite the studio's ambitious and patriotic mission statement, in which they promised to create cinema that provided "indisputable services to national greatness," and initial investment in feature-length dramas that dealt with serious social themes, Atlântida soon turned its attentions to carnival musicals, developing the comedic dimension of the foolproof formula.

In contrast to Brazil, during the so-called "golden age" of the Mexican film industry (1940 to the mid-1950s), melodramas proved to be the most popular genre at the box office—particularly those involving the Mexican Revolution and, somewhat later, domestic strife—along with the *comedia ranchera*, a genre blending comedy and romance set in northern Mexican ranches, an iconic location of national identity in the post-revolutionary era. As with the *chanchada* in Brazil, which began as a vehicle for carnival marches and sambas performed by stars of the radio and nascent record industries, popular music was central to the *comedia ranchera* as well as the so-called *cabaretera* or brothel melodramas that enjoyed widespread popularity in Mexico in the 1940s and 1950s. Similarly, Argentine cinema was dominated in the 1930s by the tango melodrama, inspired by the lyrics of the national music. As John King states, "local producers soon realized the commercial potential of tango-led national cinema," which gave rise to "investment in advanced technology and a cultivation of a homespun star system," as well as defining the output of Argentina's first two studios, Sono Film and Lumiton (King 2000: 37–38).

Even in these three countries, efforts to promote national cinema (as a domestic industry and a set of representational conventions) were not successful in dominating local markets. When Latin American audiences were not watching Hollywood imports between the 1930s and the late 1950s, however, they were going to the cinema to see homegrown comedies, melodramas, and musicals. Interestingly, the development of distinctive national traditions such as the Brazilian *chanchada*, the Argentine tango movies, and Mexico's *cabareteras* and *comedias rancheras* also allowed them to travel across national borders and attract new audiences.

The role of the state in Cuba and Venezuela

LUIS DUNO-GOTTBERG

In contrast to the "big three" national cinemas, Cuba and Venezuela illustrate the ways in which state intervention shapes film industries with small and medium-sized domestic markets. The Venezuelan case demonstrates with particular clarity the frequently porous line between public and private endeavors, and how state investments, both direct and indirect support, can influence domestic productions carried out ostensibly by private companies.

As in other countries in Latin America, cinema arrived in Cuba as an import financed by private capital—a foreign technology and cultural commodity, soon to be appropriated to convey a particular sense of modernity and identity (López 2000; Paranaguá 2003). Local entrepreneurs such as José Casasús and Enrique Díaz Quesada (1883–1923) made their first films through the sponsorship, respectively, of a local brewery (*El brujo desapareciendo* [*The Disappearing Wizard*, 1889]) and a North American company interested in promoting its local amusement park (*El Parque Palatino* [*Palatino Park*, 1906]). These vistas seem to anticipate the staging of an exotic Cuba for foreign consumption (Chanan 2004: 54), something that would be challenged by the Revolution of 1959. Domestic production would be extremely limited through the 1950s, as U.S. companies dominated distribution and exhibition, and imported films (from Hollywood, as well as some from Mexico and Argentina) ruled local screens.

While not providing support for domestic production, the state did intervene in the distribution and exhibition of films in these decades through ongoing censorship. Fulgencio Batista's dictatorship, for example, banned *El mégano* (*The Charcoal Worker*, 1955) after just one screening. A film showing the dire living conditions of workers harvesting wood to make coal in the countryside of Cuba was deemed too subversive years before the Revolution.

The weakness and dependency of the Cuban film industry persisted until the advent of the Revolution, at which time the Cuban state became the sole producer, distributor, and exhibitor of cinema. This new phase in the history of Cuban cinema rested on the explicit understanding of the medium's value as a crucial tool of the state's revolutionary politics. Indeed, almost immediately, the new government created a film department within the *Dirección de Cultura del Ejército Rebelde* (Culture Division of the Rebel Army). This was followed, in March 1959, by the *Instituto Cubano del Arte y la Industria Cinematográficos* (Institute of Cuban Cinematic Art and Industry, ICAIC), an organization that would significantly change the course of national cinema by directly investing and organizing production, distribution, and exhibition (from theaters and mobile projection units, to the influential *Festival Internacional del Nuevo Cine Latinoamericano*). This founding gesture is remarkable and speaks of the relevance of cinema for those coming into power, considering its place as the second legislative action of the revolutionary government, only preceded by land reform.

Although a governmental institution, ICAIC aimed at preserving a degree of autonomy, while at the same time enacting the Revolution's goal of creating a national cinema. This balancing act frequently led to polemical decisions and clashes not only with filmmakers, but also other representatives from the government. *PM* (1961), directed by Saba Cabrera Infante and Orlando Jiménez Leal, might be the most famous case of censorship; ICAIC interrupted its screening, deeming it untimely or inappropriate. The debates that ensued led to Fidel Castro's famous "Words to the Intellectuals." In the 1970s, in the context of the so-called *quinquenio gris*, and later in the 1980s, ICAIC delayed or restricted the release of films by Sara Gómez, Humberto Solás, Manuel Octavio Gómez, and Sergio Giral.

Nicolás Guillén Landrián offers a particularly notable case, as he experienced some of the most serious forms of censorship when his documentaries were seen as critical of the Cuban Revolution. His 1963 *En un barrio Viejo* (*In an Old Neighborhood*), for example, bears some resemblance to *PM*, censored the year before. After he was expelled from ICAIC, his films were often withdrawn from exhibition altogether. Between 1970 and 1989, the film-maker was castigated, interrogated, and imprisoned multiple times.

Nevertheless, even as it carried out such disciplinary actions, ICAIC also clashed with members of the Communist Party—for example, while defending its right to exhibit films such as Fellini's *La dolce vita* (1961). The institution was also active in defending artists cast as "social misfits," who risked being sentenced to work at the Military Units to Augment Production (UMAP).

With the collapse of communism in Eastern Europe in late 1989, Cuba entered a deep crisis known as the Special Period that greatly influenced the relationship between the state and the film industry. With greatly reduced funding, ICAIC confronted its biggest crisis, evident in the drastic fall in film production, and the forced merger with other institutions in 1991. This action coincided with the scandal of *Alicia en el pueblo de las maravillas* (*Alice in Wondertown* 1991), directed by Daniel Díaz Torres, a scatological critique of Cuban bureaucracy that confronted all sorts of institutional attacks (cf. Chanan 2004: 611; García Borrero 2013). Following the Special Period, the search for external funding became a matter of survival. Ibermedia, for example, supported Cuban cinema starting in the mid-1990s, and it was not uncommon to see co-productions that reproduced stereotypical images of the country to please international audiences. One of the most remarkable consequences of this transformation is the emergence of private producers in the last decade, some of them formerly connected to ICAIC. *Juan de los Muertos* (*Juan of the Dead*, 2011) is the most successful film produced within a commercial model and outside of the state. Along with these alternative sources of funding and distribution, digital technologies—including online distribution, with its new levels of autonomy—have granted significant freedom for a younger generation and the emergence of new subversive discourses.

As the country transitions to a more liberalized economy and film production relies more on private capital, the state continues to exercise control by regulating distribution and exhibition on the island and through subtle forms of censorship. The Ministry of Culture seems to create obstacles for some films, such as *Verde, verde* (*Green, Green*, Enrique Piñeda Barnet, 2011), *La piscina* (*The Swimming Pool*, Carlos Machado Quintela, 2011), and Carlos Lechuga's *Melaza* (*Molasses*, 2012), which received limited release and vanished from theaters. Movies such as *Memorias del desarrollo* (*Memories of Development*, Miguel Coyula, 2010) were excluded from the competition of Havana's Festival of New Latin American Cinema and would not receive an official release in the country. Other independent films have been excluded from the official catalog of Cuba's cinematheque, and thus from the archive that informs Cuba's national film history.

Venezuela's film industry has followed a different trajectory in terms of the role of the state, as government intervention has played an important role since very early on. Looking at this history, one could assert that, in general, the attempts to develop a commercially viable industry have depended on and benefited from governmental support—ranging from direct subsidies and legislation, to the construction of technical facilities and infrastructure. As in the case of Cuba, cinema arrived in Venezuela as an import and did not immediately lead to the birth of an autonomous, commercially viable film industry. Local entrepreneurs produced shorts starting in 1896, as well as numerous newsreels, and Enrique Zimmerman directed the country's first feature, *La Dama de las Cayenas* (*The Lady of the Hibiscus*) in 1916. Unlike Cuba, the state took a strong interest in film, particularly in periods in which the national economy was flourishing. Starting in 1908, dictator Juan Vicente Gómez sponsored several films, mostly devoted to promote "his" public works and other state initiatives. In 1927, when Venezuela's oil exports took off, Gómez funded the *Laboratorio Cinematográfico de la Nación* (National Film Laboratory), placing it under the Ministry of Public Works (MOP). In the years to come, variations in oil revenue would determine the many cycles of investment and divestment in the film industry: the booms of the 1970s and 2000s coincided with high oil prices and a significant expansion of state intervention in the cultural arena.

The *Laboratorio* not only supported governmental projects, but also provided assistance to some private productions. Several technical experiments took place under the sponsorship of this state institution. The first non-synchronized sound film in the country, *La venus de nácar* (*The Mother-of Pearl Venus*, Efraín Gómez, 1932), is one example. Admittedly, the authoritarian and self-serving nature of Gómez's regime makes it hard to distinguish "state sponsorship" from a private venture. Indeed, many of the newsreels produced celebrate the industrial advances of the country by showcasing Gómez's own companies, or those of his relatives. Furthermore, it was Efraín Gómez, nephew of the dictator, who directed *Laboratorio Cinematográfico*, channeling his own interest in the nascent business of cinema. In 1928, he founded Maracay Films.

After Gómez's death, the *Laboratorio* became the *Servicio Cinematográfico Nacional*, and soon after that was privatized and renamed *Estudios Ávila*, under the supervision of the well-known writer Rómulo Gallegos. The importance of this short-lived project (1938–1942) cannot be overstated: it represents a serious attempt to create a national film industry (Acosta 1997: 190). The relationship with the state was not severed completely, as *Estudios Ávila* made a significant number of documentaries for the government; in fact, these documentaries constituted the majority of its production. In revising this history, one could perhaps speak of a project of privatization that allowed outsourcing of services for the state. In 1942, facing significant challenges, the equipment was returned to the MOP. Bolivar Films followed with a more successful business model, providing services for private and public interests after 1940. Beyond non-narrative cinema produced for/with the state, the 1940s–1950s is characterized by a series of alliances with Mexican producers, leading to the development of a small industry and modestly successful commercial model.

The most visible presence of the state appears toward the late 1960s, with the creation of the *Cinemateca Nacional* (1966), under the direction of filmmaker Margot Benacerraf, and the increasing subsidies for production. The 1970s is remembered as a "golden era" and coincides with a great influx of oil revenue. This allowed significant funding for filmmakers, as well the development of protectionist legislation—such as screen quotas to guarantee exhibition. In 1975, for example, the Venezuelan government provided significant funding for the production of nine features: *Compañero Augusto* (Enver Cordido), *Los muertos sí salen* (*The Dead Do Leave*, Alfredo Lugo), *Fiebre* (*Fever*, Alfredo Anzola, Juan Santana, and Fernando Toro), *Soy un delincuente* (*I Am a Delinquent*, Clemente de la Cerda), *Sagrado y obsceno* (*Sacred and Obscene*, Román Chalbaud), *Canción mansa para un pueblo bravo* (*A Meek Song for a Fierce People*, Giancarlo Carrer), *La ruta del triunfo* (*The Triumphant Route*, Manuel Díaz Punceles), *300,000 héroes* (*300,000 Heroes*, María de Lourdes Carbonell), and *La invasión* (*The Invasion*, Julio César Mármol). This support came through unlikely state institutions: Corpoindustria (an organization devoted to modernization of national industry) and Corpoturismo (an organization devoted to tourism).

All this activity was overseen by the newly created *Comisión Nacional de Cinematografía* and led to a series of blockbuster films. As in other parts of Latin America, the 1980s was a period of deregulation and contraction. Nevertheless, institutional support was never completely absent, and in 1981 the government created the *Fondo de Fomento Cinematográfico* (FONCINE) to support national production. This institution was replaced in 1993 by the *Centro Nacional Autónomo de Cinematografía* (CNAC); at the same time, the first important legislation promoting and protecting national cinema appears—the "Ley de Cinematografía Nacional." CNAC's institutional model entailed collaboration between state entities and the private sector.

With the advent of the Bolivarian Revolution (1999), state participation increased to levels never seen before. In 2005, new legislation came into effect (*Reforma a la Ley de Cinematografía Nacional*), introducing a series of protectionist measures to benefit national production, while at the same time creating fiscal incentives for private investment (Villazana 2008). As a whole, an institutional network has been developed to support the production, distribution, and preservation of film: CNAC (Centro Nacional de Cinematografia), Amazonia Film (for distribution), Villa del Cine (for production), and the *Cinemateca Nacional* (for exhibition, research, and preservation).

This history of state support for film production would not be complete without acknowledging more repressive governmental measures, including the confiscation of films, defunding projects, censorship, and disciplining filmmakers and officials. The innovative video art project *Imagen de Caracas* (*Image of Caracas*, Jacobo Borges and Inocente Palacios, 1967) was commissioned by the Municipal Council of Caracas to commemorate the city's 400th anniversary. A month after it opened, the project was shut down by the state, due to its polemical interpretation of national history. One of the best-known cases of censorship involved Luis Correa's *Ledezma, el caso Mamera* (*Ledezma, the Mamera Case*, 1981). The director was eventually imprisoned in 1982, accused of "apology to crime." Other films, such as Carlos Azpúrua's *La pesca de arrastre* (*Trawling*, 1983) and *Caño Mánamo* (1986), were subject to different obstacles and censorship. In 2014, the government exerted undue pressure on Javier Guerrero, then President of *Cinemateca Nacional*, to influence programming the institution. His firm response to such pressure led to his ousting.

Cuba and Venezuela illustrate the ways in which state intervention shapes film industries in small and medium-sized domestic markets. It also exemplifies the pitfalls of governmental support, which can easily turn into a limiting factor when institutions dictate what national cinema ought to represent and how it should do so. One additional issue relates to the economic fluctuations affecting the state: the collapse of the Soviet Union and the collapse of oil prices radically affected the production of Cuban and Venezuelan cinemas, respectively. That being said, it would be naïve to think that private sponsorship is free from constraints, pressures, and risks.

The reinvention of the state in neoliberal Mexican cinema

IGNACIO M. SÁNCHEZ PRADO

Perhaps a testament to the historical role of the state in Mexican cinema is the publication, in 2012, by the previous administration of the Mexican Film Institute (IMCINE), of *El Estado y la imagen en movimiento*, a fairly comprehensive history of the relationship between the government and the national film industry since the beginnings to the present (*El Estado* 2012). The collection of essays tells a fascinating story that by and large periodizes Mexican cinema across the axes established by legislation, paradigms of subsidy, and the tension between the state and international factors such as Hollywood's power and trade practices. It is indeed true that the very existence of Mexican cinema between the end of the national period in the 1950s and the rise of the neoliberal period in the late 1980s owes a great deal to the different stages of state subsidy. As the authors in *El Estado* demonstrate, it would have been unthinkable for Mexican cinema in the 1960s to survive a massive decline of audiences without the support of state funding and the PRI-affiliated labor union. Indeed, the generation of directors that flourished in the 1970s, including Jorge Fons, Arturo Ripstein, and Felipe Cazals, were by and large favored by a proactive policy of film production by the administration of President Luis Echeverría (1970–1976), whose brother oversaw the institution in charge of national film at the time. It is also true that the support of populist genres by the government of President José López Portillo (1976–1982) and the subsequent withdrawal of the state from film funding as a result of the economic crisis of 1982 were devastating for the structures and paradigms that sustained the Mexican film industry for the previous half-century. Canonical accounts of Mexican cinema in the 1980s and early 1990s describe the period as a crisis (Pelayo 2012), or even as the "end" of the Mexican film industry (Saavedra Luna 2007), since the decline of state support was directly tied to the radical reduction of film venues and to the lack of film directors engaging in social issues or artistic pursuits. This crisis was not necessarily an industry crisis (which at the time had a thriving private sector based on vehicles for TV stars and raunchy comedies), but rather the end of a social contract: the true traumatic event was the idea of a "cinema without the state," which reached its pinnacle during the near-extinction of the industry in 1995, when production declined to a paltry eight films per year as a result of the 1994 financial crisis.

When we speak of the relationship between the state and cinema in Mexico during the neoliberal era, the core element to consider is not so much the withdrawal of the state, but rather a fundamental reconstitution of its role in the industry. During the post-golden age decades, the state exercised what one could consider a near-monopoly over all stages of cinematic production and consumption. Yet, as neoliberalism became the operative state ideology in the 1990s, its role in Mexico's culture industries changed in significant but uneven ways. Distribution was one of the places where the transformation was most profound. A significant percentage of screens in Mexico were operated by the Compañía Operadora de Teatros S.A. (COTSA), a state-owned entity that notoriously kept its theaters in awful condition. There was little encouragement for the private sector to enter the market, since price controls kept ticket prices artificially low and the workforce was mostly bound to the Sindicato de Trabajadores de la Industria Cinematográfica (STIC), an old and all-encompassing union whose strict seniority rules prevented younger generations of filmmakers and workers from entering the industry. The administration of President Carlos

Salinas de Gortari (1988–1994) dismantled a significant part of this infrastructure, by closing COTSA and selling many of the theaters, and by liberalizing the price of the ticket. As the 1994 crisis hit, private investors used the absence of the state to launch the modern multiplex system, with the opening of the first Cinemark, which was closely followed by two companies: Cinemex and Organización Ramírez, which rebranded itself as Cinépolis. Misha MacLaird, who wrote one of the most concise and complete English-language accounts of the process, shows that it was part of a neoliberal framework that favored entrepreneurialism in culture industries, as well as the transformation of cultural audiences into target markets (MacLaird 2013: 21–74). In this, cinema followed general trends in the neoliberalization of media aligned with the elevation of consumption into a form of citizenship (García Canclini 2001).

More importantly, this had a fundamental effect on film aesthetics. Privatization led to a demographic change in film spectatorship in Mexico, which went from predominantly working class to predominantly middle and upper class. In turn, to cater to these new audiences, Mexican cinema, particularly the one intended for commercial audiences, dramatically and visibly shifted into genres and ideologies aligned with the new ticket-paying audiences (Sánchez Prado 2014). The effects of this were visible particularly in the first Mexican blockbusters of the late 1990s, such as *Sexo, pudor y lágrimas* (*Sex, Shame and Tears*, Antonio Serrano, 1998), *Todo el poder* (*Gimme Power*, Fernando Sariñana, 1999), and *Amores perros* (*Love's a Bitch*, Alejandro González Iñárritu, 2000). These films, different as they may seem, were all aimed at the new audiences through advertising schemes novel to the Mexican industry (such as the proactive use of the film soundtrack and the inclusion of well-known media figures in casts and publicity campaigns), and clearly reflected ideological concerns of the emerging middle class, including the idealization of creative work, a feeling of vulnerability in relation to urban crime, and the sense of unequal modernization that accompanied the neoliberal era. They were also examples of films that in different ways sought to dissociate themselves from the legacies of state-sponsored production in film.

The paradox here is that, as distribution and exhibition became predominantly private, and as film catered more directly to this commercial market, the size of the state's footprint in film production did not significantly diminish. An analysis from the 1970s recovered by Carl Mora showed that the overwhelming number of film productions between 1971 and 1976 were either produced by the state or by private entities financed through schemes of the state-owned Banco Cinematográfico (Mora 2005: 122). In the 1970s, at the height of cinematic statism, 37 out of 42 films were produced by the state, a whopping 88 percent. In 2015, according to numbers furnished by IMCINE (Carmona Álvarez and Sánchez y Sánchez 2012: 13), 70 percent of film production (98 out of 140 films) had some form of state support. It is possible that Mexico could have a viable industry without state support. After all, the top-grossing films are generally funded by two private production juggernauts, Televisa's Videocine and Pantelion enterprises, and the multinational AG Studios, which includes producers and distributors such as Lemon Films and Ítaca. But it is equally true that Mexico's amazing output and its diverse cinematic ecosystem (which includes considerable festival fare, a healthy documentary output, and a well-established art cinema circuit) would be unthinkable without state support. The key factor is that in most cases, governmental backing exists in the form of co-productions through a fellowship system that allows filmmakers to get different percentages of their funding through state funds, supported by legislation aimed at state-sponsored artistic production (Lay Arellano 2005).

The consequence of this scheme has not been the withdrawal of the state from film production, but rather the ability of sectors of the film industry to create a diversified industry precisely because they are not bound by either the narrow criteria of commercial cinema nor, as happened in the past, by a state agency with great power to censor film through funding restrictions.

Nonetheless, there is no better place to see how crucial state support is to cinematic ecosystems in the neoliberal era in Latin America than in Mexico's exhibition system. Over 90 percent of screens in Mexico are controlled by the Cinépolis-Cinemex duopoly, and other than the Cineteca Nacional, the state does not sustain any major exhibition space. In this situation, per IMCINE data, only 6 percent of all audiences goes to Mexican films; 19 percent of film releases are Mexican (and only 80 out of 140 films produced get any release at all, meaning that as much as 40 percent of films never actually reach theatrical audiences); and only 7–12 percent of screens show Mexican cinema in general, with a whole season (the summer, flooded with Hollywood releases) in which it is impossible to see a Mexican film in a multiplex. A new threat is emerging, as the Trans-Pacific Partnership (TPP) has a clause that forces Mexico to cap the number of screens devoted to national cinema at 10 percent, in direct contradiction to the industry's stated goal of 30 percent (Gutiérrez 2016). Should the Mexican government subscribe to this clause, it would radically damage the industry and undermine the state's crucial legacy, discarding the notion of the state as a protector of national cinema in favor of a new role guaranteeing the distribution of Hollywood film through trade policy.

Contemporary cinema in Argentina, Brazil, and Chile: the curious role of the state in a neoliberal era

JOANNA PAGE

In the midst of a wave of academic interest in border crossings, migration, the global, and the transnational, it can be easy to underplay the continued importance of the state in Latin American filmmaking. Paradoxically, public policy and state funding have gained a renewed significance in the current neoliberal era. Throughout the Southern Cone, government policies over the past two decades have had an enormous impact on the availability of film funding and exhibition space for national films. In Argentina, Brazil, and Chile, the introduction and enforcement in the mid-1990s of laws designed to protect and stimulate the national film industry are universally considered to have been the most significant enabling factors in the boom in film production that dates from that period. The timing of these laws is, at first sight, puzzling. As Gonzalo Aguilar points out, "cinema, in an era in which state protectionism was a bad word, was an activity that was subsidized and promoted by the State" (Aguilar 2008: 200). Why should cinema have been singled out for protectionist policies by a rampantly neoliberal regime? Mapping some features of the complex role of the state in the boom of cinema in Brazil and Argentina since 1995, and in Chile since 2005, will shed some light on this question.

A recognition of the vital role of government policies and public funding in Latin American filmmaking does not mean underestimating the extent to which the industry also benefits from foreign funding. While international co-productions still represent a minor fraction of the total films produced in any year by Argentina and Brazil, for example, a great number of productions are financed with the help of funds associated with international film festivals, notably Hubert Bals and Sundance, or with other European or transatlantic programs, such as Fond Sud Cinéma and Ibermedia. These grants, however, generally cover a relatively low proportion of the cost of making a film. As a typical case, Gustavo Taretto's *Medianeras* (*Sidewalls*, Argentina, 2011) was made with the help of Ibermedia and Germany's World Cinema Fund, but the bulk of its budget was covered by Argentina's INCAA (Instituto Nacional de Cine y Artes Audiovisuales); Taretto readily affirms that "Without [the INCAA] it would be impossible to have a film industry in Argentina" (Naderzad 2011).

The considerable power wielded by the INCAA over the past decades is clearly to be seen in the stimulation of certain kinds of film production over others, which has resulted from shifts in its policies and modes of operation. As César Maranghello observes, in the last years of the Menem government, the INCAA reserved its funds for the biggest players in the industry; at the beginning of the 2000s, however, changes to loan policies created new opportunities for young directors, bringing in "a real change in generation," with *operas primas* representing 60 percent of the films released in 2001 (Maranghello 2005: 257–258; see Falicov 2007: 92–93, 115 for INCAA policies in the 1990s). While a few directors have pursued a career independently of INCAA support (notably Raúl Perrone and Mario Llinás), it continues to provide indispensable backing for almost all films produced in Argentina.

Public policies have also played a dramatic role in the resurgence of Brazilian cinema since President Fernando Collor de Mello's dismantling of the state film enterprise, Embrafilme, in 1990. In particular, new tax incentive laws implemented in 1992 paved the way for private corporations to invest in national films, and the creation of ANCINE (Agência Nacional do Cinema) in 1993 has led to the expansion and greater enforcement of legislation to protect the national film industry (Rêgo 2011: 35–39). Alessandra Meleiro gives the example of the blockbuster *Cidade de Deus* (*City of God*, Fernando Meirelles, 2002), with over 20 percent of its funding raised by means of the incentive laws. As Meleiro suggests, "Cases like this confirm the importance of the incentive laws and government policies in nurturing domestic film production" (Meleiro 2013: 188). Similarly, in his study of the film and audiovisual industries in Chile, Roberto Trejo Ojeda signals that the role played by the state should be seen as the single most important factor in the sector's recent growth (Trejo Ojeda 2009: 128). The consequence of a reliance on state support, of course, is that national film industries are peculiarly exposed to economic downturns. Dependence of this kind, as Trejo Ojeda suggests, marks both the condition of possibility of a national cinema and the limits of its development (p. 129).

Although public policy and state support for national film industries have often been important in Latin America, marking the rhythm and tempo of its silences and revivals, a change in rhetoric and practice has taken place in recent years. Instead of being conceived as a form of public spending, with the aim of protecting a national industry, state funding for cinema is now increasingly understood as an *investment* (Trejo Ojeda 2009: 119). This shift takes place as a result of the abandonment (or radical rewriting) of the "social contract" that had existed between the state and the national film industry in previous decades, as Sánchez Prado points out in the Mexican context (p. 53). Among other things, it means that the state becomes a powerful sponsor of national films, with the aim of promoting tourism but also to attract foreign companies to film in the country. This can bring significant benefits to local economies: for example, crew members of the James Bond film *Quantum of Solace* (2008) are estimated to have spent US$8 million on hotels, food, and tourism during their brief visit to Chile's Atacama Desert (Long 2009).

The development of a national film industry becomes vital because it provides the skills and technologies needed to support foreign filmmaking in the country. Chile in particular has developed a high-quality post-production industry and is now the Latin American leader in this regard.

An expansion in national filmmaking is seen as crucial to Latin America's insertion into the global market more generally, with governments conscious that "a country without its own images might not seem to exist in the contemporary culture market," especially as audiovisual industries represent an important and growing sector within the world economy (Trejo Ojeda 2009: 9–10). Between 2013 and late 2014, "culture" had the third greatest presence in the coverage of Chile in the international media, surpassed only by "politics" and "sport," and references to culture and cinema contribute a good proportion of the positive coverage of the nation abroad (Fundación Imagen de Chile 2015: 6, 10). ProChile, the arm of the Foreign Affairs Ministry (Ministerio de Relaciones Exteriores) charged with promoting Chilean goods and services abroad and stimulating tourism at home, pays particular attention to the nation's film industry. As its Director explains, promoting visual arts and other creative industries "allows Chile to show itself to the world as an educated, trustworthy and developed country, which is of benefit to all export sectors" (ProChile 2013).

The audience for Latin American films since the 1980s differs dramatically from that of the "golden age" of the 1930s and 1940s, when films were primarily made for working-class audiences rather than the metropolitan elite (Falicov 2007: 81). With state support, contemporary filmmaking has tended to focus on an increasingly middle-class and intellectual section of the population. Ascanio Cavallo and Gonzalo Maza ascribe this phenomenon to the fact that many young filmmakers in Chile (as in other Latin American countries) are film school graduates, learning their trade within an academic environment, which explains "the self-reflexive form of many of their works." This new generation may not have consciously turned their back on the general public, they suggest, but have shown greater interest in "pursuing their own language and concerns" (Cavallo and Maza 2010: 15). While more commercial filmmakers such as Argentina's Daniel Burman and Juan José Campanella succeed in appealing to an enthusiastic middlebrow public, the majority of national films in Argentina are aimed at a much more reduced audience of cinephiles. This change in focus arises in tandem with a deeper shift in the social profile of cinema spectatorship in Latin America, however, where in many countries the incursion of multinational-owned multiplexes in the 1990s and the closure of neighborhood cinemas has made moviegoing an activity for wealthy urbanites. Sánchez Prado has observed the effect of this phenomenon on the narrative modes of Mexican films, for example, which have renounced the modes of melodrama that responded more clearly to popular tastes (Sánchez Prado 2014: 82).

For a number of critics, the recent wave of "novísimo cine chileno," which dates from 2005, is characterized by individualism, an autobiographical impetus, and a retreat into private, intimate spaces that is consonant with social relations under neoliberalism, finding an easy entry into the global market. Carlos Saavedra Cerda finds that "national cinema is directed towards the inner life and becomes an expression of an *auteur*, while at the same time the films produced represent the kind of object demanded by the international market of images" (Saavedra Cerda 2013: 22). He charges these films with "depoliticizing the subject" and "validating the market in their themes" (p. 23). However, the charting by recent Chilean films of the reduction of public space to spaces of consumption, together with the social segregation that marks a grossly unequal society, is certainly not carried out uncritically. The state's failure to provide basic welfare is tragically manifest in *La buena vida* (*The Good Life*, Andrés Wood, 2008), for example, while *Huacho* (*Orphan*, Alejandro Fernández Almendras, 2009) highlights the vast inequalities that separate middle-class urban consumers from agricultural workers in the impoverished provinces. The fact that many recent productions are filmed almost exclusively in domestic, middle-class spaces, and signally fail to imagine forms of collective vision and action—examples would include *Velódromo* (Alberto Fuguet, 2009) and *Zoológico* (Rodrigo Marín, 2011)—does not imply an endorsement of their characters' narcissism and anomie.

Trejo Ojeda notes that the two elements that make up cinema's hybrid nature—at once aesthetic object and economic commodity—represent "two kinds of logic that do not always coincide and can even become contradictory" (Trejo Ojeda 2009: 18). Such divergences are abundantly evident in contemporary filmmaking in the Southern Cone, where the ideological "content" of films often renders paradoxical and even nonsensical their co-option by the state for the purposes of selling a positive image of the nation abroad and/or pursuing greater integration in the international economy. Many such films emphasize the internal fragmentation of the nation or the negligence and weakness of the state in the face of violence. One thinks of the systematic exploitation of farmworkers in *La mujer de barro* (*The Mud Woman*, Sergio Castro San Marín, Argentina–Chile, 2015), the institutional corruption rife in *El estudiante* (*The Student*, Santiago Mitre, Argentina, 2011), the discomforting critique of white privilege and prejudice in *Casa grande* (*The Big House*, Fellipe Barbosa, Brazil, 2014), or the precarious existence of indigenous communities whose rights are consistently ignored, as depicted in *El etnógrafo* (*The Ethnographer*, Ulises Rosell, Argentina, 2012).

And yet, perhaps this contradiction is less sharp, or less important, than it appears. Cinema has become an important means for post-dictatorship Southern Cone governments to project an image of a modern, technologically advanced, democratic nation. This means embracing a diversity of films, some of which may challenge the policies or even the status of the nation itself. Even the proliferation of films about repression under dictatorship serves to distance the contemporary state from such acts and to emphasize its return to democracy. During Alfonsín's regime, as Tamara L. Falicov reminds us, the circulation of "quality" films from Argentina on the international film festival circuit became a "primary vehicle" for promoting a new image of a modern, democratic country that invested in national culture (Falicov 2007: 53). Similarly, taken as a whole, films that attack the logic of the nation may merely emphasize choice, multiculturalism, and individual freedom, all of which sit comfortably within a neoliberal agenda, and provide no impediment to the marketing of a national cinema. If we have entered an era in which—as Aguilar argues—audiovisual art in a media-dominated society is not a space of resistance, but one increasingly shaped by politics and finance, many filmmakers have opted to "penetrate this machine of images," nevertheless "marking out, with their own work, a difference" (Aguilar 2008: 196). That they are able to do so is, of course, testament to the fact that democracy has prospered in the Southern Cone, while throwing light on the facility with which neoliberal marketing machines may profit even from dissenting voices or apparently uncommercial activities.

State subsidies and promotion have aided the considerable success of Latin American productions at international film festivals, while audiences at home have dwindled. Many more films are currently being produced that could never hope to recoup their costs; relying heavily on state subsidies, and in the context of very limited screening opportunities within their own countries, directors have both the freedom and the incentive to find alternative distribution routes. The past few years have seen a boom in the distribution of films from

Latin America on the Internet, either directly uploaded onto sites such as YouTube or made available on websites that often describe themselves as a kind of "free Netflix," via which viewers may stream a wide range of fiction and documentary films, including very recent ones. Examples of such sites would include the Chilean www.cinepata.com, established in 2008 by the writer and director Alberto Fuguet, and the Argentine www.cinemargentino. com, founded more recently in 2013. Both are endorsed by state bodies for film funding but receive little or no money from them; directors simply give their permission for films to be streamed free by means of Creative Commons licenses.

These sites are clearly conceived as means of circumventing the market forces of the global film industry, and often appeal to nationalist and regionalist sentiment in the celebration of what is not commercially viable. Fuguet, reflecting in 2015 on the creation of www.cinepata.com, suggests that they were able to anticipate a new trend in thinking about film in Chile: "that cinema should be part of garage culture: that is to say, stripped-down, artistic, without profit" (Orellana 2015). The distribution of Latin American cinema is important, for him, "because we feel Chilean and are Chilean, and are outside of the industry. Outside of the big circuit. It seems to us that our neighbours and allies are Latin American." Indeed, few of the films available to stream are subtitled, which reinforces the site's objectives of national and regional distribution, as an alternative to the "cinema for export" model promoted by the Chilean government.

Viewing films on the Internet rather than in cinemas or on television is fast becoming more popular across Latin America: boosted by the increase in online viewing, home video revenue is predicted to overtake cinema takings by 2018 in Argentina (Crettaz 2014). This provides significant opportunities for distribution beyond cinema circuits and a new impetus towards filming in digital formats. The growing centrality of the Internet in audiovisual entertainment is also opening up new creative possibilities in the form of transmedia projects such as *Malvinas30* (Alvaro Liuzzi, 2012) and *Tras los pasos del Hombre Bestia* (*Following the Footsteps of the Beast Man*, Roberto Igarza and Fernando Irigaray, 2013) in Argentina and *Latitudes* (Felipe Braga, 2013) in Brazil, together with alternative financing models such as crowdfunding. Yet, as Braga himself suggests, such alternatives may not bring about greater choice or liberty for the filmmaker. By comparison with Argentina and Chile, Brazil's tax incentive laws have paved the way for a greater dominance of commercial sponsors: *Latitudes* is sponsored by Procter & Gamble and Heineken, among other companies. While Braga acknowledges that every filmmaker of his generation "owes their career to the tax incentive model," he is concerned that "the categories 'audience' and 'consumer' will merge into one single thing. Brands will end up acting as curators of content" (Mango 2013). The state, as has been argued here, appears to be much less interested in "curating content" and more interested in pursuing international critical acclaim; the vigorous promotion of national cinema within the neoliberal "cinema for export" model has the ironic consequence of sheltering filmmakers from market forces and according them a surprising artistic freedom.

References

Acosta, J. (1997) "Bajo el signo del Estado." *Panorama histórico del cine en Venezuela, 1896–1993.* Caracas: Fundación Cinemateca Nacional, pp. 179–192.

Aguilar, G. (2008) *Other Worlds: New Argentine Film.* Buenos Aires: Santiago Arcos.

Carmona Álvarez, C. and Sánchez y Sánchez, C. (2012) *El Estado y la imagen en movimiento. Reflexiones sobre las políticas públicas y el cine mexicano.* Mexico City: Instituto Mexicano de Cinematografía.

Cavallo, A. and Maza, G. (2010) *El Novísimo Cine Chileno*. Santiago: UQBAR.

Chanan, M. (2004) *Cuban Cinema*. Minneapolis, MN: University of Minnesota Press.

Crettaz, J. (2014) "Medios: el video online superará al cine y crecerán Internet y el cable." *La Nación*, June 4, 2014. Available at: www.lanacion.com.ar/1698193-medios-el-video-online-superara-al-cine-y-creceran-internet-y-el-cable (accessed June 1, 2017).

El Estado y la imagen en movimiento (2012). Mexico City: Imcine/Conaculta.

Falicov, T. (2007) *The Cinematic Tango: Contemporary Argentine Film*. London: Wallflower.

Fundación Imagen de Chile (2015) *Presencia cultural de Chile en la prensa internacional*. Santiago: Fundación Imagen de Chile.

García Borrero, J. (2013) "*Alicia en el pueblo de maravillas* (1990), de Daniel Díaz Torres." Available at: https://cinecubanolapupilainsomne.wordpress.com/2013/08/31/alicia-en-el-pueblo-de-mara-villas-1990-de-daniel-diaz-torres/ (accessed June 1, 2017).

García Canclini, N. (2001) *Consumers and Citizens: Globalization and Multicultural Conflicts*, trans. G. Yudice. Minneapolis, MN: University of Minnesota Press.

Gutiérrez, V. (2016) "TPP acabaría con sueño del cine mexicano." *El Economista*, June 9.

Higson, A. (2000) "The Limiting Imagination of National Cinemas." In M. Hjort and S. MacKenzie (eds.), *Cinema and Nation*. London: Routledge, pp. 63–74.

King, J. (2000) *Magical Reels: A History of Cinema in Latin America*. London: Verso.

Lay Arellano, T. (2005) *Análisis del proceso de la iniciativa de Ley de la Industria Cinematográfica de 1998*. Guadalajuara: Universidad de Guadalajara.

Long, G. (2009) "Chile's Film Industry." *Business Chile*, April 1, 2009. Available at: www.business-chile.cl/en/comment/reply/1679 (accessed June 1, 2017).

López, A. (2000) "Early Cinema and Modernity in Latin America." *Cinema Journal*, 40: 48–78.

MacLaird, M. (2013) *Aesthetics and Politics in the Mexican Film Industry*. New York: Palgrave Macmillan.

Mango, A. (2013) "Brazil's First Transmedia Fiction 'Latitudes' Opens on YouTube." *The Hollywood Reporter*, August 30, 2013. Available at: www.hollywoodreporter.com/news/brazils-first-transme-dia-fiction-latitudes-618448 (accessed June 1, 2017).

Maranghello, C. (2005) *Breve historia del cine argentino*. Barcelona: Laertes.

Meleiro, A. (2013) "Finance and Co-Productions in Brazil." In S. Dennison (ed.), *Contemporary Hispanic Cinema: Interrogating the Transnational in Spanish and Latin American Film*. London: Tamesis Books, pp. 181–204.

Mora, C. (2005) *Mexican Cinema: Reflections of a Society, 1896–2004*. Jefferson, NC: McFarland.

Naderzad, A. (2011) "Gustavo Taretto: Argentine Director Chronicles Big-City Living in New Film." *Screen Comment*, June 24, 2011. Available at: http://screencomment.com/2011/06/interview-medianeras-director-gustavo-taretto/#sthash.Z6rWvU2H.dpuf (accessed June 1, 2017).

Orellana, N. (2015) "Cinépata: cine chileno y latinoamericano gratis, legal y en línea" (interview with Alberto Fuguet). *Red Cine Club Escolar* (Cineteca Nacional de Chile). Available at: www.ccplm.cl/redcineclubescolar/cinepata-cine-chileno-y-latinoamericano-gratis-legal-y-en-linea/ (accessed June 28, 2017).

Paranaguá, P. (2003) *Tradición y Modernidad en el cine de América Latina*. Madrid: Fondo de Cultura Económica.

Pelayo, A. (2012) *La generación de la crisis. El cine independiente mexicano de los ochenta*. Mexico City: Instituto Mexicano de Cinematografía.

ProChile (2013) "Chile apuesta por la internacionalización del arte y el diseño en importantes ferias." Available at: www.prochile.gob.cl/noticias/chile-apuesta-por-la-internacionalizacion-del-arte-y-el-diseno-en-importantes-ferias/ (accessed June 1, 2017).

Rêgo, C. (2011) "The Fall and Rise of Brazilian Cinema." In C.M. Rêgo and C. Rocha (eds.), *New Trends in Argentine and Brazilian Cinema*. Bristol: Intellect, pp. 35–49.

Saavedra Cerda, C. (2013) *Intimidades desencantadas: la poética cinematográfica del dos mil*. Santiago: Cuarto Propio.

Saavedra Luna, I. (2007) *Entre la ficción y la realidad. Fin de la industria cinematográfica mexicana 1989–2004*. Mexico City: Universidad Autónoma Metropolitana-Xochimilco.

Sánchez Prado, I. (2014) *Screening Neoliberalism: Transforming Mexican Cinema, 1988–2012.* Nashville, TN: Vanderbilt University Press.

Tompkins, C. (2013) *Experimental Latin American Cinema: History and Aesthetics.* Austin, TX: University of Texas Press.

Trejo Ojeda, R. (2009) *Cine, neoliberalismo y cultura: crítica de la economía política del cine chileno contemporáneo.* Santiago: Arcis.

Villazana, L. (2008) "De una política cultural a una cultura politizada: La República Bolivariana de Venezuela y su revolución cultural en el sector audiovisual." In J. Rabb and S. Thies (eds.), *"E Pluribus Unum" National and Transnational Identities in the Americas/Identidades nacionales y transnacionales en las Américas.* Münster: LIT Verlag and Bilingual Press, pp. 161–173.

4

UNPACKING PERIODIZATION

Laura Podalsky

Editors' introduction

This essay offers a meta-critical interrogation of the broader picture of Latin American film's place in larger understandings of cinema around the world. While much of the best contemporary scholarship on Latin American film gains its force through a methodological narrowing of areas of study (a movement, a genre, a textual affinity among a group of works), the broader methodological implications of the historical field are often left unquestioned. Podalsky addresses that paucity of "big picture" interrogations by considering the assumptions, often unspoken, about periodization (i.e. the way we choose to break up and manage the time parcels within which critical analysis takes place). She draws on the work of postcolonial historian Dipesh Chakrabarty and film studies scholar Bliss Cua Lim who question the colonial(izing) framework of "modern time consciousness." Along with Chakrabarty, philosopher Walter Benjamin provides a point of departure for her suggestions about alternate historiographical models that might reshape our understanding of Latin American cinemas' role as modern(izing) medium and cultural practice, and also problematize facile notions of "world cinema" that have gained increasing traction in Anglo-American film studies.

Her theoretically oriented argument offers a useful balance to the rich microhistories presented elsewhere in the volume. Chapter 2 (Rielle Navitski), Chapter 8 (Salomé Aguilera Skvirsky), Chapter 12 (Mariano Mestman), Chapter 13 (Masha Salazkina), and Chapter 19 (Andrea Cuarterolo) provide highly nuanced accounts of particular historical horizons. Whether explicitly or implicitly, those essays problematize cinema's supposedly linear trajectory of successive aesthetic and industrial innovations. Like those authors, Podalsky calls for greater attention to be paid to the dense temporalities (of residual, dominant, and emergent impulses) within historical horizons, as well as to promises never realized.

This essay proposes to interrogate the traditional temporal coordinates by which we understand the historical trajectory or periodization of Latin American cinemas. This broad meta-critical consideration of the historiographical frameworks underlying Latin American film criticism may appear overly ambitious given the explosion of Latin American film studies over the past 10 years and the differing scholarly traditions of Argentina, Bolivia, Brazil, Chile, Mexico, Peru, Spain, the United Kingdom, the United States, etc. Perhaps the scholarship is simply too varied for useful generalizations. Indeed, is such abstract reflection even necessary? As more than one colleague has noted, most scholars already distrust grand historical narratives about particular national cases—let alone about Latin American cinema as (if it were) a whole. All encompassing studies that promise an overview (from the arrival of the first technologies in the mid-1890s up to the present) have given way recently to more modest, in-depth examinations of particular historical horizons. In addition, many film scholars (not just film historians) have demonstrated a heightened reflexivity about the ideological, professional, and disciplinary forces that shape any and all accounts of historical "developments." Nonetheless, I would argue that it is important to tease out the conceptualization of time that undergirded those older, totalizing narratives because it *still* influences today's more self-aware microhistorical studies and also shapes how Latin American cinemas are positioned in relation to filmmaking traditions elsewhere.[1]

Traditional historiographies and the colonializing tendencies of modern temporality

Whether practiced in the US, UK, Argentina, Mexico, Brazil, or Cuba, Latin Americanist film studies have tended to privilege a "stagist" or geological model whereby the history of film as a whole has been broken into a series of distinct periods or discrete layers "separated by watershed moments of aesthetic and/or industrial rupture" (Podalsky 2011: 56–57). This is the case in both national and regional histories. Argentine film history traditionally distinguishes between the silent period, the studio era, the "new" cinemas of the 1960s (Generación del 60, Gleyzer, Cine Liberación, etc.), the cinema of re-democratization, and the new "New Argentine Cinema" of the mid-1990s to the present (España 1994, 2000, 2004). Mexican film history follows an analogous segmentation: the silent era, the "golden age" (1930s–1950s), the "fall" of the studios and the era of the *churros* (1950–1960s), the various rebirths via state support, and the New Mexican Cinema. This history is often recounted via successive *sexenios* or presidential terms (García Riera 1998). Cuban film history follows a more simplified breakdown into a pre- and a post-revolutionary cinema, and within that framework segments the latter by decades: the experimental 1960s, the "gray" 1970s, the popular 1980s, the crisis of the 1990s, and the new new Cuban cinema of the 2000s (Noguer 2002; Chanan 2004). In terms of "Latin American cinema" writ large, scholars have often distinguished between the silent, the early sound era or "old" Latin American cinema (1930s–1950s), the New Latin American Cinema (1960s–1970s or 1980s), and "contemporary" cinemas (1980s onwards) (Paranaguá 1985; Schulmann 1987; King 2000; Schroeder Rodríguez 2016). There are certain variants such as Juan Antonio García Borrero's notion of "submerged Cuban cinema" that urged scholars to rethink ICAIC-centric histories. This demanded discarding 1959 as a "starting point" for Cuban film history and recognizing filmmaking taking place alongside as well as outside state sponsorship, privileging simultaneity over teleology. In general, however, this "stagist" model of history reifies rupture—measured in terms of technological innovations (e.g. sound, digital), aesthetic tendencies, modes of production, and/or a relationship with the state. In privileging breaks, change, and difference, these models oftentimes overlook continuities as well as the complexity of given historical horizons by digging fairly narrow "pits" of analysis. This is particularly evident in English-language scholarship that, until fairly recently, has privileged film criticism over film history, a subfield that has a rich tradition and enjoyed strong institutional support in Argentina and Mexico (López 2006: 198–199, 2014: 137–138).

The consequences of this older model for the study of Latin American cinemas are far-reaching, as it has influenced objects of study, approaches, and methods. Most notably, this framework has privileged the analysis of the texts themselves (through efforts to define dominant formal conventions and recognize deviations that develop into aesthetic renovations). Particular attention is paid to modes of production through efforts to delineate the dominant industrial structures that supposedly determine particular formal conventions and that constrain change or make it possible. Other potential foci—including horizons of reception, spectatorial protocols, and intermedial connections (López 2014: 138–141)—are displaced or ignored altogether. Experimental and educational films, promotional shorts, and community filmmaking are all overlooked or marginalized. Recent scholarship has begun to address these variants in substantive ways (Schiwy 2009; Rodríguez 2011; Cusi Worthman 2013; Garavelli 2014); nonetheless, such studies tend to emerge as discrete works and, with few exceptions (Lusnich 2010), their potential to problematize larger conceptualizations of "Latin American cinemas" has not been realized.

The geological model has proven remarkably resistant to efforts to reconceptualize the trajectories of Latin American cinemas and their relationship to other cinemas. Paulo Antonio Paranaguá spearheaded such an endeavor in the mid-1980s, problematizing the notion that Latin American cinemas were derivative of the "more highly developed" US cinema. By identifying the region's shared structural limitations, he "highlighted the falsity of asymmetrical comparisons that . . . characterized productions [from the 1930s to 1950s] as inefficient copies of Hollywood films . . ." (Kriger 2014: 141; all translations by the author). In the 1990s, Alberto Elena and others furthered this project of radical reframing by underscoring "the lack of a linear, homogenous, or harmonic development of the medium and film language" (Lusnich 2010: 2). Unfortunately, these efforts have not had sufficient repercussions. Despite the widespread recognition of unequal industrial structures and their resulting influence on the creativity of filmmakers and the expectations of audiences, developmentalist rhetoric still predominates in film studies scholarship—for example, in accounts that celebrate the "maturity" or greater aesthetic complexity of contemporary filmmaking (Hart 2004: 13).

The difficulty of eschewing such tendencies—even in the work of scholars who recognize the structural challenges facing Latin American filmmakers—makes it essential to denaturalize the temporal imagination that undergirds how we place Latin American cinemas in relation to other traditions. In this regard, postcolonial theory offers a particularly illuminating framework for pinpointing the modern notions of temporality upon which traditional Western historiographies depend. Subaltern studies historian Dipesh Chakrabarty and film scholar Bliss Cua Lim can help us envision other ways of understanding spatial-temporal relations and, in so doing, deconstruct the all-too-facile models of "world cinema" (currently popular in the Anglo-American academia) as well as the "total histories" (favored at a certain moment by some scholars in Latin American academies) in more durable, long-lasting ways.

In his groundbreaking book *Provincializing Europe: Postcolonial Thought and Historical Difference*, Chakrabarty placed the Western practice of writing history (or "historicism") that emerged in the nineteenth century within the context of European colonialist ventures, arguing that it was a "way of thinking about modernity and capitalism as originating in Europe" that instantiated a "stagist theory of history" (Chakrabarty 2000a: 7–9). Europe appropriated "the adjective 'modern' for itself" and economic (and political) dynamics in that continent became a yardstick by which to measure other cultures' readiness for self-rule (pp. 8, 42). This knowledge system had an instrumental corollary, serving as a justification for the political subjugation of others who were (always already) consigned to the antechamber to modernity (pp. 8–9).

According to Chakrabarty, historicism's deep-seeded epistemological power has been difficult to dislodge during and even after anti-colonial independence movements because of the way in which it has been internalized by nationalist elites. In "Radical Histories," he traces part of this process by discussing the influence of the European Enlightenment—in particular, "the propaganda of Reason" that established equivalencies between the modern and the scientific, as well as a series of foundational binaries: modernity vs. tradition, rational vs. anti-rational, intellectual vs. emotional—on Indian intellectuals (Chakrabarty 2000b: 257, 261, 262–263). Indian historians, for example, have utilized those tenets of European rationalism to delineate their objects of study in relation to nation-building and state formation—favoring the examination of political movements (as uniquely suited to producing subject-citizens) and ignoring religious movements or characterizing them as incidental to the fight for political independence. As a result, Indian history has been written as if it were a long march toward modernity, an unfinished process of forming (rational) subject-citizens. Chakrabarty recognizes that some recent accounts, such as those of subaltern historians, have partially broken away from the stagist model (Chakrabarty 2000a: 14–15). Nonetheless, he insists on its dogged afterlife, noting that Europe remains a "silent referent in historical knowledge" (p. 28).

Although the intellectual formation of Latin Americanist film scholars differs from that of Indian historians, there is nonetheless a certain similarity in the history-telling procedures of both groups. This becomes particularly notable in dominant understandings of the relationship between cinema and modernity. For example, for scholars writing in the 1970s and 1980s, the new cinemas of the late 1950s and the New Latin American Cinema of the 1960s–1970s represent the first examples of "modern cinema" in the region (Burton 1983). Such characterizations clearly recognized the importance of breaking away from industrial modes of production deemed to be foreign to the conditions of possibility in the region. At the same time, notwithstanding the recognition of important distinctions between the "aesthetics of hunger" ("imperfect cinema," Third Cinema) and European art cinema, those critical studies tended to echo particular aesthetic concepts tied to postwar European film criticism by writers such as André Bazin, whose key essay "The Evolution of the Language of Film" proposed a teleological trajectory wherein particular formal innovations permit the fullest realization of cinema's true potential.

Despite the subsequent questioning of Bazin's phenomenological proposals, the dividing line between modern and a prior (non-modern) cinema remains in place—evident in the work of two different intellectuals who have had a strong influence on Latin Americanist film scholarship: Gilles Deleuze (in his preference for a [modern] time-image cinema) and neo-formalist David Bordwell (whose notion of "classic cinema" as determined by Hollywood has enjoyed remarkably prescriptive power). Regardless of their many differences, both of these critical-theoretical frameworks depend on a notion of evolution or development—often aesthetic—and have immense implications for attempts to conceptualize the trajectories of cinemas (often reduced to *the* trajectory of *the* cinema), as well as the relationship between traditions from different parts of the world. Argentine scholar David Oubiña makes this precise point when he says the following in terms of Deleuze:

> Everything functions as if classic cinema and modern cinema were geological layers placed one on top of the other. Modern cinema [...] overturns and buries the [old] logic of classic cinema, as if there were never any possibility of coexistence and as if the prior model simply stopped.
>
> *(Oubiña 2014: 127 n8)*

He counters this paradigm by suggesting that there is not a single modern cinema, but instead a "modern impulse that is expressed in varied forms by each filmmaker and that deviates from the classic paradigm through vectors whose disruptive intensity is quite variable" (p. 128). Given the influence that Deleuze (as well as Bordwell) have had on recent Latin Americanist film scholarship, Oubiña's remarks are particularly welcome for questioning a Eurocentric model of aesthetic innovation. That said, Oubiña himself retains the basic supposition of a (historic) rupture after which emerged (certain) films that were (finally) modern.

Unraveling these densely wrought frameworks depends upon recognizing the underlying temporal logic that generates such binaries and naturalizes a stagist model of history. Equally important is understanding how cinema also contributed to the naturalization of this particular temporal regime as well as to concomitant notions of space (and race). In *Translating Time*, Lim argues that the temporality deployed by the cinema adheres to what she calls "modern consciousness of time" (analogous to Chakrabarty's notion of "homogenous time") (Chakrabarty 2000a: 73). She traces this to epistemological regimes that emerged at the end of the nineteenth century during an era of new colonial and neocolonial projects. Although the standardization of time has long had a role in the regulation of human behavior, the International Meridian Congress in 1884 took things a step further by inaugurating a singular system of time keeping around the globe, and thus a regularized sense of time that quickly became understood as natural (Lim 2009: 11). As noted by both Lim and Fatimah Tobing Rony, it is precisely during this same period that anthropology and other new disciplines of humanist inquiry emerge—all of which depend upon the "spatialization of time"—(now) understood as linear—and propose new ways of seeing the relationship between different human groups (Rony 1996: 9–10; Rosen 2001: 89–144; Lim 2009: 13). In sum, this modern time consciousness not only became a "means of exercising social, political, and economic control over periods of work and leisure," but also "underwrites a linear, developmental notion of progress that gives rise to ethical problems with regard to cultural and racial difference" (Lim 2009: 11). As we know, those changes in the regimes of knowledge were extremely important for (neo)colonial projects that justified the domination of other groups by characterizing them as backwards or primitive—in other words, as exhibiting a prior state of human existence.

Even if we reject those models of "human development" today, modern time consciousness is still with us, and its continued dominance can help explain the difficulty of reconceptualizing the relations between cinemas from different parts of the world. The task is nonetheless absolutely vital, particularly for U.S. and U.K. academics for whom the notion of "world cinema" has gained increased traction. If this term is to have any radical potential beyond its present cache in the publishing world, we must follow the lead of colleagues such as Nataša Ďurovičová and Kathleen Newman (2010), Stephanie Dennison and Song Hwee Lim (2006), and Lucia Nagib (Nagib 2006; Nagib et al. 2012) to help transform how we write about and teach cinemas-in-relation. To do so involves rethinking the transnational linkages between Latin American cinemas by exploring the circulation of films, stars, and directors (Hershfield 2000; Irwin and Castro Ricalde 2013; Lusnich et al. 2017), the construction of interpretive communities across national borders (D'Lugo 2010), and regional circuits of production-consumption (Taboada 2015; Navitski 2017). These recent efforts to reconceptualize the spatial circuits of Latin American cinemas can benefit from complementary studies that rewire our understanding of the temporalities of production, reception, and the relationship between the two.

Of plural contemporaneity and intermittency

While helping us to interrogate existing historicist tendencies, the theoretical contributions of Chakrabarty, Lim, and Walter Benjamin also point to at least two ways that we can reconceptualize film and temporality. Chakrabarty and Lim's work encourages us to not only jettison a linear, developmentalist understanding of film (as technology, as formal system), but also to recognize any given historical horizon as temporally heterogeneous. As the Indian-born historian puts it, we must acknowledge the "contemporary as plural" (Chakrabarty 2000a: 88). Another productive option might be to craft fuller accounts of the intermittent—i.e. minor or truncated tendencies that are brushed aside in traditional narratives featuring consolidated historical horizons with moments of punctual rupture (or "development"). Here, Walter Benjamin's interest in ruins and remains becomes a useful point of departure for imagining this second proposition. These two alternate temporal frameworks can encourage us to rethink our approaches and widen our understanding of relevant objects of study. In the process, as recent scholarship has demonstrated, we can craft more complex accounts of the relationship of cinema to modernity, as well as other larger sociocultural processes. To support that contention, let us turn to a more detailed discussion of each proposal.

Heterogeneity within historical horizons

Conceiving the "contemporary as plural" involves identifying the *temporal* heterogeneity of any given historical horizon. This is not a matter of compiling a list of aesthetic tendencies or diverse modes of production that existed during the same time period—for example, noting that Horacio Coppola made his avant-garde short *Así nació el obelisco* (*Thus the Obelisk Was Born*, Argentina, 1936) within a year of the premiere of more commercial urban films such as *Monte criollo* (Argentina, Arturo Mom, 1935) and *Noches de Buenos Aires* (*Buenos Aires Nights*, Argentina, Manuel Romero, 1935). Rather, we need to present historical horizons as amalgamations of residual, dominant, and emergent technologies, aesthetic tendencies, industrial dynamics, and receptive practices. This is a difficult task; after all, the very act of crafting scholarly accounts, necessarily limited in scope and depth, helps to crystallize particular constellations by tracing particular connections and leaving out others. One way to sidestep this obstacle might be to pinpoint transitional moments (whether defined in terms of the changing structure or practices of the film industry, culture industries, or society at large) wherein such overlays are more evident, and to target our analyses at particular interfaces (e.g. between different modes of filmic production, or between film and other media).

For example, we might look at how aesthetically innovative cinema emerged alongside and *shared* certain tendencies with commercial efforts that themselves were under renovation. What might it mean that formally innovative, independently produced films such as *Prisioneros de una noche* (*Prisoners of a Night*, Argentina, 1960) and *Tres veces Ana* (*Three Times Ana*, 1961), directed by newcomer David José Kohon, appeared only two to three years before *El Club del Clan* (*The Clan's Club*, Argentina, 1964), made by established director Enrique Carreras to capitalize on the popularity of a TV show of the same name that premiered in 1962? It is certainly possible to characterize Kohon's films as cutting-edge productions, whose penchant for eschewing formulaic plots, filming on the streets (instead of the studio), and complex shot compositions contrasted sharply with the studio productions from the same era (Podalsky 2004b: 193). Yet such an account ignores evident similarities with Carreras's film. All three narratives revolve around the difficulties facing young adults, including conflicts with their parents' conservative values and finding career paths that provide adequate financial support. The films also utilize the young protagonists' spatial itineraries (within Buenos Aires or the surrounding area) to speak metaphorically about the mobility (or lack thereof) of the "next" generation in a modern era. While there is no doubt that Kohon's films offer a more radical departure from the stylistic norms of studio films, *El Club del Clan* also evinces signs of formal renovation (e.g. through the use of canted angles to adequately express the crazy antics of the young singing group) that suggest the filmmakers' interest in appearing hip and up to date. Indeed, the film's plot, foregrounding musical spectacles over narrative development, closely imitates patterns evident in another, newer technology—namely, the quick pacing of TV variety shows from the same era. Instead of characterizing Kohon's films as exemplary of a new *modern* cinema, might we not consider how *both* Kohon and Carreras's works articulate a mid-late twentieth-century modernity?

The recognition and analysis of such commonalities have several advantages. First, this approach allows us to craft a more dynamic view of the film industry in a given period as "temporally plural" (i.e. as constituted by different combinations of innovation and stasis, rather than by a simple opposition between mainstream/commercial and avant-garde/independent productions). In early 1960s Argentina, certain commercial filmmakers deployed proven formulas in ways that had assured a share of the local market; others incorporated just enough signs of renovation—tied to the growing influence of a new technology, television—to appeal to younger, emerging audiences without turning away older sectors. The recognition of the simultaneity of forward- and backward-oriented impulses of the films themselves, their interpretive protocols (dependent on the audiences' knowledge of prior texts and/or emergent fashions), and how the film industry positioned itself in relation to other media (in this case, both TV and the record industry) disrupts more linear accounts of "development."

As might be evident from the above-mentioned, this sort of scholarship demands moving away from a treatment of film texts as privileged objects and placing greater emphasis on the analysis of media networks and horizons of reception, as a number of (often younger) scholars have begun to do—among them, Rielle Navitski (film and the illustrated press in Mexico and Brazil between 1896–1930), Andrea Cuarterolo (film and photography in Argentina, 1840–1933), and Laura Isabel Serna (Mexican film culture from the late 1910s to the early 1930s). For instance, in her book *Public Spectacles of Violence*, Navitski examines the fascination with crime and violence in urban cultural production in early twentieth-century Mexico and Brazil through a comparative analysis of films and the illustrated press. Deeply interested in film's role in particular experiences of modernity in the early twentieth century, Navitski's study makes visible the contemporary as plural, most notably in her chapters on film culture outside of major cities. She does so, in part, by looking at the asynchrony of film exhibition schedules (i.e. how certain imported genres such as the adventure melodrama or westerns that were considered outdated in the capital city were still being circulated in provincial areas, where they influenced local filmmakers eager to stake a claim to *local* modernity). For example, while drawing on imported crime and adventure serials, *Retribução* (*Retribution*, Brazil, Gentil Roiz, 1925) showcased Recife's economic productivity (including a shot of the local Elixir Americano factory) as well as the picturesque landscape (Navitski 2017: 229–230). For its part, *Mocidade Louca* (*Mad Youth*, Brazil, Felipe Ricci, 1927) gained the collaboration of the Mogyana Railway Company to film a thrilling train crash whose inclusion pointed to Campinas's modern transportation system, as well as the technological dexterity of the filmmakers themselves. As convincingly discussed by Navitski, these regional productions demonstrate that the cinema was not a delivery device— traveling from Hollywood to Brazil, or from Rio to Recife—to teach provincial publics "to be modern." Provincial populations in the north were always already modern in the sense of experiencing analogous transformations to those in southern Brazilian cities and those in the US and Europe.

More generally, *Public Spectacles* calls for a different understanding of the relationship between cinema and modernity that is more in line with Miriam Hansen's arguments about film as a form of vernacular modernism. Rather than characterizing modern cinema as an aesthetic found in "independent" or avant-garde films, Hansen urges us to examine how (certain) film practices *within commercial cinema* acknowledge and engage with "the set of technological, economic, social, and perceptual transformations associated with the term modernity . . . including the cinema's own role in them" (Hansen 2010: 294–295). While Navitski's study carries out that charge, she also critiques Hansen for overestimating Hollywood's influence, arguing that her model "does not take into account the degree to which discursive tensions within the 'host' culture might shape the very terms upon which cinema's reception occurred" (Navitski 2017: 13). Like Serna's study of early Mexican cinema, *Public Spectacles* demonstrates how the reception of imported films was an active process of negotiation and appropriation. On a meta-critical level, such studies identify horizons of reception as another site through which we can disrupt linear narratives of imported cinema (as delivery device) to showcase a modernity originating elsewhere.

The new generation of Latin American film histories has utilized the paucity of extant films from the first decades of the twentieth century as a stimulus to address new objects of study and forge new methods—for example, delving into state archives of governmental bodies responsible for regulating the film exhibition (Serna 2014), or comparing the spatiotemporal dimension of nineteenth-century photography—via double exposure and seriality— to that of early films (Cuarterolo 2013). The very rich and heterogeneous nature of their primary sources has, perhaps, encouraged the researchers' skepticism toward total histories. In line with Michel Foucault, their studies underscore the danger of establishing false isomorphisms—whether between horizons of production and reception, or more broadly between discourses (about the modern) and material practices (lived transformations, varied economic structures and dynamics).

Truncated trajectories

Other scholars are disrupting established periodizations by examining minor tendencies that fail to become dominant within the historical period in which they emerge (in this volume, see the contributions of Aguilera Skvirsky and Ortega) and by exploring *infrahistorias* about private tensions and alliances between individual filmmakers that problematize institutional histories (García Borrero 2016; Palacios 2016). These critics pick up on the "historical materialist" approach outlined by Benjamin to combat historicism. In one of the most-cited sections of "Theses on the Philosophy of History," he describes a Paul Klee painting called "Angelus Novus." The central figure, whose "face is turned toward the past," helps Benjamin visualize his new historiographical model:

> Where we perceive a chain of events, he sees one single catastrophe which keeps piling wreckage upon wreckage and hurls it in front of his feet. The angel would like to stay, awaken the dead, and make whole what has been smashed. But a storm is blowing from Paradise; it has got caught in his wings with such violence that the angel can no longer close them. This storm irresistibly propels him into the future to which his back is turned, while the pile of debris before him grows skyward. This storm is what we call progress.
>
> *(Benjamin 1977: 257–258)*

Inverting standard characterizations to name modernity as a cataclysmic event, Benjamin points to the costs of imposing a singular temporal logic that privileges the new. His metaphors recognize how the socioeconomic forces behind the rapid transformation have been naturalized in ways that shape human perception, and consequently undercut attempts to craft an external vantage point. Like the angel, we cannot withstand the powerful winds called progress. Nevertheless, Benjamin suggests, by turning our gaze towards the ruins, we can recognize the fragmentary matter left behind and offer accounts of potential configurations ("making whole what has been smashed") ignored by a historiographical framework (disciplining disparate phenomena into a "chain of events") given to us by modernity itself. For Benjamin, the revelatory potential of this perspective held a utopian promise; for Latin Americanist film studies scholarship, perhaps an enhanced ability to reconceptualize change over time.

For example, what should we make of the aforementioned commercial youth films that had a brief heyday in Mexico and Argentina in the 1960s, only to re-emerge with greater success in the 1980s and 1990s, respectively? Investigating such intermittent trends can tell us a great deal about industrial dynamics (e.g. how production companies, distributors, and exhibitors perceive the market in given historical moments and the micro-maneuvers that they deploy to foster the growth of particular sectors or niche markets). This depends on the compilation of quantitative information to identify production trends (e.g. about the number of youth films made in given years) and evaluate relative commercial success (as delineated in industry magazines), as well as the analysis of advertising tactics. In the early 1960s, youth films constituted less than 10 percent of Argentine productions (per a review of the industry journal *Heraldo de Cine*). Placed within the context of larger exhibition trends, they occupied a small portion of available screen time and were not among the top box-office winners (which included, in the case of Buenos Aires, Hollywood spectacles such as *My Fair Lady*, *The Sound of Music*, and *Mary Poppins*) (*Heraldo del Cine*, December 31, 1965; December 31, 1966). Nonetheless, the industry's hopes for such films are evident in journals such as Argentina's *El Heraldo*, which regularly commented on the commercial potential of domestic and foreign films featuring young performers. In its review of the co-production *Nacidos para cantar* (*Born to Sing*, Argentina–Mexico, Emilio Gómez Muriel, 1965), starring Mexican idol

Enrique Guzmán and Argentine singer Violeta Rivas, *El Heraldo* noted that the film's value lay in "its cast, the furor over the *nueva ola*, the songs of Chico Novarro, [and its role as] youth entertainment," and recommended that exhibitors target young adults by billing the film in the following way: "Never before have so many young idols been together on screen! [. . .] Irresistibly appealing personalities, [. . .] and the music that drives young people crazy!" (*Heraldo del Cine*, May 12, 1965: 172). Placed against the relative paucity of such films and their lack of box-office success, these suggestions serve as a trace of industrial tactics—the search for new formulas and new markets—that did not consolidate in that period.

The reasons for that failure only become apparent through comparison with the youth films that (re)emerged decades later and had much greater commercial success—at least in Mexico (Podalsky 2004a). Without proposing any continuity between the two periods, it is possible to recognize analogous configurations between film and other media industries that in the 1980s (as in the 1960s) identified young people as a rela-tively untapped market sector, as well as the potential profitability of bolstering the interface between media. In the 1960s, such synergies were informal—evident in the sale of albums and films with the same name (e.g. the Palito Ortega vehicles *Fiebre de primavera* [*Spring Fever*, 1965]) and recognized by *El Heraldo* in its analysis of *Nacidos para cantar* ("With the full flowering of the market for the *nueva ola*, including record sales of albums, concerts, TV audiences and income from dances and films like *Fiebre de primavera* and *Santiago querido*, there couldn't be a better time for a film with Enrique Guzmán [and] Violeta Rivas [. . .]"). The formalization of these sorts of interfaces, how-ever, would only become possible with the rise of mass media conglomerates such as Mexico's Televisa (and its film company Televicine) and production companies such as Argentina's Patagonik linked to U.S. ventures. The former could deliberately promote particular performers such as Lucerito and Gloria Trevi across its media holdings (TV, radio, films); the latter could draw on the proven success of its partner (Disney) to make homegrown versions such as *High School Musical: El Desafío* (Jorge Nisso, 2008) of established hits.

In sum, the examination of minor trends that are truncated in one moment and then re-emerge at a later point in time can help us recognize conditions of possibility—in terms of the film industry as well as its tangled relationship with larger sociocultural and eco-nomic dynamics. In the case of Latin American youth films, we can acknowledge the significance of industrial restructuring, particularly in relation to the ongoing reconfigura-tions of larger media constellations, as well as the pivotal role of youth (as discursive figure and as social agent) in different configurations of modernity. Benjamin reminds us that this sort of analytical method "is based on a constructive principle" that contrasts sharply with historicism's "additive" method of "muster[ing] a mass of data to fill the homogenous, empty time" (Benjamin 1977: 261). I am less confident than Benjamin in the revolutionary potential of altering historiographical methods, yet nonetheless have faith that such adjust-ments can offer a forceful and productive intervention in discussions of Latin American cinemas' (spatio)temporal location.

Final thoughts

Notwithstanding the immense productivity of the alternate historiographical models dis-cussed above, this essay does not advocate throwing out traditional histories. As Chakrabarty notes in his analysis of Indian historiography, such chronologies have an important pedagogical function (Chakrabarty 2000b: 273). Clara Kriger makes an analogous point when recognizing the utility of the canons established in the 1950s by the first film histories (written by Domingo DiNubila, Alex Viany, and others) in promoting local production in a moment of industrial transition (Kriger 2014: 136–138). The counter-histories produced in the following decades by filmmakers such as Glauber Rocha and Fernando Solanas/Octavio Getino were similarly productive in generating debates about the nature of film traditions understood as national. Even today, more traditional film histories written in English—such as Dennison and Shaw's *Popular Cinema in Brazil* or Schroeder Rodríguez's *A Comparative History of Latin American Cinema*—play an extremely valuable role in helping film scholars in the Global North recognize that Latin American cinemas are not delimited by contemporary art cinema or "festival directors" such as Carlos Reygadas, Lucrecia Martel, Walter Salles, Lisandro Alonso, etc., but begin in the 1890s and encompass numerous popular traditions. In sum, it is not a question of eschewing modern time consciousness, which is "indispensable but inadequate" (Lim 2009: 10), or of throwing out traditional histories—which can have an important pedagogical function (Chakrabarty 2000b: 272–273)—but rather of recognizing their constitutive shortcomings *even as* we produce other forms of scholarship that foreground the fragmentary and heterogeneous.

Note

1 I would like to thank Ana Laura Lusnich, her colleagues in CIyNE, and Clara Kriger for commenting on an earlier version of this essay. The articles in Clara's 2016 volume of *AdVersuS* (by Kriger, Page, and Oubiña) were particularly helpful in constructing my theoretical framework, which borrows Oubiña's geological metaphor.

References

Benjamin, W. (1977) "Theses on the Philosophy of History." *Illuminations*, 4th ed. New York: Schocken.
Burton, J. (1983) "'The Intellectual in Anguish': Modernist Form and Ideology in *Land in Anguish* and *Memories of Underdevelopment*." Paper presented at the Latin American Program Colloquium, Woodrow Wilson International Center for Scholars, Smithsonian Institute, Washington, DC, April 26.
Chakrabarty, D. (2000a) *Provincializing Europe: Postcolonial Thought and Historical Difference.* Princeton, NJ: Princeton University Press.
—— (2000b) "Radical Histories and Question of Enlightenment Rationalism: Some Recent Critiques of *Subaltern Studies*." In V. Chaturvedi (ed.), *Mapping Subaltern Studies and the Postcolonial*. London: Verso, pp. 256–280.
Chanan, M. (2004) *Cuban Cinema*. Minneapolis, MN: University of Minnesota Press.
Cuarterolo, A. (2013) *De la foto al fotograma: Relaciones entre cine y fotografía en la Argentina (1840–1933)*. Montevideo: Ediciones CdF.
Cusi Worthman, E. (2013) *Indigenous Media in Mexico: Culture, Community, and the State*. Durham, NC: Duke University Press.
Dennison, S. and Hwee Lim, S. (2006) "Situating World Cinema as a Theoretical Problem." In S. Dennison and S. Hwee Lim (eds.), *Remapping World Cinema: Identity, Culture, and Politics in Film*. London: Wallflower.
Dennison, S. and Shaw, L. (2004) *Popular Cinema in Brazil*. Manchester: Manchester University Press.
D'Lugo, M. (2010) "Aural Identity, Genealogies of Sound Technologies, and Hispanic Transnationality on Screen." In N. Ďurovičová and K. Newman (eds.), *World Cinemas, Transnational Perspectives*. New York: Routledge, pp. 160–185.

Ďurovičová, N. and Newman, K. (eds.) (2010) *World Cinemas, Transnational Perspectives*. New York: Routledge.

España, C. (ed.) (1994) *Cine argentino en democracia, 1983–1993*. Buenos Aires: Fondo Nacional de las Artes.

—— (2000). *Cine argentino: industria y clasicismo, 1933–1956*, vols. I and II. Buenos Aires: Fondo Nacional de las Artes.

—— (2005) *Cine argentino: modernidad y vanguardias, 1957/1983*, vols. I and II. Buenos Aires: Fondo Nacional de las Artes.

Garavelli, C. (2014) *Video experimental argentino contemporáneo: una cartografía crítica*. Buenos Aires: Editorial de la Universidad Nacional de Tres de Febrero.

García Borrero, J.A. (2016) "Revolución, intelectual y cine. Notas para una intrahistoria del 68 audiovisual." In M. Mestman (ed.), *Las rupturas del 68 en el cine de América Latina*. Buenos Aires: Akal, pp. 249–284.

García Riera, E. (1998) *Breve historia del cine mexicano*. Mexico City: Libros sin Fronteras.

Hansen, M. (2010) "Vernacular Modernism: Tracking Cinema on a Global Scale." In N. Ďurovičová and K. Newman (eds.), *World Cinemas, Transnational Perspectives*. New York: Routledge, pp. 287–314.

Hart, S. (2004) *A Companion to Latin American Film*. Woodbridge, UK: Tamesis.

Heraldo del Cine, May 12, 1965, p. 172.

Heraldo del Cine, December 31, 1965, p. 443.

Heraldo del Cine, December 31, 1966, p. 521.

Hershfield, J. (2000) *The Invention of Dolores del Rio*. Minneapolis, MN: University of Minnesota Press.

Irwin, R.J. and Castro Ricalde, M. (eds.) (2013) *Global Mexican Cinema: Its Golden Age*. London: BFI/Palgrave Macmillan.

King, J. (2000) *Magical Reels: A History of Cinema in Latin America*. London: Verso.

Kriger, C. (2014) "Estudios sobre cine clásico en Argentina: De la perspectiva nacional a la comparada." *AdVersuS: Revista de Semiótica*, 26: 133–150.

Lim, B. (2009) *Translating Time: Cinema, the Fantastic, and Temporal Critique*. Durham, NC: Duke University Press.

López, A. (2006) "The State of Things: New Directions in Latin American Film History." *The Americas*, 63(2): 197–203.

—— (2014) "Calling for Intermediality: Latin American Mediascapes." *Cinema Journal*, 54(1): 135–141.

Lusnich, A.L. (2010) "Planteamientos de los estudios sobre cine en el marco de la carrera de artes combinadas de la Universidad de Buenos Aires." *Imagofagia*, 2. Available at: www.asaeca.org/imagofagia (accessed March 1, 2016).

Lusnich, A.L., Aisemberg, A. and Cuarterolo, A. (eds.) (2017) *Pantallas transnacionales: El cine argentino y mexicano del período clásico*. Mexico City: Cineteca Nacional.

Nagib, L. (2006) "Towards a Positive Definition of World Cinema." In S. Dennison and S. Hwee Lim (eds.), *Remapping World Cinema: Identity, Culture, and Politics in Film*. London: Wallflower, pp. 30–37.

Nagib, L., Perriam, C., and Dudrah, R. (eds.) (2012) *Theorizing World Cinema*. New York: I.B. Tauris.

Navitski, R. (2017) *Public Spectacles of Violence: Sensational Cinema and Journalism in Early Twentieth Century Mexico and Brazil*. Durham, NC: Duke University Press.

Noguer, E.G. (2002) *Historia del cine cubano. Cien anos: 1897–1998*. Miami, FL: Ediciones Universal.

Oubiña, D. (2014) "Bazin y Deleuze y la critica cinematografica en la Argentina." *AdVersuS: Revista de Semiótica*, 26: 116–132.

Page, J. (2014) "De la interdisciplinariedad a la indisciplina: nuevos rumbos en los estudios de cine en Argentina." *AdVersuS: Revista de Semiótica*, 26: 96–115.

Palacios, J.M. (2016) "Ephemerality, Epistolary, and the Historiography of Chilean Exile Cinema." *Fragmentary Archives, Contingent Histories*. Panel at the Annual Conference of the Latin American Studies Association (LASA), New York, May 27–30.

Paranaguá, P.A. (1985) *O Cinema na América Latina: Longe de Deus e perto de Hollywood*. Porto Alegre: L&PM.

Podalsky, L. (2004a) "De la pantalla: jóvenes y el cine mexicano contemporáneo." *El Ojo que Piensa*, 6 (November). Available at: www.elojoquepiensa.udg.mx (accessed October 15, 2004).

—— (2004b) *Specular City: Transforming Culture, Consumption, and Space in Buenos Aires, 1955–1973*. Philadelphia, PA: Temple University Press.

—— (2011) *The Politics of Affect and Emotion in Contemporary Latin American Cinema: Argentina, Brazil, Cuba, and Mexico*. New York: Palgrave Macmillan.

Rodríguez, C. (2011) *Citizens' Media against Armed Conflict: Disrupting Violence in Colombia*. Minneapolis, MN: University of Minnesota Press.

Rony, F.T. (1996) *The Third Eye: Race, Cinema and Ethnographic Spectacle*. Durham, NC: Duke University Press.

Rosen, P. (2001) *Change Mummified: Cinema, Historicity, Theory*. Durham, NC: Duke University Press.

Schiwy, F. (2009) *Indianizing Film: Decolonization, the Andes and the Question of Technology*. New Brunswick, NJ: Rutgers University Press.

Schroeder Rodríguez, P. (2016) *Latin American Cinema: A Comparative History*. Berkeley, CA: University of California Press.

Schulmann, P.B. (1987) *Historia del cine latinoamericano*. Buenos Aires: Legasa.

Serna, L.I. (2014) *Making Cinelandia: American Films and Mexican Film Culture before the Golden Age*. Durham, NC: Duke University Press.

Taboada, J. de (2015) "¿Cómo lo hacen? Breve guía para entender el cine regional." In J. Noriega Bernuy and J. Morales Mena (eds.), *Cine andino*. Lima: Universidad Nacional de San Marcos, Facultad de Letras y Ciencias Humanas/Pakarina, pp. 245–252.

5
OFF-SCREEN CULTURE

Maite Conde, Laura Isabel Serna, and
María Fernanda Arias Osorio

Editors' introduction

Textually oriented critical approaches continue to dominate much scholarship on Latin American cinema. Yet, in recent decades, this scholarly paradigm has given ground to historicized explorations of local cinematic experiences. Unlike many text-bound studies, these new research horizons provide vital clues about specific film audiences and the social practices, pleasures, and anxieties that were part of moviegoing at particular historical and geographical conjunctures. Similarly, paratexts, such as journalistic discussions of films, help to map the social role of cinema, showing historical negotiations and its role in broader forms of leisure activities.

In this chapter, three scholars provide exemplary case studies of this approach: Maite Conde considers *Cinearte*, a popular Brazilian film magazine of the 1920s. She argues that this harbinger of the rich fan culture that Roberto Ortiz examines in Chapter 11 helped early on in the century to consolidate Hollywood's presence in Brazil. *Cinearte* fostered a vibrant film culture as it reconfigured Hollywood's templates in Brazilian contexts. Film journals also had a material counterpart, as Laura Isabel Serna demonstrates in her consideration of the social space of cinematic viewing embodied in a number of first-run movie houses built in 1940s Mexico City. As Serna argues, the flowering of the country's film industry coincided with the construction of these mid-century "movie palaces," which offered moviegoers an idealized urban space where they could act out the gender and class ideals of modern industrial capitalism. Between the mid-1950s and 1980s, a new type of film culture developed around Colombian *cine-clubs*, groups of film enthusiasts who exhibited movies, usually on a weekly basis. They understood cinema as something different from entertainment. *Cine-clubs* catered to spectators in ways similar to those of the art house cinemas. María Fernanda Arias Osorio maintains that the evolution of *cine-clubs* in Cali shows us how complexly the cinema was experienced in a peripheral Latin American city,

(continued)

(continued)

creating a rich and contentious political and cultural landscape as films intertwined with diverse urban cultures, political positions, and scholarly trends. Foregrounding sociopolitical situations and historical moments that impinge on the interpretation of cinematic texts, this scholarship illustrates the historically embedded social forces that frame popular films and their reception.

Introduction

The early decades of cinema in Latin America saw a deep preoccupation with off-screen culture. While commentators in newspapers and magazines were attracted to the modernity of the technology recently imported from Europe (López 2000a), they were also fascinated by the ambience of the screening, commenting on the constitution of the audience and on exhibition venues (Serna 2014). This reminds us that the film text is merely "one element in a complex of factors, institutions and networks relevant to the study of film culture," and consequently that the task of understanding cinema is more than a problem of film form (Turner 2002: 11).

Latin American film scholarship, however, has until recently tended to focus on films and film production at the expense of historicized explorations of how the cinema was experienced. Critical works have bypassed issues relating to reception and exhibition to privilege a history of filmmaking, of texts and their content, to the exclusion of the contexts in which cinemagoers engaged with films. This emphasis on production was guided by theoretical discussions of cinema and national identity in the 1950s and 1960s, focused on asserting local production in the face of Hollywood's hegemonic presence. In this context, historiography sought to assert the presence of Latin American films, favoring texts that rejected Hollywood's commercial mode. In the process, the region's popular films were "dismissed as imitative of Hollywood" (López 2000b: 432).

This textually oriented approach has been re-evaluated since the 1970s. Influenced by interpretive theories, such as reception theory, audience studies, social history, and cultural studies, this re-evaluation showed how cinema is part of a broader cultural landscape and how its consumers are imbricated in discursive universes, particular political situations and historical moments that impinge in the interpretation of a film text (Ginsburg et al. 2002: 2). This "context-activated historical mode" (Staiger 1992: xi) illustrated how social forces and cultural forms beyond the screen play a part in producing the meaning of a film for spectators.

Such work led to a reinterpretation of traditions previously denigrated as imitative of Hollywood, such as Mexico's melodramas (López 1993) and Brazil's musical comedies, the *chanchadas* (Vieira and Stam 1985). More than an attempt to recuperate dismissed genres, though, this scholarship illustrated the historically embedded social forces that framed popular films and their reception, highlighting how their regime of pleasure intersected with broader cultural activities. These contextually embedded readings opened up interpretations of the region's cinematic development, and recovered a sense of agency, often elided by previous explorations. The new emphasis on agency reconfigured the spectator as a member of a social audience, understood not solely as a construct of the text, but also as a member of concrete social, cultural, and material conditions (Kuhn 2002: 18–29). This represents a shift from interest in texts and production to focus on the processes of interaction between texts, spectators, institutions, and ambient culture, challenging the previous ontology of the text. How and where films are watched and the cultural forms and institutions linked to them are an important part of understanding what cinema means within a culture and how they fit into the broader range of entertainment activities offered to audiences.

This "contextual model for film research" (Mayne 1993: 11) has brought into consideration historical intertexts that were part of the "discursive practices that constructed the social and cultural space of the cinema as an institution" (Serna 2014: 5). Scholars have explored how trade journals and magazines are a crucial index of the historical dimensions of filmgoing. The journals and magazines exemplify a Latin American cinephilia, as a phenomenon (cultural and historical), experience (collective and individual), and knowledge (reflection, fascination, and interpretation). Central to this is the physical act of viewing films, with the exhibition venue figured as a key discursive site. Studies of the architecture of movie theaters, their location and screening patterns, provide vital clues of specific film audiences and the social practices, pleasures, and anxieties that were part of moviegoing at particular historical and geographical conjunctures. Similarly, paratexts such as discussions of films in the press help to map the historical placement and reception of cinema, showing historical negotiations and how it played a part in broader forms of cultural production (Conde 2011). Such empirical research provides us with a more expansive notion of Latin American cinema. It has broadened the history of the region's cinematic development, revealing it as more than visions on a screen.

Film and fanzines in 1920s Brazil: the case of *Cinearte*

MAITE CONDE

Film became a regular feature in Brazil's popular illustrated press after 1915, when American studios started furnishing magazines with publicity material for their films. Advertisements for movies, reviews, and photographs of U.S. stars proliferated in illustrated weeklies such as *Para todos* (1918) and *Scena muda* (1921). Fostering a familiarity with Hollywood's products, this publicity aided North American studios' consolidation of Brazil, part of an aggressive strategy that aimed to make Brazilians "good" spectators of U.S. movies. By 1921, U.S. imports represented 71 percent of the total number of films screened in Brazil, a figure that rose to 86 percent in 1929 (Ramos 1987: 107).

Hollywood's consolidation in the Brazilian market was central to Brazil's first film magazine, *Cinearte* (1926), which described itself as "the natural intermediary" between the latter and Hollywood. Reviews, publicity stills, and features about U.S. actors made Hollywood familiar for Brazilian readers, allowing them to participate in its spectacular world. Materials that instructed readers how to understand U.S. movies reinforced this participation, and in so doing initiated a specialized discourse about cinema. Sections such as "The Art of Filmmaking" introduced aspects of film form, such as montage and *mise en scène*, teaching readers how to evaluate cinema's cinematography. Such sections fostered an idea of film not as a popular entertainment, but as an art form, as expressed by the magazine's name.

In its conception of film art, the magazine denigrated European cinema, dismissing its realism as "uncivilized" (Xavier 1978: 182–186). By contrast, writers such as Gonzaga praised American films as "a good cinema" (p. 182). Hollywood's glamorous stars and luxurious sets were celebrated as sophisticated and its industrial productions were elevated as a cinematic ideal. *Cinearte* thus helped to promote Hollywood and legitimized its language as universal, naturalizing its implantation in Brazil.

Cinearte also instructed its readers in the practices of fandom, encouraging an intimate investment between its consumers and U.S. stars. The magazine urged readers to write fan letters to their favorite actors and actors. Write-in sections, which published stars' addresses, facilitated this communication, encouraging Brazilians to engage directly in American film culture. Contests that invited readers to nominate "the most beautiful star" also promoted an engagement with Hollywood, stimulating fans to keep abreast of developments in U.S. cinema (1926 no. 9: 2). *Cinearte* brought American movies into the lives of Brazilian readers, domesticating its products. This was apparent in stories of stars at home. The magazine often depicted Hollywood actors "away from the screen and studio" (no. 163: n.p.). A 1929 article, titled "Wallace Beery and His Wife Rita Gilman," for instance, showed the star at home, his glamorous Hollywood lifestyle countered through the ordinariness of the domestic setting (1929 no. 160: n.p.). Such images demonstrated that Hollywood's stars are "just like us" (Dyer 1998). Indeed, Hollywood stars were often Brazilian-ized in *Cinearte*. Interviews with U.S. starlets underscored their similarities to Brazilians. A 1926 interview with Ruth Roland noted that she had "the same virtues as us" (no. 2). Images reinforced this connection between Hollywood and Brazil. February and March issues included photographs of American actresses dressed in attire "for carnival," as if they were ready to participate in Brazil's pre-Lenten festivities.

Cinearte's domestication of Hollywood helped to bring the distant world closer to consumers. In "The Work of Art in the Age of Mechanical Reproduction" (1936/2002), Walter Benjamin refers to a history of the modes of human perception and to the decay of the aura, which characterizes contemporary perception. This decay is associated with developing mass culture and with consumers' desire to bring things closer, annihilating uniqueness through reproduction. *Cinearte* functioned as part of this process. It brought Hollywood and its stars closer to readers, projecting them not as distant gods, but as ordinary—even "Brazilian"—intimately connecting them to Brazil.

Photographs added to this. Photo spreads of stars could be pulled out and collected by readers, thereby creating a personal investment in Hollywood. These images helped to bridge the space between the Brazilian readers and U.S. films. This was central to the section "From Hollywood to You," in which correspondent L.S. Marinho penned articles from Los Angeles. Marinho focused on topics such as new screenings or productions, providing *Cinearte*'s readers with a personal entry point to Hollywood. Stories of his encounters with stars emphasized this point, and they were amply illustrated. Photographs portrayed Marinho with well-known actors, placing the Brazilian correspondent in the world of the movies, and forging an image of Brazil "at home" in Hollywood. The publication of photographs of stars reading *Cinearte* strengthened this. Actresses such as Clara Bow were often depicted leafing through the magazine. Mirroring Brazilians' own act of reading the fanzine, in the images *Cinearte* became a link to the US, much like Marinho, an object that creates identification between Hollywood and Brazil (Vieira 1991: 34).

Cinearte thus helped to consolidate Hollywood's presence in Brazil. The journal's intimacy with U.S. cinema in some senses fostered a narcissistic overidentification with American film culture, which became an object of admiration. The journal played out this identification by mirroring the format of U.S. fanzines such as *Photoplay* (Salles Gomes 1974: 295; Xavier 1978: 167). For Salles Gomes and Xavier, this reflection foregrounds a passive subjection to the Hollywood industry's dream factory, which turns on the logic of reification—a mimetic empathy with American cinema. Yet *Cinearte*'s relationship with Hollywood was not simply mimetic. *Cinearte*'s specialized film discourse also encouraged audiences to engage critically with Hollywood's movies. Reviews for U.S. films were often negative. One, for example, dismissed *The Canvas Kisser* as "a puerile film" with "a weak narrative" (1927 no. 45: 29); another noted that *The Runaway* "has some good action but lacks direction" (1927 no. 45: 29). Fans participated in these critiques in letters, and they were especially damning of U.S. movies' negative depiction of Brazil. Condemning "American films that degrade us," one reader stressed the "need to eradicate the offensive productions from our screens [and] eliminate the presence of studios, like Fox, who use the seventh art to discredit our nation." The reader added, "We must support the development of Brazilian film" (1928 no. 203: 7). Far from passive, *Cinearte* and its readers actively engaged with Hollywood, and the publication opened up a space in which critics and fans began to discuss national cinema.

With its slogan "All Brazilian films must be seen," *Cinearte* defended and promoted national cinema. While Hollywood dominated Brazil during this period, domestic filmmaking did not completely cease. The 1920s saw a burst of cinematographic activity. Between 1921 and 1930, Brazilian feature film production averaged 16.7 films per year (Johnson 1987: 36). These were films mainly produced by companies in regional cities, outside of Rio and São Paulo. Alongside reports on U.S. movies, *Cinearte* reported on these developments, in its section "Brazilian Film Production," endowing the independent regional projects with a united Brazilian identity. Adopting Hollywood's template, *Cinearte* reviewed domestic movies and reported on upcoming screenings. It also published photographs of their actors and actresses, in poses that mirrored their U.S. counterparts (Salles Gomes 1974: 336). Thus, *Cinearte* created a Brazilian star system, projecting the image of a national film industry. Hollywood's ubiquity and the limited exhibition of domestic films, however, meant that the Brazilian public had little access to the films that the Brazilian stars appeared in, and their consumption of domestic movies was relegated to the pages of *Cinearte*. For Salles Gomes, the magazine "was concerned with creating a fiction with the greatest semblance of an appearance of reality, but that had little actual basis in it" (Salles Gomes 1974: 336).

Given the fictional qualities of this star system, it is hardly surprising that Salles Gomes highlights its mimetic qualities. *Cinearte* was not without commentary that reinforced this, as its writers often stressed the Hollywood patrimony of Brazilian stars. One feature referred to actress Lelita Rosa as "the national Greta Garbo" and to Lia Jardim as "the Brazilian Clara Bow" (1929 no. 56). Consequently, *Cinearte*'s star system, like the journal, has been deemed an example of "the mimicry that articulated an attempt to define a Brazilian cinema based on imported parameters" (Xavier 1978: 119). Yet *Cinearte*'s Hollywood-style stardom had practical intentions; it aimed to "make names. They will guarantee the success of our new films" (Salles Gomes 1974: 336). The magazine emphasized the importance of North America's publicity-driven strategies, which could awaken "the public's attention" (1926 no. 5: 1). Stars were fundamental to this, as they could "attract the public to our cinema, without having to count on film itself" (1926 no. 21: 5). This points to an unconditional faith in the power of publicity and in the agency of readers. Stardom did not merely project a national film industry; it could conjure it into existence with stars manufacturing a Brazilian dream factory.

Cinearte's star system, then, signified the possibilities of an industry that could capitalize on consumers' desires. These consumers were primarily women. Advertisements for female products in *Cinearte* show that women were its principal audience, which visually and textually inscribed them into its address (Vieira 1991: 34–42). *Cinearte*'s stardom also overwhelmingly focused on female starlets. Women were the objects of Brazilian cinema, as well as its target audience, and the journal's star system catered to a cinematic market in which women were key. Women's centrality to *Cinearte*'s Hollywood-inflected star system is unsurprising. In the 1920s, U.S. films explicitly addressed female spectators and Hollywood's star system was aimed largely at women. U.S. movies consequently had a profound impact on Brazilian women:

> Novel attitudes and images of female behavior arrived in Brazil from the United States in easily assimilated form through movies. Films portrayed women as independent working girls, modern heroines, and even as sexual temptresses' who stepped out of traditional roles of resignation.
>
> *(Hahner 1990: 115)*

The press often commented on Hollywood's new models of femininity. In 1923, commentarist Belmonte wrote that American actresses were "the models of the fair sex of my country" (Besse 1996: 29).

New models of femininity, however, were also imbricated with changes in women's role in Brazil. By the 1920s, women began to assume new roles in public space, challenging Brazilian women's traditional domesticity. Hollywood keyed into these changes, as did Brazilian films. Brazilian filmmakers targeted female audiences, with narratives and stars. Women played leading roles in many of the 1920s regional movies. Carmen Santos, Eva Nil, and Lelita Rosa starred in films such as *Retribuição* (*Retribution*, Gentil Roiz, 1924), *Braza dormida* (*Dormant Embers*, Humberto Mauro, 1928), and *Vício e beleza* (*Vice and Beauty*,

Figure 5.1 Brazilian actress Eva Nil on the cover of *Cinearte* magazine. Issue no. 86, October 19, 1927.

Antonio Tibiriçá, 1926). The appearance of actresses in these films emphasized Brazilian women's new public role, stressed in plots that depicted female characters in outdoor spaces.

Women's appearance on the screen, however, was not celebrated. Newspapers denigrated actresses, citing their public visibility as stimulating a sexual chaos that was precipitating a social crisis. Women's presence on-screen presented a danger to Brazilian tradition, which threatened to delegitimize Brazilian cinema, and *Cinearte*'s promotion of a national cinema carefully emphasized its female stars' traditional qualities, reconfiguring Hollywood's templates. The magazine accentuated Brazilian starlets' traditional backgrounds, which obeyed past notions of femininity. Interviews with actresses were conducted at home in the presence of parents, and supported by photographs. An article on Lia Torá, for instance, featured images of the star at home with her sister, mother, and grandmother, firmly rooting her in a domestic setting and to past generations of women (1929 no. 149: 8).

Cinearte's traditional portrayal of Brazilian actresses was markedly different to those from the US. While Hollywood stressed stars' rags-to-riches trajectory, this was absent in *Cinearte*'s depiction of Brazilian starlets, which emphasized their elite backgrounds. The magazine's depiction of domestic stars also stressed their "otherworldliness," in contrast to its promotion of the ordinary nature of Hollywood's stars. Actress Lia Torá, for instance, was described as "a saint with a halo in search of an altar" and Carmen Santos was "a star descended from heaven" (1929 no. 164: 14–15). The magazine also imbued its female stars with an elusive 'It' quality, defined as an innate attractiveness that cannot be acquired. Such descriptions countered the belief that anybody can be a star and *Cinearte* reinscribed its homemade stars within parameters that presented little threat to Brazilian tradition.

This negotiation was evident in contemporary movies. Hollywood's working women, such as Clara Bow, were absent in Brazilian films, whose stars instead played the parts of daughters from traditional families, as seen in *Braza dormida* (*Sleeping Ember*, Humberto Mauro, 1928) and *Retribuição* (*Retribution*, Gentil Roiz, 1924). Additionally, the films' ubiquitous happy endings saw the triumph of marriage, re-establishing women's domestic role. That the films' narratives reflected *Cinearte*'s promotion is expected. While the fanzine's discourse instructed readers on how to understand film, it also taught Brazilian filmmakers how to make movies. Articles about filmmaking techniques educated burgeoning filmmakers in the art of making movies. These sections were crucial to regional filmmakers, who consumed *Cinearte*'s cinematic lessons to make films that, like the fanzine, adopted Hollywood's template yet at the same time reconfigured them for Brazil. *Cinearte* helped to consolidate Hollywood's presence in Brazil; it also fostered a vibrant film culture and laid the foundations for a national cinema by translating Hollywood.

The "golden age" of Mexican movie theaters

Laura Isabel Serna

The golden age of Mexican cinema (1930s–1950s) also saw the appearance of publications devoted to national film culture such as *Cinema Reporter* and *Filmográfica*, which, like Brazil's *Cinearte*, provided a forum for the discursive construction of a national film culture. These Mexican journals had a material counterpart. In the 1940s, modern, first-run cinemas—considered appropriate venues for sophisticated, urbane audiences—emerged in Mexico City. Press coverage of these cinemas demonstrates how the social space of cinemas participated in framing Mexican films as vehicles for nationalism, even as they bore traces of the transnational underpinnings of the national industry.

Characterizing the spaces where motion pictures were screened as modern was not new. In 1896, Lumiere's *cinematographe* premiered publicly in Mexico City in the basement of a pharmacy on Plateros Street. This location was apt for the debut of a new medium considered both science and entertainment. Subsequently, existing theaters integrated film exhibition into their programs, *carpas*, or tent shows, emerged in the less elite neighborhoods of the city, and repurposed existing buildings became cinemas. After the Revolution, elegant cinemas sprung up downtown and in the commercial districts of wealthier *colonias* (neighborhoods). The exteriors of these buildings employed the neocolonial style of the period. Inside, gilt finishes, framed mirrors, and heavy curtains signaled luxury in an idiom drawn from the late nineteenth century. Though the cleanliness, comfort, and safety of cinemas came under scrutiny, the Mexican popular press framed these cinemas as evidence of Mexico's progress and modernity (Serna 2014: 47–84).

The social and political significance of movie theaters shifted with the emergence of a national film industry after the mid-1930s and the growth of the Mexican economy. In the 1940s, the Mexican state focused on economic growth through industrialization, while continuing to consolidate power in the name of the revolution. World War II, which Mexico entered in 1942, allowed the state to implement import-substitution policies that sought to increase industrial production to serve the domestic market. Under President Manuel Avila Camacho (1940–1946), Mexico's economy grew by almost 10 percent annually. This led to increased rural to urban migration, growth in professions such as advertising and architecture, and the expansion of consumer culture (Niblo 2000; Gillingham and Smith 2014).

In this context, and propelled by the introduction of sound technology, the Mexican film industry grew. Between 1940 and 1950, feature film production increased more than threefold from 38 features to 123 in 1950 (Noble 2006: 510). The flowering of the country's film industry required not only modern production facilities, supported by both investment capital (domestic and foreign) and the state, but also moviegoing venues that matched the industry's new profile. Moviegoing became a favored pastime of more Mexicans than ever as urban populations grew. Indeed, cultural critic Carlos Monsiváis argues that rural transplants learned how to be modern from the films they saw on screen (Monsiváis 1995: 145–151). Thus, the 1940s saw an upsurge in the construction of first-run cinemas, some part of chains and others independently owned.

Built in the heart of the city or along major arteries such as Paseo de la Reforma, the *Cines Teresa* (Francisco V. Serrano, 1942), *Trans-Lux Prado* (Carlos Obregón Santacilia, 1947), *Chapultepec* (S. Charles Le, 1942), and *Metropolitan* (Pedro Gorozpe Echeverria, 1943) were conceived of as examples of modern architecture and part of a city reimagined through the lens of tourism and automobile travel. Press descriptions highlighted their proximity to prominent civic spaces, other modern buildings, and landmarks. For example, the *Cine Trans-Lux Prado*, built in 1947, benefited from its "luxury location in the Hotel Prado in front of the Alameda Central" (*El Universal* 1947: 10). Similarly, the *Cine Chapultepec*, built in 1944, occupied a prominent location on Paseo de la Reforma, a boulevard built in 1860 to emulate the Champs-Élysées in Paris. Descriptions of the Chapultepec emphasized that car owners could take advantage of the wide avenues that converged on Reforma and ample parking—enough for at least 1,000 cars—while non-car owners could reach the theater via the city's modern trolley and bus system (Alcántara Pastor 1944b). Further down the avenue was the Monument to the Revolution built by the same architect, Carlos Obregón Santacilia, in a similar art deco style. The Chapultepec thus sat along a thoroughfare dedicated to Mexico's history and its future as a cosmopolitan city.

The use of art deco and modified versions of the international style signaled this cosmopolitanism in architectural terms. The international style, which became popular in Mexico in the 1930s, emphasized the use of materials such as glass and steel that had to be imported to Mexico, while art deco celebrated technology with geometric forms and linear decorative motifs (Fernández 2001: 31–45). Though sometimes eclectically applied, Mexican architects used these modern styles to reshape the cityscape in the idiom of indus-trial capitalism. In contrast to the highly ornamented theaters built during the 1920s and 1930s, first-run theaters of the 1940s featured sleek exteriors. One journalist described the Chapultepec as a building "whose façade doesn't tell the passer-by what its interior con-tains" (Alcántara Pastor 1944b: 12). Indeed, it was difficult to ascertain the location of the theater, despite the imposing vertical neon sign with the theater's name that emerged out of its marquee, because the upper stories appeared to belong to an unremarkable, if mod-ern, office building. A marquee that echoed the shape of the hotel's sleek industrial façade signaled the Trans-Lux Prado's presence and a Third Cinema also built in 1942, the *Cine Teresa*, had an art deco façade free of ornamentation other than two lighted marquees, one that hugged the flat surface of the façade and the other that hung over the entrance. These two marquees and the lighted vertical sign that connected them gave the Teresa the appear-ance of the grill of an automobile awash in neon light.

If these cinemas' exteriors signaled the machine age—flat surfaces, metal, and neon lights—the interiors offered luxurious, modern respite from the city outside. The Chapultepec, for example, "flaunt[ed] the money invested" in its design and decoration (*Mexico Cinema* 1944: 8). Press coverage described thick carpets, meters of mirrors, silk curtains, undulating walls, curved staircases, sculptures that appeared to float over foun-tains, and recessed lighting. Journalists noted that these details were executed in a modern style, "a stylization of French art," and noted they had been selected to create the experi-ence of luxury and comfort. Descriptions of the Trans-Lux Prado and the Chapultepec noted that their seats were wide and comfortable and their aisles wide. Along with the Teresa, these theaters boasted up-to-date air conditioning and ventilation systems. The Trans-Lux Prado advertised a system "to disinfect and perfume the theater daily" (Pastor 1947: 49). These amenities signaled modernity through style and technology, presenting the theaters as spaces that promised to transport patrons into an aesthetically pleasing and physically comfortable environment away from the dirt, crowding, and fast pace of the modern industrial city (Moreno 2003: 207–228).

This idealized version of urban life created an environment in which a particular type of social subject could be called into being (Capron and de Alba 2010). Anne Rubenstein observes that mid-century "movie palaces" allowed women to "pose themselves fashionably, surrounded by luxuries—especially the luxury of space" (Rubenstein 2012: 146). Indeed, descriptions of the Chapultepec emphasized that the theater had been designed to "permit women to show off their exuberantly fantastic hats, without bothering those behind them" (Alcántara Pastor 1944b: 12). The Teresa went so far as to declare itself "dedicated to the women of the metropolis [DF]" whose charms would be mirrored in the cinema's "natural and unequaled beauty" (*El Nacional* 1942: 2). Similarly, the Chapultepec's vestibules cre-ated the frame for "a magnificent spectacle" as ticket holders, men and women, had to pass through the space that in the words of one journalist bespoke "splendor, beauty, and refined taste" (Alcántara Pastor 1944a). While the mirrors and modern lighting that distinguished these cinemas from their predecessors lent themselves to the acts of display these descrip-tions suggest, these acts of performance were inflected by an assumed (or aspirational) class position. When the Trans-Lux Prado noted its management hoped it would become the "most distinguished place for women to meet in the afternoons," they imagined a middle- or upper-class woman who had both time and money to spend on leisure (*El Universal* 1947: 10). The Chapultepec was also envisioned as a "club" for "socially elegant meetings" (Alcántara Pastor 1944b). Thus, these cinemas offered moviegoers an idealized urban space where audiences could act out the gender and class ideals of modern industrial capitalism.

Each theater was touted as material evidence of Mexico City's cosmopolitanism. The Cine Chapultepec was declared "positively beautiful and worthy of the culture of its [Mexico City's] residents" (Alcántara Pastor 1944a). The Trans-Lux was compared with the toniest cinemas in New York, Hollywood, and London (Pastor 1947). The Cine Teresa was a "modern and beautiful" cinema, "the pride of Mexico" (*El Nacional* 1942: 2). Nevertheless, tensions over the national character of Mexico's film industry and film culture percolated below these pronouncements and can be seen in the discourse around the films selected for each theater's opening night. For their openings, the Teresa and Trans-Lux screened Hollywood films featuring well-known stars. The Teresa's management chose *El hijo de la furia* (*Son of Fury: The Story of Benjamin Blake*, John Cromwell, 1942), starring Tyrone Power, and *El castillo del desierto* (*Castle in the Desert*, Harry Lachman, 1942), a Charlie Chan film. The Trans-Lux Prado showed *¡Qué bello es vivir!* (*It's a Wonderful Life*, Frank Capra, 1946) and *El Engaño* (*Deception*, Irving Rapper, 1946), with Bette Davis (*Cinema Reporter* 1947: 33).

Figure 5.2   A banner advertising the film *It's a Wonderful Life* (Frank Capra, 1946) and the neon sign of the Cine Trans-Lux Prado, 1947. © (num. 293678). SECRETARÍA DE CULTURA.INAH.SINFONA.FN.MX. Reproduction authorized by INAH.

In contrast to this strategy of making popular Hollywood films available to Mexico City audiences, in 1944 the Cine Chapultepec (built with U.S. capital and designed by a well-known American theater architect, S. Charles Lee) declared that "its owners wanted to pay homage to Mexican Cinema and demonstrate their affection for the Mexican public" with their opening night program (Alcántara Pastor 1944a).

The Chapultepec was built by American expatriate businessman Theodore Gildred, who had begun to assemble a theater circuit in Mexico City under the aegis of the Compañía Operadora de Teatros, S.A. (Paxman 2008: 208). Press coverage noted Gildred's investment and architect S. Charles Lee's involvement in the project in passing, instead making Mexican engineer Miguel Giralt the project's spokesperson (Lee 1987: 54–58). Giralt cast the project as a transnational collaboration between Mexican and foreign professionals made possible by Mexican laborers. He emphasized that it would be a forum for the screening of not only *El Corsario*, but also for the "best to date" among the productions of CLASAS and other national film companies. Thus, Gildred's company carefully positioned the theater, which could have been interpreted as an imperialist project, as a conduit for the Mexican film industry's prestige.

Press coverage surrounding the opening of the *Cine Metropolitan*, which the cultural supplement, *Jueves de Excelsior*, described as a "work of architecture that will bring prestige to Mexico," cast the stakes of this negotiation into relief. Journalists emphasized that the architect, Pedro Gorozpe Echeverría, and indeed everyone on the project, was a Mexican national. According to the extensive coverage of the theater's construction, the "timeless and classical" building, with an art deco façade that contrasted with its classically inspired interior, fit easily into Mexico City's built environment. The theater's premiere screening consisted of a "grand work realized in its totality by Mexican artists and workers, with Mexican capital! With Mexican capital"—the Mexican version of *Les Miserables* directed by Fernando Rivero (Pastor 1943: 104). Coverage of the Metropolitan recognized that the design and financing of theaters had implications for the nationalist project of the Mexican film industry. Indeed, the Metropolitan positioned itself as an important conduit for the diffusion of Mexican films, criticizing the fact that it cost less to screen a foreign film than one made in Mexico (Pastor 1943: 104). Press coverage of the Metropolitan implied that patronizing the theater would be a nationalist gesture.

In the 1940s, many perceived the Mexican film industry as a bulwark against Hollywood's influence. This celebration of what amounted to import substitution in the realm of mass culture constituted part of what Seth Fein refers to as Mexico's "nationalist ideological veneer in an era of transnationalization" (Fein 2001: 160). As scholars have documented, both major U.S. studios and investors holding U.S. passports, some of whom had extensive business interests in Mexico, were deeply involved in the Mexican film industry, even as the state began offering more sustained support (Fein 2001: 279). Examining the discourse around the construction and promotion of first-run theaters allows us to see, from another vantage point, the complicated politics of the cultural nationalism that dominated and continue to dominate discussions of Mexican cinema. Rather than monuments to an autochthonous, developed film industry, the flagship motion picture theaters of the 1940s attest to the complicated web of relationships that constituted Mexican cinema as a cultural formation, even during its "golden age."

Cine-clubs in Cali, Colombia

María Fernanda Arias Osorio

Between the mid-1950s and 1980s, a new type of film culture was born and developed around Colombian *cine-clubs*, groups of film enthusiasts who exhibited movies—usually on a weekly basis—undertaking previously nonexistent educational criticism, and sometimes filmmaking activities, and assuming cinema as something different from entertainment. These clubs catered to spectators in ways similar to those of the art house cinemas analyzed by Wilinsky (2001); however, their informal and itinerant working methodology differed from that of art house cinemas and *cinematheques* in the US and Europe. While the vicissitudes of Colombia's *cine-clubs* have been chronicled (Martínez 1978), the role they played in the wider transformation of the national film cultures, the rich film culture they created, and their connections to international trends remains understudied.

We can trace the foundation of *La Tertulia*, the first *cine-club* opened in Cali in 1956 (Uribe de Urdinola 1956–1969), in different spheres: the diversification of the types of films exhibited, wider coverage of film-related information in the local press, circulation of specialized international magazines and books, growing levels of literacy and urbanization in the country, a new governmental attitude toward the social role of cinema, and increasing distribution of 16 mm films. *La Tertulia* aimed to encourage the perception of film as an art form, enhancing the average spectator's aesthetic taste. Such points of view derived from discourses and practices that defined a film culture opposed to commercial and mass culture, founded on the importance of the film director, the rescue of out-of-circulation movies, the establishment of specialized distribution and exhibition circuits and the use of formats ignored by commercial theaters. This emphasis on the aesthetic dimension of cinema called into question the two ways of valuing cinema that prevailed until the 1940s: as a modern industrial product and as a tool of Catholic moral education. In articles published in local newspapers and specialized courses, *La Tertulia* advocated for a cosmopolitan and aesthetically informed spectator. This stance did not imply a generational challenge or radical political activism; however, the appreciation of movies as aesthetic objects transformed how films were perceived in different contexts.

In the 1970s, three new clubs showed diverse and contradictory ways of understanding cinema. *La Casa de la Amistad de los Pueblos*, *Nueva Generación*, and *Cine Club de Cali* led heated debates about the aesthetic and political qualities of movies, expressed in local specialized magazines, literature, and everyday film-related practices and discussions. Coordinated by Pakiko Ordóñez and supported by the USSR and Cuba, *La Casa de la Amistad de los Pueblos* (1971–1982) screened movies every Saturday at the traditional Colón Theater and in labor unions and communal centers during the week. Strongly influenced by dependency theories, leftist politics, and the New Latin American Cinema, *La Casa* believed that film should be a tool of political denunciation, awareness, and education of the lower classes. Prior to screenings, "protest music" played on the sound system for working-class spectators convened by unions and left-wing political movements. A debate forum followed in which the movies screened were expected to have exposed the problems faced by subaltern groups in their revolutionary struggle, including the understanding of the ideological maneuvers of capitalism and imperialism. The films were acquired from embassies, the *Cinemateca Colombiana*, and informal networks of film circulation managed by unions and religious communities associated with the liberation theology (Ordoñez 1978, personal communication).

La Casa screened "anti-imperialist" films that served as pedagogical and motivational tools. Considered industrial and mass products aimed at generating ideological indoctrination, U.S. films were left aside and European art films were equally rejected, as they were thought to be focused on the aesthetic qualities of film and connected to cinephile positions. Such claims were aligned with a politically resistant periphery in opposition to an imperialist center, generator of escapism, and disguised as art or industry.

Meanwhile, the *Nueva Generación cine-club* (1972–1978), managed by Gustavo and Alfonso Zorrilla, screened movies every Saturday at the Calima Theater. Its program addressed students looking for "quality" cinema with no pretensions of being film specialists. "Classical" music played before the screenings and its cine-forum featured "friendly, polite, and intelligent dialogue resulting from the diverse opinions expressed by the audience" (*Boletín Cine Club Nueva Generación* no. 9. 1974: 1). The programs included European and American movies, shown individually or as part of series organized by topics such as contemporary youth, musical film, or political film, considered to have "artistic" values. Film director series were notoriously absent.

Despite its name, the views by *Nueva Generación* did not imply strong generational challenges, radical cinephilia, or political militancy. Its sporadic bulletins combined basic information about the movies, poems, short stories, and articles about student protests. Its members, however, were clear in standing apart from any radical leftish categorization. They also dissociated from cinephilia and the eclectic programs, and topics included in its bulletin showed a general interest in artistic expressions that never reached "cinematic specificity."

Nueva Generación and *La Casa* were diametrically opposed to *Cine Club de Cali* (1971–1977), founded by Andrés Caicedo at the San Fernando Theater. Its program was built around film series organized by directors, countries of origin, or genre. During its life span, the club published 322 mimeographed programs with original, adapted, or translated

Figure 5.3   Typical Cine-Club Cali film flyer distributed at public screenings.

information about the directors and the films scheduled. Eventually, brochures that were more elaborate were published, as well as the magazine *Ojo al Cine* (Galindo Cardona 2008, 2010). Their activities extended to film exhibition, criticism, and filmmaking activities (Caicedo 1999; Mayolo 2002, 2008; Ospina 2007).

Several characteristics set this *cine-club* apart from the rest: its passionate cinephilia (known as "cine-syphilis"), its fondness for the *politique des auteurs* and American cinema, and its interest in local and national history. According to *Cine Club de Cali*, *La Casa* was too "*mamerta*"—a derogative adjective employed to denigrate leftist militants—and *Nueva Generación* advocated for "quality cinema," a trend that the members of this club despised. The reception practices encouraged by this club expressed the search for new expressive forms and links between the different types of urban cultures and experiences. Before the screenings, they played rock, a music associated with the youth from the middle and upper classes, and Salsa, tied to the lower classes—different, yet connected through attitudes of generational rebellion. As in working class theaters, spectators "even smoked pot" (Ospina 2007; Arbeláez 2010; Vidal 2010). Rebellion was never associated with political militancy, nor with the reverence that works of art supposedly deserved, but with more hedonist and open-minded attitudes.

The members of this club showed their intention of embodying the essence of the city, while creatively intervening in local, national, and international film traditions, by making up three new terms: *Caliwood*, *gótico tropical* (tropical gothic), and *pornomiseria*. Caliwood alludes not to desire and nostalgia, but to a playful and ironic defiance to the traditional vision of Hollywood as superior and unattainable. Tropical gothic expressed a longing for putting aside the dichotomies that separated the films considered to depict artistic values and those considered "escapist" and part of mass culture, vindicating the usually despised horror genre as an important film tradition. *Pornomiseria* defined and criticized Colombian films that concealed the pornographic essence in their approach to misery and a particular geopolitical situation: the Third World selling their own images of poverty to the First World (Faguet 2009; Gómez and de la Vega Hurtado 2009).

These three terms defined not only the orientation of *Cine Club de Cali*'s exhibition and criticism activities, but also its film production, filled with ironic and hybrid codes to approach local issues. While feature films such as *Pura Sangre* (*Pure Blood*, Ospina, 1982), *Carne de tu carne* (*Flesh of Your Flesh*, Mayolo, 1983), and *La Mansión de Araucaima* (*The Araucaiama Mansion*, Mayolo, 1986) were part of the *gótico tropical* genre, *Agarrando pueblo* (*The Vampires of Poverty*, Mayolo and Ospina, 1978) was a mockumentary that hypothetically captured the production process of a *pornomiseria* documentary. These films intersect the textual strategies identified by Julianne Burton through a "critical adaptation of forms of dominant cinematic discourse in a three-part process of mimesis, negation or subversion, and substitution" (Burton 1985: 13). Far from being exclusively "textual," these strategies also permeated exhibition activities and critical production, defying the traditional limits between high and low culture, and local, national, and international cinema. The peripheral position of the country in the political and cultural world map was thus vindicated as part of its cultural specificity and richness, while the "anxiety of influence" was resolved through the negotiation of multiple aesthetical and political influences (Gómez and de la Vega Hurtado 2009).

Despite having different positions, these clubs coexisted with the common aim of criticizing the perception of cinema as mere entertainment, offering a clear example of the various, if paradoxical ways of assuming the relations between film, politics, and the nation. In her analysis of the conflictive relations between Hollywood and Latin American cinema, Ana M. López states that, in spite of the limitations of the cultural imperialism and dependency theories, those discussions "did allow for a recognition of important cultural inequalities, and pointed the way for the reconceptualization of differences and cultural specificity which constitutes the core of the globalization approach" (López 2000b: 432). The complex situation described by López was at the core of film exhibition, criticism, and production practices, and the subsequent development of cine-clubs. In the film culture of these clubs, the theories of cultural imperialism and dependency reached their peak in the 1970s. Cinephilia, however, created new ways of approaching the central/peripheral relations. As analyzed by Thomas Elsaesser (2005), by the late 1970s, new theoretical positions exposed in Screen magazine discredited the traditional cinephilia espoused by Cahiers du Cinema during the 1950s and 1960s. Also, post-structuralism, psychoanalysis, a renovated critical theory, and cultural studies weakened the theories of dependency and cultural imperialism (Supelano-Gross 2009; Campo 2010). This represented a paradoxical situation: perpetuating the perception of films as either art or ideological text, cine-clubs facilitated the entrance of cinema into the academy as an object of study. However, the renovated scholarly perspectives implied that the previous positions were incompatible with a truly critical film analysis. Interested in discovering the profound structures of power and new ways of resistance, the new trends distanced themselves from leftist ideological/political film analysis and distrusted the emotional intensity of cinephilia.

In the 1980s, several factors eroded the role of cine-clubs as active associations of spectators involved in film exhibition, production, and criticism: the softening of the tensions between divergent political and aesthetic positions, the closing of theaters and high admission prices, the monopolization of the film distribution and exhibition business, new domestic technologies related to film reception, and new consumption habits. Some leftist movements were radicalized to the point of becoming illegal revolutionary groups, diminishing their influence among the lower classes while the cine-clubs associated with them closed. In the 1990s, the still-remaining cine-clubs, linked to cultural or educative institutions, were perceived as places of high culture. In contrast to the early 1980s, when those associated with film-related activities were cine-club regulars, the new dynamics of exhibition, criticism, and audiovisual production related to this film culture became almost exclusively connected to universities and scholarship. After the late 1980s, a new generation educated in social communication schools generated new discussions regarding film and video, but already determined by new exhibition, consumption, and criticism practices immersed in new dynamics of globalization.

This brief account of the evolution of cine-clubs in Cali shows us how complexly the cinema was historically experienced in a peripheral Latin American city, creating a rich and contentious political and cultural landscape as films intertwined with diverse urban cultures, political positions, and scholarly trends. This reveals Latin American cinema as a cultural and discursive activity that engages with and indeed transcends the cinematic screen. Cine-clubs, magazines, movie theaters, and even discussions about film have played a crucial role in forging Latin America's film culture off- as well as on-screen.

References

Alcántara Pastor, A. (1944a) "Un cinema de ensueño frente a la fuente de Diana Cazadora," El Universal Gráfico, August 18, 1944.

—— (1944b) "La maravillosa fuente de marmol y onix en el nuevo cine chapultepec." El Universal Gráfico, August 23, p. 12.

Benjamin, W. (1936/2002) "The Work of Art in the Age of Mechanical Reproduction." In H. Arendt (ed.), *Illuminations: Essays and Reflections*, trans. H. Zohn. New York: Random House, pp. 211–245.

Besse, S. (1996) *Restructuring Patriarchy: The Modernization of Gender Inequality in Brazil 1914–1940*. Chapel Hill, NC: University of North Carolina Press.

Burton, J. (1985) "Marginal Cinemas and Mainstream Theory." *Screen*, 26(3–4): 2–21.

Caicedo, A. (1999) *Ojo al cine*. Bogotá: Editorial Norma.

Capron, G. and de Alba, M. (2010) "Creating the Middle Class Suburban Dream in Mexico City." *Culturales*, 6(11): 159–183.

Cinema Reporter (1947) "Sección Técnica Cinematográfica." *Cinema Reporter*, March 15, p. 33.

Conde, M. (2011) *Consuming Visions: Cinema, Writing and Modernity in Rio de Janeiro*. Charlottesville, VA: University of Virginia Press.

Dyer, R. (1998) *Stars*. London: BFI.

Elsaesser, T. (2005) "Cinephilia or the Uses of Disenchantment." In M. Valck and M. Hagener (eds.), *Cinephilia: Movies, Love and Memory*. Amsterdam: Amsterdam University Press pp. 27–43.

Faguet, M. (2009) "Pornomiseria: Or How Not to Make a Documentary Film." *Afterall: A Journal of Art, Context, and Enquiry*, 21 (Summer): 5–15.

Fein, S (2001) "Myths of Cultural Imperialism and Nationalism in Golden Age Mexican Cinema." In G. Joseph, A. Rubenstein, and E. Zolov (eds.), *Fragments of a Golden Age: The Politics of Culture in Mexico since 1940*. Durham, NC: Duke University Press, pp. 159–198.

Fernández, M. (2001) "Architecture 20th Century." In M. Werner (ed.), *Concise Encyclopedia of Mexico*. New York: Routledge, pp. 31–44.

Galindo Cardona, Y. (2008) *Cine Club de Cali, 1971–1979*. Undergraduate Dissertation, Universidad del Valle, Cali.

—— (2010) "Ojo al Cine: Revista de Crítica Cinematográfica." *Fundación Patrimonio Fílmico*. Available at: www.patrimoniofilmico.org.co/docs/ojo_al_cine.pdf (accessed June 1, 2017).

Gillingham, P. and Smith, B. (eds.) (2014) *Dictablanda: Politics, Work, and Culture in Mexico, 1938–1968*. Durham, NC: Duke University Press.

Ginsburgh, F., Abu-Lughod, L., and Larkin. B. (2002) *Media Worlds: Anthropology on New Terrain*. Berkeley, CA: University of California Press.

Gómez, F. and de la Vega Hurtado, M. (2009) "Short Film and Documentary Third Cinema in Colombia: The Case of Luis Ospina." In F. Ekotto and A. Koh (eds.), *Rethinking Third Cinema: The Role of Anti-Colonial Media and Aesthetics in Postmodernity*. Berlin: Lit Verlag, pp. 53–80.

Hahner, J. (1990) *Emancipating the Female Sex: The Struggle for Women's Rights in Brazil, 1850–1940*. Durham, NC: Duke University Press.

Johnson, R. (1987) *The Film Industry in Brazil: Culture and the State*. Pittsburgh, PA: University of Pittsburgh Press.

Kuhn, A. (2002) *Dreaming of Fred and Ginger: Cinema and Cultural Memory*. New York: New York University Press.

Lee, C. (1987) "The Show Started on the Sidewalk." Interview with Martha Valentine, University of California Los Angeles, Oral History Program, pp. 54–58.

López, A.M. (1993) "Tears and Desire: Women and Melodrama in the Old Mexican Cinema." in E.A. Kaplan (ed.), *Feminism and Film*. Oxford: Oxford University Press, pp. 505–521.

—— (2000a) "Early Cinema and Modernity in Latin America." *Cinema Journal*, 401(1): 48–78.

—— (2000b) "Facing up to Hollywood." In C. Gledhill and L. Williams (eds.), *Reinventing Film Studies*. London: Arnold, pp. 419–438.

Martínez, H. (1978) *Historia del cine colombiano*. Bogotá: América Latina.

Mayne, J. (1993) *Cinema and Spectatorship*. London: Routledge.

Mayolo, C. (2002) *Mamá, ¿qué hago? Vida secreta de un director de cine*. Bogotá: Oveja Negra.

—— (2008) *La vida de mi cine y mi televisión*. Bogotá: Villegas Editores.

Mexico Cinema (1944) "Escenas." *Mexico Cinema*, no. 26, August, p. 8.

Monsiváis, C. (1995) "All the People Came and Did Not Fit onto the Screen: Notes on the Cinema Audience in Mexico" In P.A. Paranaguá (ed.), *Mexican Cinema*. London: British Film Institute, pp. 145–151.

Moreno, J. (2003) *Yankee Don't Go Home: Mexican Nationalism, American Business Culture, and the Shaping of Modern Mexico, 1920–1950*. Chapel Hill, NC: University of North Carolina Press.

El Nacional (1942) "Hoy se inaugural el gran 'Cine Teresa'." *El Nacional*, June 9, section 2, p. 2.

Niblo, S.R. (2000) *Mexico in the 1940s: Modernity, Politics, and Corruption*. New York: Rowan & Littlefield.

Noble, A. (2006) "*Vino todo el pueblo*: Notes on Monsivais, Mexican Movies and Moviegoing." *Bulletin of Latin American Research*, 25(4): 506–511.

Ospina, L. (2007) *Palabras al viento: mis sobras completas*. Bogotá: Editora Aguilar.

Pastor, L. (1943) "El teatro 'Metropólitan' se estrena con los miserables." *Jueves de Excelsior*, September 2: 104.

—— (1947) "México cuenta con otro cine moderno." *Revista de Revistas*, March 30, 1947.

Paxman, A. (2008) *William Jenkins, Business Elites, and the Evolution of the Mexican State: 1910–1960*. PhD Dissertation, University of Austin, Texas.

Ramos, F. (1987) *História do cinema brasileiro*. São Paulo: Art editora.

Rubenstein, A. (2012) "Theaters of Masculinity: Moviegoing and Male Roles in Mexico before 1960." In V.M. Macías-González and A. Rubenstein (eds.), *Masculinity and Sexuality in Modern Mexico*. Albuquerque, NM: University of New Mexico Press, pp. 132–157.

Salles Gomes, P.E. (1974) *Humberto Mauro. Cataguases. Cinema*. São Paulo: Perspectiva.

Serna, L.I. (2014) *Making Cinelandia: American Films and Mexican Film Culture before the Golden Age*. Durham, NC: Duke University Press.

Staiger, J. (1992) *Interpreting Films: Studies in the Historical Reception of American Cinema*. Princeton, NJ: Princeton University Press.

Supelano-Gross, C. (2009) "Interview with Rubén Jaramillo." *Constelaciones. Revista de Teoría Crítica*, 1: 142–150.

Turner, G. (2002) "Introduction." In *The Film Cultures Reader*, London/New York: Routledge, pp. 1–14.

El Universal (1947) "Advertisement: Trans Lux Prado." *El Universal*, March 23, section 3, p. 10.

Uribe de Urdinola, M. (1956–1959). *Bitácora*. Cali: La Tertulia.

Vieira, J.L. (1991) "O marketing do desejo." In *Quase Catálogo 3: As estrelas do cinema mudo*. Rio de Janeiro: CIEC, UFRJ, MIS, pp. 7–19.

Vieira, J.L and Stam, R. (1985) "Parody and Marginality: The Case of Brazilian Cinema." *Framework*, 28: 20–49.

Wilinsky, B. (2001) *Sure Seaters: The Emergence of Art House Cinema*. Minneapolis, MN: University of Minnesota Press.

Xavier, I. (1978) *Sétima arte: um culto moderno*. São Paulo: Perspectiva.

Interviews with Colombian filmmakers and critics

Arbeláez, Ramiro. September 8, 2010.

Campo, Óscar. October 27, 2010.

Ordónez, "Pakiko." September 22, 2010.

Vidal, Rodrigo. January 23, 2010.

6

SPACE, POLITICS, AND THE CRISIS OF HEGEMONY IN LATIN AMERICAN FILM

Geoffrey Kantaris

Editors' introduction

In this chapter, Geoffrey Kantaris challenges dominant lines of inquiry and critical paradigms that long have guided Latin American film scholarship. In particular, he takes aim at the persistent interest in questions of representation—i.e. in how films portray a given country or social group (the indigenous, women, the working class)—as well as recurrent debates about film's relative status as national or transnational industry and art form. In an effort to reorient our conceptual frameworks, he turns our attention to analyzing film as commodity form and cinema as "desiring-machine."

Like Jens Andermann (Chapter 15), Kantaris addresses film's role in the production of space/place as part of larger socioeconomic and political processes shaping the region. In this case, however, the author takes a longer, diachronic view of three key moments of radical transformation in the spatial configuration of the region—the 1920s (as Colombia defends its [national] interests in response to the US-driven creation of Panamá), the 1950s (as Mexico undergoes a second wave of urbanization), and the 2010s (as the state attempts to manage increasing socioeconomic polarization in Buenos Aires)—through the analysis of three films: *Garras de oro—Alborada de justicia* (*Clutches/ Claws of Gold—The Dawn of Justice*, P.P. Jambrina, 1926), *El bruto* (*The Brute*, Luis Buñuel, 1955), and *Elefante blanco* (*White Elephant*, Pablo Trapero, 2012). Without any intention of characterizing the three films as typical or exemplary (of particular genres or filmmaking traditions with particular countries or periods), Kantaris suggests that the works interrogate "the construction of (popular) identity and political representation" that themselves are dependent on particular (ideal/ized) forms of spatiality. The chapter is attentive to the films' staging of crises in (political and artistic) representability while also insisting on the recognition of the medium's own status as a commodity that helps to commodify places and peoples as well as to de- and reterritorialize ("private") desires and (political) imaginaries. Like Nilo Couret's Chapter 16, Kantaris's essay reminds us that film functions within a larger geopolitical matrix, rather than merely as a means to re-present preexisting temporal and spatial configurations.

> The great obsession of the nineteenth century was, as we know, history: with its
> themes of development and of suspension, of crisis and cycle [. . .]. The present
> epoch will perhaps be above all the epoch of space.
>
> *(Foucault 1986: 22)*

It no longer seems possible to provide a predominantly historical account of "Latin American" being or becoming, let alone of the national structures and identities that emerged from the ruins of the Spanish and Portuguese Empires. This is partly because the nation-state in Latin America—from the start a precarious and, more often than not, rapacious administrator of an identitarian community that was always "yet to come"—is everywhere losing control of the economic, cultural, and biopolitical arenas over which it claimed to hold sway. It is also partly a result of our contemporary eschatology—i.e. the "end" of modernity's grand narratives of social transformation, whether these be (in Latin America) broadly statist, national-popular, or the last remnants of Marxist and Maoist insurgencies. Whereas for Hegel the end of history would come with the full realization of reason in the form of the state, overwhelming time through repetition and circularity, in the aftermath of the state it is now the never fully realized, outwardly expanding form of the market that abolishes all temporality, depth, and genealogy.

It has become something of a topos in contemporary studies of Latin American culture to label as "neoliberalism" the void that persists after the maligned end of history, and to reclaim a prior national culture as the last critical bulwark of identity, genealogy, and difference in the face of the crisis-ridden expansion of global capitalism. In Latin American film studies in particular, and partly in response to the spectacular transnationalization of "Mexican" cinema in the first two decades of the twenty-first century, the analytical terrain seems broadly divided between, on the one hand, those who tend to affirm film's continued role as a filter of historically determined national imaginaries, gaining its intelligibility largely from its critical relationship to national hegemonic processes and their periodic crises, and, on the other, those who prefer to emphasize the centrifugal forces that rupture the neat circle of aesthetic reflection and critique, prioritizing transnational circuits of production and reception, and the global circulation of even the most staunchly national films.

Yet I believe we need to think beyond the cultural deadlocks produced by the crisis of the nation-state, the neoliberal end of ideology/history, entrenched national politico-cultural interests, and the celebration of "network struggle" and global digital cultures. In line with my epigraph, I want to explore how an engagement with the national, geopolitical, and urban production of space and place can help us to move beyond the impasses and cycles of the national-popular vs. the transnational-multicultural divide, or of "identity politics [vs.] radical multiculturalism" (Beverley 2011: 39), that besets film studies as much as broader Latin American cultural studies. The questions raised by this impasse go to the heart of film's ambiguous status as both a mass-produced cultural product (especially in its golden age in Latin America) and as the inheritor of traditional functions of literature in the production of identitarian narratives, which is to say that they go to the heart of film's status as "popular" culture.

Paradoxically, the greatest philosopher of space, Henri Lefebvre, affirms that "if space is produced, if there is a productive process, then we are dealing with *history*" (Lefebvre 1991: 46, original emphasis). He goes on to caution that this history of the production of space "is not to be confused either with the causal chain of 'historical' (i.e. dated) events, or with a sequence, whether teleological or not, of customs and laws, ideals and ideology, and socio-economic structures or institutions" (p. 46). It is instead to be understood as a series of contradictions and crises in the social relations of production, which give rise to, "produce," different spatialities, different modes of relationship between people, and the spaces precipitated from the forces of abstraction. It is in this guise that, through the three films I shall be discussing here, I aim to outline a cinematic registering of the production of Latin American space, of the shifting social, economic, and political forms that are legible in the quintessentially spatial medium of film.

Although each film is taken from a different key moment in the development of Latin American cinema, and from three diverse geographical spaces, the choice is necessarily arbitrary, and they should not be taken as "representative" either of their genres nor of "national" cinemas, except in the broadest possible terms. Rather, these films are linked by how they address or force a crisis in the construction of (popular) identity and political representation through their engagement with the forces that produce what Lefebvre calls "abstract space" (Lefebvre 1991: 49ff.). This can be understood as the form of spatiality produced by the requirements of commodity production, distribution, and consumption, and it can operate at every scale from the local to the global and the virtual. It is represented in these films through: the gigantic economic forces that were reshaping national spaces and identities at the beginning of the twentieth century in Colombia and Central America; the powerful processes that led to the transformation of Mexico from a rural to a predominantly urban society in the 1950s (processes in which popular cinema itself plays a crucial role); and the chaotic spatial forces at work in the Argentine megalopolis today, together with the challenge that this space and its inhabitants represent to the historical cycles of national-popular hegemony.

How Wall Street created a nation

The cultural mobility of silent film—in terms of its themes, its actors, and its distribution—placed it from the outset in a complex and, as we shall see, tense relationship to national cultures and identities. Perhaps this is why Walter Benjamin, still in the 1930s, was able to laud film for its power to liberate us from our routine imprisonment in space-time:

> Our taverns and our metropolitan streets, our offices and furnished rooms, our railroad stations and our factories appeared to have us locked up hopelessly. Then came the film and burst this prison-world asunder by the dynamite of the tenth of a second, so that now, in the midst of its far-flung ruins and debris, we calmly and adventurously go traveling.
>
> (Benjamin 1992: 236)

There is a powerful dialectic at work here that defines the spatial contradictions operating within the outwardly expansive domain of capitalist modernity: on the one hand, film has the technological power to delve into the everyday and to explode systematically the traditions, mythologies, and habits that structure it, disembedding such belief systems from their "organic" rootedness in everyday life, their *habitus*; on the other hand, film reinscribes the local into a higher set of ideological discourses and national and supranational narratives bounded by the ongoing production of hegemony *within* the nation-state and the geopolitical competition for hegemony *among* nation-states.

A little-known Colombian silent movie made in 1926 called *Garras de oro—Alborada de justicia* (*Clutches/Claws of Gold—The Dawn of Justice*) is a perfect illustration of the spatial tensions alluded to by Benjamin, but which are here intensified by the film's location on the frontier between transnational flows of capital and their relationship to national sovereignty and hegemony. There is a very good reason why the film is little known: it was effectively censored under pressure from U.S. consular officials after a year or so of screenings in different towns in Colombia, because of fears that it would stoke up anti-Yankee sentiments among the Colombian populace. The film did not resurface until the 1980s, after some of the footage had been lost or deteriorated beyond restoration. It was financed in the wake of the foreign investment boom of 1923 by a group of Cali-based businessmen (Suárez et al. 2009: 59), who were incensed by the takeover by the United States, under Theodore Roosevelt, of the former Colombian Province of Panama in 1903, so that the US could build, control, and profit from the Panama Canal. The film is directed by one "P.P. Jambrina," a pseudonym of Alfonso Martínez Velasco.

As explained by Ovidio Díaz Espino in his book *How Wall Street Created a Nation* (Díaz Espino 2001), a Wall Street firm backed by wealthy American investors who were close to Roosevelt appears to have secretly bought a large stake of the worthless shares of the French company that had failed in the attempt to build the canal in the 1880s. The U.S. government then paid $40 million supposedly to the liquidator of the French company for the rights to continue the works. However, the newspaper publisher Joseph Pulitzer, proprietor of the *New York World*, alleged that $12 million of this sum had been paid instead to a dummy fronting company for J.P. Morgan, thus massively enriching Roosevelt's associates. An enraged Roosevelt sued the *New York World* for libel. *Garras de oro* concerns this episode, with both Pulitzer (called James Moore in the film) and Roosevelt having sent agents to Colombia to gather evidence about the "transfer" of Panama to U.S. control. In the film, one of Pulitzer's agents, an unreliable womanizer called Paterson, has fallen in love with the daughter of a Colombian consular official, Berta in "Rasca-Cielo" (New York). Paterson heads off to Colombia in a bid to prove to Berta that he is worthy of her, and to defend her nation by helping Pulitzer/Moore defend himself against Roosevelt's libel suit.

Juana Suárez points out that "national romance" in *Garras de oro*—a readily available formula in early silent adaptations of popular nineteenth-century novels in Latin America—is quite problematic, citing Doris Sommer on the fantasy nature of such "wish-fulfilling projection[s] of national consolidation and growth" (Sommer 1991: 6–7; Suárez et al. 2009: 77). The romance between Paterson and Berta "inaugurate[s] cinematically another type of accord: nations in political and diplomatic conflict no longer seek to consolidate the national but rather the international." Indeed, the belated national romance here is both unstable and quite conflicted, a rhetorical fantasy of victory for Colombian national honor and purity of motives in the face of U.S. neo-imperial ambitions. In the film, Moore's reporters are able to obtain key documents just in time to save the day for the U.S. free press and for Colombian justice and honor in the face of U.S. capitalist dissolution of its territory. Colombia in the guise of Berta, actually played by an Italian actress, tames the wayward US, in the guise of Paterson, thoroughly Colombianizing him and their offspring in a nationalistic fantasy sequence at the end of the film on the July 20 Independence Day, replete with the national anthem and a hand-tinted insert of the Colombian flag proudly flapping in the wind. Yet the intertitle immediately following this references the indemnity treaty between the US and Colombia of April 6, 1914 (erroneously recorded as 1916), in which Colombia accepted a mere $25 million for the loss of Panama, and the film's final sequence is an explicitly allegorical cameo that has Uncle Sam in his typical top hat weighing the Isthmus of Panama in the scales of Justice, played by Berta in blindfold, against the backdrop of a large map of Colombia (Figure 6.1). The scale refuses to tip, despite the heavy bags containing the sum of $25,000,000 weighing against the tiny cutout isthmus.

Figure 6.1   Uncle Sam weighs Panama against bags of gold in *Garras de oro* (1926).

While the intended meaning of this overdetermined national allegory is clear, its effects are far less straightforward. For what has really won out in the film, and in reality, are not nation-states at all, nor international diplomacy, nor Colombian national honor, but the "clutches of gold" of the title: the power of Wall Street to instrumentalize nation-states in the geopolitical shaping of Latin American space for the purposes of commercial profit, to make and unmake nations at will. Here, money quite literally produces space, carving out a new nation from an existing one for the purposes of building transportation infrastructure that will speed up the commercial trade of goods. Marx was the first to identify the tendency in capitalism to overcome spatial obstacles to the free flow of commodities through an increase in the speed of transportation, information flows, logistical organization, and turnover. By its very nature, capitalism "drives beyond every spatial barrier," and the "extraordinary necessity" it has to overcome distance by increasing the velocity of production, transport, and communication leads to what he famously termed "the annihilation of space by time" (Marx 1993: 524). Later spatial theorists, and in particular the Marxist urban geographer David Harvey, call this process "time-space compression" (Harvey 1989: 260–307) and identify it as a fundamental force at work within both urbanization (which shortens the distance between production and consumption) and, later, globalization (which drives beyond the spatial barriers represented by the nation-state system and its fragmented national markets).

Beyond the national romance, it is this annihilation of space (distance, in this case) by the need for greater velocity of trade, and the consequent deterritorialization of the nation-state system by money, that is, effectively, the principal agent at work within this film. Although Latin American territory, from the moment of its "discovery" by European powers, has always been constructed through the vicissitudes of global trading systems, from slavery, to plantations and mining, the commercial shaping of Latin American space under colonial rule had been primarily concerned with resource extraction. The gigantic financial forces at work in the carving out of Panama for the purposes of carving an interoceanic canal across the isthmus are of a different order and do not serve resource extraction per se, but reflexively serve the expansion of capital itself. It is of no little significance that this film, although considered an orphan due to its long disappearance, lies at the very origins of Colombian cinema, which was born, as it were, coincidentally with the traumatic challenge posed by modern global finance to a national sovereignty that was barely 100 years old. For film itself is not, of course, exempt from these same spatial forces that the film documents. As early as the 1920s, the projection of national space through film, its relay through mass mediatization, and the transnational star system of silent film, began to render national space simulacral, even as the national itself was becoming a commodity to be bought and sold on international capital markets.

Popular film and the production of urban space

With the advent of the "talkies," the international market that operated in the distribution and star system of silent cinema was rapidly, if not uniformly, "renationalized," as it was generally no longer possible for, say, an Italian actress to play a Colombian heroine, as in the case of *Garras de oro*. In Mexico, the advent of sound enabled the rise of a popular national film industry in the 1940s and 1950s, which nevertheless rivalled Hollywood in its popularity and reach within the Spanish-speaking world, even as it drew on, imitated, and then renationalized Hollywood genres and themes. Into the midst of this popular cinema that served the burgeoning urban population of the cities arrived a foreigner, Luis Buñuel, in exile from Spain, in 1946. He quickly set about learning the codes and conventions of Mexico's popular, often melodramatic genres, and began to produce films within the local idiom, but often also pushing the limits of that idiom. His most famous urban film is *Los olvidados* (*The Young and the Damned*, 1950), which in fact flatly defied the conventions for the idealized representation of poverty and the city in films such as *Nosotros los pobres* (*We the Poor*, 1948). The much less well-known follow-up to *Los olvidados*, in terms of its urban thematics and its working through of a number of the more challenging themes of the former film in a more popular idiom, is *El bruto* (*The Brute*) of 1953. In this film, Acevedo-Muñoz argues (Acevedo-Muñoz 2003: 126), Buñuel casts lead actor Pedro Armendáriz (who had personified the ideology of *machismo* in the films of Emilo Fernández) distinctly "against type" in the gullible, manipulated, and dim-witted figure of El Bruto, a slaughterhouse worker (called Pedro), who becomes a henchman for an ageing capitalist, Don Andrés, but ends up as a pawn in the hands of Don Andrés' young "wife," Paloma, a femme fatale played by Katy Jurado.

Buñuel's urban films are set at the beginning of what would later become known as the "Mexican miracle," a period of rapid economic expansion and urban growth that would last until the oil shocks of the 1970s. The unprecedented urban construction boom that he had recorded in *Los olvidados* (1950), and which is the cause of the immediate social conflict in *El bruto* (Don Andrés wants to redevelop the plot where his tenants live), points us towards a profound set of processes that were fundamentally reorganizing social and family relationships, and with them the conventional mappings of social power and libidinal investments. But beyond Buñuel's reflexive use of the popular star system and generic formulae in *El bruto*, what is being framed is not so much the figure of the *macho*, as the role played by popular cinema itself, particularly the urban genre of the *cine de arrabal*—a key interface between the urban populace and technological modernity—in this remapping of the libidinal economy of Mexican society. This is why my interest in the film lies not in the emasculation of its protagonist, but in the changing sexuality of *women* as an index of their pushing at the boundaries of their affective capture within the institution of the patriarchal family. The flows of affect, libido, and money that Buñuel extrapolates from popular melodrama has everything to do with the deterritorializations induced by urbanization, by national and international capital flows, and their imaginary entanglement in the vision machine of popular cinema.

El bruto begins with the staging of a typical urban land struggle between the ageing property magnate, supported by the forces of law and order, and the rebellious occupants of a tenement he owns in the Portales district of Mexico City. The (then) working-class district was an area of major real-estate speculation and development in the 1950s, with the old ramshackle houses being torn down and replaced with apartment blocks at a feverish rate, so that by 1960 the population of the area had expanded hugely and had become largely middle class. This climate of land speculation and the breakup of semi-communal living conditions makes of the film a *spatial* expression of class conflict, which is mapped out in terms of the power of money to dissolve communities while unleashing new forms of libidinal economy. By opening the film with this scene of social struggle between the abstract representation of space as exchange value and the lived spaces of the community (to use Lefebvre's terms), Buñuel is directly staging the power of money to dissolve community and *become the real community* (Marx 1993: 225–226)—i.e. substitute itself for community as an abstract expression of the relations between people, including the very nucleus of social reproduction: the family.

The film sets up a whole series of inverted family relationships: the father-and-daughter "couple" of Don Carmelo and the teenage Meche; Don Andrés himself and his "wife" Paloma, young enough to be his daughter, who live with his doddery father whom they treat as if he were an irresponsible child; and El Bruto, who lives with a woman who has brought her whole family into their two-room living space, and who is both protected and exploited by his "boss" Don Andrés as his (illegitimate) son without overt recognition of the fact. Yet El Bruto ends up sleeping with Paloma, his putative stepmother, then making "home" in a hovel on a construction site with the teenage Meche, as a substitute for her father (whom he had unintentionally killed), and finally murdering his own father (Don Andrés) in some pre-political realization of the Oedipal drama.

Through this freak show of partial or pathologically Oedipalized family structures, Buñuel mercilessly subverts the travails of family romance encoded in popular urban melodramas such as those directed by Roberto Gavaldón and Julio Bracho. However, the film has a somewhat more complicitous relationship to the thoroughly urban *arrabal* films and the related *cabaretera*/prostitute genre. Buñuel here taps into the neorealist mode he had used so effectively in *Los olvidados*, in the representation of the daily struggle for food, work, and decent living conditions of the working-class *arrabal* inhabitants, and, bizarrely at first, fuses it with the "dangerous seductress" image already associated with actress Katy Jurado (e.g. as the fallen woman "who gets up late" in *Nosotros los pobres*). He pushes to a crisis point the contradictions at work in the axiomatic that governs the *arrabal* film's compulsive cannibalization of prurient national melodrama, stylized and voyeuristic "neorealism," and contemporary Hollywood crime/noir formats. If these genres are already partially decoded by the *arrabal* films, which is to say turned by the machine of cinema itself into deterritorializing flows of desire and affect exchangeable for the price of a cinema ticket, then Buñuel, in *El bruto*, violently confronts us with the dark, explosive forces unleashed in this process. These are condensed in the powerful extrapolation of the Catholic sublimation of sexuality and death at the heart of his representation of the Mexican femme fatale, in the gigantic urban machinery that absorbs the hundreds of thousands of post-revolutionary peasants converging on the burgeoning cities, and in the violent institution of a modern biopolitical order through the capture and taming of these "brutes."

It is important to stress that Mexican film of this period does not "express" this axiomatic in some naïve representational sense; rather, Mexican film *is* the axiomatic in a very real sense, for it subjects all of the "customs" and habits, which the new urban migrants went to the cinema to "learn," according to Monsiváis (Martín Barbero 1987: 180), to the logic of the *spectacle as commodity*, and hence to the axiom of quantitative equivalence and exchange. The popular cinema can be understood as a machinery, on the one hand commodifying affects for sale, and on the other slowly but surely precipitating an avalanche of new wants, customs, and habits, forming an incipient culture of popular consumption based upon image, spectacle, and fashion. It is perhaps nowhere more true than in Mexico of the 1950s, at least in Latin America, that cinema allies itself so intimately with capitalist modernization and the urbanization of capital in a society that had been hitherto predominantly rural, and became predominantly urban by 1960. Buñuel exposes the extent to which these powerful urban processes have a de-Oedipalizing effect that begins with the inversion of family structures and family "romance," and ends in the radical decoding of feminine identity and desire, allegorized perfectly in the shift it charts from women's passivity and capture within domesticity to the assertion of active female desire.

Paloma's radical assertion of her own desire and her manipulation of the dimwit Bruto to achieve her aims unleashes a powerful force within the film, which it hardly knows how to contain by its destructive close. Although Pedro ends up sleeping with his "stepmother" Paloma and killing his father, Paloma's desire is precisely *that which exceeds her Oedipal capture* in the (Mexican) psychodrama of paternity. Indeed, Buñuel links Paloma's *excessive* desire specifically and reflexively to the cinematic desiring-machine, as well as to the urban production of space in a sequence after El Bruto has been moved, for his own safety, to a hovel on another construction site owned by Don Andrés. Paloma has come to visit him clandestinely, telling Don Andrés that she was *going to the cinema* with a friend. On the soundtrack throughout Pedro and Paloma's transgressive lovemaking, we hear the obtrusive sounds of construction machinery, so that we cannot avoid the impression that this erotic encounter, on a construction site, takes place at the center of some huge urban machine. That enormous deterritorializing machinery is the combined power of both the cinema-machine, with its dangerous decoding of affect, and the city-machine, in which the fluidity of capital circulation is transmogrified into desire, the one intertwined inseparably with the other.

Beyond populist reason

I began with an allusion to the collapse of temporal significance that, for Hegel, would occur upon the full realization of reason in the form of the state. History would collapse into repetition and sameness, since its dialectical motor would have come to a standstill. In *The Eighteenth Brumaire*, Marx famously corrected Hegel, quipping that history always repeats itself, but the first time as tragedy, and the second as farce. The historical repetition evinced in Argentine director Pablo Trapero's 2012 film *Elefante blanco* (*White Elephant*) lies somewhere in the gap between Hegel and Marx, laying great emphasis on the feedback loops through which representation and history intersect and fold into each other. For it is not only the case in this film that history, specifically the history of populism in Argentina, appears to be stuck on repeat, but also that the representational mechanisms of history as well as of the film itself are somehow blocked through this very repetition. In line with my overall theme, this blockage is given an overwhelmingly spatial form, reflecting Trapero's long-standing exploration of the urban as a condensation of economic, political, and libidinal investments (*Mundo grúa/Crane World*, 1999; *Carancho*, 2010), and suggesting, perhaps, the reversibility of Marx's aforementioned dictum regarding "the annihilation of space by time": in the twenty-first century, it is perhaps time and history that are annihilated by space.

Elefante blanco is mostly set in Ciudad Oculta ("Hidden City") or Villa 15, a shantytown in the Villa Lugano district to the southwest of Buenos Aires, which has become iconic in part due to the huge abandoned hospital that lies at the heart of the slum, the so-called White Elephant. It concerns two priests, one of them Belgian, and a social worker who work in the *villa* and find themselves caught at the intersection of the competing demands of the local people and the ecclesiastical and state apparatuses. The priests operate within the legacy of the influential Movement of Priests for the Third World, and of its former charismatic leader, the priest Carlos Mugica, who was murdered in 1974 at the hands of the secret paramilitary organization known as the Triple A, the Argentine Anti-Communist Alliance. For the priests of the movement, missionary work in the *villas* (shantytowns) in 1960s and 1970s Buenos Aires was both a continuation and radicalization of a largely proscribed left-wing Peronism, and conjoined political and theological concepts of redemption, with Perón, Christ, and the coming Revolution acting as exchangeable placeholders in an affective structure of revolutionary messianism. Mugica is at the center of a struggle for ontotheological legitimation, which is to say that he becomes the symbolic point of confluence of a desire to grant the slippery and contingent terrain of politics something of the unanswerable power of the divine, encoded as "the people." The historical repetition shown in this film, which is set in 2011 but fruitlessly repeats a story from the 1970s, has the inevitable effect of framing the history of populism in Argentina, putting it in quotation marks and forcing us to confront its contradictions. While the tone is by no means farcical, in Marx's terms, the tragedy now emerges precisely from the *repetition* of a history that has not been transcended, where the mechanisms of the articulation and translation of popular demands within social and political institutions appear to be blocked. This ideological blockage constitutes in many ways the ground upon which the film's aesthetics are based, and which revolve around a crisis of *representation* in both the political and aesthetic senses of this word.

The film's intelligent script, written by Santiago Mitre (*El estudiante/The Student*, 2011), Martín Mauregui, and Alejandro Fadel, seems fully aware of these representational aporias. If the (Kantian) sublime traditionally determines the frontier between aesthetics and politics understood as a moral or ethical duty that arises from the gap between the representable and the unrepresentable, then the sublime is repeatedly signaled as a fundamental representational frontier in this film. In the political sense, the failure of representation—of the state's duty to translate the wants and needs of the inhabitants of the *villa* into forms of political agency—is displaced onto the terrain of ethics: the almost infinite moral debt and duty of the priests, their theological calling, towards the salvation of the multitude.

But the sublime has also come to stand as a figure of the crisis of representation in the aesthetic sense in postmodern society: this is the so-called postmodern sublime discussed by Jean-François Lyotard, which grows more intense with the globalization of information and communication systems. In the film, it is the chaotic urban backwaters of the megalopolis—the "unrepresentable" and "unmappable" space of the *villa*—which takes on, for the priests and for us as cinemagoers, the terrifying attributes of the sublime. In the first daylight sequence set in Ciudad Oculta, after a series of establishing shots surveying the *villa*, the principal protagonist of the film, Father Julián, orients the new Belgian priest, Nicolás, as the pair stand on a balcony of the second floor of the abandoned hospital at the center of the *villa*, surveying the urban space below. He tells Nicolás that there is no official census of the population of the *villa*, which they estimate from their own baptismal records to be around 30,000, and that it does not appear on any map ("ni figura en el mapa"). The *villa* is thus equated from the outset with the breakdown of the process of mapping that is given strong filmic emphasis elsewhere in the film's imagery, both due to state abandonment and because its population, to use a Rancièrian formula, does not count, and therefore is not counted (Rancière 1999: 6–18). An equivalence is established here between the unmeasurable space of the *villa*, its uncountable population, and the abandoned building, with the White Elephant standing as a synecdoche for the slum and its shunned population, and the slum, with its drug-fueled gang wars, standing as a synecdoche of what Manuel Castells calls the "new urban form" of the megalopolis, "globally connected and locally disconnected, physically and socially" (Castells 1996: 437).

Effectively, the central problem of the film will revolve around a question concerning the occupation of this urban space and the demand for land on the part of these citizens, systematically abandoned by all the institutions of the state, under every political regime. Julián informs Nicolás that the building project dates from the 1930s, and it links the socialism of Alfredo Lorenzo Palacios with the populism of General Perón, under whose government a serious attempt was made to finish the building, which would have been the largest hospital in Latin America had it been completed. During the dictatorships that followed on from Perón's first two terms of office (1946–1955), the building was completely abandoned, and part of it was occupied by homeless slum residents, new migrants to the city, and, more recently, by street children and drug addicts. The current owner of the building is, in an ironic twist of history, the Foundation of the Mothers of the Plaza de Mayo.

In some ways, then, the building, although having its origins in an earlier socialism, is linked to the first wave of Peronist populism. It is a place that gathers together a nameless *plebs*, one that is not yet a "people" and which challenges the hegemonic processes of all subsequent regimes. But the building obviously represents also the failure of these systems of representation, and this idea of failure extends to all the representational systems given in the film—whether architectural, religious, or political—which are intertwined with an ethics of salvation of the multitude. It should be clear that I do not claim that the film is criticizing the intentions of those who make such salvation their vocation. The failure in the film is represented as a tragedy, repeated as a form of repetition-compulsion in the Freudian sense. In the priests' oft-declared devotion to Carlos Mugica and recitation of his words ("Lord, I want to die for them, help me to live for them, I want to be with them at the coming of the Light"), the film deliberately stages a confused mixture of pre-political, or perhaps post-political, affect, and the invocation of a transcendental ethics that attempts to capture affect under the sign of an absolute duty, in the absence of any political translation of the needs and demands of the inhabitants of the *villa*.

Yet the film clearly stages a shift from this ontotheological stance towards one of populist political praxis, gradually changing the essentialist sign of theological duty into the equivalential and differential signs of political logic, and exposing the conflicts that emerge in this shift. This is where the film plays out most obviously the formalist political analysis of

Argentine political theorist Ernesto Laclau, as laid out in detail in his *On Populist Reason* (Laclau 2002). Laclau sees Antonio Gramsci's concept of hegemony as making sense only within a "vast historical mutation" (p. 126) from concepts of "manifest destiny" (p. 127), including Marxist teleology, towards a political process governed by the articulation of a series of democratic demands by an empty signifier. The basic mechanisms of this historical mutation of populism that Laclau, throughout his career, drew explicitly from Peronism, and its basic mechanisms, are easy to outline: a series of distinct and fragmented social demands must be "articulated" by some other element; however, that element can only act as articulator of many disparate demands if it is able to act as a placeholder for each and every one of them. In order to do this, it must itself become an empty placeholder, or an empty signifier, voided of positive content of its own. As Laclau puts it, "empty signifiers can play their role only if they signify a chain of equivalences [. . .]. An ensemble of equivalential demands articulated by an empty signifier is what constitutes a 'people'" (p. 171).

An almost too obvious exemplification of Laclau's thought occurs in *Elefante blanco* during the celebration of the 37th anniversary of the "death and martyrdom" of Carlos Mugica. Julián, standing on an open-air stage with an iconic image of Mugica behind him on a backcloth, pronounces the following words to the assembled crowd:

> "For even the Son of man came not to be ministered unto, but to minister, and to give his life as a ransom for the multitude." [. . .] We are gathered today to remember a brother, a friend. And his memory unites us, unifies us. To oppose violence, to fight violence with love.

The iconography seems explicitly designed to recall that of populist political rallies in Argentina, with the image of Perón or Evita, and in more recent times that of Néstor Kirchner, substituted here with that of Mugica (Figure 6.2). In each case, the absent figure becomes the empty signifier which, in the words of Julián, "unites us, unifies us," and stages the hegemonic political process that "saves" the multitude. Yet from an extra-diegetic perspective, the film curiously retranslates and displaces populism's empty signifiers onto an image of Christian faith, and then onto a crisis of faith on the part of its practitioners, returning the ideological process of the construction of national-popular hegemony to a more basic mechanism, or at least an older one. It is precisely in the gap between the two

Figure 6.2   Padre Julián (Ricardo Darín) evokes the "death and martydom" of Carlos Mugica in *Elefante blanco* (2012).

systems, their incompatibility at the level of the diegesis, and the discomfort felt by the audience in seeing secular political processes translated back into questions of belief, and of regimes of belief in the broadest sense, that the film plays out its most fundamental critique.

Empty signifiers start to proliferate: not only Mugica and his "miracles," both present and absent at the same time in many sequences, but also the priests who repeat more or less self-consciously his story and whose faith is itself challenged by mortality and death. But in the end, it is the fundamental spatial translation of all of these processes—the very building marooned at the heart of this marooned community, the White Elephant—which powerfully calls into question the political machinery of populist reason. If the empty signifier is the Lacanian *objet petit a*, as Laclau contends (Laclau 2002: 127), then the film confronts this structural emptiness or veil, which maintains the illusion of belief, with a radically different mode of vacuity. This White Elephant, this empty, useless but enormous object, is impossible to veil despite the fact that historically the military did everything they could to erase the Hidden City, hiding it behind screens so that it would not spoil the view of the city from the main roads nearby (Bontempo 2014). By placing the White Elephant, this synecdoche of the unmappable *villa* and spatial remainder of powerful political forces, at the end of its chain of empty signifiers, as an obstacle that resists every attempt of ideological reincorporation, we arrive finally at something like the nucleus or hard core of the real, not the support of fantasy in the metonymic chain of empty signifiers that is the *objet a*, but the void of an unsymbolizable residue that disturbs and blocks the regimes of belief generated by both Church and state.

Conclusion

By the end of *Elefante blanco*, after the collapse of the priests' mission and the shooting of Julián in some senseless, "farcical," cops-and-robbers-style repetition of the assassination of Mugica (see Vezzetti 2013), the "reasoning engine" of the hegemonic processes underlying populist reason lies "huddled in dirt," as John Wilmot, Second Earl of Rochester, put it in his poem "A Satyr against Reason and Mankind." It is no accident that the film's principal theme music is taken from a transcription for brass of a score by Michael Nyman entitled "A Satire against Reason," originally released for the film *The Libertine* (2004) about the life of Wilmot. His famous satirical poem invokes the corruption of systems of governance, whose authors, "swollen with selfish vanity, devise / False freedoms, holy cheats, and formal lies / Over their fellow slaves to tyrannize" (Wilmot 2002: 102). The resounding, dissonant chords of Nyman's theme accompany the opening journey down the Amazon from Iquitos in the aftermath of the jungle massacre. But they also accompany the final evocation of the "ideal," consensual community in the Trappist monastery where Nicolás takes refuge after his traumatic foray into the *villa*. This must now appear as some ironic, final hypostatization of the logic of the empty signifier, for the image of the idyllic pastoral community, of the fully reconciled society—far from the "madding crowd" of the slum—emerges precisely from the vacuity of the signifier that establishes the full, non-hierarchical equivalence of each member of the community.

From the "noisy silence" of early silent cinema to the ironic silence after the "end" of politics, the films I have examined in this chapter point us to a series of powerful forces that call into question the dominant narratives of hegemony and representation through which Latin American identities are so often thought. Film is a popular medium that has historically accompanied the rise of, and indeed helped to form and interpellate, the modern national-popular subject. Yet as a medium, it cannot be understood fully without an awareness that it is itself imbricated in those convulsive, contradictory flows that reshape identities, places, and spaces. It is perhaps unsurprising that film is uniquely attuned to the forces that escape conventional political representation, but which powerfully act to dematerialize and rematerialize space to service the requirements of commodity production and consumption (the city, the country, the nation, the globe, and now, of course, cyberspace). For film is the most "spatial" of media, with its sets, locations, physical placing of its subjects in space, and its ability to produce virtual and imaginary spaces through which the cinemagoer "goes traveling."

References

Acevedo-Muñoz, E.R. (2003) *Buñuel and Mexico: The Crisis of National Cinema*. Los Angeles, CA: University of California Press.

Benjamin, W. (1992) *Illuminations*, trans. H. Zohn. London: Fontana Press.

Beverley, J. (2011) *Latinamericanism after 9/11*. Durham, NC: Duke University Press.

Bontempo, A. (2014) "Villa 31: el muro de la vergüenza." *Marcha: una mirada popular de la Argentina y el mundo*. Available at: www.marcha.org.ar/index.php/nacionales/ciudad/5856-villa-31-el-muro-de-la-verguenza (accessed June 1, 2017).

Castells, M. (1996) *The Rise of the Network Society*. Oxford: Blackwell.

Díaz Espino, O. (2001) *How Wall Street Created a Nation: J.P. Morgan, Teddy Roosevelt and the Panama Canal*. New York: Four Walls Eight Windows.

Foucault, M. (1986) "Of Other Spaces," trans. J. Miskowiec. *Diacritics*, 16(1): 22–27.

Harvey, D. (1989) *The Condition of Postmodernity: An Enquiry into the Origins of Cultural Change*. Oxford: Blackwell.

Laclau, E. (2002) *On Populist Reason*. London: Verso.

Lefebvre, H. (1991) *The Production of Space*, trans. D. Nicholson-Smith. Oxford: Blackwell.

Martín Barbero, J. (1987) *De los medios a las mediaciones: comunicación, cultura y hegemonía*. Naucalpan: G. Gili.

Marx, K. (1993) *Grundrisse: Foundations of the Critique of Political Economy (Rough Draft)*, trans. M. Nicolaus. Harmondsworth: Penguin.

Rancière, J. (1999) *Disagreement: Politics and Philosophy*, trans. J. Rose. Minneapolis, MN: University of Minnesota Press.

Sommer, D. (1991) *Foundational Fictions: The National Romances of Latin America*. Berkeley, CA: University of California Press.

Suárez, J., Arbeláez, R., and Chesak, L.A. (2009) "*Garras de oro (The Dawn of Justice—Alborada de justicia)*: The Intriguing Orphan of Colombian Silent Films." *The Moving Image*, 9(1): 54–82.

Vezzetti, H. (2013) "Memorias de un cura villero," *Informe Escaleno*. Available at: www.informeescaleno.com.ar/index.php?s=articulos&id=46 (accessed June 1, 2017).

Wilmot, J. (2002) "A Satyr against Reason and Mankind." In J. Adlard (ed.), *The Debt to Pleasure: John Wilmot, Earl of Rochester, in the Eyes of His Contemporaries and in His Own Poetry and Prose*. New York: Routledge, pp. 98–103.

7

ENCOUNTERS WITH THE CENTAUR

Forms of the film-essay in Latin America[1]

María Luisa Ortega[2]

Editors' introduction

Discussions of Latin American documentaries, particularly those that take place outside the region, frequently limit themselves to a small corpus: from *La hora de los hornos* (*The Hour of the Furnaces*, Fernando Solanas and Octavio Getino, 1966–1968) and *La batalla de Chile* (*The Battle of Chile*, Patricio Guzmán, 1975–1979), to *Los rubios* (*The Blonds*, Albertina Carri, 2003), *Nostalgia de la luz* (*Nostalgia for the Light*, Patricio Guzmán, 2010), and *Omnibus 174* (*Bus 174*, José Padilha and Felipe Lacerda, 2002). This singular attention to films dealing with the authoritarian past or contemporary violence overlook a long, rich history of documentary forms, from the process genre mentioned by Salomé Aguilera Skvirsky in Chapter 8 to the community-based efforts discussed in Chapter 14 by Freya Schiwy, Amalia Córdova, David Wood, and Horacio Legrás. This chapter offers a substantive meta-critical consideration of the underlying theoretical parameters and geo-cultural dynamics that have led to this tendency to associate Latin American filmmaking with a certain notion of the political—in ways analogous to Nilo Couret's reconsideration of the category of "art cinema" (Chapter 16).

The essay-film is the point of departure. Identifying the essay as a hybrid form that has had a distinctive role in Latin American cultural formations, author María Luisa Ortega insists on the importance of recognizing specific geo-cultural traditions that undergird the works themselves, as well as the theorizations of the essay-film by scholars. Her more nimble reconceptualization of the category itself allows us to acknowledge a much wider corpus—including more intimate films from the past such as Cuba's Sara Gómez's *En la otra isla* (*On the Other Island*, 1968) and *Una Isla para Miguel* (*An Island for Miguel*, 1968), as well as the Brazilian films *Industria* (*Industry*, Ana Carolina, 1969) and *Congo* (Arthur Omar, 1972) and "fake" documentaries from

(continued)

(continued)

the contemporary period. Similar to Aguilera Skvirsky's rethinking of realisms (in the plural), Ortega's identification of various genealogies of the essay-film also allows us to problematize facile periodizations that have proposed a rigid break between 1960s filmmaking and the present.

The essay is a hybrid, centaur-like genre, responding to the heterogeneity of modern culture, in all of its discordant multiplicity.

(Reyes 1944a: 58)

In 1944, Alfonso Reyes, one of the greatest Spanish-language essayists and a pioneer of Spanish-language film criticism, defined the literary essay as "the centaur of genres," a point of convergence between critical thought and literary expression, inhabiting multiple forms, a product of modern culture (Reyes 1944a, 1944b). In an era in which film and radio took over some of the functions of literature, according to Reyes, the essay became a focal point of literary reinvention in the context of a diverse culture very different from the closed, circular, harmonic sphere of earlier periods.

In 1996, Philipe Lopate published "In Search of the Centaur," a pivotal critical text on the contemporary essay-film. It is difficult to identify the connection that might explain the similarity in terminology. It might have been Aldous Huxley, who cites the centaur as one of the multi-formed hybrids that would metaphorically define the literary essay as an example of "artistically-controlled free association." Huxley is also the point of departure for Laura Rascoli and Timothy Corrigan's theoretical ruminations on the essay-film. For Huxley, "the essay moves between three poles: the personal and autobiographical; the objective, factual, concrete-particular; and the abstract-universal." According to Corrigan, in the essay-film, there are three analogous, interacting registers (personal expression, public experience, and the process of thinking) that appear in different gradations in each film (Corrigan 2011: 205–214). It is precisely those interfaces that produce the textual commitments and rhetorical strategies that construct the spectatorial experience, and in turn define an essay-film (Rascaroli 2008).

The study of these correlations subtends all contemporary writing on the essay-film and will be the basis of my mapping of essay forms in Latin American cinemas (Blümlinger 1992/2004; Arthur 2003; Weinrichter 2007; Català 2014). This theoretical tradition also provides two critical perspectives that have coexisted in tension with each other and will be useful for this analysis. Both perspectives help to establish artistic genealogies and the very criteria that define the essay form itself. The first elucidates the existence of a "cinema of ideas," as proposed by 1920s Soviet and French filmmakers and theorists. This critical position emphasizes film's capacity to produce visual thought void of literary elements, and to construct concept-images or dialectical images similar to those found in baroque art and twentieth-century photocollage, photoessay, and photomontage. Within this framework, the essayistic is associated with films without narrators or explicit enunciatory subjects, and assumes that the filmmaker's voice will express itself through editing and other rhetorical and discursive operations. This line of thought allows us to conceptualize the Latin American essay-film of the 1960s, as well as certain contemporary films that eschew explicit personal expression in favor of inscribing the filmmaker's perspective within film form itself.

The second critical position utilizes a different point of departure: a certain type of European cinema from the 1950s wherein the subject, the world, and language work together as an explicit enunciatory unit marked by the flow of thought, expressed primarily through words. Generic constrictions and alignments are rejected in favor of the asymmetric, heretical, and anti-methodical forms that, for Theodor Adorno, characterized the essay form. Such expressive tendencies would proliferate around the world in the 1970s, and by the 1990s the essay-film "burst into a recognizable international phenomenon" (Arthur 2003: 59). Within this transnationalizing process, there are a number of Latin American nonfiction films that feature a recognizable enunciatory voice, and are structured according to the free and erratic flow of experiences, thoughts, and emotions that link the filmmaker to the world and interpellate the spectator through the intersection of personal expression, public experience, and thought.

Existing scholarship on the essay-film reveals distinct tendencies, each tied to the intellectual background of the individual scholars. That said, the French (and Francophile) theoretical and cinephilic traditions have been able to forge a consensus that locates the genuine essayistic voice (starting with Montaigne) as the universal point of origin, and marginalizes other possible genealogies that might include the political essay and the editorial, briefly mentioned by Anglo-American critics. From my perspective, this dominant critical framework has cut off approaches that might account for the cultural matrices and specificities derived from geo-cultural traditions, both in terms of the practice of the essay-film and the discourses that surround it.

Perhaps for that very reason, *La hora de los hornos* (*The Hour of the Furnaces*, Fernando Solanas and Octavio Getino, 1966–1968) is the only Latin American film to be included in the diverse genealogies presented by international essay-film scholarship, and even then there is little attention paid to the film's connection to the international history of the essay-film, the two theoretical lines discussed above, or the role of other contemporaneous discourses in shaping the work's status as an essay-film. Retrospectives and film series that showcase the essay-film tend to include other Latin American documentaries such as *Chile, la memoria obstinada* (*Chile, The Obstinate Memory*, Patricio Guzmán, 1997), *Tire Die* (*Throw Me a Dime*, Fernando Birri, 1960), *Chircales* (*The Brickmakers*, Marta Rodríguez and Jorge Silva, 1972), and *Ilha das flores* (*Island of Flowers*, Jorge Furtado, 1989). This problematic selection demonstrates a lax understanding of the category itself, as well as the distant observer's preference for the political when approaching Latin American cinemas. This tendency on the part of international critics and curators has had the unfortunate consequence of conditioning academics and exhibitors within the region to overlook the plurality of essayistic tendencies in the region's cinema.

Scholars of Latin American cinemas have contributed to the problem by making little effort to chart the multiple manifestations of the essay-film in ways that approximate the critical attention given to such works by European and U.S. critics. We do not even have an initial account of how the concept of the essay-film (and its brethren) emerged or has been utilized in Latin American film criticism and historiography—a task that would help qualify or problematize the temporal frameworks and conceptualizations promoted by international scholars. Nor are there studies that use the essay-film as a vantage point from which to rethink the traditions of Latin American cinemas—at the very least, from the 1960s onward. Finally, if we are correct about the value of exploring the different cultural traditions that nurture essayistic forms in the region, we will also need to review the multiple modalities of the Latin American literary essay in order to illuminate the particularities of the filmic manifestations of that form.

Given the existing frameworks and blind spots just mentioned, the following pages will offer an archeology of past discourses and practices as the basis of a potential genealogy, as well as a map of the present moment based on interpretive possibilities that may be developed in future investigations.

About 1968: the essay-film as an archeology of the present

The term "essay-film" emerges most forcefully in Latin America around 1968. In their "Informe por el grupo Cine-Liberación" ("Report by the Cine-Liberation Group"), Solanas and Getino characterized *La hora de los hornos* as "the first Argentine essay-film about national issues and liberation" (Grupo Cine Liberación 1968/1969: 21), or, as Solanas would clarify later, it was an ideological and political essay-film. In September of that same year, the notion of the essay would be discussed in several public debates during the first "Muestra del Cine Documental Latinoamericano" in Mérida, Venezuela (Ortega 2016). For example, Oswaldo Capriles called for conceptualizing the documentary less as form of propaganda than as a genre analogous to the literary essay, with all the subgenres associated with it. For Capriles, the documentary should not be valued for the efficacy of its slogans, but rather for the quality of its argumentation, the weight of its evidence, and the clarity and beauty of its expression. In his perspective, the central issue was the question of form (Capriles 1968).

La hora de los hornos included many features that justified its characterization as an essay-film and that allow us to chart the understanding of the essayistic during that period. First, the structure of the film (e.g. the division of the first part into a prologue, 13 chapters, and an epilogue) and its inclusion of intertitles and lengthy citations lend it a bookish quality. The analogy with the written (political or historical) essay was established by Solanas himself along with other filmmakers such as Mario Handler, who characterized *La hora* as a liberated exercise in formal experimentation (Handler 1969; Solanas 1969). Second, Solanas (1969) alluded to the film's concept-images as units of knowledge generated by the editing. *La hora* rehabilitated the tradition of *montage* that, as noted earlier, certain theorists have identified as one of the points of origin for the essay-film (Arthur 2003; Weinrichter 2007; Corrigan 2011; Tracy 2013). Within this framework, Josep Maria Català reconsiders the film in light of its renovation of baroque emblems. The shots did not function as acts of witnessing, memory-images, or historical images; instead, in the interaction of voice and text, the image track transformed reality into an idea, allowing the spectator to witness the act of thinking or the thought process (Català 2014).

Analogies with literature became more complicated in other critical accounts that located the essence of the essay-film in its expressive autonomy from that written medium. This is exemplified in Louis Marcorelles's characterization of *La hora* in *Cahiers du cinéma* as an "essay, in the truest sense, written directly for the screen, without literary mediation" (Marcorelles 1969). Cuban writer-filmmaker Jesús Diaz employed a similar argument when claiming that the films of Santiago Álvarez were true incarnations of the cinematic essay, because they did not owe anything to the literary essay; editing served as a uniquely cinematic, expressive tool and the works' innovation lay in their style and formal technique rather than in their messages (Díaz 1980/2003). According to Díaz, those were the qualities that Álvarez shared with the great Spanish-language essayists (José Martí, Miguel de

Unamuno, José Ortega y Gasset, Alfonso Reyes, Juan Marinello). For Georg Lukács, it was formal innovation that differentiated the essay, an ability to reorder known things in order to reveal the truth about them (Lukács 1910/1974). Álvarez's works offer a singular example of this, as their images and sounds are invested with a materiality or thingness, which is then utilized in the editing process to create concept-images wherein the cognitive and the emotional remain irreducibly linked (Ortega 2009).

The previous discussion suggests that the two critical frameworks have at least two points in common: both establish analogies with the literary essay (in terms of formal questions) and conceptualize the essay-film as a cinema of ideas based on a visual thought process that emerges primarily through the editing process. There is also a third, implicit commonality that can be productive for our current reflections on the essay-film. Solanas and Getino affirmed the following: "Our era is an era of the hypothesis, more than thesis; an era of works-in-progress [that are] inconclusive, disordered, violent" (Grupo Cine Liberación 1969/1988: 51). For his part, Julio García Espinosa proposed that cinema should show processes, more than pre-established, close-minded judgments that impede analysis on the part of the spectator (García Espinosa 1969/1976). Here again are echoes of Lukács's words: "the essay is a judgment, [. . .] not the verdict, but the process of judging" (Lukács 1910/1974: 18).

In light of that, *La hora de los hornos*, Álvarez's documentaries, and other recognized works from that period exemplify a type of political essay-film that, like its literary counterpart, oscillates between judgment and the process of judging, from the enunciatory position of a collective (political and historical) subject. That said, the assertive and direct nature of their discourse distance them from today's more tentative, open, and fragmentary essay-films. Such characteristics were more likely to be found in the work of a filmmaker such as Nicolás Guillén Landrián, whose films were left out of canonical accounts of the Latin American documentary until recently. Deploying similar techniques to those of his compatriot Álvarez, Guillén Landrián utilized formal experimentation to open up meanings and to stage an encounter between thought and sensorial experience (Ortega 2008; Reyes 2008). From *Ociel del Toa* (1964) to *Coffee Arábiga* (1968), his work introduced elements (fragmentation, reflexivity, epistemic uncertainty, digression) that would become characteristic of contemporary iterations of the essay-film. While lacking an explicit personal voice, his films transmit a sense of intimate communication that emerges, above all else, from his approach to the bodies and voice of others. By enacting thoughts and sensibilities, his films eschewed verdicts and judgments. In ways similar to his contemporaries, Guillén Landrián's work reordered our sense of the world, but according to a different relational logic—one that enacted an archeology of the present that was not reducible to a singular system of knowledge and action.

Seeing anew today . . . other genealogies of the Latin American essay-film

The reinterpretation of certain Latin American documentaries from the 1950s, 1960s, and 1970s allows us to trace other thematic and formal sources of essayistic potential. If Alain Resnais's artistic documentaries from the 1950s are recognized as a precursor to the contemporary essay-film, we can find a similar antecedent in Latin American filmmaking of that same period. The essayistic potential of the art documentary is evident in a film such as *Reverón* (Margot Benacerraf, Venezuela, 1953). Despite its reconstruction of the Venezuelan artist's biography and professional trajectory in the form of a traditional expository documentary, the film departs from those established conventions in certain segments in order to test the tools of the medium so as to capture the creative process, and to visually evoke the vital artistic imaginary of Reverón. This occurs, for example, when the camera wanders through the artist's disturbing workshop, as if it were a *flâneur* haphazardly gathering up impressions and objects of uncertain worth and through the staging of a self-portrait made during the production of the film itself.

Reverón is also a portrayal that, akin to contemporary practices, presents the main character as an elusive figure that the film can never fully capture. Something similar occurs in *Carlos, Cine-retrato de un caminante* (Mario Handler, Uruguay, 1965), a testimonial documentary that shifts between a dialogical mode of address and a more intimate space of communication with the spectator. The effort to give a voice to a man who lacks one in his everyday life becomes operationalized at the level of form, through the asynchronic juxtaposition of the vagabond's words over an image track that is at once observational and fragmentary. In this way, Carlos's voice serves as a type of soliloquy, or internal monologue. At times, the portrayal adopts a confessional tone; in others, it situates the spectator as an interlocutor, as the protagonist directs his questions to us as well as to Handler. Through these techniques, Carlos blurs the lines of the "social type" showcased in classic documentaries; instead, he appears as a unique, irreducible subject providing us with a window into his personal experience.

Along with the dialogical and the intimate, reflexivity is another constitutive feature of the essay-film. From the time of its emergence in the 1950s, the rapid maturation of the independent documentary soon encouraged filmmakers to challenge representational conventions and the established forms of political, historical, and testimonial nonfiction films. Brazil would produce films such as *Lavra-dor* (*Work-er*, Paolo Rufino, 1968) and *Congo* (Arthur Omar, 1972) that openly question documentary representation in a number of ways. This sort of reflexivity about filmic conventions and devices becomes almost a calling card of Cuban filmmaking during this period—both in fiction and documentary. For the purposes of this essay, the medium-length *Hombres de Mal Tiempo* (*Men of Bad Times*, Alejandro Sanderman, Cuba, 1968) is illuminating given the central role of re-enactment, a particularly generative feature of the essay-film (Corrigan 2011). Sanderman crosscuts between the testimonies of ex–combatants about their memories and experiences of a battle that took place during the War of Independence, and filmmakers preparing to make a film about the conflict with the veterans' help. From the tension between these two scenes, there emerges a consideration about the limits of the filmic representation of the past and about the role of personal memories and experiences in the reconstruction of historical events. The fragmentation, tentative attitude, intimacy, and reflexivity that emerged in such films responded to the temporal, filmic, and discursive contexts in which they were made. Contemporary nonfiction films would rework those characteristics in ways that made their essayistic potential more evident.

The essayistic modes of contemporary nonfiction

The following consideration of contemporary film is not an effort to identify and sanctify "true" essay-films; that has long been a problematic scholarly enterprise. Instead, I will chart some of the predominant modes of enunciation and representation, and most notable formal and discursive devices that characterize the essayistic in the contemporary moment. The selection of films discussed below does not attempt to define a canon, but rather recognizes the circulation and visibility of certain filmmakers and films in exhibition spaces and critical and scholarly accounts.

1. Between the portrait and the self-portrait

The interface between the portrait and the self-portrait has been the point of emergence for the explicit inscription of the filmmaker's voice in contemporary nonfiction films from Latin America, with multiple antecedents, including the short *Di-Rocha* (Glauber Rocha, Brazil, 1977) (Ortega 2011). A common feature of the essay since Montaigne, self-portraiture in these films takes on forms associated with literary and pictorial counterparts. The subject does not discuss him or herself directly or present him or herself as sole author. Instead, the films show what the filmmakers perceive, situating themselves as "writing tools" and a means of expression, displacing the ego from its normative position (Guasch 2009).

As mentioned earlier, and in accordance with Corrigan, the portrait-film and similar variants that critically engage art objects, films, and other aesthetic experiences are favorable sites for structuring two modes of the essay-film: the portrait-essay and the refractive essay (Corrigan 2011). In contemporary Latin American documentaries, the portrayal of artists/filmmakers and the artistic process itself has given rise to different engagements and aesthetic dialogues between the subject of the film and the subject who films in ways that vacillate between speculative complicity and critical refraction.

The work of two Argentine filmmakers illustrates in an exemplary fashion how the essayistic "I" can express itself through the stimulus provided by another creator. In *Por la vuelta* (*For the Return*, Cristian Pauls, 2002), the portrayal of *bandoneón*-player and composer Leopoldo Federico unleashes a true essayistic, almost literary inscription, in which the musician's presence, absence, and gaze encourage the filmmaker to question his own identity and his own past. It is a text marked by mourning, and functions as an act of reparation for losses—both irrefutable (his father) and anticipated (Federico)—that have long motivated autobiographical considerations (Bergala 1998). Pauls' voice-over uses words to paint a visual self-portrait of his youth, when his love for music emerged, and at times adopts an epistolary form, as other essays have done. Yet, above all, the narrating voice is the expression of the solitary act of writing. Personal expression prevails over public expression, but the latter is implicit in the relationship established between the two generations through their shared memories and affection for tango.

Starting with *La TV y yo* (*TV and I*, 2002), Andrés Di Tella's work has explored the essayistic in different guises through family history, autobiography, and first-person address. In *Fotografías* (*Photographs*, 2007), the essay-film reaches its sharpest, most recognizable incarnation. The evocation of the figure of the mother is a mechanism that unleashes a series of cognitive and affective itineraries, erratic journeys in space and time, encounters and interactions that reanimate the meaning of visual and filmic objects and materials. Di Tella's "I" is split between the filmmaker-writer-subject and the subject who is written and screened by the film—a unique feature of the essay-film (Blümlinger 1992/2004). Unlike the previous case, however, this essayistic inscription does not seek to pattern itself after its literary counterpart. In this particular splitting, the subject acquires different valences (father/husband/son; professional documentarian and home moviemaker), to the point of encountering himself in a self-portrait that questions his own identity. Both the filmmaker-subject and the film itself present themselves as works-in-progress, as immersed in the process of becoming that unfolds through experiences in the world and with others. In *Hachazos* (2011), the essayistic takes an alternate route in the tentative portrayal of the experimental filmmaker Claudio Caldini and his creative universe. Di Tella's meditative, reflexive, doubting voice (present in his earlier films) retreats from center stage. Something similar occurs with the exploration of the socio-historical world, which is now limited to the personal and political experiences of the protagonists of the golden ages of Argentine experimental film. *Hachazos* is really a refractive essay-film. Caldini's creative processes (appearing via re-enactments, recreations of old work, and preparations for future projects), on the one hand, and the materiality and visuality of his works, on the other, allow for DiTella's own epistemic and affective self-reflections and self-inscriptions. The literal, physical, and verbal encounters of the two filmmakers in some sequences are refracted in others in which film form itself transmits their different ways of understanding the cinema and its engagement with the world.

2. Chronotopes 1: journeys in time

The subject who constitutes him/herself through the essay is always in movement, under construction, without a fixed pathway or itinerary. Thus, trips and displacement in space and time are suitable devices for the essay-film's fluid epistemology that moves between public and private sphere, between the self and the world. The articulations of time-space emerge as the product of the act of inscription itself, as chronotopes constructed by the filmmaker's endeavors.

Contemporary Latin American nonfiction films have approached the past, the present, and memory in diverse assemblages that combine autobiography, family history, and reflections about identity (personal, political, national). In addition to Di Tella's two films mentioned above, there are numerous others, including *El diablo nunca duerme* (*The Devil Never Sleeps*, Lourdes Portillo, Mexico–US, 1994), *La línea paterna* (*The Paternal Line*, José Buil and Marisa Sistach, Mexico, 1994), *Um Passaporte Húngaro* (*A Hungarian Passport*, Sandra Kogut, Brazil, 2001), *La quemadura* (*The Burn*, René Ballesteros, Chile and France, 2009), *Cuchillo de palo* (Renate Costa, Paraguay and Spain, 2012), and *La danza del hipocampo* (*The Dance of Memory*, Gabriela D. Rubalcaba, Mexico, 2014). They demonstrate the multiple pathways taken by filmmakers in order to reconsider the past and the present through family genealogies that connect the private to the public. In this context, certain films that confront the still-open wounds of the political past have given birth to essayistic forms noteworthy for their innovative discursive strategies.

There is an amazingly extensive critical bibliography about new subjective narratives about traumatic memory and the historical ruptures unleashed by authoritarian dictatorships in the Southern Cone. Among the most discussed is Albertina Carri's *Los rubios* (2003), a film that set off a heated public debate in Argentina. As a child whose parents disappeared at the hands of the military, Carri crafts her documentary as a response to previous films about and by children orphaned by the dictatorship. Much has been said about the film's highly experimental form—most notably, the use of multiple devices to confront the insurmountable fissures of memory and the impossibility of reconstructing the past through the construction of radical, complex subjectivity (Noriega 2009; Andermann 2012). The doubling of the self (in the body of Albertina herself and that of the actress who plays her in several sequences), the fragmentary structure that foregrounds process (and gives a twist to the notion of a work-in-progress), and the use of animation in particular sequences (to evoke a young child's imaginary take on loss and absence) demand an intense, cognitive engagement on the part of the spectator. In sum, through this sort of complex weaving,

Carri's film-essay eschews intimate, contemplative conversation in favor of the epistemic interrogation of modes of representation and the deconstruction of hegemonic and counter-hegemonic discourses.

The work of Chilean Patricio Guzmán has brought together the self and the collective subject in a variety of ways in his reconstructions of the memory of the political past, which at times tend toward the essayistic. In *Nostalgia de la luz* (*Nostalgia for the Light*, 2010), this emerges in a clear, original manner thanks to the subtle interweavings that do not necessarily highlight the subjective or authorial voice of Guzmán himself to express the trajectory of his thoughts and feelings. The film is a calm, contemplative consideration, at once active and open, about the nature of time on different scales (cosmological, geological, archeological, historical, human) that Guzmán links together in order to generate new constellations of ideas drawing on different forms of knowledge and expressed by different voices. Like a spiral without a predetermined shape, the film leads us through numerous displacements between two object-poles that function as time machines: at one end, the stars that astronomers and astrophysicists study from their laboratories in the Atacama desert; at the other, the bones sought in that same inhospitable environment by family members of those who disappeared during the dictatorship. Through metaphor, the film encourages us to think about the ephemeral nature of the human scale of time and memory, leaving open the question about what will happen with the memory of that traumatic past when the people who gather and curate it pass away.

3. Chronotopes 2: journeys in space

The journey and a *flâneur*-like attitude are two tropes frequently invoked as a substratum of the essayistic. Some of the films mentioned above such as *Fotografías* illustrate how the essay-film constructs itself through parallels established between the physical and mental displacements of the subject. The objects and experiences that are gathered together in such meanderings, and the filmmaker's attitude toward them, function chronotopically to generate a constellation of ideas and affects through which the subject transmits his or her relationship to the world to the spectator. This coexists with the contemporary documentary's tendency to structure itself around searches, in a variety of narrative guises: from the police investigation to the work-in-progress, the *carnet de voyage*, or the diary (whether personal or production/filmmaking) that allow for the subversion of traditional epistemologies.

Ningún lugar en ninguna parte. Apuntes para un documental sobre la ficción (*No Place Anywhere: Notes for a Documentary about Fiction*, José Luis Torres Leiva, Chile, 2002) demonstrates the essayistic potential of the figure of the *flâneur*, but it is only fully realized in *Opus* (Mariano Donoso, Argentina, 2005) through the film's intertextual, metatextual, and reflexive density. At first, Donoso's work appears to be a production diary and a travel journal about the 2002 trip that the filmmaker and his crew took to San Juan (the birthplace of the director, as well as Domingo Faustino Sarmiento, one of Argentina's founding fathers, known for his educational reforms) to document the protests occurring in local schools against budgetary cuts. The initial goal of showcasing the contemporary socioeconomic crisis through the problems afflicting public education quickly becomes unworkable. In response, the film adopts the reflexive and deconstructive rhetoric associated with today's documentary—what Paul Arthur has called the "aesthetics of failure" (Arthur 1993). This takes place through the film's very structure as a work-in-progress, as well as Donoso's reflexive voice-over, where he comments ironically on what it takes to make a "good" documentary, constantly questioning the project itself. This reflexive interrogation is further intensified through the inclusion of phone conversations and email exchanges between the filmmaker and his U.S. uncle, Jerry Rubin, who apparently is the film's producer, and whose voice at times speaks directly to the spectator. *Opus* also superimposes the structure of the literary essay over the production diary/travel journal. Chapter breaks and numerous quotes (both literary and philosophical) establish ongoing intertextual references and meditative digressions throughout the film. Despite this deconstructive reflexivity, *Opus* never gives up on thinking about the country's social and political conflicts, or encouraging the spectator to reflect on questions of identity, the sense of belonging to particular places, and the conflictive relationship with objects and symbols. The landscape and also the invocation of San Juan and Sarmiento as allegorical figures allow Donoso to trace connections between physical and mental displacement and between the past and the present. These are the chronotopes of an essayistic inscription that can never adequately grasp the object under discussion; the film's form itself echoes the tentative and incomplete nature of its epistemological position.

Essays about truth and representation

Orson Welles characterized two of his films as essays: *Portrait of Gina* (1958), which he described as "a personal essay [. . .] in the tradition of a newspaper; it is me on a given subject" (Bazin and Bitsch 1958/2008), and *F for Fake* (1973). Critics would later add another film to this list: *Filming Othello* (1979). The first and the last exemplify two of the essayistic traditions discussed previously: the portrait and the deconstruction of filmmaking-in-progress. Let us now turn to a third variation: those essay-films that interrogate the relationship between reality and fiction, truth and lies, representation and performance.

In *F for Fake*, Welles cites Pablo Picasso to affirm the following: "Art is a lie, a lie that makes us realize the truth." In the last few decades, the so-called fake documentary has taken up this paradox. As a symptom of contemporary epistemological and artistic impasses, the fake documentary has become a means to think through the institutionalizing of truth, as well as epistemologies associated with more traditional expository modes. This is precisely the locus of its essayistic potential (Català 2014: 453). Imagination and the creation of fictitious characters and situations serve to propose hypotheses about reality, and through them to arrive at a conditional truth. This tentative and provisional exploration of the truth engages the spectator in an intense intellectual dialogue with both content and form simultaneously.

All of these features are evident in *Un tigre de papel* (*A Paper Tiger*, Luis Ospina, Colombia, 2007), one of the few examples of a feature-length fake documentary from Latin America. It tells the story of Pedro Manrique Figueroa, a man who supposedly introduced the technique of the collage to the Colombian art scene.

The film relies on the usual devices of the fake: the manipulation of archival materials, the use of a rigorous investigation as organizing structure, and the inclusion of interviews that mix up what really happened with minute details and anecdotes about a totally fictitious person. This mash-up crafts a thrilling journey (from 1934 to 1981, when we lose track of Figueroa), tracing the relationship between art and politics in Colombia within the wider context of the international history of socialism and communism. Along the way, two other formal elements are put into play: Figueroa's collages (concept-images that present utopian visions characterized by the irreverence of a non-dogmatic political imaginary), and signs and graphics that undercut the functionality of 1960s political

Estas imágenes
son suyas,
poséalas.
Lo representan:
cúbrase con ellas
como los brujos
con sus mantos.
Lo explican
por encima
de las apariencias:
Tenga fe en
esta explicación
simbólica.

Figure 7.1   The "work" of the fake collagist Pedro Manrique Figueroa, juxtaposed with director Luis Ospina's commentary in *Un tigre de papel* (*A Paper Tiger*, Colombia, 2007).

cinema with ironic phrases, quotes, and meta-referential texts. Both components lead to digressions, commentaries, and references; alert the spectator to the possibility of fraud; and, in so doing, involve him or her in a ludic, stimulating communication. Pedro Manrique is a microhistorical, fictional artifact that enables the film to express the dreams, expectations, and disillusionments of the Colombian left (i.e. the experiences and dilemmas of Ospina's generation within the larger, real macrohistory). This reconsideration of the past necessitates problematizing all representational practices that monopolize truth-claims. For that reason, the film's thought process emerges through the relationship established between formal devices and the institutions (political, artistic, cinematographic) to which they refer. Ultimately, Ospina's film constructs a spectatorial position that shifts between the rhetoric of the fake and that of the (collective) self-portrait.

Jogo de Cena (*Playing*, Eduardo Coutinho, Brazil, 2008) plays with this same uncertainty about the line between reality and fiction, but does so through a very different modus operandi. It is a hypnotic essay-film about performance and storytelling that transforms the interview, a canonical documentary device, into the art of conversation. The minimalist *mise en scène*—interviewer and interviewee seated on the stage of an empty theater—gets to the heart of the film's proposal. The first shot reproduces a newspaper ad looking for women with stories to tell who want to participate in a casting call for a documentary. From that point forward, the film unfolds as a "jogo de cena" (staged play/game). Twenty-three women chat with Coutinho, telling stories about their love of the theater and performance, about motherhood and parent–child relationships, presenting scraps of lives characterized by loss, pain, and suffering. The transcendental and the trivial are woven together in the fluid and seemingly spontaneous dialogues with the filmmaker. Brazilian spectators—or those familiar with Brazilian film—will recognize the faces of certain well-known actresses mixed together with others that are completely unknown, and yet will be unable to solve the puzzle of how certain bodies tell particular stories, or whether or not the expressed emotions (both laughter and tears) are the product of the act of remembering

Figure 7.2   The same affective tale is told by multiple bodies: one an anonymous woman, the other
a well-known TV Globo actress in *Jogo de Cena* (*Playing*, Eduardo Countinho,
Brazil, 2008).

or a calculated performance. This uncertainty becomes intensified when the stories begin
to repeat themselves, when the same tale is told by another body-voice whose gestures and
emotions imbue it with different qualities.

The film never reveals what's "behind the curtain." But the flow of the stories is interrupted on occasion to allow us to see the "actress" expressing herself outside her role,
discussing her concerns about the "scenes" and the director's demands. The fake documentary's cognitively demanding reflexivity is attenuated in *Jogo de Cena* by the spectator's
pleasure in allowing him or herself to be swept away by the affective intensity of the tales
themselves, in the "the melodramatic imaginary" through which Coutinho honors Latin
American popular culture (López 2014). All of this generates an intellectual pleasure—more
aesthetic than cognitive—based on the spectator's ability to recognize re-presentations,
and the play between constants and variations that reference the very essence of filmic
dramaturgy—whether in fiction or documentary. *Jogo de Cena* exemplifies a modality of the
essay-film in which intimacy, the larger world, and thought processes are linked together in
novel ways—perhaps only as Eduardo Coutinho himself could do.

Conclusions

The emergence of the essay-film as a recognizable tendency of contemporary cinema is pos-
sibly a symptom of a certain cultural moment like the one that stimulated Alfonso Reyes'

reflections in the 1940s. Technological changes, the crisis of traditional epistemologies, and the diversity of visual culture have produced intense transformations in how the interactions within the subject and with the world are expressed while also reinventing the languages.

Contemporary Latin American cinema exhibits essayistic forms similar to those visible on the international scene, a coincidence explicable by new transnational flows in the production, circulation, and reception of nonfiction film and by the new equally transnational cinephilic cultures. Whereas Lopate's reductive model would not include many of the above-mentioned works in the category of the essay-film, Corrigan's more comprehensive, malleable theoretical propositions allow us to productively think through the formal reinventions that have taken place—from the differential deployment of personal expression, public experience, and thought processes, as well as the interface between them—and to trace lines of continuity and rupture linking the past to the present.

Such an overview brings to light the different valences that such interactions acquire, given the contexts in which subject, world, and language are rooted. The enunciatory forms of Carri and Guzmán are inseparable from the public spaces in which the politics of memory and forgetting have been enacted, and from their articulation in previous documentaries. Popular culture, orality, and melodrama nurture the formal principles of other films, from *El diablo nunca duerme* to *Jogo de cena*, and serve as the cultural matrix endowing the interactions between public and private with meaning. The formal elements of the *Un tigre de papel* dialogue with the tradition of collage as well as with the principles of *montage* featured in earlier forms of Latin American political cinema, and at the same time the film's form is also the result of the filmmaker's move to a video format in the mid-1980s to link up with international trends in the audiovisual essay. Whereas the reflexivity and fragmentation of 1960s cinema targeted the shadowy zones hidden within affirmative political discourses, these same characteristics are employed differently today to illuminate other uncertainties about the encounter between the self and the world. Recent films explore subjectivity through formal maneuvers that dialogue aesthetically and discursively with the type of essayistic nonfiction that has been legitimized in international circuits. And, yet, at the same time, the specific manifestations of subjectivity visible in Latin American essay-films crystallize different cultural, identitarian, and sociopolitical elements produced by the multiple tensions between centers and peripheries at the level of the national and the transnational.

Notes

1 This essay was underwritten as part of "Las relaciones transnacionales en el cine digital hispano-americano: los ejes de España, México y Argentina" (CSO2014-52750-P), a research project financed by Spain's Ministerio de Economía y Competitividad del Gobierno.
2 Translated by Laura Podalsky.

References

Andermann, J. (2012) *New Argentine Cinema*. London: I.B. Taurus.
Arthur, P. (1993) "Jargons of Authenticity (Three American Moments)." In M. Renov (ed.), *Theorizing Documentary*. New York: Routledge, pp. 108–134.
—— (2003) "Essay Questions: From Alain Resnais to Michael Moore." *Film Comment*, Jan/Feb: 58–63.
Bazin, A. and Bitsch, C. (1958/2008) "Interview with Orson Welles." *Senses of Cinema*, 46 (2008). Originally published in *Cahiers du Cinéma*, 84, June. Available at: http://sensesofcinema.com/2008/the-new-wave-remembered-focus-on-charles-bitsch/orson-welles-bazin-bitsch/ (accessed March 17, 2015).

Bergala, A. (1998) *Je est un film*. Paris: Éditions ACOR.

Blümlinger, C. (1992/2004) "Lire entre images." In S. Liandrat-Guigues and M. Ganebin (eds.), *L'essai et le cinéma*. Seyssel: Éditions Champs Vallon, pp. 49–66.

Capriles, O. (1968) "Mérida: realidad, forma y comunicación." *Cine al día*, 6 (December): 4–9.

Català, J.M. (2014) *Estética del ensayo. La forma ensayo, de Montaigne a Godard*. Valencia: Universitat de València.

Corrigan, T. (2011) *The Essay Film: From Montaigne after Marker*. New York: Oxford University Press.

Díaz, J. (1980/2003) "Provocaciones sobre el cine documental y la literatura (1980)." In P. Paranaguá (ed.), *Cine documental en America Latina*. Madrid: Cátedra, pp. 472–476.

García Espinosa, J. (1969/1976) "Por un cine imperfecto." In *Por un cine imperfecto*. Madrid: Castellote Editor, pp. 17–34.

Grupo Cine Liberación (1968/1969) "Informe por el grupo Cine-Liberación (enero, 1968)." *Cine del tercer mundo* 1(1): 19–23.

—— (1969/1988) "Hacia un tercer cine. Apuntes y experiencias para el desarrollo de un cine de liberación en el Tercer Mundo." In *Hojas de cine: Testimonios y documentos del Nuevo Cine Latinoamericano*. Mexico City: Secretaria de Educación Pública/Universidad Autónoma Metropolitana, vol.1 pp. 29–62.

Guasch, A.M. (2009) *Autobiografías visuales. Del archivo al índice*. Madrid: Siruela.

Handler, M. (1969) "La hora de los hornos." *Cine del tercer mundo*, 1(1): 24–32.

Lopate, P. (1996) "In Search of the Centaur: The Essay Film." In C. Warren (ed.), *Beyond Document. Essays on Nonfiction Film*. Hanover, NH: Wesleyan University Press.

López, A.M. (2014) "A Poetics of the Trace." In V. Navarro and J.C. Rodríguez (eds.), *New Documentaries in Latin America*. New York: Macmillan, pp. 25–43.

Lukács, G. (1910/1974) "On the Nature and Form of the Essay." In *Soul and Form*, Cambridge, MA: MIT Press, pp. 15–18.

Marcorelles, L. (1969) "L'épreuve du direct. F. E. Solanas: La hora de los hornos." *Cahiers du cinéma*, 210 (March): 37–39.

Noriega. G. (2009) *Estudio crítico sobre Los rubios*. Buenos Aires: PicNic.

Ortega, M.L. (2008) "El 68 y el documental en Cuba." *Archivos de la Filmoteca*, 59: 75–91.

—— (2009) "De la certeza a la incertidumbre: collage, documental y discurso político en América Latina." In S. Gomez Lopez and L. Gómez Vaquero (eds.), *Piedra, papel y tijera. El collage en el cine documental*. Madrid: Ocho y Medio/Ayuntamiento de Madrid, pp. 101–137.

—— (2011) "Una (nueva) cartografía del documental latinoamericano contemporáneo." *Cine documental*, 4. Available at: http://revista.cinedocumental.com.ar/4/articulos_04.html (accessed on June 13, 2017).

—— (2016) "Mérida 68. Las disyuntivas del documental." In M. Mestman (ed.), *Las rupturas del 68 en el cine de América Latina*. Buenos Aires: AKAL, pp. 355–394.

Rascaroli, L. (2008) "The Essay Film: Problems, Definitions, Textual Commitments, Framework." *The Journal of Cinema and Media*, 48(2): 24–47.

Reyes, A. (1944a/1997) "El deslinde." In *Obras completas*. Mexico City: Fondo de Cultura Económica XV, pp. 15–422.

—— (1944b/1997) "Las nuevas artes." In *Obras completas*. Mexico City: Fondo de Cultura Económica IX, pp. 400–403.

Reyes, D.L. (2008) "El documental reflexivo cubano: testimonio paralelo de una revolución." *Archivos de la Filmoteca*, 59: 93–103.

Solanas, F.E. (1969) "Solanas por Godard, Godard por Solanas." *Cine del Tercer Mundo*, 1(1): 48–63.

Tracy, A. (2013) "The Essay Film." *Sight and Sound*, 23(8): 44–48.

Weinrichter, A. (ed.) (2007) *La forma que piensa. Tentativas en torno al cine-ensayo*. Pamplona: Punto de Vista.

8

REALISM, DOCUMENTARY, AND THE PROCESS GENRE IN EARLY NEW LATIN AMERICAN CINEMA

Salomé Aguilera Skvirsky

Editors' introduction

Until fairly recently, the New Latin American Cinema often has been the only manifestation of Latin American cinemas to be recognized in English-language scholarship on "international film," with the manifestos of filmmakers such as Fernando Solanas and Octavio Getino, Glauber Rocha, and, occasionally, Julio García Espinosa serving as the sole examples of Latin American-based film theory and criticism to appear in film theory anthologies. It is only with the increased *external* recognition of contemporary films from the region in festival circuits that the understanding of "Latin American Cinema" has begun to shift away from its association with politically militant and aesthetically avant-garde film.

Within this broader context, Aguilera Skvirsky's chapter offers a welcome reconsideration of the NLAC by turning our attention to lesser-known films from the late 1950s—many of which showcased manual labor and the process of production (whether mining salt, weaving wicker crafts, or threshing wheat). Whereas previous scholarship has situated those documentaries as precursors to more fully realized works of the following decade, Aguilera Skvirsky argues that we need to reconceptualize these films of the "early" New Latin American Cinema. Her chapter demonstrates the importance of acknowledging the long history of the "process genre" (going back into the silent period), as well as the particular horizon within which such films re-emerged in the 1950s alongside contemporaneous debates that re-semanticized the notion of underdevelopment. The chapter also calls for the deployment of a more robust, complex model of *realisms* that allows us to reposition the films of the "early" and "late" NLAC as differential manifestations of this representational/discursive mode.

(continued)

(continued)

The chapter has important implications for Latin American film historiography and criticism. In ways that complement Mariano Mestman and Masha Salazkina's examination of the micropolitics of the NLAC (Chapters 12 and 13), Aguilera Skvirsky demonstrates the usefulness of thick, historicizing approaches and the importance of problematizing (or discarding) teleological frameworks. Indeed, her conclusion points to the reappearance of the process genre in recent documentaries and fiction films. Like the "slow" fiction films from the 2000s examined by Nilo Couret (Chapter 16), Aguilera Skvirsky notes that films such as *El Velador* can be seen as responses to accelerating work rhythms and the "instrumentalization of neoliberal life."

One of the most celebrated films ever produced in Latin America, *Memorias del subdesarrollo* (*Memories of Underdevelopment*, Tomás Gutiérrez Alea, Cuba, 1968) has, at its core, a representational paradox, crystallized in its title. While "underdevelopment" is a term that has, since its ascendance in the 1940s, conjured a vivid set of images of material immiseration and poverty (e.g. unkempt, barefoot children; swollen, parasitic bellies; houses built of cane, etc.), Alea's film features few images of this variety—and all of these have their source not in the Cuba of 1968 (the year the film was shot), but in archival newsreel footage from other countries or from other historical time periods. In Alea's treatment, "underdevelopment" shifts from a visually marked category to one whose signs are not manifest, whose effects are largely immaterial. Underdevelopment, as an invisible psychic condition, is the principal subject of the film. The paradox of the film turns on an implicit argument about cinematic realism that is virtually a truism today: seeing is not believing; appearances are deceiving; naturalist aesthetics guarantee neither truth nor political radicalism. *Memorias de subdesarrollo* definitively announced the end of what is now viewed as the first "stage" of the New Latin American Cinema tied to the realist representation of underdevelopment, which was often attributed to the influence of Italian neorealism and Griersonian documentary. Alea's film marked—in 1968, and perhaps inadvertently—a division within the history of the New Latin American Cinema (NLAC), between the early and the late New Latin American Cinema. That division has been a lasting feature of the historiography of the movement.

The subject of this essay is that first phase of production—the early films of the New Latin American Cinema, primarily encompassing documentaries made in the 1950s and early 1960s, and including such landmark films as *Arraial do Cabo* (Paulo Saraceni, 1959) and *Aruanda* (Linduarte Noronha, 1960) in Brazil; *Araya* (Margot Benacerraf, 1958) in Venezuela; *Mimbre* (*Wicker*, Sergio Bravo, 1957), *Trilla* (*Path*, Sergio Bravo, 1959), *Día de organillos* (*Barrel Organ Day*, Sergio Bravo, 1959), *Láminas de Almahue* (*Scenes from Almahue*, Sergio Bravo, 1962) in Chile; *Tire Dié* (*Toss Me a Dime*, Fernando Birri, 1956), *Faena* (*Work*, Humberto Ríos, 1960), and *Ceramiqueros de Tras la Sierra* (*Ceramicists from Tras la Sierra*, Raymundo Gleyzer, 1965) in Argentina; and *Chircales* (*Brickmakers*, Marta Rodríguez and Jorge Silva, 1967) in Colombia. This period includes a number of lesser-known films such as those by Manuel Chambi and the Cusco School; others by Jorge Prelorán in Argentina; *Las callampas* (Rafael Sánchez, Chile, 1958); and *Andacollo* (Jorge di Lauro and Nieves Yancovic, Chile, 1958). This essay will concentrate, however, on the most paradigmatic examples.

The critical reception of these films is puzzling: on the one hand, scholars have unequivocally asserted the films' historical importance; on the other, they have exhibited a striking lack of curiosity about and attention to the films themselves. Of *Aruanda* and *Arraial do Cabo*, Glauber Rocha wrote in 1960 that they "inaugurate Brazilian documentary in its phase of renewal" (Rocha 1960; this and all further translations by the author). Randal Johnson wrote of *Aruanda* in 1998 that many critics believed it had "sparked" the Cinema Novo movement (Johnson 1998: 194). Paulo Antonio Paranaguá cites the accomplished documentary filmmaker Eduardo Coutinho's comment, in 1992, after seeing *Araya* for the first time, that it was the greatest Latin American documentary made before the use of direct sound (Paranaguá 2003: 42). Pablo Piedras recently described *Faena* as one of the "key films" made outside of Fernando Birri's *Escuela Documental de Santa Fe* that "prefigured the militant cinema to come" (Piedras 2009: 61). Meanwhile, *Tire Dié* is considered the inaugural film of what historians of Argentine cinema have called "the first historical cycle" of Argentine political and social cinema (Lusnich 2009: 25).

With perhaps the exception of *Tire Dié*, this recognition and praise has not produced the reams of close analysis that one might have expected, and which have accompanied the classic political films of the next phrase of the NLAC such as *Deus e o diabo na terra do sol* (*Black God, White Devil*, Glauber Rocha, Brazil, 1964) and *Memorias del subdesarrollo*. Today, the interest in the early films of the NLAC is mostly antiquarian: the films figure as illustrations of a historical moment that is considered important because it was a "stage" in the "evolution" of the New Latin American Cinema from a derivative Latin American variant of Italian neorealism to an autochthonous contribution to world cinema (Mestman 2012; Mestman and Ortega 2014). We have lost our way into this early cycle of New Latin American Cinema; the films have become lifeless relics. This, I argue, is a function of the sedimented, taken-for-granted framework of cinematic realism that has attached itself to these films and dominated their interpretation.

What follows is a three-part meta-reflection on the early phase of the New Latin American Cinema. In the first, I assess the achievements of these films at the historical moment of their emergence, in order to account for the broad critical consensus on their historical importance. In the second part, I argue that the realism framework that has dominated the scholarship on these films is no longer a fruitful interpretative lens through which to approach them. Just as the eclipse of Bazinian realism did not lead to the abandonment of Italian neorealist production by scholars who found other aspects of these films to examine and analyze, there is more to these early NLAC films than their realism or than their representation of underdevelopment. In the third part, I propose an alternative lens through which to analyze this production, arguing that several of them share a concern for processes of production and belong to what I call the "process genre."[1] This genre is constituted not by a thematic unity (e.g. labor), but by a formal syntax that can be crudely thought of as a visual how-to. Apprehending this common feature of these films has the potential of opening them up, allowing scholars to pose new questions around their cinematic influences, their contexts of production, their relation to the changing meanings and status of labor in a region where manual labor was traditionally denigrated, and to examine their politics from a fresh perspective.

Underdevelopment

From a historical vantage point, we might argue that the most striking feature of the realist films of the first wave of the New Latin American Cinema was their representation of poverty—or what came to be known as the representation of underdevelopment. Before these films, the cinematic representation of poverty in this region had a different, sanitized look (Burton 1990: 78). Institutional entities such as Brazil's Instituto Nacional de Cinema Educativo (INCE) and Chile Films concerned about national filmic self-representation— both as a matter of strengthening national identity at home and as a matter of international branding—had employed various forms of censorship. In the case of Brazil, for example, the state regularly sent nonfiction educational films to compete in international film festivals and to participate in world's fair expositions, but was always careful to project an image of Brazil as the land of progress—a place that was quickly modernizing, where Man was succeeding in taming the environment—rather than as the land of an exuberant, tropical, free-range nature or of material deprivation (Schvarzman 2004).

By way of contrast, in the early NLAC documentaries, the representation of underdevelopment became an explicit objective, and was an innovative proposal. In his 1964 reflection on the school of documentary that he had established in Santa Fe, Fernando Birri wrote:

> Underdevelopment is a hard fact in Latin America . . . The cinema of our countries . . . presents us with a false image of both society and our people . . . Indeed, it presents no real image of our people at all, but conceals them. So, the first positive step is to provide such an image. This is the first function of documentary. How can documentary provide this image? By showing how reality *is*, and in no other way.
>
> *(quoted in Martin 1997: 93)*

His prescription: "to confront reality with a camera and to document it, filming realistically, filming critically, filming underdevelopment with the optic of the people" (Birri 1997: 94). As straightforward and simple as this prescription appears to be, its central term, "underdevelopment," was a relatively new invention—and its meaning was far from transparent. What was imagined by "underdevelopment" at the time?

The discourse of development—of which "underdevelopment" is a product—is a very peculiar discourse on economic immiseration and poverty; it constructs its object more than it describes something in the world. The discourse is generally traced back to the 1940s, to Harry Truman's 1949 inaugural address (Escobar 2011), in which he referred to the "*underdeveloped areas*." "More than half the people of the world," he noted:

> are living in conditions approaching *misery*. Their food is inadequate. They are victims of *disease*. Their economic life is *primitive* and *stagnant*. . . . Democracy alone can supply the vitalizing force to stir the peoples of the world into triumphant action, not only against their human oppressors, but also against their ancient enemies—*hunger*, *misery*, and *despair*.
>
> *(Truman 1949, emphasis mine)*

A new framework for perceiving the ills of the Global South was being announced. Not only did Truman paint a rather vivid picture of the ills of the so-called underdeveloped areas (e.g. hungry, diseased, primitive, and stagnant), his rhetoric inscribed the developed and the underdeveloped within an evolutionary, civilizational logic inherited from the Enlightenment. The underdeveloped areas were "premodern"; they were isolated, rural, traditional, not industrialized, but with the proper application of technical know-how and the requisite will, they could eventually become developed—that is, "modern," urban, industrialized (Saldaña-Portillo 2003).

The evolutionism implicit in the discourse of (under)development was not new. The roots of social evolutionism can be traced back to Immanuel Kant, Georg W.F. Hegel, Auguste

when Fernando Birri argues, polemically, that cinema's solution to underdevelopment is for "one to put herself in front of reality with a camera and to document it, to document underdevelopment," by which he has in mind nothing less concrete than the documentation of "the lack of electricity, of hygiene, the shortage of water in wells, the helplessness of the elderly . . ." (Birri and Giménez 1964: 13, 20), he puts his faith not so much in the "that-has-been"-ness of the photographic image as in the evidentiary value of the *data* provided by appearances and testimony.

By the end of the 1980s, these formulations had begun to seem inadequate. In a volume on Latin American social documentary, published in 1990, Julianne Burton wrote:

> Birri thus posits a double function for the documentary: to negate false representations of reality, and to present reality as it "really" is. This formulation testifies to a naïve faith in the direct and incorruptible communicability of a pure and passive truth that merely awaits capture by the right agency. There is a double essentialism at work here: an assumption that the essence of the nation can be apprehended with camera and tape recorder, and a related belief that what is seen (and heard) is the essence of what is, and of what is knowable about what is.
>
> *(Burton 1990: 77)*

This strain of criticism objects to both an epistemological naïveté about cinematic realism, and to the political conservatism of the discourse of "objectivity." The failure to appropriately problematize the mediated, constructed nature of the photographic image was seen as an instance of "using the master's tools," and thus as a political failing as much as an aesthetic one. From today's vantage point, the formulations of these NLAC pioneers are an index of a certain historical moment at best, and an embarrassment at worst.[2]

The assessment of the early films of the New Latin American Cinema from the point of view of the present faces another, related political critique. If, at the time they were exhibited, the most striking feature of these films was the starkness of the "national reality" of underdevelopment, today there is nothing surprising about naturalistic depictions of poverty and economic immiseration: it is now a cliché in contemporary representational treatments of the Global South. Back in the 1950s and 1960s, who could have imagined that a visceral visual depiction of poverty could be so easily packaged, branded, and sold as a commodity? By the time the Colombian filmmakers Luis Ospina and Carlos Mayolo made the mock-documentary *Agarrando Pueblo* (*The Vampires of Poverty*) in 1977, "poverty porn" (*pornomiseria*)—the film's critical target—was a staple of Colombian and Latin American cinema (Faguet 2009).

The scholarly fixation on the early documentaries of the New Latin American Cinema follows from an implicit reading of them in which their primary interest and significance is in *what* they depict (viz. underdevelopment). They have functioned as illustrations of a hitherto neglected reality of underdevelopment. But that reading had a different significance in 1965 than it did in 1977 or than it does in 2017: in 1965, the starkness of economic immiseration was a corrective to prior, escapist representations; in 1977, there was a certain saturation of this kind of depiction; in 2017, these depictions are a cliché. If this cycle of films has been largely forgotten, critically neglected, I would argue that this is because of a certain realist reading of them that became hegemonic and unwavering. But with the declining prestige of photographic realism, the degraded political promise of the representation of underdevelopment, and the postcolonial critiques of even Marxist variants of evolutionism, this hegemonic interpretative approach has become a dead end. In other words, the realist lens no longer provides a generative critical framework for the treatment of this production. But if we shift the optic, a different picture emerges, one that could potentially breathe new life into this body of films.

The process genre

The shift I propose would interpret these films through the lens of the process genre.[3] The process genre is a ciné-genre (Gunning 1995) defined by its employment of a definite filmic syntax in which practical activity—processes of doing and making (artisanal and industrial)—are represented as a series of chronological, sequentially ordered steps. The filmic presentation of the stages of production provides an intelligible visual account of the beginning, middle, and, crucially, end result of the process. It is often experienced as filmic how-to manual, even though many films that belong to the process genre were not intended as actual guides to action. The genre has been associated with the early sponsored or indus-trial film, in which companies employ processual syntax to sell commodities (Kessler and Masson 2009). Indeed, a numerically significant number of the films made between 1906 and 1917 were process films. In these films, the steps in the industrial production of com-modities such as biscuits or Christmas crackers or walking sticks are rendered in order: for example, in *The Manufacture of Walking Sticks* (Heron, 1912), the raw material arrives, the sticks are shaped, the cane handles are bent, the sticks are fired in kilns, and finished walk-ing sticks are packaged for export. Intertitles are used to preview the steps (e.g. "Pimento Trees arriving from West Indies," "Shaping of Hazel by Bandsaw"). The final shot is often a tableau depicting a scene of a middle-class family consuming the commodity we have just seen fabricated, as in *A Day in the Life of an English Coal Miner* (Kineto, 1910) (Gunning 1997). But the process genre is a term that can be usefully applied more capaciously to other kinds of cinema from ethnographic films such as *Nanook of the North* (Robert Flaherty, 1922), in which we see Allakariallak engage in a series of processes, including the memora-ble construction of an igloo window made of ice, to art films such as *A Man Escaped* (Robert Bresson, 1956), in which the entire film is devoted to how the man escapes—that is, *how* he constructs a chisel from a spoon, *how* he uses the improvised chisel to dislodge the wood planks of his prison cell door, and *how* he crafts a rope from bed wire and shredded sheets.

Several of the films of the first cycle of the NLAC belong to the process genre. They are organized around productive activity, which is then treated processually. *Aruanda* depicts the fabrication of ceramic housewares in a modern-day quilombo community in a remote part of the Paraíban sertão; *Araya* presents the process of salt mining on the Arayan penin-sula in Venezuela; *Mimbre* is about a wicker craftsman in the Quinta Normal commune of metropolitan Santiago; *Arraial do cabo* treats traditional fishing and fish-salting in a small municipality on the coast of the state of Rio de Janeiro; *Trilla* depicts traditional methods of wheat threshing in the community of Calquinhue in the province of Concepcíon in Chile; *Faena* is about the process of meat production at a Swift slaughterhouse on the outskirts of La Plata; *Láminas del Almahue* presents the making of wheels in the region of Larmahue, Chile; *Ceramiqueros de Traslatierra* is about the fabrication of clay figurines for the tourist market in the small community of Mina Clavero, in the province of Córdoba; *Chircales* depicts the traditional brick-making activities of a family of migrants from the countryside living on the outskirts of Bogotá.

What do I mean when I say that these productive activities are treated processually? Let me give an example. *Aruanda* is a 22-minute film, most of whose screen time is devoted to depicting a series of production processes: the construction of a home from mud and branches, the planting and harvesting of cotton, the craft in ceramics. In rendering these processes, the film employs a peculiar formal syntax—what I call "processual representation." Eight minutes of the film are devoted to showing the making of ceramic housewares—from the preparation of the dirt, to the collecting of well water, to the mixing of the water and the dry dirt, to the formation of the vessels, to their firing, to their transport by donkey on market day. One 30-shot subsection of this process, taking up close to three minutes of screen time, follows the formation of a single jug, beginning with a shot of a woman collecting water from a well and ending with the fully formed prefired jug (Skvirsky 2011) (Figure 8.2). This sequence is a paradigmatic example of processual representation. While the series of steps are not filmed in real time—each shot is about 10 seconds long—the sequence has been filmed and edited in such a way that the spectator can easily assess the progress of the work from one shot to the next. The high-angle close-up shots of disembodied, skilled hands working their magic on the nascent jug's clay coils and the use of form cuts that maintain scalar consistency across shots train the spectator's attention on the micro-drama of jug fabrication rather than—in the more usual ethnographic fashion—on the bodies or lined and sun-kissed faces of the artisans. The sequence engenders the signature effect of the process genre—absorption—as the spectator becomes, first, aroused by the unfolding narrative of the trajectory of matter from mud to vessel, and then sated by seeing the narrative resolve itself in the final display of a well-crafted, finished clay jug.

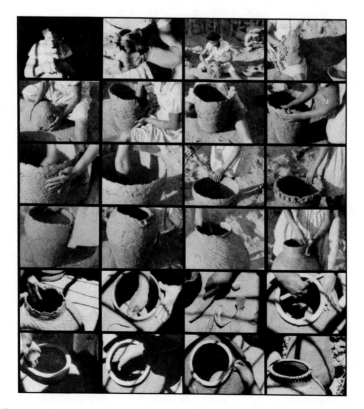

Figure 8.2 Fragment from the ceramic sequence ending with a shot of the completed jug. Each frame enlargement corresponds to a single shot (*Aruanda*, Linduarte Noronha, 1960).

127

To a greater and lesser degree, the deployment of processual representation is a feature of all the films I list above. They are all structured by a process with a definite beginning, middle, and end, and they all present the steps in that process sequentially—with more and fewer digressions—so as to produce a sense of involvement in the logical and causally linked progression of action. *Araya*, for example, traces the steps in the production of salt, from the extraction of rock salt from the lagoon, to the natural drying process, to the piling, to the weighing, to the packaging, to the transport, etc. *Mimbre*, which is more digressive than *Aruanda* or *Araya*, recounts the steps in the artisanal process of crafting life-sized wicker animals, from the preparation of wicker fibers, to the weaving of strands over and under upright stakes, to the bending of stakes in the creation of undulations, to the approximation of bird feathers and fish and horse tails, to the animation of these life-sized farm animals by children putting the figures to use, etc.

While there is much to be said about the Latin American process genre, I would like to restrict myself in this essay to two questions: Why has the processual character of this first wave of NLAC films been unremarked in the historical scholarship? And what is to be gained by focusing on it now? It is worth bearing in mind that from the vantage point of the historical moment that produced the early documentaries of the New Latin American Cinema, their innovation would not have been their processual syntax, for process genre films were the standard for nonfiction films at the time in much of the region. In Chile, for example, by the early 1940s, process films were becoming the dominant mode of nonfiction filmmaking. Between 1941 and 1957 (the year *Mimbre* was made), of the approximately 57 documentaries exhibited nationally, at least 24 could be considered process films and several others incorporated processes (Vega 2006). The process films featured titles such as *La pesca en alta mar* (*Fishing on the High Seas*, Armando Rojas Castro, 1941), *Carbon Chileno* (*Chilean Coal*, Pablo Petrowitsch, 1944), *Salitre* (*Salt Mine*, Pablo Petrowitsch, 1946), *Acero* (*Iron*, Patricio Kaulen, 1950), and *Petroleo chileno* (*Chilean Oil*, Armando Parot and Fernando Balmaceda, 1955). Most of these films were focused on industrial processes and factory production, and in one form or another touted Chilean modernization and industrialization. Almost all of these films were supported by private companies such as Braden Copper and Carbonífera Lota-Schwager and Nestlé, or by public entities such as the Instituto de Cinematografía Educativa de la Universidad de Chile and the Ministry of Agriculture, and many were produced by private publicity companies such as Cinep, and Emelco, an Argentine company. Between 1957 and 1969, process films continued to account for a large proportion of nonfiction production—approximately 25 process films of the 83 exhibited (Vega 2006).

In Brazil, on the other hand, nonfiction film emerges not within the context of sponsored corporate films, as in Chile, but within the context of the state's first film institution, the Instituto Nacional de Cinema Educativo (INCE). Most of the 358 produced by INCE between 1938 and 1967 either by Humberto Mauro (who was director of production) or overseen by him were process films. Processual representation was Mauro's preferred filmic syntax during the first part of his time at INCE. The ideological thrust of the productions of this period—not unlike the Chilean publicity films—cast Brazil as a *modernizing* country with its share of brilliant men—scientists, inventors, statesmen, industrialists, etc. Among these process films, there was a heavy emphasis on scientific and technical films with titles such as *O Telegrapho no Brasil* (*The Telegraph in Brazil*, Humberto Mauro, 1936), *A Screw* (Humberto Mauro, 1936), *Lição Pratica de Taxidermia* (*Practical Lesson in Taxidermy*, Humberto Mauro, 1936), and *Graphite* (Humberto Mauro, 1943). In addition, there were industrial films such as *Toque e Refinação do Ouro* (*Gold Refining*, Humberto Mauro, 1938), *Fabricaçao de ampolas* (*Fabrication of Bulbs*, Humberto Mauro, 1946), and *Lentes oftálmicas—industria* (*Ophthalmic Lenses—Industry*, Humberto Mauro, 1953).

Thus, processual representation was not an innovation in the 1950s in this region. Rather, what was new was the representation of underdevelopment, and as a result *it* became the focus of critical commentary. Perhaps it is only possible to apprehend the processual character of these early NLAC films as a significant feature of their aesthetics and their politics now, today, because processual representation has returned as an organizing aesthetic conceit in global cinema from slow cinema (e.g. Lisandro Alonso, Lav Diaz) to recent observational documentary (e.g. Lucien Castaing-Taylor and Véréna Paravel, Harun Farocki, Sharon Lockhart, Kevin Jerome Everson, Eugenio Polgovsky). The Latin American film context has also seen a resurgence of art cinema process films, some of which even establish an explicit intertextual dialogue with the process films of the first, realist cycle of the NLAC. Recent Latin American process films or films mediating on the process genre include *La Libertad* (*Freedom*, Lisandro Alonso, Argentina, 2001), *Abril Despedaçado* (*Behind the Sun*, Walter Salles, Brazil–France–Switzerland, 2001), *Trópico de Cáncer* (*Tropic of Cancer*, Eugenio Polgovsky, Mexico, 2004), *Los Herederos* (*The Heirs*, Eugenio Polgovsky, Mexico, 2008), *Parque via* (Enrique Rivero, Mexico, 2008), *El Velador* (*The Night Watchman*, Natalia Almada, Mexico, 2012), and *Resonancia* (Mateo Herrera, Ecuador, 2013).

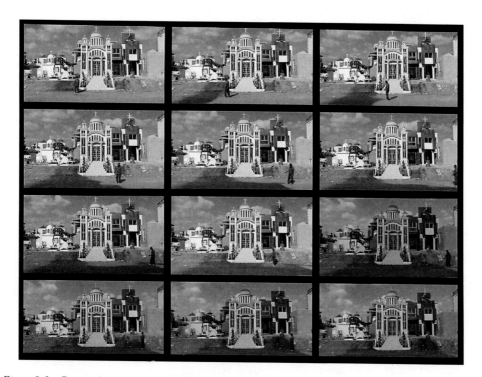

Figure 8.3   Recent Latin American process film. The process of watering the ground in the shape of a perfect square. The shot is five minutes long from beginning to end; it has no cuts. It is represented here with frame enlargements in order to give the reader a sense of the processual character of the shot (*El Velador*, Natalia Almada, 2009).

To take just one example from this list, *El Velador* is an observational documentary about mausoleum construction in a Sinaloa cemetery favored by drug lords. The film contains a processual sequence that has become renowned. In the sequence, which is a single shot that ends the film, the main character, a night watchman, waters the dusty road in front of a baroque mausoleum in the shape of a perfect square. Over the course of the five-minute take, the seemingly menial labor of Martín hosing down the ground is revealed as skilled, technical labor comprised of a set of sequential, logical steps. Meanwhile, the extreme long shot image of Martín with his hose making his way within a large canvas of moistened dirt evokes the labor of the action painter—perhaps like Jackson Pollock—wielding a paintbrush, hunched over a canvas resting on the floor of his studio (Figure 8.3). The process genre is making its presence felt—perhaps not surprising for a historical moment in which the meaning and the character of work seem to be changing with continuing automation, deskilling, and the migration of labor into spheres that were once private. Moreover, the new production is paradoxically mining the conventions of the process genre—one of the seemingly most instrumentalist of genres—in its refusals of the instrumentalism of neoliberal life.

***

Once we adjust our perspective and see the earlier, historical production of the late 1950s and early 1960s through the prism of the process genre, new questions arise about the aesthetics and politics of these films. The questions I have in mind pertain, first, to influence. Besides Italian neorealism and Griersonian documentary, what were the other relevant cinematic influences—both local and international—such as the Institut des hautes etudes cinématorgraphiques (IDHEC) where Margot Benacerraf and Humberto Ríos studied in the 1950s? Second, what is the status of labor in these films? And what is the significance of the emphasis on material popular culture in the films rather than on other, more traditional preoccupations of folklore studies such as storytelling and ritual? Third, to what extent do these films temper the romanticism of the European and U.S. process genre exemplars such as *Nanook of the North* by their concomitant insistence on the materiality of underdevelopment?

Notes

1 The process genre is the subject of my manuscript-in-progress, titled *The Aesthetic of Labor: Cinema and the Process Genre*.
2 I take it as symptomatic that recent scholarship has attempted to recuperate *Tire Dié* and Fernando Birri's Escuela Santa Fe project, at least by responding to the charge of naïve realism. These re-evaluations of Birri's so-called "naïve realism" have comprised the requisite first step in the reassessment of the politics of this production. Still, most of the other films of this period have not experienced a similar reassessment (see Bernini 2004; Aimaretti et al. 2009; Fradinger 2013; Sadek 2013).
3 Tom Gunning coined the term "process film" to refer to early films about the production of commodities. I consider myself to be building on his observations about early cinema by: (1) extending the concept to cover other periods, other film forms, and other media such as pictorial instructions, craft demonstrations, and motion studies; and (2) beginning to theorize it more systematically (see Gunning 1997).

References

Aimaretti, M., Bordigoni, L., and Campo, J. (2009) "La Escuela Documental de Santa Fe: Un Ciempiés Que Camina." In A.L. Lusnich and P. Piedras (eds.), *Una Historia del Cine Político y Social en Argentina: Formas, Estilos, Registros (1896–1969)*. Buenos Aires: Nueva Librería, pp. 359–394.

Bernini, E. (2004) "Politics and the Documentary Film in Argentina during the 1960s." *Journal of Latin American Cultural Studies*, 13(2): 155–170.

Birri, F. (1997) "Cinema and Underdevelopment." In M. Martin (ed.), *New Latin American Cinema, Volume One: Theory, Practices, and Transcontinental Articulations*. Detroit, MI: Wayne State, pp. 86–94.

Birri, F. and Giménez, M.H. (1964) *La escuela documental de Santa Fe*. Santa Fe: Editorial Documento del Instituto de Cinematografía de la U.N.L.

Burton, J. (1990) "Democratizing Documentary: Modes of Address in the New Latin American Cinema, 1958–1972." In J. Burton (ed.), *The Social Documentary in Latin America*. Pittsburgh, PA: University of Pittsburgh Press, pp. 49–84.

Carneiro, R. (2003) *Evolutionism in Cultural Anthropology: A Critical History*. Boulder, CO: Westview Press.

Escobar, A. (2011) *Encountering Development: The Making and Unmaking of the Third World*. Princeton, NJ: Princeton University Press.

Faguet, M. (2009) "Pornomiseria: Or How Not to Make a Documentary Film." *Afterall: A Journal of Art Context and Enquiry*, 21: 5–15.

Fradinger, M. (2013) "Revisiting the Argentine Political Documentary of the Late 1950s and Early 1960s." *Latin American Perspectives*, 40(1): 37–49.

Gunning, T. (1995) "'Those Drawn with a Very Fine Camel's Hair Brush': The Origins of Film Genres." *IRIS-PARIS*, 20: 49–60.

—— (1997) "Before Documentary: Early Nonfiction Films and the 'View' Aesthetic." In D. Hertogs and N. de Klerk (eds.), *Uncharted Territory: Essays on Early Nonfiction Film*. Amsterdam: Stichting Nederlands Filmmuseum, pp. 9–24.

—— (2007) "Moving Away from the Index: Cinema and the Impression of Reality." *Differences*, 18(1): 29–52.

Harris, M. (1968) *The Rise of Anthropological Theory: A History of Theories of Culture*. New York: Crowell.

Johnson, R. (1998) "Documentary Discourses and National Identity: Humberto Mauro's Brasiliana Series and Linduarte Noronha's Aruanda." *Nuevo Texto Crítico*, 11(1): 193–206.

Kessler, F. and Masson, E. (2009) "Layers of Cheese: Generic Overlap in Early Non-Fiction Films on Production Processes." In V. Hediger and P. Vonderau (eds.), *Films That Work: Industrial Film and the Productivity of Media*. Amsterdam: Amsterdam University Press, pp. 75–84.

Lusnich, A.L. (2009) "Introducción: Orígenes y Desarrollo Histórico Del Cine Político y Social En Argentina." in A.L. Lusnich and P. Piedras (eds.), *Una Historiad Del Cine Político y Sociale en Argentina: Formas, Estilos, Registros (1896–1969)*. Buenos Aires: Nueva Librería, pp. 25–41.

Margulies. I. (2003) *Rites of Realism: Essays on Corporeal Cinema*. Durham, NC: Duke University Press.

Martin, M. (1997) *New Latin American Cinema, Volume 1: Theories, Practices, and Transcontinental Articulations*. Detroit, MI: Wayne State University Press.

Mestman, M. (2012) "From Italian Neorealism to New Latin American Cinema." In S. Giovacchini and R. Sklar (eds.), *Global Neorealism: The Transnational History of a Film Style*. Jackson, MI: University Press of Mississippi, pp. 163–177.

Mestman, M. and Ortega, M.L. (2014) "Grierson and Latin America: Encounters, Dialogues and Legacies." In Z. Druick and D. Williams (eds.), *The Grierson Effect: Tracing Documentary's International Movement*. London: British Film Institute, pp. 223–238.

Morgan, D. (2006) "Rethinking Bazin: Ontology and Realism Aesthetics." *Critical Inquiry*, 32(3): 443–481.

Nagib, L. (2011) *World Cinema and the Ethics of Realism*. New York: Continuum.

Nagib, L. and Mello, C. (2009) *Realism and the Audiovisual Media*. Basingstoke: Palgrave Macmillan.

Paranaguá, P.A. (2003) "Orígenes, Evolución y Problemas." in P.A. Paranaguá (ed.), *Cine Documental en América Latina*. Madrid: Catedra, pp. 13–78.

Piedras, P. (2009) "Cine Político y Social: Un Acercamiento a Sus Categorías a Través de Sus Debates y Teorías." In A.L. Lusnich and P. Piedras (eds.), *Una Historia del Cine Político y Sociale En Argentina: Formas, Estilos, Registros (1896–1969)*. Buenos Aires: Nueva Librería, pp. 43–64.

Rocha, G. (1960) "Documentários: Arraial Do Cabo E Aruanda." *Jornal Do Brasil, Suplemento Dominical*, August 6. Available at: www.contracampo.com.br/15/documentarios.htm (accessed June 1, 2017).

Sadek, I. (2013) "Contesting the Optic of (under) Development: Tire Dié and the Emergence of Independent Documentary Cinema in Argentina, ca. 1958." *Social Identities*, 19(3–4): 287–305.

Saldaña-Portillo, M.J. (2003) *The Revolutionary Imagination in the Americas and the Age of Development*. Durham, NC: Duke University Press.

Salinas, C.M., Stange, H.M., and Salinas, S.R. (2008) *Historia del cine experimental en la Universidad de Chile, 1957–1973*. Santiago de Chile: Uqbar Editores.

Schvarzman, S. (2004) *Humberto Mauro e as imagens do Brasil*. São Paulo: Fundação Editora da UNESP.

Skvirsky, S.A. (2011) "Quilombo and Utopia: The Aesthetic of Labor in Linduarte Noronha's Aruanda (1960)." *Journal of Latin American Cultural Studies*, 20(3): 233–260.

Truman, H. (1949) "Inaugural Address." Available at: www.trumanlibrary.org/educ/inaug.htm (accessed June 1, 2017).

Vega, A. (2006) *Itinerario del cine documental chileno, 1900–1990*. Santiago: Centro EAC, Estudios y Artes de la Comunicación.

PART II

Interrogating critical paradigms

9

COSMOPOLITAN NATIONALISMS

Transnational aesthetic negotiations in early Latin American sound cinema

Adrián Pérez Melgosa

Editors' introduction

Film historians have often favored an emphasis on national cinemas as a way to organize historical views of Latin American film development. Whether working on regional surveys (King 1990; Paranaguá 2003) or particular domestic contexts (García Riera in Mexico; Di Núbila in Argentina; Salles Gomes in Brazil), scholars have conveyed the impression of a coherent chronology. In the process, such studies suppress the nuanced complexity of the historical evolution of the cinematic institution and foreground a narrow geopolitical matrix for understanding film production in the region. Films that appear to deviate from a constructed national aesthetic are frequently characterized as outliers, deviations from dominant norms. In attempting to frame a "big picture" view of film development, scholars have often failed to take into account both the social and cultural diversity, as well as the strategies through which particular films address both national and cosmopolitan audiences.

Adrián Pérez Melgosa helps illuminate this suppressed dynamic as he historicizes the contexts of production of the work of producers and filmmakers during the first crucial decade of the sound era. As he argues, some of the notable films of the early sound period need to be seen as efforts to create domestic markets as they also involve a recognition that those same local audiences craved the narrative and cultural attractiveness that foreign films delivered. What was really at stake in the effort to take into account the multifaceted nature of audiences of the period is an appreciation for the deeper struggle to resolve the ideological tension between the defense of national tradition and the fascination with the spectacle of modernity.

In developing this more subtle and nuanced picture of the dynamics of film development in the region, Pérez Melgosa explores the first sound feature films made in Brazil, Mexico, Argentina, and Chile that highlight the cinematic strategies employed to forge a "cosmopolitan nationalist" aesthetic based on the creative use

(continued)

(continued)

of allusion to international films, genre bending, creative cinematography, and the incorporation of local popular traditions. The source of this style, he contends, is traceable to the presence of a group of émigré film technicians who collaborated with local producers and talent, thereby further breaking down the simplistic notion of cultural homogeneity in presumed early national cinema. In unpacking this early instance of transnational stylistics, the chapter further illuminates the methodological processes reflected in Juan Poblete's treatment of Chilean cinema in Chapter 1 and Rielle Navitski's discussion of early national cinema in Mexico and Brazil in Chapter 2, as well as the more theoretical questions of writing film history presented by Laura Podalsky in Chapter 4.

When Latin American films began to talk, they adopted the voice of experience, gravely warning their audiences against the dangers of a "modernity" they depicted as deeply deceptive, morally decadent, and dangerously enthralling to the senses. In these early talkies, dialogue generally praised local traditions and the sheltered spaces of home, village, *barrio*, and nation. At times, we see the protagonists of these films deride foreign fashions, dances, and customs, as in *Acabaram-se os otarios* (*No More Suckers!* Luiz de Barros, 1929), the first Brazilian feature talkie, and in *Los tres berretines* (*The Three Amateurs*, Equipo Lumiton, 1933), the second feature sound film produced in Argentina. At other times, the story warns about the dangers that befall those who contravene tradition and venture into the modern city, a lesson that the protagonist of the first Mexican feature sound film, *Santa* (Antonio Moreno, 1932), experiences in her own body after being betrayed, prostituted in a city bordello, and ravaged by cancer. Yet another group of films depict the prodigal return to a sheltering home space. "After seeing it all, nothing seems better to me," explains Alberto (Alberto Gómez) about his return to his *barrio* in *¡Tango!* (Luis Moglia Barth, 1933), the first Argentine film to use optical sound. A similar feeling motivates the protagonist of the now lost first Chilean talkie, *Norte y Sur* (*North and South*, Jorge Delano, 1934). Here, Hilda Sour portrays a woman who abandons her wealthy husband in the US to return to her first love and her birthplace in Chile. Commenting on this film, the Chilean magazine *Ecran* advanced the hope that talkies would "liberate us from the tyranny of foreign productions" ("Norte y Sur" 1934: 16). Each of these early talkies served as an outlet for their producers' desire to disrupt their audiences' fascination with foreign films and convince them symbolically to follow the example of the protagonists and "return home," to watch their national films.

The images of these first Latin American talkies, however, convey a very different message. The cameras are captivated with the bustle of modern life and the rhythmic motion of the automobiles, streetcars, and other new machines that were rapidly changing the urban landscape. Their characters work in emerging industries as popular singers, tango composers, radio broadcasters, engineers, detectives, and gangsters. Insistently, they appear dressed according to the latest international fashion while dancing in swanky cabarets, attending film theaters, riding mechanical attractions, or watching sports events at massive stadiums. At home, they listen to their radios, talk on the phone, and smoke stylish cigarettes in rooms carefully decorated with fashionable furniture.

This chapter explores the ideological tension articulated in these early talkies between the defense of national tradition and the fascination with the spectacle of modernity.

It reviews the first sound films produced in Brazil, Mexico, Chile, and Argentina, including a detailed discussion of *La fuga* (*The Escape*, Luis Saslavsky, 1937), an aesthetically complex attempt to solve the marketing and ideological riddle at the heart of national cinemas in Latin America: how to create a faithful national audience for domestic talkies out of spectators whose taste and conception of the filmgoing experience had been profoundly shaped by the modernist ethos of Hollywood.

Through his combination of nationalist plots and dialogues with cosmopolitan images that effectively adapted and transformed Hollywood techniques and visual tropes, these early talkies provide evidence of the emergence of what Miriam Bratu Hansen has termed "vernacular modernism." That is, a set of distinctive aesthetic processes through which cultures around the world received Hollywood and European films. Film, Hansen concludes, "is the single most inclusive cultural horizon in which the traumatic effects of modernity were reflected, rejected or disavowed, transmuted or negotiated" (Hansen 1999: 68). While Hansen underscores the creativity stemming from local popular appropriations of the modernist language conceived in the global centers of power, a close analysis of these early Latin American talkies allows us to trace other less noted transnational processes: those centripetal paths through which aesthetic innovations originating in the cosmopolitan environment of early Latin American film studios became reappropriated by Hollywood and eventually by world filmmaking. By analyzing both of these vectors of transnational influences, I will trace the emergence of a set of cultural and industrial practices we could term cosmopolitan nationalism. This complex process began as entrepreneurial cosmopolitan elites from Latin America conceived the idea of replicating locally the studio production system, importing technologies, technicians, and other talent from Hollywood and European film industries. These early sound film studios provided an expansive climate of creative experimentation. Some of the innovations developed there would later find their way to Hollywood and other film industries as directors, cinematographers, and actors continued their itinerant careers.

Reconstructing the early sound period: both sides of the camera

Only a few fragments survive of *Acabaram-se os otarios* and no known copies have survived of *Norte y Sur*. Full copies exist, however, of the first Mexican talkie, *Santa*, and of the first two Argentine feature films to use optical sound, *¡Tango!* and *Los Tres Berretines*. In 1929, *Acabaram-se* follows two gullible immigrants to São Paulo: Bentinho Samambaia (Genésio Arruda) from the provincial interior, and Xixilio Spicafuoco (Tom Bill) just arrived from Italy. After a series of misadventures in which they are cheated out of their money, Bentinho and Xixilio decide to leave the city and its deceitful modernity. As a farewell, they visit a cabaret where guests are dancing Argentine tango and North American black bottom. Offended by the sight of fellow Brazilians dancing to these foreign rhythms, Bentinho scolds the audience by singing "Deixei de ser Otario" ("I am done with being a sucker"). But the "sucker" label he intends as an insult to the audience turns back to the immigrants themselves when the cabaret audience laughs at Bentinho's unrefined appearance and performance. Thus, while the narrative is in sync with the traditionalist views of the two immigrants, the images ridicule them. This ambivalence allows the film to occupy both sides of the tradition/modernity divide and appeal to the complex allegiances of audiences conflicted by nationalist emotions and cosmopolitan tastes.

Santa shows how modernity is more unforgiving with the trespasses of female characters. Moreno's film depicts the transformation of an innocent peasant girl into the most famous prostitute in Mexico City. After being seduced by a deceitful army officer, Santa (Lupita Tovar) is pushed out of her home village. She only finds shelter in a bordello and becomes a prostitute. After a series of lovers and admirers, Santa falls sick with cancer and everyone abandons her. By contrast, the male protagonist in the first Argentine talkie, *¡Tango!*, fares much better in his journey to and back from the urban centers of the world. Alberto succeeds as a tango singer, and enjoys fame and success in Buenos Aires and Paris. Along his journey he has experienced all the luxury of modernity and a succession of deceitful friendships and love betrayals. Unlike Santa, he manages to return to his childhood's "barrio" and reconnect with his first love Tita (Tita Merello). From distinct national perspectives, the plots of these talkies reiterate a single message: the characters' curiosity for modernity will bring them grief, financial ruin, disappointment, and even death.

While opening only two weeks after *¡Tango!*, the second Argentine talkie, *Berretines*, depicts a much more nuanced take on this dilemma. In the film's opening dialogue, Don Manuel captures the fears of film producers when he protests to his customers that "This is a hardware store, not Metro-Goldwyn. Even to buy heaters they seek models from the movies." Some spectators may have heard a fair critique of cinema and modernity in these words. But his characterization as an old man with a Castilian accent adds another layer of meaning, recasting Don Manuel's opinion as a trite complaint from a cranky old immigrant unable to fully understand Argentine culture. *Berretines* reframes the tradition vs. modernity dilemma as a generational and nativist question. In the end, the film shows the immigrant parents embracing their children's fascination with soccer, tango, and film, the three cultural "whims" the film identifies as the trademarks of Argentine national culture. *Norte y Sur* avoids ambiguity in its nationalist perspective through its protagonist's happy return to her home country. Yet the film cannot fully escape the irony at work in the protagonist's forced choosing between economic affluence in the US and her nostalgia for home. In order to critique modernity, the film ends up showing the main sources of its appeal.

These plots recycle a series of commonplaces found in popular genres of the time. Once adapted into films, however, such narrative tropes acquired one more layer of significance as critiques of Hollywood's worldview and of its use of film to celebrate and disseminate modernity worldwide. By punishing those characters who abandon their home and their culture and rewarding the prodigal ones, even when leaving room for irony and ambiguity such as in *Acabaram-se* and *Berretines*, these narratives attempt to interrupt the strong affective attachment their national audiences had developed with Hollywood films and the worldview they projected (Schnitman 1984: 21).

In the Mexican context, Carlos Monsiváis has shown how the country's early talkies both reflected and modeled solutions to the social conflicts arising from Mexico's national reorganization in the aftermath of the Mexican Revolution (Monsiváis 1977: 173–176). Writing about this same period in Argentina, Mathew Karush connects early nationally produced sound film with an existing "deeply melodramatic mass culture" that had already been disseminated through a media cluster formed by radio, popular magazines, and tango songs. This melodramatic mass culture praised the nobility of the working class and denigrated the rich as selfish and immoral, creating what Karush terms a "national culture of class" (Karush 2012: 3). More ambivalent in their moral predicaments, early Brazilian talkies attempted to appeal to both recent immigrants and seasoned urbanites through an ambiguous laughter that simultaneously targets national inadequacies and foreign pretentiousness. This may have instilled in Brazilian audiences the idea that the way to deal with the difficulties presented by modernity was to "laugh them off."

Figure 9.1   Posters for *Acabaram-se os otarios* (Luiz da Silva, 1929) and *¡Tango!* (Luis Moglia Barth, 1933) convey these films' intention to bridge national and cosmopolitan cultures.

There is an essential contradiction in the way these films mix traditional, folkloric, and romantic nation-building narrative tropes with images, sounds, and even conditions of production and processes of reception intimately aligned with modernity. "Populist" messages were embedded within, and marketed along with, a cosmopolitan discourse of taste, highlighting the appeals of modernity and of the media that disseminated it. Cosmopolitan tastes and intermedial networks of influence were not mere contributors to the emergence of the Latin American sound-film industry. Rather, they represented the very environment in which studios, technicians, talent, and film techniques emerged. Clearly traceable in the biographies and ideology of the people who made these early sound films, cosmopolitanism left its mark on the visual and sound techniques through which these films were composed.

Cosmopolitanism behind the camera: transnational aesthetic flows

As theoretical categories, both cosmopolitanism and transnationalism have raised heated debates among critics not only within historical discussions of national identity, but also as part of current debates about globalization and universalism. The term cosmopolitan, meaning "at home in the world," simultaneously connotes fluid border crossings and universalist ambitions, an ambiguity that stands at the center of debates about this term. Within the Latin American context, defenders of historic cosmopolitanism, such as Gonzalo Aguilar (2014), define the cosmopolitan subject as the necessary mediator between center and periphery, and between repertoire and innovation. By contrast, detractors of cosmopolitanism such as Timothy Brennan, who articulates his critique within an inter-American context, denounce it as part of a constellation of relativist theoretical terms such as transnationalism, hybridity, and multiculturalism, which he sees as forming the ideological global arm of the American empire (Brennan 1997: 109, 125).

In early Latin American talkies, cosmopolitanism is a category born out of a very specific historical context, especially in regard to our understanding of the nature of local audiences. Their cinematic taste had been educated by the visual codes and style of foreign films, and they craved technical sophistication, visual exoticism, and novelty. Producers found in the importation of talent the most efficient and timely way to bring their films to stand technically on par with those from abroad. Cosmopolitanism, both from world-traveling elites and from migrants, presented itself as the answer to the technical and aesthetic portion of the riddle.

To study the cosmopolitanism surrounding these early talkies requires a transnational analytical perspective. If read through a nation-centric lens, these films become disconnected entities, too heterogeneous in their aesthetics and themes. Chronological proximity appears as the only reason to group them together. From this point of view, the song performances in *Acabaram-se* and *¡Tango!*, for example, become valuable only as testimonies of a seminal time in Brazilian and Argentine popular music, while their plots are dismissed as either inconsequential comedy or trite melodrama. Similarly, *Santa* and *Los tres berretines*, two films that make a special effort to display the public spaces of modernity, become from this perspective successful attempts to project Mexico City and Buenos Aires onto the list of modern world cities (Poppe 2009: 53). The technical innovations introduced by Delano in *Norte y sur*, such as the much commented scene where he superimposed the image of a fighting cock upon the figure of a man dancing *cueca* (Chile's national dance), or his dramatic use of the sounds of a bouncing punching ball to naturalize the transition from a scene of boxing onto one of a moving train, become evidence of the creative talent of the director (Godoy Quezada 1966: 161). On the other extreme, a global perspective collapses these films into an undifferentiated group of peripheral derivatives, unpolished copies of their Hollywood and European counterparts. This is the perspective Monsiváis adopts to define Latin American films in the 1930s and 1940s as displaying "a mix of incoherent plots and excess of songs" (Monsiváis 2010: 65). It is also the perspective that informs Octavio Getino's characterization of all 1930s Argentine films as sharing in one industrial and ideological project with those cinemas they were in competition with (Getino 2005: 28).

Adopting a transnational mode of reading, aiming our critical lens at that space that Kathleen Newman has defined as lying "above the national but beneath the global," opens up the in-between spaces in which these films were produced, which remain invisible both to the discourses of national specificity and of global uniformity (Newman 2010: 11). It is in these spaces in which we can explore "how motion pictures register, at the formal level of narrative, broad and long-term social transformations, that is, changes in the capitalist world economy" (p. 9). Some existing readings of the first two Argentine talkies hint in this direction, but rather than developing them beyond the nation, end up using their insights to further build a national cinematic perspective. When, for example, Karush observes the emergence of a "culture of class" in early radio and sound-film, he sees it as a local adaptation of the trends towards melodrama and populism that dominate the transnational marketplace (Karush 2012: 42). Similar to Hansen's perspective in "vernacular modernism," Karush's argument uses the transnational as an origin to depict national adaptations and explain nationalistic politics. Other critics have complicated this nationalist argument by suggesting that one of the goals of early Argentine sound films was "to export Buenos Aires as the principal capital of the Spanish speaking world" (Posadas et al. 2005: 12). Here, the reasoning travels from Buenos Aires to a transnational Hispanic space, and eventually back to construct nationalist pride.

Both of these arguments gain support from Beatriz Sarlo's idea of peripheral modernity in regard to the Argentine avant-garde of the 1920s and 1930s, a modernity characterized by a culture of "mixing" native and imported material goods and symbolic practices (Sarlo 2003: 28). This idea may be easily extended to describe Brazilian, Mexican, and Chilean contexts. Looking at these films through a transnational lens, however, allows us to see how the cluster of cosmopolitan influences that made early sound films possible were simultaneously nationalistic, cosmopolitan, and transnational.

While it is impossible to reconstruct how producers, filmmakers, and audiences lived these negotiations of the local with the transnational, traces of this process may be elicited from existing archival information, and, most importantly, from the films themselves. The fragmentary information we have about the people who made possible *Acabaram-se* already points toward the cosmopolitan identity of director Luiz de Barros. Before directing, he had studied art in Europe and worked as an intern at the Gaumont Studios in Paris. The Syncrocinex system employed in this film, hailed as Brazil's autochthonous film-sound technology, also has transnational origins. It was built in São Paulo at the workshop of Pathé distributor Gustavo Zieglitz by modifying imported equipment (Freire 2013: 108).

We know significantly more about the group of producers who collaborated to make *Santa*. They were an ideologically heterogeneous sampling from the Mexican cosmopolitan upper class, who in 1932 joined their financial and cultural capital to form the Compañía Nacional Productora de Películas (CNPP). Leading the group was Juan de la Cruz Alarcón, a Spanish-born entrepreneur who pioneered distribution of Hollywood and European films in Ciudad Juárez, El Paso, and other towns along the US–Mexico border. He associated with Gustavo Sáenz de Sicilia, a silent film director and former Mexican foreign service officer, and they enlisted the help of Carlos Noriega Hope, a journalist and avant-garde writer who had worked between 1919 and 1930 as a Hollywood reporter for the Mexican newspaper *El Universal*. At first sight, their political views demarcate mutually conflicting territories. Cruz Alarcón was a supporter of the Mexican Revolution and of President Madero, while Sáenz de Silicia was a right-wing aristocrat activist who had co-founded the Mexican Fascist Party in 1922. Noriega Hope was an intellectual actively promoting the aesthetic avant-garde of the *Estridentista* artist collective, which sought to transfer revolutionary ideals to literature, painting, and other arts. From different positions, they shared a belief on the need to develop and promote nationalism: Alarcón saw it as the way to expand his business, Sáenz de Sicilia as a way to advance his fascist political vision, and Noriega Hope as a source of artistic inspiration. The core of *Santa*'s cast and crew (from Spanish-born director Antonio Moreno, through Mexican-born stars Lupita Tovar and Donald Reed [née Ernesto Avila Guillén], to assistant director Ramón Peón from Cuba) also had extensive Hollywood experience, having worked in Fox and Paramount's Spanish-language talkies

(Kohner 2011: 169–188). Moreno's direction in *Santa* shows the influence of D.W. Griffith and Josef von Sternberg, with whom he had worked as leading actor.

Traces of these transnational experiences became embedded within several elements of *Santa*'s aesthetics and ideology. Marvin D'Lugo finds the earliest example of the deployment of film music to articulate a communal transnational Hispanic identity in the amalgam of bolero, foxtrot, tango, and flamenco songs that make up its soundtrack (D'Lugo 2010: 181). One of the most intriguing aspects of D'Lugo's theorization is his tracing the origins of this trope to the use of music in a second wave of Hollywood's *films Hispanos*. These films employed music strategically to disguise the jumble of accents stemming from the multinational casts of Hollywood and Joinville Spanish productions (D'Lugo 2010: 166–168). The transnational Hispanic soundscape of early Latin American sound films, it turns out, has a transnational Anglo-Latino origin. Frequently, this perception of *Santa* as a trans-Hispanic production has led critics to describe it reductively as borrowing its narrative and compositional technique from Spanish silent film with a peppering of technical influences from Hollywood filmmaking of the time (Hershfield and Maciel 1999: 19). Closer analysis shows a much more complex network of allusions, repurposing, and reappropriations of motifs and techniques from films from around the world. Early in the film, we see a subtle homage to the Lumiére Brothers in a scene that shows workers coming out of a paper mill. Soon after, *Santa* alludes and reworks another key scene in the history of cinema from Griffith's *The Birth of a Nation* (1915), the controversial sequence in which Gus (Walter Long), a black soldier, follows a white woman, Flora Cameron (Mae Marsh) into the woods and tries to seduce her. Like Flora, Santa appears strolling happily in a bucolic forest that reflects her innocence and beauty: both embrace trees, see crystalline streams, and run into playful animals. Each is pursued by a soldier whose point of view is adopted by the camera. In Griffith's movie, race is the origin of dramatic tension. Fearing that the soldier will rape her, Flora jumps off a rocky cliff. *Santa* relocates the tension to the struggle between modernity and tradition, as she falls in love with her pursuer and is betrayed by the soldier, precipitating her "fall" into prostitution. A visual metaphor foreshadows the future sufferings of the protagonist: as the soldiers ride away, the close-up shot lingers on their horses' hooves as they repeatedly trample a bunch of flowers. Cinematically, this montage scene parallels one in Eisenstein's *¡Qué viva México!* (*Thunder over Mexico*, 1931), in which a group of horsemen trample the heads of three workers.

Santa's cinematography also converses with Dziga Vertov's *Man with a Movie Camera* (USSR, 1929) in the scene that introduces Mexico City. A turning wheel of fortune at the center of the screen dissolves to a moving Ferris wheel first, and later to a circling merry-go-round, to finally land on a Mexican hat. As the camera moves away, we see the hat among many others hanging from a market stall. In the context of Santa's misfortunes, Vertov's analogical montage, conceived to celebrate modern life, turns into a moralizing critique of the ups and downs of fortune that the images evoke. Influences of German expressionism appear when Santa seeks shelter in a church, during her first night in the city. A high-angle shot of a massive wooden Christ enveloped in darkness acquires tones of supernatural judgment, and a single lamp creates a triangle of light pointing to the center of the screen while Santa's diminutive body enters the frame from the darkness on the bottom left and never advances past the lower half of the screen. The emphasis on emotion and spirituality characteristic of expressionism are employed here to underline the real and merciless power of the institution of the Church. *Santa*, the most Mexican of films, is therefore the transnational meeting point of a wide swath of world film influences, and a laboratory of

Figure 9.2 This sequence of shots from *Santa* (Antonio Moreno, 1932) depicts, through analogical montage, the protagonist's feeling of vertigo and disorientation upon her arrival in the big city.

developing talent and technicians that would then transfer their formative experience back to Hollywood and to other Latin American film industries.

In Argentina, the significant array of cosmopolitan, international, and intermedial influences that led to the emergence of sound-film during the early 1930s are well documented. As Ana López has argued, "the mid-1930s, as radio became a mass-medium, and cinema begun to speak in Spanish and Portuguese—was a profoundly intermedial moment with broad transformative consequences" (López 2014: 139). Critical literature, however, consistently diminishes extra-national and non-cinematic influences as colorful anecdotes to an otherwise solidly national and media-specific landscape. The Argentine case clearly shows how central these connections were. The four upper-class entrepreneurs that founded the Lumiton studios in 1933—Enrique Susini, Miguel Mújica, César Guerrico, and Luis Carranza—had lived and been educated in Europe and the United States. In 1920, they collaborated in producing the country's first radio broadcasting, and would later become the founders of one of its first phone companies. In fact, they funded Lumiton by reinvesting the capital they obtained by selling their early radio and telephone companies (Ulanovsky et al. 1997: 19–25).

Critical to the development of local film crews was the arrival in Argentina of a group of emigré film pioneers. Many of them further developed their film technique while in Argentina and would take these lessons with them as they moved to other countries and other cinemas: people such as Hungarian-born cinematographer John Alton, who was instrumental in the opening of the Lumiton studios and later worked for Argentina Sono Film, German-born cinematographer Gerald Huttula (frequently credited as Gerardo Huttula), who worked alongside Alton for a time and would return to Germany in the late 1930s, and film directors Catrano Catrani and his wife Vlasta Lah, both of whom studied at the Centro de Cinematografía Esperimentale di Roma before coming to Argentina in 1937 to start the San Miguel Studios (Trelles Plazaola 1989).

Particularly significant is the role of John Alton, who emigrated to the US in 1919, and in 1932 directed for Paramount the camera department in Joinville (Paris). Alton's own account of his entrance into the Argentine film industry illustrates the ease with which cosmopolitan film pioneers came to the country: "I met some Argentine million-aires who were planning to build a studio in Argentina. They asked me to come design it for them, so I asked for one-year leave-of-absence from Joinville. I went to Argentina, we built a studio, and I made one film" (Alton 1995: xiii). This film was *Los tres ber-retines*. Alton, a flamboyant individual, continues, "I did everything. They didn't know what a prop man was, so I had to show them. I had to set up the lab" (p. xiii). Alton also seems to have learned new tricks in Argentina. Through his work in the 20-some films he directed, photographed, and/or illuminated there, Alton developed many of the mood lighting conventions that later, upon his return to Hollywood in 1939, would became his signature techniques, and the foundation of the cinematography of film noir. Through the almost seven years (1932–1939) he spent working at both Lumiton and Argentina Sono-Film studios, he trained and became a model for many of the country's first cinema-tographers. These sound-film studios were crossroads of transnational and intermedial networks of capital and technologies. Yet they also developed within a particularly nationalistic political environment in Argentina, at a time when a right-wing alliance between conservative and new nationalists implemented a mixture of traditionalist and fascist-inspired policies.

The second talkie released in Argentina, *Los tres berretines*, relied on comedy, melo-drama, and a skillful camera style to negotiate this same dilemma. The newly arrived John Alton was part of the Lumiton team credited for directing the film. With this in mind, we can imagine the cosmopolitan nationalism emerging in this film as the result of behind-the-camera negotiations between Alton's technical savvy, his and the producer's cosmopolitan experiences, and the nationalist rationale that justified the emergence of the new studios. Like the other early talkies, the film borrows from a variety of international film sources. The credit scene introduces Buenos Aires as a modern, vibrant metropolis through a succession of shots of buildings, crowded streets, policemen directing traffic, and streetcars advancing towards the audience. The editing choreographs them into a complex dance using techniques developed in the "city symphony" genre in films such as *Berlin: Symphony of a Great City* (Walter Ruttmann, 1927). The film complicates the represen-tation of the world of soccer, tango, and cinema by presenting them not only as cultural manifestations, but also as industrial products: the camera enters into the "backstage" spaces where the characters toil to compose and market a tango song, draw the plans for a soccer stadium, train and negotiate their contracts, and audiences discuss the films they watch. These elements—the borrowings from foreign film genres, techniques, and films, together with the emphasis on locating the film on spaces of production—performatively communicate the same process of "adaptation" to the modern through "making it work to your advantage" that Don Manuel experiences throughout the film.

Figure 9.3   Right column: four frames from *Los tres berretines* (1933) depicting Buenos Aires'
city life. Left column: four frames from *Berlin: Symphony of a Great City* (Walter
Ruttmann, 1927).

La fuga: between cosmopolitan crime and rural patriotism

Luis Saslavsky's *La fuga* (*The Escape*, 1937) illustrates the level of formal complexity and
aesthetic sophistication that some directors had achieved in their efforts to balance the tensions between cosmopolitan aspirations and nationalistic sentiment in their work. *La fuga*
opened at a time when, as Jorge Luis Borges summed it up in his review of Saslavsky's film,
"nobody wanted to see national films" (Aguilar and Jelicié 2010: 43). The plot dramatizes
this struggle between cosmopolitan and national allegiances through the story of a cynical
dapper Buenos Aires gangster, Daniel Benítez (Santiago Arrieta), who, fleeing from the
police, ends up impersonating a school teacher in the small traditional town of Puerto
Esperanza, on the Argentine border with Paraguay. Its production, however, showed how
intricately connected were transnational and national elements in this film. *La fuga* was the
first release of Pampa Film, a local subsidiary of Warner Bros. The camerawork is credited to
Gerardo Huttula, a cinematographer trained in film advertising and animation in his native
Germany. While uncredited, by his own testimony John Alton was responsible for much of
the lighting, cinematography, and *mise en scène* work (Alton 1995: xvi).

Warner's representatives compelled Saslavsky to change the film's original title, *Dream
of a New Life*, to *La fuga*. The resonances of crime and marginality in the final title erased

the romantic references to migration and redemption implicit in the original. The film itself evidences other transnational influences. Its opening follows the conventions of a gangster film: credit titles flow over a dimly lit interior scene showing a mysterious man in a fedora and raincoat selling some jewels. Outside, three men wait on a motorboat ready to depart. Further away, four policemen hide behind a group of trees. As the man in the fedora, later identified as Benítez, exits the small shack, a shoot-out ensues. Leaving his hat on a bush as a decoy, the gangster escapes. Robles (Francisco Petrone), a hard-nosed and scrupulously honest detective identifies Benítez by his hat, but has to give up the chase. Both men are in love with Cora Moreno (Tita Merello), a sophisticated and successful cabaret singer who loves and protects Benítez, but is officially Robles's fiancé.

When Daniel flees Buenos Aires and arrives in Puerto Esperanza, the film abandons its gangster film style and becomes a mellower melodrama reminiscent of a comic *sainete*. The action moves among scenes of family meals, school lessons, and daily farmer's chores. As the somber mood of the opening scenes and their atmosphere of immorality and vice disappear, so does the high-contrast light as the scenes fill with broad daylight. Gradually, Daniel grows more appreciative of the mission of a schoolteacher and of the simple lifestyle of the countryside. By the time Robles finally catches up with him, the gangster has fully embraced his new way of life, has developed deep affection for his students, and fallen in love with Rosita (Niní Gambier), the naïve, practically minded, and kind-hearted daughter of his genuinely patriotic host family. This genre transformation from gangster film to romantic comic melodrama completes the film's narrative journey from cosmopolitanism to nationalism. The aesthetic journey is not as linear, however, and complicates this clean progression of the exemplary national redemption narrative. The gangster scenes that introduce and end the film are more than a mere cosmopolitan wrapping. Saslavsky and his crew wanted to construct an original narrative and visual style by utilizing a wide repertoire of cinematic rhetorical tools from a variety of sources.

Other creative genre transformations and transgressions abound in the film. The little hideout where Daniel's gang retains Sr. Pallerjac (Augusto Codecá), the actual teacher they expected in Puerto Esperanza, becomes a very peculiar schoolroom. Here, the kidnapped teacher educates his gangster captors and treats them as naughty schoolchildren, using his ruler against their guns to impose discipline. In the countryside, a group of comedic scenes drawn from the *sainete* tradition focusing on characters feigning cosmopolitans taste while secretly craving things socially considered vulgar: once the school principal relents from dipping bread in her coffee in pubic but eagerly dunks it when alone. The most elaborated of these comedic devaluations of cosmopolitan aspirations appears in a sequence that directly quotes Charles Chaplin's *The Pilgrim* (1923), in which an escaped inmate who remains at large by impersonating a preacher gets stuck to a sheet of flypaper. Saslavsky, who acknowledged Chaplin as a source, gets Daniel to sit on the sticky paper at the house of the richest family in Puerto Escondido. Rosita and the housemaid rescue him. Here, the visual metaphor goes well beyond the significance of the scene in Chaplin's film, showing the sophisticated city predator trapped in the charming simplicity of the countryside.

The intermedial context in which Argentine sound cinema developed takes front stage in Saslavsky's film. Nightly, a live radio broadcast of Coral's performance at the Olimpo cabaret travels through the airwaves from from Buenos Aires to Puerto Esperanza. The film builds on its spectator's familiarity with the radio experience to naturalize its transitions between modern and traditional cultures, cosmopolitan and nationalistic views, and between the gangster and melodrama genres. The radio as a trope acquires further symbolic strength by becoming a narrative-bound motif: Coral's tango songs contain coded messages to Daniel about the progress of Robles' investigation. But foregrounding the visual presence of the radio and its seductive modernity along with the film's contrasting aesthetics implicitly contains an affirmation of, and admiration for, cosmopolitanism. The complex and seductive depiction of urban scenes on highly polished high-contrast cinematography, probably one of Alton's contributions, casts an aura of seductive mystery over the actors, their words, actions, and the spaces where they live. The *mise en scène* surrounding urban characters consists of multilayered arrangements of luxurious objects illuminated by a single light source. Simple devices are used to maximum effect: a lampshade foregrounded to occupy one full quarter of the frame provides a sense of depth to the actors' presence on screen. Various arrangements of peculiarly designed tables, chairs, staircases, lamps, and mirrors manage to convey in one shot the multiple and contradictory allegiances of each character.

These elements, together with mood lighting and multilayered composition techniques, would later become specifically associated with John Alton's contribution to the film noir style during his Hollywood career. They help create film noir's signature paradox: the ability to denounce the corruption of a world that has lost a sense of justice and to represent that same world as an aesthetically and intellectually fascinating universe. *La fuga* anticipates this paradox as it reserves its more aesthetically appealing scenes for the Buenos Aires cosmopolitan nightlife, a world that the narrative morally condemns. Thus, when one of Daniel's associates, uncertain about whether Cora is working for the gangsters or the police, shoots her as she sings her nightly tango/message, we cannot help but see in her a beautiful sacrificial victim who might be morally compromised but intensely appealing in her passionate elegance. The cosmopolitan nationalism repertoire of *La fuga* includes

Figure 9.4 *La fuga* (Luis Saslavsky, 1937). John Alton experiments here with venetian blind lighting to create an atmosphere of moral tension.

genre mixing, resignification of Hollywood motifs, creative use of sharply differentiated cinematography, thematic inclusion of intermediality, and creative repurposing of Hollywood scenes. With its complex set of cinematic tools, *La fuga* manages to compartmentalize taste and ideology as if they belonged to different spheres of identity, implying that, as in the film, it was possible to construct a strong nationalist character while participating in a cosmopolitan sphere of taste.

Conclusion

In their search to bridge the gap between the nationalist imperative to create domestic markets and audiences, and the cosmopolitan tastes of filmgoers and producers, early Latin American talkies developed a cosmopolitan nationalist aesthetic: a dynamic process that developed an evermore complex and creative engagement with Hollywood and European films. Key to this process were a group of technicians, directors, and talent that brought their expertise to the newly created sound studios in Argentina, Mexico, Brazil, and Chile, and who also enjoyed broad creative freedom to experiment with new techniques and narrative modes. As they returned to work in Europe and Hollywood, many of the cinematic tropes they explored in their Latin American films would become the seeds for styles such as film noir, and would reinvigorate genres such as melodrama.

References

Aguilar, G. (2014) "Cosmopolitanism in the Era of Globalization." *Mardulce Magazine: Revista de Mardulce Editora*, 6. Available at: www.mardulceeditora.com.ar/magazine/articulo.php?id=36&n=6 (accessed May 2, 2016).

Aguilar, G. and Jelicié, E. (2010) *Borges va al cine*. Buenos Aires: Libraria.

Alton, J. (1995) *Painting with Light*. Berkeley, CA: University of California Press.

Brennan, T. (1997) *At Home in the World: Cosmopolitanism Now*. Cambridge, MA: Harvard University Press.

D'Lugo, M. (2010). "Aural Identity, Genealogies of Sound Technologies, and Hispanic Transnationality in Screen." In N. Durovicova and K. Newman (eds.), *World Cinema: Transnational Perspectives*. New York: Routledge, pp. 160–185.

Freire, R. de L. (2013) "*Acabaramse os otários*: Compreendo o primer longa-metragem sonoro brasileiro." *Rebecca: Revista brasileira de estudos de cinema e audiovisual*, 2(3): 104–128.

Getino, O. (2005) *Cine argentino: entre lo posible y lo deseable*. Buenos Aires: Fundación CICCUS.

Godoy Quezada, M. (1966) *Historia del cine chileno: 1902–1966*. Santiago de Chile: Fantasía.

Hansen, M. (1999) "The Mass Production of the Senses: Cinema as 'Vernacular Modernism'." *Modernism/Modernity*, 6(2): 59–77.

Hershfield, J. and Maciel, D.R. (1999) *Mexico's Cinema: A Century of Film and Filmmakers*. Oxford: Scholarly Resources Books.

Karush, M.B. (2012) *Culture of Class: Radio and Cinema in the Making of a Divided Argentina 1920–1946*. Durham, NC: Duke University Press.

King, J. (1990) *Magical Reels: A History of Cinema in Latin America*. London: Verso.

Kohner, P. (2011) *Lupita Tovar: "The Sweethart of Mexico."* Bloomington, IN: Xlibris.

López, A. (2014) "Calling for Inter-Mediality: Latin American Mediascapes." *Cinema Journal*, 54(1): 135–141.

Monsiváis, C. (1977) *Amor perdido*. Mexico City: ERA.

—— (2010) *Aires de familia: Cultura y sociedad en América Latina*. Barcelona: Anagrama.

Newman, K. (2010) "Notes on Transnational Film Theory: Decentered Subjectivity, Decentered Capitalism." In N. Durovicová and K. Newman (eds.), *World Cinema: Transnational Perspectives*. London/New York: Routledge, pp. 3–11.

"Norte y Sur: Primer exponente de la nueva cinematografía chilena" (1934) *Ecran* (Chile), 5(174): 16.

Paranaguá, P.A. (2003) *Tradición y modernidad en el cine de América Latina*. Madrid: Fondo de Cultura Económica Española.

Poppe, N. (2009) "Sightseeing Buenos Aires in the Early Argentine Sound Film *Los tres berretines*." *Journal of Cultural Geography*, 26(1): 49–69.

Posadas, A., Landro, M., and Speroni, M. (2005) *Cine Sonoro Argentino 1933–43, Vol. 1*. Buenos Aires: El Calafate.

Sarlo, B. (2003) *Una modernidad periférica: Buenos Aires 1920–1930*. Buenos Aires: Ediciones Nueva Visión.

Schnitman, J. (1984) *Film Industries of Latin America: Dependency and Development*. Norwood, NJ: Ablex.

Trelles Plazaola, L. (1989) *South American Cinema/Cine De America Del Sur: Dictionary of Film Makers*. Río Piedras: Editorial de la Universidad de Puerto Rico.

Ulanovsky, C., Panno, J., Merkin, M., and Tijman, G. (1997) *Días de radio: historia de la radio argentina*. Buenos Aires: Espasa Calpe.

Further reading

Areco, M. and Lizama, P. (2015) *Biografía y textualidades, naturaleza y subjetividad: Ensayos sobre la obra de María Luisa Bombal*. Santiago: Universidad Católica de Chile.

Collier, S. (1988) "Carlos Gardel and the Cinema." In J. King and N. Torrents (eds.), *The Garden of the Forking Paths: Argentine Cinema*. London: British Film Institute, pp. 15–30.

Dolkart, R.H. (1997). "The Right in the Década Infame: 1930–43." In S. McGee Deutsch and R.H. Dolkart (eds.), *The Argentine Right: Its History and Intellectual Origins, 1910 to the Present*. Lanham, MD: SR Books, pp. 65–98.

Elena, A. and Díaz López, M. (2006) *The Cinema of Latin America*. London: Wallflower Press.

España, C. (1984) *Medio siglo de cine: Argentina Sono Film. S.A.C.I.* Buenos Aires: Heraldo del cine.

Ferreira, F. (1995) *Luz, cámara, memoria. Una historia social del cine argentino*. Buenos Aires: Corregidor.

Gopalan, L. (2002) *A Cinema of Interruptions: Action Genres in Contemporary Indian Cinema*. London: British Film Institute.

Jarvinen, L. (2012) *The Rise of Spanish-Language Filmmaking: Out from Hollywood's Shadow, 1929–39*. New Brunswick, NJ: Rutgers University Press.

López, A. (1985) "A Short History of Latin American Film Histories." *Journal of Film and Video*, 37(1): 55–69.

López, A. and Tierney, D. (eds.) (2014) "In Focus: Latin American Film Research in the Twenty First Century." *Cinema Journal*, 54(1): 108–142.

Lusnich, A. L. (2005) *Civilización y barbarie en el cine argentino y latinoamericano*. Buenos Aires: Editorial Biblos.

Poppe, N. (2014) "Approaching the (Trans)National in Criticism of Early Latin American Film." *Cinema Journal*, 54(1): 115–120.

Shaw, L. and Dennison, S. (2007) *Brazilian National Cinema*. London/New York: Routledge.

10

GENRE FILMS THEN AND NOW

Gerard Dapena

Editors' introduction

Critical appreciation of the social and political significance of genre films in Latin America has been slow in coming. While functioning for decades as a staple of film industries across the region, musicals, comedies, melodramas, westerns, and other formula films were dismissed by critics and scholars as merely low-grade mimicry of Hollywood styles and narratives. The earliest modification of that attitude came about in the later 1960s as European scholars, expanding the elite auteurist canon, "discovered" the subversive strategies that shaped Luis Buñuel's aesthetic assault on Mexican potboilers of the 1940s and 1950s. Critics derided such films as "*churros*," a name that likened them to fried crullers, since they were quick and cheap films that were eagerly consumed by popular audiences. His *anti-churros* were metaphorically hard to digest and aimed at subverting the audience's passivity to genres. It was not until the 1990s, however, that studies in Latin American melodrama as a subversive feminist discourse attracted new critical scrutiny and inspired a new wave of critical scholarship on popular cinema in the region.

In this chapter, Gerard Dapena expands in detail the argument first presented by Victoria Ruétalo and Dolores Tierney in their groundbreaking collection, *Latsploitation* (2012), which focused on the uses of genre as a marketing tool for distributors and exhibitors, a framework for artistic innovation, and finally a purveyor of ideology and sociopolitical commentary. Continuing that line of development, Dapena identifies the inventive hybridity of filmmakers who began mixing genres in ways that cumulatively have kept genre films alive and flourishing despite changes in technology and even audience tastes. This creative reworking of genre has thus allowed cinema from the region to develop a commercial and even artistic presence overseas. The chapter puts special emphasis on two genres in particular that have become imbued with a newfound social, artistic, and even political vitality: the western, perhaps the quintessential Hollywood genre, which has been translated into various national contexts (from *ranchero* films in Mexico to *cangaceiro* films in Brazil and *gaucho* films in

Argentina), and the horror genre, once arguably the most reviled of popular genres. The horror genre, in fact, has become a kind of aspirational model for filmmakers seeking strong box-office appeal in home markets and artistic recognition and audiences at international festivals.

At one time, genre in film was a category used to describe movies made on the cheap, following formulaic scripts, and lacking in any artistic or authorial vision. Genre would later become a way to describe and group films based on "repeated plot motifs, recurrent image patterns, standardized narrative configurations and predictable reception conventions" (Altman 1997: 277). Nowadays, the concept has been broadened, so that genre refers not only to an industrial practice predicated upon the interplay of standardized repetition and differentiation, but also encompasses multiple functions as a critical category: a marketing tool for distributors and exhibitors; a framework for artistic innovation; a purveyor of ideology and sociopolitical commentary; and finally as a tacit contract between audiences and the film industry (Langford 2005: 2). All of these critical concepts can be applied to the study of Latin American genre cinema. This chapter presents an overview of recent trends shaping the production and worldwide exhibition of Latin American genres films, emphasizing the ways earlier genre formations in Latin America have evolved from what film historians had long viewed as the mimicry of Hollywood styles and narratives of the early sound period.

Since we cannot speak properly of film industries in most of Latin America, film genres here originated and evolved in a haphazard manner. Yet this ad hoc approach to production allowed for a greater margin of inventiveness when it came to mixing conventions from different genres, engendering movies that were porous and fluid in generic terms. Although Hollywood's studios did release films combining codes from different genres, Latin America's classic cinema often exhibits an exceptional degree of genre hybridity. The beloved *Nosotros los pobres* (*We the Poor*, Ismael Rodríguez, Mexico, 1948), for instance, transitions almost seamlessly from humor to pathos to the joy of song and dance, while *Carnaval no fogo* (*Carnival in Fire*, Walter Macedo, Brazil, 1949), a typical *chanchada*, weaves together humor, romance, suspense, and several musical numbers in a story about gangsters plotting a heist during Rio's carnival. This cinematic hybridity mirrors such characteristic transculturation processes of Latin America's *criollo* culture as *mestizaje*, syncretism, baroque multiplicity, and carnivalesque strategies of inversion and mockery (Kantaris and O'Bryen 2013: 10).

Yet while the popularity of film genres arriving from Europe and Hollywood among Latin American audiences compelled producers, screenwriters, and directors to emulate them, they nevertheless sought to adapt these genres to each national context through the incorporation of locally inflected cultural signs of identity. A brief look at how Latin American filmmakers reworked the Western and translated it into various national contexts illustrates this transculturation of genre conventions. Northern Mexico's affinities to the American Southwest made the western a natural genre to exploit and adapt; films such as *Los Hermanos del Hierro* (*My Son, the Hero*, Ismael Rodríguez, 1961) showcased the region's cultural identity. Although Mexican westerns rarely escaped their B-movie status, in the 1960s director Alberto Mariscal brought an auteur-like, personal vision to the genre that fused Mexican themes with the hyperbolic visual style popularized by Sergio Leone's Eurowesterns. Argentine films such as *Pampa bárbara* (*Savage Pampa*, Hugo Fregonese, 1945) and *El último perro* (*The Last Dog*, Lucas Demare, 1956) took up the Hollywood western's thematic opposition between wilderness and civilization to portray the life of the gauchos and the interior's settlement (García 2011). Across the border, *O Cangaceiro* (Lima Barreto, 1953) combined the regional folklore of the Brazilian northeast with the iconography of the American western to depict the historical phenomenon of banditry in the early twentieth century, while *Matar ou Correr* (*To Kill or to Run*, Carlos Manga, 1954) subjected the western to the *chanchada*'s parodic treatment.

In the 1960s, a new generation of Latin American film critics, inspired by their European peers from *Cahiers du cinema*, promoted auteur theory and international art cinema. Yet while they followed the steps of their French counterparts in praising certain Hollywood directors as auteurs and championing minor film genres such as the western, they rarely discussed Latin American genre films (the attention that *Nuevo Cine* paid to Buñuel's films from the 1950s for their subversion of melodrama's conventions being one of the few exceptions). The Latin American filmmakers who entered the scene during those years maintained an equally fraught ambivalence to their commercial film industries and the notion of genre. Influenced by the aesthetics of the European New Waves and driven by a radical left-wing worldview, they sought to formulate a cinematic language that was revolutionary in both form and ideology. Hollywood cinema and its Latin American imitations became the declared enemy.

In this vein, leading figures of Brazil's *Cinema Novo*, such as Glauber Rocha, openly voiced their contempt for the *chanchada* (Simonard 2006: 37–41), but key films from this movement such as *Macunaima* (Joaquim Pedro de Andrade, 1969) and *Xica da Silva* (Carlos Diegues, 1977) clearly invoked its parodic and carnivalesque spirit. Rocha would eventually alter his view on the *chanchada*, recognizing its significance as a national cinematic expression that connected with the Brazilian people (Rocha Melo 2005). In Cuba, Julio García Espinosa used Brechtian audiovisual disjunctions in *Las aventuras de Juan Quin Quin* (*The Adventures of Juan Quin Quin*, 1967), a parody of American adventure films, in order to provoke awareness of the ideological machinations behind this genre's conventions. Yet other Cuban filmmakers chose to embrace the generic structures of Hollywood cinema, creating straightforward action films where revolutionary heroes confronted counterrevolutionary villains, as exemplified in Octavio Cortázar's two youth-oriented box-office hits: *El brigadista* (*The Teacher*, 1978) and *Guardafronteras* (*The Border Guard*, 1980).

The brutal dictatorships that seized power across Latin America in the 1970s suppressed most critical cinematic practices. In Argentina, there was little room then for filmmakers other than the likes of Emilio Vieyra, a proficient craftsman at home in the most disparate genres. After launching Argentine pop singer Sandro in a 1960s trilogy of musicals—which, like those starring Angelica María in Mexico, were geared towards the growing youth segment of the audience—Vieyra directed spy and crime thrillers, adventure films, westerns, and soft-core exploitation films. In Mexico, René Cardona, Jr, best known for his thriller *Tintorera* (*Killer Shark*, 1977), showed a similar versatility through the 1970s onwards, helming disaster movies, horror and sci-fi films, westerns, teenage musicals, and erotic comedies. In fact, exploitation fare became virtually the norm in Mexico's film industry in the late 1970s, especially after the unexpected success of *Bellas de noche* (*Beauties of the Night*, Miguel M. Delgado, 1975), which updated the *cabaretera* subgenre by combining plenty of nudity and salacious humor with catchy boleros. The wave of imitations that followed, although trashed by critics (Sánchez 1975: 8–9) for their vulgarity, low artistic pretensions, and moral hypocrisy, kept filling Mexico's movie theaters well into the 1980s. Their heyday coincided with the rise in Brazil of the *pornochanchadas*, sexed-up comedies

interspersed with some musical numbers. Isabel Sarli and Libertad Leblanc, two sex god-
desses from Argentina, had already paved the way for this franker attitude towards nudity
and sexuality in the 1960s, starring in lurid melodramas and crime thrillers—several of
which were co-productions between various Latin American film industries—that managed to break into international sexploitation circuits and turn sizable profits (Ruétalo
2009: 211–212).

Although the turn to sexploitation movies helped revive local film industries, families
seeking wholesome entertainment gradually turned away from the cinema into the arms
of television. The other staples that dominated 1970s film production in Mexico—crime
thrillers, chili westerns, and action B-movies—were no more palatable due to their increasing levels of on-screen violence. Here, one must give special mention to the notorious
yet immensely popular *narcofilms*; inspired by folk ballads from northern Mexico about
the lives and exploits of smugglers and drug traffickers (*narcocorridos*), movies by Rubén
Galindo Aguilar such as *La banda del Carro Rojo* (*The Red Car Gang*, 1976) and *La Muerte
del soplón* (*Death of a Stoolie*, 1978) set the paradigm to be followed by numerous other titles.
As Ryan Rashotte remarks, genre hybridity also runs rampant in *narco* cinema: musical
numbers pop up between gunfights and car chases and melodramatic situations alternate
with violent action sequences (Rashotte 2015: 2–4). When, by the early 1990s, changes
in the film business forced the closing of theaters in working-class neighborhoods, the *nar-
cofilm* migrated to late-night television and the home-video format, where it retained its
popularity, especially among the Mexican–American community in the US. Daily head-
lines spotlighting the horrors of Mexico's drug war, alongside rumors about the drug trade
laundering their profits through the production of *narcofilms*, have kept this subgenre in
the limelight.

Unlike the New Latin American Cinema movement, the filmmakers of the 1980s and
1990s were less opposed to working with established genre formats, as their priority was
to reconnect with audiences alienated by the modernist experimentation of auteur cinema. In their hands, the established conventions of a specific genre were often rearticulated
to express critical perspectives on contemporary issues. In some cases, the turn towards
genre was the reflection of a profound cinephilia, as in the case of film critic José Carlos
Huayhuaca, who adapted the codes of the detective genre to the Peruvian milieu for his
debut film *Profesión: detective* (1986). On the other hand, his fellow filmmaker Francisco
Lombardi, an established figure in the arthouse circuit, reached wider audiences by resorting
to film noir conventions in *Bajo la piel* (*Under the Skin*, Peru, 1996). Similarly, Sebastián
Cordero's debut feature film *Ratas, ratones, rateros* (*Rodents*, 1999), a story about delinquent youth, leveraged its generic affiliations into the biggest box office in the history of
Ecuador's cinema. Given the entrenched legacies of violence that have impacted so many
Latin American communities, it is not surprising that Latin American filmmakers from
this era found in the thriller a means to generate affect through "a generic apparatus particularly suited for queries about a past that troubles the present" (Podalsky 2011: 64). For
instance, Adolfo Aristarain, an admirer of classic Hollywood cinema, directed two well-
received crime thrillers—*Tiempo de revancha* (*Time for Revenge*, 1981) and *Últimos días de
la víctima* (*Last Days of the Victim*, 1982)—that exposed political corruption and corporate
malfeasance during the Argentine dictatorship's last gasps.

The progressive film critics behind the Colombian magazine *Ojo al cine* had shown
a keen taste for horror cinema, paying homage to George Romero, Roger Corman, and
B-horror movie queen Barbara Steele. It would then seem appropriate that editors Luis
Ospina and Carlos Mayolo would in time become directors of genre films. The latter coined

the term "gótico tropical" (tropical gothic) to describe his films *Carne de Tu Carne* (*Flesh of Your Flesh*, 1983) and *La Mansión de Las Araucaimas* (*The Mansion of the Araucaimas*, 1988). Ospina, for his part, conveyed his love of horror movies in his debut feature film *Pura sangre* (*Pure Blood*, 1982), the tale of an infirm plantation owner who survives on the blood of children, and his passion for film noir in his sophomore film, *Soplo de vida* (*Breath of Life*, 1999).

The presidency of Carlos Salinas de Gortari (1988–1994) renewed state involvement in the production of Mexico's films, and as the cinema's centennial approached, stepped up promotional efforts at home and abroad, culminating in a retrospective of Mexican cinema held at the Centre Georges Pompidou in Paris in 1992, which raised awareness of Mexico's illustrious cinematic past and revived interest in its classic film genres. Alfonso Arau's blockbuster adaptation of Laura Esquivel's bestseller *Como agua para chocolate* (*Like Water for Chocolate*, 1992), one of the biggest international film hits of the era, repurposed the melodramatic sensibility of Latin America's classical cinema for contemporary audiences the world over. This premise, however, had already been successfully explored by women directors such as María Luisa Bemberg and María Novaro, who injected a feminist sensibility into their respective revisions of the woman's picture: the costume melodrama *Camila* (1984) and the romantic musical *Danzón* (1991). A feminist parodic perspective also underlies Carla Camurati's reappropriation of the *chanchada* in *Carlota Joaquina: Princesa do Brasil* (*Carlota Joaquina: Princess of Brazil*, 1995), a box-office smash credited with spearheading the contemporary renaissance of Brazilian cinema.

The implementation of new protectionist policies by many Latin American film industries in the late 1990s has resulted today in an unprecedented boom in film production; the re-emergence of genre films is one notable aspect of this recovery (Hopewell 2014; Rey Mallén 2014). More than ever, Latin America's cinemas are deeply implicated in the global flow of media products and funding sources (Alvaray 2013: 69), yet Latin American film producers and directors still face the challenge of finding a public at home and making their films profitable. The turn towards genre films constitutes a strategy that addresses these two goals: they draw domestic viewers and—inasmuch as they are exportable because they appeal to audiences all over the world—generate income in international markets, as producers Oscar Kramer and Alejandro Suaya observe (Newberry 2008). Perhaps this explains why the divide between auteur cinema and genre filmmaking is no longer as impermeable as in the past, since several successful art films have couched their narratives in a familiar genre format. Moreover, filmmakers who started their careers making independent films have now transitioned into mainstream genre films (e.g. Pablo Trapero) and art house production companies such as Mantarraya have opened subsidiary labels devoted to genre films.

If in the twenty-first century the melodrama has seemingly found a more favorable haven in television's wildly popular soap operas (*telenovelas*), it still appeals to movie directors interested in deploying its polarized worldview and heightened emotions in order to question the social and political status quo. The success of films such as *El crimen del padre Amaro* (*The Crime of Father Amaro*, Carlos Carrera, Mexico, 2002) or *Arráncame la vida* (*Tear This Heart Out*, Roberto Sneider, Mexico, 2009) suggests that melodramas are still capable of drawing big audiences to the theater. The hit biopic *2 Filhos de Francisco* (*Two Sons of Francisco*, Breno Silveira, Brazil, 2005) set a true-life tragic story to the sounds of *música sertaneja*, music from the Brazilian backlands, updating the combination of melodrama and music for contemporary audiences. Though radio continues to play an important role, music video channels such as MTV now mediate the relationship between the recording industry and the cinema. The music video format has impacted such Latin American movies as the musical comedy *¿Qué le dijiste a Dios?* (*What Did You Tell God?*, Teresa Suarez, Mexico, 2014) or soundtrack films such as *A beira do caminho* (*Along the Way*, Breno Silveira, Brazil, 2012), a road movie set to Roberto Carlos' songs. Targeting teenage pop music fans, Patagonik and TV Azteca produced for Argentina and Mexico, respectively, a remake of the American hit *High School Musical: El Desafio* (*The Challenge*, Jorge Nisco, 2008), the first Disney-branded feature film made in Latin America. Conceived with distinct scripts, separate local casts, and an original soundtrack for each version, their tremendous success prompted a remake for the Brazilian market.

Due to the popularity of Hollywood-style crime thrillers and action films, their production has been quite uniform across Latin America. Using the crime thriller as a generic framework is one way for first-time filmmakers to get their projects made and seen or for directors from countries without a film industry to attain some visibility in the international marketplace, e.g. *7 cajas* (*Seven Boxes*, Juan Carlos Maneglia and Tana Schémbori, Paraguay, 2011). The thriller format can facilitate co-productions and enhance the possibilities of distribution in other Latin American markets, as in the case of *Secretos de confesión* (*Secrets of the Confessional*, Henry Rivero, Venezuela and Colombia, 2013). With its scathing portrayal of the ties between paramilitary groups, corrupt politicians, and drug lords, José Padilha's box-office smash *Tropa de elite 2* (*Elite Squad 2*, 2010) exemplifies how contemporary Latin American thrillers can pair fast-paced violent action sequences with the indictment of state institutions and still rake in box-office gold.

Robert Rodriguez and Quentin Tarantino's postmodern mix of action, humor, and horror and their stylish, hyper-violent tributes to 1970s exploitation cinema have exerted a strong influence on many young directors from Latin America, setting the pattern for films such as *Diablo* (*The Devil*, Nicanor Loretti, Argentina, 2011) and Ernesto Díaz Espinoza's knowing homage to Peckinpah's classic, *Tráiganme la cabeza de la mujer metralleta* (*Bring Me the Head of the Machine Gun Woman*, Chile, 2012).

Figure 10.1   Fernanda Urrejola in *Tráiganme la cabeza de la mujer metralleta* (*Bring Me the Head of the Machine Gun Woman*, Ernesto Díaz Espinoza, Chile, 2012).

Over the course of a decade, Díaz Espinoza, in collaboration with his fetish actor Marko Zaror, has carved a niche as a director of cult action films that have won international awards and played in U.S. movie theaters: the first South American martial arts movie, a superhero picture, an espionage thriller, etc. With the action comedy *Santiago Violenta* (2014), winner of the Audience Award at the Valdivia International Film Festival, he has moved from the margins to the center of Chile's film scene.

Garcia's Espinosa's switch to comedy is not fortuitous, since the genre, as James Young (2014) remarks, is enjoying a tremendous renaissance across the continent. Antonio Serrano's *Sexo, pudor y lágrimas* (*Sex, Shame and Tears*, 1999) was credited with bringing spectators back to Mexico's movie theaters in the late 1990s. The same can be said 15 years later of such popular films as *Cásese quien pueda* (*Get Married If You Can*, Marco Polo Constandse, 2014) and *Amor de mis amores* (*Love of My Loves*, Manolo Caro, 2014). In fact, eight out of the 12 highest-grossing Mexican and Brazilian films released between 2010 and 2014 could be described as comedies. Undoubtedly, television exerts the biggest influence on the development of contemporary Latin American comedy. For one thing, renowned actors from sketch-comedy shows and sitcoms have leveraged their popularity into successful movie careers. TV comedian Leandro Hassum has starred in many of Brazil's biggest movies, whereas Chilean impressionist and TV personality Stefan Kramer scored two megahits in a row: first by playing himself and multiple other characters in *Stefan v/s Kramer* (2012) and then by running for political office in the satire *El ciudadano Kramer* (*Citizen Kramer*, 2013). Also in Chile, the presence of performers from the TV show *El club de la comedia* (*Comedy Club*) fueled the box-office success of *Barrio Universitario* (*University Neighborhood*, Fernando Vidal, 2013) and *Fuerzas especiales* (*Special Forces*, José Miguel Zúñiga, 2014). Mexican TV personality Eugenio Derbez merits a special mention. His breakthrough film *No se aceptan devoluciones* (*Instructions Not Included*, 2013) mixed humor and pathos and Spanish and English (the story moves from Acapulco to Hollywood), thereby creating the perfect transnational commodity: it broke all box-office records in the history of Mexican cinema while becoming, at the same time,

Figure 10.2   Loreto Peralta and Eugenio Debrez in *No se aceptan devoluciones* (*Instructions Not Included*, Eugenio Debrez, Mexico, 2013).

through its pull with the Hispanic community, the highest-grossing Spanish-language film ever exhibited in the US. (Cervantes 2013).

Although Ignacio Sánchez Prado (2014) argues that romantic comedies generally embody the neoliberal worldview of their middle-class viewers, the rare film that lampoons the values of this social class, such as *Nosotros los nobles* (*We, the Nobles*, Gary Alazraki, 2013), can become a media sensation. A remake of Buñuel's *El gran calavera* (*The Great Madcap*, 1949), which in turn was remade in Colombia as *Malcriados* (*Daddy's Kids*, Felipe Martínez, 2016), Alazraki's film became the second highest-grossing film in the history of Mexico's cinema, couching its critique in the visual language and performative style of a sit-com. Political satires, too, have done quite well at the box office in recent years, perhaps in response to the ongoing revelations of corruption at the highest levels of government. Thus, Luis Estrada's *La dictadura perfecta* (*The Perfect Dictatorship*, 2014) and Roberto Santucci's *O Candidato Honesto* (*The Honest Candidate*, 2014) were the top 2014 domestic releases in Mexico and Brazil, respectively. Parody remains equally alive and well in contemporary Latin American cinema; for instance, in Venezuela, comedian Benjamín Rausseo (aka El Conde de Guácharo) has struck box-office gold with his irreverent spoofs of American action films. The search for this kind of profit is also propelling the practice of producing sequels with the goal of generating as much cash as possible out of a successful property: in Colombia, the team of producer Dago García and director Harold Trumpetero followed up on their comic road movie *El paseo* (*The Trip*, 2010), which drew almost 1.5 million spectators, with equally successful sequels in 2012 and 2013.

With his first three films, each more successful than the previous one, Juan Taratuto refined a contemporary version of the classic romantic comedy format that was warmly embraced by Argentina's moviegoers. His debut feature *No sos vos, soy yo* (*It's Not You, It's Me*, 2004) grossed nearly $500,000; his next effort, *¿Quién dice que es fácil?* (*Who Said It's Easy?*, 2007), almost tripled that figure, and *Un novio para mi mujer* (*A Boyfriend for My Wife*, 2008) became the top Argentine film of 2008, exceeding $5 million in ticket sales. With its roots in the tradition of Italian film comedy, on the one hand, and Woody Allen's work from the 1970s, on the other, Taratuto's reimagining of the romantic comedy has transcended its national context, inspiring a number of foreign remakes. In Argentina, Taratuto's success opened the door to an explosion of romantic comedies, from Hernán Goldfrid's *Música en espera* (*Music on Hold*, 2009) to Emilio Tamer's *Un amor en tiempos de selfies* (*Love in the Age of Selfies*, 2014), echoing trends elsewhere in the region. In Mexico, three domestic comedies surpassed $10 million each in ticket sales during the first half of 2014, while seven comedies have exceeded $5 million each since 2013 (Young 2014). These positive box-office results indicate that comedies are a viable option for drawing Latin American audiences back to their national cinemas and shoring up the fragile local film industries: comedies are inexpensive to make and rely on the charisma of the performers rather than on costly production values (Staff Cine Premiere 2008). Taratuto and fellow director Ariel Winograd have defended their predilection for the romantic comedy format as a serious and challenging enterprise (*La Nación* 2007). Actor Pablo Echarri, star of Taratuto's comedy *Papeles en el viento* (*Papers in the Wind*, 2014), has argued that genre films, beyond the high box-office returns that help cement local film industries, help renew audiences' affection for their national cinemas (Bardesio 2015).

Unlike romantic comedies' mainstream pull, horror and fantasy appeal primarily to a niche fan base, yet I would argue that this is the most vital area in Latin American genre filmmaking today, casting an ever-wider net among audiences (De Pablos 2014; Valenzuela 2014). Various factors have contributed to this development. On the one hand, a new generation of film school graduates who are passionate about this genre now has access to affordable digital technology and, on the other, adventurous, independent film producers are interested in financing movies that can find audiences abroad. It is no secret that in the past 15 years, there has been a worldwide renaissance of horror and fantasy; riding this wave, Latin American filmmakers have eagerly followed in the footsteps of Guillermo del Toro, seeking to cross borders by creating movies in a globally recognized transnational style that showcases their talent.

Latin America boasts a rich history of horror cinema. Mexico's film industry launched a successful cycle of horror/fantasy films that lasted well into the 1970s; many of these titles circulated internationally. Between 1965 and 1968, at the start of his career, Vieyra participated in an interesting experiment in the transnational exhibition of Latin American horror cinema, directing five horror movies and thrillers for the U.S. Hispanic market, which, later dubbed into English, also circulated in the North American sexploitation circuit (Dapena 2009). The boundaries between horror and exploitation blurred in the highly personal cinematic universes of two self-taught, micro-budget filmmakers: José Mojica Marins, based in São Paulo, invented and played the sinister figure of Zé do Caixão (i.e. Coffin Joe), while Jairo Pinilla, operating from Cali, conjured delirious storylines about zombies, Satanists, extraterrestrials, carnivorous plants, and marijuana-crazed snakes. In recent years, both directors have emerged from obscurity thanks to retrospectives in specialized festivals that have brought them legions of new fans (Tierney 2009: 122; Hoyos 2013).

While horror and fantasy films are being made today in many Latin American countries, Argentina and Chile enjoy the most thriving scene, alongside Mexico, where several of Carlos Enrique Taboada's classic supernatural thrillers have been remade with the youth market in mind. This recycling of successful film properties extended to the Mexican legend of *La Llorona*, first brought to the cinema in the 1930s and updated for contemporary consumption in the box-office smash *Km 31* (Rigoberto Castañeda, 2006); its sequel opened in 2015. While lacking Mexico's tradition in the genre, Chile has nevertheless been turning out a steady stream of horror films, and Jorge Olguín is the genre's unquestionable pioneer. After achieving cult status with his first two features and a U.S. distribution deal with his third feature—the English-language zombie thriller *Solos* (*Alone*, 2009)—Olguín moved on to bigger budgets in his last two bilingual ventures: *Caleuche: el llamado del mar* (*Caleuche: The Call of the Sea*, 2010) and *Gritos en el bosque* (*Whispers in the Forest*, 2012). His decision to shoot these fantasy/horror films based on Chilean legends in English exemplifies the new interplay between the local and the global. The enterprise known as Chiliwood, a collaboration developed between the Chilean production company Sobras International Pictures (headed by filmmaker Nicolás López) and American film director, actor, and producer Eli Roth, further confirms that when it comes to horror cinema, the transnational relationship between center and periphery is no longer unidirectional.

If horror films once struggled to find audiences in Latin American countries with no tradition in this type of filmmaking, they now land at the top of the box office. Witness the success of *Juan de los muertos* (*Juan of the Dead*, Alejandro Brugués, Cuba, 2010), *El Páramo* (*The Squad*, Jaime Osorio Márquez, Colombia, 2011), *Cementerio general* (*General Cemetary*, Dorian Fernandez Morris, Peru, 2013), or *La casa del fin de los tiempos* (*The House at the End of Time*, Alejandro Hidalgo, Venezuela, 2013). Horror films are even being made in countries with a bare-bones film industry such as Costa Rica—e.g. *El sanatorio* (*The Sanatorium*, Miguel Alejandro Gómez, 2010). Moreover, remakes of horror films have created avenues for transnational exchanges—e.g. the Colombian supernatural thriller *Al final del espectro* (*At the End of the Spectra*, Juan Felipe Orozco, 2006) was remade several years later in Mexico as *Espectro*

(*The Demon Inside*, Alfonso Pineda Ulloa, 2013) with Spanish actress Paz Vega in the leading role. The quality and originality of this new crop of horror films has also attracted the attention of film programmers and producers outside of Latin America (Perasso 2012), resulting in American remakes of Jorge Grau's *Somos lo que hay* (*We Are What We Are*, Mexico, 2010)—a film that played at Cannes and other prestigious film festivals—and Gustavo Hernández's *La casa muda* (*The Silent House*, Uruguay, 2010), and a Bollywood remake of the psychological thriller *La cara oculta* (*The Hidden Face*, Andrés Baiz, Colombia, 2011).

Visual style in Latin American horror production reflects the same dichotomy between commercial and independent filmmaking found elsewhere in the movie business. A film such as *Km 31* revels in high-tech digital effects and the fast-paced, montage-driven aesthetics typical of mainstream international horror cinema. *La casa muda*, on the other hand, creates its unsettling effect through a minimalist aesthetic: a cast of four inside one set, a handheld camera style of long, highly mobile takes, and a chill-inducing soundtrack at the service of a true-story narrative suspended between the real and the imagined. Moreover, Latin American horror films often convey critical perspectives, reflecting deep-seated anxieties about societal violence, urban squalor, marginalized groups, or environmental degradation, among other issues.

The new respectability of the horror genre and its concurrent recognition in institutional circles that previously shunned it is one example of how attitudes towards genre films have drastically changed in Latin America. Decades ago, critics and festival programmers dismissed them while prominent directors approached generic conventions with suspicion, attempting to subvert or deconstruct them. Today, Latin American filmmakers wholeheartedly embrace genre films for both artistic and economic reasons: if cinephilia draws them to genre, there is also the desire to fill movie seats and generate income to sustain their own careers and the chronically underfinanced film industries they work in. If at one time Latin American musicals, melodramas, and sexploitation traveled all over the world, today horror, thrillers, and romantic comedies are opening new doors to international funding and distribution, reaching audiences both at home and abroad, and spinning off remakes. Yet in an ever-competitive media marketplace, the dilemma that Latin America's film industries faced in the past and once bedeviled Argentina's Sono Film or Brazil's Vera Cruz studios—to nationalize foreign genres or to produce films in an international style so as to access global markets—again occupies center stage, and has perhaps become evermore pressing.

References

Altman, R. (1997) "Cinema and Genre." In G. Nowell-Smith (ed.), *Oxford History of World Cinema*. Oxford: Oxford University Press, pp. 276–285.

Alvaray, L. (2013) "Hybridity and Genre in Transnational Latin American Cinemas." *Transnational Cinemas*, 4(1): 67–87.

Bardesio, M. (2015) "Sigo siendo un tipo de barrio." *El Pais* (Montevideo), January 18. Available at: www.elpais.com.uy/divertite/cine/pablo-echarri-sigo-tipo-barrio.html (accessed September 7, 2015).

Cervantes, J. (2013) "Las películas mexicanas más taquilleras de la historia." *Forbes*, December 17. Available at: www.forbes.com.mx/las-peliculas-mexicanas-mas-taquilleras-de-la-historia/ (accessed February 6, 2015).

Dapena, G. (2009) "Emilio Vieyra: Argentina's Transnational Master of Horror." In V. Ruétalo and D. Tierney (eds.), *Latsploitation: Exploitation Cinemas and Latin America*. New York/London: Routledge, pp. 87–101.

De Pablos, E. (2014) "Brazil Locals Embrace Sci-Fi and Scary Films." *Variety*. Available at: http://variety.com/2014/film/festivals/brazil-locals-embrace-sci-fi-and-scary-films-1201182443/ (accessed February 6, 2015).

García, A. (2011) "Hombres de a caballo." *Radar.Pagina 12*, June 19. Available at: www.pagina12. com.ar/diario/suplementos/radar/9-7127-2011-06-19.html (accessed September 7, 2015).

Hopewell, J. (2014) "Horror Movie Production Gets Boost from Argentine Government." *Variety*, August 30. Available at: http://variety.com/2014/film/markets-festivals/horror-movie-production-gets-boost-from-argentine-government-1201294759/ (accessed February 6, 2015).

Hoyos, A. (2013) "'Hago cine con las uñas . . . y sin ellas': Jairo Pinilla." *El Tiempo* (Colombia), November 12. Available at: www.eltiempo.com/archivo/documento/CMS-13180776 (accessed February 6, 2015).

Kantaris, G. and O'Bryen, R. (2013) "The Fragile Contemporaneity of the Popular." In G. Kantaris and R. O'Bryen (eds.), *Popular Culture: Politics, Media, Affect*. Woodbridge: Tamesis Books, pp. 1–42.

La Nación (2007) "Hacer reír es una cosa seria." *La Nación* (Buenos Aires), February 5.

Langford, B. (2005) *Film Genre: Hollywood and Beyond*. Edinburgh: Edinburgh University Press.

Newberry, C. (2008) "Argentina Tries to Shed Arthouse Image." *Variety*, February 7. Available at: http://variety.com/2008/film/markets-festivals/argentina-tries-to-shed-arthouse-image-1117980429 (accessed February 6, 2015).

Perasso, V. (2012) "América Latina exporta caníbales y zombies a Hollywood." Available at: www. bbc.com/mundo/noticias/2012/03/120324_cine_de_terror_latinoamericano_auge_vp.shtml (accessed February 4, 2015).

Podalsky, L. (2011) *The Politics of Affect and Emotion in Contemporary Latin American Cinema*. New York: Palgrave MacMillan.

Rashotte, R. (2015) *Narco Cinema: Sex, Drugs, and Banda Music in Mexico's B-Filmography*. London/New York: Palgrave Macmillan.

Rey Mallén, P. (2014) "Alfonso Cuarón, Box Office-Breaking Comedies and an Academy Award: The New Golden Age of Mexican Cinema." *International Business Times*, February 28. Available at: www.ibtimes.com/alfonso-cuaron-box-office-breaking-comedies-academy-award-new-golden-age-mexican-cinema-1558108 (accessed February 4, 2015).

Rocha Melo, L.A. (2005) "A chanchada segundo Glauber." *Contracampo*, 74. Available at: www. contracampo.com.br/74/glauberchanchada.htm (accessed August 31, 2015).

Ruétalo, V. (2009) "Temptations: Isabel Sarli Exposed." In V. Ruétalo and D. Tierney (eds.), *Latsploitation, Exploitation Cinemas and Latin America*. New York/London: Routledge, pp. 201–214.

Sánchez, F. (1975) "Un largo viaje del churro a la fotonovela." *Otrocine*, 5(5): 6–11.

Sánchez Prado, I.M. (2014) "Regimes of Affect: Love and Class in Mexican Neoliberal Cinema." *Journal of Popular Romance Studies*, 4(1). Available at: www.jprstudies.org (accessed August 25, 2015).

Simonard, P. (2006) *A geração do cinema novo: para uma antropologia do cinema*. Rio de Janeiro: Mauad X.

Staff Cine Premiere (2008) "La 'nueva' comedia romántica argentina." Available at: www.cinepremiere.com.mx/la-nueva-comedia-romantica-argentina.html (accessed February 4, 2015).

—— (2009) "José Mojica Marins and the Cultural Politcs of Marginality in 'Third World' Film Criticism." In V. Ruétalo and D. Tierney (eds.), *Latsploitation: Exploitation Cinemas and Latin America*, New York/London: Routledge pp. 115–128.

Valenzuela, A. (2014) "Una pasión que crece a pura sangre." *Página12*, November 30. Available at: www.pagina12.com.ar/diario/suplementos/espectaculos/5-34117-2014-11-30.html (accessed February 4, 2015).

—— (2015) "Mexican Movies Show Broader Success in 2014." *Variety*, March 9. Available at: http://variety.com/2015/film/global/mexican-movies-show-broader-success-in-2014-1201448715/ (accessed September 7, 2015).

Young, J. (2014) "As Mexican Auds Embrace Local Comedies, Filmmakers Hope Dramas Can Cash in Too." *Variety*, October 24. Available at: http://variety.com/2014/film/global/mexico-audiences-embrace-local-comedies-1201336021/ (accessed February 6, 2015).

Further reading

Acevedo Muñoz, E. (2003) *Luis Buñuel: The Crisis of Nationalism in Mexican Cinema.* Los Angeles, CA: University of California Press.

Alvarez, P. (ed.) (2007) *Tango y cine nacional: una fusión de origen.* Rosario: Editorial Ciudad Gótica.

Augusto, S. (1989) *Este mundo é um pandeiro. A chanchada de Getúlio a JK.* São Paulo-SP: Companhia das Letras, Cinemateca Brasileira.

Aviña, R. (2004) *Una mirada insólita: Temas y géneros del cine mexicano.* Mexico City: Editorial Océano.

Ayala Blanco, J. (1993) *La aventura del cine mexicano.* Mexico City: Grijalbo.

Chanan, M. (2004) *Cuban Cinema.* Minneapolis, MN: University of Minnesota Press.

Cine Latino Americano Años 30–4–50 (1990) Mecio City: UNAM.

Colina, E. and Diaz, D. (1971) "Ideología del melodrama en el viejo cine latinoamericano." *Cine cubano*, 73(5): 14–26.

Conrich, I. and Tincknell, E. (eds.) (2006) *Film's Musical Moments.* Edinburgh: Edinburgh University Press.

Costanzo, W.V. (2014) *World Cinema through Global Genres.* Malden, MA: Wiley-Blackwell.

Couret, N.F. (2013) *Peripheral Humor, Critical Realism: Latin American Film Comedy, 1930–1960.* Dissertation, University of Iowa.

D'Lugo, M. (2009) "Early Cinematic Tangos: Audiovisual Culture and Transnational Film Aesthetics." *Studies in Hispanic Cinemas*, 5(1–2): 9–23.

—— (2010) "Aural Identity, Genealogies of Sound Technologies and Hispanic Transnationality." In N. Durovicova and K. Newman (eds.), *World Cinemas: Transnational Perspectives.* New York/London: Routledge, pp. 160–185.

Dennison, S. and Shaw L. (2004) *Popular Cinema in Brazil.* Manchester: Manchester University Press.

Díaz-Zambrana, R. and Tomé, P. (eds.) (2012) *Horrofílmico: Aproximaciones al cine de terror en Latinoamérica y el Caribe.* San Juan: Isla Negra Editores.

España, C. (ed.) (2000) *Cine argentino: industria y clasicismo 1933–1956.* Buenos Aires: Fondo Nacional de las Artes.

—— (2005) *Cine argentino: modernidad y vanguardias 1957–1983.* Buenos Aires: Fondo Nacional de las Artes.

Falicov, T. (2007) *The Cinematic Tango: Contemporary Argentine Film.* New York: Wallflower Press.

Fein, S. (1994) "Hollywood, U.S.-Mexican Relations, and the Devolution of the 'Golden Age' of Mexican Cinema." *Film Historia*, 4(2): 103–135. Available at: http://revistes.ub.edu/index.php/filmhistoria/article/view/12234/14985 (accessed August 3, 2015).

Foster, D.W. (2014) "*Carlota Joaquina* (1995), de Carla *Camurati*: el lado femenino/feminista de la formación de la nación. *Literatura y Cine*." In J.H. Valdivieso and E. Ruiz-Fornells (eds.), *Bicentenario de la Independencia de Iberoamérica y de la Constitución de Cádiz.* Turlock, CA: Editorial Orbis Press, pp. 33–39.

Gamboa, J.L. (2012) "Siete grandes Westerns mexicanos." Available at: www.letraslibres.com/blogs/en-pantalla/siete-grandes-westerns-mexicanos (accessed September 7, 2015).

García Canclini, N. (2005) *Hybrid Cultures: Strategies for Entering and Leaving Modernity.* Minneapolis, MN: University of Minnesota Press.

García Mesa, H. (1983) "El cine negado de América Latina." *Cine Cubano*, 104: 89–96.

García Riera, E. (1992–1997) *Historia documental del cine mexicano*, 18 volumes. Guadalajara: University of Guadalajara.

Gonçalves Pereira (2004) "O Western americano na poética de Glauber Rocha e 'Deus e o Diabo na Terra do Sol'." *Contracampo*, 10/11. Available at: www.uff.br/contracampo/index.php/revista/article/view/529 (accessed August 3, 2015).

Greene, D. (2005) *Mexploitation Cinema: A Critical History of Mexican Vampire, Wrestler, Ape-Man and Similar Films.* Jefferson, NC: McFarland & Co.

—— (2007) *The Mexican Cinema of Darkness: A Critical Study of Six Landmark Horror and Exploitation Films, 1969–1988.* Jefferson, NC: McFarland & Co.

Herlinghaus, H. (2002) "La imaginación melodramática." In H. Herlinghaus (ed.), *Narraciones anacrónicas de la modernidad: melodrama e intermedialidad en América Latina*. Santiago: Editorial Cuarto Propio, pp. 21–59.

Hopewell, J. (2013a) "Latin America Film Industry Surges." *Variety*, September. Available at: http://variety.com/2013/film/global/latin-america-surges-1200662574/ (accessed February 6, 2015).

—— (2013b) "Latin American Horror Booming at Blood Window Market." *Variety*, November 20. Available at: http://variety.com/2013/biz/global/scarefare-surges-in-latin-america-1200857018/ (accessed February 6, 2015).

Karush, M. (2012) *Culture of Class: Radio and Cinema in the Making of a Divided Argentina, 1920–1946*. Durham, NC: Duke University Press.

Kriger, C. (2009) *Cine y peronismo: el estado en escena*. Buenos Aires: Siglo XXI.

López, A.M. (1991) "The Melodrama in Latin America: Films, Telenovelas, and the Currency of a Popular Form." In M. Landy (ed.), *Imitations of Life: A Reader on Film and Television Melodrama*. Detroit, MI: Wayne State University Press, pp. 596–606.

—— (1993) "Tears and Desire: Women and Melodrama in the 'Old' Mexican Cinema." in J. King, A.M. López, and M. Alvarado (eds.), *Mediating Two Worlds: Cinematic Encounters in the Americas*. London: British Film Institute, pp. 147–163.

—— (2000a) "Early Cinema and Modernity in Latin America." *Cinema Journal*, 40(1): 48–78.

—— (2000b) "Crossing Nations and Genres: Traveling Filmmakers." In C. Noriega (ed.), *Visible Nations: Latin American Cinema and Video*. Minneapolis, MN: University of Minnesota Press, pp. 33–50.

—— (2010) "Mexico: La Hacienda y el Cabaret: Musical Spaces of the Classical Mexican Cinema." In C. Creekmuer and L. Mokdad (eds.), *The International Film Musical*. Edinburgh: University of Edinburgh Press, pp. 121–140.

"Luis Buñuel" (1961) *Nuevo Cine* I (Mexico), pp. 14–15.

Millones, C. (2014) "Historias locales, atractivo universal." *La Nación* (Buenos Aires), November 6. Available at: www.lanacion.com.ar/1741553-historias-locales-atractivo-universal (accessed February 4, 2015).

Monsiváis, C. (1993) *Rostros del cine mexicano*. Mexico City: IMCINE.

—— (1994) "Se sufre porque se aprende (el melodrama y las reglas de la falta de límites)." In C. Monsiváis and C. Bonfil (eds.), *A través del espejo: el cine mexicano y su público*. Mexico City: Ediciones El Milagro, IMCINE, pp. 99–224.

—— (1995) "Mythologies." In P.A. Paranaguá (ed.), *Mexican Cinema*. London: British Film Institute, pp. 117–127.

Moyano, H. (2013) "'Malditos Sean!' y la cuota de pantalla." Available at: http://hernanmoyano.com.ar/2013/01/04/malditos-sean-y-la-cuota-de-pantalla/#more-172 (accessed February 6, 2015).

Oliveira Dias, R. (1993) *O mundo como chanchada: cinema e imaginário das classes populares na década de 50*. Rio de Janiero: Relume-Dumará.

Oroz, S. (1992) *Melodrama: O cinema de lagrimas da America Latina*. Rio de Janeiro: Fundo Editora.

Paranaguá, P.A. (1995) *Mexican Cinema*. London: British Film Institute.

Pedelty, M. (1999) "Bolero: The Birth, Life and Decline of Mexican Modernity." *Latin American Music Review*, 20: 71–110.

Pinazza, N. (2014) *Journeys in Argentine and Brazilian Cinema: Road Films in a Global Era*. London: Palgrave Macmillan.

Phillips, W.D (2014) "*O Cangaceiro* (1953) and the Brazilian Northeastern: The Western in the Land of the Sun." In C. J. Miller and A. Bowdoin Van Riper (eds.), *International Westerns: Re-Locating the Frontier*. Plymouth, UK: Scarecrow Press.

Raña, M. (2011) *Guerreros del Cine: Argentino, Fantástico e Independiente*. Buenos Aires: Fan Ediciones.

Sadlier, D.J. (2005) "Introduction: A Short History of Film Melodrama in Latin America." In D.J. Sadlier (ed.), *Latin American Melodrama: Passion, Pathos, and Entertainment*. Urbana-Champaigne, IL: University of Illinois Press, pp. 1–18.

Sarzynski, S. (2009) "The Popular, the Political, and the Ugly: Brazilian Nordesterns in a Comparative Cold War Context, 1960–1975." In F. Ekotto and A. Koh (eds.), *Rethinking Third Cinema: The Role of Anti-Colonial Media and Aesthetics in Postmodernity*. Berlin: Lit Verlag, pp. 81–105.

Shaw, L. (2000) "The *Chanchada* and Celluloid Visions of Brazilian Identity in the Vargas Era (1930–45)." *Journal of Iberian and Latin American Studies*, 6(1): 63–74.

"Sigo siendo un tipo de barrio." (2015) *El País* (Montevideo), January 18.

"Tiempo de Morir. La primera película colombiana que barre con los premios en un festival internacional." *Semana*, January 6, 1986. Available at: www.semana.com/cultura/articulo/tiempo-de-morir/7269-3 (accessed August 3, 2015).

Tierney, D. (2007) *Emilio Fernández: Pictures in the Margins*. Manchester: University of Manchester Press.

Tuñón, J. (1998) *Mujeres de luz y sombra en el cine mexicano: la reconstrucción de una imagen, 1939–1952*. Mexico City: El Colegio de México.

Wessels, C. (2015) "An 'Imperfect' Genre: Rethinking Politics in Latin American Westerns." In M. Higgins, R. Keresztesi, and D. Oscherwitz (eds.), *The Western in the Global South*. New York: Routledge, pp. 183–197.

"Year in Review: The Top Grossing Latin American Films of 2012." Available at: www.cinema tropical.com/Cinema-Tropical/the-highest-grossing-latin-american-films-of-2012.html (accessed February 4, 2015).

"Year in Review: The Top Grossing Latin American Films of 2013." Available at: www.cinema tropical.com/Cinema-Tropical/year-in-review-the-top-grossing-latin-american-films-of-2013. html (accessed February 4, 2015).

"Year in Review: The Top Grossing Latin American Films of 2014." Available at: www.cinema tropical.com/Cinema-Tropical/year-in-review-the-top-grossing-latin-american-films-of-2014. html (accessed February 4, 2015).

11

NEW LATIN AMERICAN STARDOM

Dolores Tierney, Victoria Ruétalo, and
Roberto Carlos Ortiz

Editors' introduction

The Latin American star system, like that in other regions, has emulated the Hollywood model in large measure because of its power to mobilize moviegoing audiences. Various contributors to this collection have underscored particular ways in which regional film cultures have borrowed certain of Hollywood's strategies to promote local star culture. Maite Conde's discussion of fan magazines in Brazil in the 1920s (see Chapter 5), for instance, provides an early example of the ways the Hollywood star paradigm self-consciously served local interests in shaping a Brazilian national audience. Similarly, in Chapter 20, Alejandro Kelly Hopfenblatt's focus on photography in star construction and the commercial promotion of particular stars helps us better appreciate the rich visual influence of cinema in shaping popular tastes and commodity culture in the region.

In recent decades, with seminal works by Vieira, López (1993; 1994; 1998), Paranaguá, and Tuñón, Latin American star studies have expanded their scope, generating sophisticated discourses on the ways in which individual stars maneuver their celebrity persona within the social, cultural, and even moral projects of national and transnational communities. The authors of this chapter argue for a substantive alteration of that meta-discourse on stardom in which key Latin America actors are seen not merely as "star texts," but to extend the metaphor, as centers or "constellations" of intermedial artistic and market networks in ways that transcend their status as mere entertainers. While defined by the box office, their real value lies in the ways these contemporary icons engage in forms of ethnic identity politics, thereby displacing old stereotypes on international screens. Notably, all three of these "new" stars considered here occupy the porous media spaces that enable them to move between mainstream commercial cinema in their own countries but also the wider global art house film circuit.

Once exclusively aimed at mass marketing and publicity apparatuses directed at broad national and international markets, today's Latin American stars pose a much more nuanced political and social persona as they reflect the trajectory of recent cinema from the region, moving across geopolitical borders and enjoying recognition both within mass markets as well as art house cinema circles. As a result, stardom is no longer the extraneous marketing supplement to films from Latin America it once was.

This chapter analyzes contemporary film stardom in Latin America through three stars who represent not just a gender and geographical sweep of the continent (Brazilian Sônia Braga, Mexican Gael García Bernal, and Argentine Ricardo Darín), but also the key discourses that define how Latin American stardom currently works. Although this chapter relates these discourses to individual stars and their careers, it also acknowledges that these concepts apply as well to other contemporary Latin American stars (e.g. Salma Hayek, Wagner Moura).

Existing scholarship suggests Latin American stardom is defined in four key ways: regionally, transnationally, ethnically, and televisually. First, as Ana M. López (1994) points out, Latin America's stars have historically been regional stars, appealing to the shared values and tastes of a pan-continental audience stretching between Latin America and the Spanish-speaking United States. Second, and both historically and in the contemporary era, stardom is also defined transnationally and in transatlantic contexts, expanding to include the US and Spain in a star system (and co-production models) that ensures the financial viability and distribution of Spanish-language films (see Ruétalo in this chapter). Third, Latin American and Latino/a stardom is further determined by the production and circulation of films in the United States and by the particular racial and ethnic negotiations that fit within the racial hierarchies of Latin America and the United States (López 1998; Beltrán 2009; Tierney 2012). Lastly, another key element in Latin American stardom, and equally important to the early careers of Braga, Darín and Bernal, is the role television plays in determining stardom in national contexts. This is particularly the case in Latin American television's most popular format, the *telenovela*, which is how our three stars initially found fame. In Mexico and Brazil, for example, the national star system is defined principally by actors from this format. But across the continent, stardom may also be further determined when established *telenovela* stars (such as Braga or Moura) move on to work in national film industries and then subsequently transnationally (in Hollywood or Europe).

This notion of nationally defined televisual stardom, which then shifts into national filmmaking and beyond, is also exemplified by other contemporary Latin American stars. Like Braga, who became a star with *Gabriela* (1975), Mexican actress Hayek, also achieved stardom in a *telenovela* (*Teresa*, 1989), before moving into film in Mexico (*Callejón de los milagros*, *Midaq Alley*, Jorge Fons, 1995) and simultaneously to the US, where she became a star through a variety of film and television projects, including both acting and producing roles (*Frida*, Julie Taymor, 2002; *Ugly Betty*, 2006–2010; *30 Rock*, 2009–2013). This chapter's selection of Braga, Darín, and Bernal over other contemporary Latin American stars such as Hayek, Brazilian Moura, or Argentine Federico Luppi is a strategic one. It represents the three major industries in Latin America (Mexico, Brazil, and Argentina), and a sweep that is both gender (two men and two women—Alice Braga is also studied alongside her aunt) and generationally based. Braga comes from an earlier generation of Latin American stars of the 1970s, whereas Darín and Bernal come from the post-2000 boom— even though Darín, like Braga, is middle-aged. Additionally, these three actors' star texts and careers mobilize *both* existing (regional, transnational, and ethnic) and emergent discourses of Latin American stardom: the abandonment of the local/shift into the global and eventual return (Braga), the tension between art house and mainstream cinema, national and international stardom (Darín), and ethnic stardom (Bernal). Moreover, the choice of stars focused on is further determined by the fact that most of them appeared in Latin America's major art house successes. In addition to precipitating a still ongoing new "golden age" for Latin American cinema, it is our contention that these successes have shaped the forms their subsequent stardom has taken: Alice Braga in *Cidade de Deus* (*City of God*, Fernando Meirelles and Kátia Lund, 2002), Darín in *Nueve reinas* (*Nine Queens*, Fabián Bielinsky, 2000), and Bernal in *Amores perros* (*Love's a Bitch*, Alejandro González Iñárritu, 2000), *Y tu mamá también* (*And Your Mother Too*, Alfonso Cuarón, 2001), *El crimen del padre Amaro* (*The Crime of Padre Amaro*, Carlos Carrera, 2003), and *Diarios de motocicleta* (*Motorcycle Diaries*, Walter Salles, 2004).

Sônia Braga: The Resistant Star

ROBERTO CARLOS ORTIZ

Sônia Braga is arguably the most important movie star produced by Brazilian cinema. In the 1980s, the actress became the Brazilian movie star with the most international projection since Carmen Miranda in 1940s Hollywood cinema. Despite lengthy absences from Brazilian productions, Braga is still considered a Brazilian cinema star and has taken part in more emblematic film and TV projects than Miranda. Whereas her predecessor's glamorous star image in Brazilian radio was replaced with the tropicalized stereotypes in her Hollywood musicals (López 1993: 73–77), Braga's star image has remained tied to her work in Brazilian media. The press often calls her "the eternal Gabriela," after the 1975 Rede Globo soap opera that first made her a national star, or "the Spider Woman," after the 1985 Brazilian/U.S. co-production credited with consolidating her international stardom. Notwithstanding her uneven trajectory, Braga's lengthy career in Brazilian and U.S. cinema and television offers an interesting case study about changing paradigms in post-classical stardom.

In April 2016, Braga attended the Cannes Film Festival premiere of *Aquarius* (Kleber Mendonça Filho), her first starring role in Brazilian cinema since *Tieta do Agreste* (Carlos Diegues, 1996). The 65-year-old actress was the star attraction at the red carpet event, dazzling photographers in a stylish gown by famed Cuban–American designer Narciso Rodríguez. At the steps of the Grand Théâtre Lumière, the event took a political turn when cast and crew and pulled out signs denouncing the ousting of Brazilian President Dilma Rousseff. Braga joined her colleagues and helped to hold a sign that read: "A coup took place in Brazil." The *Aquarius* screening earned a lengthy standing ovation and Braga's performance became a critical favorite. However, the protest provoked a social media backlash in Brazil, including a Twitter campaign with the hashtag #BoicoteAquarius. Braga's Facebook page was filled with nasty comments that questioned her right to protest since the actress has been living in the United States. Weeks later, the newly appointed Minister of Culture, Marcelo Calero, also criticized the Cannes protest, claiming on Brazilian TV that it damaged the country's image abroad. In a June 6, 2016 Facebook post, Braga responded with a "history lesson" that informed the 33-year-old minister of her contributions to Brazil's international image: "[A] Brazilian actress was Brazilian cinema's box-office champion and held that title for 30 years—also winning, with Brazilian films, besides international projection, many awards abroad, that way promoting the name of Brazil and of our culture."

Figure 11.1   The aging star as symbol of resistance: Sônia Braga in *Aquarius* (Kleber Mendonça Filho, 2016).

Scholarly articles on Braga have emphasized the construction of her star text, especially her image as a Brazilian sex symbol, in relation to issues about race, sexuality, and nation (Dennison and Shaw 2004; Da Silva 2014; Legg 2015). Looking beyond the intertextual star images, more recent star studies have considered the evolving media contexts in which stars must work to remain relevant. In "Re-examining Stardom," Christine Geraghty (2000: 187–188) proposes a distinction between three kinds of contemporary stardom: celebrity, professional, and performer. Braga has mostly worked within the star-as-professional category, which is akin to the classic Hollywood studio star system. The Brazilian actress has given audiences a more or less consistent star image through her work in different media contexts. Since Hollywood has generally represented the ideal for movie stardom, the Oscar-winning success of *Kiss of the Spider Woman* (Hector Babenco, 1985) is generally credited with consolidating Braga as an international movie star. After reviewing her career in Brazilian film and television, however, *Kiss* seems more like a turning point in Braga's transnational stardom and her subsequent career illustrates the challenges faced by Latin American female stars of her generation.

Braga made her professional debut with the São Paulo staging of *Hair* (1969), which led to small parts in underground cinema and a starring role in the musical literary adaptation *A Moreninha* (*The Little Brunette*, Glauco Mirko Laurelli, 1970). Her rise to stardom, however, happened under contract to Rede Globo. Braga first became known as a cast member of the Brazilian version of *Sesame Street* (1972) and as a supporting actress in trailblazing soap operas. She achieved full stardom and sex symbol status with the title role in *Gabriela* (1975), an adaptation of a bestselling Jorge Amado novel that was part of Rede Globo's strategy to elevate their programming quality. With her small stature, big smile, and long, frizzy "wild hair," Braga as Gabriela offered viewers a more accessible ideal of Brazilian beauty, overcoming criticism for naturally lacking the literary character's "clove and cinnamon" skin color (and achieving it instead through a mix of suntans and makeup). Gabriela's childlike behavior and earthy sexuality endeared her to viewers. In the soap opera's most famous scene, a barefooted Gabriela climbs to grab a child's kite caught on a tiled roof while town

167

members congregate below to watch and cheer. Oblivious to the impropriety of her action and to the desires she awakens, Gabriela is only concerned with bringing the kite down to stop a child from crying.

In 1976 came the widely publicized theatrical release of *Dona Flor e seus dois maridos* (*Dona Flor and Her Two Husbands*, Bruno Barreto, 1976), a big-budget adaptation of another Jorge Amado bestseller. Braga's (brief) sex scenes were highly anticipated after the film's publicized problems with censors. The advertising catered to the viewers of low-budget sex comedies with female nudity (*pornochanchadas*) that dominated the national box office during the period of the right-wing dictatorship. One poster showed Braga in bed with her two male co-stars, smiling with her arms over their necks and her naked legs crossed. The tag line played on the double entendre of the verb *dar* (to give): "Ela dá a receita certa para amar dois homens" ("She 'gives' the correct recipe to love two men"). Released in November 1976, *Dona Flor* held (until late 2010) the record for most ticket sales by a national film.

Two years later, the sexually explicit *A Dama do Lotaçao* (*Lady on the Bus*, Neville D'Almeida, 1978) told the story of Solange (Braga), a frigid upper-class woman who, after being raped by her husband on their wedding night, starts picking up men on local buses for sex. Ostensibly a Brazilian *Belle de Jour* (Luis Buñuel, 1967), adapted from a Nelson Rodrigues story, the movie's contradictory messages about female sexuality (Buckley 1998) make it Braga's most ideologically muddled star vehicle. Critics panned the movie, but *A Dama* was the first Brazilian film to premiere simultaneously around the country and to sell a million tickets in its initial week. Advertised with a poster that only showed the glammed-up star provocatively dressed in red, *A Dama* established Braga as Brazil's "box-office queen."

Braga's stardom began to assume an international dimension during this period, when Rede Globo started to export their soap operas and Embrafilme (Brazil's national film company) offered financial assistance for the U.S. release of *Dona Flor*, which fit their plans to support "quality films that will also have mass appeal" (Lifsher 1977: B11). *Gabriela* was the first Brazilian *novela* broadcast in Portugal and became a national phenomenon. The following year, news of *Dona Flor*'s box-office success in the United States traveled to Brazil. Marketed as an erotic comedy for art house audiences, the film was the most successful Latin American release in the US, and Braga's sensual image—"a heavy-lidded, full-lipped beauty that moves from timid girl to ripe woman without a blemish" (Christiansen 1978: A6)—even impressed critics who disliked the movie. A deglamorized Braga also starred in *Dancin' Days* (1978), a milestone soap opera blending maternal melodrama, social commentary, disco music and trend-setting fashions, which became one of Rede Globo's most successful exports.

Eu te amo (*I Love You*, Arnaldo Jabor, 1981) was the first Braga film to screen at Cannes, during the "Un Certain Regard" sidebar. After watching it there, *Newsweek*'s film critic ecstatically proclaimed Braga "the first true post-Sophia Loren star, a woman of blazing beauty who combines the comic verve of Carole Lombard with a courageous sexual explicitness" (Kroll 1982: 83).

With the international success of *Eu te amo*, Braga seemed poised to fulfill her desire to promote Brazilian cinema abroad: "I want more than international stardom for myself, [. . .] I want Brazilian cinema to become a star" (Wolf 1982: 70). Even though it fared better abroad, *Gabriela* (Bruno Barreto, 1984), an MGM and United Artists production that paired her with Italian superstar Marcello Mastroianni, lacked the soap opera's charm and failed to repeat *Dona Flor*'s success. Taking part in the promotional campaign for *Kiss of the Spider Woman* (1985), filmed in English, increased her international visibility, but Braga's parts were secondary to the two male leads (Oscar-winning William Hurt and Raúl Julia). Still, Braga maintained her international star image through extra cinematic elements, such as being a jury member at the 1986 Cannes Film Festival or presenting at the 1987 Oscars ceremony. After moving to New York City, Braga began to work mostly in the United States.

As a Brazilian woman with imperfect English, a former soap opera actress who posed nude for *Playboy*, a sex symbol in her mid-30s, Braga defied 1980s Hollywood movie star standards. Within Hollywood's Eurocentric casting norms, her light skin and dark hair meant she could portray only multiple Latin American nationalities, but she had to contend with being typecast as a Latina and older character. Since turning 40, Braga was often cast in Latina mother roles that suppressed the sensuality that had been the basis of her star image since *Gabriela* and *Dona Flor*. Her best opportunities have all been as a guest star on popular TV series such as *Sex and the City* (2001), *Alias* (2005), and *Brothers and Sisters* (2010). Though she has regularly traveled back to Brazil, Braga's frequent absences from Brazilian cinema and television have become a recurring question in frequent TV interviews.

The mobility between countries and genres and the Latino visibility in the media have increased significantly since Braga's move to the United States in the 1980s. There has been a shift in the mode of stardom among the younger generation of international Brazilian movie stars. Stars-as-performers such as Wagner Moura or Alice Braga (Sônia's niece) do not attempt to build a consistent star image. They emphasize the acting work—such as gaining weight and learning Spanish for *Narcos* (2015-)—and draw attention away from their personal lives. This approach has allowed them to play more diverse roles, but they lack the mythical quality of their predecessor, whose star image added a layer of signification to *Aquarius*, Sônia Braga's critically acclaimed return to Brazilian cinema.

Divided in three parts, *Aquarius* is a character study of Clara, a retired music critic in Recife who stubbornly refuses to sell her apartment to developers. The first part, Clara's Hair, refers to the protagonist's survival of cancer treatment. However, it could also be interpreted in relation to Sônia Braga's own long "wild hair," central to her sex symbol image. Though mostly worn tied up, Clara lets her hair down in key scenes about her sexuality: revealing her mastectomy scar while undressing for a shower, dancing to a Roberto Carlos song after being sexually rejected for lacking a breast, and satisfying her sexual needs with a gigolo. In the 1970s, Sônia Braga's body (and hair) symbolized freedom and supplied sexual fantasies during the Brazilian dictatorship. In the 1980s and 1990s, she embodied sexualized stereotypes about Brazilians and Latinos in U.S. media. In the 2010s, Braga's performance as Clara has given her star image a more political dimension as symbol of survival and resistance. And that image has been supported beyond cinema, through political views shared on Facebook and her brief role as a fierce Latina mother in the race-conscious Netflix series *Luke Cage* (2016).

Gael García Bernal: updating ethnic stardom and mobility

Dolores Tierney

Gael García Bernal's stardom has been determined from its beginnings by border crossings. His early film roles, *Amores perros* and *Y tu mamá también*, which had relatively huge crossover success in the United States and Europe, catapulted him from national prominence and what would have been a small art house circuit to Hollywood/global stardom *before* he had appeared in any major English-language roles. This border crossing and crossover appeal has necessarily produced a certain kind of "ethnic stardom" that continues through his more contemporary roles. By ethnic stardom I mean the transborder positioning of his identity as a Latin American in the Hollywood film industry and U.S. imaginary, and the ways Gael fits into the formation of stardom for U.S. audiences even though his early career and critically successful roles (until *Mozart in the Jungle*) happened largely elsewhere.

In order to understand the dynamics of his ethnic stardom, we might productively contrast his career outside of Mexico with that of the earlier experiences of another Mexican actor, Pedro Armendáriz, who played a variety of different ethnicities during his Hollywood career, including Turkish, Mongol, Cuban, and Cherokee, but only consistently played his own Mexican ethnicity in John Ford films—as a Mexican in *The Fugitive* (1948) and a Mexican-American in *Three Godfathers* (1948) and *Fort Apache* (1948) (Tierney 2012). Unlike Armendáriz's "otherness," performed mostly within the Hollywood industry, Gael achieves a transnational star status even before entering the Hollywood star constellation, and ironically does not appear in a high-profile American film until the lead role in the recent *Rosewater* (Jon Stewart, 2014). Notably, he has yet to play the role of a Mexican in a fully "Hollywood" film—although he has played Mexican characters in the co-production *La casa de mi padre* (*The House of My Father*, Matt Piedmont, 2012, Panteleon/Lionsgate) and in the independent *Babel* (Alejandro González Iñárritu, 2006). Nonetheless, he occupies a unique variation of Mexican cinematic identity in Hollywood, presenting Taymor's *Frida* as one of the nominees for Best Picture at the 2003 Oscars ceremony, and posing for an interview with *People*—a prominent U.S. publication—in 2004 (Sánchez Prado 2013: 147). In effect, his career seems to have updated the kind of ethnic stardom that characterized Armendáriz, and, by analogy, earlier Americanized Latin American actors, including Carmen Miranda, Fernando Lamas, etc., by virtue of a series of transnational media connections.

To add a further layer of complexity to his ethnic stardom, we note how it is often Latin American/Spanish directors who have called on Gael to play different (Latin American) others, albeit directors funded by U.S. (Sundance) and European (Film Four, Canal+, TVE) institutions. As these films circulate in the US through art house circuits, they reinforce the interstitial nature of his unique updating of ethnic stardom. Viewing his career in these terms, we are better able to appreciate the importance of his winning a coveted Golden Globe in 2016 for his portrayal of Rodrigo de Souza, the conductor of the fictional New York Symphony in *Mozart in the Jungle*, the Amazon Prime series that also won the Golden Globe for Best Comedy. Gael's win was a fitting climax to the previous two years of continued (ethnic) and transnational mobility. These included sitting on the prestigious jury of the Cannes Film Festival and starring as a mysterious forest-dwelling activist in *El Ardor* (*The Burning*, Pablo Fendrik, Argentina, 2014), which also showed at the festival. He starred as a migrant in *Desierto* (*The Desert*, Jonas Cuarón, 2015), a chase thriller set in the New Mexico desert, and had a new term coined (by Daniela Cabrera of the digital publisher *Remezcla*) for his own press coverage: "Gaelindura" (Chavez 2014). A play on words, *Gaelindura* translates literally as "pretty Gael," but it could also be taken to mean "Gael appeal."

From his film debut in the critically and commercially successful *Amores perros*, followed by major roles in three of the region's other highest-grossing films—*Y tu mamá también, El crimen del padre Amaro*, and *Diarios de motocicleta*—Gael (whose individuality is highlighted by the fact that he is often referred to by just his first name) has been credited with "creating a buzz around [not just] Mexico's new cinema," but also contributing hugely to the successes

Figure 11.2 *Diarios de motocicleta* (Motorcycle Diaries, Walter Salles 2004). *Gaelindura*, or "Gael appeal."

of a new wave of Latin American cinema of the early 2000s (De la Mora 2006: 169). These four successful films roles in a four-year period launched him to global (Hollywood) stardom.

Since appearing in *Diarios de motocicleta* and *La mala educación* (*Bad Education*, Pedro Almodóvar, Spain, 2004) in the same year, Gael has continued to move between act-ing projects in Mexico (*Rudo y Cursi*, Carlos Cuarón, 2008), France (*La science des rêves*, *The Science of Sleep*, Michel Gondry, 2006), Spain (*También la lluvia*, *Even the Rain*, Icíar Bollaín, 2010), and the US (*Babel; Letters to Juliette*, Gary Winick, 2010; *La casa de mi padre*; *Mammoth*, Lukas Moodyssen, 2009; *Rosewater; A Little Bit of Heaven*, Nicole Kassel, 2011). As a result of this multiplicity of national and transnational contexts in which he works and his "performance of characters from diverse national and cultural origins," Gael's stardom, Ignacio Sánchez Prado argues, has become "deterritorialized" into a kind of "post-Mexico" Mexicanness (Sánchez Prado 2013: 148).

In casting Gael in a variety of different Latin nationalities, Salles, Larraín, and Bollaín are likely tapping in to Gael's regional/transnational appeal, as well as the financial/box-office security his star status brings, while simultaneously catering to the homogenizing tendencies of their U.S. and European backers. Despite his presumed deterritorialization, Gael's stardom is never completely dislocated from his Mexicanness or Latin Americanness, and never de-racial-ized or de-ethnified. His un-bordered stardom might facilitate his deliberate de-racination from any national bonds in films such as the English-language *Mammoth*, which is set in a variety of international locations (New York, Bangkok) and made by a Swedish director. Conversely, these dislocations also facilitate his flat but successful mimicking of Argentine (*Diarios de motocicleta*), Spanish (*La mala educación*), and Chilean accents (*¡No!*, 2014 and *Neruda*, 2016, Pablo Larraín). These country-specific performances are balanced by the allegorical *Blindness* (Fernando Meirelles, 2008), in which Gael's non-specific Latin Americanness (along with a number of other features) is important in anchoring the film in a Latin American context.

There is, of course, another way to interpret the variety of ethnicities and nationalities in Gael's career: in relation to the notion of ethnic stardom. The variety of non-white nation-alities (excepting of course his Frenchness in *The Science of Sleep*), which Gael and other

Mexican actors before him were called upon to perform, could be considered emblematic of the practice of homogenizing all "others," as in Hollywood's predominantly Eurocentric vision "otherness" is not considered significant in itself, and is therefore interchangeable.

Taking into consideration the history of Latino/a American representation in Hollywood, Gael's most current role (*Mozart in the Jungle*) represents progress in the US/Hollywood's ethnic representation. From the second season onwards, his character is defined as specifically Mexican, whereas in the first season he was presented as a pan-Latin American who had a Brazilian-/Portuguese-sounding last name (De Souza), drank mate, and was soundtracked by a number of different "Latin" musical genres, including samba. That he can play his own ethnicity in a U.S. project suggests a progressive shift in Gael's stardom as it is conceived in the United States. A further progression in the future would be if he gets to perform a character whose ethnicity is not an issue, or merely to continue to play his own ethnicity (Mexican) consistently (as with other ethnic stars such as James Cagney, who as a star constantly played Irish Americans). Although, as Diane Negra points out, even playing one's own ethnicity does not cancel out Hollywood's tendency to "absorb and commodify" ethnicity (Negra 2001: 1).

A key factor in Gael's ethnic Latin American stardom as it has evolved over time is the connection to politics and his social commitment. Although not all of his films buttress this aspect of his stardom, political roles are still the ones for which he is most well known and the ones most mentioned in his star text (Rapkin 2014). In addition to playing a young Che Guevara in the moment of his awakening to radical consciousness in *Diarios de motocicleta*, and Zahara, a transgender woman in *La mala educación* abused and silenced by the Catholic Church, he has recently appeared in *Desierto* as a young migrant hunted by a murderous anti-immigration vigilante, in *Rosewater* as a political prisoner, and in *El Ardor* as a mythical Kai fighting developers who seek to destroy the jungle in northern Argentina. Gael's political commitments are also clear from the numerous "issues"-based films he chooses to act in, even though the characters he plays are not, the films emphasize, sympathetically political. In *También la lluvia*, for instance, he plays a film director, Sebastián, who wants to make a historical epic about the colonial era's mistreatment of indigenous people, but balks at getting involved in the contemporary indigenous rights conflict in Bolivia. In *¡No!*, he plays advertising executive René Saavedra, who successfully sells the "no" campaign in the 1988 plebiscite that ended the Pinochet dictatorship with the same kind of vacuous marketing spiel used to sell a bottle of Coke.

Extra-textually, Gael's stardom is buttressed by political activism that it is frequently cited in press coverage of his films and in interviews (Rickett 2015). But in contradistinction to what Toby Miller suggests in "Why Coldplay Sucks" (Miller 2013), about the political activism of many U.S. and U.K. stars and celebrities, Gael's activism amounts to more than a Twitter account and paying lip service to causes. He is involved in direct action for the issues (principally migration) he is committed to, action that more often than not takes the form of cinema-related activities, producing and appearing in *¿Quién es Dayani Cristal?* (*Who Is Dayani Cristal?*, Marc Silver, 2013), about how tighter border controls are literally killing many Central American migrants attempting the crossing into the United States, and producing and part-directing *Los invisibles* (*The Invisible Ones*, Marc Silver, 2010) about the terrifying and dangerous experiences of Central American migrants crossing through Mexico to the US.

Gael's political activism is also about allying social causes with the cause of Mexican cinema itself, which he pursues through a variety of producing and directorial projects. In 2006, with fellow Mexican actor Diego Luna and producer Pablo Cruz, he set up CANANA

Films, which produces films that are overwhelmingly focused on social and political issues. These include the Mexican films *Las elejidas* (*The Chosen Ones*, David Pablos, 2015), an exposé of forced prostitution among teenage girls, *Revolución* (2010), an anthology film that commemorates Mexico's 1910–1920 Revolution and highlights ongoing instances of social exclusion and marginalization in which Gael directs one of the shorts, "Lucio," and *Miss Bala* (Gerardo Naranjo, 2011), about political corruption at the heart of Mexico's drug wars. As well, CANANA co-produced the Chilean film *¡No!*. Gael also co-founded Ambulante, with Luna and Elena Fortes, the moving festival of documentaries that "promot[es] social and educational concerns" (MacLaird 2013: 68), and is now into its 12th year. In 2007, Gael made his feature film directorial debut with *Déficit*, a film focused on social inequality and the gap between rich and servant classes in Mexico.

A recurring comment in press coverage about Gael focuses on the evident contradictions between his commitment to political and issue-based films and his good looks and sex appeal (Rapkin 2014; Rickett 2015). It has been suggested (by seminal theorist of star studies) Richard Dyer, however, that such a "degree [of] *opposition* or *contradiction*" is common in the elements of a star's signification, and that consequently "the star's image is characterized by attempts to negotiate, reconcile or mask the difference between the elements" (Dyer 1998: 64, my emphasis). In Gael's image, the reconciliation between sex appeal and politics seems to be worked out through a particular form of ethnic stardom that takes on ideas about Latin America as seen and homogenized from a U.S. perspective. In these terms, his star persona connects his Latin Americanness with an imagined post-1960s political radicalism that is particular to Latin America and its history of revolution *and* a more classical version of Latin stardom: the sensual *Latin lover*. Rather than politics detracting from his sex or Gael appeal, it is crucially defined by his connection to politics.

Indeed, politics and sex appeal are often connected by his much-commented-upon charisma, which is discernible not just in his star persona off-screen, but also, and very importantly, in certain *on-screen* roles as well, particularly when he plays real-life characters famous for their charisma and politics. For instance, at one point in the Robert Redford-commissioned *Diarios de motocicleta*, Gael as the young Ernesto Guevara greets and talks to various stallholders at the market in Temuco, Chile. The effectiveness of these moments in the film, in which the stallholders (who, following director Walter Salles' common practice, are played by nonprofessional actors) appear awkward and bashful as they speak to Ernesto (Gael), relies both on Gael's acting out of Ernesto's legendary charisma (Niess 2003: 58) but also on the actor's own charisma. Gael is and is perceived as simultaneously his real charismatic self (the famous Mexican/Latin American actor) and an actor playing a charismatic historical individual communicating with real people.

Some journalistic accounts (Rapkin 2014; Heawood 2015; Rickett 2015) cite the fact that Gael has not moved to Hollywood to work purely within its parameters as proof of his political credentials and appeal:

> He could have taken those good looks, which have barely changed over the years, climbed aboard the Hollywood gravy train and never looked back, but instead he has chosen to make, for the most part, Latin American films. Not just as an actor, Bernal is also a producer, writer and director, bringing zeal to a range of politically charged human-interest stories.
>
> (*Rickett 2015*)

What these accounts perhaps do not take into consideration is that working and residing in Latin America (most recent interviews and articles note he is based between Mexico City and Buenos Aires) (Rapkin 2014; Rickett 2015) is part of the Gael appeal/*Gaelindura* that fuses politics with his national/regional origins. What happens in his continuing role in *Mozart in the Jungle* (Season 4 is out December 2017) however—where, as Rodrigo he plays a good-looking, charismatic, and unconventional character who is not (yet) political—may mean a renegotiation of the terms on which Gael's ethnic stardom is based.

The secret in Ricardo Darín's eyes

Victoria Ruétalo

Although arguably the most important star in contemporary Argentine cinema, Ricardo Darín's stardom is also defined by a transnational space that is not Hollywood, but the Spanish-speaking and global art cinema markets (Garavelli 2015). The star in fact turned down the possibility of a Hollywood career when he discovered the role on offer was that of a drug dealer in *Man on Fire* (Tony Scott, 2004) (Darín 2013). This section looks at the construction of Darín's stardom in relation to key local elements: Argentine masculinity, the New Argentine Cinema, and the tension between his status as an exemplary figure and star of domestic cinema and of international successes. Through close textual analysis of some of his key films, including *Nueve reinas* (*Nine Queens*, Fabián Bielinsky, 2003), the metacinematic *Delirium* (Carlos Kaimakamian Carrau, 2014), *El aura* (*The Aura*, Fabián Bielinsky, 2005), and *El secreto de sus ojos* (*The Secret in Their Eyes*, Juan José Campanella, 2009), and their increasingly deliberate framing that focuses on his expressive eyes and face, I want to argue that his star text is defined as representative of a new era of Argentine masculinity.

Of the 21 features he has starred in since his breakthrough success in *Nueve reinas* 16 are co-productions, 15 (including the Oscar-winning *El secreto de sus ojos* have Spain as a co-producer, and two are only Spanish, including *Una pistola en cada mano* (*A Gun in Each Hand*, Cesc Gay, 2012). The high numbers of co-productions and productions with/in Spain in Darín's recent filmography, including the recent phenomenally successful *Relatos Salvajes* (*Wild Tales*, Damián Szifrón, 2014), which broke box office records in Argentina and earned $27 million worldwide, make Darín a star in both local (Argentine) *and* international (Spanish) markets. Indeed, as John Hopwell points out in relation to his casting in *Relatos Salvajes*, Darín is enough of a name actor in Spain and Argentina to sell a film in both territories (Hopwell 2013).

Although a unique national star in Argentina (in 2011 he won the Konex Foundation Diamond Award as the most influential and distinguished personality in the entertainment industry), Darín's film performances in predominantly big-budget mainstream films are in many ways outside the dominant critical trend in Argentine cinema: New Argentine Cinema pursues a politics of (an anonymous) face and body and prefers to use nonprofessional performers who can bring a sense of authenticity rather than performativity to film acting (Aguilar 2008: 209). New Argentine films such as *La ciénaga* (*The Swamp*, Lucrecia Martel, 2001) seek to denaturalize acting and outwardly reject melodrama (Gundermann 2005: 258). Although *Nueve reinas* has been folded into the ideological aims of the New Argentine Cinema, Darín's work in it and in films such as *Hijo de la novia* (*Son of the Bride*, José Juan Campanella, 2000) and *Luna de Avellaneda* (*Avellaneda's Moon*, José

Juan Campanella, 2004) is perceived as much more commercial, and more a part of both mainstream Argentine and international cinema. In contrast to the non-performativity of New Argentine Cinema, Darín's stardom is based precisely on the expressiveness of *his* face, which since his first important hit, *Nueve reinas*, has become his trademark.

Darín's face, which is increasingly the focus on in his post-2000 films, is key to the way he embodies a new Argentine middle-aged man. Different to a previous generation of actors whose careers peaked in the 1990s (e.g. Miguel Ángel Solá, Héctor Alterio, Federico Luppi) and who personified a tough and straightforward middle-aged man emasculated by the neo-liberal shift that took place in the Menem era (Rocha 2012: 16), Darin communicates through his face, and in particular through his eyes. These add a layer of complexity, depth, and vulnerability to his star persona (Andermann 2012: 133), and express a masculinity that is more thoughtful and analytical than that of male stars of previous generations.

Darín began acting on television at the tender age of 3, worked in *telenovelas* throughout the 1970s, 1980s, and 1990s, and in the theater during most of his life. He also starred in a series of popular films for the Argentine production company Aries Cinematográfica, two of which were directed by Adolfo Aristarain, *La playa del amor* (*Love Beach*, 1980) and *La discoteca del amor* (*Love Disco*, 1980), which helped to solidify the "galancito" (young

Figure 11.3   Darín is an attentive observer with penetrating eyes that often hide a secret.

Figure 11.4   Darín's eyes express a masculinity that is more thoughtful and analytical than that of male stars of previous generations.

"galán," handsome, eligible sex symbol) status he acquired in *telenovelas* such as *Ayer fue mentira* (*Yesterday Was a Lie*, Canal 9, 1975). Although he received some recognition for his early films, it was not until *Nueve reinas* that he began to register as a star in Spanish-language markets. *Nueve reinas* was a landmark film that grossed over $12 million worldwide (Alvaray 2008: 53), and marked a new phase in the actor's career that coincided with increases in co-productions and better distribution practices, and consequent success of Argentine cinema in international markets. It was as much these industrial shifts as the particular qualities of Darín's face and acting abilities that made him a staple of Argentina's domestic cinema (particularly as seen from the global art cinema market), and ushered in a new era in his career as a versatile transatlantic middle-aged star.

Clara Garavelli suggests that between 1994 and 2012, as Darín becomes a star, there's a shift in both his publicity shots and how he is framed by the camera, from predominantly medium shots to mainly close-ups (Garavelli 2015: 422). Following Garavelli, we can see that in *Nueve reinas*, shots of Darín's character, Marcos—as he cons his way through a variety of scenarios—focus on his head and face, and consequently emphasize both that he is performing and his character's untrustworthiness. The film opens at an Esso station when Juan (Gastón Paul) tries to cheat the clerk. In this scene, Marcos' profile in close-up observes the exchange from behind the aisle before he steps in to rescue Juan, highlighting the character's actorly feigning while simultaneously focusing on the actor's good-looking face. Marcos remains an actor for most of the film (indeed, the film is about acting itself), with close-ups reinforcing the fact that he is always acting with his face. Only at the end does the film unveil a "true" Marcos, when he returns from the bank, his face bloodied and without the money. He turns to Juan, who walks off in (feigned) disgust.

There's a similar focus on shots of the character's/Darín's face in Bielinsky's *El aura* (2004). Darín plays Esteban, a quiet and reserved taxidermist who suffers from epilepsy, but who also has a photographic memory. This ability is emphasized in a key moment through close-ups of Esteban's face witnessing a crime. Bielinsky sets up characteristics in both *Nueves reinas* and *El aura* that establish the kinds of roles that characterize Darín's subsequent career, making him not just a "catchy face" (Garavelli 2013: 24), but also an attentive observer with penetrating eyes that are hiding a secret.

Other directors (Juan José Campanella and Pablo Trapero) who frequently cast Darín in their movies make similar use of his eyes. *El secreto de sus ojos*, the fourth produced with Campanella, tells the tale of a writer, Benjamín (Darín) who attempts to solve a mystery after 25 years. The film reconstructs the case through flashbacks as Benjamín attempts to write it down in a novel. The film focuses on Benjamín's face when he is writing, often lingering on his eyes (Rocha 2014: 10). Near the end of the film when he is driving away from Morales' house (the victim's husband), shots of Benjamín behind the wheel are crosscut with his thoughts and flashbacks. When he remembers Morales' words "don't think anymore," all the pieces of the case/puzzle start to fit together. The camera then closes in on his face and lingers until we see his eyes at the moment of understanding. The scene brilliantly exemplifies the characterization of Darín as an analytical thinker, who works through the past to recreate the present and eventually solves the mystery.

This emphasis on Darín's face, particularly his piercing eyes, continues in his more recent work, signaling his role as witness in *Elefante blanco* (*White Elephant*, Pablo Trapero, 2012), analytical thinker in *Carancho* (*Vulture*, Pablo Trapero, 2010), modern-day detective in *Tesis sobre un homicidio* (*Thesis on a Homicide*, Hernán Goldfrid, 2012), and perceptive observer in *Un cuento chino* (*Chinese Takeout*, Antonio Llorens, 2011). In all of these instances Darín's nuanced facial expression draws us constantly to his eyes as the locus of meaning.

The combination of the shots of Darín's face and eyes across his *oeuvre* is even more calculated in *Delirium*—a self-conscious and self-referential exploration of both his "star image" (Dyer 1998: 62) and the many complexities of his on- and off-screen persona during the post-*Nueve reinas* era. It features three friends, Federico, Mariano, and Martín, who decide to liven up their dull lives and gain instant wealth and fame by making a "New Argentine" film. They approach the "big star" "Darín" (who plays himself) to help them achieve this goal, but accidentally kill him early in the shoot. To cover their tracks, they arrange to leak to the press footage that suggests that "Darín" is leaving Argentina. "Darín's" suspicious disappearance leads to a national crisis when Susana Giménez (TV personality and Darín's real-life partner for nine years) appears on TV as the president of Argentina, trying to alleviate the chaos and demands "Darín's" return.

Delirium initially reinforces the on- and off-screen characterization of Darín as the "guy next door" (Urraca 2014: 359; Garavelli 2015) when one of the filmmakers refers to him as "un tipo común" ("a common man") and "Darín" agrees to work on the low-budget production because he (mistakenly) believes he knows Federico's family. And yet "Darín's" celebrity-like behavior on set contradicts the "guy next door" type. When he first arrives to meet the filmmakers, he wears an ascot, which paints him as pretentious. During filming, he makes so many demands that the filmmakers proclaim "que no se haga la Estrella" ("he shouldn't act like such a prima donna"). In addition to being about the making of a "New Argentine film", *Delirium* consciously identifies itself as a new Argentine film, but also plays with some of the movement's central tenets. For instance, it casts three unknown and deliberately under-acted performers who provide the kind of access to the "real" experiences of the everyday that the movement so values, alongside a professional, melodramatic actor (Darín). This injection of the "real," which is so central to the mythos of New Argentine Cinema, ironically also happens in the slippage between Darín and the version he plays of himself, "Darín." This perpetual reflexive exercise of Darín's presence in the film reveals an obsession with performance that clearly distances "Darín" from this "guy next door" public persona and makes him a less ordinary and more exceptional presence. The film makes clear that "Darín" is a star, but makes fun of his analytical thinker star persona that is so often embodied by the frequent close-up (across his *oeuvre*) on his eyes. In *Delirium*, the extreme close-up of his eyes (showcasing him "thinking") happens ironically only when he is lying dead and gazing sightlessly into the camera.

The recurring close-ups of Darín's familiar face, particularly those of his unique and distinctive eyes in his post-*Nueve reinas* career, indicate not just the slightly vulnerable and thoughtful new Argentine middle-aged man, but also trace the influence of (his early career in) television. To a certain extent, the excessive focus on his face and eyes post-2000 also fossilize his star image for Argentine audiences. He remains frozen in the local imagination even as he coexists and becomes a star in transnational markets.

Conclusion

From the above discussion and analyses of three exemplary star discourses, it seems Latin American stardom cannot exist without a necessary external axis of production/consumption and distribution. There are, however, also some telling differences among the career paths of Braga, Bernal, and Darín. Braga and Bernal are evidently constrained in their choice of roles by their Latin Americanness/ethnicity when they work outside their country of origin. Despite this, Braga has stayed away from Brazil and been criticized for it, whereas Bernal has managed to shift easily back and forth between U.S./European and

Latin American industries without ever seeming to leave Mexico. Darín, on the other hand, has rejected the idea of ever working in Hollywood.

What seems most interesting contemporaneously in these three star studies, and a useful avenue of future research, is how and whether Latin American stardom will continue to shift as more and more Latin American stars are courted and continue to work in U.S. television. Moura has just finished appearing in the Netflix production *Narcos*. Mexican Demián Bechir has been in *Weeds* (2008–2010) and *The Bridge* (2013–2014), and Bernal appears next in season four of *Mozart in the Jungle*. For a star system with its local beginnings in television, this move suggests Latin American stardom is coming in a (kind of) full circle.

References

Aguilar, G. (2008) *Other Worlds: New Argentine Film*. New York: Palgrave Macmillan.

Alvaray, L. (2008) "National, Regional, and Global: New Waves of Latin American Cinema." *Cinema Journal*, 47(3): 48–65.

Andermann, J. (2012) *New Argentine Cinema*. London: I.B. Tauris.

Beltrán, M.C. (2009) *Latino/a Stars in US Eyes: The Makings and Meanings of Stardom*. Chicago, IL: University of Illinois Press.

Buckley, C. (1998) "Gender Troubles in Neville D'Almeida's *Dama do Lotacao*." *Studies in Latin American Popular Culture*, 17: 129–138.

Chavez, D. (2014) "Gael Garcia Bernal Learned Portuguese in Bed and Other Highlights from 'The Year in Gael'." *Remezcla*. Available at: http://remezcla.com/lists/gael-garcia-bernal-learned-portuguese-bed-highlights-year-gael/ (accessed January 15, 2015).

Christiansen, R. (1978) "'Dona Flor'—Sexy Brazilian Exotica." *Chicago Tribune*, July 31: A6.

Darín, R. (2013) "Interview with Alejandro Fantino." *Animales Sueltos*. América TV, LS86. Buenos Aires, September 17. Available at: www.youtube.com/watch?v=izOatvH5vPk (accessed August 1, 2015).

Da Silva, A. (2014) "Sônia Braga: la beauté latine de la 'vraie femme brésilienne' des années de la dictature." *Mise au point*, 6. Available at: http://map.revues.org/1748 (accessed February 15, 2015).

De la Mora, S. (2006) *Cinemachismo: Masculinities and Sexuality in Mexican Film*. Austin, TX: Texas University Press.

Dennison, S. and Shaw, L. (2004) *Popular Cinema in Brazil, 1930–2001*. Manchester/New York: Manchester University Press.

Dyer, R. (1998) *Stars*. London: Routledge.

Garavelli, C. (2013) "A Shared Star Imagery: The Argentine Actor Ricardo Darín through Spanish Film Posters." *Ol3Media*. Available at: http://host.uniroma3.it/riviste/Ol3Media/Stardom_files/Ol3Media%2013%20Stardom.pdf (accessed August 25, 2015).

—— (2015) "Conquering the Conquerors: Ricardo Darín's Rise to Stardom in Spanish Film Culture." *Bulletin of Hispanic Studies*, 92(4): 411–428.

Geraghty, C. (2000) "Re-Examining Stardom: Questions of Text, Bodies and Performance." In C. Gledhill and L. Williams (eds.), *Re-Inventing Film Studies*. London: Arnold, pp. 183–201.

Gundermann, C. (2005) "The Stark Gaze of the New Argentine Cinema: Restoring Strangeness to the Object in the Perverse Age of Commodity Fetishism." *Journal of Latin American Cultural Studies*, 14(3): 241–261.

Heawood, S. (2015) "Gael Garcia Bernal: 'Donald Trump Calls Mexicans Rapists and Drug Dealers. It's Hate Discourse'." *The Guardian*, December 30. Available at: www.theguardian.com/tv-and-radio/2015/dec/30/gael-garcia-bernal-donald-trump-mexicans-hate-discourse-mozart-in-jungle (accessed June 1, 2017).

Hopwell, J. (2013) "Telefonica Studies Ups Production Slate." *Variety*, September 23. Available at: http://variety.com/2013/film/global/telefonica-studios-ups-production-slate-1200662004/ (accessed November 3, 2015).

Kroll, J. (1982) "Sex Goddess from Brazil." *Newsweek*, May 3: 83.

Legg, B. (2015) "The Bicultural Sex Symbol: Sônia Braga in Brazilian and North American Popular Culture." In S.J. Albuquerque and K. Bishop-Sanchez (eds.), *Performing Brazil: Essays on Culture, Identity, and the Performing Arts*. Madison, WI: University of Wisconsin Press, pp. 202–223.

Lifsher, M. (1977) "Attracting Brazilians: Brazilian Movies Getting Better." *Los Angeles Times*, June 25: B11.

López, A.M. (1993) "'Are All Latins from Manhattan?' Hollywood, Ethnography and Cultural Colonialism." In J. King, A.M. López, and M. Alvarado (eds.), *Mediating Two Worlds: Cinematic Encounters in the Americas*. London: BFI, pp. 67–80.

—— (1994) "A Cinema for the Continent." In C.A. Noriega and S. Ricci (eds.), *The Mexican Cinema Project*. Los Angeles, CA: UCLA Press, pp. 7–12.

—— (1998) "From Hollywood and Back: Dolores Del Rio, a Transnational Star." *Studies in Latin American Popular Culture*, 17: 5–32.

MacLaird, M. (2013) *Aesthetics and Politics in the Mexican Film Industry*. New York: Palgrave Macmillan.

Miller, T. (2013) "Why Coldplay Sucks." *Celebrity Studies*, 4(3): 372–376.

Negra, D. (2001) *Off-White Hollywood: American Culture and Ethnic Female Stardom*. London: Routledge.

Niess, Frank (2003) *Che Guevara*. London: Haus Publishing.

Rapkin, M. (2014) "Gael Garcia Bernal: The Intellectual Women's Heartthrob." *Elle*, September 17. Available at: www.elle.com/culture/celebrities/a14776/gael-garcia-bernal-interview/ (accessed June 1, 2017).

Rickett, O (2015) "Gael Garcia Bernal: 'I Feel Hopeful and Naively Optimistic'." *The Observer*, June 7. Avaialble at: www.theguardian.com/film/2015/jun/07/gael-garcia-bernal-interview-film-latin-america (accessed June 1, 2017).

Rocha, C. (2012) *Masculinities in Contemporary Argentine Popular Cinema*. New York: Palgrave Macmillan.

—— (2014) "*El secreto de sus ojos*: An Argentine Melodrama." *New Cinemas: Journal of Contemporary Film*, 12: 3–15.

Sánchez Prado, I. (2013) "The Neoliberal Stars: Salma Hayek and Gael García Bernal and the Post-Mexican Film Icon." In D.C. Niebylski and P. O'Connor (eds.), *Latin American Icons: Fame across Borders*. Nashville, TN: Vanderbilt University Press, pp. 147–156.

Tierney, D. (2012) "Latino Acting on Screen: Pedro Armendáriz Performs Mexicanness in Three John Ford Movies." *Revista Canadiense de Estudios Hispánicos*, 37(1): 111–134.

Urraca, B. (2014) "Rituals of Performance: Ricardo Darín as Father Julián in *Elefante blanco*." *Revista de Estudios Hispánicos*, 48: 353–372.

Wolf, W. (1982) "Flying Up From Rio." *New York*, May 17: 70, 73.

12

RADICAL RUPTURES IN THE CINEMA OF LATIN AMERICA AROUND "1968"

Mariano Mestman

Editors' introduction

Problematizing the easy symbiosis between "the long 1960s," typically crystallized in the term "1968," and the complex movement known as the New Latin American Cinema (NLAC), this chapter interrogates the historical trajectory of the movement vis-à-vis two axes of inquiry: the interplay between national/regional experiences and transnational flows around 1968, and the links between the NLAC movement, Latin Americanism, and Third Worldism in general. While not arguing for a return to unproblematic "national" cinema studies, Mariano Mestman emphasizes that the ruptures with cinematic and political traditions that occurred in the late 1960s were simultaneously linked with transnational flows while also deeply rooted in national historical, political, artistic, and cinematic specificities. On the flip side, and pointing to a series of broad geopolitical exchanges, Mestman details how Latin Americanism came to be understood and adapted locally and the influence of the Federation of Pan-African Filmmakers (FEPACI) on the organization of the Latin American Filmmakers Committee. Together with Chapter 13 (Masha Salazkina), this chapter begins a much-needed interrogation and contextualization of the complex political, ideological, and aesthetic flows of "1968."

The protests that took place in and around the symbolic year "1968" represent a historic moment of dialogue about the national and transnational dynamics of politics and culture. In Latin American political cinema, we can see this process in a series of ruptures with tradition that we identify with "1968," but which, as the following try to clarify, actually precedes and follows it (1967–1974). This essay will explore these dynamics framed by a few initial questions. Are there, in fact, commonalities between the ruptures of Latin American cinema and those associated with "1968" in other latitudes? If so, what common features and meanings can be identified? How can these be interpreted outside the Eurocentric perspective, which appears embedded in the very idea of "1968"? What dialogues were established between the Latin American, European, or North American "1968," and between Latin America and other parts of the so-called Third World? To what extent can we speak in broad terms of Latin America as a region without delving into the unique characteristics of each country?

1968, the "long 1960s," and the New Latin American Cinema

Mostly, "1968" was studied and imagined as a First World (French, European, or American) phenomenon. But recent scholarship has begun to highlight global events outside the First World, thus expanding our understanding of the processes of revolt, rebellion, and revolution in "1968," both geographically and chronologically (Rutherford et al. 2009; Christiansen and Scarlett 2013; Sherman et al. 2013).

As we know, "1968" is part of a vaster "epoch," the "long decade of the 1960s." In an early and now classic essay on how to characterize this decade, Fredric Jameson (1984: 16) spoke of a "rhythm" and "dynamics" characteristic of a period that, in his view, extends from the second half of the 1950s until some point between 1972 and 1974. Per Jameson's argument, important events occurring in Latin America and the Third World justified extending this period from the 1950s into the 1970s. Other scholars have proposed that the 1960s started with the Algerian War (1954) and/or the Conference of Bandung (1955), and view it as reaching as far as the war against the Nicaraguan Contras in 1980 (Rutherford et al. 2009: Introduction).

Bibliography on cultural and intellectual production in Latin America has frequently addressed the topic of the long decade. Eric Zolov (2008, 2014), for example, emphasizes the transnational and cultural dimension of the 1960s protests in Latin America and acknowledges the limitations of considering these processes within the chronologically imposed 10-year period (1960–1969). In an important book on the radical Latin American writers in the 1960s, Claudia Gilman (2003) has justified the use of the idea of an "epoch" to refer to a period spanning the 1960s and 1970s (from 1959 until around 1973 or 1976, in her model). According to Gilman, there are several common features to this period, such as a strong interest in politics and the expectation and belief in radical and imminent transformations at all levels. In terms of film, this "epoch" (from the mid-1950s through the mid-1970s) is most frequently associated with the New Latin American Cinema (NLAC). Extensive scholarship has been produced about this period, with academic research increasingly focused on its transnational influences and exchanges.

Although we know what the term NLAC refers to, it has never been easy to establish an exact timeline for this movement or its geographical reach. Some scholars (e.g. Paranaguá 2000, 2003a, 2003b; more recently León Frías 2013) have insisted on the restrictive and increasingly canonical use of the term NLAC—especially when it is associated with more politicized film directors and movies. They have also noted the limits of the term, as the conditions and exclusions implicit to NLAC leave out other equally innovative or groundbreaking films of the period. I am very aware of the risk of simply repeating a narrative that privileges a broader vision of the NLAC phenomenon as though to somehow justify it. My goal, however, is not to discuss the "selective traditions" (to use Raymond Williams' term) that were created by the filmmakers' discourses and manifestos during those years. These formulations reflected a type of discursive construction typical of almost any group intending to make a cultural or political intervention, and thus should be understood as a type of (political) rupture. Of course, this was not the only rupture during such radical times, but it was perhaps the most significant.

A more in-depth examination must start by shifting away, at least temporarily, from the broadest definitions of the NLAC and from the sweeping, integrative narratives that, canonical or otherwise, continue to appear in many essays and doctoral theses. Instead, I am particularly interested in perusing the broader visions of the NLAC phenomenon, as well as interpreting the influences and processes of transnationalization within political film. That is to say, research should start by focusing on the dynamic nature of this cinema and the diverse meanings and values that accompanied the ruptures in each place. Thus, this analysis requires a focus on the specific cultural configurations in each country and how transnational influences were received and processed where the films of rupture were ultimately made. This isn't a new idea, as many of the books written about NLAC have noted how important it is to consider the unique features of each country. More than a new approach, then, this perspective involves shifting the emphasis to the ruptures—a key concept used in the plural to highlight the fact that there is not a single categorical rupture—and the way these ruptures evolve into a singular here and now in "1968."

In the following pages, I will deal with two issues: the different types of ruptures (both countercultural and political) and their local or national singularities. Then, I will analyze how some imaginaries of the period, such as "Latin Americanism" or "Third Worldism," functioned in different Latin American countries (also in the First World) in "1968" and the "long 1960s."

Between countercultural and political cinematic ruptures

The ruptures of "1968" were built upon ideologies and social imaginaries that incorporated and reworked the avant-garde impetus of the early twentieth century (since the Russian Revolution) in politics and art. This recovery of radical traditions in a search to define an idea of "revolution" was common across the world in the 1960s, as exemplified by the left or national "new lefts," the Leninists, Third Worldists, Christians, Fanonists, Maoists, Trotskyists, etc. It often appeared in conjunction with processes of cultural renovation and experimentation, along with the incorporation of "global" countercultural trends visible in music, art, and new youth cultures.

Considering this historical context, we can recognize, at a minimum, two discernible facets in the cinematographic transformations of "1968" in Latin America, at least from an analytical perspective. The first involves countercultural trends and is associated with the new sensibilities of the decade, while the second is more directly related to the radical politics of the Third World, working-class struggles, and/or guerilla warfare. While the manifestation of the latter one is more obvious and extended among the films of those years, the presence of countercultural dimension and/or experimental practices are more frequent in certain groups or national cultural configurations than in others. In any case, we can examine this countercultural trend in both the films where it is most evident or decisive, as well as in films that are often read either mainly in terms of their political dimension. One such example is the documentary *El grito* (*The Shout*, Mexico, 1970), coordinated by Leobardo López Arretche. Because it denounces the Tlatelolco massacre of October 2, 1968, *El grito* has usually been interpreted as a political film. However, the very process of filming the protests by film students from the National University (UNAM) and the depiction of a variety of expressions among the youth participating in the movement reveal the strong countercultural dimension of the rupture. The last section of the film focuses on the

October massacre and shows us, in a rather martyred plaintive tone, the harshest side of the repression. The sections on August and September, however, amply demonstrate the countercultural deployment of the student movement: the massive festive spirit and the generational character of the movement, in synergy with an internationalist avant-garde. In these sections, we can discern facets of the new 1960s subjectivity associated with the arts in the sequences of youth at the UNAM esplanade milling around the collective productions of improvised murals created by students, in the sociodramas about the repression, in the creation of large cardboard figures of the agents of repression (such as the gorilla/grenadier), which were then set on fire in the Zócalo, in street graffiti, and in the hundreds of ingenious posters and prints illustrating that classic "1968" graphic style that interpellates the government in anger but also demonstrates an irony and humor that sustained the irreverent spirit of the movement.

Along with this countercultural dimension of the rupture, in other instances we can also analyze the areas of experimentation in film language in the more political films of the period. This is the case of the work of some of the best-known filmmakers of the 1960s, such as the Cuban Santiago Álvarez, who combined visual and sound experimentation through the montage of his films and his use of collage, the Argentine director Fernando Solanas in the first part of *La hora de los hornos* (*The Hour of the Furnaces*, 1968), and others. Yet these were not the filmmakers who actually represented the counterculture or experimentation, innovations and ruptures in this period. In some countries, experimental groups emerged as an alternative to the film industry and to the state, but also against political-militant

Figure 12.1   Moments of the countercultural deployment of the student movement in *El grito* (*The Shout*, Leobardo López Arretche, Mexico, 1968).

183

films. We can identify a political dimension in the practices of these experimental groups that confronts authoritarian regimes of dictatorships by frequently alluding to the country's situation in indirect, allegorical ways. Yet these kinds of groups were primarily interested in formal exploration and searched for innovations of cinematic language. In Argentina, for example, there was a group of avant-garde filmmakers centered around Alberto Fischerman, as well as, later, others linked to the work of the Insituto Di Tella and the CAYC (Oubiña 2016). In Mexico, a good number of the filmmakers associated with the larger Super 8 movement also exhibited marked experimental tendencies (Vázquez Mantecón 2012). Meanwhile, in Brazil, as Ismail Xavier (1993) noted in a now classic essay, there was an emphasis upon the exploration of cinematic language in the service of allegory. In this context, Xavier commented upon filmmakers such as Júlio Bressane and Andrea Tonacci, among others, who rejected the historical teleology associated with the great hopes prior to the 1964 coup—as magnificently exemplified by Glauber Rochas's *Deus e o diabo na terra do sol* (*Black God, White Devil*, 1964)—and instead promoted a break with previous narrative strategies and transformed their anti-teleology into a formal principle.

In the case of Cuba, Juan Antonio García Borrero (2016) has noted how around 1968, the national film institute (ICAIC), with its relatively high level of autonomy, not only promoted political-historical films commemorating the centennial of Cuba's fight for independence, but also premiered feature-length films such as *Memorias del subdesarrollo* (*Memories of Underdevelopment*, Tomás Gutiérrez Alea, 1968), along with shorts such as *Coffea Arábiga* (Nicolás Guillén-Landrián, 1968) and Sara Gómez's *Una isla para Miguel* (*An Island for Miguel*, 1968) and *La otra isla* (*The Other Island*, 1968). With notable amounts of skepticism, these films offer a surprisingly critical view of revolutionary Cuba.

Thus, the "1968" scene in Latin American film includes more than one type of innovation and rupture, with singular features in each country as well as diversity within.

Local, national, and transnational dynamics

In the 1960s, new independent films circulated among the different countries of Latin America with the help of key figures in film distribution and production such as the Uruguayan Walter Achugar and the Argentine Edgardo Pallero, among others. Some filmmakers made the move from one country to another or exchanged materials thanks to the efforts of pioneering institutions such as the Noticierio ICAIC Latinoamericano, organized in Cuba by Santiago Álvarez. Examples of these exchanges include the documentaries Álvarez made in several countries of Latin America and in Vietnam; the Argentine group known as the Escuela Documental de Santa Fe, which participated in the documentary film project "Caravana Farkas" (the Farkas caravan) in Brazil; the films of Raymundo Gleyzer in Brazil and Mexico, as well as his projects for Chile and Bolivia; and the films of Ugo Ulive in Cuba and Venezuela. The same can be said of the films made in exile such as the work of Jorge Sanjinés in Peru and Ecuador; Miguel Littín in Mexico; or many Latin American filmmakers in Cuba. At the same time, the reach of several of these films and other filmmaking projects expanded across Latin America and even worldwide: Cuban film in general, Brazilian filmmaker Glauber Rocha, and an ambitious, internationalist project (entitled "Por muchos Vietnam"/For Many Vietnams) laid out by Fernando Solanas and Octavio Getino after the broad response to the premiere of *La hora de los hornos* at the Pesaro Film Festival (Italy) in June 1968.

Although these and other projects and exchanges across borders reflected common interests, most of the films made reflected a reality specific to the country in question.

That is to say, while these films often addressed problems afflicting all of Latin America—underdevelopment, dependence, or insurrection—they generally focused on the country where they were made or where the filmmaker was from, and its specific contexts and conflicts. In any case, focusing on the importance of each "country context" in the social imaginary reflected in the political films of this period does not mean thinking in terms of a naturalized or essentialized "national identity"—even though some of the films and manifestos did so during those years—but instead entails a review of more dynamic and complex national "cultural configurations" (Grimson 2011).

Moreover, in some cases, the different local features within each country are also relevant when configuring the ways in which the changes of "1968" were processed. To the degree that the question of the national remained a priority, and to the degree that the continental and transnational grew in importance, the local became the axis through which to access these different regimes. In this regard, we could consider the importance of the NLAC in certain smaller cities across Latin American, including the many sites where *Cinema Novo* appeared across Brazil; the group of documentary filmmakers in Santa Fe, Argentina; the documentary films made by the Escuela de Cusco in Peru; the Viña del Mar film festival in Chile; the *cineclubismo* (film clubs) and critics in Cali, Colombia; the Film Department at the Universidad de los Andes in Mérida, Venezuela; and others. These "local" trends often resulted in peculiar dynamics of innovation and rupture within a "national context." While these local dynamics interacted fluidly with the transnational and national, the national was not always a mandatory point of departure for film projects. This is the case, for example, of certain key festivals such as the 1967 Viña del Mar Festival in Chile that, focusing on its transnational dimension, became known as the "watershed moment" of the New Latin American Cinema. To study the ruptures in Chilean cinema history, however, it is also necessary to examine the festival's local history around Valparaíso and Viña del Mar and its impact on Chilean filmmakers. The festival dated back to the beginning of the decade and

Figure 12.2   A meeting of filmmakers at the Viña del Mar Festival in 1969. From the collection of Sergio Trabucco.

already had an identity honed by Dr. Aldo Francia and his team. It is a history that is not exclusively Chilean, but nonetheless reflects the new film culture that had been materializing in that country in the decade before Viña '67 and Viña '69.

Thus, while we can read the interventions by Chilean filmmakers in the many meetings held during the festivals (such as the famous polemic between Raúl Ruiz and Fernando Solanas in 1969) as part of the debates of the New Latin American Cinema, we can also read them in relation to the search for an innovative cinematic language within Chilean cinema itself.

In addition, it is important to bear in mind that not every film director who participated in the ruptures of "1968" had the same experience of "making film" or defined the very notion of "filmmaker" in the same way. The knowledge of film history—and more specifically of the innovations of post-World War II cinema—was common to the Latin American filmmakers of the period, many of whom had studied abroad, participated in international film festivals, and also worked as critics. In each country, however, filmmakers constructed different types of relationships with the production apparatus of the state and/or industry and with the circuits for promoting contemporary cinema. Thus, filmmakers cultivated different practices with regards to cinema. At times, this meant promoting programs for a national (or Latin American) cinema; at others, it meant adopting the latest trends in the visual arts or in advertising. Finally, in some cases, the focus was on amateur filmmaking, with plenty of variations and combinations of all these different practices. In other words, the word "cinema," whose general meaning is evident, does not necessarily refer to an identical practice or one common to all. At the very least, filmmakers had different relationships to hegemonic "film production." These relationships were not only based on the myriad discourses surrounding "poor cinema" or "imperfect cinema" (García Espinosa 1969); they did not merely entail swapping "auteur film" for "collective filmmaking" (Solanas and Getino 1973; Sanjinés and Ukamau Group 1979); they went beyond the debates on avantgarde, experimental, and political filmmakers discussed, for example, in Argentina, Brazil, or Mexico. They were also based on the diverse practices of the filmmakers themselves, including the choice of short films, medium-length and feature films, documentary or fiction, and available technologies (Super 8, 16 mm, 35 mm, etc.).

Latin Americanism and national singularities

Just as the "new cinemas" of Latin America drew on languages and aesthetics developed in other regions (the avant-garde films of the first decades of the twentieth century, the interwar realisms, Italian neorealism after World War II, the new European cinemas, sometimes the new American cinema, diverse trends in documentary filmmaking, etc.), they also entered into dialogue with the 1960s discourses and social imaginaries of "Latin Americanism."

But what "Latin Americanisms" are reflected in the political cinema of each country? How was Latin Americanism articulated in countries such as Argentina with strong political movements (Peronism)? What about its relationship to past or contemporary cultural movements such as modernism, anthropophagy, and tropicalism in Brazil? And what of the importance of aboriginal communities or the *indigenista* discourse in the Andean region? How did these relate to that influential trend of the period, Third Worldism? In other words, what does Latin Americanism mean in films that arise from national and cultural configurations or contexts in which blacks, aboriginals, *mestizos*, and mulattoes have different meanings due to the consolidations of different historical processes of hegemony and subordination? And finally, what does Latin Americanism mean in countries with widely different political situations in "1968"?

The singular features of each country that I propose to emphasize here—once again, this is a question of emphasis, and not an argument that they are the only aspect to consider—can be seen in how each film approaches the figures of this Latin Americanism, the representatives or symbols of armed insurgency or of the everyday, subaltern heroics. In previous works (Mestman 2010, 2013), I have written about how filmmakers from different countries appropriated in different ways the images of shared revolutionary figures such as Ernesto "Che" Guevara, assassinated in October 1967, and perhaps the most unifying figure of the revolutionary Latin American process in 1968. I have also examined how political film also incorporated the testimony of subaltern figures, configuring an epic account marked by the historic struggle for liberation and the daily struggle for survival, but with each country providing its own variation on the different kind of hegemony or otherness these testimonies evoke.

Here, I will focus on one example related to this last issue. The appearance or expansion of testimony in Latin American film (as well as in culture and literature) at the end of the 1960s aimed to "resolve" one of the major issues of political film of the period, that of "giving a voice to the people." In some cases, the sectors that were represented or which lent their voice demonstrate a greater "integration" to politics or to the hegemonic culture. Depending on the case, this can be attributed to processes of homogenization—using this concept with care, and considering its contradictions—in relation to formal schooling, unionization, acquired social rights and citizenship, and the penetration of modernization or of the cultural industry. Yet there are cases in which the incorporation of these other voices is inscribed within what are more complex histories, where the construction of non-hegemonic imaginaries requires a greater focus on details, even within the shared context of Latin American and global revolution. For example, let's consider societies characterized by colonial tales of the subjugation of originary peoples and cultures, most of which notably managed to survive, albeit as majorities forcibly ousted from national politics and dominant culture. This is the focus of Jorge Sanjinés and the Ukamau group in Bolivia. Their cinematic search around "1968"—and until at least 1971—involves the challenges of a revolutionary filmmaker who also has to deal with the colonial issue. Both problematics (revolution and coloniality) can be seen in *El coraje del pueblo* (*The Courage of the People*, 1971), where the indigenous/common people's world vision is presented through testimony, the fictional staging of real events by the people who lived them, and the reconstruction of a collective memory.

It might be useful to ask, however, why we emphasize a "national" uniqueness in a case where the construction of a modern nation entailed the destruction of an ancestral culture and its history, that of the Quechua and Aymara communities, whose idiosyncrasy Jorge Sanjinés attempts to recover through his films. This recovery via film unfolds in a time and place—the 1960s, Bolivia—and "converses" with an idea of world revolution—the revolution of the twentieth century, the revolution of "1968"—but also with a Bolivian revolution, that of the Revolutionary Nationalist Movement (MNR) in 1952. It also takes place within a given institutional framework of active interventions of state entities such as the Bolivian Film Institute (ICB, its Spanish acronym). Perhaps for all these reasons, these cinematic constructions of the national imaginary neither ignore nor exclude originary people but incorporate them via the hegemonic *indigenista* imaginary and its variations. Naturally, this process mutates in relation to the different moments in power of the MNR. Sanjinés's films disrupt that hegemonic imaginary, "negotiating" instead the incorporation of the Andean-common people's culture

Figure 12.3 Recovering the miner community via the fictional staging of real events by the people who lived them. *El corage del pueblo* (*The Courage of the People*, Jorge Sanjinés, Bolivia, 1971).

with the topics of Western revolution. Between the films *Yawar Mallku* (*Blood of the Condor*, 1969) and *El coraje del pueblo*, the biggest challenge is to create a decolonial perspective (taking a stand against the cultural logic of colonialism, in an anti-capitalist as well as anti-Western stance) within a new revolutionary context both in Bolivia—around the presidency of General Juan José Torres—and across Latin America (Sanjinés, 2004).

Third Worldism in Latin American films

Finally, we need to consider the dialogues and the convergences between NLAC and the Third Worldist discourses and imaginaries in all the myriad forms they took in this period, when it was present "everywhere" around the world. Along with Latin America's historic place in the Third World in both material and immaterial terms, I will focus on the workings of this political/cultural/cinematographic trend that we refer to as Third Worldism in the respective countries of Latin America and their political films. The dialogue between transnational trends and local/national dynamics must also be carefully examined.

In the introduction to the book on the celebrated Edinburgh Third Cinema conference of 1986, Paul Willemen suggests that "in Europe, most Third Cinema products have definitely been consumed in a Second Cinema way, bracketing the politics in favor of an appreciation of the authorial artistry" (Willemen 1991: 9) Yet, at the same time, important political films of Latin America and of the Third World were used and consumed in a militant and Third Worldist sense on a parallel European (and American) circuit. Without denying the type of reception/consumption Willemen refers to, it is still important to acknowledge this other militant circuit that was carried out by groups such as Spaniards, Italians, French, British, Canadians, or Americans. These groups gave a political use to key films from the Third Worldist imaginary such as *The Hour of the Furnaces*, among others.

I have recently presented a series of previously unreleased audiovisual documents that revealed how this Third Worldist trend functioned in Latin America, not only at the level of discourse or social imaginary, but also for a brief time in a material form (Mestman 2014). In 1973 and 1974, Latin American political cinema was connected and articulated in three successive meetings with the Pan-African Federation of Filmmakers (FEPACI). The first two were working meetings of a Third World Cinema Committee in Algiers (December 1973) and Buenos Aires (May 1974); these were followed by the Rencontres Internationales pour un Nouveau Cinéma in Montreal (June 1974), perhaps the largest and most controversial event of global political cinema during this period. More than 250 people associated with political filmmaking in 25 different countries came together at this meeting to debate Third Cinema (among other topics, of course) as a possible alternative to mainstream movies. It is important to consider that even at that historic moment, at the close of the "long decade of the 1960s," Third Worldism was still an important trend, with a radical agenda and getting plenty of attention in world geopolitics, as seen in the IV Conference of the Non-Aligned Countries in Algiers (September 1973).

The Association of Latin American Filmmakers was created in a close dialogue with the Pan-African Federation of Filmmakers during the meeting in Montreal in June 1974, and as a corollary to the Algiers/Buenos Aires/Montreal circuit mentioned. Some of the figures who promoted the founding of this association in Montreal also participated in the creation of the Latin American Filmmakers Committee in Caracas (Venezuela) three months later. These men, including Walter Achugar (Uruguay), Edgardo Pallero (Argentina), and Miguel Littín (Chile), would also be named to the executive committee of this new association. A representative of the Cuban ICAIC also attended both of these events (Julio García Espinosa in Montreal and Manuel Pérez in Caracas). However, the involvement of Latin American political cinema in these gatherings before Caracas (September 1974)— and especially the creation of a common association in Montreal in a dialogue with the Africa FEPACI—is almost overlooked in both the literature and the memory of the New Latin American Cinema.

We already know that before this last moment (1973–1974), Third Worldist film forged a path at international gatherings and festivals, and that its reach can be traced into the First World during the 1960s. In addition, the concept of "Third World" or "Third Cinema" had been progressively developed in manifestos and in the films, books, documents, and alternative movie houses of the NLAC. We need, however, to delve more deeply into the workings of the idea of the "Third World" within each of the Latin American political groups or filmmakers during these years. We should inquire about the meanings and values attributed to this term in Latin America during the different periods that comprised the "long decade of the 1960s." Until the first half of the decade, Third Worldism appears sporadically in the NLAC as a phenomenon that can be described at best as emerging, without playing a significant role in the configuration of its identity. However, it later appears to earn its spot in the cinema of the region thanks to certain key filmmakers. On the one hand, it was about rejecting the image of Latin America and the Third World that was fostered in the so-called core countries (of the First World). This image was built on "nostalgia for primitivism," to cite Brazilian filmmaker Glauber Rocha in his manifesto "The Aesthetics of Hunger" (1965). Rocha's perspective was aligned with the search for a political and aesthetic break with a language associated with cultural colonialism and with mainstream Western filmmaking styles. On the other hand, Third Worldism in film was a configuration of a militant/combative notion (*La hora de los hornos, Tercer Mundo, Tercera Guerra Mundial*, the Santiago Álvarez documentaries about Vietnam, the creation of the Third

World Cinémathèque in Montevideo, etc.). Yet, in both cases, to the best of our knowledge, the specific bonds between Latin American and African (or Asian) filmmakers were forged throughout the European "1968" scene. Perhaps it is not until a third moment that the ties between segments of the NLAC and African political film are at last constructed in relation to the different gatherings referred to above (Algiers–Buenos Aires–Montreal, between 1973 and 1974). This would be, then, the moment when the Third Worldist trend establishes a certain presence in the imaginary that permeates filmmaking policies and even television experiences in certain countries. The aim behind such trends would be "cultural decolonialization" and the "decolonialization of taste."

During each of these moments, the Third Worldism that permeates Latin American political films generally had socialist overtones (with varying degrees of nationalism) associated with global milestones in the struggle against imperialism (Algiers, Cuba, Chile, Vietnam, etc.). However, the scope of this Third Worldist tendency in each of the political group or filmmakers in Latin America was not necessarily homogeneous and deserves further analysis.

These notes on different aspects of the "1968" ruptures in Latin American cinema are part of a larger research agenda to better understand this crucial moment in Latin American film and politics. They only begin to address the questions that arise from investigating macro- and micro-moments of rupture in deeply contextualized instances that cut across the region/local, the national, and the global.

References

Christiansen, S. and Scarlett, Z. (eds.) (2013) *The Third World in the Global 1960s*. New York: Berghahn Books.

García Borrero, J.A. (2016) "Cuba: Revolución, intelectual y cine. Notas para una intrahistoria del 68 audiovisual." In M. Mestman (ed.), *Las rupturas del 68 en el cine de América Latina*. Buenos Aires: Akal, pp. 249–284.

Gilman, C. (2003) *Entre la pluma y el fusil. Debates y dilemas del escritor revolucionario en América Latina*. Buenos Aires: Siglo XXI.

Grimson A. (2011) *Los límites de la cultura*. Buenos Aires: Siglo XXI.

Jameson, F. (1984) "Periodizing the 60s." In S. Sayres, A. Stephanson, S. Aronowitz, and F. Jameson (eds.), *The 60s without Apology*. Minneapolis, MN: University of Minnesota Press, pp. 178–209. The volume corresponds to a special issue of *Social Text* (1984), 3(3) and 4(1).

León Frías, I. (2013) *El nuevo cine latinoamericano de los años sesenta. Entre el mito y la modernidad fílmica*. Lima: Universidad de Lima.

Mestman, M. (2010) "The Last Sacred Image of the Latin American Revolution." *Journal of Latin American Cultural Studies*, 19(1): 23–44.

—— (2013) "Las *masas* en la era del *testimonio*. Notas sobre el cine del 68 en América Latina." In M. Mestman and M. Varela (eds.), *Masas, pueblo y multitud en cine y televisión*. Buenos Aires: Eudeba, pp. 179–215.

—— (2014) "Estados Generales del Tercer Cine. Los Documentos de Montreal, 1974." *Cuaderno de la Red de Historia de los Medios*, 3: 18–79.

Oubiña, D. (2016) "Argentina: El profano llamado del mundo." In M. Mestman (ed.), *Las rupturas del 68 en el cine de América Latina*. Buenos Aires: Editorial Akal, pp. 65–123.

Paranaguá, P.A. (2000) *Le cinéma en Amérique Latine. Le miroir éclaté. Historiographie et comparatisme*. Paris: L'Harmattan.

—— (2003a) *El cine documental en América Latina*. Madrid: Cátedra.

—— (2003b) *Tradición y modernidad en el cine de América Latina*. Madrid: FCE.

Rocha, G. (1965) "An Aesthetic of Hunger." In M.T. Martin (ed.), *New Latin American Cinema*, vol. 1. Detroit, MI: Wayne State University Press, 1997, pp. 59–61.

Rutherford, S., Mills, S., Krull, C., and Dubinsky, K. (eds.) (2009) *New World Coming: The Sixties and the Shaping of Global Consciousness*. Toronto: Between the Lines.

Sherman, D.J., van Dijk, R., Alinder, J., and Aneesh, A. (eds.) (2013) *The Long 1968: Revisions and New Perspectives*. Bloomington, IN: Indiana University Press.

Vázquez Mantecón, Á. (2012) *El cine súper 8 en México. 1970–1989*. Mexico City: Filmoteca UNAM.

Willemen, P. (1991) "The Third Cinema Question: Notes and Reflections." In J. Pines and P. Willemen (eds.), *Questions of Third Cinema*. London: British Film Institute, pp. 1–29.

Xavier, I. (1993) *Alegorias do subdesenvolvimento. Cinema novo, tropicalismo, cinema marginal*. São Paulo: Editorial Brasiliense.

Zolov, E. (2008) "Expanding Our Conceptual Horizons: The Shift from an Old to a New Left in Latin America." *Contra corriente: A Journal on Social History and Literature in Latin America*, 5(2): 47–73.

—— (2014) "Latin American in the Global Sixties (Introducción)." *The Americas*, 70(3): 349–362.

Further reading

Burton, J. (1990) *The Social documentary in Latin America*. Pittsburgh, PA: Pittsburgh Press.

Chanan, M. (1985) *The Cuban Image*. London: BFI Books.

Elena, A. and Díaz López, M. (eds.) (2003) *24 Frames: The Cinema of Latin America*. London: Wallflower.

García Borrero, J.A. (2009) "Cine cubano post-68: los presagios del gris." in *Otras maneras de pensar el cine cubano*. Santiago de Cuba: Editorial Oriente.

Guevara, A. (2008) *¿Y si fuera una huella? Espistolario*. Madid: Ediciones Autor.

Higbee, W. and Lim, S.H. (2010) "Concepts of Transnational Cinema: Towards a Critical Transnationalism in Film Studies." *Transnational Cinemas*, 1(1).

King, J. (1990) *Magical Reels: A History of Cinema in Latin America*. London: Verso.

López, A.M. (1997) "An 'Other' History: The New Latin American Cinema." In M.T. Martin (ed.), *New Latin American Cinema*. Detroit, MI: Wayne State University Press, pp. 135–156.

Lusnich, A.L. (2011) "Pasado y presente de los estudios comparados sobre cine latinoamericano." *Comunicación y medios*. Santiago de Chile: Universidad de Chile.

Martin, M.T. (ed.) (1997) *New Latin American Cinema*. Detroit, MI: Wayne State University Press.

Pick, Z.M. (1993) *The New Latin American Cinema: A Continental Project*. Austin, TX: University of Texas Press.

Ross, K. (2004) *May '68 and Its Afterlives*. Chicago, IL: University of Chicago Press.

Sanjinés, J. (2004) "Transculturación y subalternidad en el cine boliviano." *Revista Objeto Visual*, Cuadernos de Investigaciones de la Cinemateca Nacional de Venezuela, 10: 11–29.

—— (2009) *Rescoldos del pasado. Conflictos culturales en sociedades postcoloniales*. La Paz: Fundación PIEB.

Stam, R. (1980–1981) "The Hour of the Furnaces and the Two Avant-Gardes." *Millennium Film Journal*, 7(9): 140–150.

13

TRANSNATIONAL GENEALOGIES OF INSTITUTIONAL FILM CULTURE OF CUBA, 1960s–1970s

Masha Salazkina

Editors' introduction

This chapter continues the historical interrogation of the New Latin American Cinema movement (NLAC) begun by Mestman in Chapter 12. Although ostensibly focused on the cultural practices and policies of Cuba's ICAIC in the 1960s and 1970s, it performs a crucial historiographical operation that should serve as a model for further inquiries of the intellectual influences and negotiations that formed the NLAC in general. Carefully unpacking the layers of intellectual influences from Soviet theorists such as Vsevolod Pudovkin and well-known Italian theorists Umberto Barbaro and Guido Aristarco, the chapter presents a far more complicated scenario of intellectual and political confrontations and negotiations than has ever been acknowledged in the formation and social and political longevity of the ICAIC as the premier Cuban cultural institution. As an exemplar of film theoretical history, the chapter confirms our understanding of particular transnational intellectual flows while igniting our scholarly curiosity for more research of this kind into the other intellectual strands that formed the theoretical basis of the amorphous, regional, and multifaceted NLAC and the Third Worldist movement in general.

It has been a commonplace of the scholarly literature on the New Latin American Cinema to point out the movement's stylistic indebtedness to both the Soviet cinematic avant-garde and Italian neorealism (Willemen 1997: 225; Stam et al. 2015: 149). This claim is hard to debate, yet it coexists uneasily with the known ideological orientation of the radical Latin American filmmakers who constituted this movement, which, like most of the

New Left movement in Latin America and elsewhere, stood in opposition to the political and aesthetic hegemonies of Cold War-enforced binaries. In addition to the problematic status of the Soviet Union within the leftist cultural discourses of the 1960s, New Latin American Cinema made great efforts to differentiate itself from European art cinema—to which Italian neorealism was seen as a precursor. This was made most explicit in the formulation of Third Cinema, whose very definition entails an opposition to both Soviet cinema (as an example of a "First," or studio-system, form of filmmaking), and to "Second" cinema, which would include Italian neorealism (Solanas and Getino 1976). Glauber Rocha, in 1970, was even more direct, claiming that "Fox, Paramount, and Metro are our enemies. But Eisenstein, Rossellini, and Godard are also our enemies. They crush us" (Johnson and Stam 1995: 88). The importance of cinema as an expression of national (and regional) consciousness at the heart of the New Latin American Cinema is certainly key to understanding this anxiety of influence (López 1988; Pick 1993). Moreover, both the avant-garde aesthetics and the documentary impulse (associated with the Soviet montage and Italian neorealism, respectively) have their own rich indigenous histories in Latin America (Mestman 2011).

Such difficulties of constructing transnational genealogies of Latin American (and other) film cultures are, in fact, paradigmatic: all too often, they risk subjugating the specificities of the local, national(ist), and regional ideologies to the larger picture, which only supports the still-predominant Eurocentric vision of film history. The relationship between New Latin American Cinema and its Soviet and Italian influences, however, is firmly embedded in the political cinematic discourses of the 1960s. These discourses often emphasized the now largely ignored "Third Wordlist" aspects of political cinema in Latin America as linked to its contemporary liberation movements of Africa and Asia, as well as to the realities of transnational circulation of film culture in prior decades (Vincenot 2004; Gabara 2006; Rozsa 2017). As part of this shared internationalist culture, early Soviet cinema and Italian neorealism served as shared symbolic place markers for the historical locations of the transmission of knowledge about political organization of the cinematic apparatus, which shaped the institutional histories of Latin American film culture of the 1960s. The reception of Soviet and Italian (mostly Marxist) film criticism and films associated with it played an important role in several locations within Latin America in the late 1950s through the 1960s, perhaps most notably in the Santa Fe School in Argentina (De Pascale 1994) and the criticism emerging from *Revista de Cinema* in Brazil (Xavier 2011). This essay focuses attention on the relationship of Cuba's famous film institute (ICAIC) to the ideas of Vsevolod Pudovkin in Russia, and Umberto Barbaro and Guido Aristarco in Italy. The debates they engendered in Cuba in the 1960s provide an additional context for understanding the work of such key Cuban cultural figures as Alfredo Guevara, Julio García Espinosa, and Tomás Gutiérrez Alea, and Cuban film culture of the 1960s and 1970s more broadly. An analysis of the historical alliances and tensions between the European and Cuban Marxist intellectuals and artists further illuminates paradigmatic moments of crisis on the Cuban cultural sphere such as the Padilla affair, and sheds light on the larger problem of the seemingly privileged status of film institutions in Cuba. This historical narrative traces the transmission of ideas and aesthetic ideologies by placing them in their concrete institutional and material sites of exchange—film schools, festivals, and other international meetings—emphasizing the importance that specific cultural actors—filmmakers, critics, curators, and institutional heads—exercised over this process. The institutions serve in this history as contact zones, embodying existing power hierarchies, establishing clear relations between center and periphery, inside and outside, formal and informal practices.

The dynamic displayed by the status of ICAIC vis-à-vis the state is historically mirrored in the institutions to which it is historically connected—the Moscow Film School ([V]GIK) and the *Centro Sperimentale di Cinematografia* in Rome. In all these instances, the state's modernizing agenda assigns cinema a unique status, a heightened political and social role, actively supporting and promoting the institutions that advance it. The privileged status and international prestige enjoyed by these institutions legitimizes some forms of alternative public spheres, however fleetingly and temporarily. Thus, their cultural production can travel further, enabled by the freer circulation within the networks they created.

One of the first acts of the Cuban revolutionary government, in March 1959, was to establish the *Instituto Cubano de Arte e Industria Cinematografica* (ICAIC). From that point on, it enjoyed an exceptional status on the Cuban cultural scene, both as a tool for revolutionary education (in explicitly political and broadly cultural senses) within the country and as a de facto diplomatic representation of the radical success of the Cuban Revolution abroad. As such, it could rely on state material support, which included international travel for its top representatives. A close relationship between Fidel Castro and the appointed president of ICAIC, Alfredo Guevara, allowed for direct access to political power, which led to greater independence to achieve the material, intellectual, and aesthetic priorities of the institute, which far surpassed those of any other sphere of culture (Douglas 1996: 153; Chanan 2004; Pérez 2006: 248). Consistent with Michael Chanan's claim that "The case of Cuban cinema suggests . . . [that] the public sphere does not simply dissolve, but finds an active and vicarious surrogate on the film screen" (Chanan 2004: 16), the critical apparatus developed at ICAIC by its two artistic directors, Julio García Espinosa and Tomás Gutiérrez Alea, reflected the broader Marxist preoccupation with a materialist aesthetic—but one that would engender true social liberation through cinematic experience (Chanan 2001). These filmmaker-theorists emphasized the materialist apparatus that sees the cinematic process itself as an expression of collective creativity (as involving many people, including nonprofessionals), thus turning the modernist debate inside out: it wasn't that the artist was an exemplary or special individual, but that every individual was a repressed artist. True social liberation advances under the slogan that everyone is an artist—and thus real civil society is an artistic collaboration. To quote a brief passage from García Espinosa:

> [Imperfect cinema] is not only an act of social justice—the possibility for everyone to make films—but also a fact of extreme importance for artistic culture: the possibility of recovering . . . the true meaning of artistic activity. *Then* we will be able to understand that art is one of mankind's "impartial" activities. That art is not work, and that the artist is not in the strict sense a worker.
>
> Imperfect cinema cannot lose sight of the fact that its essential goal as a new poetic is to disappear . . .
>
> Art will not disappear into nothingness: it will disappear into everything.
> (*García Espinosa 1979: 82, my emphasis*)

For the historian, then, there are two planes that must be investigated in order to fully understand this dense conceptual formation: the particular synchronic fields that come into prominence are the discourse on "Third Cinema," where the question of aesthetic labor is posed within the matrix of issues specific to the postcolonial experience, and a wider historical shift towards postindustrialism in Europe and the US, which raised new political realities, theoretical frameworks, and artistic practices. These synchronic fields are only now beginning to be fully investigated, and I will touch upon some of these issues briefly in my conclusion. For its part, the diachronic/historical plane, discussed here, takes these theories back to their precursors in the Soviet Union and Italy starting in the 1920s.

Both Italy and the Soviet Union provided a significant critical and theoretical apparatus that shaped the curriculum of many postwar film educational institutions internationally. Both also became important centers for the training of filmmakers in the postwar period, especially for the aspiring cinéastes from Latin America, Africa, and Asia. Much of this apparatus was shaped in the course of the 1920s, 1930s, and 1940s—and despite the oft-assumed cultural autarky of both totalitarian states, it was a transnational process.

In correspondence to the policies of modernization aggressively pursued by both states, many of the Soviet–Italian cinematic exchanges in the 1920s and 1930s centered around problems that arose in noncommercial cinema (educational, political, scientific, and indus-trial) and the organization of the film industry around experimental educational projects. While direct exchanges were limited, Italian institutional and cultural discourses and prac-tices relied heavily on Soviet examples, creating a rich site for transmission and translation of Soviet cinema and theory in Italy during the first phase of the fascist regime, from the 1920s up to the Spanish Civil War. The spaces for this cultural circulation were almost entirely situated outside of commercial structures, and Soviet cinema became the cor-nerstone of cinematic education in 1930s Italy, primarily through the work of the *Centro Sperimentale di Cinematografia* (Salazkina 2012, 2014).

The role that the Centro played in the history of Italian cinema is well known. But of equal historical and cultural importance is its function as a major site of international cultural dialogue both in the pre- and postwar periods. Umberto Barbaro was one of the first professors at the Centro, responsible for much of the cultural and ideological diversity in the 1930s and 1940s (Brunetta 1969). A fervent Marxist, Barbaro trans-lated Eisenstein, Pudovkin, and Timoshenko, along with Balázs and Arnheim, and used Soviet cinema extensively in his teaching and essays, providing a pro-Soviet voice as the co-editor of *Bianco e nero*, the official journal of the Centro. He saw Soviet cinema explicitly as "the starting point and as an example for the rebirth of Italian cinema" (Brunetta 1993: 170).

Barbaro assimilated and synthesized seemingly disparate aesthetic and ideological approaches under the title of a realism that had freed itself from the bourgeois mimetic moment of the nineteenth century. As part of his debates on realism, Barbaro took up Pudovkin's writings as a secret weapon against the prevailing Crocean idealism (whose champion was his colleague, protector, and director of the Centro, Luigi Chiarini), while operating within a rhetoric that was acceptable to the fascist state. This idealism, extend-ing themes generated in the romantic age of the nineteenth century into the twentieth, understood art in terms of individual expression that transcended the routines of every-day life without attempting to change them in any critical or systematic way. Under this aesthetic program, according to a Marxist perspective, cinema's revolutionary potential is diverted into an affirmation of social hierarchies, and film theory is replaced with connois-seurship: the writing of appreciations and evaluations. What Barbaro found in Pudovkin above all else was a way of looking at the construction of the art object that stripped away the individualistic notion of the artist and marking the process of its production: its insti-tutional setting, its network of distribution, and its reception (insofar as the art object can apprehend it). Pudovkin's conclusion, however, did not undermine the organizational role played by the film director; rather, his position carved out a role for cinema education as the process by which the film director learned how to create a critical distance from naïve, class-bound visual and narrative impulses. In his early work, Pudovkin emphasized the collective and collaborative nature of filmmaking:

> Collective work is what makes every part of the work a living and organic part of the larger goal/task. The nature of filmmaking is such that the more people take a direct and organic involvement, the more varied their involvement in the work, the better the final product of this process—the film—becomes.
>
> *(Pudovkin 1974a: 129)*

Contrary to what this quote would seem to imply through the idea of "direct and organic involvement," Pudovkin insisted on the importance of a script as a way of centralizing the work of the creative collectivity:

> It is not a lone director who is called upon to resolve the creative tasks [required by the filmmaking process]. Only a collective/community united by a shared idea and a unified understanding of a goal, creative and self-directed, can do the work [of real filmmaking].
>
> *(Pudovkin 1974b: 47)*

The transition from script to filming was further mediated through the collectivity of self-reflexive cinematic production in order to remain coherent. Thus, Pudovkin's theories were "technical" enough to account for the medium specificity of cinema (which was one of the central issues of film theory at the time), and practical enough to function as a didactic tool, which was particularly important to the development of film education. Finally, Pudovkin's version of realism redeemed the figure of the artist, not on bourgeois individualist terms, with its cult of the genius, but on class-based terms, with its transparent need for some critical organizing force. In this iteration, what central planning was to industrial policy, the director would be to the production of film. Realism was as much a matter of such an organizational approach as an aesthetic stance.

For Barbaro, then, the natural consequence of this understanding of realism was that it became a term for the transformative function of cinema: art "is not limited to making an interpretation of the world, but intends to actively transform reality" (Pudovkin 1932, quoted in Brunetta 1969: 28). This point is sometimes buried under the criticism of the general "political ineffectiveness" of neorealism as politically engaged cinema. However, it was Barbaro's politicized representation of Italian neorealism in terms of the potential of cinematic expression—rather than describing a specific film movement—that strongly influenced the global theorists and practitioners of political modernism of the 1950s and 1960s (including Gillo Pontecorvo, Fernando Birri in Argentina, and theorists and cinéastes of Cinema Novo such as Alex Viany and Nelson Pereira dos Santos in Brazil). Barbaro's approach to neorealism particularly resonated with the Cuban artists and theorists who were first exposed to it in Rome, where García Espinosa and Gutièrrez Alea studied at the Centro, and Alfredo Guevara spent considerable time in the late 1950s.

The importance of Barbaro's (and therefore Pudovkin's) conceptions of realism to the development of Cuban film theory and criticism can be evidenced by the fact that Barbaro was one of the theorists translated and published by the ICAIC publishing house (Barbaro 1965). His relevance, however, seems contradicted by the total paucity of any secondary research on this connection. How are we to understand the complex relationship critics and filmmakers in Cuba had to this particular intellectual genealogy? To answer this question, we again need to turn to what was happening in Italy in the 1950s, as well as the Cuban cultural debates of the 1960s, to trace the changing discourse surrounding Soviet cinema in both countries.

Because of the importance of Soviet film theory in establishing film culture in Italy in the interwar period, the status of Soviet cinema in postwar Italy became a particularly controversial and hotly debated subject with the emerging critiques of Stalinism, socialist realism, and Zhdanovism in the 1950s. While the position of the European communist parties towards these discoveries and their resulting attitudes towards the Soviet Union marked the division between the Old and New Left in Europe and the UK, the debunking of the "myth of the Soviet Cinema" in Italy was especially traumatic because of the associations between Stalin's cult of personality and Italy's own fascist legacy. The very overlap between fascist and early Soviet rhetoric that originally enabled the dissemination of Soviet film culture in Italy in the 1930s and 1940s, and in turn contributed to the articulation of the neorealist aesthetic by figures such as Barbaro, is also what determined a strong response against socialist realism from many of the Italian leftist film cultural figures in the aftermath of World War II. Thus, in postwar Italy, the critical stance by the left against socialist realism, and Soviet cinema in general, was inseparable from the anxiety over the fascist roots of the very film institutions that after the war meant to represent the "reformed" post-fascist Italy. So when in 1968 Aristarco becomes one of the first to receive an academic position as a chair in the History and Criticism of Cinema in Italy, the other person to receive the same honor was Luigi Chiarini, further underlining the very historical continuity in film institutions Aristarco so passionately critiqued.

Much of what resonated between Soviet cinema and the Italian cinema of the fascist era—the epic mode and triumphalist narrative structure, the representation of the leader as "the father of the people"—became grounds for the strong ideological and aesthetic rejection of Soviet cinema in the 1950s and 1960s (Misler 1973; Aristarco 1981). The cultural figures who were strongly associated with it—and this meant, above all, Barbaro, who remained an unwavering supporter of the Soviet Union for the rest of his life—became synonymous with everything the newer generations of cineastes rejected. Aristarco along with Cesare Zavattini were the earliest critics of socialist realism in Italian leftist film culture, and both played an important role in the formation of the post-revolutionary film culture in Cuba (García Espinosa 2005: 62). While Zavattini's role in the history of Cuban cinema deserves a separate study, Aristarco's role in it is even less known.

The Italian debates on Soviet cinema began with particular force on the pages of the journal *Cinema Nuovo* as early as 1956, when the journal was in the first years of its existence. Founded by Aristarco in 1952, the title of the journal was meant to reference *Cinema*, one of the key film publications in 1930s–1940s fascist Italy. Subsequently, the term "New Cinema" ("Cinema Nouvo") in 1960s Italy would become synonymous with a new international aesthetic emblematic of the famous Pesaro Film Festival (*Il nuovo cinema* 1989). This particular conceptual constellation allowed for the inclusion in the festival of militant filmmaking from Latin America alongside both West and East European "auteur" and art cinemas—the festival famously awarded its main prize in 1968 to *La hora de los hornos* (Fernando Solanas and Octavio Getino, 1968), making Pesaro one of the key sites for the exchanges among the various factions of the European leftists and the Third Worldist artists. Despite personal and ideological disagreements with the organizers of the Pesaro festival, Aristarco's journal sets the stage for this development. The debates concerning the revisionism of Soviet cinema occupied its main pages throughout the 1950s, before the focus shifted towards discussing the "new cinemas" emerging both in Europe and beyond (in particular, in Latin America and Eastern Europe). By the 1960s, *Cinema Nuovo* was one of the first journals that systematically included accounts of the New Latin American Cinema, and especially the Cuban film industry, playing an important role in its dissemination around Europe and promoting Cuban cinema as an exemplary case of the "New Cinemas." Just months after the victory of the Cuban Revolution in 1959, Aristarco began corresponding with the future heads of ICAIC. In addition to responding enthusiastically to their questionnaires and calls to help establish the new film institute, he provided them with additional contacts throughout Europe among film critics and cinematic functionaries. He also provided an analysis of his own institution-building experience in Italy (see Fondo 2, Box 10, Biblioteca Luigi Chiarini, Centro Sperimentale di Cinematografia, Rome) and his sense of the theoretical and critical canon of the study of film as the author of the highly influential *History of Film Theories* (1951) and editor of the first definitive collection of film theory and criticism, *L'arte del film: antologia storico-critica* (1950), both of which were subsequently translated into Spanish and circulated all over Latin America (Aristarco 1950, 1951, 1968). In 1964 and 1965, *Cinema Nuevo* even had its own Latin American edition, published in Argentina.

While ICAIC's international projection emphasized institutional cohesion and film-making achievements, Cuban cinema's internal history was plagued with fissures, conflicts, and polemics. From the outset, the issue of socialist realism was a point of contention between ICAIC representatives, who preferred a more open approach to artistic creation and interpretation, and the Old Left cultural critics and bureaucrats, whose strict parameters had a lasting effect in other areas of cultural production. Within the cultural sector, the most orthodox Marxists clustered within the Department of Culture (later reformed as the National Council of Culture, CNC). Their credentials as long-standing Communist Party members gave them great leverage in the existing situation, and the CNC competed with ICAIC as to which organization would have greater control over the film culture of the island (Rojas 2009). The CNC regarded ICAIC's film acquisition and programming choices with suspicion, and throughout the 1960s the relationship between the two institutions was fraught with conflicts, which manifested themselves in a series of public debates. The underlying problematic was whether the socialist realist model was appropriate for Cuba. Concerned by the increasing valorization of the Soviet model and CNC's encroachment, the ICAIC representatives defended the value of formal plurality in artistic practice, and reacted against the superficial attribution of class character to specific formal features in artistic expression (Pogolotti 2007).

Yet, while fully sharing the rejection of the socialist realist model, the theoretical stance represented by the ICAIC critics differed significantly from Aristarco's (Lukaczian) notions of critical realism. The emphasis on the cultural revolution informs the theoretical foundations of García Espinosa's work, which indeed rejects the primacy of any prescriptive formal principle, focusing instead on how film can function as a political and social event in the struggle for liberation. Similarly, Solanas and Getino's conceptual grounding of the notion of Third Cinema rejects any formally prescriptive notion of "progressive" or "radical" Marxist filmmaking in favor of an approach in which the production methods (rather than a specific aesthetic formula) are at the center of the debate.

ICAIC's ability to articulate this position from within the Marxist aesthetic discourse (however unorthodox) allowed them to successfully reconcile (however temporarily) political pressures with a more sophisticated and clearly modernist approach to filmmaking and the question of artistic labor as such. At the same time, it successfully affirmed ICAIC's own hegemonic power within the Cuban cultural and artistic sphere. ICAIC mobilized the theoretical apparatus of participatory, mobile, and engaged cinema combined with a re-evaluation of its aesthetic function and potential as a public sphere and heterogeneous space of reflexive social interaction (through filmmaking, film viewing, and criticism). The attention of the foreign observers was particularly important as the public sphere for the ICAIC theorists was ambitiously conceived of as international, linking the audiences and the liberatory struggles around the world. Through its production and dissemination of images and ideas about Third World struggles (in particular through its famous newsreels), ICAIC was instrumental in the promotion of the tricontinental cinematic project as envisioned in the late 1960s. This vision was further supported by the European leftists, and Italian Marxists in particular: from the Latin American Film festivals taking place in the early 1960s in Liguria, to the International Festival of Free Cinema in Porretta Terma and the Pesaro International Festival of the New Cinema, Italian film institutions promoted Cuban film and the image of Cuba as a model for postcolonial liberation struggles around the world. This alliance, however, proved to be somewhat short-lived, and by the 1970s some of the divergences between European Marxist cultural critics and their Cuban counterparts became more pronounced, culminating in the famous Padilla affair in 1971. As Irene Rozsa deftly summarizes the events:

> On April 9, key thinkers, writers and artists who had initially supported the Revolution signed an open letter addressed to Fidel Castro expressing their unease with the poet's arrest. In a second letter, dated May 20, they linked Padilla's public session of "self-criticism" to the Stalinist trials, and cautioned against further instances of these tendencies of the Soviet model of communism. Initially published in the French newspaper *Le Monde*, these letters promptly circulated in other languages and other publications.
>
> (*Salazkina and Rozsa 2015: 74*)

The divisions triggered by these revelations took shape in the little-known debate between Julio García Espinosa and Guido Aristarco, one of the most heated moments of altercation during one of the last, and still the least explored, gatherings of the international Third Worldist film community, the *Rencontres Internationales pour un Nouveau Cinéma* in Montreal in June 1974.

The debate occurred after Aristarco's presentation at the very end of the event, where he briefly criticized the Cuban film *Girón* (*Bay of Pigs*, Manuel Herrera, 1972) for what he saw as its "triumphalist" aesthetic at the expense of any critical exploration of the conflict inherent in the contemporary moment.

Aristarco used this critique as an occasion to advocate for a return to what he proposed to be a true Marxist artistic method of critical realism. This proclamation was joined by Guy Hennebelle, one of the key French scholars of Third Worldist cinema, who shared Aristarco's concerns about the film as "inspired by the film aesthetics of American imperialism." He also added more explicitly that he did not agree with "certain alliances that Cuba practices with certain countries such as the Soviet Union." In response, García Espinosa attacked Aristarco's ideas as lacking any historical concreteness and undermining the centrality of the transformative—rather than interpretive—role of Marxist analysis. He claimed that the choices made by Cuban filmmakers were determined not by a desire to revolutionize film aesthetics, but by a need to contribute to a cultural revolution, which had

Figure 13.1   *Rencontres Internationales pour un Nouveau Cinéma.* Courtesy Cinémathèque Québécoise.

Figure 13.2   Aristarco's presentation in Montreal at the *Rencontres Internationales pour un Nouveau Cinéma.*

its own specific historical and political needs. García Espinosa argued that Aristarco's (and, implicitly, the "European") position demonstrated a lack of understanding of the concrete realities facing the Third World and Latin America in particular.

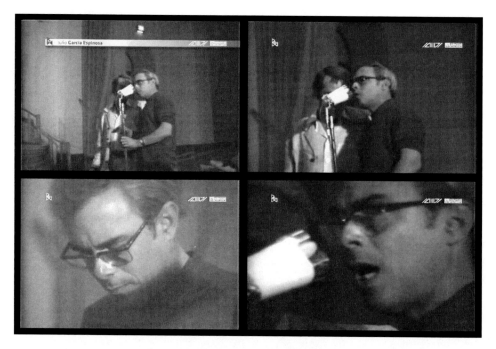

Figure 13.3 Montage of García Espinosa's interventions during the debate at the *Rencontres Internationales pour un Nouveau Cinéma*.

This was supported by an intervention from Fernando Solanas, who was another partici-pant at the event. Solanas spoke for the Latin American filmmakers, maintaining that they were actively opposing "any approach which in the abstract criticizes the concrete march of history of the revolutionary processes." This, according to him, led to an "abstract and misinformed critique" (see reels 20 and 29 of the event, archived at the Cinémathèque Québécoise).

This was one of the few moments of open disagreement between the different factions of what could be loosely defined as a Third Worldist movement represented at the con-ference by demonstrations of unity and solidarity. As such, it crystallized with particular force some of the tensions—both political and historical—that came into play within this cluster. In some ways, the animated debate (recorded and preserved at the Cinémathèque Québécoise, along with all the other audiovisual documents from the Rencontres) lays bare certain tensions that existed between the European and Latin American groups represented at the meeting. These tensions rhetorically took the shape of disagreement over theoretical issues in Marxist aesthetics, and can be mapped onto the difference in critical film discourse in Europe during that period, which was primarily concerned with issues of aesthetics and textually based ideological critique, vis-à-vis the strand of Latin American critical tradi-tion, which was rooted in the analysis of material conditions of production and reception of cinema. While taking place at the same time as the Western European rediscovery of early Soviet film theory as foundational for what David Rodowick famously popularized as the "political modernist" turn in film theory (referring to exclusively European and North American discourses as "theory"), this debate crystallized the divergent trajectories of film theory and its appropriations of Soviet film theory. Aristarco represented an earlier, pre-structuralist and largely humanist strand of Marxism, concerned with critical realism. By the 1970s, this tradition was perceived as intellectually outmoded as the European and North American film criticism followed a structuralist route, grounded in textual readings, with Eisenstein's dialectical image/montage as a model. At the same time, Latin American film criticism—especially in Cuba—followed the path of materialist apparatus theory, but importantly the Third Worldist, and more specifically Latin American-centered geopolitics, also discursively and politically shaped it. Fundamentally, therefore, these theoretical dissonances reflected the divergent historical experiences and political goals of European and Latin American Marxists of the period. As these intellectual paths diverged, they also succeeded in rhetorically separating any shared transnational genealogies, each insisting on its unique "origins." Similarly, as the cultural institutions that allowed for these exchanges—namely, (V)GIK, Centro Sperimentale, and ICAIC—became firmly associated with nationalist interests (which they were always, indeed, created to serve), the rhetoric of their historical and cultural exceptionality came to better serve these goals. These developments retrospectively obscured the internationalist goals and translational dynamics of many of their theoretical and artistic productions. The former came to appear passé with the demise of Marxist internationalism, while the latter risked subsuming cultural and political specificities under what to many looked suspiciously like an intellectual version of globalization. From our historical vantage point, the work of disentangling these histories, so profoundly shaped by the very dialectics of the local and the global, the national(ist) and the international(ist) is only just beginning.

References

Aristarco, G. (1950) *L'arte del film: Antologia storico-critica*. Milan: Bompiani.
—— (1951) *Storia delle teoriche del film*. Turin: Einaudi.
—— (1968) *Historia De Las Teorías Cinematográficas*. Barcelona: Lumen.
—— (1981) *Sciolti dal giuramento. Il dibattito critic-ideologico sul cinema negli anni Cinquanta*. Bari: Dedalo Libri.
Barbaro, U. (1965) *El Film Y El Resarcimiento Marxista Del Arte*. Havana: Ediciones ICAIC.
Brunetta, G.P. (1969) *Umberto Barbaro e l'idea di Neorealismo*. Padua: Liviana.
—— (1993) *Storia del cinema italiano, v.2*. Rome: Edizioni Riuniti.
Chanan, M. (2001) "Cuba and Civil Society, or Why Cuban Intellectuals Are Talking about Gramsci." *Nepantla*, 2(2): 387–406.
—— (2004) *Cuban Cinema*. Minneapolis, MN: University of Minnesota Press.
De Pascale, G. (1994) *Fernando Birri, L'Altramerica*. Naples: Le Pleiadi.
Douglas, M.E. (1996) *La tienda negra: El cine en Cuba, 1897–1990*. Havana: Cinemateca de Cuba.
Gabara, R. (2006) "'A Poetics of Refusals': Neorealism from Italy to Africa." *Quarterly Review of Film and Media*, 23: 201–215.
García Espinosa, J. (1969) "For an Imperfect Cinema." In M.T. Martin (ed.), *New Latin American Cinema*, Detroit, MI: Wayne State University Press, 1997, pp. 71–82.
—— (1979) "For an Imperfect Cinema." *Jump Cut*, 20: 24–26.
—— (2005) "Recuerdos de Zavattini." *Cine Cubano*, 155 (November): 60–65.
Il nuovo cinema: venti anni dopo, Pesaro 1984. Per una nuova critica: i convegni pesaresi 1965–1967 (1989) Venice: Marsilio.
Johnson, R. and Stam, R. (1995) *Brazilian Cinema*. New York: Columbia University Press.
López, A.M. (1988) "An 'Other' History: The New Latin American Cinema." *Radical History Review*, 41: 93–116.

Mestman, M. (2011) "From Italian Neorealism to New Latin American Cinema." In R. Sklar and S. Giovacchini (eds.), *Global Neorealism: The Transnational History of a Film Style*. Jackson, MI: University Press of Mississippi, pp. 163–177.

Misler, N. (1973) *La Via italiana al realismo: La politica culturale artistica del P.C.I dal 1944 al 1956*. Milan: Gabriele Mazzotta Editore.

Pérez, L. (2006) *Cuba: Between Reform and Revolution*. New York: Oxford University Press.

Pick, Z. (1993) *The New Latin American Cinema: A Continental Project*. Austin, TX: University of Texas Press.

Pogolotti, G. (2007) *Polémicas Culturales de los 60*. Havana: Editorial Letras Cubanas.

Pudovkin, V. (1932) *Il soggetto cinematografico*. Rome: Eizioni d'Italia.

—— (1974a) "Kollektivizm—baza kinoraboty." In *Sobranie sochinenii v trekh tomakh*. Moscow: Iskusstvo.

—— (1974b) "O scenarnoi forme." In *Sobranie sochinenii v trekh tomakh*. Moscow: Iskusstvo.

Rojas, R. (2009) "Apuntes para una historia intellectual." In C. Naranjo Orovio, A. Crespo Solana, and M.D. González Ripoll Navarro (eds.), *Historia de Las Antillas: Historia de Cuba*. Madrid: Consejo Superior de Investigaciones Científicas, pp. 405–416.

Rozsa, I. (2017) "Film Culture and Education in Republican Cuba: The Legacy of José Manuel Valdés-Rodríguez." In R. Navitski and N. Poppe (eds.), *Cosmopolitan Visions: The Transnational Horizons of Latin American Film Culture*, pp. 298–323.

Salazkina, M. (2012) "Moscow–Rome–Havana: A Film Theory Roadmap." *October*, 139 (Spring): 97–117.

—— (2014) "Soviet–Italian Cinematic Exchanges: *Transnational Film Education in the 1930s*." in M. Hagener (ed.), *The Emergence of Film Culture: Knowledge Production, Institution Building, and the Fate of the Avant-Garde in Europe, 1919–1945*. Oxford: Berghahn Books, pp. 180–198.

Salazkina, M. and Rozsa, I. (2015) "Dissonances in 1970s European and Latin American Political Film Discourse: The Aristarco—García Espinosa Debate." *Canadian Journal of Film Studies*, 24(2): 66–81.

Sanjinés, J. and Ukamau Group (1979) *Teoría y práctica de un cine junto al pueblo*. Mexico City: Siglo XXI.

Solanas, F. and Getino, O. (1973) *Cine, cultura y descolonización*. Buenos Aires: Siglo XXI.

—— (1976) "Towards a Third Cinema." In B. Nichols (ed.), *Movies and Methods: An Anthology*. Berkeley, CA: University of California Press, pp. 44–64.

Stam, R., Porton, R., and Goldsmith, L. (2015) *Keywords in Subversive Film/Media Aesthetics*. Oxford: Wiley-Blackwell.

Vincenot, E. (2004) "Germán Puig, Ricardo Vigón et Henri Langlois, Pionniers de la Cinemateca de Cuba." *Caravelle*, 83: 11–42.

Willemen, P. (1997) "The Third Cinema Question." In M.T. Martin (ed.), *New Latin American Cinema*. Detroit, MI: Wayne State University Press, pp. 221–251.

Xavier, I. (2011) "Bazin in Brasil." In D. Andrew and H. Joubert-Laurencin (eds.), *Opening Bazin: Postwar Film Theory and Its Afterlife*. Oxford: Oxford University Press, pp. 308–315.

14

NEW FRAMEWORKS

Collaborative and indigenous
media activism

Freya Schiwy, Amalia Córdova, David Wood,
and Horacio Legrás

Editors' introduction

Latin American film studies has constituted itself as a field primarily through the analysis of film as an art form and as an industrial practice. Within this framework, its primary object of study has been feature-length fiction films and documentaries made by professional filmmakers and artists—from *Ganga Bruta* (Humberto Mauro, 1933) to *El Velador* (*The Night Watchman*, Natalia Almada, 2011). Aesthetic and industrial analyses have been the principle critical approaches: the former taking aim at the workings of film form, the latter at the changing structures and dynamics of filmmaking practices. Largely left out of this framework are numerous other modes of filmmaking, including educational films, most experimental as well as ethnographic films, and community-based audiovisual projects.

Since the mid-2000s, some pioneering scholars have begun to scrutinize those modes, and in the process have broadened our critical scaffolding (Schiwy 2009; Garavelli 2013; Wortham 2013). Those who have studied indigenous and collaborative media activism, like the authors in this chapter, have helped us to recognize the role of film- and video-making in the self-representation of social groups at the subnational level, as well as the significance of alternative distribution and exhibition networks within and beyond Latin America. In this chapter, Córdova, Wood, Schiwy, and Legrás also widen the scope of Latin American film studies by accounting for film/video's interface with other media, from community radio, to television, to digital technologies. The chapter also helps us to reassess film history in the region by utilizing the discussion of contemporary indigenous and collaborative media activism to help us reassess the relationship between film and political militancy—an interface long defined by the New Latin American Cinema of the 1960s and 1970s.

Latin America is awash with activist video. No social protest goes unrecorded; myriads of video shorts and still photos form part of cultural activism throughout the hemisphere. Some of these recordings are part of now decades-old processes of claiming access to communication networks; others are more ad hoc responses to acute social uprisings or other quotidian forms of creativity. They speak to a vision that the Cuban filmmaker Julio García Espinosa had articulated in the early 1970s in his famous manifesto "For an Imperfect Cinema". Anticipating technological advances, he envisioned that Art would become *art*, an expression of daily creativity rather than the purview of those with means and formal education. In this chapter, we ask: What does it mean to make revolutionary film and video in Latin America today? How has the understanding of revolution changed since the 1960s, and what has that meant for the role of audiovisual media? How have film policies and institutional sites limited and enabled the emergence of different kinds of activist film and video? What is the importance of technological innovation, such as VHS and digital production and distribution technologies? How important is film aesthetics, and how relevant are the styles of collaboration? Have priorities changed?

In this chapter, we review some of the enormous variety of collaborative activist film- and video-making emerging with the advent of digital recording and editing possibilities. Focusing on Brazil, Bolivia, Colombia, Argentina, and Mexico, as well as the transnational space of indigenous media festivals, we find parallels and differences in the contemporary processes in these locations, as well as continuities and ruptures with respect to earlier forms of militant filmmaking. We begin with Amalia Córdova's overview of the particularities of indigenous film and video production, its precarious funding sources, and its international circulation networks, including the role of international indigenous film and video festivals. In the subsequent section, David Wood traces a historical genealogy of indigenous and collaborative film- and video-making that highlights the personal and institutional connections to 1960s militant filmmaking and an array of alternative film and video initiatives emerging in the 1980s, especially in the Andean context. Both Córdova and Wood highlight the pivotal role played by Coordinadora Latinoamericana del Cine y Video de los Pueblos Indígenas (Latin American Council of Indigenous Peoples' Film and Communication, CLACPI) in collaborative media-making in indigenous languages.

The third section points to parallels between indigenous media processes and the *piquetero* activist video that arose in Argentina in the context of protests against neoliberal government policies. Named for the street demonstrations that took place, *piquetero* film is highly diverse, yet as a whole also indicates a rupture between traditional and current understandings of filmmaking and revolutionary action. Much of the "estrangement" that Horacio Legrás detects emerges from a current disregard for aesthetics, which had been such a central part of film as revolutionary action in the past. While indigenous media resists stable definitions in terms of genre, topics, or aesthetics, and its production and distribution is extremely diverse across the hemisphere, both *piquetero* film and the diversity of indigenous media take a critical stance regarding the effects of global capitalism. *Piquetero* media activism is also linked with grassroots organizations such as the EZLN (Ejército Zapatista de Liberación Nacional, National Zapatista Liberation Army). Indeed, in the last section, we suggest that, as the case of Oaxaca has shown, there are instances when the strands of indigenous decolonial media activism join together with other media activist and artist groups in a broad-based search for alternatives to current race, class, and gender relations, inventing new grassroots forms of democracy, partially elaborated in the very process of activist media production and distribution. Freya Schiwy traces the centrifugal lines of media activism evoked in a creative commons documentary about the 2006 Oaxaca uprising. She shows how physical and virtual spaces are articulated in the encounter between indigenous movements, anarchists, feminists, transnational alter-globalization, and Indymedia activists. These linked spaces suggest that the relation between film and revolutionary action has shifted away from conceiving of film as inciting action as a response to injustice. Today's revolutionary action is in large part articulated in media activism itself, informed by decolonial struggle, and produces a joyous affect that is quite distinct from traditional militant cinema.

Indigenous video, transnational networks, and indigenous festivals

AMALIA CÓRDOVA

The forms of resistance and organization through which indigenous peoples respond to settler-state impositions vary widely, with political and media representation increasingly becoming a key part of the struggle. Indigenous video or *video indígena* often manifests community perspectives on abuses and violations of indigenous rights. The motivation and ethics that guide its producers are evident, but because the circumstances of production vary widely, there is no strict and fast definition of indigenous video. In other words, *video indígena* results from collaboration among diverse social agents, including non-indigenous and indigenous/first nation media makers, subjects, and actors, but does not subscribe to a particular genre, topic, or mode, and much less a set of common aesthetic preferences. Similarly, the relationships with state film policies, support, and co-optation vary across the hemisphere and have changed over time, with several indigenous video production groups rejecting any relationship with the state in favor of international nongovernmental funding or the support of grant foundations. A shared concern that has persisted over recent decades, however, is the creation of respectful, insider perspectives on the great diversity of indigenous and first nation lives and concerns. The relatively inexpensive recording and editing possibilities of video technologies has made them the common means to transmit those perspectives.

As Salazar and Córdova (2008) explain, there is a range of production capacity, from prolific production centers with a long-standing history of indigenous media production, collectives with more limited output and more sporadic productions. Video nas Aldeias/ Video in the Villages (VNA) in Brazil, the Plurinational Communication System of the Indigenous and Aboriginal Peoples in Bolivia, and several media collaborations in Mexico (Ojo de Agua Comunicación, Chiapas Media Project/Promedios, and the Turix Collective) have been producing indigenous media over several decades. Other indigenous political organizations, both regional and national, such as CONAIE (Confederación de Nacionalidades Indígenas de Ecuador/Confederation of Indigenous Nationalities of Ecuador) and ONIC (Organización Nacional Indígena de Colombia/National Indigenous Organization of Colombia), have produced a smaller number of works and house important media archives in precarious conditions. A growing number of other smaller-scale indigenous and collaborative production efforts are dispersed across Abya Yala (the Kuna name for the Americas, now widely used in public discourse by indigenous leaders and advocates), including Argentina, Chile, El Salvador, Guatemala, Panama, Paraguay, Peru, and Venezuela. Indigenous video is even being produced in less documented areas such as

Figure 14.1 Xavante filmmaker Divino Tserewahu from the Video Nas Aldeias project.

Nicaragua, Suriname, and Paraguay, despite fragile structures of production and different forms of organization and representation. In all of these areas, indigenous producers remain fairly autonomous and isolated, as there are no established nationwide media centers to coordinate the effort of indigenous media-makers.

As with most independently produced film and video, funding is the first hurdle, and for indigenous producers it often becomes the first instance of transnational mediation. A handful of dedicated indigenous video organizations make ends meet, but few videographers make a living from their media skills; moreover, they consistently lack sufficient equipment and infrastructural support. The basic financing has come from five major sources or a combination of them: self-generated funds (*autofinanciamiento*); local fundraising by grassroots, indigenous, or media organizations; state or national funds and grants geared to support indigenous "development"; international film or indigenous-designated funds; and foundations, nonprofits, and nongovernmental organizations. Of course, the existence of these funding sources does not guarantee securing sufficient financing given the parameters and priorities of the agencies themselves.

For example, financial support for *video indigena* is notably limited, even in organizations that ostensibly support indigenous, social, and rural development. Despite existing mandates and recommendations from the United Nations, major nongovernmental organizations involved in indigenous or community development in the "Third World" have not invested in media or seen indigenous communication as a funding priority. For their part, national governmental bodies have often declared self-generated, locally circulated media such as community television and radio illegal, further restricting potential revenue streams.

Traditional film funding circuits have supported indigenous film and video, but only in limited ways. Institutes associated with US-based film festivals such as the Sundance Institute's Native Forum (founded in 1994) and the Tribeca Film Institute's Latin America Fund have awarded fellowships to filmmakers in Latin America. To date, TFI has included 10 indigenous video-makers in their fellowship programs, among them Vincent Carelli

(VNA trainer), Juan José García (Zapotec), Crisanto Manzano (Zapotec), Emigdio Julián (Mixtec), Pedro Daniel López (Tsotsil), and Carlos Efraín Pérez Rojas (Mixe). However, these are minor investments; mainstream film funding circuits favor auteurs with individually driven projects and academic or artistic credentials from formal institutions. Indigenous film and video projects, in contrast, may be based on traditional stories that have a collective authorship, or may be produced through group training workshops that are subject to organizational or community approval. Negotiating these factors with foundations' application processes can be frustrating and challenging; even when indigenous communities do pursue external funding opportunities, their work is often political and may conflict with the views of funders, especially state funders.

Few national film offices and arts councils support these efforts in substantive, ongoing ways. For example, Mexico's Instituto Nacional Indigenista launched an indigenous video training program in the early 1990s. However, it has had waning impact and been criticized by practitioners and scholars for its inconsistency, patronizing politics, and tendency to shape and depoliticize the content and style of self-representation (e.g. Ramos and Castells Talens 2010: 83–94; Wortham 2013; Wammack Weber 2017).

There are exceptions; some governments and state agencies have offered effective support for limited periods. The Brazilian state, whose multicultural policies were originally designed to target racial inequality affecting its Afro-descendant population, applied a best-practice model of support to nongovernmental social and cultural agencies, with positive results. In effect, this favored Video nas Aldeias. In Mexico, arts councils—including the Consejo Nacional de la Cultura y de las Artes and Fondo Nacional de Creación Artística—have provided occasional funding for particular productions, such as the collaborative Tsostil documentary *La pequeña semilla en el asfalto* (*The Small Seed in the Asphalt*, Pedro Daniel López López, 2009). Ecuador's 2015 film fund includes a specific fund for community-produced works as well as—for the very first time in South America—a separate, competitive fund for indigenous shorts, features, and television productions (Consejo Nacional de Cinematografía del Ecuador 2015).

Given the precarious funding situation, it is not surprising that most video projects across Abya Yala depend heavily on international cooperation or are completely reliant on the committed fundraising work of civil societies and the media centers devoted to the production of indigenous film and video. In Latin America, these include the partnership between the Bolivian Indigenous-Aboriginal Audiovisual Council (CAIB) and the Centro de Formación y Realización Cinematográfica (CEFREC), known as CEFREC-CAIB, Promedios/Chiapas Media Project, Oaxaca's Ojo de Agua Comunicación, and now also Brazil's Video nas Aldeias, among others. Endowments from international agencies such as the Basque solidarity agency Mugarik Gabe, the Basque government, and the Spanish Agency for International Cooperation (Agencia Española de Cooperación Internacional, AECI) have supported the indigenous media training process in Bolivia, along with nongovernmental funding from grassroots indigenous organizations and in-kind support raised by the CEFREC-CAIB partnership. AECI's indigenous program also has funded targeted workshops and various film festivals in other Latin American countries.

These sorts of partnerships also exist at the level of exhibition and distribution. Indigenous film and video festivals have sought to convene all parties in solidarity with indigenous peoples and their rights. Thanks to the rich content and steady production of indigenous-themed works, and a great deal of outreach and advocacy work, indigenous film and video started to circulate at small gatherings, coalescing into a specialized transnational community in the mid-1980s. The first hemispheric indigenous-themed film festival was the Native American Film and Video Festival, held in New York City at the privately owned Museum of the American Indian (MAI) in 1979. It was put together by the Smithsonian's National Museum of the American Indian when it took stewardship of the MAI, and took place every two to three years in various venues across the city from 1989 until 2011. Since 2000, the ImagineNative Film & Media Arts Festival (www. imaginenative.org/profile/) held annually in Toronto, Canada, has offered a similar space for gathering and exchange, and is now the largest festival of its kind. In Latin America, documentary filmmakers and advocates of indigenous peoples, including Venezuelan anthropologist Beatriz Bermúdez and Mexican documentary filmmaker Juan Francisco Urrusti, among others, convened at the first Festival Latinoamericano de Cine de los Pueblos Indígenas (Latin American Film Festival of Indigenous Peoples) in Mexico City in 1985. The most important outcome of this festival was the founding of CLACPI.

From that point forward, the organization has played a pivotal role for indigenous media production, coordinating indigenous media projects across Abya Yala. CLACPI's support network for indigenous media production in Latin America is transnational in more than one sense: it is a hemispheric, inter-indigenous exchange between indigenous nations, confederations, or collectives, as well as an example of North–South partnerships beyond nation-state frameworks. CLACPI has helped establish strategic alliances with agencies such as Mugarik Gabe and AECI, thus raising additional training funds and opportunities. The first leaders of CLACPI were activist anthropologists who hosted the festival in their own countries. Anthropologist Claudia Menezes organized the second CLACPI festival in Rio de Janeiro, Brazil, in 1987, in the midst of political battles over the Amazon region and strong local indigenous activism. Bermúdez organized the third CLACPI festival in Caracas, Venezuela, in 1990. As indigenous filmmakers began participating in CLACPI, they criticized the organization's lack of indigenous leadership and their challenges led to new approaches and initiatives.

Founded by indigenous directors who broke away from CLACPI, the first indigenous-directed film festival in Latin America was the Festival de Cine y Video de las Primeras Naciones de Abya-Yala, held in Ecuador in 1994. Organized by the Confederation of Indigenous Nationalities of Ecuador (CONAIE) and initially under the leadership of Mexican-trained Kichwa director Alberto Muenala, this new effort reconceived the purpose of an indigenous festival by introducing community screenings along with socially committed award categories and a video-library component. "We couldn't organize a film festival that would screen just in the capital. First we had to take it to the communities so community members could enjoy the creations that speak of sister nations/peoples from other latitudes," stated Antonio Vargas, organizer of the third Abya Yala festival and president of CONAIE at the time (Lucas 1999). This ambitious biannual festival fell apart after its fourth version in 2001, but it had a lasting impact by irreversibly transforming the narrative and expectations surrounding the exhibition of indigenous films and videos in the region and globally, as is apparent in more recent components of Toronto's ImagiNative festival.

The CLACPI festival and its offshoot, the Anaconda Award to Indigenous Video of the Amazon and Tropical Rainforests of Latin America (founded in 2000), continue to provide prime gathering places for an otherwise immensely dispersed and disenfranchised community of indigenous filmmakers with trainers, producers, funders, and advocates. Since its creation, CLACPI has organized 12 festivals, as well as innumerable training workshops and communication seminars devoted to strengthening the development of indigenous media in Latin America. CLACPI has also collected a vast video archive in La Paz, Bolivia. Its most recent festival was held in 2015 in Wallmapu, the Mapuche territory that straddles the national border of Chile and Argentina. It included community screenings, children's screenings, and counted primarily on indigenous organizational leadership (CLACPI 2015).

Hemispheric indigenous film and video festivals such as the Native American Film and Video Festival in New York and the CLACPI festival have also created selection criteria that respond to the needs of indigenous media-makers, rather than the expectations of mainstream industrial or independent film and festival audiences. They seek to offer a wide spectrum of films instead of merely the "best" or "most representative" works by region, nation, or genre. Because so many works focus on matters of human and territorial rights, the film programs tend to be thematic rather than regional. Perhaps most importantly, these festivals create a space for forging alliances of local, national, and global nature.

The growing indigenous video movement in the Americas maintains its flow through indigenous film and video festivals that become meeting grounds for the far-ranging community of

Figure 14.2   The 2006 CLACPI festival at the Teatro Macedonio Alcalá in Oaxaca City, Mexico.

video-makers, serving as a locus for recognition, potential fundraising, and building awareness on pressing social and political concerns faced by indigenous communities. This circuit of festivals is where indigenous media reaches urban, regional, and international audiences, and at the same time has given rise to a new sensibility among indigenous producers that "we are our own international market" (Ginsburg 1994: 177). These gatherings offer rare opportunities for exchange among members of different indigenous nations and for building networks of solidarity with the struggles of indigenous peoples.

Militant and audiovisual praxis in the Andean and Amazonian regions: ruptures, continuities, and the question of validation

DAVID WOOD

By the early 1980s, both mainstream film production and the alternative, auteurist, and militant tendencies loosely gathered under the term "New Latin American Cinema" were at a point of crisis or transition in much of Latin America. Across the continent—not least in the coastal, Andean, and Amazonian regions of Colombia, Ecuador, Peru, Bolivia, and Brazil—a series of broader ongoing ideological, cultural, and technological shifts helped reshape moving image production and consumption in the region. This enabled an array of community-based and activist media projects, as outlined in the previous section, to arise and, in many cases, to flourish. On the political/ideological front, this scenario responded to a petering-out of the radical left-revolutionary projects that many filmmakers had underwritten in prior decades (foreshadowing Cuba's Special Period of the 1990s). It also responded to a corresponding wane in the revolutionary orientation of surviving guerrilla organizations, such as those in Colombia and Peru, transitions towards (neo)liberal democracy in much of the region, a shift towards identity politics, multiculturalism and *interculturalidad*, and a heightened role of social movements. Other factors included a marked decline in many national filmmaking and film exhibition businesses, both in Latin America and beyond; corporate and/or state strangleholds on national television and media spectrums; local and transnational NGO funding for alternative media projects; and the rise of video technologies that brought with them new political and expressive possibilities, as well as dramatic changes in viewing habits.

Such developments have been widely celebrated for democratizing moving-image production and consumption (e.g. Aufderheide 1993; Gumucio Dagron 2012). In this sense, collaborative and activist video from the 1980s inherited and deepened the agendas of militant filmmaking collectives of the previous decade, such as those by Marta Rodríguez and Jorge Silva in Colombia and Jorge Sanjinés in Bolivia, Peru, Ecuador, and beyond, who sought by various means to convert their indigenous, proletarian, or otherwise "popular" collaborators into both co-authors and the primary audiences of their films. The same is true for the work of French/Brazilian documentarist Vincent Carelli in Brazil, who worked with Amazonian communities from the late 1960s, subsequently collaborated with the government-run Fundação Nacional do Índio, and founded the Centro de Trabalho Indigenista in 1979. These image-makers' efforts to break down filmmaking hierarchies is displayed in work such as the militant testimonial documentary *El coraje del pueblo* (*The Courage of the People*, Jorge Sanjinés, Bolivia, 1971), in which members of the highland mining community of Siglo XX (including Domitila Barrios de Chungara, some years before publishing her celebrated testimonial book in 1977) reconstruct and re-enact massacres of mineworkers by the Bolivian state, or *Nuestra voz de tierra, memoria y futuro* (*Our Voice of the Land, Memory and Future*, Marta Rodríguez and Jorge Silva, Colombia, 1980), in which members of the Consejo Regional Indígena del Cauca (CRIC) participated in the documentation and dramatization of political, educational, and mythological aspects of the indigenous struggle to recover both land rights and historical memory in southwestern Colombia.

As discussed in the following sections, however, the turn to video in the 1980s brought with it a series of profound changes in the nature of the activist and militant audiovisual sphere. The undoing of authorship on the part of the vanguard intellectual is only partial in those projects informed by revolutionary Marxist thought, by the didactic impulse of the documentary cinema project, and, in Silva and Rodríguez's case, by visual-anthropological methods adapted from Jean Rouch's *cinéma vérité*. Like the published testimonial literature of Moema Viezzer and Domitila Chungara (1977) or Elisabeth Burgos-Debray and Rigoberta Menchú (1983), such films are marked by a tension between the expressive subjectivities of popular protagonists and those of their lettered advocates, which inevitably carried through into the indigenous and community video projects that arose in the 1980s. Mestizo filmmakers such as Rodríguez, Carelli, and Iván Sanjinés (son of Jorge) were instrumental during that decade in training and promoting the work of indigenous moving-image makers both in their home countries and across Latin America during the 1980s and 1990s, holding video workshops and participating actively in the 1985 Mexico City festival mentioned above, and founding CLACPI alongside Bermúdez, Urrusti, and other social and media actors from across the continent. Such activities entailed a process of technology transfer that echoes the ethical problems inherent in ethnographic filmmaking: the material technologies, the technical expertise, and the cultural capital that "outsider" filmmakers pass on to their "native" collaborators become contested categories that are, variously, necessary tools for creating coherent and attractive narrative vehicles for audiovisual communication, or colonial impositions that undermine the perceived authenticity or autonomy of originary peoples' cultural expressions. Concepts such as collaborative filmmaking or "shared anthropology" (again, borrowing from Rouch) thus raise the inevitable but sometimes uncomfortable question of discursive power: in the words of Guatemalan visual anthropologist Carlos Y. Flores, the question of "the way in which the power to act and to propose are established, and the manner in which the outcomes are distributed among the different participants" (Flores 2007: 222). As Sarah Elder points out, reflecting on her own ethnographic documentaries with native peoples in Alaska, such projects may well create an "open space for making meaning," but this is also a space that produces moral dilemmas: "if I as director give over power to my subjects, is their power real or is it a colonial hoax?" (Elder 1995: 96). Although the filmmakers/teachers mentioned here do not always theorize overtly on these issues, their praxis suggests a reflexive response, aiming to strike a balance between cultural sensitivity and the need to share technical expertise. Some video documentaries achieve a critical engagement with the cultural, technological, and ethical problems raised by collaborative media projects by triangulating indigeneity, modernity, and moving-image technologies: for instance, *A festa da moça* (*The Girl's Party*, Vincent Carelli, Brazil, 1987), *O espírito da TV* (*The Spirit of TV*, Vincent Carelli, Brazil, 1990), or *Viaje a Kankuamia* (*Trip to Kankuamia*, Erik Arellana, Colombia, 2006), which use audiovisual technologies as structuring narrative devices; *Memoria viva* (*Living Memories*, Marta Rodríguez and Iván Sanjinés, Colombia, 1993), which juxtaposes different forms of audiovisual register filmed by indigenous and *mestizo* filmmakers working collaboratively; or the CEFREC-produced fiction short *Ángeles de la tierra* (*Angels of the Land*, Patricio Luna, Bolivia, 2003), with its arch, decolonizing use of mainstream television and cinema aesthetics.

As Córdova points out in the previous section, CLACPI has played an important role in the growth, continuity, and internationalization of indigenous video from the late 1980s forward. CLACPI has supported and collaborated with institutions, projects, and networks such as Vídeo nas Aldeias in Brazil (founded in 1986 by Vincent Carelli, who has been a member of CLACPI); the communications department of CONAIE; and CEFREC (directed by Iván Sanjinés, also a member of CLACPI) and CAIB. With support of the leading national indigenous and *campesino* organizations in Bolivia, both organizations collaborated in shaping an Indigenous-First Nations Plan for Audiovisual Communication. Since its beginning in 1996, CEFREC-CAIB's work has evolved and expanded exponentially, now supporting the work of the Sistema Plurinacional de Comunicación de los Pueblos Indígenas Originarios Interculturales de Bolivia, a vast multimedia network that maintains video, radio, television production, workshops, and other leadership training centers, as well as an active website that streams radio and television productions (www.apcbolivia.org) (Figure 14.3). CLACPI also collaborated with the Fundación Sol y Tierra in Cauca, Colombia, in 1991, and more recently with the Tejido de Comunicación Pueblo Nasa in 2001 (whose roots go back to Rodríguez and Silva's previous collaborations with the CRIC). This expansion in indigenous video infrastructure—which builds to a great extent upon existing social movements and political structures through which originary groups have historically articulated their negotiations with nation-states—has considerably strengthened local, national, and transnational funding, production, and exhibition networks for indigenous media production. It has also enabled indigenous audiovisual communicators to remain conversant with dominant structures while operating in a transformative context of relative cultural and political autonomy: an area termed by Schiwy (2009: 15) as "the border of dominant centers."

The emergence of the field of indigenous video should then not be seen as existing in a vacuum; rather, it should be understood in the broader historical context of the 1970s and 1980s, which saw a plethora of popular and collective film (mainly Super 8 mm), video, television, and media production initiatives arise and consolidate throughout the region: a phenomenon that Bolivian media scholar Alfonso Gumucio Dagron refers to as "decentralized communication." Key examples from that era include the miners' radio stations in Bolivia dating back to the early 1960s and beyond; the feminist media collectives Cine Mujer in Colombia (1976–1993), São Paolo-based Lilith Video, begun in 1983 and working for almost a decade (Marsh 2012: 136–137), and more recently Mujeres Creando in Bolivia (since 1992); the Associação Brasileira de Vídeo Popular (1984–2004); and the

Figure 14.3   A photograph of filmmakers in the production process, from the website of Bolivia's Agencia Plurinacional.

Grupo Chaski in Peru, which was founded in 1982 initially as an alternative film distribution and exhibition project via a network of *microcines*. Local, popular, or alternative television networks have also provided valuable counterpoints to mainstream media discourse since the 1970s and 1980s, such as the university television channels in Bolivia or the Brazilian TV dos Trabalhadores (established in 1986), while in Colombia the creation of regional television networks such as Telepacífico, Teleantioquia, and Telecaribe in the 1990s, following the dismantling of the centralized film-funding mechanism FOCINE, opened up new broadcasting fronts for alternative media. Of course, this is only a very selective handful of examples from a broad, diverse, and evolving field of alternative, independent, community-based, and collaborative media projects and processes in and beyond Latin America (e.g. Aufderheide 1993; Bermúdez Rothe 1995; Noriega 2000; Gumucio Dagron 2001, 2012; Coyer et al. 2007; Atton 2015). Meanwhile, diverse filmmakers and collectives have sought to use audiovisual media to promote human rights and environmentalist agendas; and to enfranchise or express the challenges faced by marginalized urban groups (e.g. Víctor Gaviria's auteurist work with street children in Colombia; or the Central Única das Favelas in Brazil since 1999) or prisoners (e.g. the Cine al Patio project in Bogotá led by lecturers and students from the National University of Colombia since 2002).

The rapid growth and decreasing costs of digital technologies in recent years, as well as the increasingly vernacular nature of audiovisual production tools and online distribution and communication platforms, have allowed such projects to multiply. However, the deep digital divide that still afflicts the region (due in good measure to corporate telecom strangleholds), together with uneven access to skills and cultural capital, means that the digital commons is not exempt from vertical power relations, even as it remains a powerful and valuable concept: the inequalities that framed militant film and video production in previous decades are by no means surpassed. A number of debates and problems relating to the production, consumption, distribution, preservation, and study of collaborative film and video underpin this power relation. One of them, as Horacio Legrás explores below in more detail, arises from the question of aesthetics: the extent to which alternative moving image production should or should not use, appropriate, or subvert hegemonic or vanguard modes of representation; the need or otherwise for militant advocacy to harness poetic or artistic transformation. For many indigenous video-makers the search for a "decolonized" and autonomous video medium entails a particular mode of aesthetic creativity that is grounded in the cultural specificity of the community—what Ginsburg (1994) calls "embedded aesthetics." Other media producers use conventional documentary realism or creatively appropriate mainstream film genres and conventions. As Salazar and Córdova (2008) sustain, the desire for broadcast-quality video is sometimes embraced but can also become a limitation. When producing with limited funds, some of the techniques of "imperfect cinema," particularly those inherited from neorealism such as the use of nonprofessional actors and a commitment toward addressing locally important social and cultural issues, imply continuities with 35 mm or 16 mm analogue filmmaking, even as video technology significantly changes its look and possibilities.

As Córdova has indicated above for collaborative media in indigenous languages, related to these still uneven power relations is the way in which collaborative media practice is validated (or not) through mechanisms such as state or private funding initiatives, grants, and so-called "festivalization": for what audiences are films and videos intended, how do those audiences in turn appropriate alternative media productions, and to what personal or collective interests and agendas do they respond? Finally, although online platforms have some potential to act as dynamic digital media repositories, the growing volume and the precarious nature of much alternative and militant audiovisual production means that the task of preserving, curating, and analyzing its archive is fraught with practical, financial, methodological, and ethical dilemmas. At root is the thorny question of validation. But rather than collaborative image-makers being subject to external parameters of aesthetic taste, political correctness, or archival worth, they are now active participants in the generation and evaluation of such parameters.

Militant cinema and the struggle against neoliberalism in Argentina

Horacio Legrás

"*Piquetero*," or militant cinema, refers to a group of films and filmmakers whose documentaries accompanied the fight against neoliberal policies in Argentina between the mid-1990s and 2003. These groups used digital video to document social protests and the creation of alternate social forms of production, consumption, and participation such as cooperatives (industries taken over by their workers and popular assemblies). Indeed, militant cinema groups can be considered social movements in their own right. Like other social movements, video activism gathers people from different backgrounds around a common and often practical objective. Since it is the task that defines the group, the configuration of video activist groups change as they undertake new projects. In this sense, they are as estranged from traditional forms of understanding film as the groups they serve are estranged from traditional forms of understanding politics.

The geographical distribution of militant cinema within Argentina often follows the geographical distribution of social conflicts. The collective Kino Nuestra Lucha linked its production to important social movements such as the occupied Brukman textile factory in Buenos Aires in films such as *Control Obrero* (*Workers' Control*, 2002), *La fábrica es nuestra* (*The Factory Is Ours*, 2002), and *Obreras sin patrón* (*Workers without a Boss*, 2003). One of the first important productions of Cine insurgente, *Diablo, Familia y Propiedad*, documented the exploitative practices of the Ledesma sugar mill company in the north of Argentina and its ties to the last dictatorship. Collectives of militant film appeared in provinces such as Neuquén (Ojo Izquierdo, 1999), Jujuy (Wayruro, 1992), and Santa Fe (Santa Fe Documenta, 2003). Meanwhile, Buenos Aires saw the emergence of consolidated groups such as Boedo Films (1992), Ojo Obrero (2001), Contraimagen (1997), Alavío (1996), and Mascaró Cine Americano (2002), among others.

Although united by a common grassroots activism, these groups, like their indigenous media counterparts, differ widely in their composition and practices. Some of them, such as the anarchist-leaning Alavio, shun any collaboration with the state, while others—such as Ojo Obrero and Wayruro—apply for the subsidies that the national film institute (INCAA) offer on a yearly basis. Some are organically if also loosely linked to particular political organizations, while others do not have explicit party allegiances. Some collectives hold workshops on different aspects of film production. For example, Wayruro, in northern Argentina, offers regular courses on digital photography, direction, and editing, and screens the resulting production on public television. Other groups such as Alavio refuse any collaboration with state agencies but participate in projects of community television. Other collectives have specialized in historical documentary, such as Mascaró Cine Americano, which produced several documentaries between 2006 and 2008 on the guerrilla groups PRT (Partido Revolucionario de los Trabajadores/Workers Revolutionary Party) and ERP (Ejército Revolucionario del Pueblo/People's Revolutionary Party) that were very active from the later 1960s to the mid-1970s.

Fernando Kirchmar, who directed *Diablo, familia y propiedad*, pointed to the political cinema of the 1960s—specifically to the work of Cine Liberación identified with the figure of Octavio Getino and Fernando Solanas and Cine de la Base developed by Raymundo Gleyzer—as an inspiration for the more recent *cine insurgente*. This proposed continuity between an earlier militant cinema and *piquetero* cinema that share a conception of aesthetic activism forged in the urgency of immediate political demands, conceals, however, important discontinuities. Solanas or Birri—and to a lesser extent Gleyzer—conceived their films for a political public sphere that differs markedly from the intended audience of *piquetero* cinema. Solanas's *La hora de los hornos* (*The Hour of the Furnaces*) premiered in well-established commercial circuits in Buenos Aires, where it was presented as "the most seen Argentine film of all times." In 1973, a commercial ad promoting the film claimed that 40 million people worldwide had seen Solanas's film. Although very dubious, the claim illustrates how the audience for an emblematic political movie of the New Latin American Cinema differs from the one for contemporary video activism, given the latter's close-knit ties to grassroots social movements. This change in the audience also registers an important mutation in the nature of political participation. In the 1960s, the political sphere had not yet exploded into a multitude of discrete, micropolitical, and postnational entities unified only by their common opposition to the neoliberal depredation of the public and the common.

In one of the few existing academic studies of militant (*piquetero*) cinema, de la Puente and Russo (2004) characterize the movement as a series of discrete political groups (rather than directors), who, mindful of the importance that the image plays in the hegemonic structuration of modern societies, undertake a type of cinema whose main aims are counter-information, social change, and consciousness-raising. The authors see these three features as a continuity of the political cinema of the 1960s. Sometimes the groups themselves suggest this connection. The name of the collective *Argentina arde* references a legendary group of avant-garde artists based in the city of Rosario, who, in 1968, produced *Tucumán arde*, a series of texts and photographs that revealed the shocking poverty and deprivation in Tucumán, and in this way constituted a case of counter-information. However, when *Argentina arde* opens, one of its productions with the title: "vos lo viviste, no dejes que te lo cuenten" ("you witnessed it, don't let other people tell you about it"), the stress is not so much on counter-information as it is on the practices that determine the circulation of information.

Although the use of film to increase social awareness about economic or political injustices is another area in which contemporary video activists perceive themselves as heirs of the political cinema of the 1960s, avant-garde techniques of defamiliarization that are so prominent in the films of Solanas, Gleyzer (especially *La revolución congelada*) or Glauber Rocha in *Terra em Transe* (*Entranced Earth*) are largely absent from the production of video activists. As *piquetero* cinema is directed at those who are already convinced, today's militant filmmakers are not interested in the persuasive power of novel aesthetic devices. The general lack of formal ambitions in *piquetero* cinema reinforces the limited potential of this cinema to speak to those who are outside the experience of social or political mobilization.

As de la Puente and Russo (2004) note, those who critique this aspect of *piquetero* cinema conceive of film as a product whose efficacy depends on the possibility of instantiating a different language from the one used in dominant forms of cultural communication. Militant *piquetero* filmmakers see this objection as one-sided, since it is exclusively centered on the experience of the spectator and his or her individual response to the film. In their productions—they claim—the act of viewing is only one aspect of a more comprehensive process in which the community is invited to participate in the circulation and reception of the material. This can involve incorporating the film into a variety of social actions and initiatives, in ways that are very similar to the distribution practices described by Freya Schiwy in the Oaxaca uprising in the next section.

Similarly, the lack of formal ambitions (noted by Leonor Arfuch 2004, among others) has to be relativized because the charge assumes an opposition between modernist aesthetic and dominant naturalizing media that is no longer relevant, given that the modernist aesthetic of de-automatization has become the dominant language of transnational capitalism. Militant cinema can be aesthetically refreshing on grounds that do not necessarily have anything to do with a modernist historicity of culture. A short film such as *Compañero cineasta piquetero* (facilitated by Indymedia Argentina in 2002 and distributed on the Internet) is informative and entertaining even beyond any specific sociopolitical goal. Much of the freshness of this documentary comes from the voice of a resident of a slum outside Buenos Aires, who borrows a camera for one hour and records the corrupt dealings of policemen and local authorities that take place just outside the door of his house.

The explosion of militant cinema would be unthinkable without a sizable base of people with the technical knowledge to make a documentary, and an equally vast network willing to distribute and exhibit these productions. We can contrast the isolated effort of Birri's cinema school in Santa Fe in the late 1950s to the dozens of film schools and workshops that in the mid-1990s drew 7,000 film students. The prestigious Escuela Nacional de Experimentación y Realización Cinematográfica (ENERC) is the point of origin of several collectives, among them Primero de Mayo, which was formed in 1998 and produced some of the first *piquetero* films to travel outside Argentina. Boedo Films is an informal extension of the Escuela de Cine de Avellaneda from which most of its founding members graduated. Film schools often lend equipment and personnel to different collectives, making possible some of the most representative works of *cine piquetero*.

Throughout the 1990s, increasing globalization and the liberalization of the economy affected small-scale film production in several ways. The artificial exchange rate of the neoliberal period allowed access to equipment that had been prohibitively expensive in the past. In Buenos Aires alone, half a dozen self-sustaining journals and periodicals devoted exclusively to cinema began to be published. These publications widened the circle of people interested in film, a phenomenon that, combined with the establishment of university-based film programs and the increasing accessibility of film equipment, helped to foster better conditions for independent forms of cinematic production. The internationalization of film through festivals allowed subsidies to flow to local grassroots groups either through subsidies from specific festivals (Sundance, Rotterdam) or through Argentine, Latin American, or North American foundations. This increase in international connections was confirmed by the establishment of the Festival of Independent Cinema (BAFICI) in 1999. The constant support enjoyed by BAFICI is an index of the Argentine state's supportive approach to audiovisual production, which has also included passing new laws favoring national production, providing subsidies, and the integration of film production into the educational system. The state also opened up state-owned TV channels to independent productions, and on the whole encouraged a general effervescence around film that, starting in the middle 1990s, turned Buenos Aires into "a hub of film experience, filmmaking and critical review" (Stites Mor 2012: 178). Nevertheless, in ways analogous to the differential stances of filmmaking collaboratives producing works in indigenous languages, some of the *piquetero* groups ask for INCAA support and broadcast their production through public television, while others do not.

Piquetero cinema, like the social movements with which it is usually tied, is a practice that traverses different modalities of cultural production, creation, and distribution of information. It possesses multiple articulations with political parties, state organisms, and international organizations. Militant filmmakers may include links with grassroots organizations that share a more radical critique of neoliberalism (as in the case of the EZLN or video activism in Venezuela), or connect with metropolitan foundations promoting forms of cultural empowerment around the world. Beyond the unquestionable novelty of this political and participative cinema, it is also a form of expression better understood inside a larger collective, grassroots cultural industry from below—a novel form that has strong roots in Argentine history, and one which can by now be said to constitute one of the distinctive traits of cultural production in Latin America generally.

Media activist encounters and interventions from southern Mexico

Freya Schiwy

A Little Bit of So Much Truth (2007) is a feature-length documentary that focuses on the role of activist media during the 2006 Oaxaca uprising. On June 14, the governor of this mostly indigenous state violently breaks up the encampment, or *plantón*, of the Oaxacan chapter (Sección 22) of the Mexican National Teachers Union (Sindicato Nacional de Trabajadores de la Educación, SNTE) that was striking for better wages and working conditions. In response, the *plantón* resurrects itself as a broad social movement that creates an assembly, the Asamblea Popular de los Pueblos de Oaxaca (APPO). The APPO organizes the removal of garbage, creates a security force, holds lengthy meetings modeled on self-governance in Oaxaca's indigenous communities, and occupies the city of Oaxaca until the federal police violently ends the occupation in late November 2006. *A Little Bit* highlights the importance of activist radio (e.g. Radio Plantón, Radio Cacerola, Radio Universidad, etc.) and the takeover of a local television station during the six-month long uprising. Radio and television create spaces for the movement to become visible and legitimate to and for itself. They also help to coordinate the resistance by alerting the public to unfolding/imminent actions by police and paramilitary forces. Despite the bloody repression of this movement at the end of 2006, the documentary strikingly ends on an optimistic note, showing Radio Plantón back on the air and affirming that irrevocable changes have already taken place.

This documentary attests, first, to a complex site of encounter among diverse organizations and individuals joined in their opposition to the neoliberal Mexican state: indigenous organizations, anarchists, feminists, housewives, students, taxi drivers, independent media activists, and others. Second, *A Little Bit* makes visible a process of political subjectification that is linked to accessing new and old activist media. Lastly, the documentary creates an optimistic affect that is distinct from the earlier militant cinema's focus on rage in the face of neo-imperialism. Like many indigenous videos that thrive on humor and resilience, much activist video today appears to inscribe a new political mimesis, inciting hope, even joy, in socially transformative action.

Encounters

In a prime example of Indymedia-style crowdsourcing, participants in the Oaxaca movement record the uprising on camcorders and cellphones. Their footage and photos are gathered, along with reports taken from mainstream media misrepresentations, at the offices of Mal de Ojo TV. During and shortly after the Oaxaca uprising, Mal de Ojo TV produces 23 shorts ranging in length from 35 seconds to over an hour. Some of these videos are ad hoc shorts credited to the collective and intended for immediate distribution as DVDs or to be uploaded on the Indymedia Oaxaca website. Others are feature-length documentaries, directed by long-standing members of Ojo de Agua Comunicación, such as Roberto Olivares or the video artist Bruno Varela. In the informal market in Oaxaca, vendors offer Mal de Ojo TV videos along with a range of other activist videos, some credited to particular producers, others anonymous, some retrospective, others released during the uprising (e.g., *El Comal Ardiente. Qué Pasa en Oaxaca 2006–2009*, Pueblo Producción and AgAg Films; *Guerraguetza 2007. 16 de Julio en el Fortín*, Silvia Gabriela Hernández Salinas; *Oaxaca, el poder de la Comuna*, Carlos Broun, Argentina, Contraimagen, 2006). Some of the ad hoc material is also shown at occupied COR-TV, where for three weeks a diverse group of women operates and broadcasts alternative programming, until armed gunmen destroy its antenna. Mal de Ojo TV offers technical assistance to the women in the occupied television station, as well as some of the programming material, including activist videos, alternative films and documentaries, and some of the classics from Latin America's earlier revolutionary filmmaking.

Jill Irene Freidman selected footage and still photos from the materials gathered at the Mal de Ojo TV office for *A Little Bit*. She conducted interviews, edited the materials, and created a narrative commentary for her documentary. Freidman works for Corrugated Films, a US-based independent documentary producer, but footage for *A Little Bit* is attributed to 11 different independent media organizations and 18 named individuals aside from Corrugated Films and Mal de Ojo TV, including Ojo de Agua Comunicación, Canal Seis de Julio, Universidad de la Tierra, Gringoyo Production, Indymedia Oaxaca, Mario Viveros, Cooper Bates, Chiapas Media Project in Oaxaca, and Narco News. Despite their different origins and relations with militant cinema, these organizations "fit comfortably into the categories of alternative media, radical media, or citizen's media" (Magallanes Blanco 2008; Stone 2017), categories familiar from scholarship in critical communication studies (Downing 2001; Atton 2002; Couldry and Curran 2003; Rodríguez 2011).

Like the Chiapas Media Project, Mal de Ojo TV attests to a complex interrelationship between collaborative and community media in indigenous languages, earlier militant filmmaking, and current transnational media activism. Mal de Ojo TV is the temporary incarnation of Ojo de Agua Comunicación, itself an example of the double history of indigenous media in Mexico, a site of encounter among indigenous communities and diasporas with the independent video arts movement (Wammack Weber 2017) and the state-sponsored Transferencia de Medios Audiovisuales (TMA) initiative. The TMA began to create Centros de Video Indígena (CVIs) in the early 1990s, and in the case of Oaxaca held exchanges with the Smithsonian's National Museum of the American Indian in New York and received fellowships co-sponsored by the MacArthur and Rockefeller Foundations (Smith 2006: 115). As an effort to train indigenous video-makers, the TMA often failed or sought to co-opt indigenous media production by imposing standards, genres, formats, and topics. In the case of Oaxaca, at the initiative of the CVI Oaxaca staff, Ojo de Agua Comunicación became a nongovernmental organization and eventually independent from the CVI in 2002 (Smith 2006: 116; Wortham 2013). In late May to early June 2006, shortly before the uprising, Ojo de Agua Comunicación hosted CLACPI's VIII International Indigenous Film and Video Festival "Raíz de la imagen."

Like the movement it documents and of which it forms a part, *A Little Bit* joins several histories of social struggle articulated through media: Latin American cine-acción or revolutionary documentary filmmaking; video art activism; the Mexican TMA program; and the Indymedia first created at the protests against the World Trade Organization in Seattle.[1] The coming together of this diversity of social and media activists with indigenous organizations struggling for autonomy and decolonization constitutes what Bruno Bosteels has called the "precarious meeting ground" of the commune (Bosteels 2014: 184). It marks the context of activist and collaborative media production in southern Mexico and shapes the way activist video envisions revolutionary change at the beginning of the twenty-first century. This meeting ground is formed by housewives, feminists, anarchists, indigenous organizations, and others, but also includes, importantly, a plethora of independent filmmakers and media activists, some of whom have formed part of different independent, indigenous, and collaborative media and/or art collectives, who themselves may have intimate connections to transnational media art and activism, but also to the creation and transnational circuits of home, family, and fiesta video (Kummels 2017). The close collaboration between indigenous organizations and other civil society groups distinguishes media activism in southern Mexico from similar ad hoc and embedded video activism in other places. Unlike Bolivia or Ecuador, indigenous struggle does not dominate; unlike Argentina and Chile, however, indigenous decolonial struggle is also not marginalized. Yet southern Mexico is far from isolated, but instead profoundly transnational and interconnected.

Interventions

A *Little Bit* is a Creative Commons production that encourages further sourcing and re-editing and free distribution. It enters into an alternative media network that operates in physical spaces (editing centers, community screenings, and discussions during and after the events) and virtual spaces through DVD distribution and streaming on activist sites as well as YouTube. Marion Hamm calls such media intervention a concatenation of physical and virtual space (Hamm 2005: 1). In other words, revolutionary movements today are inseparable from media activism, and this overlapping space has real effects. The Oaxaca uprisings gained international visibility not only because of the intensity of video postings and updates on the Internet, but also because the U.S. citizen Bradley Will, reporting for Indymedia, was assassinated while he was filming at one of the movement's barricades. Footage of Will's death uncannily resembles Leonardo Henrickson's recording his own death at the end of Part I of the *Batalla de Chile* (1975).

As Wood and Legrás have indicated above, there are similarities between today's media activism and earlier revolutionary filmmaking in the 1960s. Solanas and Getino's notion of *cine-acción* was conceptualized in terms of a filmmaker cadre that was organized, like guerrilla struggle, as a form of radical equality among the film crew, where, ideally, members would be equally skilled and able to replace each other. The film cadre sought to incite discussion, political consciousness, and ultimately collective revolutionary action on the part of the audience. Today's activism is both broader and more integrated into the movement it documents. Activist media intervene directly by carving out alternative spaces and nodes below and beyond the global dominance of for-profit media corporations. As they intervene into the physical struggle in the streets, they provide at once a place for the exercise of self-governance, the experimenting with alternatives to the (liberal democratic) state form through the very administration of the media itself. In Oaxaca, the housewives, teachers, and other members of different women's organizations occupying COR-TV acquire technological know-how and realize their ability to be social agents (Stephen 2013; Schiwy 2017). Despite repression, the effects of participation in the physical-virtual space of media activism thus are perceived to unleash lasting changes, not only for those directly involved. For many sympathetic viewers, activist videos continue to produce effects by attesting to and documenting a sense of power whose inspirational affects transcend borders and contexts. The optimistic affect of collaborative and indigenous media (Schiwy 2017) here indicates a long horizon of struggle, a lesson learned from decolonial perspectives: revolution is a process, not a point of arrival; it cannot be sustained on rage alone.

Note

1 The creation of Indymedia was, in part, a response to Subcomandante Marcos's call to create a global alternative media network that was reiterated in New York at the Freeing the Media Teach-In, organized by various US-based alternative media organizations (Learning Alliance, Paper Tiger TV, and FAIR) in cooperation with the Media & Democracy Congress that took place between January 31 and February 1, 1997 (Subcomandante Marcos 1997).

References

Arfuch, L. (2004) "Arte, memoria, experiencia: políticas de lo real." *Pensamiento de los confines*, 15: 57–65.

Atton, C. (2002) *Alternative Media*. London/Thousand Oaks, CA: Sage.

—— (2015) *The Routledge Companion to Alternative and Community Media*. Abingdon: Routledge.

Aufderheide, P. (1993) "Latin American Grassroots Video: Beyond Television." *Public Culture*, 5: 579–592.

Bermúdez Rothe, B. (ed.) (1995) *Pueblos indígenas de América Latina y el Caribe: catálogo de cine y video*. Caracas: Biblioteca Nacional.

Bosteels, B. (2014) "The Mexican Commune: Communism in the 21st Century." In S. Brincat (ed.), *Whither Communism? The Challenges of the Past and the Present*. Santa Barbara, CA: Praeger.

Burgos-Debray, E. and Menchú, R. (1983) *Me llamo Rigoberta Menchú*. Havana: Casa de las Américas.

CLACPI (2015) "7ma. Versión. Premio Anaconda/La Paz Bolivia 2013-2014." Available at: www.clacpi.org/actividades/premio-anaconda/resenas-2/7ma-version-premio-anaconda-la-paz-bolivia-2013-2014-2/ (accessed April 10, 2015).

Consejo Nacional de Cinematografía del Ecuador (2015) *Fondo de Fomento Cinematográfico, Convocatoria 2015*, pp. 148–181.

Couldry, N. and Curran, J. (eds.) (2003) *Contesting Media Power: Alternative Media in a Networked World*. Lanham, MD: Rowman & Littlefield.

Coyer, K., Dowmunt, T., and Fountain, A. (2007) *The Alternative Media Handbook*. London/New York: Routledge.

De la Puente, M. and Russo, P. (2004) *El compañero que lleva la cámara – cine militante argentino contemporáneo*. Tesina de grado de la Carrera de Ciencias de la Comunicación. Facultad de Ciencias Sociales. Universidad de Buenos Aires.

Downing, J. (2001) *Radical Media*. London/Thousand Oaks, CA: Sage.

Elder, S. (1995) "Collaborative Filmmaking: An Open Space for Making Meaning, a Moral Ground for Ethnographic Film." *Visual Anthropology Review*, 11(2): 94–101.

Flores, C.Y. (2007) "Sharing Anthropology: Collaborative Video Experiences among Maya Film-Makers in Post-War Guatemala." In S. Pink (ed.), *Visual Interventions: Applied Visual Anthropology*. New York/Oxford: Berghahn Books, pp. 209–224.

Garavelli, C. (2013) *Video experimental argentino contemporáneo: Una cartografía crítica*. Buenos Aires: EDUNTREF.

Ginsburg, F. (1994) "Embedded Aesthetics: Creating a Discursive Space for Indigenous Media." *Cultural Anthropology*, 9(3): 365–382.

Gumucio Dagron, A. (2001) *Haciendo olas: historias de comunicación participativa para el cambio social*. New York: Rockefeller Foundation.

—— (ed.) (2012) *Cine comunitario en América Latina y el Caribe*. Havana: Fundación del Nuevo Cine Latinoamericano.

Hamm, M. (2005) "Indymedia: Concatenations of Physical and Virtual Spaces." Available at: http://republicart.net/disc/publicum/hamm04_en.htm (accessed May 13, 2016).

ImagineNative (2016) "ImagineNative Homepage." Available at: www.imaginenative.org/profile/ (accessed May 15, 2016).

Kummels, I. (2017) "Patron Saint's Fiesta Videos: Mediatization and Transnationalization between the Sierra Mixe and California." In F. Schiwy and B. Wammack Weber (eds.), *Adjusting the Lens: Community and Collaborative Video in Mexico*. Pittsburgh, PA: University of Pittsburgh Press.

Lucas, K. (1999) "AMERICA: El cine indígena se da cita en Ecuador." April 10. Available at: www.ipsnoticias.net/1999/06/arte-y-cultura-america-el-cine-indigena-se-da-cita-en-ecuador (accessed April 10, 2015).

Magallanes Blanco, C (2008). *The Use of Video for Political Consciousness-Raising in Mexico: An Analysis of Independent Videos about the Zapatistas*. Preface by Bob Hodge. Lewiston: Edwin Mellen.

Marsh, L.L. (2012) *Brazilian Women's Filmmaking: From Dictatorship to Democracy*, Champaign, IL: University of Illinois Press.

Noriega, C.A. (ed.) (2000) *Visible Nations: Latin American Cinema and Video*. Minneapolis, MN: University of Minnesota Press.

Ramos, J.M. and Castells-Talens, A. (2010) "The Training of Indigenous Videomakers by the Mexican State: Negotiation, Politics, and Assimilation." *Post Script: Essays in Film and the Humanities*, 29(3): 83–94.

Rodríguez, C. (2011) *Citizens' Media against Armed Conflict*. Minneapolis, MN: University of Minnesota Press.

Salazar, J.F. and Córdova, A. (2008) "Imperfect Media and the Poetics of Indigenous Video in Latin America." In P. Wilson and M. Stewart (eds.), *Global Indigenous Media: Cultures, Poetics, and Politics*. Durham, NC: Duke University Press, pp. 39–57.

Schiwy, F. (2009) *Indianizing Film: Decolonization, the Andes, and the Question of Technology*. New Brunswick, NJ: Rutgers University Press.

—— (2017) "The Open Invitation: Video Activism and the Politics of Affect." In F. Schiwy and B. Wammack Weber (eds.), *Adjusting the Lens*. Pittsburgh, PA: University of Pittsburgh Press.

Smith, L.C. (2006) "Mobilizing Indigenous Video: The Mexican Case." *Journal of Latin American Geography*, 5(1): 113–128.

Stephen, L. (2013). *We Are the Face of Oaxaca: Testimonio and Social Movements*. Durham, NC: Duke University Press.

Stites Mor, J. (2012) *Transition Cinema: Political Filmmaking and the Argentine Left since 1968*. Pittsburgh, PA: University of Pittsburgh Press.

Stone, L. (2017) "Romper el cerco: An Ethnography of Transnational Collaborative Film." In F. Schiwy and B. Wammack Weber (eds.), *Adjusting the Lens*. Pittsburgh, PA: University of Pittsburgh Press, pp. 151–181.

Subcomandante Marcos (1997) "Statement of Subcomandante Marcos to the Freeing the Media Teach-In." *Prometheus Radio Project*. Available at: www.prometheusradio.org/marcos_on_media (accessed Februrary 9, 2016).

Viezzer, M. and Barrios de Chungara, D. (1977) *Si me permiten hablar . . . testimonio de Domitila, una mujer de las minas de Bolivia*. Mexico City: Siglo Veintiuno.

Wammack Weber. B. (2017) "(Re) Imagining Diaspora: Two Decades of Video with a Mayan Accent." In F. Schiwy and B. Wammack Weber (eds.), *Adjusting the Lens*, Pittsburgh, PA: University of Pittsburgh Press, pp. 13–38.

Wortham, E.C. (2013) *Indigenous Media in Mexico Culture, Community, and the State*. Durham, NC: Duke University Press.

15

PRODUCTIONS OF SPACE/PLACES OF CONSTRUCTION

Landscape and architecture in contemporary Latin American film

Jens Andermann

Editors' introduction

Until recently, film studies scholars have approached the issue of space primarily in terms of representational conventions in given films, genres, and/or national traditions, often in relation to larger sociocultural dynamics. Early narratives about protagonists who journey from the countryside to the city—such as *Romance del palmar* (*It Happened in Havana*, Ramon Peon, Cuba, 1938)—could be linked to urbanization and modernization in the early part of the century; *cabaretera* films such as *Salón México* (Emilio Fernández, Mexico, 1949) could be seen in terms of the changing role of women in Mexico City; analyses of more recent films such as *Central do Brasil* (*Central Station*, Walter Salles, Brazil and France, 1998) might read the protagonists' journey northward from Rio de Janeiro as an allegory about the nation itself; or, in the case of *Dependencia sexual* (*Sexual Dependency*, Rodrigo Bellot, Bolivia and US, 2003), as an effort to examine the geographies of class, race, and sexuality in a globalized La Paz.

Jens Andermann's "Productions of Space/Places of Construction" challenges us to shift our critical frameworks, as did Chapter 6, "Space, Politics, and the Crisis of Hegemony." Whereas Geoffrey Kantaris provides a long view of how the cinema as spatial medium (through formal conventions as well as institutional praxis) bolsters or questions hegemonic formations from the 1920s to the present, this chapter delves into a single historical horizon, examining the place-making tactics deployed by a series of contemporary films from Argentina, Brazil, and Chile. While placing emphasis on the analysis of the films' formal maneuvers, Andermann also proposes a series of larger questions about how film as a medium has contributed to place-making, as

(continued)

(*continued*)

well as the limits of that process. In demonstrating how the recent films reanimate our apprehension and engagement with space and foreground local specificities, the essay situates such tactics as a response to globalization, and at the same time as part of a global conversation. In this sense, Andermann provides a useful complement to Nilo Couret's exploration of the "aesthetics of endurance" in "slow cinema." The two essays explore different aspects of how recent films respond to the contemporary time–space compression (Harvey 1989), as experienced within Latin America.

The very notion of "Latin American cinema" is predicated on a territorial imagination, one that implies not just a shared geography of production—a complex of national and regional territories *from* which this cinema harks—but also one that is being mapped out, surveyed, and inhabited by the moving image: a territory *into* which it invites its spectators. Tom Conley, studying the relationship between cinema and mapmaking, has suggested the notion of a "cartographic cinema" in order to explore the ways in which film (narrative as well as documentary) draws out and patterns an image of space, one that "can be understood in a broad sense to be a 'map' that plots and colonizes the imagination of the public" (Conley 2007: 1). Rather than the map (associated, I would argue, more with the territorial—that is, political and symbolic—organization of the diegesis), in what follows I aim to explore the notions of architecture and landscape as concepts that allow us to think about two different modes—sometimes antagonistic, sometimes complementary—of "plotting" screen space (for relations between screen and narrative space, see Heath 1981). Rather than on "representations" of architecture and landscape in Latin American cinema, then, I wish to reflect on how films lay claim to a place by way of constructing it through modes of framing and editing, as well as on the way in which the intricacy (the materiality and duration) of a locality inexorably takes on an agency of its own that dialogues with, or conspires against, these film-architectural forms of place-making (Lefebvre 2006). At the same time, landscape and architecture—as inscribed within a "cinematic cartography"— also point to opposite ends of a deep-rooted territorial imaginary, which pins "wild" or rural against urban and domestic locations, settings that, in the Latin American context, are often highly overdetermined in terms of "civilization and barbarism," of authenticity and artifice, or of indigeneity and coloniality.

If the classic films of the studio era such as Emilio "El Indio" Fernández's *Flor silvestre* (*Wild Flower*, 1945), Lucas Demare and Hugo Fregonese's *Pampa bárbara* (*Savage Pampas*, 1945), or Lima Barreto's *O Cangaçeiro* (*The Bandit*, 1953) had composed a modern "national landscape" akin to the nineteenth-century paintings of Pridiliano Pueyrredón, José María Velasco, or Pedro Américo (Baddeley and Fraser 1989; Brownlee et al. 2015), more recent fiction and documentary have turned reflexively on these deep-rooted cultural topographies to complicate and hybridize them, generating critical effects by juxtaposing the gazes of "landscaper" and "architect". Indeed, a forest can be visualized as place, as a setting for sedentary dwelling, as in Paz Encina's *Hamaca paraguaya* (*Paraguayan Hammock*, 2006), or as a space of rambling and uprootedness as in Alejandro Fadel's *Los salvajes* (*The Wild Ones*, 2012) and Ciro Guerra's *El abrazo de la serpiente* (*Embrace of the Serpent*, 2015), just as built space can turn into "landscape" by way of its framing. In the following, then, I wish to look at a series of films in which narrative or documentary engagements with landscape and architecture become at the same time occasions for reflecting on the aesthetic and political implications of cinematic space and place—in particular of the symbolic topographies constructed by modern Latin American cinema itself.

Milestones of classic and modern Latin American cinema such as Leopoldo Torre Nilsson's *La casa del ángel* (*End of Innocence*, 1957) or Tomás Gutiérrez Alea's *Memorias del subdesarrollo* (*Memories of Underdevelopment*, 1968) had already let their cameras linger on a building's interior features as well as its relation to city or countryside, in order to illustrate their characters' state of mind or allegorize their being caught up within the constraints of urban, bourgeois society. Although these connotative functions certainly remain present in more recent works, they are being accompanied or underwritten here by a parallel and almost autonomous discourse on built space, its materiality and internal correspondences, in which the camera's as well as our own gaze are tempted to dispense with the characters and the diegetic temporality of human relations. Instead, in these moments, in which architecture comes to the fore of the image, it attracts the films' interest as a would-be doppelgänger of cinema itself: a mode of framing, cutting, and editing in space that is akin to the way in which cinema breaks up and rearranges the realm of the visible. I begin with an analysis of Argentine director Lisandro Alonso's "naturalist" trilogy, featuring solitary characters in remote corners of the country, subsequently moving from Alonso's insistent deferral of the landscape form to several recent documentaries that explore the analogy between cinema and architecture as constructions of sites. Rather than to suggest an inherent affinity between the "natural landscape" and fiction, on the one hand, and between "architecture" and the documentary, on the other, what I am interested in is, on the contrary, to shed light on how the landscape form infuses the rural and "natural" margins with a documentary temporality that counteracts the fictionalizing rhetorics of journeying associated with these environments (something that is also true for the films of Carlos Reygadas, Cão Guimarães, Lucrecia Martel, or Claudia Llosa, despite their formal differences from Alonso's trilogy). Conversely, I explore how architecture provides documentary with a "storyline" for thinking about its own constructive, place-making, and thus "fictional" aspects.

Staging "nature"

In Lisandro Alonso's trilogy of films featuring taciturn loners in out-of-the-way parts of Argentina—*La libertad* (*Freedom*, 2001), *Los muertos* (*The Dead*, 2006), and *Liverpool* (2008)—any direct visual purchase on "natural space" as landscape is denied by the native protagonist, who literally *stands between* our gaze and the landscape. The relation between hero and surroundings, moreover, is one of shared opacity, the effect not just of the laconic actoral performances and of the remote locations where the action is set, but also of a particular form of shot composition. Alonso's camera in all three films remains at medium distance almost throughout, prompting us to observe his protagonists' interactions with their surroundings, never moving close enough to reveal their emotional responses nor far enough away to inscribe their actions within a wider social or natural order. Here, then, the otherness of place and protagonist stems from a visual rhetoric that binds one to the other, forcing us to infer their "meanings" from this mutual "implicatedness."

La libertad narrates in long, quiet shots the labor day of a woodcutter, from carefully choosing and preparing the trees, to cutting and transporting the trunks to the sawmill, buying provisions at a roadside gas station, and finally returning to the wood, killing, roasting, and eating an armadillo by the campfire. Alonso does not specify the spatial or temporal setting of this minimal plot; even the protagonist's full name—or rather, that of the actor playing him(self), Misael Saavedra—is only disclosed in the production credits at the end, as are the time and location of the action: "Argentina, 2001". Yet this inscription of diegetic action into national space and into the historical present has a propositional rather than affirmative character, inviting us to reflect on the extent to which Misael's existence on the outer borders of society might still participate in, or rather break free from, the nation's plight.

The question is both ethical and political: what form of contemporariness, asks Alonso, would today include urban cinemagoers as well as the woodcutter they witness onscreen? Representation seems to be his answer, as he inscribes the "documentary" footage of Misael's workmanship into a fictionalized, narrative order. Misael's working day is narrated in the form of a journey from wood to sawmill and gas station—from "nature" to "the market"— and back, which is simultaneously one from "documentary" to "fiction" (Rival and Choi 2001: 154–159). The entire first half-hour of *La libertad* consists of a mute dialogue between, on the one hand, Misael and the trees, and between his manual labor and Alonso's camerawork, on the other, always looking for the right shot to the task at hand. Thus, a series of mobile takes from the medium distance show Misael, as well as the tree on which he works with axe, spade, and electric saw, subordinating frame, depth of field, and duration almost entirely to the rhythms of Misael's woodwork. With the appearance of the voice in the second part—triggered by the minimal, market-driven exchanges between Misael, the sawmill owner, and the gas station attendant—performance and fiction come to the fore, at just the moment, moreover, in which the value of Misael's labor is at stake. "No me sirve esto —this is of no use for me," the sawmill owner refers to Misael's daywork, to justify a payment that, as we see in the following sequence, barely buys some bread and cigarettes at the store.

If the film's middle section thus approaches (albeit in a minimal fashion) a more classical action cinema, complete with shot-reverse-shot sequences showing bodies in dialogue, the final part tends more towards a cinema of affect. Here, Alonso interrupts for the first time the medium distance for close-ups of the agonizing armadillo and of Misael's face while eating. Misael's furtive look at the camera towards the end, however, briskly cuts off any empathetic affective investment, rechanneling our attention to the documentary terrain of the opening section. Camera, voice, and look—elementary forms of cinematic composition—in *La libertad* maintain a precarious balance between reality and fiction, equivalent to the one in which the film shows labor and nature to be always already subjected to exchange value and the market. Just like its protagonist, however, Alonso's film forces from this tension moments of autonomy: echoing the reduction of Misael's existence to its minimal necessities, Alonso explores the possibility of a radical ascetics in order to liberate cinema's observational powers. This strive for autonomy manifests itself most strikingly in the sequence closing the first part, in which the camera takes to the wood on its own (while Misael takes a siesta), in a strange dance or flight through trees and undergrowth, as if it were another forest animal.

Los muertos revisits this (literally) "spectacular" shot right at the beginning, yet radically changes its function. Here, apart from the thicket of subtropical rainforest, this meandering gaze encounters as if by accident the bloodied corpses of several children and, recoiling into the distance, a hand carrying a dagger. The sequence ends with a fade to green, followed by a medium-length shot of Argentino Vargas (again, played by a local man of the same name), a prison inmate, as he wakes up and gets out of bed. *Los muertos* follows Argentino's release from prison and his return journey to the family home deep in the island maze of the

Paraná River, with a similarly detached curiosity as in *La libertad*. Alonso denies us any cues for reinserting the initial sequence into the narrative, as a nightmare or flashback: the genre expectations of the prison drama and its obsession with guilt and vengeance are only called upon in order to be systematically disappointed. Yet even if left in suspension, this genre quotation infuses the film with a climate of tense expectation, as we observe Argentino's gradual reimmersion into nature: short, monosyllabic conversations with the islanders, his dexterity in collecting wild honey or in killing and disemboweling a stray goat. But as in *La libertad*, this "nature" is never outside politics, and this political dimension is likewise associated with its ambiguous status as object of documentary observation and as fictional setting.

Whereas, in Alonso's previous film, the movement from documentary observation to narrative and performance had paralleled the one from "nature" to "the market," here the sequence is inverted. Now, it is the forest setting that charges the documentary image with a fictional surplus, an excess, as the origin of an ominous, latent violence. Thus, a static shot of the nightly forest moving in and out of focus, cut against one of Argentino sleeping in a friend's family's hut not merely signals the passing of time, but also invokes a vague sense of menace, as a visual echo of the opening shot: not only for the memory of slain innocence it calls up, but for the way it introduces a gaze with no relation to the diegesis, a gaze somehow external to human affairs. Whereas the predominant camera position, just as in *La libertad*, maintains a medium distance, allowing both a proximity towards Argentino and the observation of the surroundings with which he comes into contact, this forest shot devoid of narrative function also envelops the action in the temporality of what, with Deleuze, we might call an impulse-image (image-pulsation) (Deleuze 1983: 174). For Alonso, as for Deleuze, this "prehistoric" time remains radically political, its "primitivism" being the effect of abandonment on behalf of society and the state rather than of a presocial or "natural" state of things. In *Los muertos*, this passing of the threshold of the *polis* is beautifully staged in the way Argentino—having previously been groomed at the prison for his release into civic life—gradually strips down again to near-nakedness.

Nature turns stagelike in *Los muertos* because it is still inscribed in the political as the scene of an originary exclusion: its secrecy and ominousness pose a question about the origins of power and its relation to justice and violence. Incidentally, it is at the moment of leaving polite society behind and returning to the wilderness—arriving at the waterside to board a canoe—when Argentino is challenged by an old fisherman to unravel the mystery: "So they say you've killed your brothers?" Argentino, however, claims oblivion and switches from Spanish to Guaraní—from the language of the state to that of the "interior"—before rowing off into the distance, all in a single panning shot. In fact, the compositional rhythm of *the drift* is key in *Los muertos*, providing a spatio-temporal movement that becomes one with the narrative itself, but also as the form in which Argentino's story is constantly referred back to this mysteriously charged natural setting. In one of the film's most beautiful shots, the camera drifts alongside Argentino, resting on his canoe floating downstream, finally parting ways as it drifts off into a separate current to deliver an autonomous image of river and forest.

Similarly, at the end of *Los muertos*, the camera stays behind as Argentino and his grandson enter the family hut, tilting slowly downward until it re-encounters in the dust the toy footballer Argentino had fingered just before, next to the remains of a miniature bicycle. Rather than representing an allegory (of the nation, of childhood, of poverty), the relation of this shot to diegetic action is the same as in the previous images of the natural landscape, but now extending the latter's enigmatic power to the little object, investing it with a fetishistic or talismanic quality. Moreover, this shot also signals a change in point of view, a camera staying on after the protagonist has left the frame, a shot Alonso radicalizes in *Liverpool*. The trilogy's third film concludes the paradoxical journey towards narrative and simultaneously towards the real, which Alonso had started in *La libertad*. The change here is not just one of environments—although the move from the lush, buzzing woodlands of *La libertad* and *Los muertos* to the frozen solitude of Tierra del Fuego has a profound impact, particularly on the soundtrack, which features a forbidding, almost tangible silence, instead of a densely layered tapestry of noises of the previous two films. Again, the story follows an enigmatic, taci-turn character's solitary journey: the sailor Farrel (Juan Fernández), who, as his ship docks at Ushuaia, asks for a few days' leave to visit his mother. On arrival at her village, Farrel spends the night squatting outside the village canteen and almost freezes to death before being reluctantly rescued by an elder who has taken Farrel's bedridden mother and mentally handicapped daughter into his care, telling him to piss off—which Farrel promptly does, following a halfhearted attempt to reconnect with his mother and exchange a few sentences with his daughter. Alonso's camera, in a characteristic long take, watches him walk off across a snow-covered clearing, before cutting back to the family home, the sawmill, the forest where the old man and the girl go to check their fox traps. It turns to an everyday reality re-encountered as a *social* rather than solitary world, one the film pointedly chooses over its protagonist. This is an ethical as much as an aesthetic choice, as the final sequences taking place at the backwoods community make it clear, hinting at complex, intricate relationships of tenderness, anguish, and misery: just what Farrel may have been running from.

In fact, then, even though they are set under open sky, Alonso's films seem to be less concerned with nomadic rambling than with sedentary dwelling: only Farrel partly shares the traveling foreigner's outsider's role and surveying gaze, but even his actions are those of one familiar with the location and its inhabitants. Alonso's are *anti*-road movies in their constellation of gaze, setting, and body: instead of being carried into "nature" by the gaze of an explorer who shares our disfamiliarity,[1] here we are tasked, on the contrary, with observ-ing a body *at home* in its own environment, to which Alonso—unlike "ethnofictional" films such as Lúcia Murat's *Brava gente brasileira* (*Brave New Land*, 2000) or Marco Bechis's *Terra Vermelha* (*Birdwatchers*, 2009)—never makes any effort to suture our gaze. By deliberately failing to satisfy the epistophilic desire associated with the landscape form, Alonso's work carries out a powerful critique of the idea of "nature," which is revealed to be but a social habitat in a state of marginalization and abandonment that is political rather than natural.

The arts of construction

Whereas Alonso and others have ventured out towards the spatial margins of the nation, only to find there places of dwelling, of homeliness, a string of recent documentaries have turned their attention to architecture and urbanism under the sign of displacement and uprootedness. Modern architecture, in Latin America, traditionally carried a utopian prom-ise of spatial transformation and improvement of society, from the public schools and social housing projects of Juan O'Gorman and Carlos Raúl Villanueva in Mexico and Venezuela, to Lúcio Costa's and Oscar Niemeyer's wholesale planning of Brazil's new capital city, Brasília (Fraser 2000). Documentary cinema submits such spatial arrangements of units and volumes to its own temporal grammar of framing, cutting, and (re-)editing: in this counter-rhythm, a critical archaeology of architectural place-making emerges, either as a form of memory-work that uncovers in built space a sedimentation of layers of meaning and affect or by counterpointing the different stages of the material and social process of construction with the temporality of cinematographic montage. In fact, the combination of static long takes and different kinds of panning shots exploring the dimensions of buildings' exteriors or the experience of immersion into them is already a kind of elementary grammar of this critical interrogation of architecture through film. In Jonathan Perel's *El predio* (*The Premises*, 2010), the camera's focalizing, in uncomfortably long takes with no voice-over or dialogue, on particular features of façades and interior spaces or slowly dollying down the streets and paths inside the grounds of the former Escuela Superior de Mecánica de la Armada/Naval Academy—Argentina's most notorious concentration camp during the military dictatorship, recently taken over as a space of memory by human rights organizations—works a subtle temporalization on material space. By means of the duration of the image, cinema forces the buildings to reveal layers of experience beyond the here and now of their materiality: while the long, static shots draw out the marks, stains, and traces that point to past experiences that are at once irrecoverable and ghostly present, the slow forward or lateral panning shots that alternate with these *temps morts* also offer a spatialized form of memory-work desperately searching for cues or trying to reattach to the material setting the passage of those bodies that the violence of dictatorial terror had sought to obliterate.

Other recent films similarly query the tensions between presence and absence, construction and erasure, in less extremely charged but nonetheless complex environments. Néstor Frenkel's *Construcción de una ciudad* (*Constructing a City*, 2006), Gabriel Mascaró's *Avenida Brasília Formosa* (*Defiant Brasília*, 2010), and Adirley Queirós's *A cidade é uma só?* (*One City?*, 2011) all inquire into the tension unleashed by developmentalist modernization, between the production and destruction of space, the construction of model environments, and the forced, dysfunctional, and traumatic uprooting of populations. Drawing on the memories of local interviewees and their everyday acts of resistance and complicity, as well as deploying their own, intricate cross-editing work of proper and found footage (including official archives as well as amateur Super 8 reels and videos), these films not merely "document," but also actively collaborate in the undoing of material acts of erasure. *Construcción de una ciudad* narrates the strange story of Federación, a provincial town in Argentina that was razed to the ground by the military dictatorship in the late 1970s to make way for the Salto Grande reservoir on the Uruguay River. Its inhabitants were resettled to a new model town a few miles away, planned and built according to neo-rationalist precepts. Following years of decline—not least because of material decay of homes and public utilities—the new Federación suddenly jumped to fortune in the late 1990s thanks to the discovery of thermal springs in the vicinity. Yet many residents still return to the muddy foundations of the old town, released by the lake in dry season: their mudlarking expeditions for shards of household items among the rubble of their old homes and streets, shot top-down from a crane so as to emphasize the cartographic aspect of their memory-mapping of traces near-erased by decades of flooding, are among the film's most impressive images. Yet where the people of Federación literally dig up the mud of the lake floor, Frenkel ploughs through a different sedimentation of temporal layers by cross-editing his own shots of the old and new city (their phantasmatic relationship ironically emphasized through superimpositions that make pedestrians, animals, and vehicles appear and evaporate as if time-traveling) with archival footage. The different materialities of these audiovisual memories from over 30 years—official television news and Super 8 amateur movies of the old town, its destruction, and the first days and weeks in the still-unfinished new Federación, subsequently VHS and finally digital videos of municipal ceremonies (including a local cinephile's attempt to shoot a dystopian sci-fi short among the old city's ruins)—correspond to layers of historical experience, both intimate and public. In fact, the material transition from analogue to digital that is perceptible in the grain, faded colors, and pixellation of successive samples of found footage also corresponds in political terms to the difficult and partly flawed transition from dictatorship to democracy in Argentina. The submerged city and its periodic, ruinous reappearance, as well as the affective power it still holds over residents despite the recent blessings of thermal tourism, is also a striking allegory for Argentine society's difficult relation with its traumatic past of terror and disappearance—all the more powerful for Frenkel's restraint in making it explicit.

Archival and other audiovisual materials of various kinds also feature prominently in Mascaró's and Queirós's films, both of which provide an interesting contrast to Frenkel's cinematic archaeology of (late) modern urbanism. For, whereas in *Construcción de una ciudad* the static, medium-length shots of neighbors in front of their near-identical model homes (taking advantage of their rectangular façades, akin to the shape of the screen itself) underscore the artificial and immobilizing nature of planned urban space, in *Avenida Brasília Formosa* and *A cidade é uma só?* the camera adopts the mobile gaze of city dwellers on the move. Against the verticalist, God's-eye vision of the urbanist (referenced as well as counterpointed in Frenkel's crane shots of the destroyed old Federación), Mascaró and Queirós take up the embodied, horizontal viewpoint of residents as they walk, drive and cycle through urban space (de Certeau 1988): Dildu, Nancy, and Zé Antônio, residents of Brasília's ramshackle, sprawling satellite city Ceilândia in *A cidade*, the fisherman Pirambú, the waiter Fábio, the manicurist Débora, and little Cauan in *Avenida Brasília*. The latter are residents of Recife's Brasília Teimosa neighborhood and variously affected by the former *favela's* transformation thanks to the construction of a new main road and extension of public services. Whereas Pirambú's seaside shack has been razed to make way for the new Avenida, and he himself is resettled to a distant social housing complex far away from his boat and livelihood, video amateur Fábio (whose VHS footage of the demolition is included by Mascaró) makes money on the side offering his services to neighbors aspiring to the amenities of urban middle-class society: a birthday party and video for Cauan, a Big Brother application tape for Débora. Cross-edited with the carefully choreographed reality TV rhythm of Fábio's home videos, Mascaró's fly-on-the-wall shots of everyday situations in the neighborhood chronicle the partial and contradictory "integration" into urban consumer society of a space excluded until recently from the networks of the "formal" city. For example, *Avenida* highlights the uneasy adaptation of many residents to the new reality visible in the seemingly chaotic, mutually permeable relations between insides and outsides, public and domestic spaces (enhanced by Mascaró's discontinuous editing), even while showcasing how living spaces are slowly being colonized by the amenities of middle-class life: kitchen units, TV sofas, even an rooftop swimming pool.

In Queirós's film, a similarly mobile camera, panning from the windows of cars and buses, follows the daily routines of residents of Ceilândia, Brasília's remote satellite city, where, in the 1960s, municipal authorities relocated construction workers' families who had settled on lands close to the new modernist capital. Cleaner Dildu, after a day's work and hours-long bus drive home, embarks on a quixotic one-man election campaign for municipal counselor; his cousin Zé Antônio drives him around distributing leaflets while himself looking for cheap property opportunities on the sprawling city's margins. Nancy, a singer and local activist, records for a community radio the jingle she had been chosen to perform as a child, in a public promotion campaign for resettlement to Ceilândia, effectively a mass deportation project: "A cidade é uma só"—one city for all. Queirós's film gives the lie to the song—or rather reappropriates it by following the rehearsals for its re-performance by Nancy and a group of Ceilândia schoolchildren, cross-edited with Dildu's recording of a campaign rap for the radio. The two songs also stand for the way in which *A cidade é uma só?* juxtaposes archival footage of Brasília's construction and of the resettlement of "land invaders" to Ceilândia with Queirós's own present-day material as he criss-crosses the mushrooming poverty belt where—as Zé Antônio realizes to his chagrin—hardly any unbuilt slots remain for purchasing. Here, as in *Avenida Brasília Formosa*, the formal city's clean and carefully planned spaces remain conspicuously absent: what we see on-screen is the flipside of urbanistic planning, the living spaces improvised by those for whom the architects made no provisions whatsoever, yet who, like Dildu, effectively keep the formal city running.

Just as Frenkel's, then, these two films from Brazil investigate the long-term impact of urbanistic interventions on the lives of individuals and communities. By contrast, the process of construction itself is the subject of Paola Castillo and Tiziana Panizza's *74m2* (2013) and Mariano Donoso's *Tekton* (2009). Castillo and Panizza's film follows the seven-year plight of female urban Mapuche leaders who are trying to promote a community housing project on the outskirts of Valparaíso, based on the idea of resident involvement in finishing and customizing the publicly funded base units. The idea of "participative urbanization," rehearsed at a community meeting where families are invited to color in and decorate paper models of their new homes, has won the architects prestigious awards abroad (Alejandro Aravena, the project's main architect, was the 2016 Pritzker Laureate). Yet Castillo and Panizza probe the concept by observing the women's day-to-day reality in negotiating the obstacles that keep piling up: insufficient funds, hostility from middle-class neighbors, and, once the complex has finally been built, conflicts within the community on whether to invest in weatherproofing or security fences. The film cleverly cross-edits scenes of the community dealing with these practical (and exhausting) issues, with other animated sequences that bring to life the blueprints drawn up by the architects—providing the film with a

Figure 15.1 Dildu on the campaign trail in the barren landscape of Ceilândia in A *cidade é uma só?*

baseline, a chronometric rhythm. From these abstract spaces composed on the drawing board, Castillo and Panizza cut back to the multiple and contradictory social acts of place-making these drawings trigger: from the communal Nguillatún ceremony inaugurating and blessing the grounds to the burglary alarms mushrooming among the adjacent middle-class homes and the makeshift shops that start appearing inside the new housing complex. The film's subject, then, is less the relation between architectural projection and user-driven construction of living space—moments of physical building work appear only very briefly— and more the forging of community, of affective commitment and belonging among the new settlement's residents. Being a much more strenuous, time-consuming, and emotionally demanding task than bricklaying, carpentry, and plastering, Castillo and Panizza suggest, this aspect of place-making entrusted, fundamentally, to women is systematically being devalued in a patriarchal society.

This gendered dimension becomes especially clear when contrasting *74m2* with the all-male human cast of *Tekton*, Mariano Donoso's lyrical account of the completion of the Centro Cívico, the town hall of his native city of San Juan, Argentina. Construction on the building had started in 1973, the year that Juan Perón had returned to the presidency, but was abandoned shortly thereafter. This perennially unfinished, almost instantly ruinous monument of the developmentalist state—which had promised a second "reconstruction" parallel to the one that had ushered in Peronism's golden age following the San Juan earthquake of 1944—had appeared in Donoso's debut feature, *Opus* (2005), as an emblem of the modern state's terminal crisis (Andermann 2014). What does it mean, Donoso asks, returning to the site shortly afterwards, for this building to have been effectively "completed" after all, more than 30 years after its inception? Rather than to embark on a rambling, ethnographic quest for answers to the enigma, as in *Opus*, Donoso stays put and turns to the work of construction itself, in its intricate choreography of heavy machinery, of men and materials defying gravity and bringing back iconic memories from an industrial age that seemed long gone. *Tekton* cleverly draws out these visual echoes, as when a string of workers

Figure 15.2   The film *74m2* marks the role of women in place-making.

232

leaving the site at dusk recalls the Lumière brothers' 1895 short of workers leaving the factory, or when painters dangling from ropes and carpenters laying beams high above ground
reference skyscraper construction movies by the likes of Harold Lloyd or Buster Keaton
from the 1930s. Donoso emphasizes these period references by setting the greater part of
his images—many of them in black and white—to scores of extradiegetic music (Fauré,
Ravel, Debussy), using intertitles and accelerating projection speed, in a pastiche of the
constructivist *Querschnittfilm* of silent-era German and Soviet cinema (Walter Ruttmann,
Dziga Vertov).

The documentary self-consciously replicates in its own compositional forms the mechanical rhythms of construction that seem to bring back a bygone age: in one of the intertitles,
Donoso quotes Schopenhauer on the fundamental identity between present-day builders
performing maintenance tasks on ancient Egyptian buildings and their predecessors from
pharaonic times.

The film's concern, however, is not so much with the political implications of this unexpected re-emergence of an entrepreneurial state, but rather with the ongoing validity of
the modernist idiom in architecture, and, hence, cinema: how to shoot the construction
of this late-Corbusian, functionalist monument if not through a "constructivist" aesthetic
that responds to its formal propositions? Donoso carefully paces the rhythm of his narrative according to the subsequent stages of construction, each of which takes the form of a
theatrical—or perhaps rather operatic—act, complete with its individual stage decoration,
dramatic climax, and curtain. In this way, his film also goes against the grain of the other
documentaries' "anthropological critiques" of architecture (to paraphrase James Holston's
1989 influential polemic against Brasília). Instead, he reintroduces the dimension of the
aesthetic in architecture, as akin to that of beauty in film. In one particularly delicate (and
lucky) moment, Donoso's camera shoots the hoisting-up of rooftop air conditioning units,
the iron rafters of which, as they sail through the air, appear to reflect the cloud patterns in
the sky, as if the landscape were talking back to the structures erected within it. Donoso registers this correspondence with subtle irony (expressed through the piano score underlying
the sequence), but concedes architecture its moment of grace: "El edificio está terminado—
the building is complete," recognizes one of the film's last intertitles. Perhaps, Donoso seems
to imply, there is still room after all for realizing some of modernity's promises.

Figure 15.3 The constructivist aesthetic of Mariano Donoso's *Tekton.*

Jens Andermann

Donoso's sweeping pan across the roof of the Centro Cívico towards the surrounding mountains and sky is also the moment where, in the visual rhetoric of *Tekton*, architecture falls over into landscape. It inscribes building work (including its cinematic framing and re-editing) within a space that calls back to the scene the agency and intricacy of the site: the way in which "construction" cannot but respond to, and thus reinscribe, a series of "natural elements" registered by the camera. Film's very character of a (photographic) register set in motion through discontinuous editing of shots makes it akin to the work of the architect and urban planner, whose interventions into material places are at the same time the product of a symbolic representation of these in and through the building or the plan. Contemporary Latin American cinema, both in the genre of documentary and in narrative, reflects precisely on this double gesture of (re-)inscription: What happens in the conversion of the location into a setting? Can its place-ness be retained, even as it must be enframed and reinserted, both spatially and temporally, into the editing sequence? Or is there something out there in the singularity of place that resists formal capture and reinscription? Recent films from Latin America bear witness to the difficulty of locating singularity in a world in which idiosyncrasies and particularities have been leveled under the onslaught of "globalization." Yet it is precisely their shared attempt to force out such localized singularity that makes these films so interesting, as well as establishing them as part of a conversation that is global in scope.

Note

1 Angela Prysthon (2014) argues that this "geographical imagination" characteristic of the traveling naturalist's or surveyor's gaze is what distinguishes Alonso's latest film, *Jauja* (2014), from the previous trilogy.

References

Andermann, J. (2014) "Exhausted Landscapes: Reframing the Rural in Recent Argentine and Brazilian Films." *Cinema Journal*, 53(2): 50–70.
Baddeley, O. and Fraser, V. (1989) "Mapping Landscapes." In *Drawing the Line: Art and Cultural Identity in Contemporary Latin America*. London: Verso, pp. 9–39.
Brownlee, P.J., Piccoli, V., and Uhlyark, G. (eds.) (2015) *Picturing the Americas: Landscape Painting from Tierra del Fuego to the Arctic*. New Haven, CT: Yale University Press.
Conley, T. (2007) *Cartographic Cinema*. Minneapolis, MN: University of Minnesota Press.
de Certeau, M. (1988) "Walking in the City." In *The Practice of Everyday Life*, trans. S.F. Rendall. Berkeley, CA: University of California Press, pp. 91–110.
Deleuze, G. (1983) *Cinéma I. L'image-mouvement*. Paris: Minuit.
Fraser, V. (2000) *Building the New World: Studies in the Modern Architecture of Latin America, 1930–1960*. London: Verso.
Harvey, D. (1989) *The Condition of Postmoderity: An Enquiry into the Origins of Cultural Change*. Oxford: Blackwell.
Heath, S. (1981) "Narrative Space." In *Questions of Cinema*. London: Macmillan, pp. 19–75.
Holston, J. (1989) *The Modernist City: An Anthropological Critique of Brasília*. Chicago, IL: University of Chicago Press.
Lefebvre, M. (2006) "Between Setting and Landscape in the Cinema." In M. Lefebvre (ed.), *Landscape and Film*, London/New York: Routledge, pp. 19–59.
Prysthon, A. (2014) "Paisagens sonhadas: imaginação geográfica e deriva melancólica em *Jauja*." *Devires*, 11(2): 230–255.
Rival, S. and Choi, D. (2001) "Última tendencia del cine argentino." *Kilómetro*, 111(2): 154–159.

16

ENDURING ART CINEMA

Nilo Couret

Editors' introduction

Long equated with aesthetically experimental works and frequently situated in opposition to mainstream cinema, "art cinema" is an increasingly vexing term. Starting in the 1960s, the notion became associated in the minds of many US-based scholars with French, Italian, German, Japanese, and, at times, Latin American films made by "independent" director-artists (*auteurs*) seemingly less concerned with commercial profit. In this chapter, Nilo Couret unpacks the concept of art cinema, revealing its contradictory usages through a concise overview of its deployment in different historical periods and different geo-cultural sites. Unlike traditional discussions of the term, Couret traces its use back to 1920s–1930s Brazil and Argentina, and then moves forward to the 1960s and the present day. In so doing, he enriches our understanding of how Latin American critics and filmmakers in different eras have employed the notion of "art cinema" to situate domestic productions against the larger landscape of imported works. Like Geoffrey Kantaris in Chapter 6, Couret insists on the importance of recognizing the geopolitical underpinnings of the cinema (as a set of socioeconomic institutions), *as well as*, in this chapter, of the conceptual/theoretical categories used by film critics and scholars.

While recognizing these multiple valences, Couret argues that "the real" has been "an enduring aesthetic concern for art cinema"—*if* we broaden our understanding of how the real can be made manifest. In a way similar to Salomé Aguilera Skvirsky's discussion in Chapter 8, he contends that our narrow understanding of realism has created a series of blind spots in Latin American film scholarship. He draws on the work of U.S. scholars Fredric Jameson and Lauren Berlant to proffer a new critical framework on the manifestation of the real in contemporary Latin American cinema. In so doing, he locates the conditions that make films such as *Fantasma* (Lisandro Alonso, 2006) and *Heli* (Amat Escalante, 2013) intelligible to foreign critics while also identifying formal maneuvers used by Latin American filmmakers to speak about the specific experience of neoliberalism in the region.

When José Padilha's *Tropa de Elite* (*Elite Squad*, 2007) won the Golden Bear in the 2008 Berlin International Film Festival, the Brazilian film became the second Latin American film to win the prestigious award in the festival's history precisely 10 years after Walter Salles's *Central do Brasil* (*Central Station*, 1998). The victory came as a surprise after mixed to negative reactions from members of the international press—*Variety* notoriously panned the film as "a recruitment film for fascist thugs" that celebrated "Rambo-style heroes" (Weissberg 2008) — but controversy was nothing new to the film. Set in the months preceding the papal visit of 1998, *Tropa de Elite* follows an ambitious captain of the Batalhão de Operações Policiais Especiais (BOPE) spearheading a pacification campaign in the slums of Rio de Janeiro. The film's subject matter made it the target of debates both aesthetic (a continuation of the "cosmetics of hunger" (Bentes 2001), exemplified by the earlier *Cidade de Deus* (*City of God*, Fernando Mereilles and Kátia Lund, 2002), and political (the BOPE's methods had been the subject of an Amnesty International report in 2005 and the Unidade de Polícia Pacificadora would be launched in 2008) (Amnesty International 2005).

Despite its polemical subject matter, the film was the domestic box-office champion of 2007, with over 2 million spectators during its three-month theatrical release ("Tropa" 2008), and estimates of another 11.5 million pirated copies sold ("Tropa" 2007b). Its festival success seems even more surprising given that a national jury would select *O ano em que meus pais saíram de férias* (*The Year My Parents Went on Vacation*, Cao Hamburger, 2006) as the country's representative for the Academy Award for Best Foreign Language Film. The national jury, which ironically included Héctor Babenco and Bruno Barreto, whose respective *Pixote* (1982) and *O que é isso, Companheiro?* (*Four Days in September*, 1997) also exploited violence and poverty, defended its decision, claiming that it was not selecting the best film of the year, but the best film for international consideration. *O ano* had "a standard of quality more attune to that type of awards process [with Academy members] who are over 60 years old with pre-conceived ideas and who do not really like violence" (Pimental 2007). How did *Tropa de Elite*, a film deemed too reminiscent of American-quality TV by a national jury, later become a film festival darling? The film's international distributor, the Weinstein Company, withdrew the film from Sundance and submitted it to Berlin and Cannes with the hopes of collecting laurels and better pitching the film to *art cinema* audiences ("Tropa" 2007a).

From box-office receipts to festival success, the debates about the film's content and the particular history of its reception and exhibition open onto a series of questions about the status of art cinema. Can we call a box-office champion, which spawned an even higher-grossing sequel, an example of art cinema? Does festival or awards success necessarily designate art cinema? Is there a particular "standard of quality" or film content that makes something art cinema? Does being representative of a nation or region matter in art cinema content or art cinema circulation? Further, the differences between the 1998 Golden Bear winner *Central do Brasil* and the 2008 winner *Tropa de Elite* suggest that the answers to these questions change over time. Studying art cinema necessarily entails reflecting on our criteria—whether industrial, generic, and/or aesthetic—for conferring the status of art cinema and understanding the conditions of emergence of art cinema as a category.

Discussing art cinema in Latin America requires a further caveat: the status of art cinema within film practice and film studies has its origins in postwar European cinema. Within this context, art cinema designates "feature-length narrative films at the margins of mainstream cinema, located somewhere between fully experimental films and overtly commercial products," and usually with "foreign production, [and the] overt engagement of the aesthetic, unrestrained formalism, and a mode of narration that is pleasurable but loosened from classical structures" (Galt and Schoonover 2010: 31). As Rosalind Galt and Karl Schoonover argue, the differentiation from both mainstream cinema production models and reception sites, as well as from classical structures and representations, implies a "geographically organized force field, centered around a Euro-American critical and industrial infrastructure" (p. 29). An early taxonomic attempt by David Bordwell argues that art cinema is "a distinct mode of film practice, possessing a definite historical existence, a set of formal conventions, and implicit viewing procedures" (Bordwell 1999: 716). Bordwell defines art cinema in opposition to the causal construction of the classical narrative mode—"we are to watch less for the tale than the telling"—reducing postwar European cinema to a realist film practice with an (auteur's) expressive style that yields ambiguous legibility (p. 722). Steve Neale expands Bordwell's narratological emphasis and argues for art cinema as an institution indexed to industrial and political changes occurring in European countries "to counter American domination of their indigenous markets in film and also to foster a film industry and a film culture of their own" (Neale 1981: 11). Art cinema, for Neale, is less a question of particular textual characteristics or aesthetic devices than the space for the development of indigenous cinema through the adoption of signs of art from established cultural institutions (p. 14). The production and circulation of Latin American cinema within these spaces and its broader discursive opposition to Hollywood cinema might help explain why so much Latin American cinema, regardless of differences in form, style, and context, is received (if not branded) as art cinema within these Euro-American infrastructures.

Taken together, Bordwell and Neale delineate a discursive field that relates the aesthetic to the geopolitical. Art cinema becomes a useful site through which to engage how the evolving economics of cinema intersect with changes in film form: "art cinema [is] both an active aspect of global film culture and an indispensable category of its critique" (Galt and Schoonover 2010: 30). Turning to Latin America complicates the geopolitical given the region's triangulated relationship to Europe and the United States, and discussing its art cinema aesthetics must accordingly reckon with this added complexity (Paranaguá 2003: 93). Asking "What is art cinema?" or "How is cinema art?" in the region means also asking "What is Latin America?" If European art cinema follows a "shift from European *films d'art* to global cinema," then how do the intersections of art and cinema play out in Latin America (Galt and Schoonover 2010: 30)?

This chapter attempts to answer that question by offering an account of how *art cinema endures* as a discursive category, tracing the shifts from prewar debates staged in film journals to the postwar emergence of new waves, and finally to contemporary film festival distribution and art house exhibition. This thumbnail history demonstrates not only how art cinema is a shifting discursive category in film production and reception, but also how these shifts map onto different geopolitical frameworks in the discipline. This means that studying art cinema cannot result in a bullet-point list of aesthetic traits because "the art film's long term differentiation depends on its ability continually to transform the means of demarcation, shifting them to compensate for stylistic cooptation, technological innovation, shifts in access, and ever-morphing tastes and fashions" (Galt and Schoonover 2010: 19). This chapter avoids codifying or prescribing the characteristics of art cinema; instead, it proposes identifying art cinema aesthetics in a particular context, which means also identifying how that very context is writing itself in relation to a global market. In other words, a film's claim to art cinema is an opportunity to elucidate the intersection of the aesthetic and the geopolitical at a particular conjuncture. To that end, this chapter uses art cinema as a heuristic, concluding with an analysis of selected contemporary films in order to propose a notion of art cinema as an *aesthetics of endurance* particular to the geopolitical condition of neoliberalism and postnational globalization.

Art cinema endures

In pre-World War II Latin America, debates about cinema as art form were framed in high modernist terms, shaped by both European *and* American cinemas. From the reception of Italian diva films in post-revolutionary Mexico (Navitski 2015) to the circulation and influence of Soviet cinema in Argentina in the late 1920s (Wells 2017), European cinema would seem to provide an alternative to classical Hollywood in the conventional mode of art cinema as institution. And yet in Latin America, Hollywood cinema was also heralded for realizing cinema's true potential as the seventh art, in the spirit of Soviet Americanism (or, as Kuleshov referred to it, "Americanitis") (Kuleshov 1988: 72). European *films d'art* were often disparaged for their static academicism and theatrical and pictorial tendencies *pace* the more dynamic American cinema (Paranaguá 2003: 39). In the Brazilian film journal *Cinearte*, "o Cinema-Arte" has its origins in D.W. Griffith and his use of close-ups in *Broken Blossoms* (1919) ("O cinema" 1926: 22). The author marveled at how cinema had gone from sideshow attraction to "sublime art" by mobilizing the medium toward poetic and philosophical expression. These arguments set cinema on an evolutionary path analogous to those of modern literature or painting but demanded formal innovation particular to the medium and its capacity to depict the real. Furthermore, cinema as art was not necessarily opposed to commercial success. Although often lamenting the bottom-line mentality of film producers, critics characterized the cinema as an *industrial* art where the commercial and the artistic were inextricable (Momplet 1939: 39). Writing for the Argentine fan magazine *Sintonía* in 1939, Arturo Momplet suggests that differentiating the artistic from the commercial was facile and tendentious, often resulting in an untenable position where commercial gain meant ignoring quality while notions of artistic merit risked an elitist dismissal of the audience.

These medium-ontological arguments often overlapped with national-ontological projects: defining the one went hand in hand with defining the other. In other words, debates about film content and cinematic address used art to make claims about the nation:

> Todo arte nace cuando un país siente necesidad de hacerlo, cuando ese país quiere ver su vida, sus problemas, sus goces, su miseria, sublimados por obra y gracia de eso que hemos dado en llamar arte. / All art is born when a country yearns to make it, when this country wants to see its life, its problems, its delights, its misery, sublimated by the grace of that which we call art.
>
> (Baez 1943: 17)

In this example from an important Mexican film magazine, the evolution of cinema as art dovetailed with cultural nationalist claims about the nation. Cinema as art form, conceived within a high-modernist framework of aesthetic self-sufficiency, was understood through a practice of negation akin to the nation-state project in Latin America, where the nation was also conceived defensively in relation to foreign influence.

This intersection of the aesthetic and geopolitical persisted in the first decade of the postwar period. Debates about cinema as art form occur during the postwar economic boom in new forms of film production, distribution, and reception, still articulated to questions of developmentalism and broader discourses of modernization. The paulista Vera Cruz Studios provides a case in point. Founded in 1949 in order to create "quality" films within an MGM industrial studio model under the direction of the European-trained Alberto Cavalcanti, the studio's *O Cangaceiro* (Lima Barreto, 1953) won the award for Best Adventure Film at the 1953 Cannes Film Festival (Johnson 1987: 62). Film festival programming also begins in the region in the same period, articulating the question of art cinema as a national cinema in ways that seem less recognizable from a contemporary moment where international festival exhibition is a sometimes-defining criterion for contemporary art cinema. For instance, a first edition of the Mar del Plata Film Festival in Argentina in 1948 showcased national filmmaking in the early years of the first Peronist regime and commemorated the implementation of the 1947 film law. The teleological construction of an autonomous artistic field and a sovereign nation-state were intertwined (García Canclini 2005: 96). The 1948 edition, however, does not appear in subsequent histories of the festival, dismissed because it was a noncompetitive program for *national* films. Instead, histories tout the 1954 *international* edition, modeled explicitly on counterparts in Cannes and Venice, as the first in the festival's history (Neveleff et al. 2013: 45). The omission of the 1948 edition suggests how Euro-American critical and industrial infrastructures begin to determine definitions of art cinema.

With the advent of the New Latin American Cinema (NLAC), especially following the Cuban Revolution, the rejection of Hollywood cinema seems to align the region's filmmaking with postwar European new waves, both tending "to be conceived as radically and absolutely antagonistic in both theory and practice [to Hollywood]. Filmmakers borrowed their metaphors from the vocabulary of oppression and exploitation" (Elsaesser 2005: 465). Given criticism of Vera Cruz by filmmakers such as Nelson Pereira dos Santos (who faulted the studio's "mode of action" while commending its project toward a Brazilian cinema) (Johnson 1987: 78), and the rejection of the *cine de autor* of the 1950s and early 1960s in Argentina, yearning for an "art cinema" became a minefield during the more radicalized years of the NLAC. The contestation of art cinema is particularly forceful in the canonic Fernando Solanas and Octavio Getino essay "Towards a Third Cinema." Although not representative of all of the NLAC, Solanas and Getino's Third Cinema provides a useful site in this concise history to unpack the ways art cinema was contested in the period. The authors align art cinema with Second Cinema, which designated an emergent mode of distribution and exhibition taking shape in the postwar period that was different from the dominant Hollywood industrial structures. The NLAC, intimately related to the new cinemas across postwar Europe, was a participant in a broader global film project launched alongside the commercial structures of Hollywood:

> Al lado de esta industria y de sus estructuras de comercialización, nacen las instituciones del cine, los grandes festivales, las escuelas oficiales y, colateralmente, las revistas y críticos que la justifican y complementan. / Alongside this industry and its commercial structures, film institutions, important festivals, and official schools are born, as well as the magazines and critics who defend and complement these.
>
> *(Solanas and Getino 1982: 43)*

This conception of art cinema, also dubbed "cine de autor/auteur's cinema" or "nuevo cine/New Cinema," appears more akin to our contemporary understanding of art cinema. The more radicalized figures of NLAC grew suspicious of the rapid institutionalization of these alternatives to commercial cinema, particularly in their desire to compete with and dominate markets. When Solanas and Getino advocated for a Third Cinema, they not only prescribed a cinema of anti-imperialist struggle and national liberation, but also diagnosed a rearticulation of the aesthetic and geopolitical, which again occurred at the site of art cinema.

The shortcomings of Second Cinema were both aesthetic and more broadly geopolitical. With regards to the former:

> el modelo de la obra perfecta de arte, del film redondo, articulado según la métrica impuesta por la cultura burguesa y sus teóricos y críticos, ha servido en los países dependientes para inhibir al cineasta. / The model of the perfect work of art, the fully rounded film structured according to the metrics imposed by bourgeois culture, its theoreticians and critics, has served to inhibit the film-maker.
>
> (*Solanas and Getino 1982: 48*)

For these authors, the criteria for aesthetic judgment came from without. More particularly, the process of art becoming an autonomous aesthetic sphere was a political liability, a neocolonial technique of disarticulating art from lived reality in pursuit of "universal models." With regard to the geopolitical, the perceived aspiration of art cinema to compete with and overtake commercial cinema perpetuated an equal exchange market logic that never actually existed because of the dependent neocolonial condition of Latin America. As Ignacio Sánchez Prado suggests, this was a political cinema responding to "1960s geopolitical and geocultural understandings that posed non-Western cinematic traditions of social commitment as necessarily resistant" (Sánchez Prado 2014: 106). In other words, if the earlier period put stock in modernization theory (with cinema as an apparatus of nationalist consensus-building), this period understands cinema in relation to models of dependency theory popularized in the 1960s and 1970s by the likes of Argentine ECLAC executive secretary Raúl Prebisch, André Gunder Frank, and future Brazilian President Fernando Henrique Cardoso. The canonic *La hora de los hornos* (*The Hour of the Furnaces*, Fernando Solanas and Octavio Getino, 1969) borrows directly from this rhetoric when it exclaims:

> En la dependencia no hay ninguna forma posible de desarrollo. El aparente desarrollo de algunas ciudades-puerto traduce sólo la creciente expansión de las grandes potencias en el seno de nuestras economías. / In dependency, there is no possiblity of development. The apparent development of some port cities only reflects the growing expansion of the great powers within our economies.
>
> (*Olivera 2008: 252*)

Solanas and Getino cannot help but understand Art Cinema within this hierarchizing system; a cinema built atop dependent structures is necessarily dependent.

These earlier figurations of art cinema in the region complicate a simple insertion of Latin American examples within the tradition of postwar European art cinema. The complex geopolitical concerns that have shaped the region materially and conceptually play out in these debates about the intersection of art and cinema to this day. Unlike the binary terms of Bordwell's art cinema aesthetic (i.e. it's classical Hollywood or bust), debates about cinema as art form in Latin America never quite align with these commonplace binaries because of the asymmetrical power relations that have shaped the region and, in the contemporary period, the shifting geopolitical parameters that characterize the aftermath of the Cold War. The liberal economic measures initiated in the 1970s and early 1980s, particularly in the military governments throughout the region, which paved the way for the implementation of more radical neoliberal economic platforms starting in the late 1980s, had consequences both material and discursive for Latin America. The subsequent imposition of neoliberal economic measures by the International Monetary Fund and the World Bank resulted in a period of sustained economic contraction and growing wealth inequality. By the early 1990s, most national governments had imposed steep cuts to state-funded enterprises—e.g. IMCINE (Mexico), INC (Argentina), Embrafilme (Brazil), FOCINE (Colombia)—which had kept national production afloat. In addition to production resources, distribution and reception were similarly transformed by the withdrawal of interventionist film policy that had long promoted and protected local film culture. Discursively, the declining role of an interventionist state and the intensification of globalization complicated the question of national cinema and heralded the rise of the conceptual categories of global, world, and transnational cinema.

The category of art cinema is a crucial negotiating term in this conceptual shift, invoked by partisans of the national and of the translational alike who are trying to understand the new industrial and aesthetic tendencies in contemporary Latin American cinemas and the potentially new forms of circulation outside the region. Drawing explicitly from Bordwell's art cinema aesthetic, Tamara Falicov identifies what she calls a "globalized art-house aesthetic" that facilitates border crossing—art cinema is what "successfully engag[es] global art-house audiences through familiar forms of realism" (Falicov 2013: 254). She argues that art cinema is what screens and succeeds in art cinemas, using what Thomas Elsaesser calls "the logic of reception studies," where audiences decide how a film is to be understood (Elsaesser 2005: 45). Falicov gestures toward some of the problems with such a definition determined by institutional spaces of transnational collaboration and film festival acceptance because the rules of engagement are determined by OECD taste. In documenting comparable initiatives such as those of the Sundance Institute and the Hubert Bals Fund, Miriam Ross more pointedly interrogates the politics of defining art cinema by global art house success or international film festival spectatorship (Ross 2011: 267). These spaces for transnational support often demand Latin American "authenticity" while perpetuating an uneven benefactor–beneficiary relationship in production and exhibition. Whereas Ross relies on the language of dependency theory to problematize the celebration of the transnational tendency in Latin American art cinema, others insist that co-production agreements shape but do not determine filmmaking. Luisela Alvaray, for instance, describes a mediascape containing powerful corporate interests, regional organizations, and indigenous investors, where political agency is avowed via hybridity (Alvaray 2013). For her, art cinema aesthetics and genre narrative conventions imbued with local content are less a symptom of cultural imperialism within a dependent core-periphery model than an expression of particularity within a world system. Referencing Walter Mignolo and Fredric Jameson, Alvaray represents a larger turn away from understanding cinema through the language of dependency and toward understanding media within a world-systems model. The successor to dependency theory, world-systems analysis emerged in the 1970s as a way to historicize the core-periphery structure of dependency approaches. World-systems theory grounds and periodizes capitalism differently, founding it on capital accumulation and the growth of exchange (rather than mode of production) in order to locate its origins in the colonial expansion of the early modern period (Brenner 1977).

The abandonment of economic models of national development and the new emphases on deregulation and open markets coincides with the Latin American film studies discourse about art cinema. Reception studies and comparable projects that privilege distribution and exhibition, accounts of production that naturalize the market logics of Euro-American infrastructure, and the declining discursive power of the nation are markers of how world-systems approaches map the region anew (Tweedie 2013: 4–5). And yet, this chapter's historical view of the concept of "art cinema" teaches us that this seemingly new approach risks overlooking the changing valence and colonializing status of the very term. That art cinema as "globalized art-house aesthetic" is complicit with the work of neoliberalism by taking globalization as ground has led to some returns to the national as a framework and reading strategy. Whether understanding New Argentine Cinema as national allegory of the economic crisis of the late 1990s (Page 2009) or foregrounding how the domestic market's transformations in Mexico sowed the seeds for its eventual international success (Sánchez Prado 2014), these rejoinders remind us that art cinema in the region is a contested category that articulates enduring aesthetic concerns with enduring geopolitical horizons over time.

An aesthetics of endurance

The increasing visibility of Latin American cinema in art house and film festival circuits over the past two decades invites us to find common denominators, but how to reconcile the art house blockbusters of *Amores perros* (*Love's a Bitch*, Alejandro González Iñárritu, 2000) or *Tropa de Elite* with the slow cinema of *La hamaca paraguaya* (*Paraguayan Hammock*, Paz Encina, 2007) or *Fantasma* (Lisandro Alonso, 2006)? Or the new extremism of *Heli* (Amat Escalante, 2013) with the youth films of *Club Sandwich* (Fernando Eimbcke, 2013) or *Pelo malo* (*Bad Hair*, Mariana Rondón, 2013)? Or the films circulating in identity-based festivals such as *Hawaii* (Marco Berger, 2013) or *Tatuagem* (*Tattoo*, Hilton Lacerda, 2013) with the historical genre cinema of *Machuca* (Andrés Wood, 2004) or *El clan* (*The Clan*, Pablo Trapero, 2015)? These films have radically different stories of production: *Tropa de elite* received financial backing from the Weinstein Company, whereas *Hawaii* launched a successful Kickstarter campaign. These films have radically different stories of distribution and exhibition: *Tatuagem* received accolades at LGBT festivals and eventually found U.S. distribution courtesy of niche distributor TLA releasing; *Club Sandwich* has yet to receive distribution in most international markets. These films have radically different relations to classical narrative structures: from the more conventional coming-of-age tale of *Pelo malo*, to the modular *Amores Perros*, to the elliptical *La hamaca paraguaya*. The common trait that characterizes these films is an overt engagement of the aesthetic. Their intelligibility to Euro-American art house and film festival institutions is a function of a realism that also (perhaps somewhat paradoxically) allows for authorial expressivity, "retain[ing] a close association with the thematic and aesthetic impulses of [Italian neorealism]" (Galt and Schoonover 2010: 41). Our historical account makes evident how the depiction of the real is an enduring aesthetic concern for art cinema, but how do we bring together this variety of films under the aegis of realism? We need to think realism beyond the accurate depiction of an expanded representational field (i.e. what the window looks out on and how transparent the window is), and instead identity how the world viewed affects our being in the world. As Fredric Jameson explains, realism designates less an aesthetic style or a capacity to portray a state of affairs than an epistemological claim to make the historical present perceptible despite (or because of) temporal (chronological) organization (Jameson 2012: 478). Put simply, realism allows us to sense history in its elusiveness rather than hold it captive for accurate depiction, characterized by a tension between temporal flow and arrest that cannot be sublated or codified. Whether the fast-paced editing and the subjective shooter handheld camera of *Tropa de elite* or the static camera and long takes of *Fantasma*, I read these films less to differentiate them from Hollywood than to account for how these films approach the historical present; that is, how this tension in modes of temporalization plays out in aesthetic form across these films.

Lisandro Alonso's *Fantasma* is a useful point of departure because it stages art cinema spectatorship. Alonso's *oeuvre* provides a particularly reflexive example from the New Argentine Cinema, which is less a programmatic movement than a wave of films produced in the country after the mid-1990s reflecting the shifting social realities under neoliberal austerity (Page 2009: 64). The culmination of a loose trilogy, the film features the two performers from the director's first two films—Misael Saavedra from *La libertad* (*Freedom*, 2001) and Argentino Vargas from *Los muertos* (2004)—wandering around the Teatro San Martín in downtown Buenos Aires to attend the premiere of the latter film. The film follows these actors wandering the theater separately, exploring the spaces of the Teatro San Martín, which is part of the Complejo Teatral de Buenos Aires, a theater cooperative where audiences paid subsidized ticket prices to watch the great films of the postwar European art cinema canon. This phantasmagoric movie theater space alludes to the historical influence (and relative exhaustion) of art cinema models derived from the postwar period. In a film about going to the movies, the film screening should serve as privileged event, and our trajectory in the theater should emplot our narrative: We enter; we watch; we leave. Yet this film defamiliarizes the art house by suspending this trajectory. Instead, we traverse hallways and arrive at dead ends, wander into empty dressing rooms, go up service elevators, and climb down stairs. We do not arrive at the screening until the film's midpoint. The narrative that unfolds is one that encourages us to watch for paths to cross. Vargas descends the stairs and finds himself in front of his own image in the film's advertisement in the theater lobby. Subsequently, Saavedra is in a restroom staring at his reflection in the mirror before

Figure 16.1 The art house as phantasmagoric space in Lisandro Alonso's *Fantasma*.

243

leaving and descending a set of stairs. Are these the same stairs? Will he find Vargas? The editing provides the sense that the action initiated by Saavedra in the previous frame will continue into this space, but Saavedra never arrives. There is a certain similarity in completed actions, in finding images of oneself in the middle of a labyrinthine exploration of space, and yet these itineraries seldom intersect until the film screening.

This reflexive conceit, reminiscent of Abbas Kiarostami's *Koker* trilogy and Tsai Ming-Liang's *Goodbye, Dragon Inn* (2003), is characteristic of contemporary art cinema in its more contemplative mode, privileging duration over dramatic elaboration. This "slow cinema" ostensibly rejects the narrative economy of classical Hollywood in favor of unproductive meandering and wasted time (Schoonover 2012: 65). The spectator of this slow cinema grows bored, unable to consume images for either narrative information or spectacular display. Ideally, this initial frustration turns to curiosity and then to contemplation, so that "contemplation induced by art cinema's characteristic fallow time draws attention to the activity of watching and ennobles a forbearing but unbedazzled spectatorship" (p. 70). The film screening in *Fantasma* is almost a parody of the art cinema experience: practically no one in the theater watches practically nothing happening on screen. Vargas enters the empty theater and we watch him from the vantage point of fellow audience members. He sits when the lights dim. *Los muertos* begins, and we can watch the remarkable opening sequence shot projected on the screen with Vargas's silhouetted outline in our sightline. The film orchestrates this abyssal arrangement of gazes, as Vargas is also *Los muertos*'s protagonist and the possible point of view of the projected sequence shot. We continue watching Vargas watch himself for roughly 10 minutes until the lights come up (his lights, not ours). In the tension between modes of temporalization described above, *Fantasma*'s temporal arrest allegorizes broader forms of exhaustion and refusal under neoliberalism, what Galt calls in the context of New Argentine Cinema a "default cinema" (Galt 2013: 62). This "boredom on screen" not only thematizes a late capitalist mode of temporalization where time is money, but also enacts a strain on us spectators: "we are exhausted by straining to see what may or may not be immediately accessible to us, or we withdraw altogether from the pervasiveness of visual stimuli" (Schaefer 2003: 10). And yet, boredom seems ill-suited to describe a process characterized by strain and exhaustion.

Amat Escalante's *Heli* provides a case in point with its deliberate camera movement, restrained formalism, and languid pace. Trained in the International School of Film and Television in Cuba, Escalante belongs to a young generation of Mexican filmmakers working with an aestheticized approach indebted to the formal rigor of radical film auteur Carlos Reygadas (Sánchez Prado 2014: 202). After working as an assistant on Reygadas's *Batalla en el cielo* (*Battle in Heaven*, 2005), Escalante received support toward the completion of his debut *Sangre* (*Blood*, 2005) from Reygadas and art house producer Mantarraya Producciones, who would later also finance and distribute *Heli*. Despite this languor, *Heli* is not composed of meandering episodes with "nonbelabored" bodies (Schoonover 2012: 71). The film opens with a close-up of a young man, his face bleeding under the heel of his captor. The camera tracks down his body and reveals an adjoining body in the flatbed of a pick-up truck before pushing in through the truck's rear window and looking out onto the road. The remarkable long take ends with an extreme long shot from the roadside as the truck stops at an overpass. The men in the truck unload the bodies while the camera remains static at a distance. A final low-angle, extreme long shot from the flatbed frames the men hurling a noosed body off the overpass. The camera sight remains on the swinging body as the truck moves away from the scene of the crime. This opening five-minute sequence features only three takes and ends with a simple cut to a close-up of a couple mid-embrace, the young man ostensibly forcing himself on the woman until an off-screen knock interrupts. The relation of the opening sequence to these characters remains unclear, particularly because the opening obfuscates the performers' faces. Is the man one of the criminals returned from the scene? Will this man be the victim? Will the knock be someone who has come to apprehend him? Or is it someone who has come to inform him of the event we have just witnessed? Does this occur before or after the disposal of the body? The elliptical presentation of the plot makes spectators watch with an eye toward organizing events in order to make them narratively significant (i.e. to make out the relationship of violence to the everyday). We watch the first half of the film haunted by the specter of violence, following the banal parallel stories of Heli's dissatisfying marriage and manufacturing job and his sister's budding romance with a young special forces trainee in order to connect them somehow to the opening. Once Heli discovers that drugs have been hidden in the house, we begin to rearrange the pieces of the story. The corrupt special forces enter the home, killing Heli's father and taking Heli and his sister captive along with her boyfriend, Beto. Eventually, the captors take Heli and Beto into a domestic space to be tortured. The living room becomes a torture chamber with alternating low-angle point-of-view shots from Heli's seated position and handheld tracking close-up shots of the young men torturing an already beaten Beto. The sequence culminates with a long take of Beto stripped and his genitals visibly set on fire. Despite the kidnapping, the languid pace continues with sweeping camera movements and unnerving long takes. The subsequent scenes repeat the actions of the opening sequence, and we realize how the opening served as an *in medias res* introduction. The film continues after Heli survives as he searches for his sister and copes with the aftermath of his capture. The film maintains its deliberate pace, only the languor is now charged with fatigue rather than banality.

Much like *Fantasma*, banality and tedium do not suffice to make sense of *Heli*. We do not experience time as mere screen duration but as corporeal endurance. The new configuration

Figure 16.2   The regulated body in Amat Escalante's *Heli*.

245

contests the Frankfurt School's characterization of perceptual boredom as redemptive awakening wherein withdrawing (or "defaulting") from the world supposes opposing work with an absence of action (Schaefer 2003: 26). In Escalante's *Heli*, the absence of action never means leisure or wasted time. The film features a telling sequence in the middle of Heli's shift where the workers on the floor are required to perform calisthenics (Figure 16.2). The camera tracks back and forth as the line pauses from working on one type of (car) body to another. As Lauren Berlant argues, the models of shock and subsequent adaptation, as well as the *flaneur*'s paradigmatic spectatorial position, suppose a need for relief-through-mental-distance that is ill-suited to the contemporary moment. When the subject of late capitalism must develop new "habits of ordinariness" and "genres of affect management," then modes of relief or "modes of living on" require figuring a different sensorium and relation to time (Berlant 2011: 102). In *Heli*, time does not still; rather, time cannot stop. Weariness is the structuring principle in *Heli*, and tiredness has a different relationship to time than boredom. Fatigue is a sign of past actions absorbed and affecting the present, coupled with the anticipation of release to come: "a signification of expiring time and expiration's anticipation" (Gorfinkel 2012: 312). If tiredness is a threshold, then *Heli* is constructed atop thresholds—from the literal threshold of the home that we cross with Heli's wife after the attack, to the figurative thresholds of Beto's body collapsing under the strain of his physical training, or the sexual encounters that are always deferred. In this nonlinear temporality of fatigue, the ordinary is less a microcosm or allegory for preexistent norms than a space where new rhythms can emerge and the present becomes sensuously graspable.

By way of conclusion, let us return briefly to the controversial *Tropa de elite*. An interesting companion to *Heli*, *Tropa* arguably depicts a similar story from the point of view of the special forces rather than the ordinary person caught in the crossfire. The films also share a narrative structure: a disorienting violent incident that motivates a return to past actions that elucidate the present incident and bear on future story events. *Tropa* may feature more narrational cues (e.g. intertitles, voice-over narration, color-coded lens filters), but it also overtly engages the status of the image. When Capitão Nacsimento begins a live fire exercise, he explains in voice-over narration how a special forces agent enters the *favela*:

> Não entra em favela atirando, entra com estratégia. Ele progride de beco em beco . . . Progressão em favela é uma arte. É uma arte que ninguém aprende na teoria. / [He] does not enter the favela shooting, he enters with strategy. He advances slowly from one alley to the next . . . Advancing in the favela is an art; an art that no one can learn in theory.

Nascimento's explanation overlays a masterful sequence shot that follows the trainees in a demo shipping yard with a handheld camera before craning up atop a container with Nascimento barking orders and then returning to the ground in an ostensible subjective shooter shot with a shallow-focus camera. This subjective shooter perspective is less about seeing than about motion through space, about intuitive motion and action (Galloway 2006). The camera enters the shadows, but steps into the light in a different time and space alongside the trainees now in a real *favela*. Nascimento's comments might very well apply to the deliberate engagement of the aesthetic in the film, especially considering the suggestive meanings of *atirar*. The shooting of the gun and the shooting of the camera measure time and space "*de beco em beco*." This art form that cannot be reified is learned through feats of endurance, a test of trainees' stamina and a test of spectators' appetites. Like *Fantasma* and *Heli*, the film approaches the historical present not by constructing a critical position through an imagined removal from the world, but by troubling the body's self-knowledge and by questioning its endurability. If we simply characterize art cinema as opposed to the economy and efficiency of classical Hollywood narration, then films such as the histrionic *Amores perros* or the Scorsese-like *El clan* are summarily excluded. Contemporary art cinema, then, is less a cinema where "nothing happens" than where "nothing stops." The rhythms of the habitual never quite settle and we sensually grasp the historical present as unfinished, "the way the ordinary is disorganized by capitalism" (Berlant 2011: 77). Art cinema's aesthetic practices allow us to be reflexive about our contemporary historicity—not by boring us to contemplation, but rather by making our corporeal thresholds perceptible.

References

Alvaray, L. (2013) "Hybridity and Genre in Transnational Latin American Cinemas." *Transnational Cinemas*, 4(1): 67–87.

Amnesty International (2005) "Brazil: 'They Come Shooting': Policing Socially Excluded Communities." December 2. Available at: www.amnesty.org/en/documents/amr19/025/2005/en/ (accessed February 26, 2016).

Baez, E. (1943) "El extranjerismo, un peligro del cine nacional." *Cinema Reporter*, October 30.

Bentes, I. (2001) "Da estética à cosmética da fome." *Jornal do Brasil*, 8 (July): 1–4.

Berlant, L. (2011) *Cruel Optimism*. Durham, NC: Duke University Press.

Bordwell, D. (1999) "The Art Cinema as a Mode of Film Practice." In L. Braudy and M. Cohen (eds.), *Film Theory and Criticism: Introductory Readings*. New York: Oxford University Press.

Brenner, R. (1977) "The Origins of Capitalist Development: A Critique of Neo-Smithian Marxism." *New Left Review*, 104: 25–92.

Elsaesser, T. (2005) *European Cinema: Face to Face with Hollywood*. Amsterdam: Amsterdam University Press.

Falicov, T. (2013) "'Cine en construcción'/'Films in Progress': How Spanish and Latin American Filmmakers Negotiate the Construction of a Globalized Art-House Aesthetic." *Transnational Cinemas*, 4(2): 253–271.

Galloway, A. (2006) *Gaming: Essays on Algorithmic Culture*. Minneapolis, MN: University of Minnesota Press.

Galt, R. (2013) "Default Cinema: Queering Economic Crisis in Argentina and Beyond." *Screen*, 54(1): 62–81.

Galt, R. and Schoonover, K. (eds.) (2010) *Global Art Cinema: New Theories and Histories*. New York: Oxford University Press.

García Canclini, N. (2005) *Hybrid Cultures: Strategies for Entering and Leaving Modernity*. Minneapolis, MN: University of Minnesota Press.

Gorfinkel, E. (2012) "Weariness, Waiting: Undulation and Art Cinema's Tired Bodies." *Discourse*, 34(2–3): 311–347.

Jameson, F. (2012) "Antinomies of the Realism-Modernism Debate." *Modern Language Quarterly*, 73(3): 475–485.

Johnson, R. (1987) *The Film Industry in Brazil: Culture and the State*. Pittsburgh, PA: University of Pittsburgh Press.

Kuleshov, L. (1988) "Americanism." In R. Taylor and I. Christie (eds.), *The Film Factory: Russian and Soviet Cinema in Documents*. New York: Routledge, pp. 72–74.

Momplet, A. (1939) "La película comercial." *Sintonía*, December 13.

Navitski R. (2015) "Gendering the Silent Film Spectator in Mexico: Italian Divas, Moral Panics, and Female Fans." Presented to 55th Society for Cinema and Media Studies Conference, Montréal, QC, March 28.

Neale, S. (1981) "Art Cinema as Institution." *Screen*, 22(1): 11–40.

Neveleff, J.M., Monforte, M., and Ponce de León, A. (2013) *Historia del Festival Internacional de Cine de Mar del Plata: primera época: 1954–1970*. Buenos Aires: Corregidor.

"O cinema, a verdadeira arte" (1926) *Cinearte*, March 24: 22.

Olivera, G. (2008) "Dependency Theory and the Aesthetics of Contrast in Fernando Solanas's *La hora de los horns* and *Memoria del saqueo*." *Hispanic Research Journal*, 9(3): 247–260.

Page, J. (2009) *Crisis and Capitalism in Contemporary Argentine Cinema*. Durham, NC: Duke University Press.

Paranaguá, P.A. (2003) *Tradición y modernidad en el cine de América Latina*. Madrid: Fondo de Cultura Económica de España.

Pimental J. (2007) "'O ano em que meus pais saíram de férias' bate 'Tropa de elite' e é o representante do Brasil." *O Globo*, September 26.

Ross, M. (2011) "The Film Festival as Producer: Latin American Films and Rotterdam's Hubert Bals Fund." *Screen*, 52(2): 261–267.

Sánchez Prado, I. (2014) *Screening Neoliberalism: Transforming Mexican Cinema, 1988–2012*. Nashville, TN: Vanderbilt University Press.

Schaefer, C. (2003) *Bored to Distraction: Cinema of Excess in End-of-the-Century Mexico and Spain*. Albany, NY: SUNY Press.

Schoonover, K. (2012) "Wastrels of Time: Slow Cinema's Laboring Body, the Political Spectator, and the Queer." *Framework*, 53(1): 65–78.

Solanas, F. and Getino, O. (1982) "Hacia un tercer cine." In *A diez años de 'Hacia un tercer cine'*. Mexico City: Filmoteca de la UNAM, pp. 37–56.

"Tropa de Elite: Bilheteria Brasil" (2008) *Adorocinema*. Available at: www.adorocinema.com/filmes/filme-133548/bilheterias/ (accessed January 31, 2016).

"'Tropa de Elite' desaparece da competição de Sundance" (2007a) *Folha de São Paulo*, November 30.

"'Tropa de Elite' tem lançamento antecipado no Rio e SP" (2007b) *UOL*, October 4.

Tweedie, J. (2013) *The Age of New Waves: Art Cinema and the Staging of Globalization*. New York: Oxford University Press.

Weissberg, J. (2008) "Review: Elite Squad." *Variety*, February 11.

Wells, S.A. (2017) "Parallel Modernities: The First Reception of Soviet Cinema in Latin America." In R. Navitski and N. Poppe (eds.), *Cosmopolitan Film Cultures in Latin America, 1896–1960*. Bloomington, IN: Indiana University Press.

PART III

Business practices

17

TRANSNATIONAL NETWORKS OF FINANCING AND DISTRIBUTION

International co-productions

Luisela Alvaray

Editors' introduction

The traditional "mapping" of Latin American film production around rigid notions of national cinema, at best an approximation of the cultural sphere reflected in and around particular films, has become transformed over the last two decades by new patterns of transborder funding of film production and the advent of new audiovisual technologies, specifically digital. Juan Poblete, in Chapter 1, looks at the formation of a national cinema in Chile with these issues in mind, while in Chapter 24, Gonzalo Aguilar, Mariana Lacunza, and Niamh Thornton explore the impact of digital technology on contemporary cinematic experiences.

In this chapter, Luisela Alvaray takes a closer look at these emerging funding arrangements, assessing the impact of multiple intra- and transnational collaborations. Moving us beyond the mere listing of funding groups, their policies, and the amounts invested in specific films, her work here complements Tamara L. Falicov's discussion in Chapter 18 of the impact of international film festivals on Latin American film production. Alvaray's ultimate goal is to consider some of the artistic and social ramifications of these exchanges. Long unquestioned as a relevant category, not just for cataloguing films, but also analyzing them, the international dimension of Latin American cinema has now become inflected in new ways through governmental bureaucracies and the influence of regional and transborder film-funding entities such as Ibermedia.

Admittedly, the role of state has shifted, but also the roles of different stakeholders are becoming more prominent. Alvaray's discussion exposes a number of the implications that shape our perception of the contemporary identification of film within audiovisual culture. The combination of different media platforms and outlets is radically transforming industrial schemes and practices of consumption. This requires scholars to recognize and analyze economic and political systems connected to mass-media products and the relations of domination and power that they entail.

Take One. Billy Ray's English-language remake of Academy Award-winning Argentine film *El secreto de sus ojos* (*The Secret in Their Eyes*, Juan José Campanella, 2009) opened in U.S. theaters on October 23, 2015. Chiwetel Ejiofor, Nicole Kidman, and Julia Roberts played the roles originally performed by well-known Argentine actors Ricardo Darín, Soledad Villamil, and Pablo Rago. The original film had received financial support from public institutions and private companies both in Argentina and Spain. IM Global, a big player in Hollywood and in the international arena (selling both mainstream and international independent films), was one of the three producers of the 2015 remake. In 2012, IM Global had founded the international sales joint venture Mundial with production/distribution company Canana—based in Mexico City and conducted by Mexican Gael Garcia Bernal, Diego Luna, and Pablo Cruz (Hopewell 2012).

Take Two. By February 2015, *Pelo malo* (*Bad Hair*, Mariana Rondón, 2014), a Venezuelan–Peruvian–Argentine–German co-production, could be watched in the US and in Latin America through the HBO network. *Pelo malo* had had a run through film festivals the previous year, winning the "Concha de Oro" of the San Sebastián film festival. The funds to produce *Pelo malo* had come from four sources: Germany's World Cinema Fund, the

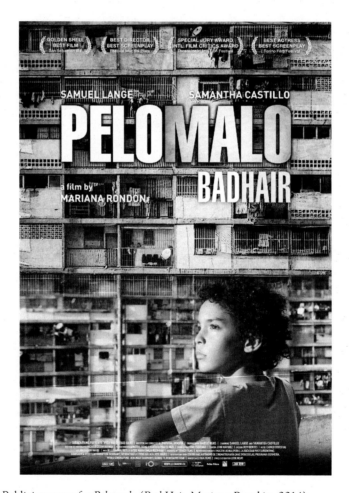

Figure 17.1 Publicity poster for *Pelo malo* (*Bad Hair*, Mariana Rondón, 2014).

US-based Global Film Initiative, Venezuela's CNAC (National Film Institute), and from Latin America's intergovernmental institution Ibermedia.

Take Three. Having spent several years researching on the Pacific coast of Colombia, and with the support of his mentor Spike Lee, U.S. filmmaker Josef Kubota Wladyka, decided to crowdfund his first feature film *Manos sucias* (*Dirty Hands*, 2014). The film investigates the lives of members of the community of Buenventura, considered one of the most dangerous cities in Colombia for its connection to the drug trade. Wladyka and his producers built a strong relationship with the people of the community, who became the actors in his story. This Colombia–US co-production is listed as a Colombian film and received backing from Colombia's Caracol Television, distributor Cine Colombia, and Proimágenes Colombia—a film fund of the Colombian government. *Manos sucias* won an award at the Tribeca Film Festival in 2014.

These examples show the intricate networks of creative, institutional, and commercial connections webbing the Latin American film industries. I use them to underscore several questions that will be central to my considerations. First, these projects confirm that numerous practices through which Latin American films are made and distributed are multidirectional. Production is not always based in one geographical region, and in fact many times occurs in unique "contact zones" where cultures, people, funds, policies, commercial strategies, technologies, and narratives intersect. This has profoundly transformed the practice of making films as much as the ways people view, define, and discuss them. Second, the proliferation of social agents involved in the production and distribution of cinema in Latin America, in and outside of the region, compels us to think each film as a node where multiple and diverse forces (local and foreign, public and private, communal and corporate) converge, destabilizing, in many ways, the prevailing "national" paradigm that informs cultural policies, critical writing, and commercial trade. Third, and as a consequence, the negotiations between creative processes, national and regional narratives, and foreign support continue to be part of an ongoing debate over the place that international co-productions have, or the way they "re-localize" national narratives vis-à-vis Latin America as a cohesive region.

With these questions in mind, my goal is to map the international networks of production and distribution of films in Latin America in the twenty-first century. As we will see, new scenarios have emerged, old institutions are changing, and new actors and media platforms are involved. State and inter-state regulations and agreements have facilitated more permeable alliances between public organizations and private companies, as much as the internationalization of production and distribution. Not only have the roles of states shifted, but also the roles of different stakeholders. New private investors—including television networks, media conglomerates, and independent producers, among others—based within and outside of the region have become essential partners in the development of the film industries. New synergies with other media industries, such as television, have emerged. A proliferation of media festivals and markets continues to bolster more traditional forms of distribution. And the Internet enabled new forms of financing and consumption that are affecting the rhythm and the ways films are made, transmitted, and received. There are, consequently, new intra- and transnational collaborations, as well as intermedial solutions that re-semanticize the idea of "film industry" itself. Ambiguous in its usage, it is a notion that is already controversial when utilized in reference to Latin America. Yet it has become even more elusive since we are continually confronted with different economies at play, grounded in the historically specific rise of the free market and the new information society. These factors influence the ways we perceive the range of private and public support in light of the shifting roles and interests of states, as much as independent (national and international) investors. They also force us to rethink the cultural product not only in relation to its producers, but also to its consumers, now more independent in their media access.

It is important to note that while Latin American cinemas have common histories, they have also differed in terms of their industrial development, financial clout, and cultural influence. In any one country in Latin America, people are socially and culturally diverse. Therefore, generalizations that would apply to all countries, communities, and industries may not be appropriate. Cinematic practices and discourses continue to multiply and change. By analyzing the relations among some of the main players, however, I hope to contribute to a reflective discourse that may help us better understand the current role of cinema in the balance of local and foreign economic powers, as well as its cultural influence toward the development of Latin American societies in the context of rising global media networks.

Productive and varied industries

In 2014, the United States produced 707 films, while production in Latin America was at a high of 477 features, and, of those, 87 percent were made in Argentina, Brazil, and Mexico—the three major industries (IMCINE 2014: 13; MPAA 2014: 21; Kanzler and Talvera Milla 2015: 13, 45). This is a ratio that has not varied much since 1930. Octavio Getino points out that between 1930 and 2000, 90 percent of the films produced in Latin America were made within the same three industries (Getino 2007: 169). These numbers are significant in several ways. First, 477 features in 2014 doubles the number of films produced in 2006 and is more than five times the number of films produced in 1997 (*Focus* 2000: 16; Kanzler and Talvera Milla 2015: 45). Those figures indicate a constant growth of film production in Latin America since the mid-1990s, contrary to Hollywood's more steady number of productions. Second, while Argentina, Brazil, and Mexico have historically been the countries with the highest number of productions, other countries in the region are fast developing their industries in noticeable ways—in terms of creative productivity, technological expertise, infrastructure, and their regulatory system of support. Third, the place of cinema in the cultural landscape in Latin America differs to a certain degree from how it is conceived by the players in fully developed, commercial industries. Whereas in Hollywood private entrepreneurs have traditionally run the industry, in Latin America the difficulty of finding financial support has historically made the states the principal players in film production, funding, and regulation, and they have thus constructed a different mediascape for film reception.

Without diminishing the significance of the relations of power that may connect certain films to economically powerful institutions and corporations in and outside of Latin America, it is important to emphasize that there are innumerable structured and unstructured ways in which films are currently produced. Thus, the notion of industry becomes a malleable one. Rather than shying away from the term, I want to characterize the stream of practices and policies related to the production and distribution of film, in order to shine a light onto the dynamics of power behind them, and to understand how films and their production practices intertwine as we give signification to them. What we see in Latin America are accumulations of many different cinematic experiences at the local level that redefine the concept of industry itself in which cultural, economic, political, and social values are regarded differently in distinct contexts.

New alliances, new roles: the rise of co-productions

After decades in which Latin American governments saw their role as creating policies and funding arrangements to promote and protect national film industries, by the early 1990s governmental approaches changed. In Mexico and Brazil, for instance, governments initiated privatization plans in sync with larger neoliberal platforms. Soon enough, it was clear that this move was unsuccessful. While Brazilian and Mexican industries produced 74 and 98 films in 1989, respectively, by 1993 production plummeted to 9 films in Brazil and, in 1994, to 14 in Mexico (Rêgo 2005: 86; Sánchez Ruiz 2004: 27). Consequently, since the mid-1990s, international collaborations and alliances have become common strategies for national cinemas. The flows of economic globalization led stronger industries, such as those in the US and in Europe, to seek better opportunities elsewhere. The US-based members of the Motion Picture Association (MPA), who had been marginally involved in distributing Latin American films, saw benefits from creating stronger alliances with local companies, thus expanding their market shares and working with new creative talent. For Spain and Portugal, Latin America seemed a natural partner, since cultural and linguistic commonalities were already an advantage to any economic expansion. For some Latin American states, entering the free flows of the market seemed an appropriate route (in hindsight, not necessarily fulfilled) for development and economic growth. For independent Latin American filmmakers and producers, as well, collaborations with companies and institutions in Europe and the US promised greater profitability and more international exposure for their work.

One of the strategies to mend the void left by the initial minimization of the state support in some film industries was the passing of national film legislation intended to protect production, stimulate private investment, and promote internationalization through co-productions. Many of these new laws mandated the establishment of state-funded National Film Institutes (where they did not already exist) to give shape to the national film culture. In Brazil, for instance, while Embrafilme, the traditional film institute, was dismantled in 1990, a 2001 decree (ratified in a 2002 law) mandated the creation of Ancine to promote, regulate, and protect national film production. But even before the creation of Ancine, the 1991 Rouanet Law (Lei 8.313) and the 1993 Audiovisual Law (Lei 8.685) served to rekindle Brazilian film production—a phenomenon that has been called the *retomada*, or the rebirth of the film industry. Both laws provide tax credits to businesses, individuals, and even foreign investors that want to finance audiovisual works made in Brazil. Moreover, there are now local institutions and organizations at other levels that also contribute with funds for filmmaking.

In July 2014, Brazilian President Dilma Roussef announced a $540 million package of government funds to subsidize the audiovisual industry—monies that would be directed towards both production of film and television content and the digitization of theaters (Hopewell 2014a). The heads of the independent production company Gullane Filmes, based in São Paulo, stated that "Today, we have the funds from the federal government, states, municipalities, television networks and distributors . . . Brazilian cinema is making up for lost time . . . the public wants to see Brazilian films. It's our time" (*Revista Filme B* 2015: 44, my translation). Founded in 1996, Gullane Filmes has been taking advantage of state support at all levels. As of May 2015, it had 24 films and six television productions in the works (*Revista Filme B* 2015: 45). Gullane Filmes works in mixed waters between auteurist films, films made for the Brazilian market, and films that the company calls "crossover projects"—those that appeal to Brazilian and international audiences alike (Hopewell 2015). Like Fernando Meirelles' production company O2 Filmes and Conspiração Filmes (two other notable private companies in Brazil), Gullane usually sends films to major international film festivals, but also collaborates with larger local and foreign corporations in producing more mainstream products. This modus operandi is not uncommon nowadays. One could argue that multiple and similar private companies throughout Latin America making co-production deals in and out of their national contexts have contributed in fundamental ways to the rise in productivity of the region. These examples illustrate the notion of innovation at the directorial as much as the producers' level, leading the way in the development of the contemporary industry. In other words, while the state is supporting film production with a favorable regulatory system, independent producers' new commercial and artistic strategies are contributing to make the system sustainable.

Tax incentives and state subsidies have also encouraged the participation of major media companies in film production. Historically, television companies in Latin America have not been interested in sponsoring cinematic activity (Caballero 2006). However, this panorama changed in the 1990s. In Mexico, Televisa had been providing minimal funds for film production since the 1970s; more recently, its cinematic activity intensified, participating in some of the most profitable titles coming out of Mexico. In Argentina, Patagonik, a joint venture between Grupo Clarín (Argentina), Telefónica Media (Spain), and Disney (US) has also been working with resources and personnel from television networks owned by Grupo Clarín (Getino 2007). In Brazil and since 1998, Globo Films, the film branch of Rede Globo, has participated in more than 165 productions, many of which have been national box-office records, such as *Tropa de Elite 2* (*Elite Squad 2*, Jose Padhilla, 2010), *Se Eu Fosse Você 2* (*If I Were You 2*, Daniel Filho, 2009), *2 Filhos de Francisco* (*Two Sons of Francisco*, Breno Silveira, 2005), *Carandiru* (Hector Babenco, 2003), and *Cidade de Deus* (*City of God*, Fernando Meirelles, 2001). Films co-produced by Globo Films have garnered four Academy Award nominations (Globo Filmes 2015; IMDb Pro 2015). More recently, *Que horas ela volta?* (*The Second Mother*, Anna Muylaert, 2015) won prizes at the Sundance and Berlin festivals and was a success both in Brazil and abroad, becoming the second most profitable Brazilian film of 2015. *Que horas ela volta?* was a joint project of Globo Films and Gullane Films. Director Muylaert, who has also been a film critic and a screenwriter, avoids easy clichés, and contrarily investigates social privilege and the relationships between peoples of different class backgrounds with complexity. This becomes one more in the list of films that have contributed to rethinking social relations in Brazil, including *O Som ao Redor* (*Neighboring Sounds*, Kleber Mendonça Filho, 2012), *Doméstica* (Gabriel Mascaro, 2012), and *Branco Sai, Preto Fica* (*White Out, Black In*, Adirley Queirós, 2015) (Silveira 2015). The fact that Muylaert is participating in this character-driven yet commercially propelled film is evidence of the intersections, or dissipating borders, between the works of independent auteurs/producers and those of larger private corporations.

National legislation that incentivizes investors to participate in film co-production has also opened the gates for the internationalization of the film industries. In particular, from 1998 until 2008, MPA companies co-produced 13 films with Mexico, 44 with Argentina, and 101 with Brazil. In addition, they distributed 78 other Latin American films (MPA Brasil n.d.). These figures suggest a shift in the MPA's priorities. In 2002, Steve Solot, the former Vice President of MPA-Latin America affirmed that:

> There is a new focus on product diversification and a new trend toward co-production and distribution of national films and television programming by [MPA] companies in foreign markets. This is not the result of any patronizing

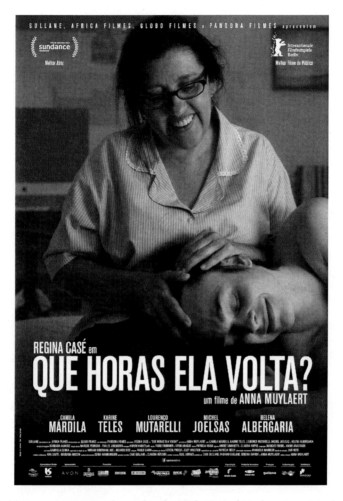

Figure 17.2   Publicity poster for *Que horas ela volta?* (*The Second Mother*, Anna Muylaert, 2015).

attitude; rather it derives from a change in internal policy at the head-office level of these studios, which allows for translation from theory into practice of the principal "think globally and act locally."

(*Solot 2002*)

The approach described by Solot continues. Because of the size of the market, and the increasing market share of Brazilian films, Paramount, Disney, and Universal, for instance, are investing more in Brazilian co-productions (Hopewell 2014b). Co-productions are also a way in which Hollywood investment can bypass film quotas in countries that have and enforce them. According to Frederic Martel, "American films take over 80% of Brazilian box office receipts. And even for the remaining 20%, you have to remember that many Brazilian films are co-produced with the Americans. Overall, it's over 85%." (Martel 2010, cited in *The American Assembly* 2012). Mexico is Hollywood's most important Latin American market and the tenth most important overall for Hollywood majors. Local

Mexican companies such as Canana, Cha Cha Cha Productions, and Lemon Films, to name a few, have agreements with U.S. companies that favor co-production and distribution of Latin American films (Alvaray 2011; MacLaird 2013). Moreover, many Hollywood patrons are recruiting Latin American talent to produce English-language works—for instance, Argentine director Damián Szifrón of the Oscar-nominated *Relatos salvajes* (*Wild Tales*, 2014) will write and direct a Mark Wahlberg film; Chilean director Sebastián Silva recently shot in Brooklyn the English-language *Nasty Baby* (2015), and *Tropa de Elite*'s José Padilha produced the television series *Narcos* (2015) for Netflix.

Knowing as we do that the U.S. film industry has historically dominated international screens, the alliances with Hollywood majors may seem suspect from a critical perspective. Their recent investments are motivated less by a desire for artistic collaborations than by a perception of business opportunities in Latin America, as has been the case in East Asia, Eastern Europe, and other regions around the world (Solot 2002). And clearly the participation of large US-based firms seems a challenge to the dissemination of local meanings, culturally specific narratives, and therefore to a diversification of perspectives. There are, however, several things to consider. First, Latin American filmmakers, producers, and film personnel have benefited from international co-productions by learning the technologies and "know-how" that people from more developed industries have shared. Second, the success of some of the filmmakers of the region, such as Alejandro González Iñárritu, Guillermo del Toro, Alfonso Cuarón, Walter Salles, Fernando Meirelles, Claudia Llosa, Lucía Puenzo, Adrián Caetano, Pablo Trapero, and José Padilha, among others, brings more exposure, and most certainly more investments to the film industries in the region. They themselves have negotiated international agreements with producers around the world. Third, the participation of MPA companies has to be framed within the larger milieu of international exchanges and agreements happening around the region. The intraregional and Ibero-American agreements have had a paramount role in promoting joint economic ventures and cultural cohesiveness in the region. As a matter of fact, co-productions have been multidirectional, as can be seen for the Mexican case in Figure 17.3.

Before referring to regional ventures, some points need to be emphasized. The fact that the Latin American governments have had to create institutions to administer and protect national cinemas is evidence of the prevalent sociocultural role that cinema has held to articulate and disseminate the countries' social and political realities. Governments invest to guarantee the existence of and control over the products of culture. Paradoxically, however, some of the policies crafted in the national film laws since the 1990s, such as the tax incentive regulations, involve processes of internationalization through co-productions, as they invite foreign investors to partake in the creation of local products. This is one of the ways in which internationalization (through financing and other forms of collaboration that derive from that) has become a prerequisite for strengthening national cultures. In Argentina, one of the countries with a high number of international co-production agreements, the only legal requisite for a film to be branded an "Argentine film" is that the INCAA (the Argentine Film Institute) have some form of participation in the production process (RECAM n.d.). But co-productions, on the other hand, have become the formula par excellence for national cinemas to survive in the free-for-all mediascape being shaped through economic liberalization and the globalization of media in the new millennium. National film cultures continue to be repositioned, reimaged, and reimagined, as national borders dissolve through economic alliances, professional collaborations, and film narratives.

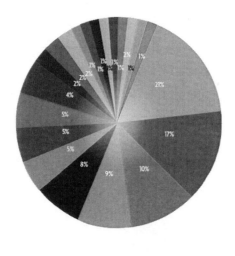

Figure 17.3   Mexican co-productions, 2007–2014, by country (for full colour image, see www.routledge.com/9781138855267).

Source: Anuario Estadístico del Cine Mejicano 2014.

Regional integration

Confronted with the uncertainty of what the global free markets would bring to the Latin American audiovisual space at the end of the twentieth century, there were some governmental initiatives to multiply the chances for the regional cinema to expand. Coalitions, or an imagined regional integration, appear to be a good path to reach more audiences and help smaller countries. In 1989, representatives from 13 Latin American governments signed an agreement to jointly formulate policies that would benefit all countries involved in terms of the financing, production, and distribution of films. The countries represented were Argentina, Bolivia, Brazil, Colombia, Cuba, the Dominican Republic, Ecuador, Mexico, Nicaragua, Panama, Peru, Spain, and Venezuela (CACI 1989). Relying on common languages, histories, and cultures, the arrangement seemed to favor not only the idea of preserving cultures, but also the possibilities for filmmakers and producers to access larger pools of funds, and for their films to travel to wider markets. The fruit of this agreement materialized with the 1997 launch of the Ibermedia program. In its mission statement, Ibermedia affirms that its charge is "to work for the creation of an Ibero-American audiovisual space," fomenting regional integration through co-productions. By April 2016, Ibermedia had a total of 19 members and had supported 636 co-production projects, helped to distribute 298 films, and awarded 2,700 training grants to people of all member countries

(Ibermedia n.d.). Some celebrated films supported by Ibermedia are *La jaula de oro* (*The Golden Cage*, Diego Quemada-Diez, 2013), *El casamiento* (*The Marriage*, Aldo Garay, 2013), *Pelo Malo* (Mariana Rondón, 2013), *No* (Pablo Larraín, 2012), *Contracorriente* (*Undertow*, Javier Fuentes-León, 2010), *Carancho* (*Vulture*, Pablo Trapero, 2010), and *Gigante* (Adrián Biniez, 2009), just to mention a few.

While Ibermedia has had a positive impact on co-production, effective systems of distribution have been slow in their establishment. Libia Villazana chronicles how, throughout the 2000s, the issue came up repeatedly in annual meetings of the organization, but the representatives never found easy solutions (Villazana 2009: 56–58). In 2009, one new possibility emerged with the launching of Ibermedia TV. Under the title *Nuestro Cine/ Nosso Cinema* (*Our Cinema*), the program broadcasts one Latin American film per week on public television channels of every member country. Thus, every year, 52 Latin American films find a way into people's homes through television. In Argentina, three public channels show the films of Ibermedia TV, including INCAA TV. Created by the national film institute in January 2011 within the framework of the 2009 Audiovisual Communication Services Law (Ley 26.522), INCAA TV is devoted to showing images connected exclusively to Argentina and Latin American cultures. Ibermedia has also promoted the program *DocTV Latin America*, which helps the production of documentaries and its distribution to all member countries (DocTV 2016). Television, thus far, has been Ibermedia's main outlet for distribution. Yet, in July 2014, the creation of Ibermedia Digital was announced as an Ibero-American educational platform (Ibermedia n.d.).

Another important intergovernmental institution that has contributed to integrate the Latin American audiovisual space is Mercosur Audiovisual. Through the creation of RECAM (Reunión Especializada de Autoridades Cinematográficas) in 2003, Mercosur has been effective in stimulating the establishment and growth of film festivals in the region, fomenting film exchanges and sponsoring meetings between producers, filmmakers, and sales agents. It has also encouraged bilateral co-production and distribution agreements between country members, as much as with some countries in Europe. Saliently, RECAM created the Mercosur Audiovisual Observatory, which has promoted research on cinemas of the region and in relation to cinemas from Europe and North America (Moguillansky 2009; Getino 2012).

Cooperation between Europe and Latin America

In Icíar Bollaín's *También la lluvia* (*Even the Rain*, 2010), the police fervently battle in Cochabamba with indigenous Bolivians who want to stop the privatization of the water supply, while at the same time a Spanish film crew is attempting to shoot a film about Columbus's arrival in the Americas. In Fernando León de Aranoa's *Amador* (2010), a Peruvian immigrant woman in Madrid becomes the caretaker of and develops a special relationship with an old dying Spanish man. In Miguel Cohan's *Betibú* (2014), a Spanish newspaper editor assigns two of his journalists to investigate the death of a businessman in a gated community outside of Buenos Aires. Bollaín's film is a co-production between companies in Spain, Mexico, France, and Bolivia. León de Aranoa's Spanish-produced film creates a narrative arc in which the relations between South Americans and Spaniards are investigated. Cohan's film, based on an Argentine novel, is co-produced and claimed in equal parts by famed companies Tornasol Films (Spain) and Haddock Films (Argentina)—the latter also produced the original *El secreto de sus ojos*.

These varied examples tell us of the collaborations between film companies in Europe and Latin America, as much as how cinematic stories are dynamically exploring a Spanish-Latin

American imaginary. They reinforce the sense of what D'Lugo refers to as a Hispanic trans-national community with shared cultural values (D'Lugo 2008: 4), or what Baqués calls the consolidation of a Euro-Latin American audiovisual space, centered on the supranational cinematic collaboration of the last 15 years (Baqués 2011). Thus, they are referring to an integration based on both the content and the production context of the co-produced films. It follows that the "national" then becomes a shared space among several nations, which mate-rializes in the existence of a single film—a contact zone subject to the labor that produced it and the imagery created within the boundaries of two or more singular national cultures. Yet the fact that co-productions facilitate the circulation of films in broader markets also has to be accounted for when referring to the malleability of the idea of national cinemas. The international flow of films provides them with a transnational quality that had been mainly connected in the past to films from larger industries. As Dennison affirms, international circu-lation dissolves the "strictly national paradigm" for contemporary films (Dennison 2013: 14).

Co-productions between Latin America and Spain began to be imagined from the 1930s, but materialized in the 1940s, during the Franco era (Caballero 2006: 4; Díaz López 2008: 26). The numbers have increased since the 1990s, as evidenced in Figure 17.4.

Clearly, Argentina and Mexico have been privileged beneficiaries of co-production agreements with Spain, which is a historical constant. Between 1978 and 2009, Spain co-produced 145 films with Argentina, and 110 with Mexico (Ciller and Beceiro 2013: 239).

Co-productions between Europe and Latin America have, to a large extent, been promoted by public policies on both sides of the Atlantic. Certainly, many public insti-tutions linked to the Spanish Ministry of Culture, the Ministry of External Affairs, and to Television Española (TVE) have been fundamental for this task (Caballero 2006: 9; Baqués 2011: 36). Yet private media corporations and independent producers with clear commercial interests—such as Tornasol Films, Wanda Visión and Wanda Films, Filmax Entertainment, Lola Films, and conglomerate Telefónica Media, in the Spanish case—have also played a vibrant role. Such exchanges generate a cinematic currency that is at the same time local and transnational. For instance, a group of prominent Latin American filmmakers and actors—such as Cecilia Roth, Ricardo Darín, Federico Luppi, Magaly Solier, Daniel Burman, Adolfo Aristarain, and Guillermo del Toro—are top players in

COUNTRY	1990-1999 (10 years)	2000-2009 (10 years)	2010-2014 (5 years)
Argentina	25	113	49
Mexico	14	45	21
Brazil	0	8	14
Chile	2	18	7
Colombia	5	8	14
Peru	4	7	6
Venezuela	3	10	9
Uruguay	0	10	7

Figure 17.4 Feature films co-produced by Spain.

Data extracted from ICAA website

Note: Some of the films accounted for may be co-produced by more than two countries, and thus, may be recorded more than once on this table.

the Spanish mediascape. But, more importantly, the cinematic space, markedly or not, combines diverse cultural values and symbolism, as much as technical and performative know-how in each one of the films.

Other kinds of film funds in Europe, many of them created since the 2000s, have also been important financial sources for co-productions. The majority of the funds are linked to film festivals, such as the "Hubert Bals Fund" (Rotterdam), "Cine en Construcción" (San Sebastián and Toulouse), "Open Doors Factory" (Locarno), and the "World Cinema Fund" (Berlin). In the manner of the recently closed French Fond Sud, these funds not only provide filmmakers with financial backing, but also give their films international notoriety and an endorsement for quality of sorts. There is also the "Foro de Coproducción" (Huelva) to connect producers, directors, and distributors with the goal of negotiating co-production deals. Since the topic of film festivals will be developed elsewhere in this book, suffice it to say that along with the funds, many of the festivals (as much in Europe as in Latin America) have developed film markets that now contribute immensely to the distribution of Latin American films. There is no doubt that these interweaving film practices contribute to reinscribe the cinema of Latin America in shared networks of signification that infuse ambivalence and amplitude in film stories and practices.

Trajectories of distribution

After its six-month run on a paid video-on-demand platform in the United States and Latin America through the HBO network (and along with 20 other Latin American feature films), the film *Pelo malo* had already guaranteed other exhibition outlets. It had been simultaneously broadcast in Europe on Canal Plus, and because of Ibermedia's support it will be broadcast on Latin American public television channels through Ibermedia TV. Then, because it received financial support from U.S. fund the Global Film Initiative, at the end of August 2015, the DVD/Blu-ray was published in the fund's collection the Global Lens and was being sold by Amazon. In addition, the Global Film Initiative organized dozens of showings of the film in festivals and around universities in the United States. Since more than a year before, French Pyramide Vidéo had already published the DVD for the European market. By August 2015, the rights to show the film had been sold to 36 countries, in many cases to countries that had never screened a Venezuelan film. In Latin America, *Pelo malo* had been sold to small independent theatrical distributors that are sprouting in different countries exclusively to disseminate Latin American works—in Colombia, Chile, Mexico, Argentina, and Uruguay. Finally, different digital portals (including some that are about to be launched) have bought *Pelo malo* for Internet distribution, namely iTunes Brazil, Imcine Mexico, Ibermedia Digital, and Scope50, the European streaming initiative of the Berlin Film Festival (Rondón 2015).

The example of this single film reflects the range of outlets that have recently emerged, or are about to emerge, and that are multiplying traditionally limited forms of distribution. In addition to the platforms already mentioned, outlets such as Netflix already have begun to show Spanish-language films made in Ibero-America, and only recently started streaming its first Spanish-language original series *Club de Cuervos* (2015), directed by Mexican Gaz Alazraki. The BAFICI film festival in Argentina recently made available for free streaming 100 Latin American films (Vargas 2015b). Argentina's INCAA TV is preparing to launch a video-on-demand service (Lampard 2015), and the Colombian Ministry of Culture is in the process of designing a digital platform to stream Latin American films (Vargas 2015a).

Digital portals promise to level the playing field in terms of people's access to culturally diverse works, while also changing the location and nature of film audiences. Local audiences are already expanding their national imaginary through the images and stories that co-productions offer, enabling them to consume films through the Internet, thereby further refiguring such an imaginary. New media platforms are arguably relocating not only audiences, but also refiguring the idea of national culture itself.

If the Internet and new media carry the torch of progress that cinema alone held in Latin America during the first decades of the twentieth century, today the combination of different media platforms and outlets is radically transforming industrial schemes and practices of consumption. This requires scholars to produce new paradigms that redefine the conceptualization of cinema as a "cultural industry," a term that has been widely utilized in Latin America since the 1960s. Referring to the production and circulation of cultural products and their contribution towards constructing a national culture, the term called on scholars to recognize and analyze economic and political systems connected to mass media products and the relations of domination and power that they entail. More generally, and since the mid-2000s, the notion of "creative industries" started gaining theoretical and practical grounds. The shift of terminology modified in other countries, such as the United Kingdom, the way in which cultural policies are written and prioritized (Garnham 2005). In Latin America, the idea of creative industries could serve to partially describe the current film industry in relation to creative production, technology, and access to information, emphasizing the importance of creativity and innovation at the entrepreneurial level, and the diversification of outlets for distribution and consumption (Getino 2012: 13–14). The term, nonetheless, has not gained universal usage, and the extant industrial panorama and cultural institutions are quite dissimilar to those in Britain. Nonetheless, the idea of creative industries goes hand in hand with the proliferation of independent production companies and distribution outlets, as we have seen in Latin America in the last two decades. But it is a contentious term that would need further analysis when applied to the realities of the industries in the Latin American context.

References

Alvaray, L. (2011) "Are We Global Yet? New Challenges to Defining Latin American Cinema." *Studies in Hispanic Cinemas*, 7(2): 69–86.

The American Assembly (2012) "The MPAA in Latin America." Available at: http://piracy.american assembly.org/the-mpaa-in-latin-america/#sthash.c9Zfql69.dpuf (accessed August 11, 2015).

Baqués, C.C. (2011) "El espacio audiovisual euro-latinoamericano: el cine como eje central de la cooperación supranacional." *Anàlisi*, 41: 27–45.

Caballero, R. (ed.) (2006) *Producción, coproducción e intercambio de cine entre España, América Latina y el Caribe*. Havana: Fundación del Nuevo Cine Latinoamericano.

CACI (1989) "Convenio de Integración Cinematográfica Latinoamericana." Avaialble at: www. recam.org/_files/documents/convenio_integr_cine_al.pdf (accessed August 10, 2015).

Ciller, C. and Beceiro, S. (2013) "Coproducciones cinematográficas en España: análisis y catalogación." *Revista Eptic*, 15(2): 234–246. Available at: https://e-archivo.uc3m.es/bitstream/handle/10016/18624/coproducciones_EPTIC_2013.pdf?sequence=1 (accessed September 1, 2015).

Dennison, S. (ed.) (2013) *Contemporary Hispanic Cinema: Interrogating the Transnational in Spanish and Latin American Film*. Woodbridge, UK: Tamesis Books.

Díaz López, M. (2008) "Connecting Spain and the Americas in the Cold War: The Transnational Careers of Jorge Negrete and Carmen Sevilla." *Studies in Hispanic Cinemas*, 5(1–2): 25–42.

D'Lugo, M. (2008) "Across the Hispanic Atlantic: Cinema and Its Symbolic Relocations." *Studies in Hispanic Cinemas*, 5(1–2): 3–7.

DocTV (2016) "DocTV." Available at: www.doctvlatinoamerica.org/ (accessed April 17, 2016).

Focus (2000) *Focus 2000: World Film Market Trends*. Publication of the European Audiovisual Observatory, Marche du Film.

Garnham, N. (2005) "From Cultural to Creative Industries: An Analysis of the Implications of the 'Creative Industries' Approach to Arts and Media Policy Making in the United Kingdom." *International Journal of Cultural Policy*, 11(1): 15–29.

Getino, O. (2007) "Los desafíos de la industria del cine en América Latina y el Caribe." *Zer*, 22: 167–182.

—— (2012) "Reflexiones sobre la situación actual de las industrias culturales en el Mercosur." *Separata Geminis*, 3(2): 8–39.

Globo Filmes (2015). "Globo Filmes." Available at: www.globofilmes.globo.com (accessed August 11, 2015).

Hopewell, J. (2012) "IM Global-Canana's Mundial Shakes Up Latin America Film Industry." *Variety*, May 12. Available at: http://variety.com/2015/film/spotlight/im-global-cananas-mundial-shakes-up-latin-america-film-industry-1201491212/ (accessed July 25, 2015).

—— (2014a) "Brazil's Dilma Rousseff Announces $540 Million Government Package for Film and TV." *Chicago Tribune*, July 2. Available at: http://articles.chicagotribune.com/2014-07-02/entertainment/sns-201407021459reedbusivarietyn1201257177-20140702_1_culture-minister-marta-suplicy-brazilian-film-industry-tv-distribution (accessed August 11, 2015).

—— (2014b) "Universal Pictures Intl. Ups Ante in Brazil." *Variety*, October 9. Available at: http://variety.com/2014/film/festivals/universal-pictures-intl-ups-ante-in-brazil-201325756/ (accessed August 11, 2015).

—— (2015) "Locarno: Films Boutique Picks up 'Violin Teacher'." *Variety*, August 11. Available at: http://variety.com/2015/film/news/locarno-films-boutique-picks-up-violin-teacher-1201567533/ (accessed August 11, 2015).

Ibermedia (n.d.) "Ibermedia." Avaialble at: www.programaibermedia.com/el-programa/ (accessed April 17, 2016).

ICAA (n.d.) "ICAA." Available at: www.mecd.gob.es/bbddpeliculas/back.do?cacheNum=2 (accessed August 20, 2015).

IMCINE (2014) "Anuario estadístico de cine mexicano." Mexico City.

IMDb Pro (2015) "IMDb Pro." Avaialble at: www.imdbpro.com (accessed August 11, 2015).

Kanzler, M. and Talvera Milla, J. (eds.) (2015) *Focus 2015: World Film Markets Trends*. Publication of the European Audiovisual Observatory, Marché du Film.

Lampard, V. (2015) "Argentina Getting its Own Video-On-Demand Service." *The Bubble*, March 17. Available at: www.bubblear.com/argentina-getting-its-own-video-on-demand-service-this-time-legal/ (accessed August 31, 2015).

MacLaird, M. (2013) *Aesthetics and Politics in the Mexican Film Industry*. New York: Palgrave Macmillan.

Moguillansky, M. (2009) "Cine, política y Mercosur. Un balance de los comienzos de una política cinematográfica regional." *Políticas Culturais em Revista*, 2(2): 137–154.

MPAA (2014) "MPAA Theatrical Market Statistics 2014." Available at: www.mpaa.org/wp-content/uploads/2015/03/MPAA-Theatrical-Market-Statistics-2014.pdf (accessed July 31, 2015).

MPA Brasil (n.d.). Accessed May 19, 2010.

RECAM (n.d.) "Informes Finales de Estudio sobre Legislación Comparada." Available at: www.recam.org/pma/contenidos/documentos (accessed August 5, 2015).

Rêgo, C.M. (2005) "Brazilian Cinema: Its Fall, Rise and Renewal." *New Cinemas: Journal of Contemporary Film*, 3(2): 85–100.

Revista Filme B (2015) May. Available at: www.filmeb.com.br/revista (accessed August 11, 2015).

Rondón, M. (2015) Interview by the Author, September 1.

Sánchez Ruiz, E.E. (2004) "El empequeñecido cine latinoamericano y la integración audiovisual." *Comunicación y Sociedad*, 2: 9–36.

Silveira, W. (2015) "Que Horas Ela Volta?" *Papo de Cinema*. Available at: www.papodecinema.com. br/filmes/que-horas-ela-volta (accessed August 11, 2015).

Solot, S. (2002) "Keynote Panel Sponsored by the Motion Picture Association." Special Issue of *Hemisphere*, Florida International University. Avaialble at: www.mpaa.org/mpa-al/FIU_Solot.htm (accessed March 2, 2005).

Vargas, A.S. (2015a) "Coming Soon: Free Netflix-Like Site Exclusively for Latin American Film." *Remezcla*, March 27. Available at: http://remezcla.com/film/coming-soon-free-netflix-like-site-exclusively-for-latin-american-film/ (accessed August 31, 2015).

—— (2015b) "Over 100 Latin American Films Are Available for Streaming, Thanks to This Buenos Aires Film Festival." *Remezcla*, August 19. Available at: http://remezcla.com/film/over-100-latin-american-films-are-now-available-for-streaming-thanks-to-this-buenos-aires-film-festival/ (accessed August 31, 2015).

Villazana, L. (2009) *Transnational Financial Structures in the Cinema of Latin America: Programa Ibermedia in Study*. Saarbrücken, Germany: VDM Verlag Dr. Müller Aktiengesellschaft & Co.

18

THE INTERLOCKING DYNAMICS OF DOMESTIC AND INTERNATIONAL FILM FESTIVALS

The case of Latin American and Caribbean cinema[1]

Tamara L. Falicov

Editors' introduction

Although the international film festival circuit, a largely European invention, has been around since the 1940s, a new paradigm for production and circulation of Latin American films has emerged over recent decades that forms a unique creative and financial symbiosis between regional and global film festivals and the films they promote. It is worth recalling that these European festivals, which serve as film distribution markets, have for decades exerted a dominant influence on the kinds of Latin American films that get screened outside of the region. In the post-World War II period, it was simply recognition through competitive awards that opened doors for Latin American filmmakers and their producers (Lima Barreto's *O Cangaceiro* [1953] and the films of Argentinian Leopoldo Torre Nilson in the 1960s).

Since the 1980s, however, various festival funds have been established at Cannes, Berlin, Toulouse, Rotterdam, and San Sebastian, to name only the most prominent, which support particular types of productions in the region. The chapter picks up from the work of Luisela Alvaray in the previous chapter, as Tamara L. Falicov, tracing the origins of the new North–South relationship that has gained prominence in film festivals since the 1980s, examines in depth some of the festivals within Latin America that have established connections with major markets. She focuses on both the economic incentives that shape regional production through the mediation of festivals, as well as the range of collaboratives that have emerged around homegrown festivals in Latin America. The essay concludes by focusing on a relatively new phenomenon: the increasingly tighter knit among film festivals both within and outside of Latin America that forge alliances, and in some cases merge the festivals.

Falicov contends that the system has become progressively more interlocked and porous, while always already structured within a system of hierarchies. Thus, film festivals are not only networked together; they are increasingly intertwining, and initiatives from European film festivals are newly grafted on to the "legitimated" Latin American ones such as the ones described.

Introduction

Film festivals make up a network with nodes and nerve endings, there is capillary action and osmosis between the various layers of the network, and while a strict ranking system exists, for instance between A-and B-festivals, policed by an international federation (FIAPF), the system as a whole is highly porous and perforated.

(Thomas Elsaesser 2005: 74)

Global film festivals have proliferated since the 1940s, and over time have become woven into a broad transnational yet highly stratified network. The concepts of "network" and "circuit" have often led scholars to invoke the anatomical metaphor employed by Thomas Elsaesser to clarify the relation of parts of the complex film festival system. As Aida Vallejo points out, "[i]t is important to understand festivals not as sum of events at the same level, but rather as interconnected where there are power dynamics and hierarchies" (Vallejo 2014: 22).

Taking Elsaesser's useful metaphor as a point of departure, one might say that the large arteries are the Class A festivals, mainly from Europe, such as Berlin, Cannes, and Rotterdam, but also the Toronto Film Festival in Canada, Sundance in the US, and Busan in South Korea. These festivals matter to Latin American filmmakers not only because access to screenings and awards clearly provide critical visibility, but also because the adjoining industry activities include small grant competitions for Global South filmmakers (such as the Hubert Bals Fund in Rotterdam and the World Cinema Fund in Berlin), as well as training programs, screenwriting labs, co-production markets, and post-production competitions and other opportunities. Perhaps more importantly, as this essay will argue, filmmakers from the periphery gather at film festivals in the Global North not only to gain access to financing and foreign distribution rights for their work; they also attend training sessions and development workshops to further network connections, refine their cultural capital, and have the potential to become further attuned to what kinds of film aesthetics tend to be favored in a European context. Gonzalo Maza calls this comprehension of aesthetics that are successful in Europe the "Hubert Bals effect," which, typically, first- and second-time directors and producers must confront when they are making films they wish to be adjudicated in Global North venues.

This chapter will present an overview of the history of European film festivals that regularly screen Latin American films and the ways in which, historically, this has marked the beginning of a North–South relationship. In addition to discussing the large, Tier A festivals, the essay will examine some of the festivals within Latin America that have established connections with major markets. I will conclude by focusing on a relatively new phenomenon: the increasingly interlocking, transnational nature of film festivals both within and outside of Latin America that forge alliances, and in some cases merge the festivals.

It is important to underscore the evolving nature of the relation between European and Latin American festivals and the film cultures they reflect. Historically, that relationship has at times been fraught with tension, such as during the period of the 1960s–1970s, when films from Latin America were "better known in Europe than in Latin America" (Bolivian director Jorge Sanjinés, cited in Hanlon 2010), much to the chagrin of progressive Latin American filmmakers. This was the period when Latin American cinema became "chic" for the Europeans; it coincided with a dangerous political climate in some parts of Latin America, marred by horrific censorship and repression in various military dictatorships in the region. Thus, organizing and attending political film screenings were potentially life-threatening activities.

Attention will also focus on the scale of "homegrown" Latin American festivals. They form part of a smaller network of national film festivals that helps fortify national film industries. Scholar María Paz Peirano details a number of Chilean festivals, for instance, and highlights the unique attributes to these lesser-known festivals, such as the Festival Internacional de Lebu (LECIL Bio Bio, Lebu International Film Festival), which originally screened work in a natural cave close to the sea (Peirano 2016: 124). More generally, larger festivals, such as Guadalajara or BAFICI (Buenos Aires International Independent Film Festival), are linking up with programs in European festivals and thereby creating another global festival convergence, or node, on the film festival circuit. Consideration of these relations will provide a more accurate sense of the increasingly interlocking, transnational nature of film festivals both within and outside of Latin America and their potential impact on the evolving nature of production and distribution of films from the region.

Historical perspectives

There are at least three distinct phases in the evolving relation of Latin American films at European film festivals: (1) an early period, running from 1937 through the mid-1960s, when major European film festivals invited sometimes token Latin American films and where these films received accolades; (2) the rise of militant cinema in the region that opposed the art house criteria of the festivals of the early phase, and consequently gener-ated alternative festivals in Europe and Latin America (Viña del Mar, Chile, Havana, the Sodre Documentary and Experimental Festival in Uruguay, Festival de Mérida, Venezuela); and finally (3) the intensification of international co-productions through the activities of international funding groups associated with European festivals (Rotterdam, Toulouse, San Sebastián, Berlin, etc.).

The initial phase begins with recognition of Mexican cinematographer Gabriel Figueroa at the Venice Film Festival (1937) for his work on Fernando de Fuentes's *Allá en el Rancho Grande* (*Over at the Big Ranch*, Mexico, 1936). In the immediate post-World War II period, another Mexican film, Emilio Fernández's *María Candelaria* (1943), won a special noncom-petitive prize at the recently revived Cannes festival. Fernández's *La perla* (*The Pearl*, 1945) won two more awards for Gabriel Figueroa's cinematography, at the Venice Film Festival in 1947 and the U.S. Golden Globes in 1949.

It was not until 1950 that Luis Buñuel's masterpiece, *Los olvidados* (*The Young and the Damned*), won a special jury prize at Cannes. In 1953, the film *O Cangaceiro* directed by Lima Barreto for Vera Cruz studios was the studio's most successful film, grossing 30 million cruzeiros ($1.5 million). The film played at that year's Cannes Film Festival, winning the Best Adventure Film Award, thereby making it the first Brazilian film to win a prestigious European festival prize (Rist 2014: 120). In the case of Argentina, the contemporary director credited with making the strongest impression abroad at international film festivals was Leopoldo Torre Nilsson. He was an art house auteur whose *La casa del ángel* (*The House of the Angel*, 1957) screened at Cannes and *La caída* (*The Fall*, 1959) at Berlin. In 1961, he was awarded a prize at Cannes by the FIPRESCI for *La mano en la trampa* (*The Hand in the Trap*). Torre Nilsson's successes at these events point to one of the essential criteria of European film festival juries of the period: the lionizing of film auteurs and, in the instance of Figueroa, the artistic creativity that is closely aligned with the auteur. In each of these instances, it may also be argued that one of the points of attraction is the imagery of the exotic and the violent as cultural markers for films from the region. This focus on what is an art cinema criterion will, in fact, be challenged in the coming decades, specifically by Fernando Solanas and Octavio Getino.

During the late 1960s and 1970s, left-leaning Latin American filmmakers used cinema as a tool to call attention to and resist a string of horrific military dictatorships in Brazil, Argentina, Uruguay, Chile, Bolivia, Peru, and others. These directors made low-budget, anti-imperialist cinema that formed a body of work and a network of filmmakers known as the New Latin American Cinema movement (NLAC). In their widely circulated manifestos and statements of theory on behalf of a new kind of film language, these artists spoke of "imperfect cinema" (Julio García Espinosa, Cuba), "Third Cinema" (Fernando Solanas and Octavio Getino, Argentina), and "an aesthetic of hunger" (Glauber Rocha, Brazil). Their films were seen by European film curators and critics, who selected Brazilian Cinema Novo films such as *Ganga Zumba* (Carlos Diegues, 1963) and *Vidas Secas* (*Barren Lives*, Nelson Pereira dos Santos, 1963), the latter of which played at Cannes, and whose director won the OCIC (International Catholic Organization for Cinema) prize in 1964 (shared with Jacques Demy's *Les Parapluies de Cherbourg* (*Umbrellas of Cherbourg*). *La hora de los hornos* (*The Hour of the Furnaces*, 1968), the most emblematic case of a "Third Cinema" film, won the top prize at Italy's Pesaro Film Festival in 1968. This has become a venerated event in contemporary Latin American cinema history given the improvised mass street protest following the film's screening, when Solanas was carried on the shoulders of the crowd and viewers engaged in street fights with police (Achugar, cited in Burton 1986: 228). In 1976, the Mexican film *Canoa* (*Canoa: A Shameful Memory*, Felipe Cazals, 1975) won the Silver Bear Special Jury Prize at the Berlin Film Festival.

While attention given to this radical political cinema by European festivals provided important visibility to films made under dangerous conditions, there were filmmakers and curators in countries such as Colombia, Chile, and Cuba, among others, also committed to "decolonizing" their conditions by relying less on European film festivals for recognition. The focus on homegrown film festivals was one reaction against the predominance of those exhibition spaces in Europe. As Mariano Mestman observes:

> from the second half of the 1960s onwards, the creation of meeting spaces for Latin American and African political filmmakers in their own region meant an incipient distinctive feature in relation to previous periods when the most usual meeting place (if any) were European Festivals or Exhibitions.
>
> (Mestman 2002: 48)

He points out that "the wording used by the Chilean Valparaíso-based newspaper *La Unión* (August 3, 1967) to title its review on the 1967 Viña del Mar Festival illustrates the prevailing spirit: 'Viña displaces Europe as a meeting point for Latin American Filmmakers'" (Mestman 2002: 49).

Thus, concurrent with the rise of the New Latin American Cinema movement was the founding of national and pan-continental film festivals where filmmakers would gather as a form of counter-hegemony and a space in which to dialogue. Political meetings and Latin American film screenings included Viña del Mar, in Chile (1969) and the Festival of New Latin American Cinema (Festival de Nuevo Cine Latinoamericano) in Havana (1979). Cuba's Festival of New Latin American Cinema, in particular, became a central hub and meeting ground for those Latin American filmmakers fleeing in exile. This festival became a sanctioned, institutionalized space for directors and moviegoers to meet and dialogue, debate political issues facing filmmakers at that time, screen films, and orchestrate roundtable discussion as a form of solidarity against the Hollywood majors, principally.

By the 1980s, however, and driven in part by the neoliberal turn in regional cultural politics, film aesthetics became less radically doctrinaire and more centered on "quality art house" cinema. With the increasingly limited state funding for national cinema, the financing quest subsequently moved abroad. As a result, a rise in co-productions and the emergence of savvy producers the likes of Mexican Bertha Navarro from Tequila Gang Productions (Guillermo de Toro), Lita Stantic (Argentina), and others entered the scene, who helped obtain funding projects vis-à-vis government agreements that were signed into law with companies in Spain, France, Germany, and Canada in the 1980s. By 1997, the Spanish government organized a reunion of national film institute heads for various Latin American countries (including Portugal) to create a co-production film finance pool, Programa Ibermedia (see Alvaray's Chapter 17 in this volume) in order to promote Ibero-American co-production and collaboration.

Financial opportunities for Latin American directors abroad, mainly in Europe, opened up theoretical debates about the kinds of aesthetics that most facilitated crossing borders and appealed to multiple audiences. Film scholars have grappled with definitions of "global art house cinema" (Galt and Schnoover 2010; Falicov 2013) and a "realignment of national cinema in new global contexts" (D'Lugo 2013) to further understand which art house films cross borders with more facility than others. Nowadays, film festivals are less of a political site for sharing oppositional cinema, and more often spaces for quality cinema to be showcased, thus building a national brand for the festival with the goal of making this temporal event unique and distinctive in some way. These "festival films" (see Falicov 2016 for more on this definition) also have a greater chance of obtaining film funds from festivals, to which we now turn.

Transnational funding and interlocked circuits in contemporary film festivals

Increasingly, film festivals throughout the world are adding supplementary industry activities such as funding competitions for Global South filmmakers, training programs for first-time directors, and others. Such benefits lend prestige to the filmmakers, who receive them and also may be a good fit for the festival's brand.

The Hubert Bals Fund of the International Film Festival Rotterdam was the first such fund founded in 1988 after the director of the festival lobbied the Dutch government for funds to support filmmakers from the developing world. He died a few months later, not knowing the fate of what he dubbed the "Tarkovsky Fund." Thus, the Hubert Bals Fund was created posthumously and named in his honor. Financed by government development aid, along with a large NGO, a foundation grant, and funds from the national lottery, the fund provides development aid money to support filmmakers in emerging film cultures "expressing and preserving their cultural diversity" (Bhalotra 2007). Films that are selected for festival development grants, for example, are given the "inside track" to be considered for selection as a "premiere" at the festival. Film premieres are the central currency for film festivals, and it has become standard practice for *Variety* magazine to review every film at its world premiere (Ruoff 2012: 5).

Festival funding is important to first- and second-time filmmakers since it symbolizes distinctive "seals of approval" by the festival juries and administrators, who are mainly responsible for selecting films to receive financial support for their production. Despite the small monetary amounts involved, these financial awards actually matter, especially in countries where local currencies are weak against the euro. But, more importantly, they often translate into large symbolic capital in that they can open the door to other cash awards and entrée into other film festivals. They help a film rise above the rest and gain a foothold in the transnational festival circuit. This privileged status cannot be overstated; in an age supersaturated with film festivals and markets, it can make a very definitive difference in whether a film gets noticed, screened, and distributed, or not.

In recent decades, with the global proliferation of film festivals, the involvement of the International Federation of Film Producers Associations (FIAPF) has increased in importance in terms of that organization's mandate to represent the economic, legal, and regulatory interests that film and TV production industries in five continents have in common (FIAPF n.d.). They have created a ranking system for film festivals around the world. Each film festival, if they are interested in being classified for "A-list" status, must undergo an accreditation process. According to film scholar Minerva Campos, the ability to host world premieres at film festivals helps ensure and maintain the ranking of the top film festivals. She found that film festivals such as those at Cannes, Berlin, and Mar del Plata had to program a minimum of 14 world premieres in order to maintain their "A-list" status (Campos 2012: 12). These premieres help further a festival's stature as a "main player" in the field. Thus, there is a never-ending quest on the part of programmers and other staff members to continually find sources of premieres.

One method to help foster new, fresh material with potential for world premieres in the future is to develop a film funding initiative or host a co-production market/forum whereby the film festival becomes a participant in funding and later in promoting and premiering projects it has helped produce. Campos argues that post-production initiatives are part of the "premieres" pipelines that festivals such as San Sebastián know will give them first look on the projects that they helped to finance (Campos 2012).

One of the implications of this pressure to find new material to satisfy the "A-list" designation is that Global South filmmakers may then opt to premiere their works at major European film festivals, thereby relegating second- and third-tier works to film festivals in their home countries (De Valck 2007: 71). Manthia Diawara concurs, stating:

> Since the best African films are screened at European and American film festivals [e.g. *Le festival trois continents* in Nantes, France, the Milan Festival of Africa, and others] not to mention the ones that get into the Cannes, Venice, Berlin, and London film festivals, filmmakers no longer look to FESPACO [the Pan-African Film Festival in Ouagadougou] for the premiere of their films.
>
> *(Diawara 1994: 386)*

Another implication of these film funds is that there is an inherent power dynamic that lies between the European/Asian/North American (minus Mexico) funders and those from the Global South seeking funds to begin or complete a project. Scholars have examined this relationship as one of neocolonialism (Halle 2010: 312), and one of Global South filmmakers having the "burden of representation" (Branston 2000: 171) to write storylines about marginalization for the benefit of wealthy viewers, or what has been deemed "poverty porn" (*pornomiseria*)[2] (Ross 2011: 262). Others have cataloged instances in which producers have been asked to make their films look more "authentic" (e.g. "more African") and pinpointed a kind of "global art house aesthetic" to which Global South filmmakers may conform (Bartlet 2000: 211). Finally, these funds may begin to create what Miriam Ross calls a "favoured group of filmmakers," after she observed that from 2005 to 2009, 7 of 20 film projects received funding both from the Hubert Bals Fund and the World Cinema Fund. Moreover, in one instance, the Chilean film *Lucía* (Niles Atallah, 2011) was given funding from Hubert Bals, Cine en Construcción, and the Global Film Initiative (the latter was suspended in 2011) (Ross 2010: 132–133). For this reason, the issue of obtaining cultural capital is crucial to the success of receiving funding. Certain directors who have the savvy and can literally "talk the talk" (e.g., English, French, or German) and understand the culture of interacting with European gatekeepers undoubtedly have a distinct advantage over others.

In terms of the criteria that Hubert Bals employs, according to their annual report, they look for "the artistic quality and authenticity of the film," and among other more standard criteria (country of production, nationality, gender, feasibility of the project both financially and artistically), there is another category that involves "the extent to which the project can contribute to strengthening the local film climate" (Hubert Bals Fund Annual Report 2014–2015). Though these categories certainly fall within the mission to help developing countries with fomenting local film culture and infrastructure, it could be argued that it is part of a discourse of development that "advanced industrialized countries" filmmakers need not concern themselves with. This observation merely points out how development aid discourses permeate funding in ways that might be limiting or reductive in narrative content to filmmakers from the Global South. Moreover, this patron relationship may potentially privilege a certain kind of filmmaker profile who delivers images the North is looking for.

When film festivals in Latin America begin to grow and expand, what are their role models? Do they imitate larger festivals or do they try to incorporate other, more home-grown models of funding? One innovative program that has begun to challenge more traditional models is Tres Puertos Cine (Three Ports Cinema), which began as a collaboration between the Australab at the Valdivia Film Festival, Chile, and the BAL Lab as part of the Buenos Aires International Independent Film Festival (BAFICI) with an affiliation with Cinemart at the Rotterdam film festival. In 2016, the workshop is now a collaboration between Australab and Distrital, an independent film festival in Mexico City and Cinemart. They promise a horizontal model, rather than a top-down vertical one. That is, rather than participants being told what they "should do," in a former Tres Puertos Cine organizer's words, they are instead, "asking filmmakers what they need" (quoted in Hopewell 2014). When Global South filmmakers are integrated into the selection processes and are asked for input, they are more invested and can claim more "ownership" of these initiatives (see Falicov 2017).

In terms of film festival models in the region that have influenced newer festivals, Gutiérrez and Wagenberg state that:

BAFICI (founded in 1999) itself has had a tremendous influence in inspiring the inception of new film festivals across the region. In Feb. 2004 the Mexico City International Film Festival (FICCO) was born (Note: it was defunct by 2010); a year later, the Santiago International Film Festival (SANFIC) began in Chile; and in 2012, the first Cali International Film Festival took place in Colombia—all festivals that model themselves on BAFICI.

(Gutiérrez and Wagenberg 2013: 300)

A counterpoint to the notion that it was BAFICI that started an "indie" trend, Chilean cultural critic Gonzalo Maza argues that these newer festivals conform to a format that only accepts work from first- and second-time filmmakers, ensuring fresh talent and a lower budget, and thus perpetuating a low-budget, grainy aesthetic, which could potentially be problematic for newer directors, such as those who do not subscribe to that aesthetic. Maza argues that festivals such as SANFIC (the Santiago International Film Festival in Chile) and later FICCO, the Mexican Contemporary Film Festival (2004–2010), were interested in being "independent" and cutting edge by showing Latin American films that might be of an aesthetic of potential interest to European film festivals. He dubs this phenomenon the "Hubert Bals Effect" (Maza 2013).

In Maza's provocative essay, he argues that these festivals may be "independent," but they wind up being, in a sense, a smaller circuit (he calls it the "kindergarten circuit") for first-tier festivals. He opines that festivals such as Cannes, Berlin, Venice, Locarno, and San Sebastián, among others, scoop up these low-budget independent films by first- and second-time filmmakers because they are inexpensive raw material that are easy to "dispose of" if their later films are not meeting expectations (Maza 2013). He later points out that these first and second films are calling cards in preparation for the third films, which hopefully do gain entrée into major festivals, or if they do not, he believes that then it becomes increasingly difficult for them to obtain co-production money, distribution deals, etc. (Maza 2013). This argument is certainly polemical, but it brings up valid arguments about why it matters so much that European and other OECD country festivals have access to new, inexpensive material to release in their festivals. One newer avenue for European festivals to have a direct conduit to fresh, new material is the increasingly interlocked industry activities between Latin American/Caribbean festivals and those in the Global North.

In the past decade, there has been an increased shift in the ways that prominent film festivals, mainly in Europe, are staking claims to smaller regional or national film festivals throughout Latin America/Caribbean in order to link up and bring vetted projects (such as those developed at Caribbean Film Mart in Trinidad, *Primera Mirada* [First Look] in Panama, and BAL Lab in Buenos Aires) to their shores (see Figure18.1, which lists many of these Latin American festival activities). In all of those cases, adjudicated films and those that have won top honors were routed directly to the *Marché du film* at the Cannes Film Festival. Recent alliances include links between the Miami International Film Festival, which vetted winning films from Ventana Sur (Argentina) to award their own competition monies in 2015; the Morelia International Film Festival (FICM), which forged two linkages in 2015: a collaboration with the Locarno film festival training academy, and with Sundance they collaborated on a workshop. In 2016, Morelia handpicked four Mexican films to screen at the Cannes Critics' Week.

This increasingly interlocked system is the harbinger of festival forms, which will increasingly rely on Global South festivals to bring projects, now filtered by transnational and

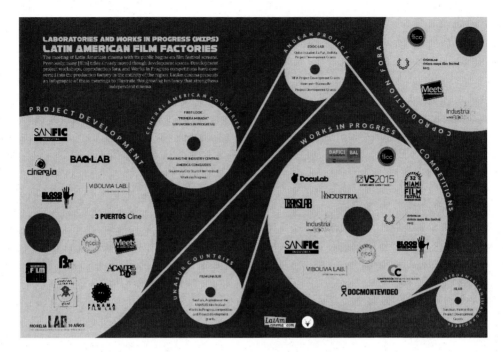

Figure 18.1 Infografia. Created by Venado, originally published in *LatAm Cinema.* English translation by the author.

local judges and juries, across borders to Europe. As Thomas Elsaesser reminds us (Elsaesser 2005: 74), the system is increasingly interlocked and porous, while always already structured within a system of hierarchies. Thus, film festivals are not only networked together, but they are increasingly intertwining, and initiatives from European film festivals are newly grafted on to the "legitimated" Latin American ones such as the ones described.

These are newer models of collaborations; some are connected through industry events such as Latin American and Caribbean film markets connecting with their counterparts in Europe. Other models relate to labs that workshop scripts, with the winning selections going on to the Cannes film market (*Marché du film*). Still others are European film festivals, which have helped to found or build out the infrastructure of a film festival, such as the case of the Curaçao film festival sponsored by the Rotterdam International Film Festival (IFFR). This special arrangement is no doubt influenced by the former Dutch colonial history, as another example of this "entrenched" relationship can be found in the case of the Suriname Film Festival in South America (now defunct). Curaçao relied heavily on funding and infrastructure from the Rotterdam International Film Festival, and Dutch development funds, as well as private foundation money in Curaçao (the Fundashon Bon Intenshon that promotes the arts locally). Officially, the Curaçao film festival is called the Curaçao International Film Festival Rotterdam (CIFFR), a clear indicator that Rotterdam plays a central role in curating and branding the festival, which will be five years old in April 2016.

Another seminal linkage occurs between the Toronto Film Festival and the Panama International Film Festival. Considered to be one of the largest in terms of films programmed and featuring a film market arguably rivaling Cannes, Toronto has historically played an important role in bringing the latest Latin American feature films and documentaries to Canada and raising awareness of these auteurs for Canadian audiences. This may or may not be incidental to the festival's co-founder, Henk Van der Kolk, who was responsible for founding an important, relatively new film festival, the International Film Festival Panama (IFFP), in 2010. The Latin American film curator for the Toronto International Film Festival, Diana Sánchez is also the artistic director for Panama, so there are criss-cross flows of films from Latin America to Canada, and back to Panama, given these key personnel who annually migrate transnationally.

Case examples between BAFICI (*BAL Lab*), *Primera Mirada* (Panama), and the *Marché du film* at Cannes

The earliest Latin America–Europe film festival relationship begins in 2013, when the Cannes film market initiated "BAL goes to Cannes" showcasing five works in progress from BAFICI's own filmmaking lab called BAL, which is over a decade old, making it Latin America's oldest "works in progress" lab. A group of 15-minute clips are first shown at BAFICI and later screened in front of sales agents and festival heads at Cannes (Hopewell and Keslassy 2013). This Cannes initiative was the first time that works in progress were selected, and emerged out of a particular industrial juncture. According to the head of the Cannes film market, Jerome Palliard, "[at a] time when the industry is wary of taking risks, works in progress offer perfect timing for sales agents, distributors and festival programmers to know pretty exactly what they'll be getting, but still have discussions with directors and producers" (Hopewell 2013). This means, theoretically, that they would prefer to see works close to completion rather than hear a pitch and invest in that manner.

The Panama International Film Festival debuted a works-in-progress competition called *Primera Mirada* (First Look) for Central American filmmakers in 2015, which offered a $25,000 grand prize sponsored by airline manufacturer Boeing. One edition of the festival later, the industry section had forged an agreement with the Cannes *Marché du film*, which would grant the winner of *Primera Mirada* an opportunity to screen the work in front of sales agents, programmers, and others at Cannes the following month, in addition to a cash prize. The 2016 edition industry award was a $15,000 cash first prize by a private, anonymous donor, which is a decrease from the previous edition (when the prize came from a corporate sponsor), clearly demonstrating how dependent festivals are on their sponsors to deliver prize money from year to year.

These linkages certainly enable newer festivals to gain prestige and notoriety, and also bolster the status of European festivals. In an interview with Curaçao chief programmer Christine Dávila, having Curaçao aligned with Rotterdam makes the island festival, in her words, "into one of the most avant-garde, experimental film festivals in the world, and at the same time [in its role as] marketplace and funder, helps filmmakers [from the Caribbean] network and have an incredible launching pad [to Europe]". By hiring Dávila to program films at the Curaçao festival, the Rotterdam staff were interested in having her promote Caribbean filmmaking in the region, first and foremost. Given her experience programming for Sundance and the Los Angeles Film Festival, and given her Latin American film expertise, they hired her to "dig deep" to help track local works by emerging directors that might not consider applying to a film festival (Dávila 2015).

Another transnational linkage that has yet to be explored in the Latin American context is the role of film festival programmers who often "wear many hats." They are invited to serve as jury members at festivals throughout Latin America/Caribbean (e.g. Christine Dávila recently served as a juror for the Central American category at the Costa Rican

Figure 18.2   Teatro Balboa: A restored theater which served as the main venue for the 2016 edition of the Panama International Film Festival. Photo courtesy of the author.

International Film Festival), while at the same time working in various other capacities at other festivals. Dávila, who is also a documentary film programmer for the U.S. festival Ambulante California (an offshoot of the nonprofit Ambulante Film Festival in Mexico founded by Gael García Bernal, Diego Luna, and Elena Fortes), also programs world cinema at Sundance. Based in Los Angeles, Dávila screens and evaluates work in her role as a juror, but theoretically could also select one of those films for her festival(s) or suggest a title for colleagues at other festivals such as the Los Angeles Film Festival, Tribeca, and San Antonio's CineFest (Dávila 2015). The presence of key gatekeepers who are assessing, vetting, and circulating work in these spaces are understudied in the field of film festival studies; these Global North programmers/jurors add another layer of mediation within festivals in the Global South.

Final thoughts

Beginning in the late 1980s, the Global North festivals helped develop, fund, and exhibit Global South films through concurrent training labs and market activities during the festival. In the 2010s, the creation of new partnerships between large European film festivals and festivals in Latin America and the Caribbean have facilitated "content conduits," thus bolstering the international profiles of festivals in Morelia, Panama, and BAFICI, to name a few, while providing a pipeline of new work for these "Class A" festivals. While this potentially gives Latin American filmmakers increased visibility, it will hopefully not hinder efforts to bring Latin American and Caribbean producers together to help forge more linkages in and among themselves. Along with these new transnational networks of content flows have come the flow of gatekeepers: programmers, jury members (who might be one and the same). These mediated relationships are worthy of further study and will help in unpacking these more deeply embedded transnational relationships that edge towards symbiosis, but which still work in hierarchical ways.

Notes

1 Acknowledgements: My thanks to Stephen Steigman, who assisted with editorial matters, Christine Dávila, who entrusted her time to me, which resulted in a wonderful interview, Giselle Anatol for her insights on the Trinidad and Tobago Film Festival, and Dolores Tierney for her posts on Emilio Fernandez films at international film festivals. Thanks as well to the editors of this volume for their insights and helpful feedback.
2 Colombian filmmakers Luis Ospina and Carlos Mayolo are credited for coining the term *porno-miseria* in a 1977 manifesto condemning European film festivals for seeking out desperate images of Third World misery and deprivation.

References

Bartlet, O. (2000) *African Cinema: Decolonizing the Gaze*. London: Zed Books.
Bhalotra, M. (2007) Hubert Bals Fund Manager, Personal Interview. January 28.
Branston, G. (2000) *Cinema and Cultural Modernity*. Buckingham, UK: Open University Press.
Burton, J. (1986) *Cinema and Social Change in Latin America: Conversations with Filmmakers*. Austin, TX: University of Texas Press.
Campos, M. (2012) "Reconfiguracion de flujos en el circuito internacional de festivals: el programa 'Cine en construccion'." *Secuencias: Revista de Historia del Cine*, 35: 84–102.
D'Lugo, M. (2013) "Pedro Almodóvar's Latin American 'Business'." In S. Dennison (ed.), *Contemporary Hispanic Cinema: Interrogating the Transnational in Spanish and Latin American Film*. Woodbridge, UK: Boydell & Brewer, pp. 113–136.
Dávila, C. (2015) Curaçao Rotterdam International Film Festival Programmer. Telephone Interview, December 22, 2015.
De Valck, M. (2007) *Film Festivals: From European Geopolitics to Global Cinephilia*. Amsterdam: Amsterdam University Press.
Diawara, M. (1994) "On Tracking World Cinema: African Cinema at Film Festivals." *Public Culture*, 6(2): 385–396.
Elsaesser, T. (2005) "Film Festival Networks: The New Topographies of Cinema in Europe." In D. Iordanova (ed.), *The Film Festival Reader*. St. Andrews, Scotland: St. Andrews Press, pp. 69–96.
Falicov, T.L. (2013) "'Cine en construcción'/'Films in Progress': How Spanish and Latin American Film-Makers Negotiate the Construction of a Globalized Art-House Aesthetic." *Transnational Cinemas*, 4(2): 253–271.
—— (2016) "'The Festival Film': Film Festival Funds as Cultural Intermediaries." In M. De Valck, B. Kredell, and S. Loist (eds.), *Film Festival Research: History, Methods, Practice*. New York: Routledge, pp. 209–229.
—— (2017) "Film Funding Opportunities for Latin American Filmmakers: A Case for Further North-South Collaboration in Training and Film Festival Initiatives." In M. Delgado, T. Hart, and R. Johnson (eds.), *Companion to Latin American Cinemas*. Jersey City, NJ: Wiley-Blackwell, pp. 85–98.
FIAPF (n.d.) "International Federation of Film Producers Associations." Avaialble at: www.fiapf.org/ (accessed December 10, 2016).
Galt, R. and Schoonover, K. (eds.) (2010) *Global Art Cinema: New Theories and Histories*. Oxford: Oxford University Press.
Gutiérrez, C.A. and Wagenberg, M. (2013) "Meeting Points: A Survey of Film Festivals in Latin America." *Transnational Cinemas*, 4(2): 295–305.

Halle, R. (2010) "Offering Tales They Want to Hear: Transnational European Film Funding as Neo-Colonialism." In R. Galt and K. Schoonover (eds.), *Global Art Cinema: New Theories and Histories*. Oxford: Oxford University Press, pp. 303–319.

Hanlon, D. (2010) "Traveling Theory, Shots and Players: Jorge Sanjines, New Latin American Cinema, and the European Art Film." In R. Galt and K. Schoonover (eds.), *Global Art Cinema: New Theories and Histories*. Oxford: Oxford University Press, pp. 351–366.

Hopewell, J. (2013) "Cannes Film Market Stages Showcase for Buzz Titles." *Variety*, May 20. Available at: http://variety.com/2013/film/features/cannes-film-market-stages-showcase-for-buzz-titles-1200483043 (accessed December 23, 2015).

—— (2014) "Buenos Aires Festival Opens Path for Local Talent." *Variety*, March 30. Available at: http://variety.com/2014/film/festivals/buenos-aires-festival-opens-path-for-local-talent-12011 49787/ (accessed October 16, 2014).

Hopewell, J. and Keslassy, E. (2013) "Cannes Reaches Out Via Market Circuit." *Variety*, May 17. Available at: http://variety.com/2013/biz/news/cannes-reaches-out-via-market-circuit-1200483230 (accessed October 15, 2015).

Hubert Bals Fund Annual Report (2014–2015) Available at: https://acceptatie.iffr.com/sites/default/files/content/hbf15_jaarverslag_lowres.pdf (accessed December 23, 2015).

Maza, G. (2013) "Porque sirven los festivales de cine? El efecto Rotterdam y la politica de la visibilidad." *La Fuga* (Chile). Available at: www.lafuga.cl/para-que-sirven-los-festivales-de-cine/304 (accessed December 6, 2015).

Mestman, M. (2002) "From Algiers to Buenos Aires: The Third World Organizing Committee." *New Cinemas: Journal of Contemporary Film*, 1(1): 40–53.

Ospina, L. and Mayolo, C. (1977) "Manifesto 'Qué es pornomiseria?'." Available at: www.luisospina.com/archivo/grupo-de-cali/agarrando-pueblo/ (accessed June 3, 2016).

Peirano, M.P. (2016) "Pursuing, Resembling, and Contesting the Global: The Emergence of Chilean Film Festivals." *New Review of Film and Television Studies*, 14(1): 112–131.

Rist, P. (2014) *Historical Dictionary of South American Cinema*. Lanham, MD: Rowman & Littlefield.

Ross, M. (2010) *South American Cinematic Culture: Policy, Production, Distribution and Exhibition*. Newcastle Upon Tyne, UK: Cambridge Scholars Publishing.

—— (2011) "The Film Festival as Producer: Latin American Film and Rotterdam's Hubert Bals Fund." *Screen*, 52(2): 261–267.

Ruoff, J. (ed.) (2012) *Coming Soon to a Festival Near You: Programming Film Festivals*. St. Andrews, Scotland: St. Andrews Film Studies.

Vallejo, A. (2014) "Festivales cinematográficos: En el punto de mira de la historiografía fílmica." *Secuencias, Revista de Historia del Cine*, 39(1): 13–42.

PART IV

Intermedialities

19

FILM AND PHOTOGRAPHY

An archeology

Andrea Cuarterolo

Editors' introduction

Photography, the medium with which the cinema is most ontologically linked, was the basis for many of the visual entertainments that most influenced the emergence of motion pictures, yet it is often overlooked in critical and historical studies. This chapter is based on the idea that a good part of the acceptance and understanding with which early Latin American cinema was received was the result of the reading competencies, representational codes, and thematic and aesthetic fashions that had been internalized by spectators during the preceding 50-year history of photography. It explores how photography and cinema were interconnected in the context of Latin America in the first decades of the twentieth century, leading the way for the exploration of film and photography intermedialities in the 1930s–1960s in Chapter 20 (Kelly and Flores).

Early cinema was intimately linked with the history of photography. Most of the medium's pioneers were professional or amateur photographers who moved between the two media. Classic film histories have traditionally approached the study of early cinema through a series of teleological foci premised upon the assumption that the early pioneering experiences were part of a primitive or preparatory period of a medium searching for artistic maturity. In its earliest days, however, the cinema did not have a definitive identity. On the contrary, it amalgamated with established visual practices, incorporating various illusionist techniques, artistic traditions, and social uses, to generate a new form of spectacle that was accessible to the public. Traditional histories of photography have minimized photography's spectacular potential, seldom if ever analyzing the medium in relation to the optical and magical spectacles that were a dominant feature of popular entertainment in the nineteenth century. The relation that "magical" photography establishes with the real world had the capacity to astound and marvel even incredulous spectators in the early years of the medium.

From the "photography of attractions" to the "cinema of attractions": the use of the image as a dispositif of the spectacular

Frank Kessler (2003) has suggested that the early years of the cinema can be divided into two periods, each characterized by a particular operation of the cinematographic apparatus. There is a first period of technological novelty, determined by the emergence of the cinema as a "spectacular dispositif" in which the medium's ability to reproduce movement and capture/restore objects was the principal attraction of the filmic spectacle. In the second period, the cinema becomes a "dispositif of the spectacular," insofar as the pro-filmic attractions (in the form of tricks, camera movements, editing, *mise en scène*, etc.) become the principal offering. In more than one sense, we can generate a similar periodization for photography. At first, realism and the iconic perfection of the photographic process were sufficient to attract potential consumers who visited photographic studios as if to view a magic show. Over time, however, it became necessary for what was represented to constitute an attraction of its own. Around 1860, the appearance of paper photography opened the photographic market to new social groups previously excluded, especially in Latin America. Going forward, photographers faced the challenge of attracting this renewed public with innovative techniques and ideas that would resuscitate the magical aura that photography had once enjoyed. Thus, we can talk about a "photography of attractions" that preceded and anticipated the "cinema of attractions" and, as we shall see, shared with it technical, aesthetic, thematic, and ideological characteristics. It appears that the first filmmakers simply rekindled the desire (already present in early photography) to astonish spectators through the intrinsic qualities of the image. In this section, we shall consider mid-nineteenth- to early twentieth-century photography in Latin America through the prism of this magical potential (later assimilated by the cinema) through four principal axes: *mise en scène*, attractions, the search for movement, and the emergence of narrative montage.

A new conception of reality—realism—characterized nineteenth-century bourgeois mentality. In the realm of aesthetics, this translated into a search for faithful representations and for visual objectivity to eliminate potential interpretations. The demand for fidelity, exactness, and legitimacy came to a head in the infant art of photography. Praising its iconic perfection and powerful verisimilitude, the Latin American bourgeoisie enthusiastically received the new technology. The potential for manipulation present in all mechanical images (so evident in today's digital era), however, was not absent from these early photographic experiences. This was even true in a genre such as portraiture, ostensibly founded upon a logic of mimesis and truth. Far from the instantaneity of contemporary photography, daguerreotype portraits demanded long exposure times that, around 1844, ranged from twenty seconds to 1.5 minutes, depending on light conditions. This meant that portraits were always posed. Through a careful *mise en scène*, which could include elements of high symbolic value, the photographic portrait transformed the subject into an object.

Costumes and sets were the two fundamental variables of the *mise en scène* of the studio portrait. In his essay "Ambientação ilusória," Brazilian scholar Carlos Lemos (1983) suggests that the photographic studios of the period provided a supply of costumes for customers who did not have the appropriate clothing to project the desired image of wealth and dignity. Similarly, photographic studios were set up like a bourgeois living room and had a great variety of objects—real and fake—that served to recreate the intimacy of an upper-class home. The use of painted backdrops was another key ingredient of the setup. Some authors (Appadurai 1997) have argued that portraitists used painted backdrops to increase the artistic legitimacy of photography by aligning it with bourgeois pictorial traditions. Others such as James Wyman (1997) affirm that painted backdrops had already appeared in other nineteenth-century fashionable entertainments such as panoramas and dioramas. Nevertheless, studio photographers embraced this decorative element in the earliest years of the daguerreotype. This scenic arrangement would also be adopted by the first fiction films, a logical consequence of the fact that throughout Latin America the cinema emerged tightly linked to these same photographic studios, rather than merely to theatrical traditions (as traditional historical accounts of Latin American film have suggested).

Another fundamental element of the studio portraiture was the pose. Most generally, the pose could be considered the subject's response to the implicit presence of an observer. Imitating a certain mental image or assuming an imaginary personality and projecting it through bodily and gestural moves, the portrait becomes, for a moment, a frozen image. Fulya Ertem (2006) suggests that there is a strong connection between photography and theater in these early images that transforms the pose into a kind of mimicry. Thus, the model's posture had to be carefully planned and rehearsed according to the expectations of subject and photographer. Connected to the pose, the look to the camera is another integral component of the portrait through which to trace points of convergence with early cinema. Looking at the camera is necessary and utterly conventional in studio photography. However, as Tom Gunning (2006: 57) explains, in the cinema of attractions this action invoked the attention of the spectator, even if it precluded any narrative illusions. Looking at the camera only became taboo in classical cinema, since it suggested a potential rupture of the fictional universe established by the film.

Figure 19.1   Painted backdrops with similar motifs. Right: *Carte de visite*, taken by G. Monegal, Buenos Aires, 1889. Left: Photogram of *Justicia criolla* (Enrique Lepage & Co, c.1907–1911). From the author's collection.

The strong influence of photography in early cinema is especially evident in the use of different types of spectacular techniques that the cinema of attractions exploited later. Important among these is the tinting of images. As would later be the case in the cinema, color functioned not only as a way to make the representation more realistic, but also as a novel and effective spectacular resource to capture the spectator's attention.

Stereoscopy was another technology that approximated photography to spectacle. As a bidimensional representation of a tridimensional subject, object, or space, stereoscopy attempted to recover that lost dimension. Like other visual spectacles of the period (such as panoramas and magic lantern views), stereoscopy also transmitted some of the perceptual sense of traveling, moving the average spectator to remote places at a time when tourism was still a costly elite proposition. Shortly thereafter, however, the genres became highly diversified. As Annette Michelson suggests:

> The number of films produced during the first fifteen years of the industry was infinitesimal compared to the vast numbers of stereographs and *cartes des visites* that were produced during the same period. However, the similarity of the important genres that were depicted in the two media is striking, and offers compelling evidence that an imitative relationship existed for some time between the early film producers and the commercial photography industry.
>
> (Michelson 1989: 39)

Jonathan Crary argues that stereoscopy submerged the spectator in a new corporal immediacy of sensations and "the body that had been a neutral or invisible term in vision was now the thickness from which knowledge of the observer was obtained" (Crary 1992: 150). These techniques demanded an active physical response from the spectator, but such responses became unacceptable with the consolidation of the "cinema of narrative integration," which was intended for a more passive spectator who would not question the artifice of image construction. The interactive contact established by stereoscopy would be, however, an integral element of the cinema of attractions.

The multiple efforts to give the image color and three-dimensionality were designed to astound the spectator by improving the mimetic abilities of the medium. Many of the spectacular resources adopted by photography in this period, however, were based upon manipulations and concrete interventions upon the image, which, far from proposing a faithful representation of reality, presaged the illusionist processes and techniques later taken up by the cinema. Close-ups were infrequent in the earliest days of photography. In addition to the technological limitations of the apparatus, there was a desire to align the new medium to the legitimate arts such as painting, in which fragmentations and magnifications of the body were still unthinkable. "Vignetting," which became very popular beginning in the 1860s, could be considered the ideological precursor of the close-up. This process made it possible to hide the background and isolate the face so that it could be the focal point of the portrait. The silent cinemas also exploited vignettes. Iris-in and iris-out shots were among the most popular variants. As with photographic vignettes, iris shots were the principal precedent of the cinematographic close-up, since they isolated or highlighted characters or objects. As Gunning suggests (Gunning 2006: 58), the cinema of attractions did not use the close-up for narrative punctuation (as would later cinemas), but rather for its spectacular and exhibitionist potential. In early films, the technique was an attraction in and of itself, a trick to incite the spectator's attention and provoke their visual pleasure.

Figure 19.2 Anonymous photograph featuring vignettes in the shape of binoculars. Buenos Aires, c.1930. From the author's collection.

Despite their representational perfection, early photographic processes were temporally limited. The required long exposure times meant that any moving object would disappear or appear blurry on the plate. Photographers also sought out ways to incorporate time and movement to the image as part of their search for additional techniques to add spectacular effects. Multiple and double exposures and multiphotography were among the most popular of these techniques in Latin America and shared the desire to communicate more complex messages than the traditional studio portrait. In these photographs, the individual immortalized by studio portraiture via stoic poses and theatrical *mise en scène* was freed from the rigid limits of representation and symbolically entered the world of the spectator. The cinematic medium quickly understood the power of these metaphors, and not only appropriated them, but also entered into a dialogue with this rich visual legacy.

It was, however, the idea of the series—popularized by photography towards the end of the nineteenth century—that had the greatest impact on the emergence of the cinema. As André Gaudreault argues, "cinematography is, without a doubt, a phenomenon that is essentially serial [and] the idea of the series is at the very heart of the decidedly photo-grammatical problematic of the process of filming" (Gaudreault 2002: 34). In the context of photography, the idea of the series and its ability to transmit the incessant flow of time emerged early, in the pioneer years of the daguerreotype. The time implicit in these early images is not visible in any one photograph; rather, it is deduced from the differences among them. The idea of the series thus initiates a new type of temporality inscribed in the spectatorial gaze:

As a device that imposes a visual trajectory that is linear and continuous, like reading, the sequence confers upon the observer an important role [in meaning-production] [. . .] It is he [the observer] who visually and mentally completes the lacunae that separate each image.

(Chik 2011:65)

Figure 19.3   Left: Multiple exposure of Don Pedro II, the Brazilian Emperor. Carneiro & Gaspar Studio, Rio de Janeiro, c.1867. From the author's collection. Right: Multiphotograph of Luvio V. Mantilla, taken by Alejandro Whitcomb, Buenos Aires, c.1898. Carlos Vertanessian Collection.

Figure 19.4   Left: The writer José Hernández. Medallion-shaped daguerreotype. Unknown author. Parana, c.1859. José Hernández Historical Museum. Right: Brazilian Empress Teresa Cristina. Mosaic created from four *cartes de visite* of the Studio Carneiro & Gaspar. Rio de Janeiro, c.1870. From the author's collection.

Thus, the figurative movement that is implicit in all these images refers to the external but real movement of the spectator's gaze.

Perhaps the first use of the series as narrative occurred mid-nineteenth century with the emergence of the photographic album and the rise of photography collecting. The popularity of the photographic series and the standardization of its methods of production, distribution, and sales were incentive for the emergence of the cinema, which, in Latin America, appeared against the backdrop of this photographic market.

The photographic series that had the closest relationship with early cinema, however, were undoubtedly the theatrical fictions. These photographic stories were very popular in the last two decades of the nineteenth century and evidence tight thematic, aesthetic, and especially narrative links to the first fictional films. Pioneer filmmakers exploited the visual styles and themes popularized by these photographic series, and above all learned narrative and editing strategies that were fundamental to the development of the fiction film.

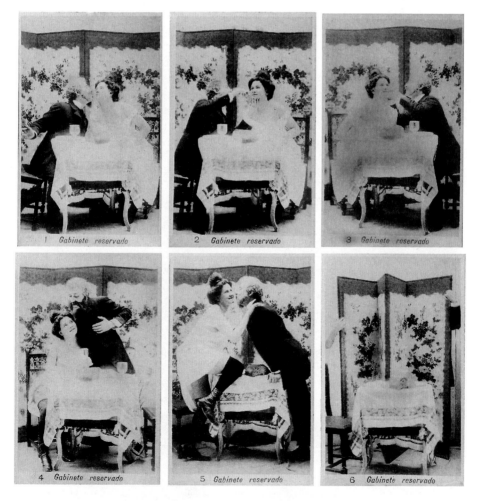

Figure 19.5 *Gabinete reservado.* Six-image theatricalized series. Unknown author. Buenos Aires, c.1898. Abel Alexander Collection.

Realistic spectacles and spectacular realities: the influence of photography in nonfiction film

The impact of photography on subsequent nonfiction cinema is quite evident on the various journalistic genres—social, political, sports, entertainment. As Mónica Dall'Asta mentions:

> [t]he vast and, upon first glance chaotic, nature of early actualities could easily fit in with the sections of an imaginary newspaper, a *visual newspaper* that, instead of describing the facts, cites them directly in selected spatio-temporal sections extracted from a basic continuum.
>
> (*Dall'Asta 1998: 249*)

In fact, images of public figures, technological or scientific novelties, national celebrations, visiting personages, and natural disasters captured in the first newsreels already had market appeal in illustrated magazines. The cinema took advantage of this interest to attract these consumers to the new business of moving images.

If studio photographers played a fundamental role in the configuration of the cinema of attractions, journalistic and documentary photographers played an equally crucial role in the emergence and consolidation of nonfiction film. It is possible to trace in early twentieth-century Latin America a parallel history between the illustrated press and film newsreels, and actualities that repeat images, points of view, aesthetic choices, themes, and even protagonists. In Argentina, photographer Domingo Mauricio Filippini, a constant collaborator of *Caras y Caretas* (the most emblematic Argentine illustrated magazine of the period), was the creator of "Actualidades Venus Film," which supplied film news about the Argentine provinces to important newsreels produced in Buenos Aires such as *Film Revista Valle*, *Sucesos Argentinos*, and the *Noticiero Panamericano*. Arturo Alexander was another Argentine film pioneer who worked both in film and photography. A descendent of the daguerreotypist Adolfo Alexander, he worked as the photo correspondent for *Caras y Caretas* and also filmed actualities (such as those produced during the centennial of the May Revolution) and early documentaries such as *Expedición Cinematográfica A. Alexander* (*Cinematographic Expedition A. Alexander*), a travelogue filmed during an expedition to Paraguay and Bolivia in 1924.

Ángel Salvador Adami, who worked for years as the photo correspondent in Montevideo for *Caras y Caretas*, is also the author of one of the first Uruguayan nonfiction films, *La Revolución Oriental* (*The Western Revolution*, 1904) about the last and bloodiest Uruguayan civil war and the book *Sangre de hermanos* (*Blood of Brothers*), illustrated with photographs shot during the conflict.

In Mexico, the links between the illustrated press and the first documentary films were especially significant. With the onset of the Mexican Revolution, the appearance of photo-reporters and filmmakers was fundamental to disseminating news of events and the legitimacy of the revolutionary leaders. One of the most notable was Jesús H. Abitia, who was responsible for an extensive filmic and photographic archive that included everything from documentary footage to portraits and postcards. A self-recognized propagandist for the constitutionalist faction headed by Venustiano Carranza and Alvaro Obregón, Abitia followed them closely and produced a complete visual dossier for their supporters and the press.

In the early twentieth century, instantaneity transformed the photojournalist into a hero of modernity, able to overcome any obstacle in order to obtain images, a privileged and ubiquitous witness of current events. The expectations generated by the aura of instantaneity, however, were difficult to satisfy. Cameras were not yet sufficiently fast and photographers logically could not always be in the right place at the right time. Thus, photojournalists and filmmakers had to resort to multiple strategies to sustain the myth of instantaneity. In 1909, the photographer Agustín Casasola recorded an interview that took place in Ciudad Juarez between U.S. President William Howard Taft and Mexican President Porfirio Díaz. His images remain fascinating today because of their air of immediacy and his apparent skill at capturing the most noteworthy moments of the event. As Daniel Escorza Rodríguez (2011) suggests, however, some of the most emblematic images were really stills from footage produced by the several camera operators also present at the event. The logo for the Casasola agency stated, "I have or will take the photo you need," a phrase that, beyond its advertising value, suggests the possibility of recurring to these tricks to maintain the illusion of an instantaneity that was more yearned for than real.

Another frequent strategy to simulate instantaneity was the reconstruction of current events in which the photographers fabricated *mise en scène* of the incident. They would often use the same locales and protagonists, or else actors or even their own colleagues to recreate the event. Images of this type were very common in the news of catastrophes or accidents, and especially in police reports, a genre that, as Lila Caimari explains, "was created out of the juncture between the chronicle of the proven and that of the imagined" (Caimari 2009: 153). These types of manipulations that constantly erased the limits between entertainment and information found their perfect expression in the so-called *fait divers*. The illustrated press periodically published all sorts of news under this rubric: from traffic accidents, crimes of passion, suicides, armed robberies, and kidnappings, to comic anecdotes, burlesque adventures, and harsh stories of cannibalism and human freaks. As Vanessa Schwartz suggests, "The *fait divers* [. . .] implied that the everyday might be transformed into shocking and sensational and ordinary people lifted from the anonymity of urban life and into the realm of spectacle" (Schwartz 1998: 36).

Illustrated magazines did not use photography until the late nineteenth century; however, the new medium became a metaphor for what the press aspired to achieve in terms of realism and impact. Photographic reconstructions had their filmic equivalents in the so-called fake actualities or reconstructed newsreels. Mónica Dall'Asta includes in this genre those films "that reconstruct, instead of filming them live, events that are particularly sensational and of a catastrophic nature" and are motivated by the desire to satisfy the growing demand of audiences for views of events "that were logically impossible to capture *in situ*" (Dall'Asta 1998: 251). Thus, for example, in 1901, the Argentine ship Guardia Nacional rescued the carpenter Federico Newmann and his 8-year-old son from Las Malvinas in the high seas. The Casa Lepage recognized the commercial potential of this rescue and took advantage of the Newmanns' presence in Buenos Aires to reconstruct their dramatic rescue to be filmed by Eugenio Py, and entitled *Salvamento de los náufragos Newmann por el transporte Guardia Nacional* (*The Rescue of the Newmann Castaways by the Ship Guardia Nacional*, 1901). The event was also covered by the magazine *Caras y Caretas* using photographic reconstructions. The existence of a filmic document, two photos that reconstruct the event, and the fact that it is highly unlikely that the shipwrecked Newmanns would have re-enacted their odyssey more than once, suggest that the reconstruction of the dramatic rescue was a joint effort by the media, among which were at least the Casa Lepage and *Caras y Caretas*.

Aurelio de los Reyes argues that "while cameramen in France, the U.S, and England opted to reconstruct current events, in Mexico they never ceased to capture real scenes [. . .] because it was probably easier and less expensive to film real events than reconstructions"

EL CUTTER NÁUFRAGO Y SUS TRIPULANTES TAL COMO LOS ENCONTRÓ EL TRANSPORT «GUARDIA NACIONAL».

Figure 19.6 "El *cutter* náufrago y sus tripulantes tal como los encontró el transporte 'Guardia Nacional'." Reconstructed photograph illustrating the article "Los náufragos de Malvinas y los del 'Munster-Castle'," *Caras y Caretas*, 146, July 20, 1901. From the author's collection.

(de los Reyes 1996: 92). However, as Escorza Rodrígues suggests, during the Revolution, photographers and camera operators frequently sought recourse in theatricalizations to represent the armed conflicts. Upon analyzing the still and moving images of the Decena Trágica (February 1913), the author concludes that they were not produced in real time. One can see a certain *mise en scène* in these images: in the photographs, forced theatrical poses, civilian clothes worn by the soldiers, and unilateral perspectives that only show the shooters, and not what they are shooting at; in the films, the protagonists' lack of concentration and their constant looks at the camera in search of approval (Rodríguez Escorza 2011).

This synthesis between authentic footage and construction also appeared in fiction films, as, for example, the case of the Mexican film *El automóvil gris* (*The Gray Automobile*, 1919), directed by Enrique Rosas, who had begun his career working on actualities and newsreels. Based on a real story sensationalized by the illustrated press, the film narrates the series of robberies committed by a band of marauders in the houses of prominent families in the capital in 1914–1915. The first part of the film told the story of the robberies in a fictional tone, while the second focused on the police investigation and the capture of the criminals, and included real footage of the execution of six of the thieves, which had been shot by

Rosas for his compilation film *Documentación histórica nacional 1915–1916* (*National Historic Documentation*, 1916). The need to harmonize the documentary parts with the fictional led the director to include other factual material in the story. Thus filming took place in the locations where the events occurred, journalist Miguel Necoechea collaborated on the script, and the police chief responsible for capturing the criminals, Juan Manuel Cabrera, provided documentation and acted as himself in the film.

The work of Colombian photographer Lino is quite similar in spirit. His book, *El diez de febrero* (*The Tenth of February*, 1906) was a graphic reportage—according to Eduardo Serrano, "the most complete produced in Colombia to that date" (Serrano 1983: 180)— that combined real images and reconstructed photographs to tell the story of a failed assassination attempt against President Rafael Reyes on February 10, 1906. The 43 photographs in the book are ordered chronologically, in the style of a photonovel, and illustrate the events and its consequences, step by step, from the moments before the attempt to the escape of the criminals, their capture, and finally their execution, which Lara was able to capture *in situ*. Almost 10 years after this photographic work, another political assassination led to another reconstruction, this time a fake documentary. Filmed by the Colombian film pioneers Vincenzo and Francesco Di Domenico, *El drama del quince de octubre* (*The Drama of October 15th*, 1915) is based on the assassination of the general, politician, and then national senator Rafael Uribe Uribe by a group of workers who had lost their jobs at the Ministerio de Obras Públicas (Public Works Ministry). With a narration that mixes documentary footage with reconstructed scenes, the film—considered the first Colombian feature-length film—recounts the details of the event, beginning with the surgery to try to save the politician's life and ending with the funeral and the commemorative acts upon the first anniversary of his death. The film included at least two scenes recreated by the Di Domenicos: the surgery and a meeting with the assassins in prison. The directors actually hired the criminals themselves to participate in the film. In his memoirs, Francesco Di Domenico wrote, "we filmed the prisoners, hiding in all the corners of the Panopticon so that we could capture them in spontaneous and not in forced poses" (cited by El'Gazi 1999). As Lila Caimari (2009) notes, the protagonists of this type of chronicle had begun to become famous in an industry that was just learning how to build fame. The celebrity of delinquents went hand in hand with the star system, sharing formal strategies—close-ups, for example—and publicity stunts.

Early cinema was intertextually voracious. Its emergence as a popular entertainment in the early twentieth century was preceded and later accompanied by the rapid growth of print culture. As we have seen, these publications had a clear thematic and aesthetic influence on actualities and early documentary cinema. The most notable coincidence between the two media, however, was their visual representation of reality as spectacle. If photographic realism allowed for the blurring of the world and its representation, then all of the world could become spectacle. Upon the appropriation of this rich visual legacy and annexing new levels of illusionism, the cinema was one of the last but most popular additions to a mass culture in which spectacles were increasingly real and reality was becoming spectacle.

A peripheral avant-garde: film and photography in the 1930s

Avant-garde movements began to impact Latin American cinema in the late 1920s and early 1930s, but unfortunately the introduction of sound and the subsequent market-driven accelerated industrialization of the medium interrupted these formal experimentations.

Nevertheless, despite the fact that there were few in number, these experimental films should be reconsidered in a broader regional context. The work of filmmakers such as Mario Peixoto (*Limite*, 1930), Humberto Mauro (*Ganga Bruta*, 1933), Rodolfo Rex Lustig and Adalberto Kemeny (*São Paulo, A Sinfonia da Metropole* [*São Paulo, Symphony of a Metropolis*], 1929) in Brazil; Emilio Amero (*777*, 1929), Sergei Eisenstein, (*¡Que viva México!*, c.1931), Paul Strand (*Redes* [*Nets*], 1934), and Manuel Álvarez Bravo (*Disparos en el Istmo* [*Shots in the Isthmus*], 1935) in Mexico; or Horacio Coppola (*Así nació el obelisco* [*Thus the Obelisk Was Born*], 1936) in Argentina exemplify a modernization of film language, which, albeit brief, set the stage for subsequent vanguard movements in the 1960s.

The main exponents of this Latin American peripheral avant-garde shared some common characteristics. First, as in the earliest years of the medium, most of these filmmakers also worked in photography. In fact, we can trace a certain parallelism between modernity in the visual arts—especially painting and photography—and in cinema in this unique moment. Second, all these avant-garde filmmakers were influenced by European (and, to a lesser degree, American) trends, which is not surprising given that most avant-garde movements that renewed photographic and filmic language emerged there. Finally, these filmmakers also participated in the creation and development of the first Latin American cine clubs. These new sites, which emerged in the late 1920s and early 1930s, were themselves avant-garde, legitimizing films outside the commercial circuit and providing the cinema with an autonomous space in the larger cultural sphere.

In Argentina, the most emblematic member of the filmic and photographic avant-garde was Horacio Coppola. The son of a prominent family, Coppola took a "grand tour" of Europe during which he sat in on courses at the Bauhaus Department of Photography, at that time directed by Walter Peterhans. At the Bauhaus, he befriended avant-garde photographers such as Ellen Auerbach and his future wife, Grete Stern. Although Coppola is most celebrated for his photography, his first contact with the avant-garde was through the cinema (Coppola 1994: 9). At an early age, he participated in the board of the Cine Club de Buenos Aires, a pioneering institution that gathered together artists and intellectuals interested in the cinema. The Cine Club de Buenos Aires closed in 1931, when its founders decided that it was more important to focus on their own filmmaking. Coppola fulfilled this objective from 1933, when he traveled to Europe and shot several documentary and experimental films. He was very influenced by the *Neues Sehen* (*New Vision*) movement in Germany, which considered photography an autonomous medium of aesthetic expression and favored experimentation to make the quotidian strange. His most important film is probably *Así nació el obelisco*, his first shot in Argentina. In sync with his photographic work of this period, the film produces a Buenos Aires in which modernity and tradition coexist peacefully.

More than a register of a real city, Coppola's film produces an urban avant-garde imaginary for a Buenos Aires in which modernity was still more of a promise than a reality. Thus, the film perfectly condenses the synthesis between classicism, criollismo, and modernity that are the dominant trait of his urban photographs.

Although Mario Peixoto was not a photographer (but rather a filmmaker and a writer), his work is also marked by photography. Like Coppola, Peixoto came from a wealthy family in the coffee business and studied abroad, in England. After returning to Brazil in 1927, his friendship with the writer Octávio de Faria led him to the Chaplin Club, the first Brazilian cine club. This group undertook a broad debate about film language in Brazil that was chronicled in the pages of the magazine *O Fan*, published until 1930. Peixoto's growing interest in the cinema led him back to Europe in 1929. According to his memoirs, while walking around Paris he ran into a photo by André Kertész on the cover of the

Figure 19.7   Still from *Así nació el obelisco* (Horacio Coppola, 1936). The city, horizontally expansive like the *pampas*, loses itself in the immense sky and mythic Río de la Plata. The film presents a romantic vision of technology in sync with the environment.

magazine *Vu* (Pereira de Mello 2007) a weekly that featured collaborations by avant-garde photographers such as Germaine Krull and Man Ray. This photograph served as the inspiration for his film *Limite* (1930), and he wrote an outline of the script that very same night. The image in *Vu*—showing a mysterious female face and, in the foreground, masculine hands bound by handcuffs—had a huge impact on Peixoto, who recreated it for the beginning of his film with the help of the well-known cinematographer Edgar Brasil. Evoking the spirit of Kertész's work, the film combines a poetic narration with a unique film syntax to tell the story of a man and two women who are caught in a small boat adrift in the sea and face imminent death.

Figure 19.8   Left: André Kertész's photo on the cover of the French magazine *Vu*, no. 74. Right: Still from *Limite* (Mario Peixoto, 1930).

Coppola and Peixoto's works are isolated examples in the history of the cinema in their countries (and in the history of Latin American cinema in general). In contrast, in Mexico, the exchanges between photography and a cinematic avant-garde were more sustained, partly thanks to the key role played by various photographers and cinematographers in the 1930s. These artists were crucial agents of the cultural expansion that took place after the Revolution, a period that was also notable for the modernization of Mexican photography.

Many filmmakers traveled to study and/or to work in the US or Europe and interacted with the avant-gardes. This was the case for Emilio Amero, one of the key precursors of experimental cinema and photography in Mexico. He was an assistant to muralists José Clemente Orozco and Carlos Mérida, and in the mid-1920s traveled to Havana and later to New York, where he worked as an illustrator for various magazines and interned with the well-known lithographer George Miller. In 1931, back in Mexico, Amero participated in the creation of the first local cine club and became very interested in filmmaking. Although little of his work has been preserved, Amero is considered one of the most radical photographers and filmmakers of the period. He was successful in producing photograms—a technique made famous by Man Ray that entailed producing images without a camera—and was the first in the country to make abstract films (Oles 2002: 93).

The encounter between Mexican photography and cinema and the avant-garde movements was, however, more profound because of the visits of several foreign artists that were entranced by the mystical aura of post-revolutionary culture. The most important of these visitors was undoubtedly Sergei Eisenstein, who arrived in Mexico in 1930 with the project of shooting a film he would call ¡Que viva México! Although the film was never fully realized, Eisenstein's work had a profound impact on the local cinematic imaginary. As Julia Tuñon argues:

> The director synthesized ideas and experiences of Mexican culture and translated them filmically, creating a paradigmatic model of the nation and of *mexicanidad* that became a model for others. [. . .] Upon his arrival in Mexico, Eisenstein interacted with intellectuals and shared the concerns of this social group, but at the same time he translated them in terms of film language and his figurations became a model: "No one escapes the influence of Eisenstein", said Carlos Monsiváis.
> (Tuñon 2003: 23, 37)

One of the cinematographers that benefited from Eisenstein's presence in Mexico was Agustín Jiménez. Originally a still photographer, in the mid-1930s he switched to cinematography. Some historians have suggested (Lozano 2002: 42) that this change was influenced by his work on ¡Que viva México! and the close relationship he established with Eisenstein. In the 1930s, Jiménez worked with a number of important directors, but his most interesting work was for Juan Bustillo Oro (*Dos monjes* [*Two Monks*], 1934; *El misterio del rostro pálido* [*The Mystery of the Pale Face*], 1935; *Huapango*, 1938) and Adolfo Best Maugard (*La mancha de sangre* [*The Bloodstain*], 1937). Both directors worked in the commercial industry, but these early films had a marked expressionist edge. Like some of his colleagues such as Gabriel Figueroa and Alex Phillips, Jiménez assimilated the style of the great expressionist German cinematographers such as Karl Freund and Fritz Arno Wagner, and incorporated it into his cinematography at a time when it was already out of fashion in Europe. Gabriel Figueroa once said, "all the photographers start from 1920's German Expressionism" (cited in Rodríguez 2008: 238), and in fact the cinematographers of this period invested in that aesthetic and applied it to a particular nationalist iconography that peaked in the 1930s and 1940s and strongly impacted audiences.

Edward Weston and Tina Modotti also spent time in Mexico. Their visit was crucial for the diffusion of new avant-garde practices in Mexican art. Modotti and Weston were part of the New Objectivity movement (a sharply focused documentary approach to photography) that emerged in the US in the 1920s as a response against the pictorialism that had previously been prevalent. Linked to the ideas of *Neues Sehen*, New Objectivity conceived of photography as an autonomous aesthetic practice with its own discursive elements. This approach strongly influenced a number of local photographers, among them Manuel Alvarez Bravo, who also worked in the cinema in the 1930s. An early member of the executive committee of the Cine Club Mexicano, Alvarez Bravo and his wife, Lola Alvarez Bravo (also a photographer), had a close relationship with Eisenstein during his Mexican sojourn. Some historians claim (De la Vega Alfaro 2002: 83) that Alvarez Bravo even participated in the shooting of ¡*Que viva México!* as Edward Tissé's assistant. In fact, Alvarez Bravo used Tissé's camera to shoot his first film, *Disparos en el istmo*. Although the film is now lost, it was described as very experimental:

> We can infer that . . . it must have been an avant-garde film that synthesized, with a language based on camera movement and movements into the frame, a contradictory vision—as picturesque as tragic—of the beliefs about life, work, and death of the inhabitants of the Oaxacan isthmus. Certainly some takes had stylistic antecedents in the photographs taken in the region by Tina Modotti and Alvarez Bravo himself as well as in the material that Eisenstein and Tissé filmed for what would have been the Zandunga episode of ¡*Que viva México!*
>
> (De la Vega Alfaro 2002: 88)

As we have seen, in the nineteenth and early twentieth centuries, photography introduced a series of formal, thematic, and ideological elements that the cinema later adopted and reformulated. In the late 1920s and early 1930s, however, it is no longer possible to speak of unilateral influences. If, as Jan Christopher Horak has argued, "the establishment of a modernist, avant-garde movement in cinema [. . .] is unthinkable without the participation of photographers" (Horak 1997: 5), the work of these photographers is equally inseparable from the influence of the cinematic avant-gardes between the wars. Although marked by their own peculiarities, the periods with which we began and end this essay are two sides of the same coin in which these media repeatedly cross-fertilize and converge.

References

Appadurai, A. (1997) "The Colonial Backdrop." *Afterimage*, 24(5): 4–7.

Caimari, L. (2009) *La ciudad y el crimen. Delito y vida cotidiana en Buenos Aires, 1880–1940*. Buenos Aires: Editorial Sudamericana.

Chik, C. (2011) *L' image paradoxale. Fixité et mouvement*. Villeneuve d'Ascq: Presses Universitaires du Septentrion.

Coppola, H. (1994) *Imagema. Antología Fotográfica 1927–1994*. Buenos Aires: Fondo Nacional de las Artes.

Crary, J. (1992) *Techniques of the Observer: Vision and Modernity in the Nineteenth Century*. Cambridge, MA: MIT Press.

El'Gazi, L. (1999) "El drama del 15 de octubre." *Revista Credencial Historia*, 112. Available at: www.banrepcultural.org/blaavirtual/revistas/credencial/abril1999/11215oct.htm (accessed September 16, 2016).

Dall'Asta, M. (1998) "Los primeros modelos temáticos del cine." In J. Talens, Jenaro, and S. Zunzunegui (eds.), *Historia General del Cine*, vol. I. Madrid: Cátedra, pp. 241–285.

De la Vega Alfaro, E. (2002) "Álvarez Bravo, cinefotógrafo." *Luna Córnea*, 24: 80–109.

de los Reyes, A. (1996) *Cine y sociedad en México 1896–1930*. Mexico City: UNAM.

Ertem, F. (2006) "The Pose in Early Portrait Photography: Questioning Attempts to Appropriate the Past." *Image & Narrative*, 14. Available at: www.imageandnarrative.be/inarchive/painting/fulya. htm (accessed October 3, 2012).

Escorza Rodríguez, D. (2011) "La imagen móvil y fija, historias paralelas. Salvador Toscano y la Agencia Casasola en el registro de temprano de la revolución mexicana, 1910–1914." *Revista Cine Documental*, 3. Available at: http://revista.cinedocumental.com.ar/3/articulos_03.html (accessed September 11, 2016).

Gaudreault, A. (2002) "Du simple au multiple: le cinéma comme série de series." *Cinémas*, 13(1–2): 33–47.

Gunning, T. (2006) "The Cinema of Attractions: Early Film, Its Spectator and the Avant-Garde." In T. Elsaesser and A. Barker (eds.), *Early Cinema: Space-Frame-Narrative*. London: British Film Institute, pp. 56–67.

Horak, J.C. (1997) *Making Images Move: Photographers and Avant-Garde Cinema*. Washington, DC: Smithsonian Institution Press.

Kessler, F. (2003) "La cinématographie comme dispositif (du) spectaculaire." *Cinemas*, 14(1): 21–34.

Lemos, C. (1983) "Ambientação ilusória." In C.E.M. de Moura (ed.), *Retratos quase inocentes*. San Pablo: Nobel, pp. 47–113.

Lozano, E. (2002) "Agustín Jiménez." *Luna Córnea*, 24: 42–73.

Michelson, A. (1989) *The Art of Moving Shadows*. Washington, DC: National Gallery of Art.

Oles, J. (2002) "El cine ausente de Emilio Amero." *Luna Córnea*, 24: 92–97.

Pereira de Mello, S. (2007) "Limite: angústia." *Alceu*, 8(15): 38–47.

Rodríguez, J.A. (2008) "Modernas sombras fugitivas. Las construcciones visuales de Gabriel Figueroa." *Luna Córnea*, 32: 233–289.

Schwartz, V. (1998) *Spectacular Realities: Early Mass Culture in Fin-de-Siècle Paris*. Los Angeles, CA: University of California Press.

Serrano, E. (1983) *Historia de la fotografía en Colombia*. Bogotá: Museo de Arte Moderno de Bogotá.

Tuñon, J. (2003) "Sergei Eisenstein en México: recuento de una experiencia." *Revista de la Dirección de Estudios Históricos del INAH*, 55: 23–40.

Wyman, J. (1997) "Introduction: From the Background to the Foreground. The Photo Backdrop and Cultural Expression." *Afterimage*, 24(5): 2.

Further reading

Bergot, S. (2013) "Cine y fotografía en la industria cinematográfica en Chile, 1900–1930." In M. Villarroel (ed.), *Enfoques al cine chileno en dos siglos*. Santiago: LOM Ediciones, pp. 79–86.

Cuarterolo, A. (2013) *De la foto al fotograma. Relaciones entre cine y fotografía en la Argentina 1840–1933*. Montevideo: CdF Ediciones.

Torello, G. (2016) "El discreto encanto de la (in)movilidad. La programación cinematográfica montevideana en las primeras décadas del siglo XX." In M. Villarroel (ed.), *Memorias y representaciones en el cine chileno y latinoamericano*. Santiago: LOM Ediciones, pp. 231–240.

Trusz, A.D. (2010) *Entre lanternas mágicas e cinematógrafos: as origens do espetáculo cinematográfico em Porto Alegre. 1861–1908*. São Paulo: Terceiro Nome/Ecofalante.

20

PROBLEMATIZING FILM AND PHOTOGRAPHY

Alejandro Kelly Hopfenblatt and Silvana Flores

Editors' introduction

Continuing the analysis of the complex intermedial relationships between film and photography begun by Cuarterlo in Chapter 19, this chapter tackles two moments in Latin American film history that have rarely been discussed in these terms: the years of studio production in Argentina, Mexico, and Brazil, and the political cinema of the 1960s and 1970s. In the first section, Kelly Hopfenblatt problematizes our standard director-driven understanding of the studio years by bringing to the fore the significant relationships between studio cinematographers and still photographers. Characterizing these relationships as marked by tensions, negations, and hybridizations, he convincingly traces the evolution of particular cinematic styles in Latin American film industries as a product of intermedial engagements. In particular, his acute analysis of the role of still star photographers and the creation of particular star images in the studio system opens up a very productive line of inquiry that merits further investigation and establishes another axis through which to approach film–audience relationships.

Focused on political filmmaking in the latter decades, Silvana Flores also problematizes how we understand this period: rather than analyze these films based on their political messages and/or effectivity, Flores carefully traces how the insertion of still photographs serves to both reinforce and unsettle the cinematic image in movement. Still photography may stop time, but its testimonial presence in these cinemas of political intervention also endow it with a kind of movement, as in the famous still of the dead Che Guevara in *La hora de los hornos* (*The Hour of the Furnaces*, 1968).

The interconnections between Latin American cinema and photography from the sound period through the 1970s reflect tensions between two allied visual media, the range of negotiations of intermedial formats, and the dynamics of assimilation/hybridization that characterized the relations. This chapter looks at exemplary sites and various case studies that dramatically underscore the creative synergies that these tensions foment. The examples are drawn from commercial fictional cinema in the early decades and the increasingly more political emergence of photographic documentaries aligned with popular social movements in the latter decades.

Tension and hybridization between film and photography in classic Latin American cinema

ALEJANDRO KELLY HOPFENBLATT

The principal Latin American film industries that emerged in the classic period (1930–1950s)—Argentina, Brazil, and Mexico—were marked by the tension between the desire to establish a national visual identity and the struggle to incorporate and transform the style and forms of Hollywood and European cinemas. The interconnections between Latin American cinema and photography in this period were a significant axis across which these tensions were worked through. This section elaborates upon three "sites" that illustrate the dynamics of hybridization and negotiation: the presence of foreign cinematographers in the early sound period and beyond, the relationships among national traditions, visual style and genres, and the function of stills and portrait photography in the consolidation of the star system and industrial production.

The need to develop cinematographic expertise led to the presence of many foreigners in these industries. European migrants and U.S. technicians hired for technical collaboration and training contributed with their advanced knowledge of filmic technique. Their presence was not foundational, but must be understood in the context of prior visual practices in these countries, ranging from the experiences of the Estudios Valle in Argentina, Edgar Brazil's experimentation in Brazil, and, in Mexico, revolutionary photography and Sergei Eisenstein's visit. This combination and the predilection for certain narrative genres led to the creation of national cinematographic traditions that alternated between aesthetic innovations and industrial standardization. Simultaneously, studio photography played a fundamental role in the consolidation of these national industries because of its role in the development of local star systems and the film publicity apparatus. Two elements were fundamental: portraits of stars and film stills. Beginning with the work of great portraitists such as Annemarie Heinrich and Armando Herrera, a stellar pantheon of Latin American photographers focused on spectacularizing national figures such as María Félix, Tita Merello, or Carmen Miranda. Working in concert with directors, these photographers brought the stars closer to spectators while at the same time shrouding them with an air of divine inaccessibility.

The foreign presence in Latin American cinemas

With the arrival of sound, Argentina and Mexico began to develop their film industries, looking to take advantage of the commercial possibilities of the Spanish-language markets. One of the tactics utilized to improve the quality of films was to import experienced cinematographers from more developed industries. The first sound films in both nations— *Santa* (Antonio Moreno, 1932) in Mexico and *Los tres berretines* (*The Three Whims*, Enrique Susini, 1933) in Argentina—already had foreign directors of photography, the Canadian Alex Phillips and the Hungarian John Alton, respectively, both imported from Hollywood.

Alongside them came other directors of photography from the US such as Bob Roberts in Argentina and Jack Draper in Mexico. In many instances, these cinematographers had themselves emigrated to the US from Europe, part of the large migratory movement in between the world wars. In Argentina, Francis Boeniger was Swiss, and Gerardo Húttula and Pablo Tabernero were German, while in Mexico, Max Lizst was from Austria and Arthur Martinelli from Italy. Prominent among them were Sergei Eisenstein and cinematographer Eduard Tissé, who worked on the unfinished production of *¡Qué viva México!* Their presence, as well as that of Paul Strand, who filmed *Redes* (*Nets*, Fred Zinnemann and Emilio Gómez Muriel, 1936), were very significant influences for directors of photography such as Gabriel Figueroa (De la Vega Alfaro 1997).

These cinematographers imbued Latin American cinema with a decisive transnational dimension that has been explored in relation to cinematography (Goity 2000; Paranaguá 2003; Higgins 2008; Lara Chávez and Lozano 2011; Lusnich 2015). The travelers brought along their accumulated experiences, but also stylistic tendencies that markedly influenced cinematographic visuality. Most of them had expressionist tendencies and their stylized treatment of images was based on very careful framing and the narrative use of the interplay between light and shadows. The films of both countries in this first period demonstrated a broad range of visual experimentation, as in the work of Agustín Jiménez in *Dos monjes* (*Two Monks*, Juan Bustillo Oro, 1934), Alex Phillips in *La mujer del Puerto* (*The Woman of the Port*, Arcady Boytler, 1934), or John Alton in *Escala en la ciudad* (*Stopover in the City*, Alberto de Zavalía, 1935), which was only later standardized and transformed.

The foundational character of these cinematographers must also be understood in the context of the national traditions in each country. In the case of Argentina, Alberto Etchebehere and Antonio Merayo had worked at the Valle studios and had years of experience, including having invented a subtitling system (Andrés de Merabelli 1995; Di Núbila 1996). Many had also had international experiences; Merayo, for example, had worked on the films of Carlos Gardel and became the perfect example of an industrial cinematographer

Figure 20.1 *Dos monjes* (*Two Monks*, Juan Bustillo Oro, Mexico, 1934). Cinematographer: Agustín Jiménez.

who delivered the visual style required by every movie in which he worked (Peña 2008). In Mexico, a country with a long history of silent film production and photography, especially during the Revolution, technicians such as Ezequiel Carrasco had already developed technical innovations and chromatic experimentation and were fundamental in the transition to sound. Furthermore, given Mexico's closeness to Hollywood, this sharing of experiences and information gave rise to the dynamism of the field.

These multidirectional circulations of knowledge, what Elena Goity has called "an educational chain" (Goity 2000: 89–90), were not limited to the nation and had a regional impact. When other Latin American countries such as Chile and Venezuela decided to embark upon industrial production, they sought the assistance of Argentine and Mexican technicians, thus continuing the cycle of knowledge transfer (Colmenares 1999; Peirano and Gobantes 2015). These flow of photographers included Spaniard José María Beltran, who worked in Argentina and Brazil and won the Best Cinematography award in Cannes Film Festival for Venezuela's *La balandra Isabel llegó esta tarde* (*The Balandra Arrived This Afternoon*, Carlos Hugo Christensen, 1951), and Argentines Alfredo Traverso and Antonio Merayo, who collaborated on many films for the national production house Chile Films.

The case of Brazil is somewhat different due to the history of its industry and the tension between national desires and regional realities. When it came time to develop an industrial infrastructure for film production, Brazilian impresarios were reluctant to recruit foreign technicians. Arthur Autran believes that this is one of the possible reasons for its unequal industrial development (Autran 2012: 124–126). Although Cinédia was the principal studio in the early sound period, the most interesting photographic work were films such as *Limite* (Mario Peixoto, 1931), which effectively ended the silent period, and *Ganga Bruta* (Humberto Mauro, 1933). Cinematographer Edgar Brazil, whom Glauber Rocha later compared to internationally renowned figures such as Tissé, Figueroa, or Gregg Toland (Rocha 1965: 19), played a fundamental role in both productions. Having obtained some distinction in the national industry, he worked in the major studios, and in 1942 founded the laboratory "A Figura" to guarantee national film production. Among his successors were the Italian Amleto Daissé, who replaced him at the Atlantida studios, and Dib Lufti, the

Figure 20.2 *La balandra Isabel llegó esta tarde* (*The Balandra Isabel Arrived This Afternoon*, Carlos Hugo Christensen, Venezuela, 1950). Cinematographer: José María Beltrán.

most important cinematographer of the Cinema Novo movement and, according to Carlos Calil, Edgar Brazil's true heir (de Noronha 2013).

In the fully industrial context, it was not until the experience of Vera Cruz in the 1950s that foreign technical talent was imported. The role of Alberto Cavalcanti, who had spent many years in Europe, was key. He brought along many of his European collaborators, chief among them cinematographer Chick Fowle, who had filmed war documentaries. According to Paulo Antonio Paranaguá, Fowle, Edgar Brazil, and the Argentine Ricardo Aronovich were responsible for creating a "Brazilian light" in cinema (Paranaguá 2003: 167). A prominent example of this visual style can be found in the internationally successful *O Cangaceiro* (Lima Barreto, 1953), where, as José Carlos Avellar has argued, Fowle combined German expressionism's artificial lighting and Italian neorealism's natural landscapes to create a flickering and unstable image of Brazil's "Nordeste" (Avellar 2000: 206).

The national and the genres

One of the principal structural challenges for the development of these industries was the search for a visual style that would condense the idea of a national identity. Generally, as a consequence of the desire to establish a difference from Hollywood and European films, the impetus of the early years was to associate the national to the rural, but in the mid-1940s urban settings became more frequent. We can identify two types of directors of photography (often working in concert with particular directors): those who worked primarily in films set in rural areas and had an affinity for landscapes (such as Pablo Tabernero and Gabriel Figueroa, and directors Mario Soffici, Lucas Demare, and Emilio Fernández) and those who specialized in urban settings, stylizing cityscapes through the tension between noir

Figure 20.3   *O Cangaceiro* (Lima Barreto, Brazil, 1953). Cinematographer: Chick Fowle.

expressionism and the later influence of Italian neorealism (such as Alex Phillips and José Ortiz Ramos, and directors Roberto Gavaldón and Carlos Hugo Christensen). Ana Laura Lusnich argues that in both cases, visual composition became vital for the development of narratives and characters. To this end, directors of photography combined German expressionist style with the depth of field cinematography of U.S. photographers such as Gregg Toland and the pictorial traditions of landscape painting and muralism (Lusnich 2015).

Within Mexican cinema, Gabriel Figueroa was a fundamental figure in the configuration of a particular visual imaginary in Emilio "El Indio" Fernández's films such as *Las abandonadas* (*The Abandoned Ones*, 1944), *La perla* (*The Pearl*, 1945), and *Enamorada* (*Woman in Love*, 1946). Figueroa had been Eisenstein's assistant and also had a working relationship with Toland (Higgins 2008). He was able to reconcile the Soviet style of cinematography in relationship to the traditions of mural painting to produce a look marked by the geometrical compositions of landscapes (Lara Chávez and Lozano 2011: 28). Although his work with Fernández is the best known, his penchant for visual abstraction, expressive use of close-ups, and careful attention to lighting were notable in his films for other directors such as *Él* (*This Strange Passion*, Luis Buñuel, 1952) and *Macario* (Roberto Gavaldón, 1960). The ending of Gavaldón's film presents one of Figueroa's most celebrated images, where the main character enters Death's cavern to find a large number of candles, each one representing a person's life. This scenario allowed him to handle different lighting sources within the same space, emphasizing the surreal nature of the sequence.

Without the international repercussion of Figueroa, Argentine cinematographers such as Antonio Merayo and Bob Roberts also created a particular vision of the Argentine pampas and northern regions of the country. Taking up the style of Argentine landscape painters of the late nineteenth century such as Prilidiano Pueyrredón, Juan Manuel Blanes, and Ángel della Valle, they took advantage of establishing shots with great depth of field and a specific iconography to dramatically emphasize the struggle between civilization and *barbarie* in films such as *Malambo* (Alberto de Zavalía, 1942), *La guerra gaucha* (*The Gaucho War*, Lucas

Figure 20.4   *Macario* (Roberto Gavaldón, Mexico, 1950). Cinematographer: Gabriel Figueroa.

Demare, 1942), or *Pampa bárbara* (*Savage Pampas*, Lucas Demare and Hugo Fregonese, 1945) (Lusnich 2015). Similarly, Pablo Tabernero in *Prisioneros de la tierra* (*Prisoners of the Earth*, Mario Soffici, 1939) and José María Beltrán in *Las aguas bajan turbias* (*Dark River*, Hugo del Carril, 1952) produced an image of Argentina's Mesopotamia that, marked by expressionist influences, highlighted the dangers of the environment. While Beltrán's landscapes recall Figueroa's compositions, enclosed spaces such as the rustic huts where the workers live are marked by striped shadows that enclose the characters in their inexorable conditions.

In Brazil, Humberto Mauro was one of the principal promoters of rural settings. Although he was a notable director, André Moncaio has proposed that he also maintains a coherent visual style in his work with various directors of photography. As Fernão Pessoa Ramos argues, his work exhibits a marked melancholy linked to the landscape and traditions of Minas Gerais that is in tension with his modern sensibility in framing and lighting (Moncaio n.d.). The final scene of *O Descobrimento do Brasil* (*The Discovery of Brazil*, Humberto Mauro, 1937), itself a recreation of Victor Meireles' painting *Primeira missa no Brasil* (*First Mass in Brazil*), encapsulates Mauro's stylistic concerns.

In contrast to these rural films that took up prior pictorial traditions, urban films since the mid-1940s were more in sync with international visual trends, particularly expressionism (through film noir) and neorealism. In the context of their rapid modernization, the city became a place for crime and perdition, as well as the increasing presence of popular masses. This is how the city appeared in the noir films that appeared in these countries in the 1940s. Alex Phillips in *La otra* (*The Other*, Roberto Gavaldón, 1946) and Alfredo Traverso in *Los pulpos* (*The Octopi*, Carlos Hugo Christensen, 1948) turned Mexico City and Buenos Aires into cities of shadows and slanted lights that trapped their protagonists. Similarly, Pablo Tabernero in *Si muero antes de despertar* (*If I Die before I Awaken*, Carlos Hugo Christensen, 1952) built the nightmarish world with internal and external chiaroscuros of a schoolboy

Figure 20.5   *Las aguas bajan turbias* (Hugo del Carril, Argentina, 1952). Cinematographer: José María Beltrán.

Figure 20.6   Left: A *Primeira Missa no Brasil*, painting by Victor Meirelles (1861). Right: *O Descobrimento do Brasil* (Humberto Mauro, Brazil, 1936). Cinematographer: Humberto Mauro.

who witnesses his friend's kidnapping. Thus, such familiar environments as the school or the house where he lives are rarefied, presenting the boy's dread and hopelessness.

In this same period, but with a less gruesome vision that attempted to communicate the changing nature of the city and its massification, cinematographers such as José Ortiz Ramos, in films such as *Nosotros los pobres* (*We, the Poor*, Ismael Rodríguez, 1947) and *¡Esquina bajan!* (*Corner Stop*, Alejandro Galindo, 1948), began to move away from

Figure 20.7   *Si muero antes de despertar* (*If I Should Die before I Awake*, Carlos Hugo Christensen, Argentina, 1952). Cinematographer: Pablo Tabernero.

the stylization then dominant (Lozano 2010). The influence of German expressionism began to wane and was overtaken by realist tendencies emerging from various countries after World War II, which were essential for the aesthetic renewal and reformulation of national cinemas of the New Cinemas that emerged throughout Latin America in the 1960s (Poirier 2011).

Photography as the foundation of the commercial framework of Latin American cinema

The relationship between photography and the cinema was not limited to film production; it also played a fundamental role in the development of the film industry beyond the screen. Film stills and star portraits were essential tools for the diffusion and consolidation of national cinema industries. Studios and specialized magazines worked to produce specific visual imaginaries for the principal stars and films. As Paulo Emilio Salles Gomes points out, the photos of stars in Brazilian magazines such as *Cinearte* worked to establish the star status of actresses Carmen Santos and Eva Nil even before the public had seen them in films (Paranaguá 1987: 199). Often, studio cinematographers would also produce still photographs of stars. This was the case of Antonio Merayo, who was responsible for producing the star image of Zully Moreno (AAVV 2008: 14–15).

Photographing stars was also an important line of work for studio photographers who specialized in this area. Notable in Argentina were photographers such as Nicolás Schonfeld, Sivul Wilenski, and especially Annemarie Heinrich, who emigrated from Europe in the early 1930s, contracted with Argentina Sono Films in 1937, and produced a large number

Figure 20.8   Andrea Palma in *La mujer del puerto* (*The Woman of the Port*, Arcady Boytler, Mexico, 1934).

of magazine covers for magazines such as *Antena* and *Sintonía* (Travnik 2004). In Mexico, Armando Herrera, "photographer of the stars," was responsible for a range of star images, from the first portraits of Cantinflas to photos of María Felix and Jorge Negrete's wedding. Working alongside the photogenic figures of the stars, his photos materialized the most important faces of the Mexican star system (Monsiváis 2012).

Before Herrera, one of the principal portrait photographers in Mexico was Gabriel Figueroa. This is how he met Alex Phillips and went on to produce stills for the industry. As Elisa Lozano argues, in this early work we can already see traces that would later characterize his cinematography such as the influence of pictorialism and expressionism and a certain tension with foreign influences. One of his principal achievements in this period was the transformation of Andrea Palma into a Mexican Marlene Dietrich, reinforcing the hybrid nature of the visual structure of Latin American cinema (Lozano 2008).

When we look at his later career and his gradual definition of a personal style that combined local traditions and foreign influences, we can once again confirm the sinuous routes of the relationship between Latin American cinemas and photography for the establishment of their own visual imaginary.

The functions of still photography in Latin American political cinema, 1960s–1970s

SILVANA FLORES

This section analyzes the relationship between film and photography in the context of Latin American political cinemas in the 1960s and 1970s through four case studies of political and social films—from Argentina, Bolivia, and Chile. By focusing on the use of still photography and its relationship to images in movement, I will illustrate the existence of a particular Latin American practice. The essay highlights the importance of photography in the training of students at the Instituto de Cinematografía de la Universidad Nacional del Litoral (Santa Fe, Argentina), the function of still photography as a tool for social critique in Chilean short films during the Popular Unity period (1970–1973) and in certain sections of the Bolivian film *El coraje del pueblo* (*The Courage of the* People, Jorge Sanjinés, 1971), and lastly the introduction of the deathbed photograph of Ernesto "Che" Guevara in *La hora de los hornos* (*The Hour of the Furnaces*, Cine Liberación, 1966/68) and its replacement for the premiere of the film after the return to democracy in 1973. All these films are visual testimonies of social realities and exploit the intermedial relationships between film and photography to do so.

Photography and cinema: tools for social testimony

In "The Ontology of the Photographic Image," André Bazin analyzed how painting struggled to "replace the outside world with its double," attempting to achieve three-dimensionality through perspective, and later, with greater difficulty, movement (Bazin 2009: 5). According to Bazin, photography, on the other hand, had a distinct advantage in its search for realism because it was a more objective art, in the sense that there was less creative intervention on the part of the photographer, beyond the selection of the photographed and a point of view. Because photography was superior to painting in terms of verisimilitude, at long last, a guaranteed objectivity had freed the pictorial arts from their will to realism. Bazin celebrated photography's ability to embalm time; it shows "lives halted in time" (p. 8). The cinema, on the other hand, with the illusion of images in movement produced by the phenomenon of persistence of vision, allows for the capture of reality to include temporality. Pascal Bonitzer argues, however, that beyond the specifics of each artistic medium, they are not antagonistic: "film is related to the still image; and painting [and we could add photography] is also related to movement" (Bonitzer 2007: 5). The cinema joins all the arts, as Riccioto Canudo argued as early as 1914 in his "Manifesto of the Seven Arts."

It is important to clarify that the cinema's approximation to the "real" and its relationship to objectivity was questioned from very early on. As Bonitzer establishes, the cinema is an artifact, "an illusion machine," and not "a transparent reflection of the real" (Bonitzer 2007: 34, 22). Nevertheless, all fictional cinema has a documentary character and the documentary can itself also be linked to a fictional configuration (Plantinga 2011). Such is the case of the cinema of political intervention (Getino and Velleggia 2002), which aims to anchor narratives, whether fictional or documentary, in contemporary social reality and linked to a social praxis.

From the photodocumentary to filmed social survey: Tire dié

The social and political Latin American films of the 1960s and 1970s combined the specificity of photography and cinema, using still images for their testimonial value in which the link with the real (historical reality, landscapes, and characters with social markers) was the principal axis. Some examples are paradigmatic of this phenomenon; the work produced by what is believed to be the first Latin American film school, the Instituto de Cinematografía founded in 1956 by Fernando Birri is one of them. In addition to being a foundational experience for the New Latin American Cinema movement, the work of Birri and his students demonstrated how photography could be fundamental for the development of audiovisual projects and social documentation. How the film *Tire dié* (*Throw Me a Dime*, 1956–1958) was developed is well known: at first, the students began their social survey via photographs; later, it became a filmed social survey. Birri and his students produced a series of photo documentaries as:

> a kind of journal of photographic notes of characters' faces, of environments [. . .] for future films, both documentary and fiction. And even if the film were never to be shot, the photo documentary has its own autonomous value, of conviction and persuasion, because of its strength as a direct-literal-visible testimony of an irrefutable reality.
>
> *(Birri 1956)*

Through the photo documentaries, Birri and his students began to photograph social realities so that they could be critically interpreted in the context of a film culture that until then had not even been able to spy upon it. Birri's pedagogical method was simple and something he had learned in his studies in Rome some years earlier: a camera and a tape recorder for interviews. Between 1956 and 1958, Birri and his students went to the neighborhoods surrounding the Salado River in the city of Santa Fe to capture the precarious lives of its inhabitants.

This closer relationship to the subjects and spaces to be filmed is a recurrent feature in the writings of those who worked on cinemas of political intervention: the intention was to go beyond the mere photographic/audiovisual register in order to produce an anthropological or sociological investigation and, in the case of *Tire dié*, a pedagogical tool (note the logo of the university in the credits). The photo documentaries produced by the institute's students promoted observation as a research tool (thus, the use of the word survey) according to an agreed upon hypothesis ("there are social marginalities in certain sectors that the media has ignored") and had concrete objectives: to create social consciousness without proposing solutions so as to invite the spectator to reflect and think of possible interventions (as the famous manifesto released upon the premiere of the film declared).

The conversion of the photo documentaries to film involved beginning "from the fragment to produce a totality" (Sadek 2008: 227). That is to say, the photo documentary registered through still images the children of the village chasing trains to get coins from the travelers, among other elements of daily life. Later, these same photographs and their corresponding captions were the raw material for the film, which allowed for their resemantization given their hypothesis and objectives. In other words, the previously produced still photographs gained an additional layer of intentional meaning when they were transposed to film. Thus, the filmic version allowed the spectator to follow the movement of the train with the children, to hear the sounds of the locomotives and the children's pleading for coins. This alternation generates a powerful comparison between the universes each represent and a greater sense of realism than that provided by the photographs alone, without sound and movement.

Juan Oliva's *Los 40 cuartos* (*The Forty Rooms*, 1962) followed the experience of *Tire dié*. Announced as the school's second social survey, it also aspired to reflect the underdevelopment that so shamed mainstream media. This was so much the case that the film was banned by presidential decree. The photo documentaries, however, were noticed by those involved in documentary film production in the period, as evidenced by the creation of a photo documentary section in the II Festival de Cine Documental y Experimental organized in Uruguay by SODRE (Servicio Oficial de Difusión Radio Eléctrica, the national public broadcasting organization) in 1956.

We can thus conclude that the work of Birri and his students linked not only film and photography, but that this intermediality extended to pedagogical practices (the debates and exhibitions of photo documentaries) and the diffusion of social testimonies that evidenced the relationship of filmmakers with communities. Beyond the autonomy of these photo documentaries, the still photograph allowed for a closer relationship to reality that produced a broader audiovisual testimony of underdevelopment. Birri continued to develop this concept in subsequent films, and would become very consequential for those involved in political filmmaking in Latin America.

Images of conviction: the films of Popular Unity

In 1950s Chile, certain tendencies toward experimentation had taken root, and by the 1960s the cinema was firmly entrenched in university and cine club circles as they promoted the new cinemas of Latin America, including new Chilean directors such as Aldo Francia, Miguel Littín, Patricio Guzmán, Héctor Ríos, Pedro Chaskel, Helvio Soto and Sergio Bravo. Several of these filmmakers were producing short political films in support of Popular Unity, the political coalition that in 1970 successfully elected Salvador Allende to the presidency. During his mandate, several directors used their cameras to capture Chile's social struggles and also made ample use of photographic archives to address social issues that were on the agenda for reform.

In many ways, these filmmakers were using manipulative techniques to make political points. They used collage and the juxtaposition of images aided by the skillful use of the soundtrack (music and voice-over narration) to reaffirm or confront specific Popular Unity initiatives. The manipulation of archival footage and photographs is common in political filmmaking. As argued by Ivork Cordido, the decision to make a documentary anchored to a particular historical moment implies taking into account that the film "is a secondary source, that is to say, that it has been manipulated before the fact" (Cordido 1972: 50), and therefore promoted a particular perspective that must be understood as an interpretative reading by its makers and not plain and simple "reality."

The Popular Unity films focus on the denunciation of capitalism and upon the need to develop consciousness about the need for change, according to the policies of the political coalition (as evidenced, for example, by the promising future offered to alcoholics in *Entre ponerle y no ponerle* (*Between Putting It and Not Putting It*, Héctor Ríos, 1971). Juxtaposing scenes via editing and inserting photographs as functional evidence of truths were among the most effective methods used to attempt to raise spectatorial consciousness. *Venceremos* (*We Shall Triumph*, Pedro Chaskel and Héctor Ríos, 1970) is notable in this respect. It makes extensive use of archival photographs, showing a veritable parade of men, women, and children in marginal situations as well as still images of newspapers and magazines. Through its editing structure, it effectively contrasts the poverty of the Chilean people with the levity of the capital consumer system and the ways of high society. The act of showing misery and hunger appears in one of the central sequences of the film constituted by the juxtaposition of a series still photos accompanied by an Ángel Parra song reclaiming the figure of "the people," *el pueblo*, and announcing the possibility of change with sequences of short shots featuring shop windows, mansions, and magazines sarcastically accompanied by happy rock 'n' roll music ("Yo quiero ser un triunfador" ["I want to be a winner"] by the Uruguayan pop group Los Iracundos), in the style of TV commercials. Although the film also uses film footage to evidence *el pueblo*, and especially its protests, the use of still photographs to denounce extreme underdevelopment and misery is particularly striking in relationship to the dynamically edited footage of the levity of the upper classes and their parties and pure breed dog shows. A frame with the words "BASTA" (Enough) against a black background that ends the appearance of stills about social inequalities in the film gives way to exuberant shots of successful protests (i.e. without military repression) accompanied by the hopeful lyrics of the Angel Parra song "Un gallo de amanecida" ("A Rooster at Dawn"): "Es el gallo que canta nuestro destino" ("It is the rooster that sings our destiny"). That destiny involved, in many ways, moving towards the formulation of a Che Guevarian *hombre nuevo* (new man), at that time a continental project.

El coraje del pueblo *and the audacity of filmmakers*

Bolivian filmmakers used still photographs as a tool for social denunciation. *El coraje del pueblo* is a clear example of how an audiovisual work can be a historical document that functionally projects to the present. In two sequences in the film—at the beginning and then towards the end—still documentary photographs appear that have a pragmatic function: to denounce those responsible for the slaughter of peasant workers that the film memorializes. The film was planned as a historical reconstruction. Produced by the Grupo Ukamau, a collective founded some years earlier by Jorge Sanjinés and Oscar Soria, the film reaffirms the testimonial spirit of politically engaged cinema of the period but does not eschew the fictional as an appropriate vehicle for that testimony and denunciation. The historical recreations were produced according to parameters that would "awaken a profound preoccupation that, beginning with the emotional shock, would continue to a state of reflection that would not abandon the spectator after the curtains drop" (Sanjinés 1980: 24). The reconstructions were also meant to approximate real social experiences and popular memory to the degree that, as the director has recounted, those from the community who watched the film "cried without distinguishing between reality and reconstruction" (p. 24).

The first sequence—film footage showing masses of people shot by government soldiers—culminates in a still photograph of a mound of cadavers. The still provides clo-sure to the dynamic tension of the previous footage and, although also a reconstruction, is accompanied by superimposed text that openly accuses the Bolivian government of having ordered the massacre. Then the denunciation becomes more specific through the insertion of archival photographs that name those responsible. In addition, other archival photo-graphs provide further evidence of later acts of violence, identifying the events and naming the responsible parties. The sequence of still photographs is accompanied by throbbing percussive music that accents the gravity of the events being documented. Thus, the film uses the indexical force of the images as evidence of their culpability and as a tool for social critique. The next sequence begins with a long shot that frames a rancho and alongside it one of the surviving victims of the massacre on a wheelchair. The camera slowly, almost imperceptibly, zooms in on Saturnino Condori, the survivor, which makes the footage feel almost like the still photographs that preceded it. This strategy is again used at the end of the film, more briefly, but with the same pragmatic intention: raising the consciousness of the people and confronting the guilty parties.

El coraje del pueblo has been celebrated for its imbrication of fictional and documentary registers and for its relentless drive to rewrite history, beyond official discourses, to incor-porate the demands of the workers. The use of nonprofessional actors who were direct or near participants in the events reinforces the impact of the desired spectatorial political engagement. Photography, as a testimonial apparatus, served a key function in this process as a trace that confirmed the need to lay bare truths that had been otherwise veiled by the media.

Beyond death: Che's face

Like many other New Latin American Cinema documentaries, *La hora de los hornos* uses stills as counterpoints and reaffirmations of the points established by the voice over narra-tion and montage editing. At the end of Part 1, "Neocolonialism and Violence," however, photography takes center stage, with the image of Ernesto "Che" Guevara's cadaver laid out in Vallegrande (Bolivia). The sequence begins with documentary footage filmed by agents of the Bolivian government to then focus on a particular photograph that reveals Che's face, with eyes open, looking out from death. As an icon of Third World revolution-ary struggles, Che is also ensconced as an icon of revolutionary cinema in the three-minute shot of this photograph. This still image, as still as death itself, has, however, a strange greater dynamism than the previous film footage. This generates a challenge for the spec-tator that coincides with the ideal of a heroic death proposed by the film. Photography, as Bazin argued, halts the instant, "embalms time" (Bazin 2009: 9), and in this instance this is reinforced by the expansion of the no time of death, which paradoxically grants the image a dynamism that it doesn't have. Roland Barthes (2006) also links photography with this paralysis of the temporal, adding that the splintering of the "real" produced by the photograph—insofar as that which is visible in the photograph no longer is—refers to "death," in which the subject photographed becomes a specter.

The series of Che's postmortem photographs were taken by the Bolivian Freddy Alborta. Together with 20 or so journalists and photographers, he arrived in Vallegrande on October 10, 1967, sent by the government to document Che's death. The images were meant to serve as a lesson to would-be revolutionaries. Instead, Cine Liberación used them to encourage people to embrace the very struggles for which Che had died. Two very different objectives for the showing of the photographs thus emerged and generate paradoxical messages. "The man who chooses his death is choosing a life" was the filmmakers' slogan that we hear via voice-over. That same choice of life or death is what the workers are unable to choose because of daily violence. As Mariano Mestman (2006) points out, the prior scene, in which we see the burial of a *campesino* from the north who died from poverty, when linked with the image of the death of a revolutionary, confirms the primordial value of the ideal. A death that is highlighted by its on-screen duration is an act of confrontation that demands reflection and the taking up of positions: three minutes within which to decide whether or not that ideal is the only option to end the inevitable deaths of the *campesinos*.

Che's deathbed photographs were also studied by Umberto Eco (1986), Susan Sontag (1977), and John Berger (2010), among others. In a 1968 article, Berger linked the photographs to the famous Rembrandt painting "The Anatomy Lesson of Dr. Nicolas Tulp" (1632) and Andrea Mantegna's "Dead Christ" (1480s). The intermediality provoked by the historic event is thus amplified, pointing not only to journalism, but also to the pictorial arts. Berger links these works to the Che photographs because of compositional similarities. For example, in one of the photographs, the soldier who touches Che's body with a finger is in the same position as Dr. Tulp and his scalpel in the Rembrandt painting. Also, there

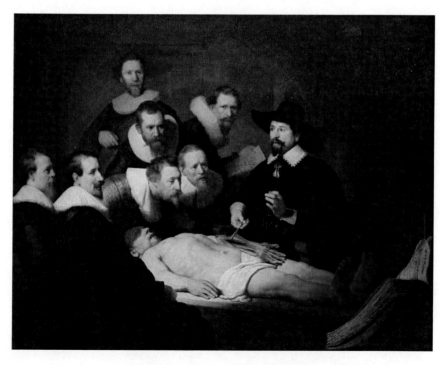

Figure 20.9 "The Anatomy Lesson of Dr. Nicolas Tulp" (Rembrandt van Rijn, 1632).

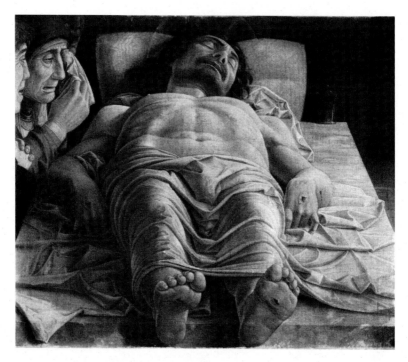

Figure 20.10 "Dead Christ" (Andrea Mantegna, 1480).

are as many anatomy students surrounding the body in the Rembrandt painting as there are onlookers surrounding Che's deathbed. Furthermore, there is in all these images the will to exhibit: from the perspective of medical education in the Rembrandt, sacrifice in the Mantegna, and the desire to prove that the myth had come to an end in the photographs (though these may have had the opposite effect). These iconographic relationships are not accidental. According to statements by the photographer, Che's open eyes—guaranteed by those who prepared his body for the photo session—likened him to someone alive. "I had the impression I was photographing a Christ [. . .] Perhaps that's why I was so careful while photographing, to show that it wasn't simply a cadaver" (Katz 2010). This beatific image of Che-Christ was appropriate in a period of great revolutionary fervor, even among certain ecclesiastical sectors who were committed to liberation theology and the Movement for Priests of the Third World. In fact, in films such as *O dragão da maldade contra o santo guerreiro* (*Antonio das Mortes*, Glauber Rocha, 1969), the *cangaceiro* Coirana is also worked into this binary that links the revolutionary with the redemptive figure who acts on behalf of the Third World dispossessed. Laying on a table, Coirana agonizes surrounded by his enemies, and, once dead, is hung from a tree with uplifted arms, as if crucified.

Solanas and Getino chose carefully from among the many photographs in the dead Che series. They opted to fragment the body, framing the photograph in a tight close-up that seems to interpellate the spectator after the doctrinaire voice-over ends, allowing Che's gaze, endorsed by death, to speak in its place. The spectator is confronted by this gaze and challenged to stop being so by becoming an active agent. This is one of the basic premises of Cine Liberación: "A cinema that emerges and works towards antiimperialist struggles is not aimed to film spectators, but to those formidable agents of this great

Figure 20.11   *O dragão da maldade contra o santo guerreiro* (*Antonio das Mortes*, Glauber Rocha, Brazil, 1969).

continental revolution" (Solanas and Getino 1973: 9). Through the *cine-acto*, the spectator would cease to be passive and move to be included in the unfolding historical process.

La hora de los hornos was at first only exhibited clandestinely and in non-Argentine film festivals. It was commercially exhibited only in 1973, but with a significant change, precisely in the final minutes of Part 1, where Che's photograph appears. According to the records, Che's face appeared together with still images and footage of historic events such as the Cordobazo and the Trelew massacre, or of historic figures such as Juan Domingo Perón, therefore diluting its centrality. As Mestman (2006) has analyzed, the idea of lessening the exclusivity of Che's photo was not unique to that historical moment in Argentina (the return of democracy). Something similar had already been discussed with Cuban authorities for the exhibition of the film there. Filmmakers such as Octavio Cortázar were not in favor of showing the cadaver, arguing that it implied defeat and represented a violent attack on spectatorial susceptibility rather than "an act for conquest" as the voice-over narration proclaims. Beyond these debates for or against its inclusion, we can nevertheless affirm that Che's deathbed image unified the specificity of film and photography: if the photograph stops time, as so may theorists have argued, when it is filmed for a significant period of time the cinematic apparatus breaks that stasis and reinserts it into time.

Conclusion

As we have observed, beyond the linkage of photography to film, as long noted by scholars and historians, there is a cultural specificity to how Latin American filmmakers have taken up the interconnection between the two media, which is rooted in the artists' heightened awareness of the historical realities of their immediate geopolitical position. We have observed two recurrent features that are informed by that self-awareness. In the earlier commercial studio period, the efforts to develop viable commercial cinema quickly moved beyond mere imitation of foreign models and negotiated a hybridized local variant of international filmmaking patterns and genres. Some of that negotiation was to be found in the ancillary fan culture that depended so heavily on the deployment of photography at the service of cinema. After the demise of the studio system, the dyad of photography/cinema took a crucial turn toward the photo documentary. By its very nature, these social and political films exploited the power of photography to reinforce the authenticity of the profilmic social reality, while creating a more intimate relationship between the filmmakers and the subjects and spaces to be filmed. This resulted in the forging of a new visual aesthetic that emphasized the ideological power of each medium to capture the images of immediate social reality through which to engage broader popular audiences.

References

AAVV (2008) *Catálogo ADF*. Buenos Aires: Asociación Argentina de Autores de Fotografía Cinematográfica.

Andrés de Merabelli, C. (1995) *Cine argentino: director de fotografía, Antonio Merayo*. Buenos Aires: El Francotirador.

Autran, A. (2012) "Sonhos industrais: O cinema dos estúdios na Argentina e no Brasil nos anos 1930." *Contracampo*, 25 (December): 117–132.

Avellar, J.C. (2000) "Memoria fotográfica." *Archivos de la Filmoteca*, 36 (October): 202–227.

Barthes, R. (2006) *La cámara lúcida. Notas sobre la fotografía*. Buenos Aires: Paidós.

Bazin, A. (2009) "Ontology of the Photographic Image." In *What Is Cinema?* trans. T. Barnard. Toronto: Cabbose Books, pp. 3–12.

Berger, J. (2010) "Che Guevara muerto." In L. Katz (ed.), *Los fantasmas de Ñancahuazú*. Buenos Aires: La lengua viperina, pp. 25–30.

Birri, F. (1956) *Fotodocumentales: 1er Cuaderno de Fotodocumentales Santafesinos*. Santa Fe: Editorial del Instituto de Cinematografía del Instituto Social de la Universidad Nacional del Litoral (UNL).

Bonitzer, P. (2007) *Desencuadres. Cine y pintura*. Buenos Aires: Santiago Arcos Editor.

Colmenares, M.G. (1999) "Industria e imitación: los géneros cinematográficos en los largometrajes de ficción de Bolívar Films." *Archivos de la Filmoteca*, 31: 122–135.

Cordido, I. (1972) *Cine y subdesarrollo*. Caracas: Ediciones Cabimas.

De la Vega Alfaro, E. (1997) *Del muro a la pantalla. S.M. Eisenstein y el arte pictórico mexicano*. Guadalajara: Universidad de Guadalajara—Instituto Mexiquense de Cultura.

de Noronha, D. (2013) "Edgar Brasil: o patrono dos diretores de fotografia brasileiros." Available at: www.abcine.org.br/artigos/?id=1285&/edgar-brasil-o-patrono-dos-diretores-de-fotografia-brasileiros (accessed September 1, 2015).

Di Núbila, D. (1996) *Cuando el cine fue aventura. El pionero Federico Valle*. Buenos Aires: El Jilguero.

Eco, U. (1986) "Lire les choses: un photo." In *La guerre du faux*. Paris: Grasset.

Getino, O. and Velleggia, S. (2002) *El cine de "las historias de la revolución."* Buenos Aires: Altamira.

Goity, E. (2000) "La fotografía en el cine argentino." In C. España (ed.), *Cine argentino. Industria y clasicismo I*, Buenos Aires: Fondo Nacional de las Artes.

Higgins, C. (2008) "Transitando lo mexicano." *Luna Cornea*, 32: 89–114.

Katz, L. (2010) "Entrevista con Freddy Alborta." In L. Katz (ed.), *Los fantasmas de Ñancahuazú*. Buenos Aires: La lengua viperina, pp. 35–43.

Lara Chávez, H. and Lozano, E. (2011) *Luces, cámara, acción. Cinefotógrafos del cine mexicano, 1931–2011*. Mexico City: Instituto Mexicano de Cinematografía.

Lozano, E. (2008) "Figueroa antes de Figueroa." *Luna Cornea*, 32: 19–30.

—— (2010) "A don José Ortiz Ramos, in memorian." Available at: http://cuartoscuro.com. mx/2010/02/a-don-jose-ortiz-ramos-in-memorian/ (accessed September 1, 2015).

Lusnich, A.L. (2015) "Transferencia de saberes y de tecnología en el cine argentino y mexicano del periodo clásico." Paper presented at "V Encuentro de Investigación sobre Cine Chileno y Latinoamericano," Santiago de Chile, April 25–30.

Mestman, M. (2006) "La última imagen sacra de la revolución latinoamericana." *Revista Ojos crueles*, 3.

Moncaio, A. (n.d.) "Humberto Mauro e a construção estética da imagem nos filmes do período do INCE." Available at: www.mnemocine.com.br/aruanda/hmauroamoncaio.htm (accessed September 1, 2015).

Monsiváis, C. (2012) *Maravillas que son, sombras que fueron: La fotografía en México*. Mexico City: Ediciones Era.

Paranaguá, P.A. (1987) *Le cinéma bresilien*. Paris: Editions du Centre Pompidou.

—— (2003) *Tradición y modernidad en el cine de América Latina*. Mexico City: Fondo de Cultura Económica de España.

Peirano, M.P. and Gobantes, C. (eds.) (2015) *Chilefilms, el Hollywood criollo: Aproximaciones al proyecto industrial cinematográfico chileno (1942–1949)*. Santiago: Editorial Cuarto Propio.

Peña, F.M. (2008) "Antonio Merayo: El fotógrafo funcional." *Filmoteca Buenos Aires*. Available at: https://filmotecaba.wordpress.com/articulos/antonio-merayo-el-fotografo-funcional/ (accessed September 1, 2015).

Plantinga, C. (2011) "Documental." *Cine documental*. Available at: http://revista.cinedocumental. com.ar/3/traducciones.html (accessed June 1, 2017). Originally published as "Documentary," in P. Livingstone and C. Plantinga (eds.) (2009) *The Routledge Companion to Philosophy and Film*. New York: Routledge, pp. 494–503.

Poirier, E. (2011) "La influencia neorrealista en los nuevos cines latinoamericanos: los límites suplantados." *El ojo que piensa. Revista de cine iberoamericano*, 4. Available at: www.elojoquepiensa.net/elojoquepiensa/index.php/articulos/181 (accessed September 1, 2015).

Rocha, G. (1965) *Revisión crítica del cine brasilero*. Havana: ICAIC.

Sadek, I. (2008) *Of Lands, Regions and Zones: The Poetics and Politics of Non-Urban Spaces in the 1960s in Brazil and Argentina*. Ann Arbor, MI: UMI Microform.

Sanjinés, J. (1980) *Teoría y práctica de un cine junto al pueblo*. Mexico City: Siglo XXI Editores.

Solanas, F.E. and Getino, O. (1973) *Cine, cultura y descolonización*. Buenos Aires: Siglo XXI Editores Argentina S.A.

Sontag, S. (1977) *Sobre la fotografía*. Barcelona: Edhasa.

Travnik, J. (2004) *Annemarie Heinrich. Un cuerpo, una luz, un reflejo*. Buenos Aires: Ediciones Larivière.

21

FILM AND RADIO INTERMEDIALITIES IN EARLY LATIN AMERICAN SOUND CINEMA

Ana M. López

Editors' introduction

This chapter illuminates the complex intermedial relation between radio and cinema during the crucial first decades of the sound era, arguing first that film historians have largely ignored or misrepresented the intermedial synergies; the chapter goes on to explore the impact of the aural dynamics that emerges from such intermedial practices on the stabilization of the audience; finally, it looks to the specific textual practices in key films of the period. The importance of López's investigation lies in two areas: First, an essential correction in our view of cinema's place within mass culture of the period; second, the long-term implictions of sound aesthetics as an agent of cultural and political meaning both for audiences and those writing about Latin American film.

Perhaps silencing the noise of the gaze we shall manage to listen, in new ways, to this long 20th Century and its contemporary legacies.

(Ochoa Gautier 2006: 8)

Radio challenges to Latin American film history

By the mid-1930s, radio and sound cinema had become commercially viable mass media in Latin America. Both were "new" media, and their parameters, powered by industrial and commercial imperatives, had yet to be fully refined. Radio and sound cinema would intersect, defining the overall mediascape of mid- to late 1930s Latin America. Therefore, this crucial decade needs to be seen as years of profound intermediality that reveal strategies of appropriation, accommodation, and, ultimately, layers of differentiation. As film scholars have noted, this was a moment of "crisis" for the cinema. But, rather than a period in which the new swept out the old, it was a period in which old and new media collided (Altman 2004: 13) and in which parallel intermedial processes served as the shifting base for the development of the "golden age" of Latin American national cinemas in the 1930s and 1940s. Focusing on the echoes of the radiophonic in early sound cinema, this chapter will explore the intersections, complements, and rivalries between sound cinema and radio in this period. Following Elsaesser (2004), it questions some of the standard historiographical assumptions through which this period has been understood. I want to interrogate a broader intermedial horizon in which we can trace the emergence of new audiovisual practices and social agents that set the stage for the regional appropriation and adaptation of sound cinema.

In standard histories of Latin American cinemas, this period of uncertainty and experimentation in between silent cinema and more industrial sound film production is typically presented as a necessary transition between almost artisanal silent cinema practices that continued through the 1930s, in some instances aligned with artistic avant-gardes (as with *Limite* in Brazil [Mário Peixoto, 1931], *La mancha de sangre* in Mexico [*The Bloodstain*, Alfonso Best-Maugard, 1937], and *Así nació el obelisco* in Argentina [*Thus the Obelisk Was Born*, Horacio Coppola, 1936]), and the institutionalization of the "Cinema" as an industrial or proto-industrial practice and an institutional mode of representation in the mid- to late 1930s and into the 1940s (King 1990: 23–36; Paranaguá 1996: 222–233). In most histories of national cinemas, the period is presented as one of "paralysis," representing the interruption of certain nation-based trajectories by the dislocating power of the new imported technologies and establishing a so-called need to "start from zero" (Machado 1987: 127; García Riera 1993: 11–15; Maranghello 2005: 64). In fact, in a teleological historiographical move, the silent cinema is often subsequently refigured as the "prehistory" of what would become the national cinema "proper." As Argentine historian Domingo Di Núbila most eloquently expressed it, "The advent of sound established the frontier between the prehistory and the history of Argentine cinema" (Di Núbila 1998: 51).

In 1930–1931, filmmaking in Latin America certainly seemed on the brink of crisis. Hollywood sound feature films had spectacularly arrived in the preceding years and profoundly changed the cultural sphere: 1928 in Havana, 1929 in Buenos Aires, Mexico City, Rio de Janeiro, and Lima, and 1930 in Santiago de Chile (Godoy Quezada 1966: 35; Vieira 1987: 140; Bedoya 1992: 87; García Riera 1993: 15; Douglas 1996: 53; España 1999: 25). In Peru, Chile, and Colombia, for example, silent film production continued haltingly through the 1930s. In Rio de Janeiro, however, film attendance declined precipitously by more than 40 percent (Vieira 1987: 135). There was little intracontinental expertise of sound film production. Only Mexico was in a somewhat better position because of its proximity to Hollywood and the constant North–South travel of film personnel. In Mexico and elsewhere, would-be sound filmmakers and creative and technical personnel traveled to Hollywood to learn about the new technology, and often to participate in the first wave of "Hispanic" films produced by the studios, which served as training for would-be national filmmakers and began to delimit the linguistic and sonic communities of a new cinematic sub-market in Spanish (D'Lugo 2010; Jarvinen 2012). Despite the appeal of the new modern technology, the appearance of sound cinema in the region also led to intense public debates about the dangers of the "Yanqui plague," that is, having to listen to English in a movie theater (García Riera 1993: 15; Morais da Costa 2008: 91–92) and the infiltration of "Yanqui" mores and ways of being in the world (Miquel 2005: 106–108). The sudden aural deluge, its potentially unintelligibility, and foreign cultural mores were not the only perceived seismic changes introduced by sound cinema. As Otávio Gabus Mendes ironically argued in Brazil, "the cinema has become an auditory spectacle [in which] audiences must be rigorously silenced . . . silence the mouth, the feet, the seats" (Gabus Mendes 1929: 20).

The few films produced in 1930–1932 in Latin America either continued with silent cinema practices, sometimes rather spectacularly, and/or experimented with mostly homegrown sound-on-disc technologies (in fact, all the larger nations experimented with domestic sound-recording technologies): *Acabarem-se os otarios* (*The End of the Simpletons*, Luiz de Barros, 1929) and *Coisas nossas* (*Our Things*, Wallace Downey, 1931) in Brazil; *Muñequitas porteñas* (*Buenos Aires Dolls*, José Agustín Ferreyra, 1931) in Argentina; and *Abismos* or *Naúfragos de la vida* (*Abysses* or *Castaways from Life*, Salvador Pruneda, 1930), *Más fuerte que el deber* (*Stronger Than Duty*, Raphael J. Sevilla, 1930), and *Santa* (Antonio Moreno, 1932) in Mexico. Many of these experimental sound-recording systems exploited existing disc recording technologies and innovated mechanisms to synchronize sound with image and to project it, a bricolage deemed necessary given the inaccessibility and expense of the imported technological apparatuses. Thus, we need to move beyond what are at best "confused chronologies" to consider the interactions between the two mass media in order to better understand the impact of both popular media on the shaping of audiences.

New intermedial chronologies

That the emergence of locally produced sound films coincides with the consolidation of radio as a mass medium is of significance on at least two levels. First, it means that the chronology of the massification of the two media follows a more intermedial path than was the case elsewhere; second, the emergence of "national" styles/idioms occurs simultaneously in radio and in the cinema. In terms of the advent of mass audiences, in the US, for example, radio was already a mass medium by the late 1920s, as evidenced by the Radio Act of 1927 and the establishment of the Federal Radio Commission to regulate the airwaves.

By contrast, the diffusion of radio set ownership and the establishment of radio stations and national networks occurred later and more slowly in Latin America. Despite the fact that radio transmissions began in the region in the early 1920s (1920 in Buenos Aires, 1921 in Mexico City, 1922 in Rio de Janeiro and Montevideo), the diffusion of the medium was sluggish by comparison to the US, and radio ownership, radio stations, and networks only began to grow exponentially in the 1930s. In 1929, for example, Argentina indisputably led Latin America in radio set ownership, but with only 525,000 sets (22.86 per 1,000 inhabitants, or with a population of almost 12 million, a penetration rate of approximately 26 percent of families, estimating average family size of six) and 22 stations. In the much larger Brazil, there were only 250,000 radio sets (6.43/1,000; penetration of 4.5 percent) and 15 stations, and in Mexico only 50,000 radio sets (3.49/1,000; penetration of 2 percent) and 19 operating radio stations (Batson 1929: 25). Other statistics suggest a somewhat higher level of penetration (Claxton 2007: 149), but the fact remains that the massiveness of radio was relative and uneven in the region. It is not until the mid- to late 1930s that Latin American radio would become a mass medium with national reach. According to an Argentine study from 1934, there were roughly 900,000 radio receivers in Latin America, two-thirds of them in Argentina (600,000), 150,000 in Brazil, and 100,000 in Montevideo (Matallana 2006: 36).

In the US, when sound fiction cinema became commercially viable c.1929–1930, radio was already a well-established medium and had already created appropriate social subjects attuned to aurality: technologically shaped *listeners*. As noted by the *New York Times* in

1930, radio had already created a "sound receptive audience" for the talkies: "The spread of radio broadcasting had . . . familiarized the general public with dramatic dialogue and high-grade music to a far greater extent than ever before" (Crafton 2004: 150). In Latin America, on the other hand, radio and sound cinema became commercially viable only in the 1930s, synergistically feeding off each other's successes and strategies. Radio and incipient sound film practices were interdependent: they shared multiple economic interests throughout the continent, as well as important crossovers and interrelationships of creative personnel (stars, singers, and actors, but also writers, producers, announcers, and comedians). In 1930s Latin America, these new social subjects—the listeners, social agents who listen—and their new activity, "listening," were produced simultaneously by both sound cinema and radio.

Throughout Latin America, radio and sound cinema reconfigured the aurality of the public sphere and the sensorial competencies of audiences. Akin to what Susan J. Douglas has argued for the US, radio redefined a culture that had been "glutted with visual stimuli":

> With the introduction of the telephone, the phonograph, and then [more definitively] radio, there was a revolution in our aural environment that prompted a major perceptual and cognitive shift in the country, with a new emphasis on hearing. Because sound is dynamic and fleeting, radio conveyed a powerful sense of "liveness."
>
> (Douglas 2004: 7)

Similarly, sound technologies also generated a renewed sense of aurality and reimagination of community that further challenged and reconfigured visual/literate culture. Douglas also emphasizes the need to recognize and identify different modes of "listening," arguing that *how* and *where* we listen and have historically listened to radio in America is crucial to understanding its impact in different eras, its particular ways of shaping individual and collective subjectivities (pp. 7–9). Although the literature on "listening" is relatively undeveloped in contrast to the literature on "spectatorship," it is clear that they constitute two different, albeit, since the 1920–1930s, complementary realms of the experience of media. In this context, then, the question is: How does the simultaneity of the perceptual revolution of radio and the redefinition of the cinema in Latin America as also an aural medium, speaking (and singing) in Spanish and Portuguese, impact the formation of "listeners" and the various modes through which Latin Americans learned and experimented with new ways of being as listeners? The construction of listening as a social practice was jointly undertaken by the two media, redefining leisure time. Radio trained listeners and created new social and social positions from which to listen: as a listening family, in the living room composed around the set; as sports fans, avidly following a game at home through the voice of the *locutor*; as a collective, in the auditorium shows in the studios where audiences could also see their favorite performers; as housewife, while busy with tasks in the house but now with a new freedom: the acoustic time to listen (and to consume). Early sound cinema simultaneously reinforced and expanded these new social agents and positions, legitimizing them even while sometimes putting them into question.

Although not really discussed by Douglas (since being "modern" was not much of a concern in 1920s–1930s America), being a "listener" in Latin America also activated a significant cultural sense of modernity. As Jonathan Sterne (2003) has traced in *The Audible Past*, technology-mediated listening—and the skills necessary to decipher and decode what is heard—had been, at least since the eighteenth century, a signpost and constitutive of an evolving and ever growing sense of modernity in the US and Western Europe, albeit not often necessarily acknowledged. Early silent cinema in Latin America allowed spectators to participate in a complex peripheral modernity centered on visuality, which resonated with the intellectual notion of a *ciudad letrada*/lettered city. Radio and sound cinema thus amplified and made accessible a new experience of modernity as "listener," appropriate for a different social and political context: a new social subject that asserts their modernity and their locality and nationess, even as they assert their cosmopolitanism and incipient globality.

What makes these comparative chronologies of radio–film culture appear confused is that the establishment of sound cinema industries in Mexico, Argentina, and Brazil took place in the context of the insistent presence of Hollywood sound cinema. Without exception, sound cinema "arrived" in Latin America and did not have an "organic" evolution (although, of course, "sound," per se had always been available in movie theaters through live and recorded music, synchronization of live voices, and other "tricks"). Contemporary studies of the introduction of sound to cinema in the US have tended to downplay the transitional nature of this period, perhaps rightly so in the U.S. context: "Sound cinema was not a radical alternative to silent filmmaking; sound as sound, as a material and as a set of technical procedures was inserted into the already-constituted system of the classical Hollywood style" (Bordwell et al. 1985: 301). Although synchronized sound did not "fundamentally change the textuality of Hollywood films, it did arguably make the system stronger and more normative" and shifted control from exhibitors to producers (Williams 1992: 128–129). In Latin America, however, even those countries that had sustained production through the 1920s were caught in a profound transitional mode and hard-pressed by the simultaneous technical and economic demands of sound cinema and the very precise and loudly proclaimed demands for nationess from critics, intellectuals, and audiences, who demanded linguistic authenticity and an imaginary national singularity from domestic producers.

Hollywood films were steadily exported to Latin America throughout this period and beyond, especially after the Hollywood studios invested in theaters in Latin America equipped with sound technology to help diffuse the "new" medium. As Gaizca S. de Usabel argues, in the early sound era Latin America was "the leading market for Hollywood films . . . and was ahead of Europe in the number of big capacity theaters" (de Usabel 1982: 80). The Hollywood studios invested heavily in updating the exhibition infrastructure of theaters in Latin American capitals, even in cities such as Buenos Aires, where some distributors, such as Max Glücksmann, who was also heavily invested in discography, were already beginning to self-finance the retrofitting of theaters (Maranghello 2005: 56). As early as 1930, 132 of the 830 movie theaters in Mexico had already been outfitted for sound (de los Reyes 1987: 118), and by 1937 there we close to 125,000 theater seats in houses outfitted for sound (Alfaro Salazar and Ochoa Vega 1997: 221–224). By 1932, 25 percent of film theaters in Latin America had been wired for sound and were ready to receive the ever-increasing output of Hollywood sound films and national productions (de Usabel 1982: 81).

This second layer of intermediality is of great importance, since subsequent "national" styles/idioms and cinematic strategies were therefore also inescapably linked to a panoply of Hollywood influences and practices. The intermedial matrix of this period is thus not only film and radio (and other sound reproduction technologies), but "film," "Hollywood film," and radio/sound reproduction. When we stop to consider that Hollywood sound films in English were initially unintelligible to most audiences unless subtitled and/or dubbed, the interrelationship among these interlocking technologies becomes even more complicated, since the standard Spanish-speaking spectator would have had to read, exercising the visual and literate, rather than fully engage in the new social and ostensibly very modern role of being a "listener" that the new technologies promised. As José Gatti suggests, an audience who must read subtitles will necessarily neither view nor hear carefully: the subtitles must be read first, and only if time permits can the eye focus on the image while the ear disconnects from foreign-language dialogue, and will at best only process music and noises (Gatti 2000: 94). How does this impact the experience and pleasure of being a modern listening subject of radio and sound cinema? Ultimately, it seems that in Latin America, being a fulfilled listening subject at the movies could only be realized through the imagined visual and sonic communities produced by national cinemas (in Spanish/Portuguese).

Finally, in smaller Latin American countries such as Chile, Uruguay, Cuba, and Colombia, in which sound national cinemas appear much later (1934 in Chile with *Norte y sur* [*North and South*, Jorge Delano Coke], 1936 in Uruguay with *Dos destinos* [*Two Destinies*, Juan Etchebehere], 1937 in Cuba with *La serpiente roja* [*The Red Serpent*, Ernesto Caparrós], and 1938 in Colombia with *Al son de las guitarras* [*To the Tune of the Guitars*, Alberto Santana and Carlos Schroeder]), the chronology is different once again. In these countries, sound cinema emerges not only under the influence of radio and Hollywood films, but also under the often more significant influence of the films of the earlier Latin American innovators, especially the more widely exported Mexican and Argentine cinemas. It is therefore not surprising that intermedial relationships are quite complex in these other national sound cinemas, few of which would obtain "industrial" status (i.e. steady production) until much later, if at all.

Echoes of the radiophonic

In general, radiophonic intermedialities are textually evidenced in three areas that remain constant throughout the period: music and the performative; diegetic, formal, and stylistic cross-fertilizations and melodramatic narrative platforms. Synergistically, the performative and the affective (sentimentalism, banality, and melodrama) were the principal registers of radiophonic intermedialities. There is also a historical progression: if, in the 1930s, music and performance are the primary sites of these intermedialities, by the end of the 1930s and into the early 1940s, films in the region exhibit more complex echoes of the radiophonic through narrative, especially through melodrama. Rather than present a catalog of filmic evidence from throughout the region to support this thesis, I will focus my analysis on key scenes from two films of the 1930–1940s (alluding to a handful of others) that point to the textual complexities of this radio–film relationship and its evolution.

Musicality and the performative

Early sound cinema and radio are linked by their dependence on music, more specifically by the development and consolidation of nationness in music. Whether tango in Argentina, rancheras in Mexico, or sambas in Brazil, radio and sound cinema found in these national rhythms a way to assert their own singularity and national imaginaries and to create mass audiences. And for sound cinema, radio itself provided a framework through which to engage the new technology. Thus, popular rhythms are the engine that drove radio as well as early sound cinema in Latin America, establishing an exciting and complex synergy that defined the national as modern and incipient and their own singularity, national imaginaries, and mass audiences. In early sound cinema, the centrality of music is most evident not only because of its presence in the soundtrack, but because it is above all visibly performed, and ostensibly experienced "live." It is not surprising, therefore, that every national cinema explored and exploited the representation of musicality by seeking recourse to radio station settings and stories and performers who were becoming media stars through their exposure through radio and recorded music. Many of these films functioned to provide what the invisibility of radio precluded: the image of the singing body and the visual re-staging of the moment of radio performance. As João Luis Vieira has argued in regard to the two first Brazilian films with direct sound (Alô, Alô Brasil [Hello, Hello Brazil, 1935] and Alô Alô Carnaval [Hello, Hello Carnaval, 1936], both directed by Adhemar Gonzaga), these films functioned as "a sort of visualized radio" that changed the position of the cinema spectator, supplementing the visual pleasure of the bodies of the singing radio starts. It was as if "had he closed his eyes, the spectator could have been sitting in front of a radio" (Vieira 2003: 48). Thus, it should not be a surprise that Latin American cinema through the 1940s and well into the 1950s privileged songs performed in their entirety rather than orchestral soundtracks. As a result, performance was always part of the diegesis, and the narrative actors were also coincidentally (and not always diegetically justified) musical performers: Libertad Lamarque in Argentina was always also a performer, even in the most lachrymose melodramas, but that Tito Guízar can sing like a radio star is never justified narratively in Allá en el Rancho Grande (Over There in the Big Ranch, Fernando de Fuentes, 1936).

In Argentina, radio had been steadily popularizing singers, comedians, tango orchestras, and announcers (locutores) since the late 1920s and already had specialized publications dedicated to medium and its stars: Radiolandia (1927), Antena (1930), and Sintonía (1933). Idolos de la radio (Radio Idols, Eduardo Morera, 1934, Argentina) premiered at the Monumental Theater in Buenos Aires on October 24, 1934, and its huge popular success was almost guaranteed by its visual display of some of the most famous radio (and theater) stars of the time—Ada Falcón, Ignacio Corsini, Pablo Osvaldo Valle, Olinda Bozán, Tito Luisardo, and Ernesto Fama, among others. It was produced by the company Productora Cinematográfica Argentina Río de la Plata, an apparently hastily put-together collaboration between tango composer/singer Francisco Canaro, radio magnate Jaime Yankelevich (owner of Radio Nacional, after 1935, Radio Belgrano), and lawyer and radio entrepreneur Juan Cossio, who aimed to maximize their radio enterprise through the new markets enabled by sound cinema. The artistic director of the production company and director of the film, Eduardo Morera (who had experience with sound film technology, having been in charge of the early Carlos Gardel shorts filmed in Buenos Aires), was in accord that their goal was to reach the same popular mass audience of Radio Nacional/Belgrano (Gómez Rial 1999: 250–260).

Certainly, Idolos de la radio fulfilled this ambition. The inclusion of more than half a dozen complete musical numbers in 100 minutes suggests that there was little time for narrative development. Although very much in the style of the musical revue films with which Hollywood had begun its incursions into sound but would soon abandon, in addition to all the musical performances, the film does have a well-developed dual focus narrative: a love plot and a rags-to-stardom (in radio) plot. As if to highlight its intermedial origins, the credit sequence is superimposed atop silhouetted images of film and radio production scenarios—cameramen holding reels, silhouetted men speaking into microphones—and still photographs of its principal stars (reminiscent of similar photographs that would have already appeared in publicity magazines). Yet in the film's very first scene, the film already announces an alleged perceptual and/or experiential superiority over the radiophonic. Despite its economy of means, the film announces its status as "cinema" with an elegant track that shows decorations and stops at a hand annotating sheet music. At this point, a female voice in off seems to be reading a job ad from the newspaper. A pan left and a cut barely concealed by a wipe effect discloses the speaker, a young woman who comments on the difficulty of finding jobs. Another fake wipe brings us to a newspaper and the original voice is revealed, when the newspaper is dropped, as that of an older woman who continues reading job ads. After economically and very cinematically establishing a family unit of an Italian immigrant grandfather and two sisters looking for work (the younger played by the great tango singer Ada Falcón in a rare screen appearance), the scene shifts in tone when the doorbell rings to introduce a man (a German/Jewish immigrant by his accent and attire) claiming to want to buy the family's radio. As they negotiate over the price of the radio, the Ada Falcón character asserts that one can hear all the stations very well and the older sister proceeds to adjust the dial, in an instructional close-up. The first station heard seems to be addressing the buyer directly: "Mr., don't let yourself be tricked, purchase cheaper!" She quickly retunes to another station airing a melodramatic *radionovela*. After alternating close-ups from the buyer and the sister to the radio apparatus as the third protagonist, a new shot focuses on the radio's electrical cord and, quickly panning left, uses the cord to establish an interesting sense of visual continuity with the cord of a microphone in a radio studio, where the actors of the *radionovela* are performing. The scene in the studio discloses that the plaintive cry of a baby in the radio drama is produced by a fat mustachioed man straddling a chair before we cut back to the living room, where the sister and the radio buyer are visibly moved by the story. Cutting back to the studio, an announcer approaches the mic to announce that we have heard episode number 2,945 of the *radionovela* "The grief of a mother, or when pain hurts." Without a break, the announcer continues with a promotional spot: "If your shoes hurt, buy Double X shoes. They are the best."

Once again in the living room, we see the sister still raptly listening as the radio announcer continues and announces a contest to select the "Queen of Tango." This radio contest will serve as the narrative motor that will propel the rest of the plot, in which Ada will sing her grandfather's compositions to become a tango star and find true love in the arms of the already established star Ignacio Corsini.

Thus, although the film is clearly intended to build upon the success and penetration of radio with popular audiences, it also rather quickly asserts its own superiority as a medium that gives the cinematic audience vision as well as sound: its authority is legitimated by the fact that it can show the workings of radio, the lies and tricks that cannot be heard by the naïve radio listener. As well, radio gives it the tools through which to establish its own

Figure 21.1   The electrical cord of the radio in the living room links to the microphone in the radio station in *Idolos de la Radio* (*Radio Idols*, Eduardo Moreira, 1934).

novel form of continuity: the radiophonic apparatus itself, the cord that visually links the receiver to the microphone through the otherwise invisible ether, narratively rationalizes the quick juxtaposition of vastly different spatial and sonic spaces through the radiophonic. Nevertheless, at the end of the sequence, the announcement of the tango queen contest is neither questioned nor doubted: the listeners in the living room "believe" and so must the narrative . . . and the audience.

Beyond musicality and the "broadcastings": the radiophonic as narrative and stylistic engine

To the degree that musicality and the performative were central to radiophonic filmic intermedialities, the establishment of a narrative platform centered on melodrama, sentimentalism, and banality was also a significant intermedial process. Melodrama was, of course, already an integral part of silent cinema throughout the region, often developing under the guise of nationalist themes and the influence of the very popular Italian diva films of the 1910s–1920s (especially in Mexico), melodramatic tango lyrics (the *arrabal* films of El Negro Ferreyra in Argentina), and Hollywood films. Early radio throughout the region, although at first focused more on music and news, quickly began to experiment with narrative modes, developing novel ways of telling stories. It had to learn how to stimulate the imagination through aurality, extremely stylized voices, music, and noises to produce the necessary excess. The process began with radial adaptations of popular literature such as Alejandro Galindo and his brother Marcos Aurelio's 1932 adaptation of Dumas' *The Three Musketeers* for XEW, "The Voice of Latin America from Mexico," or popular/folkloric themes and *sainetes* exploited by traveling theatrical companies such as Andrés González Pulido's *Chispazos de tradición* (*Sparks of Tradition*, 1931) in Argentina. Listening to narratives on the radio became a popular pastime identified as *radionovelas* (and linked to commercial sponsorships not unlike that of U.S. soap operas). *Radionovelas* emerged under the mantle of serial popular literature, the *folletín*, popular theatrical genres, and the Hollywood serial films that had already visualized these earlier forms.

In Latin America, we can trace a melodramatic radiophonic intermediality since the earliest days of sound cinema. For example, in *Madre querida* (*Dear Mother*, Juan Orol, 1934), an Ur-radiophonic melodrama, Juan Orol (who was affiliated with the XEB station, the oldest in Mexico, owned by the Compañía Cigarrera del Buen Tono) begins with a *locutor*-like preamble featuring Orol speaking directly to the spectators from behind a desk, like an embodied authoritative male radio announcer (the vast majority of *locutores* were male), dedicating the film to the *madrecitas* of the world who, as mothers, have inevitably suffered, and setting up the scene for the melodramatic excess to come. Later on, the film acknowledges and embodies the new social position of the listeners. In a crucial scene thick with longing, the boy without a mother and with a father who thinks he is widowed listen to a radio broadcast about Mother's Day in the living room. Intercut with shots of the *locutor* at the XEB studios and other unidentified families also listening to the same broadcast exalting motherhood, the film acknowledges the listeners as an invisible community and reels them into the melodrama, a shared pathos, through the mediation of the radiophonic.

By 1941, almost a decade after the convergence of sound media had begun, the relationship between the cinema and radio had changed. Radio had consolidated its popularity and had become a ubiquitous mass medium, while nationally and internationally the Mexican national cinema had also begun to hit its stride since the success of *Allá en el Rancho Grande*

Figure 21.2   Embodying the new social position of "listeners." *Madre querida* (*Dear Mother*, Juan Orol, 1934).

in 1936 and found audience niches. In the realm of filmic melodrama, the national and international success of *Cuando los hijos se van* (*When the Children Leave Home*, 1941, Juan Bustillo Oro) was seen as an engine for the increasing prestige of the national cinema and for the consolidation of the genre of suffering mothers (Bustillo Oro 1984: 193–196). It is, as Ayala Blanco argued, "the archetype of the family melodrama genre" (Ayala Blanco 1979: 50–51).

Cuando los hijos se van begins with a radiophonic frame: the film exploits the certainty that audiences already knew how to be listeners, invokes them as listeners, and gifts them with the privilege to see. After the credits, the diegesis begins with a 2.5-minute voice-over sequence introducing the setting, a colonial home in Orizaba with multiple interior enclosures, and the date: "December 24th some years ago." The doors and porticos of the house open as the resonant male voice invites us to enter "with the same emotions we felt when crossing our own thresholds." The *locutor*-like voice describes the interior patio in detail, linking specific features—the rose bushes, the trees—to the labor and sacrifice of the father and mother and laying out explicit hooks for the audience to establish affective links with the empty and still sterile space. As the camera enters the living room, for example, the voice-over asks, in a very radiophonic aural invocation of the senses, "What aroma is that? It smells like distant and happy times . . . of pine . . . of nativity scenes!" The *locutor* we never see is Manuel Bernal, a beloved XEW *locutor* famous for arguing that "in radio the voice is the image," and therefore remaining a rather mysterious public figure throughout his career; his voice would have been instantly recognizable, believable, and trustworthy to a 1940s audience in Mexico (Mota Martínez and Nuñez Herrera 1998: 149–152). This was a voice the public knew how to listen and respond to. As Bernal's voice introduces the scenario and the camera penetrates the interior spaces, he remarks, "We are invisible witnesses. No one will hear our steps or even the accelerated beats of our hearts. No one will notice our presence." Invisible, just like the radio: imagine what my voice describes, nevertheless the film will show it to you. This voiceover introduces the narrative and will interrupt the plot three other times to move the story forward, to explain temporal changes, and to comment upon the passage of time. It is the structural thread that makes sense of the temporal elisions and it invokes something else: a desire for the guidance of that ethereal radio voice that gives shape and meaning to experience. Serving the same function that would be fulfilled by a *radionovela locutor*—extensively describing locales and linking them to affective states, establishing an initial enigma to be explored, guiding and manipulating the reading, and pointing to a certain moral order to be maintained—the voiceover uses the radiophonic as an affective shortcut to effectively begin the story, having already secured the desired listening and spectatorial state and interpellating the audience as part of an affective community.

Thus, enveloped by the aura and emotional appeal of the radiophonic, the story unfolds: the threat to the sanctity of the family and its dynamics when the children, seduced by circumstances and opportunities or unfairly banished, leave home for the city. The emotional climax of the narrative curiously occurs through the radiophonic not at the end, but about two-thirds of the way through the travails of the by then reduced family unit: father Pepe (Fernando Soler), mother Guadalupe (Sara García), and compadre Casimiro (Joaquín Pardavé), who lives across the street in a space we never see. It is May 10, Mother's Day, and Casimiro brings Guadalupe a radio set as a present and a newspaper clipping announcing that her beloved favorite son Raimundo (who had been unfairly banished from the family home) is going to sing on the radio a special Mother's Day program. However, saddled by debt she has incurred to help one of the least deserving of her children, the holder of her IOUs arrives to seize her furnishings, including the new radio, for repayment. The scene is then staged (for over 10 minutes) in between staggering close-ups of Sara García weeping as she listens to her son singing and almost hugging the radio, and cutaways to Casimiro and to the men who had come to pick up her belongings (some of whom are visibly moved). Functioning as an umbilical cord that permits communication between mother and son, the radio set fulfills her oft-proclaimed desire to hear his voice again. To hear his voice, not just to see him. Once again, the film proclaims the importance of being a listener and wraps it up under the mantle of an affective miasma that sweeps all other concerns under the rug.

Figure 21.3 Sara García radiophonic apotheosis in *Cuando los hijos se van* (*When the Children Leave*, Juan Bustillo Oro, 1941).

If the valence in earlier films was dismantling the veracity of radio, that is here disavowed. Radio is both a structuring principle for the narrative and the vehicle for its most affective dénouement. The radiophonic and the filmic are one.

Conclusions

By recognizing the multivalent intermedial relationships between radio and film in Latin America as both a comparative model with the U.S. experience, and as a contrastive study of uneven development within the region, we are able to formulate a series of questions that have usually been short-circuited by most Latin American film histories. Among these is the need to question the implications of the construction of mass audiences; we are speaking here of listeners and spectators who were also social subjects and whose social positioning was stabilized, if not formed, through the technological mediation of the practice of listening. Beyond questioning how the mediascape was constructed, in tandem, by technologies that learned and competed with each other to build mass audiences, we need to further interrogate the material practices of film and radio through which "listening" as a social position was stabilized. This is not simply a question of teasing out elements of class, ideology, or political manipulation in particular texts. The interrogation of the complementarity of intermedial practices leads, perhaps inevitably, to questions of cultural/social identity formation in a period of rapid modernization.

To the degree that being modern in earlier decades meant being attuned to the spectacular visualities of the silent cinema, in the 1930s and early 1940s, that modernity had shifted and invoked listening in a new way as the crystallization of the attitudes required by the new media and their new commercial imperatives. An intermedial lens helps us to understand this period in greater depth and should also prove helpful to unravel the complexities of similar moments of "crisis" as transitions have occurred in the Latin American mediascape.

References

Alfaro Salazar, H. and Ochoa Vega, A. (1997) *Espacios distantes . . . aún vivos: Las salas cinematográficas de la Ciudad de Mexico*. Mexico City: Universidad Autónoma Metropolitana.

Altman, R. (2004) "Cinema Sound at the Crossroads: A Century of Identity Crises." In D. Nasta and D. Huvelle (eds.), *Le son en perspectives*. Brussels: Peter Lang, pp. 13–46.

Ayala Blanco, J. (1979) *La Aventura del cine mexicano*. Mexico City: Ediciones Era.

Bordwell, D., Staiger, J., and Thompson, K. (1985) *The Classical Hollywood Cinema: Film Style and Mode of Production to 1960*. London: Routledge.

Batson, L.D. (1929) "The Extent of the Development of Radio over the World." *The Annals of the American Academy of Political and Social Science*, 142 (March): 21–31.

Bedoya, R. (1992) *100 años de cine en el Perú: una historia crítica*. Lima: Universidad de Lima.

Bustillo Oro, J. (1984) *Vida cinematográfica*. Mexico City: Cineteca Nacional.

Claxton, R.H. (2007) *From Parsifal to Perón: Early Radio in Argentina, 1920–1944*. Gainesville, FL: University Press of Florida.

Crafton, D. (2004) "Mindshare: Telephone and Radio Compete for the Talkies." In J. Fullerton and J. Olsson (eds.), *Allegories of Communication: Intermedial Concerns from Cinema to the Digital*. Rome: John Libbey, pp. 141–156.

D'Lugo, M. (2010) "Aural Identity, Genealogies of Sound Technologies, and Hispanic Transnationality on Screen." In N. Durovicova and K. Newman (eds.), *World Cinemas, Transnational Perspectives*. New Brunswick, NJ: Routledge, pp. 160–184.

de los Reyes, A. (1987) *Medio siglo de cine mexicano (1986–1947)*. Mexico City: Editorial Trillas.

de Usabel, G.S. (1982) *The High Noon of American Films in Latin America.* Ann Arbor, MI: UMI Research Press.

Di Núbila, D. (1998) *La época de oro: Historia del cine Argentino, I.* Buenos Aires: Ediciones del Jilguero.

Douglas, M.E. (1996) *La tienda negra: El cine en Cuba (1897–1990).* Havana: La Cinemateca de Cuba.

Douglas, S.J. (2004) *Listening In: Radio and the American Imagination.* Minneapolis, MN: University of Minnesota Press.

Elsaesser, T. (2004) "The New Film History as Media Archeology." *Cinémas: revue d'études cinématographiques/Cinémas: Journal of Film Studies,* 14(2–3): 75–117.

España, C. (1999) "El modelo institucional: Formas de representación en la edad de oro." In C. España (ed.), *Cine Argentino: Industria y clasicismo, vol. 1 (1933–1956).* Buenos Aires: Fondo Nacional de las Artes, pp. 22–159.

Gabus Mendes, O. (1929) "De São Paulo." *Cinearte,* 183 (August 29): 20–21. Available at: http://mls.bireme.br/_popup_pdf.php?data=c|1929|08|04|0183 (accessed December 16, 2016).

García Riera, E. (1993) *Historia documental del cine mexicano: vol 1, 1929–1937.* Guadalajara: Universidad de Guadalajara.

Godoy Quezada, M. (1966) *Historia del cine chileno 1902–1966.* Santiago de Chile: Anon.

Jarvinen, L. (2012) *The Rise of Spanish-Language Filmmaking: Out from Hollywood's Shadow, 1929–39.* New Brunswick, NJ: Rutgers University Press.

King, J. (1990) *Magical Reels.* London: Verso.

Gatti, J. (2000) "Lusofonia no cinema brasileiro: notas sobre a presença de línguas no cinema." In *Estudos de cinema: SOCINE II e III.* São Paulo: Annablume, pp. 86–97.

Gómez Rial, S. (1999) "Compañía Argentina de Films Ríio de la Plata: Los románticos del micrófono." In C. España (ed.), *Cine Argentino: Industria y clasicismo, vol. 1 (1933–1956).* Buenos Aires: Fondo Nacional de las Artes, pp. 250–263.

Machado, R. (1987) "A produção paulistana de 1914 a 1922." In F. Ramos (ed.), *História do cinema brasileiro.* São Paulo: Art Editora, pp. 99–127.

Maranghello, C. (2005) *Breve historia del cine argentino.* Bardelona: Laerte, S.A. Ediciones.

Matallana, A. (2006) *Locos por la radio: Una historia social de la radiofonía en la Argentina, 1923–1947.* Buenos Aires: Prometeo.

Miquel, A. (2005) *Disolvencias: Literatura, cine y radio en México (1900–1950).* Mexico City: Fondo de Cultura Económica.

Morais da Costa, F. (2008) *O Som no Cinema Brasileiro.* Rio de Janeiro: Editora Viveiros de Castro.

Mota Martínez, F. and Núñez Herrera, M.E. (1998) *Locutores en acción: vida y hazañas de quienes hicieron la radio mexicana.* Mexico City: Asociación Nacional de Locutores.

Ochoa Gautier, A.M. (2006) "El sonido y el largo siglo XX." *Revista Número,* 51. Available at: www.revistanumero.com/51/sonido.htm. (accessed December 1, 2016).

Paranaguá, P.A. (1996) "América Latina busca su imágen." In G. Domínguez and J. Talens (eds.), *Historia General del Cine Volumen X.* Madrid: Cátedra, pp. 205–394.

Sterne, J. (2003) *The Audible Past: Cultural Origins of Sound Reproduction.* Durham, NC: Duke University Press.

Vieira, J.L. (1987) "A chanchada e o cinema carioca (1930–1955)." In F. Ramos (ed.), *História do cinema brasileiro.* São Paulo: Art Editora, pp. 129–188.

—— (2003) "Apresentação: Encontro com o cinema brasileiro." *Centro Cultural Banco de Brasil,* May, pp. 18–23. Cited in Morais da Costa, F., *O Som no Cinema Brasileiro,* p. 123.

Williams, A. (1992) "Historical and Theoretical Issues in the Coming of Recorded Sound to the Cinema." In R. Altman (ed.), *Sound Theory, Sound Practice.* New York/London: Routledge, pp. 126–137.

22

MUSIC IN LATIN AMERICAN CINEMA

Aural communities on- and off-screen

Marvin D'Lugo

Editors' introduction

A number of contributors have focused on the granular details of transnational film practices in the region. In Chapter 10, Gerard Dapena looks at the dynamics of genre films as inherently cross-border experiences. Luisela Alvary (Chapter 17) and Tamara L. Falicov (Chapter 18) review how the financing and cultural promotion of films seek to redefine local audiences in relation to international market and cultural forces. In a similar vein, Josetxo Cerdán and and Miguel Fernández Labayen (Chapter 23) view the cinema's rivalry with television in terms of the latter's success in forging national identities while negotiating broader Latin American cultural production in the global marketplace.

In this chapter, Marvin D'Lugo extends that scrutiny of the national/transnational tensions of Latin American mass media by honing in on the changing relation of music to film since the advent of sound films. He considers the affective bonds created by forms of musical address in films not always identified as movie musicals. Like Mestman (Chapter 12), he points to the watershed experience of New Latin American Cinema's practitioners, especially in Cuba and Argentina, as they engaged in experiments with musical sound as a specific subject matter of films, or as a strategy of engagement with audiences in national and cross-border contexts. Dovetailing with Ana M. López's discussion of the ideological investment of the radiophonic experience for early sound cinema's audiences (Chapter 21), D'Lugo leads us to consider the politics that underlies certain forms of musical address to audiences, beyond the institutional controls in contemporary film.

Cinematic communities of affect

The shifting relation of what Latin American audiences hear and see as mediated through sound technologies has been at the core of musical cinema almost from its inception in the early 1930s. We note this in the multilayered nature of early sound films containing popular songs, which appeared to follow the model of so-called Hollywood musicals (Altman 1999: 31–34). Though somewhat akin to *The Jazz Singer* (Alan Crosland, 1927) in their incorporation of songs with a cinematic narrative, these films were less about a musical genre than about the variations of the more dominant melodramatic mode in Latin American cinema. We see this in *Santa* (Antonio Moreno, Mexico, 1932) and *La mujer del puerto* (*Woman of the Port*, Arcady Boytler, Mexico, 1933). Even in *Allá en el Rancho Grande* (*Over at the Big Ranch*, Fernando de Fuentes, Mexico, 1936), in which songs abound, audiences as well as critics viewed the ranchera clichés as more relevant than the musical dimensions of this film. This generic ambivalence is significant insofar as it suggests that even at the outset, the alignment of popular song to film was a fluid relation, open to other stylistic and genre forces.

More to the point, a number of these musical sequences demonstrate the relationship between the music industry of this period and radio and cinema (Denning 2015: 72). Intermedial practices helped forge the impression of a mediascape in which songs were seemingly ubiquitous and connected the experiences of moviegoing with other social experiences of the new sound sensorium. Related to this was the presence of singers whose iconic status was enhanced by their seeming "mobility" across genres, as well as the social spaces of their audience's reception.

In such a multimedia context, the term "spectator" only signifies part of the story; it is more accurate in this context to use Michel Chion's term to describe the way multiple sound media conceived of their audience as "audio-viewers" (Chion 2009: 468), whose engagement with the world of the cinematic fiction mirrors their experience as mediated by popular musical sounds. The term is especially apt, as Octavio Getino argues, since the contemporary moment is characterized by the synergy among seemingly distinct audiovisual industries: radio, recordings, film, video, and their permutations through digital technologies and the Internet (Getino 2009: 19–26), which are all on display in the cinematic mediascape.

To understand the nature of musical cinema, therefore, we need to take into account not only what will be recognized as a movie musical, but also the modes of reception that frame these films. By emphasizing the role of audio-viewing, we may better appreciate the logic underpinning how certain forms of popular music are privileged in Latin American film beyond their status as mere entertainment. They hold the potential to be a unifying force of collective social and political identification in ways that recall Paul Gilroy's argument in *The Black Atlantic* (1993) for a "double consciousness" that leads black listeners to transcend the geopolitical borders of the nation as popular music shapes a transnational racial community (Gilroy 1993: 37). Gilroy's view of the psychic power of music to unify an otherwise fragmented racial community across national borders was an important intervention in postcolonial discussions of community affiliation; it serves as an important antecedent to what Tania Gentic has recently called the "aural imaginary." She argues that the cinematic incorporation of popular music involves "the spectator in space, not just the body represented on the screen, and it produces an emotional tie between them" (Gentic 2014: 201). Building on an approach to popular aural culture and the music industry first proposed by Roshanak Kheshti (2011: 724), Gentic perceives how cinema can produce "a spatialized and affective community that transcends the bordered limits of geographical space," that is, "an affective and corporeally felt notion of community" (Gentic 2014: 201).

As Claudia Gorbman reasons in more general cinematic contexts, there are affective "cultural musical codes" that will align audiences with musical sounds (Gorbman 1987: 3). In connecting the audiovisual to its audience, these bonds are never random; they involve the kind of aesthetic and technological decisions that reorder the emotional filters through which to relate to the audiovisual experience. Questions of the use of music in film therefore need to be framed in terms of how some Latin American filmmakers have conceptualized popular music texts as a negotiation with images, narrative, and the social context of their audience.

Geopolitical realignments of film musicals

During the 1950s, intensified internal migration across Latin America reordered the mass markets upon which the studio-produced movie musicals had so heavily depended. An influx into urban areas of large heterogeneous populations encountered in hybridized forms of their own music on radio a comfortable aural bridge to their adjustments to urban life (Rowe and Schelling 1991: 17–18). Cinematically, two emblematic films reflect these ongoing musical realignments that bracket the decade: *Víctimas del pecado* (*Victims of Sin*, Emilio Fernández, Mexico, 1951) and *Orfeo negro* (*Black Orpheus*, Marcel Camus, France–Brazil–Italy, 1958). Both are urban narratives, outwardly deploying the familiar formulas of musicals of the 1930s and 1940s: characters who, whether motivated or not, burst into song, or else are part of a musical show within the filmic plot. During the first quarter-century of the sound era, popular local melodies had circulated across borders in a seemingly endless series of movie musicals, enthralling local audiences beyond their country of production. Yet, owing to their imagery, narrative, and language, films such as the Mexican ranchera musical *Ay Jalisco, no te rajes* (*Ay, Jalisco, Don't Backslide*, Joselito Rodríguez, 1941), which enjoyed an unprecedented six-month run in Buenos Aires, still reinforced folkloric Mexican cultural tropes. These recent films, however, portended a different musical imaginary with a potentially more "global" rhythm and sound.

In the first musical number of Fernández's urban cabaretera narrative, as David García observes, a show-within-the-film sequence presents Cuban singer Rita Montaner voicing santería chants to the accompaniment of Dámaso Pérez Prado's band. All of this is backdrop to the gyrations of Ninón Sevilla as she leads a dance ensemble in a raucous performance (García 2012: 180). Strikingly, this sequence showcases a theatricalized Mexican *mise en scène* in which Cuban music has displaced hyper-nationalistic Mexican rhythms. While it is true that Cuban band music, especially the mambo, had lodged itself in the urban culture of Mexico City by the early 1950s, the film is less a barometer of musical tastes than a reflection of that moment when the framework of the national can no longer contain the film's characters.

This point is driven home in an early scene in *Víctimas* when the pimp Rodolfo (Rodolfo Acosta), rejecting his prostitute's baby, pressures her to abandon the infant; we see her dump her baby in a garbage can. The scene is shot against the backdrop of the Mexican Monument to the Revolution, foregrounding a post-Mexican anti-maternal image against the background of the quintessential Mexican nationalist symbol.

The pattern of transborder consciousness aligned with music became increasingly more apparent throughout the 1950s. We find evidence of an already constructed international cinema/music site for a different kind of Latin American musical cinema in the success of Lima Barreto's *O Cangaceiro* (1953) and its popular musical number "Mulher Rendeira,"

Figure 22.1   Rita Montaner with Pérez Prado's Orchestra in *Víctimas del pecado*.

which, as Ana López details, not only won special prizes at the Cannes Festival for its music, but also made particular transnational inroads in France and the US as a popular song (López 1998: 138–139). Nelson Pereira Dos Santos's *Rio Zona Norte* (*Rio, Northern Zone*, 1957), in turn, casts a reflexive spotlight of the backstory of popular Brazilian music by building a narrative around the fleeting memories of a black samba composer Espíritu, played by Grande Otelo, an actor who achieved stardom in popular *chanchadas* of the previous decade. While Brazilian film music found a responsive audience abroad, filmmakers at home began to question how music from the *favelas* has been exploited by the music industry.

Such critical foregrounding of what was once merely a form of local popular entertainment helps set the stage for a paradoxical musical film, Marcel Camus's *Orfeo negro*, an international co-production that deftly exploits its Brazilian subject matter. The film in fact displaces the rhythmically complex samba with the "cool" infectious beat and unusual harmonies of bossa nova, literally a "new way." Since the 1940s, samba had been the popular "national" sound closely identified globally with Brazil (McGowan and Pessanha 2009: 31). Owing to *Orfeo negro*'s haunting music by composers Antônio Carlos Jobim and Luis Bonfá, bossa nova elided ironically into the international popular imagination, with the idea a new Brazil, even as it focused exclusively on life in Rio's shantytowns. The film would go on to win an Oscar in the Best Foreign Film category in 1959.

After a night of lovemaking, Orfeo and Eurídice awake to the strains of Bonfá's "Manhã de Carnaval." This is, in effect, a double awakening, both the diegetic arising of the musician's lover but also, symbolically, to global audiences of a "new" musical sound from Brazil: on the one hand is the association of Orpheus in the European mythic tradition as the legendary bearer of music (Perrone 1998: 172); on the other, the cluster of tourist motifs of carnival and the natural union of local Brazilian space with border-crossing musical sounds. Bossa nova, derived from samba, but with a harmonic richness up to this point heard only in modern jazz compositions (McGowan and Pessanha 2009: 58), would in fact as a result of

Orfeo negro's success, become a national and an international craze. Like the earlier mambo, it would achieve global status as a world music genre.

No less significant in terms of its commercial appeal is the film's economy of scale that makes it congruent within the global art house film circuit that begins to take shape from the mid-1950s. The underlying implication of the early cinematic "niche market" is more than merely a reduction of scale and production costs; it implies a different type of audience, no longer defined as the nation (Galt and Schoonover 2010: 10–11). This in turn leads to a freedom of innovation in narrative construction that underscores the sense of the alternative. All of these are lessons Latin American filmmakers would soon learn on their own.

The politics and technology of new musical sounds

A newly emerging social paradigm for popular music, only hinted at in *Orfeo negro*, first comes to prominence in the 1960s, most notably in Cuba, beginning with the much-criticized *PM* (Saba Cabrera Infante and Jiménez-Leal, 1960), a Free Cinema-style documentary, with no audible dialogue, that simply records the events of nighttime frivolity of black patrons at several Havana bars. Its musical background, combined with the depiction of characters "outside the revolution," proved politically risky. It nonetheless suggests to the film's potential audience the place of popular dance music as an affective force for a population "unmediated" by other, meaning institutional, controls. That same year in *Cuba baila* (*Cuba Dances*), Julio García Espinosa proposed a more explicitly ideological project in which music and dance become models of a new mode of narration. The story of a frustrated *quinceañera* in pre-revolutionary Cuba whose celebration party goes amok is intended to suggest the alignment of social class in pre-revolutionary Cuba with popular music and dance: while the bourgeoisie are devoted to the waltz, the people engage in more nativist Afro-Cuban dance rhythms. García Espinosa's film embodies the logic of a number of Latin American films of the post-1950s that sought to "decolonize the ear" of local communities (Denning 2015: 140–147).

A subgenre of Cuban musical documentaries takes form in the 1960s and 1970s, giving textual centrality and social prominence to popular music. Rogelio París's *Nosotros, la música* (*We Are the Music*, 1964) becomes significant in its effort to expand the alignment of music and nation but, as Alexandra Vázquez argues, avoid a simplistic homogenization of all Cuban music to a single rhythmic style (Vázquez 2013: 175–176). Sara Gómez's *Y . . . tenemos sabor* (*And . . . We've Got Taste*, 1968) focuses more narrowly on the origins and contemporary nature of percussion instruments. The Cuban ideological push toward authentic popular musical forms would be rechanneled at various points with a seemingly anachronistic effort to develop locally inflected forms of musical comedy. These include *Un día en el solar* (*A Day in the Tenement*, Eduardo Manet, 1965), *Patakín* (Manuel Octavio Gómez, 1983), *La bella del Alhambra* (*The Beauty of the Alhambra*, Enrique Pineda Barnet, 1990), and *Un paraíso bajo las estrellas* (*A Paradise under the Stars*, Gerardo Chijona, 2000).

These Cuban films rely heavily on the explicitness of diegetic depictions of their popular musical themes. By contrast, in *La hora de los hornos* (*Hour of the Furnaces*, Argentina 1968), Fernando Solanas experiments with a much more sophisticated mode of musical narration that forcefully addresses the audio-viewer. One striking sequence in the first part of the film is staged in and around a record store in Buenos Aires. Here, as Craig Epplin explains (Epplin 2014: 35–37), we hear diegetic music, a popular Ray Charles song, as we see images of a group of 20-somethings mingling outside the record shop; the camera then follows them into the store where they are riffling through LPs; the popular music we hear, however, is not the music being fed through the record shop's loudspeakers. We can tell this by the rhythmic movements of the shoppers' heads. Here, we get a glimpse of Gentic's (2014) assertion of music as engaging the bodies as well as the ears of the listeners. This second strain of "semi-diegetic music," as Epplin calls it, is directed to the audio-viewer, "and stands a half-step removed from the onscreen action, which allows it to create a bridge between the store, the images that follow and the act of filming and editing" (Epplin 2014: 36).

The not-so-subtle logic of this key sequence is Solanas's critique of the neocolonial commercial imposition of popular, US-inspired music on a younger generation of Latin Americans. This brief sequence should be understood as a response to the growing presence of youth market in music and film throughout the region during this period. Youth culture connected to consumer culture had already begun to appear on screens in youth genre films in Argentina. In the chain of youth films that Enrique Carreras directs in the 1960s—*El club del clan* (1964); *Fiebre de primavera* (*Spring Fever*, 1965), *Ritmo nuevo, vieja ola* (*Old Rhythm, New Wave*, 1965), and *Mi primera novia* (*My First Girlfriend*, 1966)—musical sounds cease to be merely narrative adornment and become a soundscape containing meaning directly engaging the audience and connecting to their social milieu beyond cinema. This same paradigm also figures prominently in the Brazilian Jovem Guarda of the 1960s, with notable examples of Roberto Carlos films (e.g. *Roberto Carlos em ritmo de Aventura* [*Roberto Carlos in Tune with Adventure*, Roberto Farias, Brazil, 1967]). In Mexico, a new generation had already begun to discover their own self-image in a series of B "rocanrol" films that built on the model of earlier Mexican musical dramas and comedies (Zolov 1999: 30). Youth audiences could identify with singing heart-throb Enrique Guzmán in the chain of popular screen hits of the period that included *Twist locura de la juventud* (*Twist, the Craze of Youth*, Miguel M. Delgado, 1962), *Mi vida es una canción* (*My Life is a Song*, Miguel M. Delgado, 1963), and *La juventud se se impone* (*Youth Take Over*, Julián Soler, 1964).

For as much as these developments were rooted in local culture of youth rebellion, as Eric Zolov (1999), Julia Palacios (2005), and Laura Podalsky (2010) have argued, they also reflected a paradigm shift in sound technologies that shaped youth audiences of this new "audiotape era." The new technologies made possible new popular forms of "mobile listening," symbolized most potently by portable transistor radio (Denning 2015: 70).

Like the Cuban efforts to decolonize popular music, the subgenre of rock music films hints at a deeper shift in affective sensibilities that would redirect the use of music in Latin American films in subsequent decades. Highly individuated listening accompanies the introduction of compact disc technology in 1982 with the CD becoming the dominant industrial format for listening to reproduced music (Yúdice 2007: 49). Not only would the technology eventually uncouple music from its previous intermedial link to cinema, but it would inevitably inspire new textual strategies by filmmakers for nurturing the affective bonds that would flourish in progressively more political communities of affect in subsequent decades.

New geopolitical positioning

An essential part of that technological mobility is at the root of Carlos Monsiváis's thinking when he speaks of the twentieth century as the age of powerful and seemingly endless cultural migrations that have altered everyday life, and moved audiences both physically and virtually to new places (Monsiváis 2000: 155–180). He sees a continuum from nation-building films through modernizing television, culminating with the globalizing impact of the Internet. Within this technological sweep, the very notion of the musical film in Latin America undergoes a radical reconceptualization in its engagement with and reception by its increasingly more diverse and mobile audiences. The following discussion picks up the thread of that chronology as it traces the evolving geopolitics of music's relation to audio-viewership through the progressive expansion of sound technologies that reshape the aural imaginary.

Tangos: el exilio de Gardel (1985)

An early instance of what might be productively understood as the "reterritorialization" of the audio-viewer is Fernando Solanas's *Tangos, el exilio de Gardel* (*Tangos: The Exile of Gardel*, Argentina-France, 1985). As an international co-production, the film self-referentially pairs the global aura of the tango with its local origins, particularly as Solanas utilizes traditional and contemporary variations of the tango as a palimpsest of Argentine national politics. Working through a familiar musical repertory, one that is reinforced by the commercial availability of all forms of tango music on CD, Solanas exploits the already established affective bonds that have positioned this popular musical form with its audio-viewers.

The film begins with a highly stylized tango performed by a group of dancers on the Pont Neuf in Paris. This initial dance sequence, as it turns out, is only a bait, deployed to elicit then harness our affective response to the sensuous bodies in order to engage us in the story of the torture of Argentines at home and the political dislocation of members of the Argentine community in exile during the terrible years of the military junta.

Figure 22.2   Tango as seduction and "bait."

By the mid-1980s, a stylized performance of the tango dance had made a comeback internationally through the recent global success of *Tango Argentino*, the theatrical spectacle that was first presented by members of the Argentine exile community in Paris in 1983 (Fitch 2015: 173–174). One of the artistic supporters of that production was the famed bandoneonista Astor Piazzolla, who collaborated with Solanas on the music for *Tangos*. The plot channels the show by detailing the efforts of a group of Argentine exiles in Paris in 1979 to raise money for the production of a dramatic series of dance tableaux, a *tanguedia*, part tango, part tragedy. They have staged a dress rehearsal of the show for potential French investors. Through this on-screen audience, Solanas acknowledges the historical and commercial "trade" in tango as an entertainment commodity that has long held a special affection for French audiences, notably embodied in the evocation of the cinematic tangos of Carlos Gardel (González and Yanes 2013: 65–66). Besides staging a theatrical performance, Solanas' plot pivots on competing ideological versions of tango, pitting the nostalgic apolitical cinematic tango aligned with Gardel against the updated new tango circulated as part of contemporary cultural politics.

The conflict comes to a head midway through the film as the action halts, and Solanas foregrounds the conflicted responses of the French backers, an otherwise sympathetic community of affect engaged in aesthetic nostalgia, when they are asked to consider their literal investment in the tango show. Indirectly, we, their off-screen doubles, are also being asked about the nature of our own attraction to the reordering of the sexual bodies of the dancers in tableaux depicting the junta's state orchestrated brutality of the Argentine community.

Against the sensual affect to which it has recently been relegated in the global marketplace, the Piazzolla tango posits a more consequential political discourse about a community's resistance to political oppression. Preferring the version of the tango popularized internationally by the apolitical Gardel films, the backers are unwilling to acknowledge the troupe's assertion of a living tango, dance and music that have evolved over the century and are now imbued with contemporary political meaning. Yet such a confrontation is inevitable since the goal of the dance troupe is precisely to junk the old tango and to establish the expressive range of the *tanguedia* in order to tell the contemporary story of Argentina's political struggle. Displacing the Gardelian tango "Volver," which provides an audiovisual denouement to the film, the *tanguedia* represents an interpretive act to reshape community, according to Solanas, tied to a notion of *pueblo*, the people (González 1989: 193–194), around the affective power of a narrative of struggle against oppression embodied in the sounds.

Orfeo (1999)

A similarly politicized musical form, the samba, motivates Carlos Diegues's 1999 Brazilian production of *Orfeo*. Ostensibly a rebuttal to Camus's earlier *Orfeo negro*, Diegues's film revisits the Orpheus myth, the *favela* location, the samba school, even the Luiz Bonfá haunting Bossa Nova "Manhã de Carnaval," updating the French filmmaker's imposter Brazilianized Orpheus story (Signoreli Heise 2012: 91–92). To that end, the film looks backward to Brazilian film musical traditions—scenes of old chanchadas on a television monitor, Carnaval, and samba—but it also looks forward, with the inclusion of rap and new technologies, such as the boom box and the television simulcasts of the Samba competition, all of which have helped shape contemporary Brazilian identity. Indeed, unlike *Orfeo negro*, Diegues's *Orfeo* inscribes the presence of a local audio-viewer through whose eyes and ears contemporary Brazil is "localized" rather than "globalized," as was Camus's.

Shot in a constructed set, the "Carioca Hill" slums, designed as an amalgam of various *favelas*, underscore the contrast between the lush views of the city and the tawdry images of the slum (Signoreli Heise 2012: 98). Diegues's effort to reclaim authenticity thus produces a peculiar hybridity in the film in which the dividing line between cinematic fiction and contemporary Brazilian reality is continually erased. We see this most conspicuously in the film's opening sequence with aerial tourist views of the city and Guanabara Bay and then the immediate cut to the fictional *favela* with images of ongoing narco-related violence.

This narrative of "raw" urban reality is tellingly counterbalanced by the film's approximation of a music video rhetoric (Nagib 2007: 93–94). Diegues relocates the modern-day variant of the legend of Orpheus and Eurydice to an audiovisual *mise en scène* filled with technology that reduces the love story to mundane social reality. Cassette tapes and boom boxes predominate, as do television monitors that mix views of old chanchadas with rap music, simultcasts from Rio's Sambadrome and a pervasive radio loudspeaker, "Voz do Morro" (Voice from the Hill), a pirate radio station that punctuates pop music with announcement of local events.

The significance of the constructed cinematic *favela* lies in how it underscores the new aural imaginary for Brazilians. This communal space is more than simply the audiovisual locus of performance; it operates as a medium that provides a prosthetic ear to the characters who are literally surrounded by music; and it is music that shapes their actions as when the sounds of the samba encircles Orfeo and Eurídice after their night of lovemaking. Identification with music is how characters and actors transparently mirror the film's audience as that newly emerging audio-viewership of Brazil.

This aural *mise en scène* is further fashioned around the presence of Brazilian pop star Toni Garrido as Orfeo, the film's mythical troubadour protagonist. Indeed, Diegues's film is less about star-crossed lovers than it is about Orfeo. The fictional hero has been shaped by Garrido's own real-life biography, which included his humble roots in poverty, and his rise to fame as lead singer of the well-known *samba-reggae* band Cidade Negra that merged reggae, soul, and pop rock. Like the film, Garrido's Orfeo stands halfway between fiction and real life his hybrid identity reflects the contemporary samba's roots in the *favela* and its symbolic and real status as the spirit of the national community.

Of special note here is the recycling of "Manhã de Carnaval," which we first hear sung by young girls early on, as a lilting melody that encompasses the community's space. Later, when Orfeo returns Eurídice's dead body to the *favela* it is played again. Diegues seems to employ this crucial musical trope as part of the audio-viewers' cinematic musical memory, an auditory nostalgia that is initially affirmed only to be undermined by new and updated rhythms, voices, and songs. The repeated refrain of the song thus becomes, like the film itself, a contested site of auditory memory, ceding to the present.

Suite Habana (2003)

An analogous engagement of the audio-viewer with the power of auditory memories becomes one of the key signifying practices of Fernando Pérez's *Suite Habana*. Given the restrictive nature of Cuban society in the 1980s and 1990s, the film poses a subtle approach to the transborder political alignment of music and film, playing with a repertory of musical memories of audio-viewers from both on the island and beyond. As its title suggests, the film is shaped by the concept of the musical suite. Moving beyond the cinematic tradition of the city symphony, Pérez deploys what Salomé Aguilera Skvirsky calls the postcolonial "uncanny," that is, following Freud, urban space that one experiences as the "return of something once familiar but now repressed" (Aguilera Skvirsky 2013: 428). Indeed, the film's unvoiced politics is fashioned around the interplay between historically rooted musical rhythms aligned with instances of the island's repressed political past and contemporary images of Havana. Musical sounds shape various affective positions, pushing our engagement beneath and beyond the surfaces of the contemporary views of Havana to the site of historical consciousness displaced from the officially sanctioned images of the city during the "*Período especial*." Like Pérez's earlier films that document the Special Period—*Madagascar* (1994) and *La vida es silbar* (*Life is to Whistle*, 1999)—*Suite Habana* builds its view of the city as a community of survivors of national misfortune through a semantic play with the meanings of the word "sentir," which in Spanish can mean both to feel and to hear. Elliot Young has suggested that Pérez's long experience in circumventing state censorship in his decades of work as a documentary filmmaker (Young 2007: 36) enabled him to internalize an expressive register to circumvent any explicit political statement, leaving these formulations to audiences.

The potential for the audio-viewer's political recoding of musical material is built into the heterogeneous range of Cuban musicals sounds. The film features Habaneras, the *Contradanza habanera* with which the film begins, and more recent songs such as the 1960s ballad "Mariposas," heard on a TV and sung by popular musical artist Silvio Rodríguez, identified with the protest songs of the *nueva trova* artists of the era (Holmes 2015: 129). The absence of expository voice-over and the near total blockage of speech by any of the "characters" thwart possibility of direct articulation of a political message. As Tania Gentic argues, "resisting language as the basis for meaning" shifts the audio-viewer's attention to the need for a nonverbal supplement of meanings, which the film provides in four pivotal narratives involving musical affect and historical consciousness (Gentic 2014: 203). These include the story of Ernesto, a young man who repairs his parents' crumbling house by day and dances in Tchaikovsky's *Swan Lake* at night; Herberto, a railway worker who nightly plays the saxophone in a local church; Iván, a cross-dressing torch singer who lipsynchs Cuban Salsa singer Celia Cruz's version of "Ya no hace falta"/"There's no need anymore"; and finally, a group of nameless caretakers standing vigil over the statue of John Lennon in the memorial park honoring the fallen Beatles composer and performer. In their composite, these individuals underscore off-screen spaces and times that counter the omnipresent contemporary sense of contained Cuban space.

Fragments of an implied soundscape function as auditory reminders of earlier transborder movements of music that inevitably locate those sounds and spaces within a broader cultural and geopolitical community. Gentic argues that "[r]eading into the context of the music evoked from several different periods, these songs can be reinserted into a narrative structure of history, politics, and semantic coding of sound as meaning that corresponds to a collective national identity" (Gentic 2014: 211). While broadly speaking this is true, the "emotional work" that is involved here is pointedly directed toward bringing the audio-viewer to imagine in a historical mode the notion of community that has been lost, except on those of a particular generation. Thus, for example, "Mariposas," a song whose very lyrics echo the theme of the passage of time ("Qué maneras más curiosas de recordar tiene uno"/"What curious ways one has of remembering") is heard and viewed by 97-year-old Natividad, providing a complex intertextual critique of the Revolution that serves as a backstory to the film. A similarly unvoiced musical margin is created by the strains of *Swan Lake*, which accompanies Ernesto's ballet performance as it evokes both the historical period prior to the isolating Special Period, and the Cuban communion with a broadly defined international culture (Holmes 2015: 133).

Figure 22.3 John Lennon's "tears."

The expanding dynamics of historical traces and transnational consciousness conclude in the two final sequences that express musically the underlying tension between affective memories and constraining contemporary social reality. In the first, the silent caretaker is seated at night in the rain protecting the statue of John Lennon, erected after his death. We hear only the sound of rain, but in close-ups of Lennon's head with spectacles, the rain suggests that the singer is crying. The nearly silent *mise en scène* of the Lennon sequence underscores the apparent isolation of the statue and caretaker. Though there is no musical accompaniment to the images, Amanda Holmes reminds us of the phrase from Lennon's song, "Imagine" ("You may say I'm a dreamer, but I'm not the only one," are inscribed in Spanish at the foot of the statue), which embodies a utopian idealism (Holmes 2015: 130).

In the second sequence Pérez constructs what amounts to a coda to the entire film: Gonzalo Roig's bolero standard "Quiéreme mucho" is played over images of the deserted malecón in Havana on a rainy day, with the powerful waves crashing against the rocks in a movement synchronized with the rhythm of the song. This very same scene performed by Cuban bolero songstress Omara Portuando, "Quiéreme mucho," was first used in Pérez's fictional film of survival in the Special Period, *Madagascar* (1994). The composition dates back to 1911. Over the intervening 90 years, the melody has remained something of a standard of popular Cuban music, often associated with tourist images of the island. Here, however, its combination with footage of the waves hitting the stone barriers, effectively transforms the human lover into patria, the nation as the battered community. Especially noteworthy is the particular recording of the song in which the revered Portuando, a prominent musical persona in Cuba since the 1960s and nostalgically associated with Ry Cooder's *Buena Vista Social Club* (1999), is joined briefly by a chorus. The suggestion is not merely historical, but also opens up the sense of the unseen, otherwise unvoiced community.

The audiovisual mixing in the final sequence unifies the voiced and unvoiced fragmented lives affectively into a single aural community. The largely nonverbal musical flow of the preceding sections now cedes to the verbal through Portuando's voice and Roig's music, transposing the music into a sensorial dimension (Gentic 2014: 209) within which meaning is produced by the affective register in combination with the visual track. The result, though never verbalized, directs the community of listeners—here, both those in Cuba and off the island, as well as to foreign cultural tourists—to an unspoken political theme.

Cobrador: In God We Trust (2006)

Since the 1980s, Paul Leduc has explored strategies to subvert audiences' passive relation to cinema and to bring them to experience through the aural imaginary the projection of a borderless Latin America as a "*Patria Grande*." That vision first became apparent in Leduc's *Barroco* (1988), an adaptation of Alejo Carpentier's novella *Concierto barroco*. Retelling the history of interactions between Latin America and Europe, the film displaced all dialogue with the distinctive songs and rhythms that served to narrate five centuries of contact between American and European cultures.

In *Cobrador: In God We Trust*, Leduc mobilizes popular music for a political reading of the cultural politics of Latin America in the age of globalized economics. He constructs a transborder narrative of political resistance to the commercial exploitation of Latin America by the plunderers from the North. The film's protagonists, a radicalized Brazilian mine worker turned assassin, Cobrador, and his lover and accomplice (an Argentine photographer named Ana) move across the American continent, avenging the exploitation of the *pueblo*. The sprawling geopolitical narrative begins in Manhattan and moves in progressive tableaux to Miami, Mexico City, Buenos Aires, Rio de Janeiro, and finally a mineral mine in Belo Horizonte.

The credit sequence announces part of the film's strategy by posing a contagious Latin rhythm over shots of fog-laden Manhattan, effectively resignifying the presumed capital of U.S. trade as a Latinized urban space. This is decidedly not the gleaming global metropolis; rather, it is seen in cloud-shrouded tenements, which, in effect, locate the Latin community as underclass. Leduc employs that image as an enunciative strategy through which to position his audio-viewer to see and hear the contemporary soundscape as the product of commercial appropriation of American space. Unlike his earlier *Barroco*, in which music was seen as the unifying agency of a common culture, in *Cobrador* popular music and song become the diegetic agents of foreign exploitation. We see this most pointedly in the Mexico City sequence, in which we hear rhythmic pop music that coincides with our first view of the iconic main square, the Zócalo. The sound–image juxtaposition suggests the historical motif of invasion as we observe secular music and dance performed on the site of past and present religious space. The rock music also signifies in its own right the massification of that intrusive sound, made all the more striking as we discover what looks like a rehearsal for a rock concert being filmed against the backdrop of the Metropolitan Cathedral.

Gradually, we come to recognize that our perspective of this scene is being mediated through the camera eye of Ana, a professional photographer who is focusing on the on-screen audience of passersby who have stopped to view the rehearsal. We identify her as a distanced observer of this bizarre spectacle unfolding before the cathedral, its grotesqueness originating from a deformed syncretism of secular and religious rituals (conquest, colonial, and neocolonial commerce) in which, finally, mass-mediated popular music has totally

Figure 22.4   Secular music and dance performed on the site of past and present religious space, in Paul Leduc's *Cobrador*.

erased all prior history. The materiality of the urban terrain has been transformed into a soundscape, the locus of an exploitative spectacle shaped by musical sounds.

Leduc's intricate and layered staging of the scene involves first the sensorial engagement with the rhythmic music, then a visual distancing from the filmic *mise en scène*. This seems designed to promote in the audio-viewer a double range of interrogation involving first, affective engagement with the on-screen musical performance, then a questioning of the origins of the cultural politics that has reduced a community to the role of mere consumers of musical "merchandise." This eventually leads us to recognize the dystopian nature of the borderless community. The scene thus crystallizes one of the central themes of *Cobrador*: how mass-mediated popular music serves to control the movement of bodies, and how the industries behind that product have dissolved all geopolitical or cultural borders, producing a chaotic view of the communal Latin American space produced by the forces of global commerce.

The ambitious and complex nature of the project of *Cobrador* continually proposes a different kind of relation between film, music, and audio-viewer from the political models Solanas, Diegues, and Pérez have developed. This is a political consciousness at odds with the affective bonds that earlier engaged the aural community. Indeed, Leduc's on-screen audience of onlookers is posed as victims. Ultimately, the film folds back on earlier musical traditions because it makes music not simply the protagonist it was in other films, but the agent of invasion, aggression, and, more pointedly, the sound of the "other."

In the complex finale, which involves a muted Cobrador viewing the destruction of the World Trade Center in Manhattan from a television monitor somewhere in Brazil,

Leduc employs the cardinal event of September 11 as a moment of reflection, a pause at which to question the meaning of commercial exploitation and its violent effects. In a similarly paradoxical musical coda, he reframes that contemplative reflective stance by way of a musical sound of an earlier period. We hear the voice Tom Zé, popular Brazilian singer of the Tropicália movement, intoning one of his protest songs in Portuguese, "Quém é que tá botando dinamite na cabeca do século" ("Who Is Throwing Bombs at the Head of the Century?"). The film ends with a freeze-frame close-up of the terrorist Cobrador as a mine-worker toting a huge bag of rocks on his head and shoulders. The song and the image, like the film that precedes it, are posed as a call to the audio-viewer to question the socioeco-nomic situation in which political and economic violence threatens the community. The coda, in effect, is an affirmation of a community of resistance.

Audio-viewing now

As the previous discussion has argued, Latin American musical cinema since the 1950s has been the site of an evolving sense of audio-viewing built on the heightened recognition of newly formed communities of affect. As the shift in musical recording and film produc-tion technologies and funding has transformed our sense of what cinema is, filmmakers have embraced a radical reconceptualization of the audience and market of popular music, with profound effects on aesthetic strategies for reshaping audio-viewing. We have thus discerned the emergence of a new "economy of creativity" affecting the way films are made (digitally), how they circulate (the global art house model), and finally how they are viewed (in formats and locales outside the confines of movie theaters).

As a result, images and sounds once produced as commodities for cultural consumption have taken on a more complex and often political "afterlife." The presumed hegemony of mass culture, built into the earlier paradigm of audiences as market, has been displaced by the growing realization of postindustrial autonomy for audio-viewers. George Yúdice, for one, sees the power of downloads and "sharing" of audiovisual texts as an empowering sense of choice that displaced the static forms of imposed collective viewing and listening (Yúdice 2007: 49–51). Writing presciently at the end of the 1980s, John Mowitt argued that the new structures of listening confirmed that primacy of looking was in decline (Mowitt 1987). The progressive evolution of musicalized Latin American films thus appears aligned with politics precisely at the intersection between technologies and cultural discourses. To recognize this development is also to acknowledge the fundamental refiguring of the nature of the multiple audiences and forms that have arisen from the growing centrality of the aural imaginary. Musical gestures, like the ones chronicled by the filmmakers discussed here, and others, have further unsettled what has been, since the advent of sound films, an ambivalent relation.

References

Aguilera Skvirsky, S. (2013) "The Postcolonial City Symphony Film and the 'Ruins' of *Suite Habana*." *Social Identities*, 19(3–4): 423–439.
Altman, R. (1999) *Film/ Genre*. London: BFI Books.
Chion M. (2009) *Film: A Sound Art*, trans. C. Gorbman. New York: Columbia University Press.
Denning, M. (2015) *Noise Uprising: The Audiopolitics of a World Musical Revolution*. London/New York: Verso.
Epplin C. (2014) "Sound and Space in *La hora de los hornos/The Hour of the Furnances*." *Studies in Spanish and Latin American Cinema*, 11(1): 25–41.

Fitch M (2015) *Global Tangos: Travels in the Transnational Imaginary*. Lewisburg: Bucknell University Press.

Galt, R. and Schoonover K. (2010) "The Impurity of Art Cinema." In R. Galt and K. Schoonover (eds.), *Global Art Cinema*. Oxford/New York: Oxford University Press, pp. 3–27.

García, D. (2012) "The Afro-Cuban Soundscape of Mexico City: Authenticating Spaces of Violence and Immorality in *Salón México* and *Víctimas del pecado*." In L. Shaw and R. Stone (eds.), *Screening Songs in Hispanic and Lusophone Cinema*. Manchester/New York: Manchester University Press, pp. 167–188.

Gentic T (2014) "Beyond the Visual City: The Sound of Space in Fernando Pérez's *Suite Habana*." *Hispanic Review*, 82(2) (Spring): 199–220.

Getino O. (2009) *Industrias del audiovisual argentine en el Mercado internacional: el cine, la television, el disco y la radio*. Buenos Aires: Ediciones Ciccus.

Gilroy, P. (1993) *The Black Atlantic: Modernity and Double Consciousness*. Cambridge, MA: Harvard University Press.

González, H. (1989) *Fernando "Pino" Solanas: La Mirada: Reflexiones sobre cine y cultura*. Buenos Aires: Puntosur Editores.

González, M. and Yanes, M. (2013) *Tango: Sex and Rhythm of the City*. London: Reaktion Books.

Gorbman, C. (1987) *Unheard Melodies: Narrative Film Music*. Bloomington, IN: Indiana University Press.

Holmes A. (2015) "Backstage Pass to the City: The Soundscape of Suite Habana." *Studies in Spanish and Latin American Cinemas*, 12(2): 123–137.

Kheshti, R. (2011) "Touching Listening: The Aural Imaginary in the World Music Culture Industry." *American Quarterly*, 63(3): 711–731.

López A.M. (1998) "The São Paulo Connection: The Companhia Cinematografica Vera Cruz and O Cangaceiro." *Nuevo Texto Crítico*, 11(21/22): 127–154.

McGowan, C. And Pessanha, R. (2009) *The Brazilian Sound: Samba, Bossa Nova, and the Popular Music of Brazil*. Philadelphia, PA: Temple University Press.

Monsiváis, C. (2000). *Aires de família: cultural y sociedade en América Latina*. Barcelona: Editorial Anagrama.

Mowitt, J. (1987) "The Sound of Music in the Era of Its Electronic Reproducibility." In R. Leppert and S. McClary (eds.), *Music and Society: The Politics of Composition, Performance and Reception*. Cambridge: Cambridge University Press, pp. 173–197.

Nagib, L. (2007) *Brazil on Screen*. London: I.B. Tauris.

Palacios, J (2005) "Evocaciones de una era: Usos y desusos de la memoria en la construcción del rock en México." In M. Ulloa and A.M. Ochoa (eds.), *Música popular na América Latina*. Porto Alegre: Ufros Editora, pp. 134–151.

Perrone C.A. (1998) "Don't Look Back: Myths, Conceptions and Receptions of *Black Orpheus*." *Studies in Latin American Popular Culture*, 17: 155–177.

Podalsky, L. (2010) "El cine,el rock, la television y las culturas juveniles en los 60s en La Argentina." *Actas del II Congreso de ASAECA*. Buenos Aires: ASAECA, pp. 1482–1491.

Rowe, W. and Schelling V. (1991) *Memory and Modernity: Popular Culture in Latin America*. London/New York: Verso.

Signoreli Heise, T. (2012) *Remaking Brazil: Contested National Identity in Contemporary Brazilian Cinema*. Cardiff: University of Wales Press.

Vázquez, A. (2013) *Listening in Detail: Performances of Cuban Music*. Durham, NC: Duke University Press.

Young, E. (2007) "Between the Market and a Hard Place: Fernando Pérez's *Suite Habana* in a Post-Utopian Cuba." *Cuban Studies/Estudios Cubanos*, 38: 26–49.

Yúdice, G. (2007) *Nuevas tecnologías, música y experiencia*. Barcelona: Editorial Gedisa.

Zolov, E. (1999) *Refried Elvis: The Rise of the Mexican Counterculture*. Berkely, CA: University of California Press.

23

FILM AND TELEVISION[1]

Josetxo Cerdán and Miguel Fernández Labayen

Editors' introduction

Until fairly recently, Latin American film historians have largely ignored cinema's relation to television. Built into their silence may well have been a disdain for the commercialized medium whose appeal to the masses has often been premised on attracting the broadest audience, seemingly without concern for artistic content. Yet precisely because of this mass appeal, as this chapter argues, television has succeeded in stabilizing and disseminating the idea of national identity where earlier efforts by cinema have failed; by contrast with cinema, television has shaped national audiovisual landscapes and serves as a means of social cohesion, able to reach an entire country.

Yet Cerdán and Fernández Labayen suggest a broader view of television's social impact, contending that, due to the resounding international impact of the *telenovela* abroad, television as exclusively a national phenomenon has given way to multifaceted approaches that seek to map the local/global and intermedial projects through which film and television have collaborated. Thus, by the millennium's end, we find critical discussion of film and television subsumed under a single rubric: "audiovisual culture." In this contex, the authors present a persuasive case for redefining the once adversarial relations between film and television as more accurately a collaborative one. They argue for a wider appreciation of the developmental history of television's evolution in the region that diminishes the tired paradigm of Latin America vs. the US in terms of artistic influence and commercial viability. Out of this recognition, they maintain, comes an appreciation of a new geopolitics occasioned by the influence and intervention of European television in local productions, as well as a more nuanced view of the appeal of new subject matters that are taken from public as well as private commercial television.

The relationship between film and television has been a subject of study since television was first commercialized on a mass scale at the end of World War II. In this chapter, we do not seek to consider all the consequences of the interaction between these two media, which would be an impossible task. Rather, we focus on a few specific aspects of their relationship in Latin America through two main lenses. First, we examine the synergies between the two media on a geopolitical level, both inside and outside the region. We present the primary political and economic axes of the expansion of television in Latin America and television's importance for processes of modernization and transnational dissemination, in which cinema has also taken part. Second, this chapter presents an analysis of ways in which filmmakers have constructed their relationships to TV. In this section, we analyze four films that exemplify the aesthetic and sociocultural dimensions of the tensions between film and television in Latin America.

Geopolitics, film, and television: between state politics and transnational logics

We begin with the assumption that the cultural industries of cinema and television have played and continue to play an important role in Latin America. Since the mid-twentieth century, their appearance and development have been crucial to the consolidation of national identities, as well as a diffuse, multiple Latin American identity, and the two media share some common traits in terms of their transnational circulation and reception. As George Yúdice observes, "the height of radio and popular music around 1930, of film in the 1940s and 1950s, and then television beginning in the 1960s had the double benefit of creating employment and generating the cultural imaginary of the nation" (Yúdice 2002a). National brands, however, have functioned not only on a national level, but also contributed to the idea of a Latin American and even Ibero-American identity, both inside and outside the region (Díaz López 2005; D'Lugo 2010).

If something definite can be said about national cinematographic and television projects in Latin America, it is basically: that television succeeded in stabilizing and disseminating the idea of national identity where cinema failed. Even though "the relationships between film and politics have been close in Latin America, especially during certain periods and regimes" (Paranaguá 2003: 221), television—and previously radio—was the mass medium that created the idea of the nation which, with time, could be exported. It is clear that during certain periods (the golden age of cinema or the period of the New Latin American Cinema), the cinematographic projects of some countries (principally, Argentina, Mexico, and Brazil) were able to take hold, and more importantly national and regional audiences were able to recognize themselves in their national cinemas. These film projects, however, have been frustrated over and over for economic, political, and/or social reasons. Television, by contrast, has shaped national audiovisual landscapes and serves as a means of social cohesion, able to reach an entire country. At the same time, television has an international presence and resonance, principally through the *telenovela* (soap opera). This is true for Brazil, Mexico, and Colombia, and to a lesser degree Argentina and Venezuela. Certainly, the other countries in Central and South America, as well as the Caribbean, require individual attention.

We take as our point of departure two crucial aspects of the relationship between cinema and television in Latin America. The first has to do with the role television plays in the region: "From its origins in the 1950s, television had a commercial purpose, but within a public legal framework" (Albano and Lima 2014: 1913). Of course, the relationship between Latin American governments—often populist and nationalist—and television—which lies in the hands of private investors—is complex. Though it is true that the media are under private control, it is also true that Latin American governments—including the most populist, from those of Juan Domingo Perón in Argentina and Getúlio Vargas in Brazil, to later ones such as those of the Kirchners in Argentina and Álvaro Uribe in Colombia—have maintained good relationships with the owners of the dominant cultural industries in their respective countries. It is no coincidence that in Colombia, the meteoric rise of Caracol Televisión coincided with Uribe's government (2002–2010), or that in Brazil most media (Organizações Globo, among others) supported the 1964 coup. Once the military took power in Brazil (1964–1985), it was they who positioned television, and TV Globo in particular, as the ideal medium to create a strong sense of national identity, controlling political information through censorship and developing a consumer society in Brazil's large urban centers. Uribe's government has also used television as an element to create stability for itself.

Our second point has to do with flows of production, programming, and consumption. We first consider the models and ideals of television that influenced the development of the medium in Latin America. Then, we examine the specific narrative and aesthetic forms that arise in the region, focusing on the *telenovela* as a vernacular form of melodrama. As happened with film, many Latin American television projects developed in tension with the poles of influence of Europe and the United States, which at least during the early years of television in Latin America shaped television's educational, cultural, and economic project. For a long time, looking to Europe meant aspiring to (utopian) models of a strong public, but independent television that could provide filmmakers with a place to experiment and also provide a source of institutionally protected financing for national cinematographic production. Scholars such as Octavio Getino continue to come back to this issue today, always with similar arguments (Getino 1998, 2007). Regardless of government interference, however, the television model for most Latin American countries has followed that of the United States, leaving the management of television channels in private hands. The immediate result of the adoption of the American model was the promotion of an idea of modernization based on *gringophilia*, disseminated through a television whose power lie in advertising and entertainment, the main axes of TV made in the US (Monsiváis 2005; Rivero 2015).

If we focus on the two giants of television in Latin America, Globo and Televisa, it is important to remember that both migrated to television from other media. Globo started with the press: the newspaper *O Globo* was founded by Irineu Marinho in 1925, and its leap to the airwaves took place relatively late, in 1944. Televisa's beginnings, meanwhile, can be found in the concession Emilio Azcárraga Vidaurreta obtained in 1930 to establish the radio station XEW-AM, known as *The Voice of Latin America from Mexico*. Today, Globo and Televisa are large transnational corporations able to compete with the omnipotent American networks for audiences, including in the United States. The Azcárraga family's ties with the Spanish International Network (SIN)—established in the 1960s in the United States, becoming Univision in 1987—provides the clearest example of Televisa's internationalization and penetration in the airwaves of its neighbor to the north.

Any analysis of Latin American film and television thus must take into account the complex relationship that both film and television (as well as the music and radio industries) have with the United States. Miami, for example, plays a strategic role in the dissemination of Latin American content throughout the greater United States and reaches many other markets from there. As George Yúdice argues, from the 1980s onward, Miami has served as a strategic point for the circulation of economic and human capital between Latin America, Europe, and the rest of the United States, in addition to cultural capital (through both television and film, but also music and tourism, among other forms). Yúdice does not exaggerate when he titles one of the subchapters of his book *El recurso de la cultura. Usos de la cultura en la era global* (*The Expediency of Culture: Uses of Culture in the Global Era*) (Yúdice 2002b: 239) "Miami: capital cultural de América Latina" ("Miami: Cultural Capital of Latin America"). Nor does he overstate the case when he denounces the process of gentrification that this state of being a cultural capital has unleashed in Miami, to the detriment of many Latin Americans who live and work there (Yúdice 2005). The lines dividing the national, continental, and transnational have faded due to the interaction between producers, capital, and talent among the global media conglomerates that act from and for the region (Piñón 2014).

Television, understood as a transmodern medium capable of uniting premodernity, modernity, and postmodernity (Hartley 1999), has accelerated and popularized the processes of transnationalization that cinema had already begun, especially in elite and exclusive circles. In the last third of the twentieth century, flows of human capital toward the Global North increased notably from peripheral countries, including those in Latin America. From the end of the 1970s onward, the deregulation of television and the implementation of retransmission via satellite have made television an essential medium by which these new imagined, dislocated communities of migrants can remain connected with their places of origin. In this context, the processes of de- and reterritorialization allow serial narratives, such as *telenovelas*, to play a role that cinema has never been able to play in the same way.

One of the most impressive phenomena among recent *telenovelas* is *Yo soy Betty, la fea* (Radio Cadena Nacional, 1999–2001). This production, made by Caracol Televisión's most direct competitor, generated approximately 30 adaptations during the first decade of the twenty-first century, most of them successful, and has been sold in approximately 70 countries, both in Latin America and in culturally distant places such as Poland and India. There is a large body of academic literature about these adaptations. Many of these academic studies emphasize how this modern-day Cinderella story has been re-localized in spaces recognizable for the television viewer (Zhang and Fung 2014), while at the same time activating discourses about gender and ethnicity (Murillo Sandoval and Escala Rabadán 2013). Many also signal how the original *telenovela* already contained a series of hybrid elements that moved between the melodramatic and the comic, which for their part allowed for different hybridizations in other national adaptations (Mikos and Perrotta 2011; Rivera-Betancur and Uribe-Jongbloed 2011). However, the re-localization of this series and its consequences must be understood as part of a new context accelerated by global exchange:

> Whether she is named Betty, Lisa, or Jassi, and whether she speaks Spanish, German, Hindi, or English, Betty serves as a window through which to look at the telenovela industry not as a South-to-North counter-flow of culture but as a global network of culturally-specific content with both local and global appeal.
>
> (Miller 2010: 214)

Yo soy Betty, la fea is not an isolated case: other *telenovelas* from the last decade have led to similar dialogues and hybridizations, for example, through the adaptation of *Sin tetas no hay paraíso* (*Without Tits There Is No Paradise*, Canal Caracol, 2006) for the Spanish market (Tortajada et al. 2011).

Historical tensions between cinema and television:
from competition to partnership

Latin America did not have a film industry that could readily fight against the incipient medium of television. This status placed Latin American filmmakers in a position of uncertainty and discomfort, if not defeat. The arrival of television in Europe and the United States meant that cinema there had to seek new areas in which to develop, whether as spectacle (a new cinema of attractions) or auteur cinema. In Latin America, television's arrival coincided with the radicalness of the New Latin American Cinema. This radicalness was no doubt a response to industrial genre cinema (Hollywood) and political auteur cinema (European). The arrival of television, however, also generated a change in cinematic discourse, especially in countries where television became a mass phenomenon and where a particular form of serial fiction, the *telenovela*, became its defining element, not only on a local but also on a global level. If the traditional enemy of national and Latin American cinemas was Hollywood, the new situation transformed the enemy from without into an enemy from within. Despite the survival of popular cinema inherited from the studio era in some countries, new models of production kept this popular cinema from competing with the television industry, which was much more effective and better organized in industrial terms.

Ismail Xavier explains the situation through the Brazilian context:

> [A]t the beginning of the 1970s, a sense of a crisis in history and cinema emerged, which contrasted with the hopes of the beginning of the 1960s. This moment is best understood through the question of "internal threat" that television posed in a media system that clearly grew more complicated for filmmakers after 1969, since prior to that point they were completely overwhelmed by the larger nightmare of Hollywood's domination of the market. Television's "threat" was effective not only because of the peculiar hypertrophy of television in Brazilian society, but also because of its divorce, favored by Brazilian laws, with local cinema, which commercially lost a great deal because of it.
>
> (Xavier 2000: 78–79)

Thus, television placed many Latin American filmmakers in an uncomfortable situation. Essentially, television realized cinema's dream of creating a popular serial production that defeated the colonizer, Hollywood, within the region and even stood up to it outside Latin America.

If we use the Brazilian case as an example, cinema grew increasingly distant from its most popular modes of mass-mediated entertainment, both formally as well as in terms of sociopolitical and cultural factors. In Brazil, Cinema Novo was succeeded by Marginal Cinema, which was followed by a period of lackluster *pornochanchadas* and popular comedies. Essentially, production was dependent on the largesse of the state through the agency Embrafilme (founded in 1969). Shortly after taking office in 1990, however, Fernando Collor de Mello (Brazil's first democratically elected president in 30 years) dismantled Embrafilme and other state film agencies and Brazilian cinema virtually disappeared. In 1992, only two feature-length national films were shown in Brazil. It is no coincidence these years of decline in cinema were also the years of Rede Globo's greatest expansion. As television became the medium that defended the national and the popular, cinema drifted into increasingly marginal forms. In the 1970s and 1980s, the relationship between television and cinema became conflicted in Brazil and in Latin America more generally. The processes of radicalization and rejection of cinema often had to do with the impossibility of establishing a fluid relationship between filmmakers and television. Meanwhile, the mass closure of movie theaters across the continent and the spectacular descent of traditional film consumption during the 1980s exemplified intense changes in the audiovisual market (Getino 1998: 69). Some changes regarding the reconfiguration of the film industry and film audiences would be irreversible.

If in the 1970s and 1980s cinema and television functioned as two independent, autonomous spheres, in the 1990s there was a clear flow of cultural, human, and economic capital from television to cinema. Brazil again serves as a good example. During the second half of the 1990s, the well-known *retomada* took place, thanks to the policies of film development promoted under the governments of Itamar Franco and Fernando Henrique Cardoso. These policies allowed new elements to enter into Brazilian cinema—elements that, paradoxically, were none other than its traditional enemies: Hollywood, the enemy from without, and television, the enemy from within. On the one hand, the government promoted fiscal incentives (the Rouanet Law in 1991 and the Audiovisual Law in 1993), following a model that had been implemented with successful results in the record industry in the 1980s. These policies led large global media groups (basically Grupo Globo and the Motion Picture Association—MPA) with a significant presence in the film industry to invest in Brazilian film (Flaksman 2005; Johnson 2005). In 1997, the television network Rede Globo launched its film production arm, Globo Filmes, putting one of its most respected *telenovela* directors, Daniel Filho, at the helm. However, this move from television to cinema should not be viewed in isolation. Rather, it was part of the diversifying strategy that Grupo Globo had been developing for some time and was accelerating at this moment of digital convergence. The result of the investment in cinema of new local and global media groups was that in 2003, 21.4 percent of movie tickets sold in Brazil were for national films. Both applied their production know-how to films, giving them a more professional and competitive technical finish, and returning to popular narratives with which most of the public could easily identify. At the same time, they reverted to a television star system, following a process that had already begun in the 1970s (Johnson 2005: 27). But perhaps their most noteworthy development was in the area of promotion (P&A). The large international groups used big launch strategies for some films, in terms of publicity as well as number of copies distributed. Globo Filmes, for its part, benefited from featuring its films in all the group's media, especially television, through both direct advertising (the broadcast of trailers) and publicity (interviews on programs with celebrities that took parts in the films). Not less important in this process is the role of the MPA. Basically Columbia, but also Warner, Fox, and UIP, were more and more involved in the co-production and distribution since the middle of the 1990s: if in 1996 they distributed three Brazilian films (co-producing two of them), in 2003 they announced the co-production and distribution of 14 (Johnson 2005: 24).

Filmmakers watch television

We would like to turn now to some of the ways in which filmmakers have looked concretely at the relationship between cinema and television. We do not seek to be exhaustive in any way, including in its portrayal of Latin American filmmakers' attitudes toward television, but rather to signal some undercurrents of filmmakers' positioning with regard to television in terms of the two major modes of television production: televised fiction (and with it, the great Latin American television genre, the *telenovela*), and factual, informative, and educational television.

We have already noted how television discursively usurped Hollywood's position as an enemy of national cinemas and, as such, of filmmakers. This idea of television as an enemy from within is associated with the idea of television as entertainment. Filmmakers' position with regard to this often has not differed from that of many of the region's intellectuals, whose prejudices against television repeatedly have been denounced (Martín-Barbero and Rey 1999: 15–19). Beginning in the 1980s, these tensions would be replaced with a reassessment of television as re-energizing popular culture and mass culture. This reassessment would prove important for studies in communication and culture in all of Latin America, and would allow for fundamental work to be done on the *telenovela* and the melodrama by scholars such as Jesús Martín-Barbero and Néstor García Canclini (Varela 2010).

Below, we examine four exemplary films, each corresponding to different spatio-temporal and cultural coordinates that can lead to more complex, less deterministic discourses about television as a form of popular entertainment: *Misterio* (*Mystery*, Marcela Fernández Violante, Mexico, 1979); *Aventurera* (*Adventuress*, Pablo de la Barra, Venezuela, 1988); *The Devil Never Sleeps* (*El diablo nunca duerme*, Lourdes Portillo, Mexico, US, 1994); and *La television y yo* (*TV and I*, Andrés di Tella, Argentina, 2002). Each of these filmmakers has grasped in their own way the fundamental idea that political, national, and cultural projects are contained in entertainment television, which cannot and should not be underrated. Overall, they provide different perspectives of how feature fiction films but also personal and autobiographical documentaries have addressed the impact and legacy of television in Latin American cinema.

Misterio is a movie that came to Marcela Fernández Violante, the director of *Cananea* (Mexico, 1978), indirectly. The film was part of an effort by Margarita López Portillo—put in charge of Mexican television and cinema by her brother, José López Portillo, then President of Mexico—to make a series of three films adapting books by highly regarded novelists in order to cover up the situation of paralysis that characterized film production at that moment. The novel that *Misterio* adapts is *Estudio Q* (*Studio Q*, 1965) by Vicente Leñero, who had worked as a *telenovela* scriptwriter for both radio and TV. Like the novel that inspired it, the film tells the story of Alex, a famous *telenovela* actor who can't escape the fiction that the director and scriptwriter construct around him: every time he thinks he's made a decision, he finds it has been previously written. For all his efforts, he is incapable of escaping the fiction. *Misterio* anticipates later films such as *The Truman Show* (Peter Weir, 1998) and *Birdman* (Alejandro González Iñárritu, 2014). It also echoes the evident narrative relationships between the novel and existentialist postwar European theater. The most interesting aspect of the film, however, is how this superposition of real life and the *telenovela* signals television as a place of intimate, first-person experiences (beyond those of the characters). Although the film is generally pessimistic about the human condition, very much in line, for example, with *El ángel exterminador* (*The Exterminating Angel*, Luis Buñuel, 1962), it is not, as has been said, a criticism of Televisa or of *telenovelas* and television in general (Ramírez Berg 1992: 114). This is demonstrated by the change that Fernández Violante makes in the original text's ending. Leñero's novel ends with Alex's suicide, the only action that truly allows him to escape the director's control and take control of his life. In *Misterio*, however, Alex does not put a gun to his head, as he does in the novel. Rather, he turns his gun on the director and kills him instead. As such, and beyond its use of the banalities proper to the world of the spectacle, the film does not necessarily

Figure 23.1 Misterio (Mystery, Marcela Fernández Violante, 1980).

show itself to be critical of television. Rather, it puts forth an idea of television that was already being developed in theoretical terms. By the end of the 1970s, television drama interwove with the lives of its viewers and sometimes merged with their daily reality to the point that people made decisions based on the lessons TV shows articulated. Fernández Violante's ending proposes that, in the end, the viewer can carry out his or her own readings of resistance of different media texts, just as Alex can confront the director.

The second film to be considered here, *Aventurera*, is the first feature-length film that Pablo de la Barra, a Chilean exiled in Venezuela, made in his adopted country. De la Barra, who began his career in political cinema, was forced into exile by Pinochet's coup. *Aventurera* is a comedy ostensibly about the assassination attempt on Venezuelan President Rómulo Betancourt in 1960. In reality, the film is a portrait of a series of picaresque, popular characters who survive as best they can in a changing country. After an initial sequence that shows the preparations for the assassination attempt, the film then moves to a television studio in the minutes before the broadcast of the contest *Buscando a Agustín Lara* (*Looking for Agustín Lara*), a show that consists of choosing Lara's best imitator. Here, the film portrays television as a false world characterized by glitter and fixed prizes. Interestingly, however, this world does not differ from that of other popular spectacles, such as *lucha libre* or even politics. Although de la Barra comes from militant cinema, in this comedy he clearly draws on more popular forms (e.g. the golden age of Mexican cinema). The placement of television with other products of Latin American popular culture, such as *bolero* or *lucha libre*, even if in a brief initial sequence, is not insignificant. *Aventurera* was made during a brilliant time for Venezuelan cinema, when directors such as Román Chalbaud were at the national and international forefront, one of the few directors to have maintained a balance between his film and television work. The Fondo de Fomento Cinematográfico (Fund for Film Development, or Foncine) was created in 1980, and the 1980s would be a time of recognition for Venezuelan cinema both inside the country, where it would connect with its national audience, as well as outside, through its presence in film festivals. *Aventurera* was one of the last productions to benefit from this pivotal moment.

The third case to be considered here is the 1994 film by the Chicana filmmaker Lourdes Portillo, *The Devil Never Sleeps*. In this first-person documentary, the director narrates her return to her native Chihuahua upon learning of her Uncle Óscar's death. The film uses the structure of a police investigation that Portillo herself carries out in order to find the cause of her uncle's death. Television first appears in the film in the sequence preceding the credits. In this sequence, the narrator states in Spanish, "I had to go to Mexico to discover what had really happened," and then the film's first image appears: a satellite dish, presumably located in Mexico. The first images of Chihuahua are that of a nostalgic journey through the city. The film soon turns ironic, however, with a long shot of an old building while the director states in voice-over, in Spanish: "It's nice to see some places haven't changed." Then Portillo appears on-screen and speaks in English for the first time in the film, as if wanting to demonstrate distance, and states: "Cine Azteca, the first place where I saw a film." The film then cuts to the inside of this Cine Azteca, where we see it has become a parking lot, though one end maintains the curtain that covered the screen, framed by a pre-Colombian style molding. Lourdes Portillo parks, and the film then cuts to a close-up of her rolling down her car window. A new cut provides a panoramic shot of the interior of the room again, until it reaches the movie screen. The voice-over continues, once again in Spanish: "All these years, I was submerged in melodrama, in that magical darkness that would obsess me for the rest of my life: cinema." When she says *cinema*, the image turns black, to open once again on a completely different scene. First, we see the profile of the director with her back to the camera, looking at a television screen surrounded by the same pre-Colombian molding that frames the screen of Cine Azteca. The images on the television belong to a *telenovela*, and Univision's logo is visible in the lower right corner of the screen. The melodramatic tone of the *telenovela* sequence intensifies, and Portillo turns her head to look at the spectator questioningly. The film cuts again to a pair of hands holding a photograph of the Mexican Revolution against a cloudy sky, and the voice-over once again speaks: "Here, history resembles a melodrama." Not five minutes of the film have passed, and Portillo has already made a series of connections between cinema and television, her personal memory and Mexican history. The Univision *telenovela* reappears throughout the film to remind us of the melodramatic structure present not only in Portillo's film, but also in her family history, and, by extension, Mexican history.

The last film to be considered here, *La televisión y yo* (2002), by the Argentine filmmaker Andrés Di Tella, shares some characteristics with Portillo's film. It is also a first-person documentary that takes on the question of displacement, though in this case a politically motivated displacement. The film opens with a direct statement: "I wanted to make a movie about television, all that television means in a person's life, but something else came out." Soon after, the film identifies Di Tella's first television memory, from when he was 7 years old: the televised speech General Juan Carlos Onganía gave when he took power with the 1966 coup. Di Tella then explains how this coup meant exile for his family for the next seven years, in which his family lived in several countries. The director's summary of these years of exile is categorical: "I lost seven years of television. I'm missing half of my generation's collective memories." Thus begins his attempt to recover this loss, a loss connected to those entertainment programs that, as he states, comprise generational cultural universes that exile prevented him from accessing.

Figure 23.2   *The Devil Never Sleeps* (Lourdes Portillo, 1994) watching a telenovela on a pre-Colombian style framed TV set.

Figure 23.3   *La television y yo* (Andrés Di Tella, 2002).

In these four films from four different decades, we have seen how television interweaves with popular culture and a sentimental education, as well as with great moments in history and politics. Each film shows this in a different way, although it seems clear that as time passes, there is a greater awareness of the centrality of television's role in people's sentimental education, and there is a corresponding loss of fear of articulating this idea, even in the first person.

The other conception of television—that of its informative and educational character, more connected to what have been identified as discourses of sobriety—has also generated a series of responses that cannot be reduced to simple categorizations. The New Latin American Cinema very much took to Roberto Rossellini teachings in regard to neorealism. It continues, however, to be necessary to demonstrate how neorealism in Latin America was also nourished by other sources and how it evolved into something that might be better discussed in the plural, as neorealisms (Paranaguá 2003). It also seems these filmmakers did not take as much to Rossellini's ideas from after 1963, when he turned his attention toward television's didactic and educational potential (Quintana 1995), even though the idea of educational television was quick to catch on in Latin America. For example, in El Salvador, beginning in 1969, the United States, under the Lyndon B. Johnson administration, provided large injections of capital to create a pilot model of educational television for all of Latin America. As had previously happened in Samoa, in El Salvador educational television became a method of penetration to end the most traditional communities' resistance to embracing modern society's new forms of consumption (Lindo-Fuentes 2006). Today, the educational television projects that survive in the region are grouped in the Asociación de Televisiones Educativas y Culturales Iberoamericanas (Association of Ibero-American Educational and Cultural Television Channels, or ATEI), which in turn cooperates with Televisión Educativa y Cultural Iberoamericana (Ibero-American Educational and Cultural Television, or TEIb) and was founded at the second Ibero-American Summit in Madrid in 1992. As can be deduced, educational television in Latin America has a strong institutional accent. In any case, from the 1970s through the present, educational television has not awoken interest among most filmmakers. In fact, many educational television broadcasts only survive today thanks to the proliferation of channels and platforms on the Internet.

Beyond educational television, however, is the role of the journalist and his or her commitment to reality, and moreover to the film's subjects. Paranaguá recalls how Cinema Novo, through films such as *O desafio* (*The Dare*, Paulo César Saraceni, 1965) or *Terra em transe* (*Entranced Earth*, Glauber Rocha, 1967), constructed journalist characters who "were archetypical intellectuals, whose condition as men of the press did not lead to any discussion of media" (Paranaguá 2003: 271). This figure of the journalist, constructed nostalgically, has been questioned over time as journalists' discourses themselves have been contaminated by the methods of commercial television fiction. Paranaguá cites various examples of the changes in this figure in film, analyzing one in detail: *Como nascem os anjos* (*How Angels Are Born*, Murilo Sales, 1996). The film essentially opens and closes with two supposedly serious television interventions. The first scene shows a German team filming the film's protagonist in the Santa Marta *favela* in Rio de Janeiro, where she lives. In the final scene, the crime reporter for a local television channel reports on the protagonist's death, misinterpreting it. This film moves into the territory of what the Colombian filmmakers Carlos Mayolo and Luis Ospina denounced years before with their fake documentary *Agarrando pueblo* (*The Vampires of Poverty*, 1978). In Mayolo and Ospina's movie, which stages the crudest strategies of *pornomiseria* (misery porn), the fictional film crew says it works for a German television station. Mayolo and Ospina thus signal the contamination Paranaguá denounces, as well as the parasitic role that German (and European) television stations have regularly played in Colombia (and Latin America). About a decade after this film's release, from October 31 to November 2, 1989, Carmen Guarini and Marcelo Céspedes organized a seminar at the Goethe Institute in Buenos Aires with the suggestive title "Media from the

North—Images from the South: First Argentine-German Encounter about the Production, Distribution, Coproduction, and Development of Documentary Cinema." Taken in its broader context, it is not surprising that this seminar ended up producing lukewarm conclusions at best, "such that if the topic of financing itself implied subordination to European criteria and tastes, the new technological scene would again locate Latin America in a situation of disadvantage" (Margulis 2014: 237). The displacement of the respected figure of the journalist and the journalist's relocation alongside postcolonial practices does not pass through televised drama, at least not uniquely. Rather, this relocation has much to do with the politics of dependence that began in European cinema festivals and have continued with television reportage from European countries.

In the twenty-first century, the complex relationships between cinema and television in the territory of factuality continue to be fertile. Eduardo Coutinho remains an exemplary figure with regard to the documentary in terms of his use of the basic tools of staging and testimony, which have been taken up by Ismael Xavier in the context of the relationships between film and TV: "[t]he valorization of orality, the mode of combatting one's own limitations in the usual situations that cinema and TV present, is the way to combat asymmetry in the distribution of power" (Xavier 2012: 33–34). Meanwhile, the questions that lie at the heart of the documentary *Ônibus 174* (*Bus 174*, José Padilha and Felipe Lacerda, 2002), based on television footage of a bus taken hostage in Rio de Janeiro in 2000, remain at the opposite extreme of Coutinho's strategies. Even further from Coutinho's strategies is melodramatization of these events in Bruno Barreto's 2008 film *Última Parada 174* (*Last Stop 174*).

Other Brazilian productions that address these questions include more recent films such as *Avanti Popolo* (Michael Wahrmann, 2012) and *Branco Sai, Preto Fica* (*White Out, Black In*, Adirley Queirós, 2015). Even though these films present themselves discursively as documentaries, they explore different *mise en scène* strategies that not only use the tactics of contemporary television, but also those of the wider variety of audiovisual formats available today. Among these tactics, the performativity driven by the proliferation of social networks is the most prominent. Journalists are unlikely to recover their lost prestige; however, in exchange, a number of unprejudiced filmmakers will have learned to work in the intermediary spaces that the new media landscapes offer, unafraid to stage their protagonists' dreams. Any reduction in the richness that intermediality implies for the pairing of film and television is tremendously impoverishing. As Ana López has observed, "intermediality can help us better understand the development and evolution of Latin American mediascapes and crucial moments in its historical trajectory" (López 2014: 135).

Note

1 Josetxo Cerdán and Miguel Fernández Labayen have written this chapter in the context of the Research Project CSO2014-52750-P, financed by the Spanish Ministry of Economy and Competitiveness and co-financed with FEDER funds.

References

Albano, S.G. and Lima, M.E.O. (2014) "Book Review: John Sinclair and Joseph Straubhaar, *Latin American Television Industries*." *International Journal of Communication*, 8: 1912–1914.
Díaz López, M. (2005) "Cierta música lejana de la lengua: Latinoamericanos en el cine español, 1926–1975." *Secuencias*, 2: 76–106.

D'Lugo, M. (2010) "Aural Identity, Genealogies of Sound Technologies, and Hispanic Transnationality on Screen." In N. Durovicova and K. Newman (eds.), *World Cinemas: Transnational Perspectives.* New York/London: Routledge, pp. 160–185.

Flaksman, A. (2005) "Brazilian Cinema's Shining Moment." In *Contemporary Brazilian Cinema.* Brasilia: Departamento Cultural Ministério das Relações Exteriores, pp. 148–152.

Getino, O. (1998) *Cine y televisión en América Latina. Producción y mercados.* Santiago de Chile: Lom.

—— (2007) "Los desafíos de la industria del cine en América Latina y el Caribe." *Zer,* 22: 167–182.

Hartley, J. (1999) *Uses of Television.* London/New York: Routledge.

Johnson, R. (2005) "TV Globo, the MPA and Contemporary Brazilian Cinema." in L. Shaw and S. Denninson (eds.), *Latin American Cinema: Essays on Modernity, Gender, and National Identity.* Jefferson, MO: McFarland Press, pp. 11–38.

Lindo-Fuentes, H. (2006) "La televisión educativa en El Salvador como proyecto de la teoría de la modernización." *Cultura. Revista del Consejo Nacional para la Cultura y el Arte,* 93: 52–73.

López, A. (2014) "Calling for Intermediality: Latin American Mediascapes." *Cinema Journal,* 54(1): 135–141.

Margulis, P. (2014) *De la formación a la institución. El documental audiovisual argentino en la transición democrática (1982–1990).* Buenos Aires: Imago Mundi.

Martín-Barbero, J. and Rey, G. (1999) *Los ejercicios del ver. Hegemonía audiovisual y ficción televisiva.* Barcelona: Gedisa.

Mikos, L. and Perrotta, M. (2011) "Traveling Style: Aesthetic Differences and Similarities in National Adaptations of *Yo soy Betty, la fea.*" *International Journal of Cultural Studies,* 15(1): 81–97.

Miller, J.L. (2010) "*Ugly Betty* Goes Global: Global Networks of Localized Content in the Telenovela Industry." *Global Media and Communication,* 6(2): 198–217.

Monsiváis, C. (2005) "Would So Many Millions of People Not End Up Speaking English? The North American Culture and Mexico." In A. Del Sarto, A. Ríos, and A. Trigo (eds.), *The Latin American Cultural Studies Reader.* Durham, NC: Duke University Press, pp. 203–232.

Murillo Sandoval, S.L. and Escala Rabadán, L. (2013) "De *Betty, la fea* a *Ugly Betty*. Circulación y adaptación de narrativas televisivas." *Cuadernos.Info,* 3: 99–112.

Paranaguá, P.A. (2003) *Tradición y modernidad en el cine de América Latina.* Madrid: Fondo de Cultura Económica de España.

Piñón, J. (2014) "A Multilayered Transnational Broadcasting Television Industry: The Case of Latin America." *The International Communication Gazette,* 76(3): 211–236.

Quintana, A. (1995) "El camino del cine didáctico de Roberto Rossellini." In J. Pérez Perucha (ed.), *Actas del V Congreso de la AEHC.* A Coruña: CGAI, pp. 219–226.

Ramírez Berg, C. (1992) *Cinema of Solitude: A Critical Study of Mexican Film, 1967–1983.* Austin, TX: University of Texas Press.

Rivera-Betancur, J. and Uribe-Jongbloed, E. (2011) "La suerte de la fea, muchas la desean. De *Yo soy Betty la fea* a *Ugly Betty.*" In M.R. Pérez-Gómez (ed.), *Previously On. Estudios interdisciplinarios sobre la ficción televisiva en la Tercera Edad de Oro de la Televisión.* Sevilla: Biblioteca de Comunicación de la Universidad de Sevilla, pp. 825–838.

Rivero, Y. (2015) *Broadcasting Modernity: Cuban Commercial Television, 1950–1960.* Durham, NC: Duke University Press.

Tortajada, I., Araüna, N., Capdevila, A., and Cerdán, J. (2011) "*Sin tetas no hay paraíso.* La representación de las relaciones entre hombres y mujeres en la adaptación española de un serial colombiano." In M.R. Pérez-Gómez (ed.), *Previously On. Estudios interdisciplinarios sobre la ficción televisiva en la Tercera Edad de Oro de la Televisión.* Sevilla: Biblioteca de Comunicación de la Universidad de Sevilla, pp. 567–583.

Varela, M. (2010) "Intelectuales y medios de comunicación." In C. Altamirano (ed.), *Historia de los intelectuales en América Latina. Vol. II. Los avatares de la "ciudad letrada" en el siglo XX.* Buenos Aires/Madrid: Katz Editores, pp. 759–781.

Xavier, I. (2000) "El cine moderno brasileño." *Archivos de la filmoteca*, 36: 56–79.

—— (2012) "Indagaciones sobre Eduardo Coutinho y su diálogo con la tradición moderna." In M. Campaña Ramia and C. Mesquita (eds.), *El otro cine de Eduardo Coutinho*. Quito: Corporación Cinememoria, pp. 16–35.

Yúdice, G. (2002a) "Las industrias culturales: más allá de la lógica puramente económica, el aporte social." *Pensar Iberoamérica. Revista de cultura*. Available at: www.oei.es/pensariberoamerica/ric01a02.htm (accessed October 13, 2015).

—— (2002b). *El recurso de la cultura. Uso de la cultura en la era global*. Barcelona: Gedisa.

—— (2005) "Miami: Images of Latinopolis." *NACLA Report of the Americas*, 39(3): 35–40.

Zhang, X. and Fung, A. (2014) "TV Formatting of the Chinese *Ugly Betty*: An Ethnographic Observation of the Production Community." *Television & New Media*, 15(6): 507–522.

24

LATIN AMERICAN FILM IN THE DIGITAL AGE

*Gonzalo Aguilar, Mariana Lacunza,
and Niamh Thornton*[1]

Editors' introduction

The significance of technological change has been a central issue of Latin American film scholarship, evident in accounts of cinema's earliest years (see Navitski, Chapter 2 and Cuarterolo, Chapter 19), as well as those dealing with the repercussions of television (see Cerdán and Fernández Labayen, Chapter 23) and, most recently, of digital technologies. Such interrogations often entail two interrelated questions: (i) What do technical innovations mean for audiovisual production and circulation within the region? (ii) What (if anything) distinguishes those transformations within Latin American from analogous shifts occurring elsewhere in the world?

In this chapter, Gonzalo Aguilar and Mariana Lacunza respond to those queries, in part by showcasing how professional filmmakers in Chile and Bolivia utilize digital capture to turn their attention to the contemporary reconfiguration of collectivities and subjectivities. Lacunza detects a similar tendency in the work of TAFA, a filmmaking collective whose efforts provide an interesting counterpoint to the audiovisual productions by indigenous and community-based organizations discussed by the authors in Chapter 14.

Even as the authors recognize the opportunities made possible by digital technologies, their contributions caution us against viewing the new horizon as the realization of Julio García Espinosa's dream of audiovisual production as a truly democratic practice. The economic and geopolitical frameworks that always have influenced regional media industries are still present. Niamh Thornton's contribution reminds us that even as (certain) Latin American producers have forged agreements with Netflix and other online platforms, the circulation of Latin American films is still constrained.

Since the early 2000s, digital technologies have transformed motion picture production, distribution, and reception worldwide. Unlike other technological innovations, which have been slow to be incorporated in Latin America, the so-called "digital revolution" arrived quickly to the region and became an essential part of film culture. Digital film-making inspired and empowered a generation of younger filmmakers by providing them low-cost access to the means of quality film production. In Mexico, for instance, much of the art house cinema of filmmakers such as Carlos Reygadas, Michel Franco, and Nicolás Pereda has been produced by low-budget digital technology and widely distributed through the Internet. With the advent of streaming, film viewing has become increasingly mobile; instead of being tied to public exhibition venues or domestic spaces, spectators can now watch films on their cell phones while traveling on the subway.

While suggesting a new golden age for film production and consumption, scholars, film historians, and social commentators have been moved to reflect on the political, social, and aesthetic impact of the rapid dispersion of digital technologies across all aspects of audio-visual culture in the region. This chapter provides three interrogations of the implications of digital transformation of film culture. Gonzalo Aguilar takes the long view by placing the digital within a much wider context of radical transformations in human perception linked to capitalist imperatives and the reconfiguration of the political. In particular, he exam-ines the impact of digital technologies on the politics of representation, by interrogating how contemporary Chilean filmmakers deploy the digital to reject the notion of a collec-tive subject: "el pueblo." Mariana Lacunza analyzes the impact on production in a small national cinema, that of Bolivia, by tracking the differential uses of digital technologies by young auteurs, new documentarians, and community-based collectives. Her contribution places particular attention on the ways in which all of those filmmakers take advantage of the aesthetic possibilities of the digital format. Finally, Niamh Thornton, considering the underlying politics of the image–culture relationship first raised by Aguilar, looks at the digital technologies involved in online streaming. She focuses on the "curatorial" role of online commercial providers who serve as gatekeepers circumscribing viewers' access to films. In so doing, she exposes the underlying geopolitics of the digital, a theme that, as Lacunza demonstrates in the case of Bolivian filmmaking, continues to have ramifications for small and presumed peripheral film cultures.

Analogue *pueblo*/digital *pueblo*: the contemporary image confronts today's politics

Gonzalo Aguilar

In critiquing the notion of representation, I want to argue that film is a technological appa-ratus that *produces* a people, rather than one that simply makes them visible as seemed to be the case in the Latin American cinemas of the 1960s. Since the 1980s, cinema's interface with politics has changed given the increased power of television. In order to better under-stand this new logic, we must acknowledge two points of departure. First, we must forgo a more traditional notion of film in favor of a more capacious object of study: the circulation of images, which spurred the conceptualization of what I have called elsewhere the "*bio-image*," a notion directly tied to the impact of digital technologies:

> The desperate proliferation of biopics (Leonardo DiCaprio is growing out his beard in preparation for his latest role as Lenin) is a traumatic, digressive response to that ambivalent desire to link together the image with the real and the living. Reality shows (in which everyday life is captured to allow its protagonists to live through the image), the biodrama, the boom of the documentary and diverse home

movies that circulate on the internet – indeed, our coexistence with the internet's ever-available flow of images of everyday life, or momentous events such as birth and death, are no longer fictional, but full of life. In this context, first-person and even third-person accounts are nothing less than a struggle by live organisms to leave behind a trace or mark: the camera itself is transformed into an organism or prosthesis because life doesn't exist outside the image.

(*Aguilar 2015: 77–78*)

This leads to my second point, about the transformations wrought by digital production. One of the most successful recent films in Argentina, *El secreto de sus ojos* (*The Secret in Their Eyes*, Juan José Campanella, 2009) includes a sequence shot that opens in a packed soccer stadium and ends with a police chase. Filmed with a Red One digital camera, the sequence depends upon digital effects that go beyond the usual color corrections or image adjustments. The filmmakers did not merely erase particular objects, but also created digital multitudes: 42,000 soccer fans that appeared as real as those shown on the nightly newscast (Messuti 2016: 49).

Does that mean that there is a digital "*pueblo*"? Or that digital technologies "create" new groupings, and allow for the circulation on the Internet of collectivities and community networks that have not yet defined themselves, making rhizomatic connections that have not yet been consolidated? Are we witnessing a struggle between such rhizomatic interfaces and the huge, arboreal corporations that oblige us to navigate through Google, Instagram, Facebook, and Twitter? How does the digital image influence the new ways in which politics are constituted? And finally, how does the cinematic gaze manifest itself in postglobal capitalism and shape politics? What new nodal points can the cinema forge and how might it invent other circuitries that produce alternatives, resistances, and counter-narratives?

I want to amplify the scope of these questions by focusing on Jonathan Beller's argument in the *Cinematic Mode of Production* (2006), when he posits a reading of the "gaze" as a mode of production in capitalism. His book speaks of the gaze in filmic terms; here, I want to address this concept more broadly in terms of our everyday habits. Academics and other adult professionals generally sit in front of the computer screen to work, but this labor has unique features; it is conjoined with moments of distraction, as we surf the Net according to our eyes' journeys that themselves participate in the reproduction of economic value: publicity flyers, posts that are little more than paid ads, trolls employed by a company or a political party, links that take us to sites asking us for our credit card numbers. On our screens, numerous smaller boxes vie for our attention and encourage us to click, a type of new coin that once again demonstrates the triumph of the optic over the haptic.

If we were to trace a genealogy of the gaze as capitalist hieroglyph, there would be a first qualitative leap with the appearance of broadcasting and the network era of radio and television that programmed our consumption but also entered our homes, producing a crisis between the intimacy of private life and the performativity of public life. This cohabitation with images (seen on television as we eat, before we go to bed, together with our families) comes close, according to Hannah Arendt's celebrated formula, to labor (i.e. necessity) more than to work (Arendt 2005: 98–106).

In another qualitative leap in the history of the gaze as merchandise, the Internet made home-based work grow, and this can be verified in the acquisition of communications devices (most notably, starting with 3D printers). Work on the computer is mixed together in an intrinsic way with the eye's labor, a process whereby an act of production can slide easily into leisure. In the process of sending an email, a quick glance at our inbox allows us to take in the ads showcased on the sides of the screen.

The commercialization of the act of looking becomes more associated with consumption than with production. But it comes at a cost, just like the banners on our computer screens. In other words, rather than being tied to an apparatus of production, our gaze is trapped in the world of consumption, becoming our point of access to global capitalism. The means to get our attention, to detain our eye on the image, have reached a paroxysm with cellular devices. But more than anything else, we hold in our hand a community—a virtual one that nonetheless can be contacted, composed of friends but also of contacts with indeterminate status. Is each cell phone a potential *pueblo*?

As an institution, the cinema has not been untouched by these transformations and has incorporated them in films themselves, as well as in modes of distribution and consumption. Digitalization has quickly become a dominant presence in theaters and satellite transmission is not far off—a situation that places the special relationship between film and theaters in crisis, as those venues are now able to host the transmission of all sorts of events. Film aesthetics have also changed. Mainstream films have doubled down on spectacular special effects while the *indies* have slowed down time, bolstering the sensuous nature of the image over its informational potential. In some cases, independent filmmakers have turned away from the theatrical film to work elsewhere. With museum installations, important directors such as Chantal Ackerman, Abbas Kiarostami, Pedro Costa, and Harun Farocki, as well as Albertina Carri and Lisandro Alonso, among Latin American artists, have spatialized and reterritorialized filmic images in relation to the spectator's body in nontraditional locations.

But what can be said about *el pueblo*, or the masses? Has *el pueblo* changed or been eclipsed in this world of digital convergence? How have the many been made visible, and how do the masses see themselves within this new scenario? Two footnotes in Walter Benjamin's celebrated and much-cited essay "The Work of Art in the Age of Mechanical Reproduction" offer some insights:

1. In response to advertisements, Benjamin affirms that:

> [i]n big parades and monster rallies, in sports events, and in war, all of which nowadays are captured by camera and sound recording, the masses are brought face to face with themselves. . . . Mass movements are usually discerned more clearly by a camera than by the naked eye.
>
> *(Benjamin 2009: 684)*

2. In the opposition between the magician-painter and the surgeon-filmmaker, Benjamin affirms that while the former places his hands on the body, the latter penetrates it (we should remember that Benjamin is contemporaneous with the appearance of the stethoscope, the ophthalmoscope, the laryngoscope, and X-rays). In otolaryngology, during the "so-called endonasal perspective procedure," the surgeon must carry out "acrobatic tricks"—according to Benjamin—that depend upon mirrors and his corporal agility (Benjamin 2009: 678).

When Benjamin wrote those footnotes, drones did not exist, nor did endoscopic procedures that use fiber optics to film the body from within. There were no selfies that, like a figurative endoscopy, captured a street demonstration from within through the insinuating camerawork of a single participant subsumed within the multitude.

The *bioimage*, in all of its manifestations, modifies the place of cinema as well as the forms of collectivity. In this new moment, some films can help us to reflect on the new status of the image and *el pueblo*—among them, Patricio Guzmán's *Nostalgia de la luz* (*Nostalgia for the Light*, 2010) and Pablo Larraín's *No* (2012).

Guzmán's film begs the question: How do you populate a desert? In the film, the dialectical relationship and interaction between the one and the many emerges in an absence of cosmic dimensions. The desert is not only a geographical space, but also the image itself, marked by absence and lack. No human figure appears in the first 10 minutes, and the first face (of Gaspar Galaz) appears on screen in the fourteenth minute. Quite intentionally, the people who show up in interviews are limited to groups of two or three. The film privileges vacant spaces in which the human never arrives on time. The only "many" who appear in the film are in archival footage of miners or a mural lined with photographs of those who disappeared during the Pinochet dictatorship, in images that have withered with the passage of time. In a melancholic vision, in a present marked by the pain of those who are not there (of those who never returned), as suggested by the very etymology of "nostalgia," *el pueblo* is the past. And yet, through elusive means, *Nostalgia de la luz* evokes the many, and gestures toward the future possibility of a multitude, a community, in the agglomeration of particles, the clouds of residue and the dust of stars. The incommensurability of that stardust contrasts with the astronomers' obsessive measurements of space, whose work is akin to that of the architect imprisoned in Pinochet's concentration camp who now meticulously sketches those cells from his own apartment. As Irene Depetris Chauvin argues in "Una comunidad de melancólicos," "There is, in the scalar play of *Nostalgia de la luz*, a way of producing relationships of proximity and distance; and establishing new affective bonds" (Depetris Chauvin 2015). But what sort of technological apparatus makes this scalar play (and its potential for fostering affective bonds) possible?

"Why do we want bones?" asks Violeta Berríos, who searches for the remains of family members buried in the desert, in one of the film's most moving testimonies. It's the nexus between the horrors of the past, the pain of the present, and—because of the shared element of calcium—the stars in the sky. The ideal camera or optical device, according to Guzmán, is the telescope, not only because it reminds him of his youth, or because of Chile's renowned starry sky, but also because the telescope allows us to *see the past*. The powerful lenses of the Hubble and James Webb telescopes in space can advance our knowledge of the origin of the universe. I turn again to Berríos, who says in the film:

> I wish the telescopes could look at something besides the sky, that they could pierce through the layers of the earth to find the bones. It would be like sweeping away the dirt with a telescope and later, thanking the stars for having found them. That's my dream.

In *Nostalgia de la luz*, the telescope—just like the drone and the endoscope—peers down at us from above and penetrates the earth, making possible a stereoscope of the past and the present, even though the bodies are ghosts, the space is a desert, and it is all only a dream.

Guzmán's strategy of "emptying out" contrasts sharply with that of "saturation" deployed in Pablo Larraín's *No*. In her 2014 essay on the film, Franco-Chilean critic Nelly Richard contests the film's conception of historical time that seems more "mimetic-contemplative" than "critical-transformative" because of its use of U-matic video. She offers a corollary critique, arguing that *No* replaces "the macro-narrative of the [collective] revolution with individual micro-fantasies of private consumption." The consequence of this shift is the disavowal of historicity. For her, what Larraín's film ultimately does is "flatten the volume and density of the anti-dictatorial struggles of the past as well as today's citizen-activism in order to offer us up a replica of the past that freezes that present as a *simulacrum* of memory" (my emphasis). The term "simulacrum" is not incidental; it synthesizes a chain of attributes that for Richard define marketing and have infected film. In other words, "the *appearances of* 'publicity' (its stylistic repertoire promoting the visual consumption of images) trump the *underlying kernel* and the *representational content* of 'ideology' (the antagonisms of power and domination; the disputes over hegemony and social struggles)" (original emphasis). I ask myself whether it is possible to sustain such a categorical differentiation between publicity and ideology, between appearances and depth, between consumption and struggle.

In light of such critical anxiety, I prefer to see *No* as an exercise with digital forms and their ability to instantiate the conditions for the emergence of *el pueblo* or of new collectivities. Because what the film's protagonist does is not a matter of de-ideologizing his position or renouncing his convictions. If his journey demonstrates anything, it is the impossibility of hiding ideology behind fancy packaging or touch-ups, and that commercialization is the very condition of possibility of the ideological statement.

Before Saavedra (Gael García Bernal) joins the "No" campaign, the opposition to the dictatorship makes a publicity short that exemplifies how *el pueblo* has traditionally appeared on film through a dialectic between the one and the many (although in this case the inspiring leader is absent), the collective choreographies—of repression unleashed against fiery rebellion and organized protest, and the majestic plural (in this case, through the use of Inti Illimani's song "Vuelvo"). In contrast, in Saavedra's alternate short ("happiness is on the way"), the editing mimics the video clip and the inspiration comes from a Coca-Cola ad. Certainly, there is something lost in that shift, in the idea that the short film has to "sell" a political position. Nonetheless, what is most powerful is that the "No" side wins the election, something that would have been impossible using more traditional techniques for representing *el pueblo* (or so the film suggests). Indeed, the film insists that such tactics are not without cost, and in this way its historicity acquires a critical edge.

Similar to Guzmán's film, Larraín's *No* does not erase the present, but rather reveals its technological dimension by performing an archaeological study of the technical underpinnings of the microwave, video games, and even electric trains. It is not a matter of simply using U-matic, but also a whole series of throwback elements, including poor-quality images, others that are overexposed, live-action shots, and other digital archives. In his essay about Larraín's *oeuvre*, critic Wolfgang Bongers notes that "the images manage to trick us about temporal change, but not about the traces of bodies," arguing for the need to interpret the casting of García Bernal as "an indicator of fictionality" (Bongers 2016: 96). The actor is the body of global spectacle (which includes Latin America, and particularly Mexico), the one to whom the many must refer in order to conceive the means of their own visibility.

Despite the notable differences in what they say, the two films share something: in the desert of *el pueblo* (or the people as deserted), the goal is inventing new collectivities within existing conditions. *El pueblo* can only be reanimated through a gaze that has already been commercialized, and yet through this process stops being a collective. The films offer two responses to this commercialization of the gaze in capitalist globalization—two modes of thinking about the new situation: through a hollowing out or through a saturation of image(s).

In 1895, the Lumière brothers exhibited a pioneering film: *Workers Leaving the Lumière Factory*. Today, we can say that what the camera's lens registered then was something more than the departure at the end of the workday. The workers had abandoned the factory in favor of another form of work that would gradually become dominant: the work of the eye.

Digital Bolivia and new subjectivities

MARIANA LACUNZA

Unlike Mexico, Argentina, or Brazil, Bolivia has a small film industry that was never consolidated, owing to the lack of state support. As a result, very few domestic films could ever reach a wide national audience. The absence of screen quotas made it impossible for filmmakers to recover their investments, particularly after having to pay almost 50 percent to exhibitors and additional screening taxes. Since the mid-2000s, filmmakers and others involved in the audiovisual sector have tried, without much success, to create legislation that would provide greater support for the country's audiovisual production. Surprisingly, despite these underlying conditions, the production of Bolivian films increased notably in the early 2000s to the point that, for a time, people began to speak about a second "boom" of Bolivian film (following the one in 1995 associated with directors such as Marcos Loayza and Juan Carlos Valdivia). The growth was spurred by new digital technologies employed by a younger generation of filmmakers, and developed along three main axes: (a) auteur fictional cinema; (b) documentary cinema; and (c) films made by and from marginal communities in collaboration with the filmmaking collective Taller Ambulante de Formación Audiovisual (TAFA), which works outside the limits of the official industry. The following discussion illustrates how new aesthetic currents are emerging from these three groups of digital films in their attempt to explore cultural identity.

Between 2003 and 2008, production totaled 28 feature-length films, or approximately five per year. Of those, only six were shot on celluloid; the rest were on digital, with four transferred to 35 mm for exhibition on international circuits. It is noteworthy that 15 of the 22 films shot through digital capture during this period were *operas primas* (Espinoza and Laguna 2009: 190–191). Between 2008 and 2009 alone, there were a significant number of digital premieres, including four feature-length films in 2008 and 10 medium- and feature-length films in 2009. Unfortunately, this growth in production did not always equate with artistic merit nor guarantee box-office success. Although regional critics celebrated the quality of films such as *Zona Sur* (*South District*, Juan Carlos Valdivia), *El ascensor* (*The Elevator*, Tomás Bascopé), *Hospital Obrero* (*Working Class Hospital*, Germán Monje), *La chirola* (*The Prison*, Diego Mondaca), and *Rojo, amarillo y verde* (*Red, Yellow, Green*, Rodrigo Bellot, Martín Boulocq and Sergio Bastani) in 2009, the following year witnessed a surprising lack of quality productions. Sixteen features (both fiction and documentary) premiered in mainstream theaters that year, but with little commercial success (*La Razón* 2010). Between 2010 and 2015, digital shorts and documentaries have shown the greatest level of artistic growth, as evidenced by their inclusion in international festivals. These achievements demonstrate that digital filmmaking has been commercially successful within domestic circuits and has become the preferred format for new filmmakers.

A new auteurist cinema has recently taken advantage of digital technologies to distinguish itself from the thematics of the militant cinema of the 1960s by exploring the subjectivities of white elites as well as those in Bolivia's provinces. Operating within a globalized framework and making a strong mark on the international festival circuit, this new auteurist cinema is personalist, and represents an effort to break with the status quo (Lacunza 2011: 52). Auteurist cinema in Bolivia is part of a larger Latin American filmmaking effort to distinguish itself from Hollywood by not using digital technologies for special effects, but instead developing new types of narratives, as evident in films from many other countries in the region, including the Cuban films *Video de familia* (*Family Video*, Humberto

Padrón, 2001) and *Suite Habana* (Fernando Pérez, 2003), the Mexican *Así es la vida* (*Such is Life*, Arturo Ripstein, 2000), and the Argentine *Fuckland* (José Luis Márquez, 2001). As with digital productions in Mexico, Argentine, and Cuba, these films use digital filming practices to develop a targeted aesthetic, a subjective vision, and a strong perspective.

This "subjective vision" emerges in part as a recurrent concern for mapping the subjectivities of the protagonists on-screen. In this sense, digital technologies are used to further explore a subjective language that traces personal narratives, emotions, mental states, etc. within and through the filmic image. Like those other recent Latin American films, contemporary Bolivian cinema links an authorial project with new technologies in ways that explore digital's potential as a language and aesthetic.

In the Bolivian context, auteurist cinema is dismantling and deconstructing older notions through the use of a digital language to make visible personal dynamics involving sexuality, friendship, love, and the family. It takes particular aim at dominant discourses and social hierarchies. For example, trapped women have become a recurrent trope of this new cinema. In Rodrigo Bellot's *Dependencia Sexual* (*Sexual Dependency*, 2003), one of the most tension-filled sequences includes a split screen (Figure 24.1). The left side features the male characters eating their dinner and talking about the women who are in the kitchen. Whereas in a more traditional film the two women would be off-screen, in Bellot's film they appear on the right side of the screen. And, unlike the more traditional use of split screen in classic Hollywood cinema, wherein both sides were the same size, in *Dependencia sexual* the left screen expands during the sequence, minimizing the "female space" on the right, in order to comment critically on the oppressive force of patriarchal norms.

In another break with established norms, Boulocq and Bellot's films interpellate the spectator in ways that challenge the "male gaze" that dominated classic Hollywood. Bellot's particular use of the split screen undermines the male gaze by making the spectator aware of his or her own positioning; rather than merely aligning us with the male character's perspective, the sequence destabilizes this sight line by confronting us with another (female) gaze. Rather than privileging a male gaze, the film foregrounds multiple gazes/perspectives; akin to a computer screen, the film frame offers us multiple "windows" in order to perceive social dynamics in new ways. The two "windows" amplify the audience's field of vision increasing the amount of information in terms of what is narrated.

Figure 24.1   The split screen in *Dependencia Sexual* (2003) showcases the place of overpowering machismo in Bolivian society.

At times, the juxtaposed screens complement each other, one narrating what the other one is missing. At others, they offer sharp contrasts to challenge and complicate meaning. Such moments highlight a polyphony and dissidence that distinguish the juxtaposed "windows" in digital films such as *Dependencia sexual*, from the split screen technique used in older (analogue) productions.

While the new authorial cinema has interrogated upper-class characters, Bolivian independent documentary has privileged the exploration of other subjectivities, in particular those living on the margins of urban life. These digital documentaries offer microhistories that reconstruct marginalized subjectivities and transform them into sites of power and resistance. In some cases, the films articulate a counter-hegemonic discourse of national identity in opposition to an internal foe (the administration of President Evo Morales) or an external one (Western culture). *La chirola* (2008), director Diego Mondaca's *opera prima*, is a case in point. The film's themes and formal structure—a long monologue that oscillates between the confession of ex-guerrilla Pedro Cajías and the reconstruction of certain events—signal a break with the dominant currents of Bolivian documentary associated with Jorge Ruiz's work in the 1960s about indigenous peoples as collectives. Mondaca has noted how his team had to work differently with the digital camera because of its particular apprehension of lighting conditions, the flatter depth of field, and the different texture of the image. The digital camera allowed them to play with diverse elements, including what was out of focus and slow-motion capture at 60 frames/second; create high contrasts with light and shadow; and utilize color to achieve a greater level of texture/density of the image, even when the final film would appear in black and white (Mondaca 2010).

In *La chirola*, Mondaca captures Cajías' body moving through the crowd using high contrast to make him look more like a specter than a living being (Figures 24.2 and 24.3). The lighting and composition express Cajías' feelings of abandonment as neither the state, family, nor religion cares for him any longer. The contrastive monochrome photography, silhouetting, and lack of focus seem to explore a subjectivity that prefers to remain at the

Figure 24.2   High-contrast lighting in *La chirola* (2008).

margins of society and that resists being framed, absorbed, and appropriated. These visual techniques resonate with Cajías' final, cynical reflection at the end of the film: freedom is the ability to choose your own jail. This thought, and his determination to leave the city-space and find a piece of land in the countryside, represent his empowerment in the marginal space in which he has chosen to live. On an allegorical level, Cajías' assertion of agency echoes the counter-hegemonic project of Bolivia's new digital documentary, claiming a space on the margins of the industry.

In a different way, documentaries such as *El corral y el viento* (Miguel Hilari, 2014) challenge the older, *indigenista* documentaries and those that explored the indigenous as collectives. In the film's opening, a 12-year-old Aymara boy tortures a cat in a small room. This portrait of violence allows the film to break with the romanticized and paternalist representations of indigenous subjects present in earlier documentaries, and to distance itself from the attributes associated with ethnographic film. At the same time, the tensions between innocence and violence and between civilization and barbarism are present throughout the film in the on-screen coexistence of children and animals, and of the boy with a girl. In a self-conscious gesture of performativity, the children act in front of the camera. "Are you filming, Miguel?" asks the boy on numerous occasions, addressing the filmmaker directly (Figure 24.4).

In thinking about such exchanges between filmmaker and subject, Hilari notes that filming is a violent act, especially in places such as the countryside, and that it is important to capture people's responses to being filmed (Lacunza 2016). This is particularly so in a tight space with little light, such as the scene mentioned above, where the digital camera's presence affects the natural flow of everyday life. In the second half of the film, Hilari's uncle approaches the camera and asks, "It's a camera, right?" to which the director responds, "Yes, it is" and keeps on filming. He then shows his uncle his captured image on screen, and we see the older gentleman's surprised smile. "It's like a photo, but filmed," Hilari tells him. In this way, the scene showcases how people respond to being filmed, and at the same time underscores filmmaking as "gaze-making," as establishing a particular distance (or proximity) between the camera and the filmed subject.

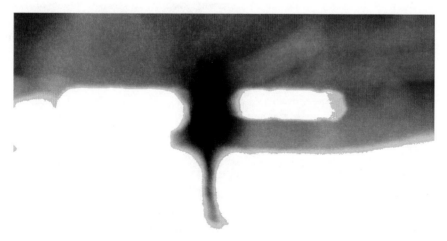

Figure 24.3 The use of lack of focus in *La chirola* (2008).

Figure 24.4   Performativity in *El corral y el viento* (2014).

Finally, there are several community-based filmmaking projects in Bolivia that have taken advantage of the new digital technologies and circulate through alternative distribution and exhibition networks. Created in 2008, TAFA, for example, works with youth from marginalized communities, utilizing digital cameras to explore Bolivian identity in new ways that differ from the older binaries (rich vs. poor, white vs. indigenous, man vs. woman, eastern vs. western provinces) in order to underscore the country's cultural diversity. Through the audiovisual exercises carried out by their young collaborators, TAFA enables the exploration of youthful subjectivities shaped less by class issues than by questions of ethnicity and gender difference.

The animated fiction *Quri Tunqu* (*Gold Corn*), produced with the Cha'lla community, is an example of how digital technologies serve as a vehicle to raise awareness and educate children in the civic principles of recycling and waste classification. During the 1–1.5 weeks of filming, the crew and their collaborators gathered 500 kg of plastic bottles for recycling. In a more general sense, the project helped to reanimate and reconfigure indigenous identity and the community's relation with the local environment. At first glance, the short seems to fit into the modern-urban superhero genre. In the narrative, defenseless children acquire superpowers in the manner of Clark Kent or Spider-Man. Special garments with powers are granted to them by the sun and transform fearful and average children into superheroes. The clothes, however, are not Superman's cape or Batman's mask, but rather indigenous garments: the *aguayo* (mantle), *chulo* (hat), and *cinto* (belt) (Figures 24.5 and 24.6). Thus, the film resemanticizes the figure of the superhero, locating the source of special powers in ancestral tradition.

While the authorial cinema frames marginality as a condition from which one must escape, most of the "marginal" subjectivities that appear in TAFA's films do not present themselves as imprisoned; rather, they exercise agency by paving their own pathway. Whereas authorial cinema invites us to gaze at and get to know "the subaltern" within the space of dominant culture, TAFA's more subjective filmic exercises

Figure 24.5 A young boy donning clothes with superpowers in the animated fiction film *Quri Tunqu.*

Figure 24.6 Animated child-heroes fighting against the garbage-monster in *Quri Tunqu.*

do not recognize this subordinate position. The youthful subjects-as-directors do not rely on comparisons with the dominant culture, nor do they create their films for other audiences. Instead, they take advantage of the portability of the digital camera to create autobiographical portraits in intimate environments (bedrooms, hallways, etc.) (Figure 24.7).

For these reasons, digital filmmaking in Bolivia undermines John Belton's (1999) contention that the new format has not instantiated a technological revolution. Both the authorial and community-based projects carry out reflexive aesthetic exercises that encourage us to "see" and "perceive" cinema (and the world around us) in new ways.

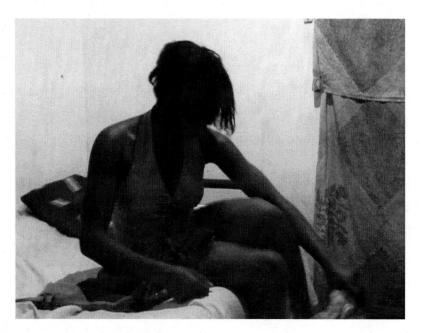

Figure 24.7 An Afro-Bolivian teen in her room.

Online distribution and access: the case of Netflix

Niamh Thornton

As a result of new technologies for delivering (amateur and professional) films for home viewing, digital distribution forces us to consider new ways of conceptualizing the curatorship and categorization of film. Streaming services, such as Netflix, MUBI, Amazon Prime, and Curzon Home Cinema, provide distinct selections of Latin American films, under categories that challenge scholarly labels for national and transnational cinema and its consumption. MUBI and Curzon Home Cinema show a carefully curated selection of films aimed at those who, in earlier eras, would have attended art house cinemas, but now can access films outside of the cosmopolitan centers where these theaters are located. Another key player is Amazon Prime, which has a growing market share and is a direct competitor with Netflix.

These services provide a limited and ever-changing offering based on their own, often oblique and usually well-guarded, decisions about what the market desires. In the case of Netflix, the company determines what can be seen based on geographic location due to territorial rights and their perception of market demand. Therefore, Netflix in the US has a healthy range of Latin American films available, yet in the UK and Ireland it is quite narrow. Given the growth in these services and the shrinking DVD market, what they show, where it gets seen, and how this determines the viewers' understanding of Latin American film, makes this a particularly fecund area for new research.

I wish to explore the application of digital technologies built around streaming services as they highlight geopolitical positioning and, as we shall see, are built around the specific commercial practice associated with geo-blocking. This section will focus more narrowly on the availability of Latin American film on Netflix across two territories—the UK and Ireland (legally one territory) and Argentina—to explore how this streaming service challenges academic labels for national and transnational cinema.

Of the above-mentioned streaming services, Netflix is the one with the most aggressive corporate policy, dividing territories by licensing agreements and employing geo-blocking to restrict access to content according to geographical location, which is often determined by territorial rights. The company also targets "unblockers" (i.e. individuals or devices that transgress territorial licenses). In January 2016, Netflix threatened "to bring the hammer down on people who circumvent country-based content licensing restrictions" using these tools (Spangler 2016). David Glance has suggested that punishing unblockers would be difficult and would be more likely to harm the streaming service's brand and push viewers either to other services or to torrent sites (Glance 2016). Glance is writing from an Australian perspective, where this debate has been a particularly live one due to the limited content available on Netflix there compared to other territories. His speculation on the consequences may not come to fruition; however, what is interesting in the geo-blocking debate is that it is not just a topic of interest to area specialists and academics, but to a wider viewership.

To discuss Latin American film in the light of its commercial distribution through streaming services calls into question how we talk about this region and group the multiple differentiated large and small cinema-producing countries into a single category. Much discussion has taken place among scholars such as Deborah Shaw (2007) and Stephanie Dennison (2013) regarding the value of using Latin America as a label in recent years. Both make strong arguments for its validity by carefully qualifying their decisions. In the light of the growing work on the transnational flows of finance and talent, their interventions are helpful in reminding researchers of the need to frame the discussion carefully. In addition, what my research on streaming services shows is that the human- and machine-generated algorithms further complicate the category (Wu 2015).

Netflix is well known for its unusual categories and "complex ecosystem of algorithms" (Vanderbilt 2013). These can be a mix of the generic, "Popular on Netflix", "Trending Now", and "Recently Added"; to the specific, "Top Picks for"; to those that are particular to Netflix, such as "Dark US TV Dramas", "Witty Comedies", or "Independent Films Featuring a Strong Female Lead." In the UK and Ireland, under the site's browse function, there is an "International Movies" category with "Latin American Films" as a searchable subcategory under the "Subgenre" field. Only 18 films were available between January and February 2016. In another study (Thornton 2018), I focused on Mexican and Cuban films across the different platforms. Of the 18, none was Cuban and four were "Mexican": *Días de gracia* (*Days of Grace*, Everardo Valerio Grout, 2011), a fiction film about three violent kidnappings during pivotal football World Cup games; *Miss Bala* (Gerardo Naranjo, 2011), a story of a beauty pageant winner caught up in drug violence; a horror, *Ahí va el diablo* (*Here Comes the Devil*, Adrián García Bogliano, 2012), which premiered at the Toronto International Film Festival; and *No se aceptan devoluciones* (*Instructions Not Included*, Eugenio Derbez, 2013), a comedy that has had the biggest box-office earnings in Mexico to date and is currently the highest-grossing foreign language film in the US (Cervantes 2013). *Miss Bala* and *Ahí va el diablo* both got festival and art house distribution. Of these, *Miss Bala* had some academic attention, while the rest, as with many genre films from Mexico, have been largely overlooked. This disparity reveals the hierarchical nature of knowledge consumption and the tendency by academics to write about films that are likely to appear on curricula, few of which are conventional or high-grossing genre films. At the same time, these genre films are the ones available to see and study on streaming services, and may challenge academics to rethink what they include on their curricula as exemplary works of "Mexican" or "Latin American" cinema?

Netflix takes a more conventional approach to country ascription than do MUBI and Curzon Home Cinema. The broader hemispheric Latin America label goes some way to explaining this. But it does offer a very small selection of films that go beyond the typical art house offering, with an emphasis on genre films, in particular horror, action, war, and comedy. There are films available during this time on Netflix that are excluded from this "Latin American" category. For example, *Babel* (2006) by the Mexican director Alejandro González Iñárritu is not included, even though one of its four narratives is set in Mexico. Likewise, *Narco Cultura* (2013) by the Israeli documentary filmmaker Shaul Schwarz is not labeled as "Latin American," although it is specifically examining drug gangs in Mexico. The labels are not comprehensive, and fail to flag the (trans)national boundaries that often determine how film is researched.

There is a general predominance of English-language offering across UK and Irish Netflix, although there is some variation, particularly under TV, with the increased popularity of Scandi-Noir, such as the Danish version of *The Killing* (2007–2012) and the Danish–Swedish *The Bridge* (2011–). On the Argentine Netflix, there is a considerable range of English-language film and TV available, but there is a greater mix, and, Spanish-language film and TV is unevenly marked by language. For example, there are categories such as "Dark Spanish-language Drama" and "Spanish-language TV Dramas", and yet under other categories there is a mix of film and TV in Spanish and other languages that are not labeled according to language. Language is not a defining category, and may work more as an invitation to browse than a delimiter.

In the browse function on Argentine Netflix, there are distinct subcategories. Some of these that bear closest comparison to that of the UK and Irish Netflix and are of interest to those studying Latin American film are "Argentinian Film" and a separate "Latin American" category. There is also an "International" section. This is similar to the categorization of films in the few DVD shops in Buenos Aires, or the more frequently found bookshops, where there are "Argentine," "Latin American," and "Universal" categories. Although I have given little space to the study of TV in this analysis, it is worth noting that there is a "Telenovelas" section that is separate from the "Spanish-language TV Dramas" section, between which there are some overlaps.

Under the Argentinian section, there are 50 films. These are varied and include: children's animated features such as *La canción del Zoo* (2013); three documentaries on the Argentine-born Pope Francis; art house favorites that are absent from UK and Irish Netflix: *El aura* (Aura, Fabián Bielinsky, 2005), *La ciénega* (*The Swamp*, Lucrecia Martel, 2001), and *Historias mínimas* (*Intimate Stories*, Carlos Sorín, 2002); and a selection of genre films. In Argentina, "Argentinian" is a broad category that includes films of Argentine interest (some of the Pope films and a selection of nature documentaries), as well as films made in Argentina of all types.

Under "International," there is a preponderance of Spanish-language films, most of which are made or set in Spain, including films by Pedro Almodóvar; the hit romantic comedy, *Ochos apellido vascos* (*The Spanish Affair*, Emilio Martínez Lázaro, 2014); and the transnational film set during the large tsunami in 2004, *The Impossible* (J.A. Bayona, 2012). These films by "Spanish" directors sit alongside kung fu films, genre thrillers, and romantic comedies. Where "International" is more suggestive of art house in the UK and Ireland Netflix, it has a broader meaning in Argentinian Netflix.

Under "Latin American," there are 228 films with a further drop-down menu entitled "Sub-genres": "Mexican" (163 films), "Brazilian" (16 films), "Venezuelan" (11 films), and "Colombian" (16 films). These are varied from documentaries, such as *Gimme the Power* (Enrique Renteria, 2012); children's animated features; a number of 1970s and 1980s Mexican films largely dismissed by academics and difficult to obtain elsewhere, such as *Paraíso* (*Paradise*, Luis Alcoriza, 1970) and *Huevos rancheros* (René Cardona Jr., 1982); a number of sex comedies; and a large range of genre and art house films, such as *El Ataúd del vampiro* (*The Vampire's Coffin*, Fernando Méndez, 1958) and the difficult to source *Tlatelolco: verano del 68* (*Tlatelolco, Summer of 68*, Carlos Bolado, 2013). The last of these touches on a controversial topic, and I was unable to find it in any brick-and-mortar shop in Mexico or in any of the usual online stores. These examples are all of Mexican films, which is the majority source country for films.

As demonstrated above, Netflix's curatorship suggests certain trends and choices. It is equally important to think about how subscribers respond to those guidelines, even though it is difficult to do so. Given that the company does not release viewing figures, it is impossible to know what is watched, although comments and ratings can give some indication. For example, *Tlatelolco: verano del 68* has three stars and, as yet, no reviews, while *El Ataúd del vampiro* has four stars and six reviews. This may say as much about genre viewers' inclination to comment as about the viewers' responses to the film.

Netflix is a private company that both responds to and determines local markets. Of concern to scholars is that what is available to screen is being determined more and more by online curatorship that lacks transparency or apparent recourse to current academic categories in its decision-making process. All of these issues bring to the fore questions that complicate the conventional interpretations of distribution and access as read through film festivals or production companies, and shifts it towards a need to source and understand algorithms and human preconceptions that are beginning to determine content on streaming services.

While there is no expectation that streaming services are required to follow scholarly labels in their curatorial decisions, nor for academics to take up their (sometimes eccentric) categories, there is potential for a global conversation about location and what that means for audiences. It brings to the fore issues of access that have always been present in the consumption of film and have been studied in relation to cinema spaces, their quality, cost, and offering (e.g. see McKee Irwin et al. 2013; Sánchez Prado 2014), but now requires new research into what online audiences can view, how streaming services are determining what is being seen, and the potential effects of content curation on scholarship and curricula.

Note

1 The sections authored by Gonzalo Aguilar and Mariana Lacunza were translated by Laura Podalsky.

References

Aguilar G. (2015) *Más allá del pueblo. Imágenes, indicios y políticas del cine.* Buenos Aires: Fondo de Cultura Económica.

Arendt, H. (2005) *La condición humana.* Barcelona: Paidós.

Beller, J. (2006) *Cinematic Mode of Production.* Hanover, NH: University Press of New England.

Belton J. (1999) "Digital Cinema: A False Revolution." In L. Braudy and M. Cohen (eds.), *Film Theory and Criticism: Introductory Readings.* New York: Oxford University Press.

Benjamin, W. (2009) "The Work of Art in the Age of Mechanical Reproduction." In L. Braudy and M. Cohen (eds.), *Film Theory & Criticism*, 7th ed. New York: Oxford University Press, pp. 665–668.

Bongers, W. (2016) *Interferencias del archivo: cortes estéticos y políticos en cine y literature*, Frankfurt: Peter Lang.

Cervantes, J. (2013) "Las películas mexicanas más taquilleras de la historia." *Forbes*, December 17. Available at: www.forbes.com.mx/las-peliculas-mexicanas-mas-taquilleras-de-la-historia/ (accessed March 3, 2016).

Dennison, S. (2013) "National, Transnational and Post-National: Issues in Contemporary Filmmaking in the Hispanic World." In S. Dennison (ed.), *Contemporary Hispanic Cinema: Interrogating the Transnational in Spanish and Latin American Film*. Woodbridge: Tamesis, pp. 1–24.

Depetris Chauvin, I. (2015) "Una comunidad de melancólicos: Cartografías afectivas en dos documentales de Raúl Ruiz y Patricio Guzmán." *Amérique Latine Histoire et Mémoire. Les Cahiers ALHIM*, 30. Available at: https://alhim.revues.org/5314 (accessed June 1, 2017).

Espinoza, S. and Laguna, A. (2009) *El cine de la nación clandestina. Aproximación a la producción cinematográfica boliviana de los últimos 25 años (1983–2008)*. La Paz: Fautapo, Gente Común.

Glance, D. (2016) "Even if Netflix Is Serious about Blocking VPNs, It Is Unlikely to Succeed." *The Conversation*, January 15. Available at: https://theconversation.com/even-if-netflix-is-serious-about-blocking-vpns-it-is-unlikely-to-succeed-53246 (accessed March 3, 2016).

Lacunza, M. (2011) *Estéticas digitales y nociones de identidad en el cine boliviano contemporáneo*. Doctoral Thesis, Ohio State University.

—— (2016) Personal interview with Miguel Hilari, September 2016.

McKee Irwin, R. and Castro Ricalde, M., with M. Szurmuk, I. Álvarez, and D. Sužnjević (2013) *Global Mexican Cinema: Its Golden Age 'el cine mexicano se impone'*. London: BFI Palgrave Macmillan.

Messuti, P. (2016) "Cine argentino y nuevas tecnologías. Modelos productivos en la ficción 1994-2012." Doctoral Thesis, Universidad de Buenos Aires.

Mondaca, D. (2010) Personal Interview, February 5.

La Razón (2010) "El 2010 se produjeron 16 peliculas nacionales, pero con baja taquilla." *La Razón*, December 26. Available at: www.larazon.com/version.php?ArticleId=123073&EditionId=2388 (accessed May 30, 2016).

Richard, N. (2014) "Memoria contemplativa y memoria crítico-transformadora-sobre la película *No* de Pablo Larraín." *La fuga*, 16. Available at: www.lafuga.cl/memoria-contemplativa-y-memoria-critico-transformadora/675 (accessed June 1, 2017).

Sánchez Prado, I. (2014) *Screening Neoliberalism: Transforming Mexican Cinema, 1988–2012*. Nashville, TN: Vanderbilt University Press.

Shaw, D. (2007) "Latin American Cinema Today: A Qualified Success Story." In D. Shaw (ed.), *Contemporary Latin American Cinema: Breaking into the Global Market*. New York/Plymouth: Rowman & Littlefield, pp. 1–10.

Spangler, T. (2016) "Netflix Vows to Shut Down Proxy Users Who Bypass Country Restrictions." *Variety*, January 14. Available at: http://variety.com/2016/digital/news/netflix-shuts-down-proxy-access-1201680010/ (accessed March 3, 2016).

Thornton, N. (2018) "Bridges, Streams and Dams: The Multiple Negotiated Strategies of Distribution and Access in Latin American Cinema." In S. Baschiera and A. Fisher (eds.), *World Cinema On Demand: Global Film Cultures in the Era of Online Distribution*. New York/London: Bloomsbury.

Vanderbilt, T. (2013) "The Science Behind the Netflix Algorithms That Decide What You'll Watch Next." *Wired*, July 8. Available at: www.wired.com/2013/08/qq_netflix-algorithm/ (accessed March 3, 2016).

Wu, T. (2015) "Netflix's Secret Special Algorithm Is a Human." *New Yorker*, January 27. Available at: www.newyorker.com/business/currency/hollywoods-big-data-big-deal (accessed March 3, 2016).

INDEX

Note: Page numbers in *italic* refer to pages with illustrations. Page numbers in **bold** refer to tables. Film titles in English have a *see* reference to the Latin American title. Definite articles in Latin American titles, e.g. *La agonía del Arauco*, have been ignored in the sorting order.

Guerra, Ciro 224
Guerrero, Javier 52
Guerrico, César 143
guerrilla groups 182, 215
Guevara, Alfredo 193, 194, 196
Guevara, Ernesto 'Che' 170, *171*, 172, 173, 187; photography and 297, 310, *311*, *312*, *313*
Guillén Landrián, Nicolás 50, 109, 184
Guimarães, Cão 225
Gullane Filmes 255, 256
Gumucio Dagron, Alfonso 213
Gunche, Ernesto 36–37
Gunder Frank, André 240
Gunning, Tom 33, 130n3, 283
Gutiérrez Alea, Tomás 2, 4, 184, 225; documentaries 120, 123; institutional film culture 193, 194, 196
Gutiérrez, C.A. 272–273
Guzmán, Patricio 24, 308, 362–363; *film-ensayo* (essay films) 107, 113, 117; national cinema 22, 24

Hachazos (Andrés Di Tella, 2011) 111
'Hacia un Tercer Cine' ('Towards a Third Cinema') (Solanas and Getino) 21
Haddock Films (Argentina) 260
Hahner, June 80
Hamburger, Cao 236
Hamm, Marion 220
Handler, Mario 10, 108, 110
Hansen, Miriam Bratu 19, 20, 69, 137, 140
Harvey, David 96
Hassum, Leandro 156
Hasta después de muerta (*Until after Her Death*, Eduardo Martínez de la Pera and Ernesto Gunche, 1916) 37
Havana Film Festival (Cuba) 6, 268
Hayek, Salma 165
HBO network 252, 262
hegemony: space/place 93, 94, 102, 103
Heinrich, Annemarie 298, 305
Heli (Amat Escalante, 2013) 235, 242, 244, 245, 246
Hello, Hello, Carnival! see *Alô, alô, carnaval!*
Hennebelle, Guy 199
Henrickson, Leonardo 220
Heraldo de Cine (journal) 70, 71
 Los Hermanos del Hierro (*My Son, the Hero*, Ismael Rodríguez, 1961) 151
Hernández, Gustavo 159
Hernández, José 286
Hernández Salinas, Silvia Gabriela 219
Heron Films 126
Herrera, Armando 298, 306
Herrera, Manuel 199
Herrera, Mateo 129
Hidalgo, Alejandro 158

high art films *see* festival films
High School Musical: El Desafío (*The Challenge*, Jorge Nisco, 2008) 155
Higson, Andrew 45
Hilari, Miguel 367, 368
historicity 3, 9–12
History of Film Theories (Aristarco) 198
Hollywood: art house cinema 237, 238, 239; *cine-clubs* 87; cosmopolitan nationalisms 137; fanzines 76, 77, 78; genre films 152; motifs 148; movie theatres 84, 85; national cinema and 18, 19, 20, 21, 22, 24, 26, 27; periodization 64, 69, 70; silent and early sound cinema 33, 38, 40, 320; stardom and star system 164; state agencies 47, 48, 55; *see also* United States
Holmes, Amanda 339
Hombres de Mal Tiempo (*Men of Bad Times*, Alejandro Sanderman, 1968) 110
Hopwell, John 174
La hora de los hornos (*The Hour of the Furnaces*, Fernando Solanas and Octavio Getino, 1966–1968) 10, 197, 216, 333; art house cinema 240; *film-ensayo* (essay films) 107, 108, 109; photography and 297, 310, *311*, *312*, *313*; political cinema 183, 184, 188
Horak, Jan Christopher 295
horror films 24, 25, 26, 151, 153–154, 157–159
The Hour of the Furnaces see *La hora de los hornos*
How Angels Are Born see *Como nascem os anjos*
How Wall Street Created a Nation (Ovidio Díaz Espino) 95
Huayhuaca, José Carlos 153
Hubert Bals Fund 241, 262, 267, 270–271, 272, 273
Huelva (film festival) 5–6
Hugo Christensen, Carlos 300, 303, *304*
human rights 214
humour *see* comedies
El húsar de la muerte (*The Hussar of Death*, Pedro Sienna, 1925) 35, 36
The Hussar of Death see *El húsar de la muerte*
Huttala, Gerald (Geraldo) 144, 299
Huxley, Aldous 106

I Lost My Heart in Lima see *Yo perdí mi corazón en Lima*
I Love You see *Eu te amo*
Ibermedia 50, 56, 270; co-production 251, 253, 259, 260, 262
Ibero-American Educational and Cultural Television *see* Televisión Educativa y Cultural Iberoamericana (TEIb)
ICAIC *see* Instituto Cubano del Arte y la Industria Cinematográficos
ICB *see* Instituto Cinematográfico Boliviano